The Life of
SAMUEL TAYLOR COLERIDGE

A Critical Biography

Rosemary Ashton

BLACKWELL
Publishers

First published 1996

2 4 6 8 10 9 7 5 3 1

Blackwell Publishers Ltd
108 Cowley Road
Oxford OX4 IJF
UK

Blackwell Publishers Inc.
238 Main Street
Cambridge, Massachusetts 02142
USA

British Library Cataloguing in Publication Data
A CIP catalogue record for this book is available from the British Library.

Library of Congress Cataloging-in-Publication Data
Ashton, Rosemary, 1947–
The life of Samuel Taylor Coleridge : a critical biography / Rosemary Ashton.
p.   cm.—(Blackwell critical biographies: 7)
Includes bibliographical references and index.
ISBN 0–631–18746–4
1. Coleridge, Samuel Taylor, 1772–1834.   2. Poets, English—19th century—
Biography.   I. Title.   II. Series.
PR4483.A85   1996
821'.7—dc20
[B]   95–2820
                                                                    CIP

Typeset in 10 on 11pt Baskerville
by Best-set Typesetter Ltd., Hong Kong
Printed in Great Britain by T.J. Press (Padstow) Ltd, Padstow, Cornwall.

This book is printed on acid-free paper

Contents

Illustrations

Acknowledgements

I am grateful for advice, suggestions, and information to the following friends and colleagues: Nicholas Büchele, Peter Cadogan, Warwick Gould, Dan Jacobson, Danny Karlin, Hilton Kelliher, Tom Mayberry, Andrew McNeillie, J. C. C. Mays, Karl Miller, Angela Minshull, Gerard O'Daly, Claude Rawson, Fred Schwarzbach, Michael Slater, Ginny Stroud-Lewis, Guilland Sutherland, John Sutherland, Henry Woudhuysen.

For permission to make use of published and unpublished material I thank Mrs A. H. B. Coleridge; Lord Coleridge; The British Library; The Librarian of Heythrop College, London; The Wordsworth Trust, Dove Cottage, Grasmere, Cumbria; The Harry Ransom Humanities Research Center at the University of Texas at Austin; Oxford University Press; Routledge.

My greatest debt is to Gerry Ashton, to whom I give my warmest thanks.

A note on extracts from Coleridge's works

Extracts from Coleridge's works reproduced without any silent correction of his idiosyncratic usage. For example: his spelling of 'Shakspeare', his use of 'it's' for 'its', and of obliques (\\), his strange accents on non-English words and inconsistent capitalization.

Introduction

He holds him with his glittering eye –
The wedding guest stood still
And listens like a three year's child;
The mariner hath his will.

The wedding guest sate on a stone,
He cannot chuse but hear:
And thus spake on that ancyent man,
The bright-eyed Marinere.

'The Rime of the Ancyent Marinere' (1798)

One of the many curious facts of Coleridge's extraordinary life is that when he wrote 'The Ancient Mariner' for inclusion in his and Wordsworth's collection of *Lyrical Ballads* (1798), he had never been abroad, never sailed across the sea. It was immediately after publication of the volume that he first crossed the Channel. In September 1798 he set off, with Wordsworth and his sister Dorothy, for a prolonged stay in Germany. Coleridge was then almost twenty-six years old. In one sense, the world was all before him; he was a young man full of genius and promise, who habitually made such a strong impression on new acquaintances that they responded with wonder and amazement and, as often as not, the offer of financial help. Two such acquaintances, the brothers Thomas and Josiah Wedgwood, were financing this trip in the hope that their brilliant protégé would come back equipped to benefit mankind from the added stores of knowledge, particularly of the sciences, that some months at a German university could furnish.

The omens were not uniformly favourable, however. The young poet who had conjured up the mariner's nightmare voyage – 'perhaps the most marvellous any navigator has ever taken', as E. M. Forster said[1] – was a creature subject to excessive feelings of guilt, dread and insecurity. As an unsympathetic acquaintance, John Rickman, complained in 1804, when

Coleridge was contemplating his second long voyage, this time to Malta, his sensitivity was such that he was 'excitable by objects to other men scarce visible or feelable'.[2] By 1804 Coleridge, though still a relatively young man, was in despair. Ill, in thrall to opium, convinced that the poet in him was 'dead',[3] unable to continue living with the wife he had carelessly married in a rush of youthful enthusiasm and for whom he now felt an alarming aversion, Coleridge set off for Malta in a somewhat despairing search for health. He feared that he was dying.

It was during the journey to Malta that Coleridge became fixed on the idea of himself as the ancient mariner of his own creation. Life seemed to be imitating art. He felt himself to be in the clutches of the ghastly figure of his own conjuring which plays a game of dice with Death for possession of the mariner's soul: the unnamed woman with skin 'as white as leprosy' to whom in editions of the poem from 1817 onwards he gave the name 'Life-in-Death'.

Coleridge survived; he was to live on until 1834. Helped by a succession of friends who were struck by his genius and his plight, he emerged from the depths of his personal hell to live a life of comparative serenity and solid achievement. Inevitably, in view of the enormous expectations raised by his early promise, his later life was marked by disappointments. Much has been said, and written, about how far short Coleridge fell of fulfilling his own and others' hopes of him. His friend and brother-in-law Robert Southey, echoing Ophelia's lament for Hamlet's lost sanity, declared in 1810, 'O what a mind is here overthrown!'[4] Coleridge's more forgiving friend Charles Lamb described him to Wordsworth in 1816 as 'an Arch angel a little damaged'. Yet despite Coleridge's illness and prevarication, and the destructiveness of his habits, Lamb, who had first known and wondered at him when they were schoolboys together at Christ's Hospital, was still able to say of his old friend, 'Tis enough to be within the whiff & wind of *his* genius, for us not to possess our souls in quiet.'[5]

The man of whom this could still be said must needs be an object of great interest. The biographer – and there have been several biographers of Coleridge[6] – is faced with a daunting task. Here was a man who enchanted people with his brilliance in conversation and with his magical, mysterious, musical poetry. From his earliest days he held listeners in thrall; in the last years of his life he was known as the Sage of Highgate.[7] Younger men – Carlyle, Emerson, James Fenimore Cooper, Coleridge's disciples J. H. Green, John Sterling, and many others – visited to hear the stream of eloquence that was known to flow for hours on end from his revered lips.

Yet his friends and admirers routinely expressed their disappointment too. It seemed to them that Coleridge *only* talked, too rarely giving his brilliance permanent expression in writing. When he did publish, they complained of his obscurity and fragmentariness. A slightly mocking, though not unkind, description of him in the *New Monthly Magazine* in 1831 is characteristic of contemporary irritation with Coleridge. Employing what was by this time a common strategy, the writer of this sketch identifies Coleridge with his own mariner:

> The author of 'The Ancient Mariner' . . . should be delineated after the poet's definition of him, as a 'noticeable man with small grey eyes'. A crowd of listeners should be around him, catching up with eagerness and ecstasy every syllable as it falls from his lips; and in a corner of the room there might be one or two persons reading his works, apparently puzzled at times to make out his meaning. On the walls should be representations of a giant devoting his life to catching flies; of a philosopher straying on the sea-shore to pick up shells, while the sails of the vessel that was to waft him to his home are scarcely to be descried in the distance.[8]

The picture is that of a brilliant poet and philosopher who failed to fulfil his potential, by a propensity on the one hand to 'spawn plans like a herring'[9] but leave too many of them unrealized, and on the other to publish works like his periodical *The Friend* (1809–10 and 1818), his *Biographia Literaria* (1817) and his *Aids to Reflection* (1825), which many found impossibly obscure. Of Coleridge's flurry of publications in the years 1816 to 1818 after a long silence Byron commented famously in the Dedication to Canto I of *Don Juan*:

> And Coleridge, too, has lately taken wing,
> But like a hawk encumber'd with his hood, –
> Explaining metaphysics to the nation –
> I wish he would explain his Explanation.[10]

Everyone agreed that Coleridge's works did not amount to a full and true expression of his intellectual and imaginative powers. But opinion was divided – it still is – over whether his achievement is *nevertheless* to be accounted a great one, or whether his prose writings contain such a mass of chaotic thinking and his poetry verse of such variable quality that he is a writer whose works ultimately fail to satisfy the reader. What holds good for an opinion of his works applies also to an observation of his life. Coleridge wrote as he lived – compulsively, brilliantly, confusingly, contradictorily. Responses to his person and to his work are bound to be connected and bound to be problematic. We might do well to bear in mind E. M. Forster's words on Coleridge:

> He seldom did what he or others hoped, and posterity has marked him as her prey in consequence. She has never ceased to hold up her plump finger to him, and shake it and say that he has disappointed her. And he has acquiesced because he is a darling. But if one turns on posterity and says, 'Well! what else do you want him to do? Would you rather have Comberbacke [Coleridge] as he is or not at all?' she is apt to be silent or to change the conversation.[11]

In his lifetime Coleridge alienated many who had begun by loving him:

his brothers, his wife Sara, the Wordsworths and Mrs Wordsworth's sister Sara Hutchinson, with whom Coleridge was guiltily in love, Southey, Hazlitt, Josiah Wedgwood. Only Lamb, to whom Coleridge was a kind comforter in the domestic calamity which befell him in 1796, held fast despite a break in friendship. In November 1796 Lamb, after his sister Mary had killed their mother in a fit of insanity, addressed Coleridge as 'My Brother, my Friend', and poured out his troubles to him.[12] In 1834, writing after the shock of Coleridge's death, Lamb declared that he was haunted by 'his great and dear spirit'.[13]

Wordsworth, whose relationship with Coleridge went from enraptured brother poet to estranged ex-friend to amicable but cool acquaintance, allowed himself a poetic expression of warmth in 1835:

> Nor has the rolling year twice measured,
> From sign to sign, its steadfast course,
> Since every mortal power of Coleridge
> Was frozen at its marvellous source;
>
> The rapt One, of the godlike forehead,
> The heaven-eyed creature sleeps in earth.[14]

Wordsworth's comment to a friend on hearing of Coleridge's death was that Coleridge was 'the most wonderful man' he had ever known. He possessed, said Wordsworth, 'great originality of mind' and 'a perfect mastery' of poetic form; on the other hand he had, in Wordsworth's view, spoilt or misused his gifts by becoming 'captivated' by 'German metaphysics'.[15]

Philosophy, in particular German philosophy, was often seized upon as one of the chief culprits in the spoiling of Coleridge's genius. This argument was advanced not only by Wordsworth, but also by Hazlitt and by a majority of reviewers of Coleridge's works during his life.[16] Complaints were made about his obscurity, mysticism and unfortunate 'Germanisation' through his reading of, and dependence on, the work of Kant, Schelling and other German philosophers. To these accusations were added, from essays by De Quincey which began appearing only a month after Coleridge's death to the book, *Coleridge, The Damaged Archangel* by Norman Fruman in 1972, further charges – alas often indisputable – of dishonesty in his unacknowledged 'borrowings' from German writers, particularly Schelling and the critic August Wilhelm Schlegel.[17] Coleridge himself led the way in the disparagement of his own achievements. From 1800 he began to compare himself unfavourably with Wordsworth, who, he told Francis Wrangham in December of that year, 'is a great, a true Poet – I am only a kind of a Metaphysician'.[18]

But Coleridge did not always think of philosophy as something which came between him and his poetic genius. In 1802, referring to Shakespeare, he declared that 'a great Poet must be implicitè if not explicitè, a profound Metaphysician'.[19] We should not, therefore, accept too readily the version of his life story which asserts that Coleridge was diverted from his true *métier* – poetry – by an unfortunate interest in metaphysics. On the other hand, it is possible to claim too much for Coleridge the philosopher. Great claims were made by his disciple J. H. Green and by his nephew (and son-in-law) Henry Nelson Coleridge, joint literary executors of his works after his death.

Coleridge's posthumous influence was certainly enormous. Through his late prose works, particularly *Aids to Reflection* and *On the Constitution of Church and State* (1830), he helped shape the Broad Church Movement of the Church of England of which Dr Thomas Arnold was a prominent leader.[20] John Stuart Mill, a philosopher of quite a different cast of mind from Coleridge, famously named him in 1840 as one of the two most significant representatives of early nineteenth-century thought, the other being Mill's own teacher and mentor Jeremy Bentham. Mill saw Coleridge, astutely, as the spokesman for ideas and principles in philosophical, political and religious matters. Unfussed by thorny questions of plagiarism, deception and obscurity, he took a broad, clear view of what he called 'the Germano-Coleridgean doctrine':

> It expresses the revolt of the human mind against the philosophy of the eighteenth century. It is ontological, because that was experimental; conservative, because that was innovative; religious, because so much of that was infidel; concrete and historical, because that was abstract and metaphysical; poetical, because that was matter-of-fact and prosaic.[21]

Mill's is an intelligent and generous account. He stops short, however, of treating Coleridge as a *systematic* philosopher, and he is right to do so. Coleridge's importance as a thinker must not be underrated, but it should be considered in the light of the absence of any other contemporary name one could put forward as an English philosopher of note in the first quarter of the nineteenth century – except for the very name Mill invokes as a worthy opponent of Coleridge, that of Bentham. Coleridge's daughter Sara put it well when helping her husband Henry Nelson Coleridge to edit Coleridge's *Literary Remains* in 1836:

> It does not seem as if the writer was especially conversant with this or that, as Babbage with mechanics, and Mill with political economy; but as if there was a subtle imaginative spirit to search and illustrate all subjects that interest humanity.[22]

If the pursuit of metaphysics was regretted by some observers of Coleridge's life and work and welcomed by others, there is one matter on which there could be no disagreement. This was the misfortune of his addiction to opium. Opinions vary about the reasons for his resorting to opium, the date from which he could be said to have moved from its use to its misuse, and the extent to which he succeeded in bringing his addiction under relative control. There is also a wide variation in the degree to which

Coleridge's critics take opium into account in analysing his works and his descriptions of how those works came into being.

'Kubla Khan' is the best known example of a poem supposed to have been composed, but not written down, during an opium-induced dream. The poem, or fragment, as Coleridge called it, presents huge difficulties of interpretation, beginning with the need to question Coleridge's very assertion that it was unfinished. Accounting for the part played by opium in its creation seems a sheer impossibility. And yet no study of the poem can ignore the opium question altogether. Coleridge's explanation of its composition in his apologetic preface on its publication in 1816, nearly twenty years after it was written, only compounds the problem of interpretation. He introduces the famous 'person on business from Porlock' who is supposed to have interrupted the wonderful reverie and thus rendered it impossible for the poet to remember more than the fifty-four lines which constitute the *written*, as opposed to the *dreamed*, poem.

Not only the poem, but also the story of its composition, attained the status of myth. For Stevie Smith, in her mocking poem, 'Thoughts about the Person from Porlock', Coleridge's visitor is a metaphor for any welcome interruption of a writer who is unable to complete his or her poem:

> As the truth is I think he was already stuck
> With Kubla Khan.

Showing fellow-feeling for the Coleridge of her poem, she continues:

> I am hungry to be interrupted
> For ever and ever amen
> O Person from Porlock come quickly
> And bring my thoughts to an end.[23]

Stevie Smith's amusing poem raises, rather sympathetically, the question of Coleridge's truthfulness, which we have seen is also an issue when considering his debts to German thinkers. Here an almost intractable problem arises for the student of Coleridge. Addicts, we know, lie. They lie in order to procure the drugs they need; they lie about the extent of their addiction; they get into a habit of lying. Coleridge often lied. Most of his untruths can be related directly to his opium habit, having their origins in both self-torturing guilt about his inability to throw off the habit and reluctance to admit, even to himself, that he was powerless to do so. But lying may well have become a self-protective habit long before he began to take large doses of opium. Indeed, his insecure, boastful, anxious, self-deprecating nature is likely to have disposed him towards drug dependency in the first place.[24]

So, then, Coleridge's statements, particularly as regards his own affairs, are often not to be trusted. But even habitual liars, we must suppose, do not lie all the time. In studying Coleridge's life and work the fair, though difficult, way seems to me to try to avoid falling into either of two extremes.

One is to ignore opium and untruth altogether, taking at face value statements of Coleridge's which are sometimes demonstrably untrue. The other
is to view Coleridge as a kind of criminal, to look always for the negative or
diminishing explanation of his sayings and doings. Better, surely, to maintain an alert scepticism without sneering or sinking into the kind of 'droll
patronising tone which every man feels called upon to adopt as soon as he
writes about Coleridge', as an astute reviewer of James Dykes Campbell's
biographical sketch of 1893 put it.[25] It is all too tempting to fall into such a
tone, since in Coleridge we have combined in sometimes comic and frequently irritating fashion a childish, neurotic need for the approval of
others with a sharp consciousness of his intellectual superiority to those on
whom he was thus dependent.

It is Coleridge's genius that demands the biographer's best efforts in this
respect. Whatever we may argue about the cause of the decline in his poetic
powers, it is undeniable that in his best poetry we have some of the finest
poems in the English language. Though he never wrote the thorough-
going aesthetic treatise he so often promised, his critical remarks on Shakespeare, Milton and Wordsworth in *Biographia Literaria* and elsewhere are as
fine and suggestive as those of any other critic, English or European.
Obscure as his prose style became in his later years, he nevertheless inspired generations of English critical, religious and philosophical thinkers,
from Arnold of Rugby, Matthew Arnold, Carlyle and Emerson to T. S. Eliot,
I. A. Richards and the American school of New Criticism in the 1940s. If he
was often devious and self-pitying, he was also often charming, humorous
and loving.

In December 1796 Coleridge wrote to the radical reformer John
Thelwall that he was 'not *fit* for *public* Life; yet the Light shall stream to a far
distance from the taper in my cottage window'.[26] The prophecy was to come
true. The epithet 'Coleridgean' is as much a part of our linguistic currency
as 'Shakespearean' or 'Dickensian'. As we might expect from its application
to such a myriad-minded man, it may mean many things and be spoken in
many different tones of voice. It is the task of the critical biographer to tell
the Coleridgean story with an openness to these differences.

As daunting almost as the problems just outlined is the further fact that
whatever criticism one might think of making of Coleridge, there is usually
at least one person who has been beforehand with it, and that is Coleridge
himself. If we pity his loneliness and insecurity as a child, so does he; if we
disapprove of his indolence and procrastination, so does he; if we are
irritated by his paradoxical habits of self-aggrandisement and self-deni-
gration, then his other habit of self-analysis is in evidence too, pointing the
way for us. As Virginia Woolf brilliantly remarked after reading his letters:

> He holds a looking-glass in his hand. He is a man of exaggerated self-
> consciousness, endowed with an astonishing power of self-analysis . . . He is
> the forerunner of all who have tried to reveal the intricacies, to take the
> faintest creases of the human soul.[27]

'The child is father of the man', as Wordsworth said. In a minor poem published in the 1800 edition of *Lyrical Ballads* he described 'A Character' – Coleridge – in a series of paradoxes:

> I marvel how Nature could ever find space
> For the weight and the levity seen in his face:
> There's thought and no thought, and there's paleness and bloom,
> And bustle and sluggishness, pleasure and gloom.

Wordsworth sums up the enigma thus:

> What a picture! 'tis drawn without nature or art,
> – Yet the man would at once run away with your heart.[28]

In Coleridge's early years he seems to have had just such an effect on all who crossed his path. And yet – and here is surely a clue to his neurotic personality – the one group of people he seems not to have charmed and delighted is the group most important to his early development: his own immediate family. It is to this group, and to the beginning of the life of the 'marvellous' Samuel Taylor Coleridge, that we now turn.

Part One
1772–1803

1

Inspired Charity Boy 1772–1791

Who knows the individual hour in which
His habits were first known even as a seed,
Who that shall point as with a wand, and say
'This portion of the river of my mind
Came from yon fountain'?
. . .
Hard task to analyse a soul, in which
Not only general habits and desires,
But each most obvious and particular thought –
Not in a mystical and idle sense,
But in the words of reason deeply weighed –
Hath no beginning.

Wordsworth Prelude (1805) II, 211–15, 232–6

Having written these lines with their salutary scepticism about the difficulty of reaching back to origins and assigning causes in the course of recording a life, Wordsworth paradoxically follows them immediately with an expression of certainty that all human lives *are* to be traced back to their beginnings in infancy in order to make sense of later manifestations of character:

Blest the infant babe –
For with my best conjectures I would trace
The progress of our being – blest the babe
Nursed in his mother's arms, the babe who sleeps
Upon his mother's breast, who, when his soul
Claims manifest kindred with an earthly soul,
Doth gather passion from his mother's eye.

(237–43)

Coleridge also wrote movingly in prose and poetry about the beauty and importance of a mother's love for her infants. Indeed, this was perhaps the only aspect of his married life in which he allowed his wife unqualified praise. However, he himself seems to have been denied in infancy the 'passion of his mother's eye'. Though his accounts of his early childhood are sometimes contradictory, most of his comments on his mother – they are remarkably few – as well as the evidence of his adult personality, suggest that his early relationship with her lacked warmth. By contrast, his memories of his father were extremely fond. The beloved father died in 1781, when Coleridge was not quite nine years old. By all accounts the Revd John Coleridge was a delightful man, but of course his death while Coleridge was a child meant that he did not live long enough to test and be tested by the difficulties which are inevitable between a father and a growing son. Coleridge's mother, on the other hand, lived until 1809, not much visited by her youngest child, and certainly not loved by him. Coleridge did not attend her funeral.

The Coleridge family is interesting for the spectacular rise in fame and fortune which took place in the few generations between Coleridge's grandfather, a Devonshire weaver, and the poet's nephews and great-nephews, who numbered among them two bishops, a judge, and a Lord Chief Justice of England, the first Baron Coleridge. The accounts we have of the family come chiefly from the second Baron,[1] augmented by Coleridge's own sketch of his early life in an irregular set of 'autobiographical letters' sent to his friend Tom Poole in 1797–8, and by his recollections as told to Dr James Gillman during his last eighteen years as a resident in Gillman's house in Highgate and published in Gillman's *Life of Coleridge* (1838).

In Coleridge's own words, his grandfather, John Coleridge, 'was dropped, when a child, in the Hundred of Coleridge in the County of Devon; christened, educated, & apprenticed by the parish'.[2] He may have been the illegitimate child of a Miss Coleridge who 'refused to marry' the father.[3] This John Coleridge settled in Crediton with his wife Mary. He was a most unusual weaver. Coleridge told William Godwin that he was

> half-poet and half-madman, who used to ask the passing beggars to dinner in oriental phrase, Will my lord turn in hither, & eat with his servant? & washed his feet – he wrote to a judge a wild letter, reasoning on the case of a condemned prisoner: the prisoner was pardoned, the judge asked the humourist to dine, & seated him at the head of the table –[4]

In 1719 their son, also John, Coleridge's father, was born. He, too, was an eccentric. When his father went bankrupt, 'young John his son, who had been one of the scholars at the Grammar School, Crediton, and had obtained there an Exhibition of the yearly value of £6 13s.4d.', as Lord Coleridge wrote in *The Story of a Devonshire House* (1906), 'walked off at the age of fifteen to seek his fortune'.[5] As John Coleridge sat by the roadside weeping at his plight, he was approached by a gentleman from a neighbouring town who took pity on him and found him a job as an usher in a local school. John became a good scholar and schoolmaster, married and had four daughters. In 1747, at the age of twenty-eight, he matriculated at Sidney Sussex College, Cambridge, a triumph for a young man of his humble background. He became a distinguished classical and Hebrew scholar, and might have had a fellowship if he had not been married. John Coleridge returned to schoolteaching in Devon, where a proverbial saying apparently arose to commemorate his luck in being plucked from obscurity to achieve academic success – 'as fortunate as the Coleridges'.[6]

John Coleridge's first wife having died, he married a second, Ann Bowdon, or Bowden, in 1753. Of her family Coleridge said, in the offhand tone he often adopted when describing his mother, 'the Bowdens inherited a house-stye & a pig-stye in the Exmore Country, in the reign of Elizabeth, as I have been told – & to my own knowledge, they have inherited nothing better since that time'.[7] By Ann Bowden John Coleridge had ten children, one daughter and nine sons, the youngest of whom was Samuel Taylor Coleridge, born on 21 October 1772. By this time his father was fifty-three years old and held the prestigious posts of headmaster of the King's School at Ottery St Mary in Devon and vicar of the parish church there.

The Church of Ottery St Mary, standing on a hill overlooking the small market town, twelve miles east of Exeter, is no ordinary church. It is a large, imposing building, acknowledged to be the finest parish church in Devon, second in importance only to Exeter Cathedral, on which it was closely modelled (see plate 1). Built in the mid-fourteenth century, it had been a collegiate church with a small community of priests, clerks, masters and choristers. After the dissolution of the monasteries in the reign of Henry VIII, the community was broken up, but a new school, the King's School, was established with local residents as governors. John Coleridge held the two posts of master and vicar from 1760 until his death in 1781.[8]

Though Coleridge's father remained poor, his position was prestigious, and he could claim friendship with the local baronet, his neighbour Sir Stafford Northcote, who was to figure prominently in an adventure which befell Samuel Taylor Coleridge as a child. John Coleridge published various learned works by subscription: a Latin grammar, some sermons, and 'Miscellaneous Dissertations' on the Book of Judges. The stories about him which came down to his sons and grandsons may have been apocryphal or at least embellished in the telling, but their very persistence puts it beyond doubt that he was a man of scholarly habits, careless of his appearance, absent-minded, and liable to misadventure. Coleridge took pleasure in considering himself to be his father's son in these respects.

His father, Coleridge said more than once, was 'a perfect *Parson Adams*', an allusion to the naive, benevolent character in Fielding's novel *Joseph Andrews*. He was 'an Israelite without guile',[9] a lovable eccentric of whom it was told that he once appeared before his bishop with shaven head, having forgotten to put on his wig; on another occasion he apparently stuffed most of his female neighbour's apron down his trousers at dinner, thinking it to be his own shirt.[10]

This amiable man, with his colder, managing wife, brought a remarkable family into the world. The mother may have been a remote figure to all her sons. It has often been remarked that Coleridge, when writing to members of his family (which he did infrequently), sent his love to his brothers and later to their wives but invariably conveyed only his 'duty' to his mother. This is striking, but it is worth noticing that his brothers also regularly sent love to their siblings and duty to their mother when writing home from their various outposts.[11] Nevertheless, Coleridge, the youngest child, felt his mother's coldness most. In his later years he told Gillman that she was a good housekeeper, intent on managing the large household, but perhaps over-thrifty – emphatically not a trait passed on to him – and with too obvious an ambition for her sons.[12] To Poole Coleridge wrote briskly in 1797 that she was 'an admirable Economist' with a 'spirit of aggrandizing her family'.[13]

It becomes clear from what we know of Coleridge's childhood misadventures that he sought to provoke his mother into giving him more attention. Though he told Poole that he was the favourite child of both his parents, he was also insecure. Bullied by Frank, the brother just above him in age, he became 'fretful, & timorous, & a tell-tale', but also 'very vain':

> Before I was eight years old, I was a *character* – sensibility, imagination, vanity, sloth, & feelings of deep & bitter contempt for almost all who traversed the orbit of my understanding, were even then prominent & manifest.[14]

With that astute perception about the contradictions in his own make-up he also told Godwin about his position in the household:

> The youngest son, & on that account treated by the nursemaid of his next older brother, as an intruding rival – beaten & sickly, takes refuge in early & immoderate reading, particularly the Arabian Nights – accustomed only to the conversation of grown persons, he becomes arrogant, & conceited.[15]

The story he told most often – and whether true in detail or not it has the same truth of feeling for the young hero–victim as the story of the blacking factory had for Dickens – concerned a childhood running away after an argument with Frank when Coleridge was about seven years old. It seems to have been a routine piece of domestic discord which became serious enough for him to fear punishment. What is interesting is that Coleridge remembers the incident with reference to his mother rather than his father. Only at the (happy) end of the story does the loving and beloved father enter the picture to receive his errant son with joy. It was the mother from whom the boy expected punishment; it was she whom he hoped to punish by running away. Coleridge told the whole story to Poole:

> I had asked my mother one evening to cut my cheese *entire*, so that I might toast it: this was no easy matter, it being a *crumbly* cheese – My mother however did it –/ I went into the garden for some thing or other, and in the mean time my Brother Frank *minced* my cheese, 'to disappoint the favorite'. I returned, saw the exploit, and in an agony of passion flew at Frank – he pretended to have been seriously hurt by my blow, flung himself on the ground, and there lay with outstretched limbs – I hung over him moaning & in a great fright – he leaped up, & with a horse-laugh gave me a severe blow in the face – I seized a knife, and was running at him, when my Mother came in & took me by the arm –/ I expected a flogging – & struggling from her I ran away, to a hill at the bottom of which the Otter flows – about one mile from Ottery. – There I stayed; my rage died away; but my obstinacy vanquished my fears – & taking out a little shilling book which had, at the end, morning & evening prayers, I very devoutly repeated them – thinking *at the same time* with inward & gloomy satisfaction, how miserable my Mother must be!

The episode, which Coleridge retold in the minutest detail, ended with his staying out all night, being *'cry'd* by the crier in Ottery' and sought by a search party:

> I might have lain & died – for I was now almost given over, the ponds & even the river near which I was lying, having been dragged. – But by good luck Sir Stafford Northcote, who had been out all night, resolved to make one other trial, and came so near that he heard me crying – He carried me in his arms, for near a quarter of a mile; when we met my father & Sir Stafford's Servants. – I remember, & shall never forget, my father's face as he looked upon me while I lay in the servant's arms – so calm, and the tears stealing down his face: for I was the child of his old age.[16]

Thus did young Samuel succeed in drawing the attention of his family, the town, and the nobility to himself. Naturally he never forgot the episode; indeed, on a hot July night in 1803 he relived the experience by association. On his hearing a calf bellowing 'there instantly came on my mind that night, I slept out at Ottery – & the Calf in the Field across the river whose lowing had so deeply impressed me – Chill + Child + Calf-lowing'.[17]

Coleridge not only told the story to several friends; he reproduced its situation in transposed forms in his poetry,[18] perhaps most tellingly in the 1829 version of his 'Monody on the Death of Chatterton':

> Lo! by the grave I stand of one, for whom
> A prodigal Nature and a niggard Doom
> (*That* all bestowing, *this* withholding all)
> Made each chance knell from distant spire or dome

> Sound like a seeking Mother's anxious call,
> Return, poor Child! Home, weary Truant, home![19]

Coleridge associates himself with the unhappy genius Chatterton, as Wordsworth also did in certain gloomy moods.[20] Here Coleridge conjoins that figure of pathos with his own traumatic childhood experience. The occasion was also the first of many on which Coleridge, as boy and – less acceptably – as man, was to run away from intolerable pressures.[21]

The loving and beloved father died suddenly in October 1781, thus ensuring that his son's memory of him would remain rose-tinted. But the effect on Coleridge's life was shattering in both the immediate and the longer term. His happiest memories from childhood centred on his father. When describing their relationship to Poole, Coleridge was consciously seeking for the origins of his own character, the twin tendency of what Basil Willey has called his 'believing temper' and his 'questing intellect'.[22] Coleridge told Poole:

> I read every book that came in my way without distinction – and my father was fond of me, & used to take me on his knee, and hold long conversations with me. I remember, that at eight years old I walked with him one winter evening from a farmer's house, a mile from Ottery – & he told me the names of the stars – and how Jupiter was a thousand times larger than our world – and that the other twinkling stars were suns that had worlds rolling round them – & when I came home, he shewed me how they rolled round –/. I heard him with a profound delight & admiration; but without the least mixture of wonder or incredulity. For from my early reading of Faery Tales, & Genii &c &c – my mind had been habituated *to the Vast* – & I never regarded *my senses* in any way as the criteria of my belief.[23]

By the time his father died, Coleridge was the last son remaining at home. All his brothers had gone out into the world at a remarkably young age. In 1781 his oldest brother John, born in 1754, was already in India, in the army. From there he immediately took on the role of protector of his 'tribe of brothers', sending home money and advice, buying a commission in the army for the third oldest brother James, and concerning himself even with the welfare of his youngest brother Samuel, whom he had never seen. John, who died in 1787 while suffering from malaria and depression, also looked after Frank, the villain of Coleridge's childhood adventure. The Rcvd John Coleridge had died the day after returning from taking eleven-year-old Frank to Plymouth to enlist as a midshipman. Frank's ship sailed to India, where he met his oldest brother and left the Navy to join John in the Indian Army. The precocious Frank, known as the 'handsome Coleridge', died by his own hand while feverish, during preparations for the Siege of Seringapatam early in 1792.[24]

Of Coleridge's remaining brothers William, the second son, was to become a schoolmaster and clergyman like his father and to die at the age of twenty-three. James, born in 1759, pursued a successful career in the army, becoming a Lieutenant-Colonel in 1807, and fathering six sons who were to have brilliant undergraduate careers at Oxford and Cambridge in the 1810s. One of them, Henry Nelson Coleridge, became very important in Coleridge's own later life.

Edward, born in 1760, lived a long life, marrying a woman '20 years older than his Mother' and settling at Ottery St Mary as 'an idle Parson', in Coleridge's disparaging words.[25] Next came George, born in 1764, who eventually succeeded his father as clergyman and headmaster of the King's School at Ottery. George also became, to his credit and often to his discomfort, 'father, brother, and every thing' to his little brother Samuel (see plate 2).[26] Coleridge's last brother – one having died in infancy – was Luke, seven years his senior and a doctor. In 1790 Luke died aged twenty-four, having walked the wards at the London Hospital in the later 1780s, when Coleridge was at Christ's Hospital School in the capital.

The only Coleridge sister, Ann (known as Nancy), was five years older than Samuel. She died shortly after Luke, early in 1791. The successive deaths of Luke and Nancy prompted Coleridge's schoolboy sonnet 'On Receiving an Account that his only Sister's Death was Inevitable', which begins:

> The tear which mourn'd a brother's fate scarce dry –
> Pain after pain, and woe succeeding woe –
> Is my heart destin'd for another blow?
> O my sweet sister! and must thou too die?

This poem, unremarkable as we might expect from an eighteen-year-old, was not published until 1834. The manuscript has an interesting, perhaps significant, variation. Lines 9–12 of the printed version run:

> Say, is this hollow eye, this heartless pain,
> Fated to rove thro' Life's wide cheerless plain –
> Nor father, brother, sister meet its ken –
> My woes, my joys unshared!

In the manuscript, by a slip of the pen, the poem lists 'mother' instead of 'father' among his dead relatives in line 11.[27]

The Coleridges were a family remarkable for their intellectual precocity, their various talents and, according to Coleridge – though he excepted himself – for their good looks.[28] What they did not possess was wealth. John in his letters from India was most worried about the effect of his family's poverty on his sister. He was horrified to hear of a plan to send the sixteen-year-old Nancy to Exeter in 1783 to learn a trade, writing vehemently to James:

> I would rather live all the rest of my days on Bread and Water than see my Sister standing behind a Counter where she is hourly open to the insults of

every conceited Puppy that may choose to purchase a Yard of Ribbon from her, horrid Idea! chucked under the chin, &c., &c., too bad to mention, for God's sake get her back, don't let her go to destruction, as some others have.[29]

John alludes here to the millinery trade, which was associated in the public mind with prostitution. When Coleridge met and became engaged to Sara Fricker in 1795, she and her mother and sisters were living in similarly reduced circumstances after the death of Mr Fricker, and they made a modest living by needlework. Sara seems to have compensated for the potential embarrassment of her occupation by an assumption of genteel manners which was a source of irritation to Coleridge and of humour to his family.[30]

The immediate result of his father's death was that Coleridge and his mother and sister moved out of the large schoolhouse into the Warden's House nearby. Thus the loss of the father was compounded by a loss of the family home, of income (however modest), and of status. Once more, the size and importance of the Church and School of Ottery St Mary should be borne in mind. The Coleridge pride, of both mother and son, must have taken a heavy blow. A few months later Coleridge was sent for by a former pupil of his father's, Judge Buller, who arranged for him to attend Christ's Hospital School, the famous school in Newgate Street, in the City of London, founded to educate the sons of poor gentry. The family pride may have suffered even over this arrangement. Coleridge's friend Henry Crabb Robinson heard in 1812 that Judge Buller had originally offered to send him to Charterhouse, and that the family felt degraded by his final settlement at a school for poor orphans, however prestigious it might be academically. According to this account, which may have originated with Coleridge himself, Coleridge's brothers were ashamed to have him visit them in his school uniform and Judge Buller himself was so snobbish in the matter that the sensitive schoolboy stopped visiting at his London house too.[31] The story has the ring of truth when we read Coleridge's accounts of his extreme loneliness as a schoolboy.

So the nine-year-old Samuel left Devon and his family for the rigours of a great London boarding school. He already felt himself to be special; he was a 'character', a prodigy in learning, inclined to be solitary but desperate for affection, a boy of keen sensibilities, easily frightened – 'haunted by spectres' on reading fairy stories and the *Arabian Nights* – yet bold and with 'a memory & understanding forced into almost unnatural ripeness', as he told Poole.[32] He combined, as gifted children often do, an advanced intelligence with emotional immaturity. His sojourn at school was unlikely to be a completely happy one.

A story is told of Coleridge at the age of three or four which, like many such anecdotes, may not be entirely trustworthy. Whether true or not, however, it catches perfectly the ambition, the fancifulness, and the reckless courting of danger which characterized Coleridge both as a precocious boy and as a grown – though in many respects immature – man. Coleridge's first publisher, Cottle, is the source of the account:

> Little Sammy Coleridge had heard of fishing, and thought he could catch fish as well as his elders. With this impression strong on his mind he went to his sister Ann, (older than himself) and asked for a hook and line, when she crooked a pin, and tying it to a piece of thread, told him to go and bring home all the fish he could catch in the gutter flowing through the street. Little Sammy thought he should never be able to catch any thing better than eels, in that ignoble current, and having an ambition to catch a whale, he hurried off toward the River Otter. The evening was coming on, and not finding a whale, in one part of the river, he posted off further down; and proceeding still in his lofty pursuit, he wandered to a great distance; till, overcome with weariness, he lay down on the bank of the river, and there fell fast asleep.[33]

On 28 March 1782 Coleridge's mother wrote her petition to the Governors of Christ's Hospital, supported by her husband's successor as vicar, the Revd Fulwood Smerdon, and by Coleridge's godfather, Samuel Taylor. The form of admission required that she 'humbly beseech your Worships, in your usual Pity and Charity to distressed Men, poor Widows, and Fatherless Children, to grant Admission of [here she filled in her son's name and his age – 'nine Years and six Months'] there to be Educated and brought up among other poor Children'.[34]

Coleridge was accepted, and began his studies in September 1782, with six preliminary weeks at the preparatory school in Hertford. But first he spent some two or three months living with his mother's brother in London. Perhaps his mother thought the visit would accustom him to London and being away from home; perhaps she was not sorry to lose him. Coleridge is silent on this point, but his brief sketch to Poole of his sojourn with his uncle is written in that proud, ironic, defensive-aggressive tone he often adopted to mask feelings of rejection or anxiety. He turns the episode into a mock-heroic one, with his nine-year-old self at the centre. It is worth noting that his maternal uncle was a tradesman, and so a cut below the Coleridges. Young Sam probably felt himself – and was apparently treated as – a rather superior creature:

> I accordingly went to London, and was received by my mother's Brother, Mr Bowden, a Tobacconist & (at the same time) clerk to an Underwriter. My Uncle lived at the corner of the Stock exchange, & carried on his shop by means of a confidential Servant, who, I suppose, fleeced him most unmercifully. – He was a widower, & had one daughter . . . He was generous as the air & a man of very considerable talents – but he was a Sot. – He received me with great affection, and I stayed ten weeks at his house, during which time I went occasionally to Judge Buller's. My Uncle was very proud of me, & used to carry me from Coffee-house to Coffee-house, and Tavern to Tavern, where I drank, & talked & disputed as if I had been a man –/. Nothing was more common than for a large party to exclaim in my hearing, that I *was a prodigy*, &c &c &c

– so that, while I remained at my Uncle's, I was most completely spoilt & pampered, both mind & body.[35]

Here we witness the first, but by no means the last, scene in Coleridge's life in which he holds an audience in thrall. He was not yet ten years old.

Christ's Hospital was founded in 1552 by Edward VI – 'the boy patron of boys', as Charles Lamb called him[36] – on the site of an earlier Franciscan monastery (see plate 3). It was intended for orphans and the children of the poor. When Coleridge arrived, it was a free establishment for the children of poor gentry, but one which, for all its association with poverty and misfortune, inculcated pride in its pupils. As Lamb wrote in one of two essays recalling his and Coleridge's time there, 'the Christ's Hospital boy feels that he is no charity-boy; he feels it in the antiquity and regality of the foundation to which he belongs', and in the ancient privileges accorded to pupils, such as special dispensation to visit the Tower of London and solemn processions through the City at Easter with treats from the Lord Mayor.[37] According to Leigh Hunt, who joined the school in 1791, just after Coleridge had left, the feeling among the boys was that their school was 'a medium between the patrician pretension of such schools as Eton and Westminster, and the plebeian submission of the charity schools'.[38]

Coleridge himself wrote sometimes with pride, sometimes with loathing, about his nine years at the school. His most positive memory came very late in his life, and was obviously carefully adapted to the recipients. Writing a testimonial for Dr Gillman's son to the Worshipful Company of Haberdashers in the City, he described his education in formal terms as having taken place at an 'honored and unique Institution' where he was 'under the tutorage and discipline of the Revd James Bowyer who has left an honored name in the Church for the zeal and ability with which he formed and trained his Orphan Pupils to the Sacred Ministry'.[39]

His descriptions of the Revd James Boyer (or Bowyer) were not always so polite. Though he praised his old headmaster's sense and severity in *Biographia Literaria* (1817), expressing amused appreciation of Boyer's merciless criticism of his and his schoolmates' efforts at verse, he also confessed that Boyer's cruelty and flogging haunted his dreams. In a sentence typical of Coleridge's divided mind at the time of writing *Biographia*, he showed himself torn between reverence and loathing for Boyer. The balance ultimately tips, somewhat fulsomely, in favour of reverence:

> The reader will, I trust, excuse this tribute of recollection to a man, whose severities, even now, not seldom furnish the dreams, by which the blind fancy would fain interpret to the mind the painful sensations of distempered sleep; but neither lessen nor dim the deep sense of my moral and intellectual obligations.[40]

Lamb and Hunt were more frank in their published recollections, describing Boyer as an ardent flogger and petty tyrant. Indeed in 1820 Lamb wickedly countered Coleridge's 'ample encomium' in *Biographia* by quoting a 'pious ejaculation' made by Coleridge himself on hearing that his old master was dying. 'Poor J. B.!' he apparently said, 'may all his faults be forgiven; and may he be wafted to bliss by little cherub boys, all head and wings, with no *bottoms* to reproach his sublunary infirmities'.[41] Though in 1830 Coleridge could describe with equanimity a flogging he received at thirteen for having declared that he could not become a clergyman because he was an infidel,[42] we can imagine that it was not at all to the liking of the proud, sensitive boy at the time.

In two lectures on education, one delivered at the Royal Institution in 1808 and the other in Bristol in 1813, Coleridge spoke out strongly against humiliating punishments such as making children sit in the 'dunces' row', as he had once had to do. He also attacked the 'barbarous ignominious punishments' advocated by a contemporary educationalist, Joseph Lancaster, which included fastening wooden shackles to a boy's neck or from elbow to elbow behind the desk.[43] Though he was inclined to accept that flogging could spur boys to 'Spartan fortitude', he also declared roundly that 'little is taught or communicated by contest or dispute, but every thing by sympathy and love'.[44]

Christ's Hospital was divided into five separate departments: a grammar school, a mathematical or navigational school, a writing school, a reading school, and a drawing school. Boys were prepared for the Navy and East India service at the navigation school and for trade and commerce at the writing school. The best scholars attended the grammar school, and the very best three or four of these, known as Grecians, were prepared by Boyer himself for University. In due course Coleridge, already precocious and soon to be fabled for his schoolboy learning, became a Grecian, and was looked up to then, and for the rest of his life, by at least one junior schoolfellow, the Deputy Grecian Charles Lamb.

But at first Coleridge was just one nine-year-old among many, thrown into a tough regime of scanty diet, hard work, and that severe hierarchy conducive to cruelty which prevailed at most public schools. (Southey had an equally deprived time at the more favoured Westminster School, from which he was expelled for publishing a schoolboy magazine, *The Flagellant*, in protest against the practice of flogging.) Boys who lived in London and had a family to go to at weekends and holidays were luckier. Lamb was one of these. In his essay, 'Christ's Hospital Five and Thirty Years Ago' (1820), he performs an act of sympathy towards his old friend Coleridge by writing the essay largely from Coleridge's point of view. The food given to the boys, from 'Monday's milk porritch, blue and tasteless' to Friday's 'scanty mutton scrags', could be supplemented for a boy like Lamb by tea, hot rolls, and plates of roast beef brought to the school every day by a maid or a kind aunt. But 'I was a poor friendless boy', writes Lamb, posing as Coleridge:

> My parents, and those who should care for me, were far away. Those few acquaintances of theirs, which they could reckon upon being kind to me in the great city, after a little forced notice, which they had the grace to take of me on my first arrival in town, soon grew tired of my holiday visits . . . I felt alone among six hundred playmates.
>
> O the cruelty of separating a poor lad from his early homestead! The yearnings which I used to have towards it in those unfledged years! How, in my dreams, would my native town (far in the west) come back, with its church, and trees, and faces![45]

Lamb's sympathy was genuine and well placed, as was the implicit criticism of Coleridge's family and friends for their neglect. Coleridge seems to have gone home to Ottery only three or four times in nine years. He told Godwin that at school he was treated 'with contumely & brutality', and that he took refuge 'in a sunny corner, shutting his eyes, & imagining himself at home'.[46] In notebooks, though not in print, Coleridge remembered the utter misery of the periodical whole-day holidays the boys 'enjoyed'. With no friends to visit – had he offended his jovial uncle Bowden, or was he too ashamed of him to go to his house? – Coleridge was let loose to fill these days as best he could. Lamb writes for him:

> The long warm days of summer never return but they bring with them a gloom from the haunting memory of those *whole-day*-leaves, when, by some strange arrangement, we were turned out, for the live-long day, upon our own hands, whether we had friends to go to, or none . . .
>
> It was worse in the days of winter, to go prowling about the streets objectless – shivering at cold windows of print-shops, to extract a little amusement; or haply, as a last resort, in the hope of a little novelty, to pay a fifty-times repeated visit (where our individual faces should be as well known to the warden as those of his own charges) to the Lions in the Tower – to whose levée, by courtesy immemorial, we had a prescriptive title to admission.[47]

There is a telling notebook entry of 1802, in which Coleridge discusses the importance of

> breeding up children *happy* to at least 15 or 16 illustrated in my always dreaming of Christ Hospital and when not quite well having all those uneasy feelings which I had at School/ feelings of Easter Monday &c.[48]

In another note Coleridge recalled how he had been moping about the City on one holiday, when, in a fine recapitulation of his father's adventure by the wayside, he was taken up by a Samaritan:

> From 8 to 14 I was a playless Day-dreamer, an Helluo Librorum [devourer of books], my appetite for which was indulged by a singular Incident; a stranger who struck by my conversation made me free of a great Circulating Library in King's Street, Cheapside – & I *read thro'* the whole Catalogue, folios and all.[49]

In 1785 Samuel's loneliness was relieved somewhat by the arrival in London of his brothers Luke and George, Luke to study medicine and George to teach at a school in Hackney. Coleridge's earliest letters are to these brothers; they show him fond of them and dependent on their good will and approval. He scarcely mentions his mother in these schoolboy letters, noticeable for their precocity and striving for effect. The one extant letter to his mother was written when he was twelve and a half years old. It is a cool document, concerned mainly with the business of thanking her and other friends for sending handkerchiefs, half-crowns, and plum cake, and ending with greetings from 'your dutiful son, S. Coleridge'.[50]

When Luke returned to Devon to practise medicine, young Samuel missed him. He had a schoolfriend, Charles Valentine Le Grice, but he was no substitute for the company of a brother with whom he had walked the wards at the London Hospital on free Saturdays, becoming, as he later told Gillman, 'wild to be apprenticed to a surgeon'.[51] After Luke had left London Coleridge wrote to him rather forlornly in May 1787:

> Legrice, and I, are very polite, very civil, and very cold. So that I doubly lament your absence, as I have now no one, to whom I can open my heart in full confidence. I wish you would *remedy* that evil by keeping up an epistolary correspondence with me.[52]

This letter is the first to enclose a poem he has written, in this case one called 'Easter Holidays', in which the fourteen-year-old poet (suppressing the horrors of those lonely Easter Monday leave days) celebrates in sub-Miltonic fashion 'festal Easter' with its processions and joyful anthems – 'jocund noise' – and piously compares present mirth with future sorrows: 'dire Misfortune's varied smarts,/ Which youthful years conceal'.[53]

This is also the first letter in which Coleridge apologizes for not replying sooner. His elaborate excuse is ominous. He has sat down no fewer than five times to write, but has torn up his efforts five times, because 'all was STUFF, as Mr Boyer phrases it'.[54] It was in a letter to Godwin in 1802 that Coleridge best described his failings as a correspondent and in general:

> In plain & natural English, I am a dreaming & therefore an indolent man. I am a Starling self-incaged, & always in the Moult, & my whole Note is, Tomorrow, & tomorrow, & tomorrow.[55]

If this penetration into his own character, especially its shortcomings, came later, Coleridge already showed a propensity as a youth to present himself in a slightly mocking way, usually in order to pre-empt a criticism he expected from others. Thus in a letter of May 1791 to his brother George he wrote lightly of his poor record as a letter writer:

> I intended to have written to my Brother James – but Mr Pitt and I have the honor of resembling one another in one particular – he in his *bellatory*, and I in my *epistolary* department – we are both men of *Preparations*.[56]

The reference is to the warnings by William Pitt, the Prime Minister, that revolutionary France was intending to invade Britain. This is Coleridge's first reference to Pitt, but by no means the last, and by no means the most critical.

Coleridge's progress at Christ's Hospital was relatively smooth. Though he spent much time in the school sanatorium – he remembered being in a 'continual low fever' at the age of fourteen – his precociousness was soon noticed. He carried on the solitary reading and dreaming habits already established at Ottery St Mary. Indeed, the common metaphor of devouring books is given a freshness and intensity by the adult Coleridge when he recalled this time:

> My whole being was, with eyes closed to every object of present sense, to crumple myself up in a sunny corner, and read, read, read; fancy myself on Robinson Crusoe's island, finding a mountain of plumb-cake, and eating a room for myself, and then eating it into the shapes of tables and chairs – hunger and fancy![57]

The description has a Dickensian dimension; one remembers how David Copperfield describes himself, a virtual prisoner in the home of his callous stepfather, being saved by having books to read. Many of the books Dickens lists are ones we know Coleridge to have enjoyed at Ottery and Christ's Hospital. *Roderick Random, Peregrine Pickle, Humphrey Clinker, Tom Jones, The Vicar of Wakefield, Don Quixote, Robinson Crusoe,* the *Arabian Nights,* 'came out', writes Dickens-as-Copperfield, 'a glorious host to keep me company'. David Copperfield read, at this time, 'as if for life'.[58] The same might equally be said of the boy Coleridge.

But Coleridge did not confine himself to works of the imagination. He was an excellent classical scholar, and soon began to read works of classical philosophy. In *Biographia Literaria* he wrote half-boastfully, half-regretfully, 'At a very premature age, even before my fifteenth year, I had bewildered myself [note the apologetic verb] in metaphysicks, and in theological controversy'.[59] His claim is corroborated by Lamb, who remembered Coleridge as one of the top boys – the Grecians – during his last years at Christ's Hospital. Famously, and movingly, Lamb conjures up a picture of his admired friend in his 1820 essay on the school:

> Come back into memory, like as thou wert in the day-spring of thy fancies, with hope like a fiery column before thee – the dark pillar not yet turned – Samuel Taylor Coleridge – Logician, Metaphysician, Bard! – How have I seen the casual passer through the Cloisters stand still, intranced with admiration (while he weighed the disproportion between the *speech* and the *garb* of the young Mirandula), to hear thee unfold, in thy deep and sweet intonations, the mysteries of Jamblichus, or Plotinus (for even in those years thou waxedst not pale at such philosophic draughts), or reciting Homer in his Greek, or

Pindar – while the walls of the old Grey Friars re-echoed to the accents of the *inspired charity-boy!*[60]

Once more Coleridge is at the centre of an admiring group, though here he is the hero of another's narrative, not his own. The precocity; the ability to astonish, even transfix, onlookers and listeners; the slovenliness of his appearance contrasted with the elegance of his speech; all these details recur in descriptions of Coleridge in his most natural mode – talking. Lamb resorted of necessity to describing Coleridge in legendary terms when he wrote, after the shock of his friend's death: 'Never saw I his likeness, nor probably the world can see again.'[61]

Though later one of Coleridge's closest friends, Lamb appears to have been, at Christ's Hospital, an admirer at a distance. Coleridge's best friends were Le Grice and Robert Allen, both of whom continued the friendship after leaving school.

It was with Allen that Coleridge began to visit the hospitable London home of a younger boy, Tom Evans, in 1788. Tom had three sisters, Mary, Anne and Elizabeth, 'and of course I fell in love with the eldest', said Coleridge much later.[62] He was to continue 'in love' with Mary until after he had met his future wife, Sara Fricker, but Mary did not fully return his feelings. In any case, he was probably more sentimentally than passionately attached to her, having met her when he was only fifteen or sixteen. The deeper attraction of the Evans household was the widowed Mrs Evans, who presented a more maternal figure than Coleridge's own mother. It was to Mrs Evans's 'care' that he betook himself for a fortnight at Christmas 1791 after his first term at Cambridge, not to Ottery. As he told his brother George, rather pompously, after that visit, 'I have indeed experienced from her a tenderness scarcely inferior to the solicitude of maternal affection'. He urged George to visit her at Villiers Street, assuring him that he would find the family 'not only a very amiable, but a very sensible' one.[63]

It is interesting that he sought to appease his brother with such assurances. He did so not least because Mrs Evans's daughters worked in a milliner's shop in Jermyn Street, and Samuel knew how his brothers viewed *that* lowly profession. His letters to Mrs Evans herself indicate that he enjoyed the company of her family so much more than that of his own because he could indulge his sense of fun and foolishness at her house. In February 1792 he wrote her a letter full of happy and flirtatious self-exposure:

> You and my Sisters have the very first row in the front box of my Heart's little theatre . . . In short, my dear Mrs Evans! my whole heart shall be laid open like any sheep's heart: my Virtues, if I have any, shall not be more exposed to your view than my Weaknesses. Indeed I am of opinion, that Foibles are the cement of Affection, and that, however we may *admire* a perfect character, we are seldom inclined to love or praise those, whom we cannot sometimes

blame. – Come Ladies! will you take your seats in this play house? Fool that I
am! Are you not already there? Believe me, You are.[64]

Referring to a forthcoming journey of Mrs Evans and Mary to their
native Wales, Coleridge sends a poem, 'To Disappointment', in which he
allows himself to imagine her his mother:

> Then haste thee, Nymph of balmy gales!
> Thy poet's prayer, sweet May! attend!
> Oh! place my Parent and my Friend
> 'Mid her lovely native vales.

There follows a promise to join them if possible: 'I may steal down
from Cambridge about the beginning of April just to look at you'.[65]
'Steal' suggests the pleasurable frisson of planning something slightly
treacherous.

Coleridge could clearly unbutton his language with the Evanses in a way
which was impossible with his own family. He ends his letter with a parody
of girlish chit-chat (as found in Sheridan's plays or Jane Austen's novels),
and a naughty pun on 'making water':

> La! it will be so charming to walk out in one's own *garding*, and sit and drink
> Tea in an arbour, and pick pretty nosegays – To plant and transplant – and be
> dirty and amused! – Then to look with contempt on you Londoners with your
> mock gardens at your smoky windows – making a beggarly shew of withered
> flowers stuck in pint pots, and quart pots, and chamber pots – menacing the
> heads of the passengers below. Foh! Oh! 'twill be very *praty* to make water –
> I meant to say – to water the *garding* morn and eve – O La! give me your
> advice.[66]

All his life Coleridge was to be attracted to circles of women, often
mothers and daughters with no male protector. The Evanses were the first;
when Coleridge met the Fricker women in 1794 – a mother with five
daughters – he was happy to act once more as surrogate son-cum-brother-
cum-wooer. Later he was to seek comfort from the women of the
Wordsworth–Hutchinson family, then the Morgan family, and finally Mrs
Gillman. He was ever seeking the perfect female family he had not known
in his youth. As for the need to love a woman sexually, that seems to have
been invariably confused with these yearnings to be mothered and be-
friended. As ever, though he was to behave with staggering lack of sympathy
towards both his wife and Sara Hutchinson, he diagnosed his own problem.
In a notebook of April 1805 he mused indirectly on his disastrous propensity to idealize women, half-echoing Miranda's wonder – 'O brave new
world/ That has such people in't' – in *The Tempest* on first seeing men other
than her father and Caliban. Coleridge wrote:

> But so it would be with a man bred up in a Wilderness by unseen Beings, who
> should yet converse and rationalize – how beautiful would not the first other

man appear, whom he saw, & knew to be a man by the resemblance to his own image seen in the clear Stream/ he would in like manner attribute to the man all the divine attributes of humanity, tho' haply it should be a very ordinary or even almost ugly man, compared with a hundred others. Many of us have felt this with respect to women, who have been bred up where few are to be seen/ and I acknowledge that both in persons and in poems it is well *on the whole* that we should retain our first Loves, tho' alike in both cases evils have happened as the consequence.[67]

Coleridge was aware of the muddle in his feelings towards women. Not only was he guiltily in love with Sara Hutchinson, Wordsworth's 'sister' and therefore a kind of sister to him too; he also confessed to a feeling of horror at having sexual intercourse with his wife: 'I freeze and am horrified at the thought of conjugal meeting', he told Morgan in 1812, in a Latin postscript to a letter, 'as though my wife were my very own sister'.[68]

Coleridge's juvenile poetry, most of it not published until after his death, gives little foretaste of what was to come only a few years later. The poems written at Christ's Hospital are composite imitations of some or all the usual models: the *L'Allegro, Il Penseroso* and *Lycidas* of Milton; the abstract odes of Gray; and the 'progress poems' of Thomson, Gray and Collins, those allegorical tours tracing an abstraction such as 'Poetry' or 'Liberty' from birth in classical civilization up to its present apogee in the England of the eighteenth century.[69] In Coleridge's earliest poems a large proportion of the nouns are personalised, capitalised abstractions. Every noun, abstract or not, has its attendant adjective, or sometimes two, with the noun sandwiched between them or, for variation, with the noun preceded by a double epithet. 'Feather'd songsters', 'smoothly-flowing Thames', 'dire Misfortune', 'much-lov'd Friend', 'with frequent slaughter red', 'soft Compassion', 'wildly-working visions', 'meek-eyed Power', 'red-hot pincers dread' are but a few examples.[70]

As Coleridge remembered it, his headmaster had been fierce about such bombast, exclaiming, '*Harp? Harp? Lyre? Pen and ink, boy, you mean! Muse, boy, Muse? your Nurse's daughter, you mean! Pierian spring? Oh 'aye! the cloister-pump, I suppose!*'[71] If Boyer did offer the sensible advice to drop such affectations, his star pupil was conspicuously slow to follow it. Though he began to find his own poetic voice in 1794, he was still capable of writing examples of 'turgid ode and tumid stanza' – to quote Byron's swipe at his early style in 'English Bards and Scotch Reviewers' (1809) – for some years to come.

Conventional though his schoolboy poems are, there are one or two which give some indication of his feelings and concerns between the ages of fourteen and eighteen. His resented but admired brother Frank, the precocious midshipman, is the likely addressee of his 1787 poem 'Dura Navis'. Frank had set sail six years before, at the impressively young age of eleven, and Coleridge, himself only fourteen or fifteen, enjoys imagining Frank's loneliness and homesickness and exposure to danger:

> To tempt the dangerous deep, too venturous youth,
> Why does thy breast with fondest wishes glow?
> No tender parent there thy cares shall sooth,
> No much-lov'd Friend shall share thy every woe.
> Why does thy mind with hopes delusive burn?
> Vain are thy Schemes by heated Fancy plann'd:
> Thy promised joy thou'lt see to Sorrow turn
> Exil'd from Bliss, and from thy native land.

Not only does Coleridge here project on to Frank his own sense of exile and friendlessness, placed as he was in a school founded for orphans. He also fancies, with some relish, Frank facing 'the horrors of a Naval Fight,/ When thundering Cannons spread a sea of Gore':

> What dreadful scenes appear before my eyes!
> Ah! see how each with frequent slaughter red,
> Regardless of his dying fellow's cries
> O'er their fresh wounds with impious order tread![72]

There is more. Should the young sailor survive the battle, Coleridge conjures up for him 'a fate more cruel still' – to eat or be eaten when the desperate crew resorts to cannibalism in order to survive.[73] Coleridge can settle a personal score in the relative safety from reproach or retaliation offered by the poetic medium.

While still at school, Coleridge bemoaned in a sonnet, as we have seen, the deaths of Luke and Nancy, and morbidly identified himself with the luckless suicide Chatterton in his 'Monody' copied in 1790 into a Christ's Hospital book of poetry kept by Mr Boyer. In 1790, too, he wrote his response to the destruction of the Bastille in July 1789, the event which enthused all radicals and liberals, schoolboys and students, before the onset of the Terror a few years later. Coleridge himself was to become a much more fiery radical in the years from 1792 to 1795, in Cambridge and Bristol, than he showed himself to be in this schoolboy ode.

The abstractions Freedom, Tyranny, Oppression, Anguish, Liberty, and Power are much in evidence in 'The Destruction of the Bastile'. Coleridge welcomes France's 'wild' breaking of the 'triple chain' in terms not very different from the Whig progress poems he was still imitating. In other words, rather than events in France suggesting to his mind the necessity for, or desirability of, a similar revolution in England, those events are subsumed by the smugly patriotic schoolboy into the language of historical parliamentary independence and the wise use of power in 'favour'd Britain', 'First ever of the first and freest of the free!' He expresses the hope (not to be fulfilled by Pitt the Younger's government) that Britain will exert herself to help Belgium in her efforts to gain freedom from Austrian power. But his praise of 'glad Liberty' is a mere conventionalism.[74]

The sonnet 'Pain', subtitled 'Composed in Sickness', was probably written during Coleridge's last year at school, when, as he remembered it, he spent 'full half the time in the sick-ward of Christ's Hospital, afflicted with jaundice and rheumatic fever' brought on partly by his recklessness in swimming fully dressed across the New River and keeping on his wet clothes afterwards.[75] Coleridge writes conventionally enough about 'Life's gilded scenes' and delight chased away by the 'Tyrant Pain'.[76] But he was already acquainted not only with bereavement, but also with chronic illness, for which he had been prescribed – as was common – opium for the relief of feverish symptoms. He mentions opium as an old friend in a letter from Cambridge to his brother George in November 1791. Describing 'a fit of Rheumatism' which has 'nailed' him to his bed, he writes blithely, 'Opium never used to have any disagreeable effects on me, but it has upon many.'[77]

The addictive properties of opium were not understood in Coleridge's lifetime, or even for several decades after that. It was widely prescribed for a variety of complaints which are now treated by aspirin and other analgesics.[78] Like Wilberforce, Sir James Mackintosh, Dean Milner, De Quincey and other well-known 'opium-eaters', Coleridge first took the drug under medical advice. That he soon became aware of pleasurable sensations after taking opium is clear from his early, guilt-free references to its effects in addition to giving relief from pain.

Even sober, respectable George Coleridge apparently enjoyed these pleasurable side-effects. Coleridge wrote to him in 1798, cheerfully describing having taken laudanum (tincture of opium) to alleviate toothache:

Laudanum gave me repose, not sleep: but YOU, I believe, know how divine that repose is – what a spot of inchantment, a green spot of fountains, & flowers & trees, in the very heart of a waste of Sands![79]

The vocabulary echoes that of 'Kubla Khan', written only a few months before.

By the time Coleridge wrote this letter to George, though he could still mention laudanum in the same breath with pleasure, he was already discovering what De Quincey, in his *Confessions of an English Opium-Eater* (1822) calls 'The Pains of Opium'. From about 1801 he would refer to his habit in letters to friends as 'the ACCURSED habit', 'this detested poison', 'this wretched vice', and in his published works more obliquely as 'mismanaged sensibility'.[80]

In 1789, when Coleridge was in his seventeenth year, an older Grecian, Thomas Middleton (later Bishop of Calcutta), gave him an edition of William Lisle Bowles's *Sonnets, Written Chiefly on Picturesque Spots, During a Tour*, published in Bath that year. These sentimental but attractively direct poems exercised an immediate, if not lasting, influence on Coleridge, who addressed a sonnet of his own to Bowles in 1794, praising his 'soft strains'.[81]

Bowles's gentle influence joined with that of another, better, living poet, William Cowper, to add to the Pantheon of dead poetic predecessors. Cowper, whose conversational poem, *The Task*, was published in 1785, was, with Bowles, Coleridge said in *Biographia Literaria*, 'the first who combined natural thoughts with natural diction; the first who reconciled the heart with the head'.[82] In a letter to John Thelwall in December 1796, in which he consciously laid himself bare, much as he did to Poole, he described his 'style of Writing' as both his own and deriving from many models:

> But do not let us introduce an act of Uniformity against Poets – I have room enough in *my* brain to admire, aye & almost equally, the *head* and fancy of Akenside, and the *heart* and fancy of Bowles, the solemn Lordliness of Milton, & the divine Chit chat of Cowper.[83]

This is rather a good summing up of the conglomerate of influences on Coleridge the schoolboy poet during his last year at Christ's Hospital. They lie behind his sonnet 'On Quitting School for College', in which, as befits such an exercise, he takes a fond farewell of school, and also of his Ottery home which he had left long before, in terms more positive than were his actual feelings about both places:

> Farewell parental scenes! a sad farewell!
> To you my grateful heart still fondly clings,
> Tho' fluttering round on Fancy's burnish'd wings
> Her tales of future Joy Hope loves to tell.
> Adieu, adieu! ye much-lov'd cloisters pale!
> Ah! would those happy days return again,
> When 'neath your arches, free from every stain,
> I heard of guilt and wonder'd at the tale!
> Dear haunts! where oft my simple lays I sang,
> Listening meanwhile the echoes of my feet,
> Lingering I quit you with as great a pang,
> As when erewhile, my weeping childhood, torn
> By early sorrow from my native seat,
> Mingled its tears with hers – my widow'd Parent lorn.[84]

School was to recur in some of Coleridge's worst nightmares, especially in the terrible, opium-ridden years 1802–3.[85] His warm feelings towards school relate undoubtedly to his friendships, to his out-of-school activities with the Evanses, and to his early love of learning. Both he and Wordsworth, who drew on the differences in their upbringings in *The Prelude*, presented his schooldays as a time of deprivation:

> For I was reared
> In the great city, pent 'mid cloisters dim,
> And saw nought lovely but the sky and stars
> (Coleridge, 'Frost at Midnight', 1798)

Compare:

> Of rivers, fields,
> And groves, I speak to thee, my friend – to thee
> Who, yet a liveried schoolboy in the depths
> Of the huge city, on the leaded roof
> Of that wide edifice, thy home and school,
> Wast used to lie and gaze upon the clouds
> Moving in heaven, or haply, tired of this,
> To shut thine eyes and by internal light
> See trees, and meadows, and thy native stream
> Far distant – thus beheld from year to year
> Of thy long exile.
>   Wordsworth *Prelude* (1805) VI

Both poets here exploit the country-versus-city topos, but both allow a certain beauty, even a positive formative influence, to the scene at Christ's Hospital. Coleridge also connected his schooltime visits to the roof with his first stirrings of love for 'a Maiden' – Mary Evans – in the verse-letter to Sara Hutchinson of 4 April 1802 which in its scaled-down version was to become the famous 'Dejection' ode. This particular verse, dropped from the published poem, is interesting for several reasons. In it, Coleridge is looking back to early feelings of love for a woman, and there is a pointedness in the fact that he addresses this poem to *another* woman. (Both Mary Evans and Sara Hutchinson were unavailable to him.) He also refers back to a time of hopefulness about his future as both lover and poet; now, in 1802, he bewails his failure in both roles. Yet the voice of the poet in this poem – or at least in parts of it – is as strong as it had ever been.

True to the complexity of his feelings towards Christ's Hospital, Coleridge paints a verbal picture of his days there which beautifully contains the paradox of a sorrowing nostalgia for a past time when he had looked forward in hopes of future happiness. Coleridge shows himself master of the varied stanza and line length and the loose syntax and rhyme scheme of the ode as the verse moves rhetorically through several related but different moods:

> Feebly! O feebly! – Yet
> (I well remember it)
> In my first Dawn of Youth that Fancy stole
> With many secret Yearnings on my Soul.
> At eve, sky-gazing in 'ecstatic fit'
> (Alas! for cloister'd in a city School
> The sky was all, I knew, of Beautiful)
> At the barr'd window often did I sit,
> And oft upon the leaded School-roof lay,
>   And to myself would say –
> There does not live the Man so stripp'd of good affections
> As not to love to see a Maiden's quiet Eyes

Uprais'd, and linking on sweet Dreams by dim Connections
To Moon, or Evening Star, or glorious western Skies –
While yet a Boy, this Thought would so pursue me
That often it became a kind of Vision to me![86]

There is a boldness and flexibility about this writing that confirms
Wordsworth's assertion that Coleridge had 'a perfect mastery' of the poetic
medium. The boy who left Christ's Hospital, aged eighteen and a half, in
the summer of 1791, was still some years away from demonstrating to
himself and others that he was a real poet. First he had some living and
learning to do. In September 1791 he went up to Jesus College, Cambridge,
on a Christ's Hospital scholarship, full of academic promise.

2

Cambridge and Pantisocracy
1791–1794

Where graced with many a classic spoil
CAM rolls his reverend stream along,
I haste to urge the learnèd toil
That sternly chides my love-lorn song.
　　　　　　Coleridge 'Absence: A Farewell Ode on Quitting
　　　　　　School for Jesus College, Cambridge' (1791)

On 16 October 1791, a few days before his nineteenth birthday, Coleridge wrote to his brother George (still teaching in Hackney), 'Here I am – Videlicet – Jesus College'.[1] He had an Exhibition worth £40 a year; by November 1791 he would have another £30 from a Rustat Scholarship, awarded to him as a clergyman's son of exceptional academic ability.

Already in his first letter from Cambridge, however, Coleridge complains of poverty; he cannot afford to buy furniture, having 'received nothing but sixpences' from the Governors of Christ's Hospital. George was to have many more letters from his brilliant younger brother in which lack of money was a main theme. Gillman repeated a story Coleridge had often told which cast his younger self as an innocent abroad. According to this account, soon after his arrival at Jesus he was visited by 'a polite upholsterer' who offered to furnish his rooms. Thinking the man to be an employee of the College, Coleridge gave him a free hand, only to be astonished when presented with the bill. Gillman adds, speaking from his acquaintance with the older Coleridge, that debt was something Coleridge dreaded, 'and he never had the courage to face it'. 'I once', continues Gillman, 'and once only, witnessed a painful scene of this kind, which occurred from mistaking a letter on ordinary business for an application for money.'[2] In his darkest days Coleridge was to fall into the habit of not opening letters lest they contain bad news of some kind – including requests for the payment of debts – a habit which caused his family and friends great pain.

A more amusing story, also told by Gillman, and also emanating from Coleridge himself, describes him in terms similar to those which circulated about his father. His fellow students progressively cut off the tail of his gown when he attended lectures, with the result that he was accosted by the Master of Jesus while crossing the quadrangle one day, with the exclamation: 'Mr Coleridge! Mr Coleridge! when will you get rid of that shameful gown?' Coleridge, glancing over his shoulder and realizing the state of his dress, apparently replied, 'Why, sir, I think I've got rid of the greatest part of it already!'[3] Shades of Parson Adams.

Coleridge's old schoolfellow, Thomas Middleton, a student at Pembroke College since 1788, took the newcomer under his wing, becoming 'my patron and protector'.[4] After a lonely start at Jesus, he soon settled down to student life. To George he wrote of attending chapel twice a day, which was required, and of hearing lectures in maths and classics. He was eager to demonstrate both his intellectual prowess and his conscientiousness, though his tone is also bantering and slightly self-mocking:

> If I were to read on as I do now – there is not the least doubt, that I should be Classical Medallist, and a very high Wrangler [prize-winning mathematician] – but *Freshmen* always *begin* very *furiously*. I am reading Pindar, and composing Greek verse, and shall try hard for the Brown's Prize ode. At my Leisure hours I translate Anacreon . . .[5]

It sounds excessive and exaggerated, but Coleridge *was* studying hard; he did in fact win the Browne Gold Medal for his Greek Sapphic ode – an honourable attack on the slave trade – in July 1792; in December 1792 he entered for the prestigious Craven Scholarship and was placed in the last four, though the scholarship finally went to a rival.[6] It is understandable that he should emphasize his hard work and glittering achievements to his brother, who acted as a surrogate father to him. Again as to a father, Coleridge assured George that he was 'an Oeconomist. I keep no company – that is, I neither give or receive invitations to wine parties'.[7]

If Coleridge naturally stressed his spartan regime to George, he just as naturally played up his devil-may-care, student-about-town image in letters to his chosen surrogate family, the Evanses. To them he wrote of attending wine parties and enjoying silly drunken escapades with other freshmen.[8] He also wrote in high spirits to Mary of a walking adventure with Middleton which ended with the two students stumbling around in the fens after dark on a February evening. 'We feared the Ghosts of the night – at least, those material and knock me down Ghosts, the apprehension of which causes you, Mary (valorous girl, that you are!) always to peep under your bed of a night.' Still in playful-Gothic mood, he conjures up for her the ghost of the poet Gray, who, he assures her, greatly values her judgement of his poetry. As for Coleridge himself, Gray's ghost has advised him to 'write no more verses – in the first place, your poetry is vile stuff; and secondly (here he sighed almost to bursting) all Poets go to —ll'.[9]

In the same letter Coleridge encloses some indifferent verses described as 'a lover's complaint to his Mistress, who deserted him in quest of a more wealthy Husband in the East Indies':

> Ah! will you, cruel Julia! will you go?
> And trust you to the Ocean's dark dismay?
> Shall the wide wat'ry world between us flow?
> And Winds unpitying snatch my Hopes away?

This was no doubt a delicious game of playing at being tortured by the imagined loss of Mary.

Coleridge spent Christmas 1791 in Villiers Street with the congenial and admiring Evans family. After winning the Greek Ode prize the following July, he passed the long summer vacation on a series of duty visits to his relations in the West Country. First he stayed in Salisbury with Edward and his elderly wife, 'who', wrote Coleridge amusedly to George on a later visit, 'by all the Cupids! is a very worthy old Lady'.[10] Then he went to his mother's house in Ottery before joining the family of his brother James, 'the Colonel', in Tiverton. Back in Ottery at the end of August, he practised for the University Craven Scholarship by writing letters in Latin to George, in which he expressed his impatience with the narrow-mindedness of his mother's circle in their attitude towards current political events.

1792 was a difficult year for British reformers and supporters of the French Revolution. Early in the year a bill calling for the abolition of the slave trade – the very topic of Coleridge's prize poem – failed in Parliament. British societies which had long agitated for the reform of Parliament, the abolition of restrictions on Roman Catholics and Dissenters, and other liberal causes, and which had welcomed the revolution in Paris, now found themselves labelled 'Jacobins' after the leading group of revolutionaries which was becoming increasingly repressive in France. Pitt's Tory government exploited every opportunity to associate British reformist groups with the alarming violence in Paris as an excuse to clamp down on civil liberties at home. In May 1792 came a Royal Proclamation against Seditious Writings and Publications. When Louis XVI was taken prisoner by the National Assembly on 10 August, royalists at home were outraged.[11]

Tom Paine, who published the second part of his republican work *Rights of Man* in 1792, was outlawed in December. He had already left England for France, where he was treated as a hero until he opposed the execution of Louis in January 1793. Those who published and sold Paine's work at home were subject to prosecution under the Royal Proclamation of the Previous May.[12] A typical conservative cartoon of 1792 shows two medals, one inscribed 'English Liberty', the other 'French Liberty'. On the former, Britannia sits peacefully, holding the scales of Justice, the British Lion at her feet and a tall ship sailing in the distance. Underneath the medal are the words Religion, Morality, Loyalty, Obedience to the Law, Independence, Personal Security, Justice, Inheritance, Protection, Property, Industry, National Prosperity, Happiness. The French medal has a wild female harpy (a caricature of the French revolutionary drawings of Liberty) with a severed head on a pole, while in the background an aristocrat hangs by the neck. Here the key words are Atheism, Perjury, Rebellion, Treason, Anarchy, Murder, Equality [!], Madness, Cruelty, Injustice, Treachery, Ingratitude, Idleness, Famine, National and Private Ruin, Misery.[13]

Coleridge, who was to become increasingly radical during his time at Cambridge, naturally did not alarm George with fighting talk, but he did allow himself some irony, in his Latin letter of August 1792, at the expense of a local worthy, a Mr Hodge:

> He is made quite low by a sort of ravenous hunger for news from France. The reports of these matters that we receive are very sad: the people of Paris were not burned alive when the city was captured, and Payne [ie Tom Paine] was not cut to pieces at Canterbury when he was making his way to France.[14]

While the good burghers of Ottery were thus lacking in enthusiasm for reforming causes, Coleridge's mother was inclined to exaggerate the successes of her sons, except, it seems, her youngest. Coleridge tells George that he has written to 'our brother Francis' – the family had not yet heard of Francis's death in India in February – and that a Mr Kesell is to ensure that the letter reaches him. Kesell, says Coleridge, has boasted of his high connections in India and has promised Mrs Coleridge to put in a word for Francis with the Governor-General of India. Having made fun of this 'puffed-up creature', Coleridge adds, a little sourly, 'our mother positively drinks in his long-winded speeches, and dreams of the most wonderful prospects'.[15]

For all his scorn of his mother's ambition for Francis, Coleridge very much hoped for success in his own candidature for honours. On his return to Cambridge in October 1792, he prepared for the University Scholarship, submitting himself to six days of examination at the end of the year. He was disappointed not to win.[16] He had worked hard, and his aptitude was not in doubt. Years later, George allowed that his youngest brother had been excellent in 'the facility with which he construed the most difficult classics' both as a Grecian at Christ's Hospital and as an undergraduate at Cambridge.[17]

George Coleridge was rather worried, however, by his brother's equal facility in making debts. Replying in 1808 to a letter from his brilliant nephew, John Taylor Coleridge, then head boy at Eton, he warned the boy against two Coleridgean sins: the imprudence of getting into debt and the plausibility in excusing himself by 'specious argumentation (which weed, by the way, grows spontaneously in the hot-bed of quick wit and strong appetite)'. 'By that sin', wrote George in solemn admonition, 'fell your Uncle Sam, and I trust that you will have too much sense, and enough religion, to prevent *you* from hoping to win by it.'[18]

While 'Sam' wrote apologetically to George about his money troubles, he expressed himself less cautiously to Mary Evans, telling her in February 1793 of the 'army of Misfortunes' that had beset him: 'Item – my head akes – Item – the Dean has set me a swinging Imposition for missing Chapel – Item – of the only two coats, which I am worth in the world, both have holes in the elbows.'[19] It is not clear exactly how he overspent his allowance. Wine was undoubtedly one expense; opium was another. Towards the end of this skittish letter to Mary he confessed, 'I have administered rather a strong Dose of Opium' (to relieve the headache? for the giddy pleasure that followed from taking it? or both?).

It seems, too, that about this time Coleridge succumbed to another traditional temptation – the attractions of prostitutes. In 1801 he told Humphry Davy that 'the period that comprizes my Unchastities' embraced his nineteenth to his twenty-second year, namely his time at Cambridge.[20] In later life his guiltiest dreams were to hark back to this period. The most elaborate description of such a dream, confided to his notebook in December 1803, includes a further flashback to Christ's Hospital, where he may have experienced homosexual advances.[21] The 1803 dream, or nightmare, is complex. As with many dreams, but perhaps particularly with opium-induced dreams like this one, the dreamer is a victim, terrified, assaulted on all sides, exquisitely sensitive to pain and humiliation, and paralysed to prevent the onslaught. Coleridge the dreamer is attacked by members of both sexes and by friends turned enemies:

Wednesd. Morn. 3 o'clock, Dec. 13, 1803. Bad dreams/ How often *of a sort/* at the university – a mixture of Xts Hospital Church/ escapes there – lose myself/ trust to two People, one Maim'd, one unknown/ insulted by a fat sturdy Boy of about 14, like a Bacchus/ who dabs a flannel in my face, (or rather soft hair brown Shawl stuff) (was this a flannel Night-cap?) he attacks me/ I call to my Friends – they come & join in the Hustle against me – out rushes a university Harlot, who insists on my going with her/ offer her a shilling – seem to get away a moment/when she overtakes me again/ I am not to go to another while she is '*biting*' – these were her words/ – this will not satisfy her/ I sit down on a broad open plain of rubbish with rails & a street beyond/ & call out – whole Troops of people in sight –.
[. . .]
In the early part of the Dream, Boyer, & two young Students, & R. Allen: Legrice & I quizzing . . . The Harlot in white with her open Bosom certainly was the Cambridge Girl . . . remembered a former Dream, in which I had suffered most severely, this wretch leaping on me, & grasping my Scrotum/ – I therefore most politely assured him of the 3 guineas, but I meant only to get rid of him . . . My determination to awake, I dream that I got out of bed, & volition in dream to *scream*, which I actually too did . . .[22]

In 1793 such dreadful nightmares were still in the unknown future. Writing to Mary Evans, Coleridge made light of his debts and joked about not attending chapel. He also began to show a keen interest in politics. Naturally, he was by inclination a radical; in February 1793 an event drew him into radical politics in Cambridge in a serious way. One of the Fellows of Jesus College was William Frend, a clergyman who had declared himself a Unitarian, no longer believing in the Trinity or the divinity of Christ. He could therefore no longer subscribe to the Thirty-Nine Articles of the Church of England, as was required of all University dons.

Because of this change in his religious views, Frend had ceased to be a College Tutor in 1788. Soon he was deprived of his fellowship as well, in consequence of his writing a pamphlet, published in February 1793, called *Peace and Union Recommended to the Associated Bodies of Republicans and Anti-Republicans.* In it he advocated the abolition of the Test and Corporation Acts in order to enable Dissenters and other non-Anglicans to enter the professions or hold Government appointments.[23] Frend also argued for reform of the Established Church, and, for good measure, urged political reform as well. In April the Fellows of the College voted to expel him. Frend appealed to the University Senate; for the whole of May he stood trial before the Vice-Chancellor. Finally he was found guilty of violating the statutes of the University and was 'banished' from Cambridge.[24]

The students followed the trial with interest; many sat in the gallery and noisily supported the rebel. Prominent among them, as his old school-fellow Valentine Le Grice recalled, was Coleridge: 'Frend's trial was then in progress. Pamphlets swarmed from the press. Coleridge had read them all; and in the evening, with our negus, we had them *viva voce* gloriously.'[25]

Of course Coleridge did not tell his brother about these stirring events and his part in them. He had already mentioned Frend in an early Cambridge letter to George, assuring him that Frend's company was 'by no means invidious', and adding with unnerving facetiousness, 'No! Tho' I am not an *Alderman,* I have yet *prudence* enough to *respect* that *gluttony of Faith* waggishly yclept Orthodoxy.'[26] In fact, Coleridge came so much under the influence of both Frend's rational religious belief and his political radicalism that, after leaving Cambridge for Bristol in 1794, he himself became a lecturer in radical politics and a lay preacher in Unitarian chapels.

Meanwhile, however, he wrote to George of other matters. On hearing of Frank's death nearly a year after it occurred, he romanticized, turning Frank from villain to 'hero of all the little tales, that make the remembrance of my earliest days interesting'. Thinking of these early days, he became a little spiteful about his family and acquaintances, indirectly venting his deep-seated resentment at having been sent away from home by an unloving mother (who is carefully not mentioned specifically in his complaint):

I quitted Ottery, when I was so young . . . and when at last I revisited Devon, the manners of the Inhabitants annihilated whatever tender ideas of pleasure my Fancy had pictured to my Expectation. I found them (almost universally) to be gross without openness, and cunning without refinement.

After thus expressing his disdain for Ottery society, he continued with frank criticism of his two surviving brothers (other than the addressee), Edward and James. He had scarcely known them as a child, and now presumed to declare Edward vain and thoughtless and James pompous.[27] George must have felt uneasy on reading these words. But he sent money to cover Coleridge's debts and was thanked fulsomely, and in Latin, for his 'truly paternal' love and care.[28]

After the excitement of the Frend trial and his failure to win the Browne Medal of 1793 for his Greek ode (on astronomy) – he came second this time – Coleridge repeated his summer vacation schedule of doing the rounds of his Devon relations. He was writing very little poetry (except in Latin) at this time, and what there was is, as he acknowledged to George, 'of the namby pamby Genus'. One example, 'The Rose', sent to George in July 1793, begins cloyingly:

> As late each Flower that sweetest blows
> I pluck'd, the Garden's pride;
> Within the Petals of the Rose
> A sleeping Love I spy'd.[29]

During this vacation Coleridge accompanied 'a party of young ladies' to a cave near Ottery known locally as 'the Pixies' Parlour'. Here he and his brothers had cut their initials into the rock as children. Now he wrote a sentimental ode, 'Songs of the Pixies', celebrating this summer visit. Ostensibly the ode leads up to a climax in which one of the young ladies is declared 'Fairy Queen'. Really its high point is the fourth stanza, in which Coleridge fancies himself as 'the youthful Bard' soon to be crowned with the traditional laurel wreath:

> Thither, while the murmuring throng
> Of wild-bees hum their drowsy song,
> By rapture-beaming Fancy brought,
> A youthful Bard, 'unknown to fame',
> Oft wooes the Queen of Solemn Thought,
> And heaves the gentle misery of a sigh
>   Gazing with tearful eye,
> As round our sandy grot appear
> Many a rudely-sculptur'd name
>   To pensive Memory dear!
> Weaving gay dreams of sunny-tinctur'd hue,
>   We glance before his view:
> O'er his hush'd soul our soothing witcheries shed
> And twine the future garland round his head.[30]

Though not good, the verse is interesting for more than one reason. Firstly, it acknowledges that for this young poet success in poetry is yet to come; it therefore combines modesty and self-criticism with hope and pride. Secondly, the language, though derived from Milton and his eighteenth-century imitators, holds out a faint promise of something more original with its 'sunny-tinctur'd' dreams and the 'soothing witcheries' of the pixies. Moreover, Coleridge shows signs of learning to control the strong rhythms and irregular line length of the ode form.

All this light-hearted epistolary and poetic activity was intended to cover up Coleridge's acute anxiety about the state of his finances. By the summer vacation of 1793 he had debts of nearly £150. Surviving letters are very few between July 1793 and February 1794, by which time Coleridge was no longer at Cambridge, but at Henley-on-Thames. The radical student and opponent of Britain's war with post-revolutionary France – a war begun in February 1793 – had suddenly transformed himself into Silas Tomkyn Comberbache, a new recruit in His Majesty's Fifteenth Light Dragoons.

So desperate did Coleridge become about his debts, and so fearful of the probable reaction of his sensible older brothers, that he abruptly left Cambridge for London in November 1793. Here he sank his last cash in a ticket in the Irish Lottery, sending off a poem on the subject to the *Morning Chronicle*, which duly published it on 7 November. The poem expresses the writer's despair – 'my pale cheeks glow' – and his last clutching at hope – 'O Fortune! . . . yield the unsunn'd stranger to the western gale!'[31]

On the same day that his poem was published Coleridge was back in Cambridge reading another poetic effusion to a party of students at Trinity College. This was 'Lines on an Autumnal Evening', for which Coleridge himself apologized in a note to the 1796 edition of his poems in which it was ill-advisedly included, calling it 'intolerable stuff'.[32] The 'Lines', with the cloying rhetoric of 'the dewy locks of Spring', 'the streamlet's brink,' 'the paly radiance', and other random expressions, were read out by Coleridge in the rooms of William Rough. Another Trinity student, Christopher Wordsworth – younger brother of William, who had left Cambridge in 1791, some months before Coleridge went up – recorded the occasion in his diary, with a wry comment on Coleridge's sickly diction.[33]

The Irish Lottery draw took place late in November. Coleridge was not a winner; he told George in a wildly self-reproachful letter of February 1794 that he had been on the brink of suicide – 'the dernier resort of misery' – but was prevented by 'an accident of a very singular kind'.[34] We do not know what this accident was. Coleridge's accounts of his desperate behaviour during November 1793 swing between extreme exaggeration and extreme understatement of his feelings and actions.

Writing to his brothers in a mood of guilt and fright, he talked of the 'strange Combination of Madness, Ingratitude, & Dishonesty' in his behaviour towards them.[35] To George he confessed not only to debts and drinking, to 'Debauchery' and 'a tempest of Pleasure' in London, but also – surely exaggerating now – to extreme laziness during his time in Cambridge. 'I became a proverb to the University for Idleness', he declared; 'even for the Un. Scholarship, for which I affected to have read so severely, I did not read three days uninterruptedly – for the whole six weeks, that preceded the examination, I was almost constantly intoxicated! My Brother, you shudder as you read.'[36] This seems highly unlikely, given how well Coleridge did in the examinations for the Scholarship. But he had got into confessional mode, and panic and a desire to abase himself and by that means win pity appear to have driven him to overstate his vices.

By contrast Coleridge later wrote in a perhaps disingenuous note, quoted by Gillman, that though his time in London in November 1793 was indeed 'that week of my existence, in which my moral being would have presented to a pitying guardian angel the most interesting spectacle', it was *not* a time of 'debauchery of all kinds'. 'God knows, so intense was my mental anguish, that during the whole time I was physically incapable even of a *desire*.' The sole root of his problem he claimed, was his debt.[37] Whatever the exact nature of his behaviour during his toings and froings between London and Cambridge in November 1793, it culminated in a rash act of despair, even near-madness: not suicide, but enlisting.

On 2 December Coleridge allowed himself to be 'crimped', or pressed into joining a regiment in order to assure himself of his next meal and a bed for the night. It was a spectacular act of escape, doubly crazy because once in the army, he was trapped in it until he could be bought out, by the use of both money and influence, neither of which he could be sure would be forthcoming on his behalf from his brothers, and also because, with Britain at war with France, there was every chance of his being sent into battle abroad. He might thus end up killing or being killed in a war of which he, as an anti-Pitt, anti-Tory liberal, in any case disapproved.

Fortunately, it did not come to that. Silas Tomkyn Comberbache, as he improbably called himself (Cottle said he noticed the surname over a door in Lincoln's Inn Fields or the Temple while walking the streets of London[38]), proved a very poor horseman and the very oddest of recruits. He was marched to Henley, where he was set to nurse a fellow soldier with smallpox. He had not been picked out for foreign duty, as some others in the regiment were, because he was 'a very indocile Equestrian'.[39]

Stories naturally accumulated about his escapades during his three months in the Fifteenth Dragoons, most of them stemming from Coleridge himself. In return for being helped to groom his horse by others more expert, he wrote letters for them to their wives and sweethearts.[40] His natural eloquence, which had singled him out among his peers at Christ's

Hospital and Cambridge, brought him astonished attention in the army. Cottle tells a tale in his not entirely trustworthy recollections of the young Coleridge, which are nevertheless based on a close friendship with the young genius. According to his account, Coleridge had been standing sentinel at a public place when two of his officers went past, talking about Euripides, whom one of them quoted. The classically gifted sentinel no sooner heard the Greek than he intervened to tell his superiors that the quotation was not accurate and the line not from Euripides but from Sophocles.[41]

We can well believe that some such exchange took place. It may also be the case that Coleridge experienced in the army one of its more unpleasant punishments. In 1798 Lamb's friend Charles Lloyd published an indiscreet *roman à clef, Edmund Oliver*, in which the eponymous hero, a man of 'excessive sensibility' and 'impetuous desires', resorts to laudanum and alcohol when things go badly with him. He finds himself a recruit in circumstances similar to Coleridge's. After getting drunk and going on parade in an unfit state, Edmund is 'picketted' by his Colonel: 'I [was] obliged to stand a whole hour, suspended by one thumb with the hollow part of my foot, bared for the purpose, upon a piece of wood not larger than a sixpence, to gratify the loathsome whims of this pampered mountebank.'[42]

Luckily Coleridge had told some of his Christ's Hospital friends about his enlistment. One of them, G. L. Tuckett, lost no time in informing George Coleridge of his whereabouts. George wrote calming letters to his frenzied younger brother and set about getting James, 'the Colonel', to arrange his 'emancipation'. He also contacted Coleridge's College Tutor, who expressed his willingness to have him back. George paid the debts.[43] Letters flew between Hackney and Henley. Coleridge's old school friends Le Grice and Allen helped too. The latter sent him tea, sugar, and money from Oxford, where he was a student; he even visited Henley 'and wept over "the thought-bewilder'd Man" [Coleridge here quotes from his own sonnet to Bowles] with tears of brotherly affection'.[44]

The discharge took some time to arrange, as the army at first insisted on a substitute recruit being found; and this, George was told, 'the *Gentlemen Crimps* will not undertake under 25 Guineas'.[45] Meanwhile Coleridge was moved from Henley to High Wycombe, 'on the Baggage Cart', and then to Reading. Here he was visited by an Ottery man, George Cornish, who encouraged him to hope for his release and 'behaved with great delicacy', i.e., gave Coleridge a guinea.[46]

The army dropped its request for a substitute recruit, accepting instead the plea of insanity put forward by Coleridge's commanding officer. The regimental muster roll reads: 'Discharged S. T. Comberbach/Insane/10 Apl'.[47] His brothers certainly thought him mad, but Coleridge was all gratitude and eagerness to please. He promised to go straight back to Cambridge, not travelling through London, where George may have feared he would take up drinking again, or perhaps visit the Evanses, though Tuckett was sure he was too ashamed to try to see them.[48]

Some time in 1799 Coleridge summed up the whole episode for Godwin, and Godwin noted it down. This may be the most accurate of all the accounts which have survived of Coleridge's misadventure:

> 1793   wins a prize for the best Greek ode [actually in 1792] – never told his love – loose in sexual morality – spends a night in a house of ill fame, ruminating in a chair: next morning meditates suicide, walks in the park, enlists, sleeps 12 hours on the officer's bed, & upon awaking is offered his liberty, which from a scruple of honour he refuses – marched to Reading – dinnerless on Christmas day, his pocket having been picked by a comrade
> 1794   discharged by Lord Cornwallis, after having been 4 months a horse-soldier – returns to Cambridge –[49]

Coleridge duly reported to George on 11 April that he had arrived in Cambridge.[50] By 1 May he could tell George that the Fellows of Jesus College had let him off with a reprimand, and that he was working on yet another Greek ode for the Browne Prize; indeed, 'I mean to write for all the Prizes.'[51] He seemed ready to settle down and study quietly for his degree, taking prizes and honours as befitted his brilliance, and preparing himself for the Church of England clergyman he was expected to become.

On 14 June 1794 the *Cambridge Intelligencer* carried an advertisement for *Imitations from the Modern Latin Poets*, which Coleridge hoped to publish by subscription. The next day he set out with a travelling companion, Joseph Hucks, on a pedestrian tour of Wales. They were to stop at Oxford on the way to pay a visit to Robert Allen. Here something happened which had the immediate effect of postponing the Welsh trip for three weeks, the middle term effect of pushing aside the Latin imitations (which were never finished), and the longer term effect of deflecting Coleridge irrevocably from completing his Cambridge career. It was an event which threw even longer shadows over Coleridge's future life, contributing to shape his career, his marriage, his greatest joys, and his worst miseries. The momentous event was Coleridge's meeting, through Allen, with Robert Southey.

Coleridge and Southey became friends instantly. Southey, two years younger than Coleridge, and a student at Balliol College, released in Coleridge a whirlwind of energy, emotion, poetical and political ideas. To read Coleridge's first letter to Southey, written from Gloucester after he and Hucks had torn themselves away from Oxford and started their walking tour at last, is to be struck by the sudden freedom of tone and manner, the open expressions of joy, excitement, even dizzy rapture. Coleridge had found a soulmate. Having made no truly congenial acquaintance at

Cambridge, he had hit on one at the other University. From this moment on, Cambridge would have no further hold over Coleridge.

Suddenly, too, Coleridge found encouragement to express his political radicalism, hitherto kept out of sight in his letters to the conservative George and only hinted at in sentimental vein to Mrs Evans and her daughters. A new door was opened to him, and he could not wait to step over the threshold. After less than three weeks' acquaintance with Southey, he was talking in capital letters about Democracy, Republicanism, Philanthropy, Pantisocracy and Fraternity.

Though Coleridge was intellectually more precocious than Southey, his career so far – he was nearly twenty-two – seems almost retarded when compared to that of his younger friend. Southey had been born in Bristol in 1774, the son of a linen draper. From an early age he lived with a wealthy aunt, Miss Tyler, from whom he could expect to inherit a comfortable fortune. At her expense he was sent to Westminster School, from which he was expelled during his final year for publishing, with his friend Grosvenor Bedford, the provocatively-named magazine, *The Flagellant*.[52] Because of this he was turned down by Christ Church, Oxford, but Balliol accepted him and in October 1793 he began his studies there, being destined for a career in the Church. Southey's time at university, like Coleridge's, was to end without his taking a degree.

For Southey's rebelliousness did not die with his expulsion from Westminster. He was unhappy about the idea of becoming a clergyman; as he wrote robustly to a friend in December 1793, 'I am not stupid enough to be orthodox. Doubts will intrude . . . the very existence of a priest is wrong.'[53] Having read Godwin's *Enquiry concerning Political Justice*, which came out in 1793, he quickly adopted Godwin's views on the depravity of society, the iniquity of private property, and the cruelty and hypocrisy of the judicial system. Southey's brisk summing up of Godwinian ideas and what they attacked ran as follows: 'We are born in sin and the children of wrath – says the catechism. It is absolutely false. Sin is artificial – it is the monstrous offspring of government and property. The origin of both was in injustice.'[54]

Southey was all the more receptive to Godwin's work, with its heady ideas so soothingly expressed in lucid, rational prose, because he felt strongly the injustice which existed in his own family in respect of property. His father had been ruined in 1790, had gone to debtors' prison, despite having a wealthy brother who could have helped him, and had died in 1792 'of a broken heart', as Southey told Horace Bedford, brother of his schoolfriend Grosvenor. Southey's mother, with several children dependent on her, had to open a lodging house in Bath, where Southey was forced 'to associate with fools and to know they think it condescension'.[55]

At the age of nineteen Southey was already connected with 'some young women, sisters, with whom I was partly educated and whose histories are as melancholy as my own'.[56] These were the Frickers, whose circumstances were not unlike those of Coleridge's London family, the Evanses. Mr

Fricker, a wine merchant in Bristol, had failed in business and died leaving his wife and her six surviving children: Sara, born in 1770, Mary, Edith, Martha, Elizabeth, and George, the youngest, born in 1785. By August 1794, when he had just turned twenty, Southey was intending to marry Edith; his friend Robert Lovell was already married to Mary; another friend, George Burnett, had hopes of Martha.[57] It only remained that Coleridge, once introduced to Southey's circle, should propose to the oldest sister, Sara.

Southey had been fired by Godwin's philosophy, grounded, like Rousseau's, in optimism about the benevolence of human nature when not forced to live under repressive laws and governments. Thus a plan arose, with Southey as the leading spirit, for the group to emigrate to America to start a utopian community free from the pressures and pre-judices of British society. The plan was lent impetus by the fact that Joseph Priestley, a leading scientist and Unitarian preacher, the discoverer of oxygen and carbon monoxide, had lately settled in Philadelphia, where he owned land.

Priestley had suffered even more than William Frend for his agitation to have the Test and Corporation Acts repealed. Edmund Burke, in his famous anti-revolutionary *Reflections on the Revolution in France* (1790), had identified him as a subversive 'Jacobin', and Priestley had replied in pamphlets in which he quoted provocatively from the Bible about having 'drawn the sword and thrown away the scabbard'. He also proposed parliamentary reform and universal suffrage, and was associated with the Constitutional Society's controversial meeting at Birmingham on 14 July 1791 to celebrate Bastille Day. A mob shouting 'Church and King' gathered outside the meeting, then followed Priestley home. His house, his laboratory, and his chapel were burnt down. He and his family left Birmingham for Hackney, where he preached and taught at the newly established Dissenting Academy. By February 1794, however, he had become tired of his notoriety and the restrictions on his activities, and set sail for America.[58] His son-in-law, Thomas Cooper, published a pamphlet in London later in 1794, *Some Information Respecting America*, in which he sang the praises of the Susquehanna Valley, where Priestley had settled.[59] Coleridge read Cooper's work in October and recommended it to Southey, who had already thought of the Susquehanna as the place to settle in. Indeed, Southey had first contemplated emigrating to America as early as December 1793.[60]

This was the remarkable young man Coleridge met in June 1794. Southey's self-confidence and his strong convictions, underpinned by a propensity to self-righteousness, undoubtedly formed a good part of the attraction he immediately exercised on Coleridge, who was drifting, buffeted, still alarmed by his army experience, in fear and awe of his brothers, yet aching to rebel. Now he was introduced to one whose credentials as a radical were impeccable, but who combined youthful enthusiasm with an unusual maturity and stability of character. Small wonder that Coleridge was bowled over.

And so Coleridge, with his head full of Southey and his plans, went walking with Hucks. From Gloucester he wrote in a flourish of high spirits on 6 July: 'S. T. Coleridge to R. Southey – Health & Republicanism! When you write, direct to me to be left at the Post Office, Wrexham, Denbighshire N. Wales. I mention this circumstance *now*, lest carried away by a flood of confluent ideas I should forget it.' Then he proceeds to let himself be indeed – the phrase is highly appropriate to his letter-writing style from now on – 'carried away by a flood of confluent ideas'. First he compliments Southey the poet: 'Verily, Southey, I like not Oxford nor the inhabitants of it – I would say thou art a Nightingale among Owls', and 'thy soaring is even unto heaven'; 'Or let me add (for my Appetite for Similies is truly canine at this moment) that as the Italian Nobles their new-fashioned Doors, so thou dost make the adamantine Gate of Democracy turn on it's golden Hinges to most sweet Music.'

Mimicking his less interesting companion Hucks, whom he describes to his new friend as 'a Man of cultivated, tho' not vigorous, understanding', he describes an incident:

> It is *wrong*, Southey! for a little Girl with a half-famished sickly Baby in her arms to put her head in at the window of an Inn – 'Pray give me a bit of Bread and Meat'! from a Party dining on Lamb, Green Pease, & Sallad – Why?? Because it is *impertinent & obtrusive*! – I am a Gentleman! – and wherefore should the clamorous Voice of Woe *intrude* upon mine Ear!?

So unfeeling was the otherwise kindly Hucks, under the influence of the 'lingering Remains of Aristocracy'. But

> when the pure System of Pantocracy [soon to be renamed Pantisocracy] shall have aspheterized the Bounties of Nature, these things will not be so –! I trust, you admire the word 'aspheterized' from α non, σφετερος proprius! We really *wanted* such a word – instead of travelling along the circuitous, dusty, beaten high-Road of Diction you thus cut across the soft, green pathless Field of Novelty! – Similies forever! Hurra![61]

New ideas damand a new use of language. Here Coleridge, without himself being yet conscious of it, declares a manifesto for his own future prose and poetry. It is significant, too, that he tells Southey in this letter that he has bought 'a little Blank Book, and portable Ink horn' so that he can record his observations of the natural scene through which he is passing, and also 'ever and anon pluck the wild Flowers of Poesy'. This was the first of those notebooks to which he was to confide his closest thoughts and feelings.

It has often been said that Coleridge's first visit to Wordsworth in June 1797 marked the symbolic beginning of English Romanticism. That was indeed a wonderful moment, full of promise and significance. But for

Coleridge we could propose an alternative beginning, dating it from this letter to Southey. From now on he was to be poetically alive to his surroundings; his notebooks and his poetry from 1794 testify to his having become, *before* the momentous meeting with Wordsworth, a poet of nature. (Wordsworth himself recognized this, declaring in the two-part *Prelude* of 1799 that Coleridge was 'one/ The most intense of Nature's worshippers'.[62])

Everything came together – philosophical and political excitement, accurate observation of nature, enthusiasm, and fluency – as a result of Coleridge's having someone to love and be loved by. He was to express again and again, usually plaintively, the belief that love and the security and happiness brought by being loved, were necessary to the success of all his endeavours:

> To be beloved is all I need,
> And whom I love, I love indeed.[63]

Southey was the first human being – apart from his father – for whom Coleridge felt an emotional warmth that was not dictated by duty or guilt or fear. He was gloriously liberated by this, his first great friendship.

Southey, too, though by nature less impulsive than Coleridge, knew he had encountered a phenomenon. He told Grosvenor Bedford that he had met 'a Cantab; one whom I very much esteem and admire tho two thirds of our conversation be spent in disputing on metaphysical subjects'.[64] Soon he was talking of Coleridge as his co-author, both of the Pantisocracy scheme for America and of joint poetical productions. Southey's poems to date had been more politically radical than his friend's, not forgetting 'The Destruction of the Bastile' and the anti-slavery ode. Southey had written 'Botany Bay Eclogues' about transportees sent to 'barbarous climes,/ Where angry England sends her outcast sons', and had addressed stirring words of support, in a poem which he later suppressed from his published works, to the so-called 'Edinburgh Martyrs'.[65]

Four reformists, Joseph Gerrald, Thomas Muir, Thomas Palmer, and Maurice Margarot, stood trial for sedition in Edinburgh between August 1793 and March 1794. Under the notorious Judge Braxfield – famous for his reply to Gerrald's comment at his trial that Jesus, too, had been a reformer: 'Muckle he made o' that; he was hanget'[66] – the defendants were found guilty and sentenced to several years' transportation each.[67] Only one of them, Margarot, survived to return to England after serving his sentence. The crime they had committed was to attend a meeting at Edinburgh of various reforming societies calling for universal suffrage and annual parliaments.[68] When Robert Burns heard of Muir's sentence to fourteen years' transportation, he responded with his apostrophe to Scottish patriotism and radicalism, 'Scots wha hae'.[69]

Southey's poem 'To the Exiled Patriots' was written in the spring of

1794, immediately after the men were sentenced. It opens with a bold apostrophe:

> Martyrs of Freedom – ye who firmly good
> Stept forth the champions in her glorious cause,
> Ye who against Corruption boldly stood
> For Justice, Liberty, and equal Laws.

It so impressed Coleridge that he rather boldly gave it a public airing in a 'Moral and Political Lecture' delivered at Bristol early in 1795, a lecture which was printed as a sixpenny pamphlet shortly afterwards.[70]

No sooner had Southey filled Coleridge full of his plans than the latter was buoyantly dictating the course of events. Drawing on his extra two years in age, and on his ghastly experiences at Cambridge and in the army, he admonished Southey in a letter written from Wrexham on 13 July not to give way to despondency. 'I once shipwrecked my frail bark on that rock . . . Be you wise by my experience – and receive unhurt the Flower, which I have climbed Precipices to pluck'. And, as Southey was talking desperately of having to become a clergyman after all, 'For God's sake, Southey! enter not into the church.'[71]

To encourage Southey to contemplate instead a life of poetry and friendship, Coleridge adapts a few lines from his effusion 'Happiness', first sent to his brother George in June 1791. It gives a hint of the fine flexible poet Coleridge was shortly to become, while comprehensively transferring the positive part of his feelings for his brother to his new-found friend:

> 'Tis thine with faery forms to talk,
> And thine the philosophic walk,
> And (what to thee the sweetest are)
> The setting Sun, the Evening Star,
> The tints, that live along the Sky,
> And Moon, that meets thy raptur'd eye . . .[72]

Even Coleridge's love for Mary Evans had become a secondary thing now that he had met Southey. He had probably avoided Mary and her family during his months of debt, debauchery, and despair, and he seems to have given up any hope of presenting himself as a serious suitor. Now, with his head full of Southey, he had a chance meeting, or near-meeting, with Mary. Had he really forgotten that Mary's sister Eliza lived with her grandmother in Wrexham, where he was now staying overnight with Hucks? He told Southey that, to his 'utter surprise', he saw Mary at Wrexham Church, whereupon 'I turned sick, and all but fainted away!' Coleridge avoided confronting her, and announced to Southey that he could never 'even in a whisper avow my passion, though I knew she loved me', for 'where were my Fortunes? and why should I make her miserable?' In a verbal or imagined act of heroic self-sacrifice he announced, 'Almighty God bless her –! Her Image is in the sanctuary of my Heart, and never *can* it be torn away but with the strings that grapple it to Life.'[73]

It seems likely that Coleridge thus put Mary out of his mind – though not finally – from a complex set of motives. His love for her was of early date; it was tied up inextricably with quasi-filial feelings towards her mother. Though he had continued to need the Evans women during his first year in Cambridge, he had since then gone through his student misbehaviour, and he probably felt guilty towards Mary. As Coleridge was to show time and time again, his response to his own (often excessive) feelings of guilt was to run away from, or punish, those towards whom these feelings were directed. In any case, Coleridge was now excited by a whole new set of enthusiasms, centred on Southey, and he may have found that it was not so difficult to face the future without her as he had imagined when all his emotional hopes had focused on her alone. This he seems to have determined, with a suitable romantic flourish – to *Southey* – to do.

In the same letter from Wrexham Coleridge entertains his friend with a traveller's tale of an encounter with some fiery Welsh democrats, from one of whom he thought he might have caught 'the Itch' (scabies) – 'he grasped my hand with flesh-bruising Ardour – and I trembled, lest some discontented Citizens of the *animalcular* Republic should have emigrated.' Then he tells Southey how he and Hucks, conscious of the good democratic mode of transport they were using, namely their own legs, had 'laughed famously' when they met two fellow Cambridge men. 'These rival *pedestrians*' were 'vigorously pursuing their tour in a *post chaise*', their excuse being that one of them had 'got *clapped*' (i.e. caught venereal disease).[74]

By the middle of August Coleridge had arrived in Bristol, where Southey now was. Together the two friends spent a week walking to Bath, Wells, and the Cheddar Gorge, all the way 'talking philosophy like two poets' and alarming the local people with their scruffy appearance. Southey told Grosvenor Bedford of a night sharing a bed with Coleridge in a 'poor pothouse' near Cheddar. Not only was Coleridge 'a vile bedfellow'; when they woke up in the morning they found they had been locked in by the inn keeper, who 'certainly took us for footpads, and had bolted the door on the outside for fear we should rob the house'.[75]

The companions visited the Somerset village of Nether Stowey, where they were kindly received by Tom Poole, a wealthy tanner, local philanthropist, and notorious democrat – 'the patron of democrats', as he was sarcastically called by the vicar of neighbouring Over Stowey, William Holland, who became apoplectic at the thought of Poole's political views.[76] Poole, noted for his generosity, his hot temper, and his vanity, was an enlightened employer and landowner. He was anxious to improve methods of tanning, hitherto a disgustingly dirty trade involving steeping hides in pits and rubbing them with brains and dog faeces, among other unpleasant procedures. And he experimented with new ways of growing wheat to ensure better crops.[77] Stowey Book Club was founded by Poole in 1793 as a means to educate his Somerset neighbours politically.

Coleridge and Southey made an immediate stir in Nether Stowey. Poole's conservative cousin, John Poole, noted in his diary for 18 August 1794 that they were 'shamefully hot with Democratic Rage as regards politics, and both Infidel as to religion'.[78] Poole himself more accurately described Coleridge as 'in religion a Unitarian, if not a Deist; in politicks a Democrat, to the utmost extent of the word'; while as for Southey, 'in Religion, shocking to say in a mere boy as he is, I fear he wavers between Deism and Atheism' (as befitted a true disciple of Godwin).[79]

Poole recognized Coleridge's exceptional intelligence, and, interestingly in view of Southey's having recently put the Pantisocracy plan into Coleridge's head, he called Coleridge 'the Principal in the undertaking'. He had already 'heard much' of Coleridge before meeting him – were his army exploits, or his precocious abilities, or both, the talk of the West Country? – knew that he was 'a shining scholar', and observed for himself that Coleridge spoke 'with much elegance and energy, and with uncommon facility'. Southey, Poole noted more briefly, was 'of the University of Oxford, a younger man, without the splendid abilities of Coldridge [sic]'.[80]

Poole took the two friends' Pantisocracy scheme seriously, though he resisted the temptation to make one of the party himself, and was aware of the unlikelihood that their perfect system of society could be made to work in practice. 'Could they realise [their ideas] they would, indeed, realise the age of reason', he told an acquaintance who had asked for details of the plan. According to Poole, the most difficult part of the scheme was how to decide on 'the regulations relating to the females'. The question – an ominous one for Coleridge – was 'whether the marriage contract shall be dissolved if agreeable to one or both parties'.[81]

During their weeks together in Somerset, the two friends bolstered one another's resolve. America beckoned to the group, which was to include Southey's mother; Edith Fricker, to whom he was now engaged; Mrs Fricker and the other Fricker sisters; Lovell, who was married to Mary; Burnett, Coleridge, and probably Robert Allen too. 'Should the resolution of others fail', Southey reported determinedly, 'Coleridge and I will go together, and either find repose in an Indian wigwam – or from an Indian tomahawk'. The place fixed on was 'the banks of the Susquehannah'.[82]

Southey showed clear signs of having been touched by the Coleridgean magic. He told Horace Bedford that with Coleridge gone (back to London, not Cambridge), he felt as if he had lost a limb. The letter is full of Coleridge: 'whilst Coleridge is absent it devolves upon me to keep all our party in spirits'; 'Coleridge and I wrote a tragedy upon [Robespierre's] death in the space of two days!' 'Coleridge says "[Robespierre] was a man whose great bad actions cast a disastrous lustre over his name".' Southey becomes quite carried away by the mental picture he and Coleridge have drawn of their idyllic future in America. 'When Coleridge and I are sawing down a tree we shall discuss metaphysics; criticise poetry when hunting a buffalo, and write sonnets whilst following the plough.' And, momentously, 'Our females are beautiful amiable and accomplished – and I shall then call Coleridge my brother in the real sense of the word.'[83]

It seems that Coleridge had been introduced to the Fricker girls in whirlwind fashion, and had expressed a willingness to marry Sara and thus make one more couple proceeding into the Pantisocratic ark. He had known her for no more than a couple of weeks. The plan was that he should find a publisher for *The Fall of Robespierre*, and that they should raise enough money by publishing their poetry to 'quit England in March next'.[84] According to Coleridge, they were also to fill the time before their departure in learning 'the theory and practice of agriculture and carpentry', their education at public schools and Oxbridge not having prepared them for such labours.[85]

The Fall of Robespierre, Coleridge's first collaborative poetic venture, can hardly be called a play. Though subtitled 'An Historic Drama' it is really, as Coleridge says in his dedication to Henry Martin, a friend at Jesus College, a 'Dramatic Poem'. Its three acts are in fact three declamatory scenes, of which Coleridge wrote the first and Southey the second and third. Since Robespierre had been executed very recently, the friends had little time to reflect on the importance of his sudden fall. He had gradually ousted the moderates from the National Assembly after the French Revolution; he had sanctioned huge numbers of executions in the name of liberty, taking supreme power to himself in July 1793. He and twenty-one associates went to the guillotine themselves on 28 July 1794, but the first English report of his death appeared in *The Times* on 16 August. By 18 August the *Morning Chronicle* had printed his last speeches to the Assembly, as well as those denouncing him. Coleridge and Southey did little more than transpose these reports into enthusiastic blank verse.[86]

Coleridge succeeded in getting Benjamin Flower, editor of the *Cambridge Intelligencer*, to publish the work as an octavo pamphlet under Coleridge's name, because, as he airily explained to Southey, his name would cause it to sell 'at least a hundred Copies at Cambridge'.[87]

The leading idea of this callow work is that of a good man turned tyrant after having been instrumental in ridding France of its previous tyranny under an absolute monarch. References to Brutus and Mark Antony are prominent, and the whole play is loosely speaking 'Shakespearean'. But both its young authors write in one vein only, the heroic, rhetorical, 'public' style of declamation. Thus not only do the politicians speechify about liberty and tyranny from the Tribune, but everyone else appears to be addressing a meeting too. This includes the one supposedly domestic scene, written by Coleridge, in which Adelaide, the wife of one of Robespierre's enemies, Tallien, sings the praises of 'domestic peace' as against public quarrels.[88] Though Coleridge's lines are often strong and sinuous, they are inappropriate to the action and setting:

> The peaceful virtues
> And every blandishment of private life,
> The father's cares, the mother's fond endearment,
> All sacrificed to liberty's wild riot.[89]

This is only slightly varied rhetorically from the language that fills the rest of the play: 'elemental wars', 'perfidious Traitor', 'restless turbulence of guilt', 'long train of hideous horrors', 'patriot murderers', 'blood-cemented throne', 'dastard despot', and so on. One phrase of Coleridge's, though made up of another cliched personification, achieves a near-Shakespearean rhythm in the last line with the expert placing of 'intoxicate' (used as an adjective):

> Thought Barrere so, when through the streaming streets
> Of Paris red-eyed Massacre o'erwearied
> Reel'd heavily, intoxicate with blood?[90]

In an age noted for the absence of new plays that were truly dramatic, this dashed-off effort was no better than might have been expected of two tyros. It received a few tolerant reviews; the writer in the *British Critic* prophesied that 'the Author might, after some probation, become no unsuccessful wooer of the tragic muse'.[91] Both Southey and Coleridge did try their hand at writing drama in future years. Coleridge even achieved brief, but notable, success with *Remorse* in 1813.

It is customary to view the Pantisocracy plan as nothing more than a madcap scheme by a group of hopelessly idealistic young men and women which was bound to be adandoned before any firm arrangements could be made. Southey and Coleridge themselves later looked back on the project with amused superiority; while travelling in Germany in 1799 Coleridge 'discoursed about it very entertainingly', according to one of his companions, Clement Carlyon.[92] Certainly their frenzied letters during the winter of 1794–5 make entertaining reading. But it is worth remembering that emigration to America was the chosen path for Priestley and his family, and for Tom Paine, as well as for thousands of economic, rather than political, migrants from Britain in the 1790s. When we think of conditions at home in 1794, we should not be surprised at the desperation felt by many for whom the 'land of liberty' had become a country of starvation and repression.

England in 1794 was an uncongenial place for those who wished for reforms, whether of the law, the Church, or the system of political representation. Since 1792 constitutional and reforming societies had been subject to harassment, suspicion, infiltration by spies and informers, and prosecution. Burke's masterly *Reflections* of 1790, the execution of Louis XVI and Marie Antoinette in 1793, the Reign of Terror under Robespierre,

Revolutionary France's aggression towards her neighbours, and the state of war existing between France and Britain since February 1793 all combined to fuel reactionary measures at home.

Pitt suspended Habeas Corpus – always a touchstone of individual liberty for Britons – in May 1794 because of a supposed seditious plot by the London Constitutional Society and the London Corresponding Society. Reformist pamphlets were suppressed; publishers and booksellers were prosecuted; and an attempt was made to follow the example of the Edinburgh Trials and clamp down brutally on extra-parliamentary opposition. Meantime, in Parliament the Whig opposition led by Charles James Fox was damagingly divided, though Fox himself was assiduous in opposing the war with France as unnecessary and in complaining about the erosion of British civil liberties. He stoutly defended the Edinburgh Martyrs, raising their case in the House of Commons, and finally showing his solidarity with them in defeat by dining with them on their prison ship before their transportation to Australia.[93]

Another famous trial was soon to follow, this time in London. Twelve men were arrested and charged with high treason following the suspension of Habeas Corpus. Among them were Thomas Hardy, a London shoemaker and founder of the London Corresponding Society; John Horne Tooke, a clergyman, political candidate, and philologist; Thomas Holcroft, a playwright and strolling player; and John Thelwall, perhaps the most courageous of all the radicals, with whom Coleridge was to have a most intense, if short-lived, friendship.[94] The court eventually found there was no case to answer, the defendants not having plotted the overthrow or death of George III, and the accused were released in November and December 1794. This was much to the discomfiture of Pitt, who had himself been called as a witness and expertly cross-examined by Horne Tooke.[95]

But at the time that Coleridge and Southey were planning their escape in the summer of 1794, Hardy, Tooke, Thelwall and the others were languishing first in the Tower of London, then in Newgate, with their lives at the mercy of the judicial system. Both Tooke and Thelwall became chronically ill from the conditions in which they were kept; Hardy's shop was attacked and his wife lost the baby she was expecting and herself died soon after. Thelwall was asthmatic, and after five months in the Tower and two more in Newgate awaiting trial – thanks to the suspension of Habeas Corpus – his health was permanently broken.[96]

As he sat in prison Thelwall wrote poetry to keep his spirits up, prefacing his small collection, *Poems written in close confinement in the Tower and Newgate, under a charge of High Treason* (1795) with Milton's lines from *Comus*:

> Fool, do not boast;
> Thou canst not touch the freedom of my mind
> With all thy charms, although this corporal rind
> Thou hast immanacled.

The poems were sold by three brave London booksellers, themselves no strangers to prosecution: J. Ridgeway, H. D. Symonds, and Daniel Isaac Eaton.[97] While incarcerated in the Tower in the autumn of 1794, Thelwall may have been sent a copy of *The Fall of Robespierre* by his and Coleridge's mutual friend, George Dyer.[98]

It is against this background of real persecution and prosecution that we should consider the Pantisocratic venture which preoccupied Coleridge and Southey after their exciting summer together. We should also remember that they had both decided against taking their degrees and entering the Church or the law – the armed forces were out of the question given their views on Pitt's Government – so that it is difficult to imagine what careers were left open to young men with scruples but no private fortune. On 7 September Southey wrote to his younger brother Thomas, a reluctant recruit to the Navy, offering him the job of 'Admiral of a cock boat' on the Susquehanna, for he, too, was now included in the plan:

> Coleridge was with us nearly five weeks and made good use of his time – we preached Pantisocracy and Aspheterism every where. There Tom are two new words, the first signifying the equal government of all – and the other – the generalization of individual property, words well understood now in the city of Bristol.[99]

But Bath and Bristol gossip got going, making things unpleasant for the Fricker sisters, and Southey had to stiffen their resolve to ignore it. 'The people talk strangely of us! so let them; can you not smile at the envy and absurdity of the many?' he asked Sara Fricker.[100] Southey himself had to weather the storm that broke over him when the aunt with whom he lived, Miss Tyler, discovered the Pantisocracy scheme and her nephew's intention of marrying Edith Fricker, whom Miss Tyler looked down on socially. He was turned out of her Bristol house on a wet October night, and had to walk the nine miles to Bath in the rain and wind.[101] His aunt never communicated with him again.

Nevertheless, Southey kept his spirits up, contemplating the 'most delectable society' to be formed in America, writing a play about another Tyler, the peasant rebel Wat Tyler, and waiting in keen anticipation for Coleridge to return to the West Country. 'Most ardently do I long to see him', he told Sara Fricker on 25 October; and to Horace Bedford he wrote on 12 November, 'I am in hourly expectation of Coleridge, a man most worthy of all esteem and love.'[102]

Coleridge did not return. He, like Southey, had parted at the end of the summer full of resolution and enthusiasm. He went first to London, where he put up at the Salutation and Cat in Newgate Street, just opposite Christ's Hospital. Here he hobnobbed with some old school friends, most notably Lamb, drinking 'Porter & *Punch* round a good Fire' and talking Pantisocracy with gusto. In his first letter to Southey since their parting he sent rather lukewarm greetings to those with whom he was to be connected by marriage: 'Remember me to your Mother – to our Mother – am I not affiliated? I will write her when I arrive at Cambridge – To Lovell and Mrs Lovell my *fraternal* Love – To Miss F *more.*'[103]

Here ostensibly was the family he had been searching for since childhood; in its bosom he meant to find a multiple role as son, brother and husband. Yet his spirits were low. By 11 September he was talking of being 'seriously unwell', 'heavy of head & turbulent of Bowells' – symptoms of opium addiction/withdrawal – and he put off his journey to Cambridge for a week.[104]

Instead of writing to his fiancée, he sent a short note to *Edith* Fricker. On his arrival in Cambridge he wrote on 18 September one of his wild letters – probably after taking opium – to Southey. One can hear him working himself up to the proper pitch of enthusiasm for 'America and Miss Fricker', a package for which he had opted in haste and which now caused him to panic:

> I am at last arrived at Jesus. My God! how tumultuous are the movements of my Heart – since I quitted this room what and how important Events have been evolved! America! Southey! Miss Fricker! – Yes – Southey – you are right – Even Love is the creature of strong Motive – I certainly love her. I think of her incessantly & with unspeakable tenderness – with that inward melting away of Soul that symptomizes it.

Then in capital letters, referring to the servant at Miss Tyler's house, Shadrach Weeks, who had been Southey's boyhood playmate:

SHAD GOES WITH US. HE IS MY BROTHER![105]

It is impossible not to think that Coleridge, once separated from Southey's inspiriting presence, was full of doubts about his feelings and his future. Admonished by Southey for not writing to Sara, he resorted in his next letter, written the following day, to injured self-defence and counter-accusation. The excuses were those familiar to his brothers, but they were undoubtedly dismaying to the 'stern serious philosophic Robert Southey', as Southey characterized himself.[106] Coleridge was ill, 'very ill'; he had run out of money; there were good reasons (unspecified) for deferring writing to Sara. He was hurt: 'I ought not to have been *suspected.*'[107]

In Coleridge feelings of guilt and of righteous indignation were often closely entwined, as here. Southey had to read a criticism of his own rectitude, even his virtue – Coleridge had been impressed by his strong moral sense, by his 'confirmed Habits of strict Morality', in particular by the fact that Southey was sexually pure[108] – as if Southey himself were to blame for Coleridge's failings. A pattern was set for their future relations. Southey was upright, exemplary, accusatory; Coleridge responded with infuriating facility, shifting the blame by means of that 'specious argumentation' which his brother George, whom it was now Southey's fate to replace in

Coleridge's emotional life, so deplored in him. Here is how Coleridge brilliantly sloughs off blame, returning it to the sender with interest:

> Southey –! Precipitance is wrong. There may be too high a state of *Health* – perhaps even *Virtue* is liable to a *Plethora*! I have been the slave of Impulse, the Child of Imbecility – But my inconsistencies have given me a tarditure & reluctance to think ill of any one – having been often suspected of wrong, when I was altogether right, from *fellow-feeling* I judge not too hastily from appearances. Your undeviating Simplicity of Rectitude has made you too rapid in decision – having never erred, you feel more *indignation* at Error, than *Pity* for it.[109]

A week later Coleridge told Southey he had now written twice to Sara; described some flirting with Miss Brunton, a member of a touring company of actors from Norwich, to whom he also addressed two of his more posturing poems attacking tyranny and praising 'peaceful virtue'; [110] and announced that *The Fall of Robespierre* was 'printed all but the Title page'.[111]

As if Coleridge were not already inclined to disintegration, he now received a letter from, of all people, Mary Evans. She had heard about the Pantisocracy plan. She had also been told – '*indeed* I do not believe it' – that he had become an atheist. She wrote now, in a 'sisterly' way, to beg him to change his mind, or she would be forced to exclaim 'O what a noble Mind is here *o'erthrown*' (the words Southey would find himself using about Coleridge in 1810). Her letter, her name, the mere idea of her unsettled Coleridge completely. 'I loved her, Southey! almost to madness.' His attempt at a cure was not to fix his mind on Sara Fricker, or even America, but 'to be perpetually with Miss Brunton – I even hoped, that her Exquisite Beauty and uncommon Accomplishments might have cured one Passion by another'.[112] This letter to Southey was written on 21 October, Coleridge's twenty-second birthday.

Coleridge had heard from his brother George, too, 'who has been Friend, Brother, Father – 'Twas all remonstrance, and Anguish, & suggestions, that I am deranged!!'[113] If George had seen Coleridge's letters to Southey at this time, he would have been convinced that his suspicion was correct. Protestations, exclamations, excuses, accusations, half-promises to go down to Bath to see Southey (and presumably Sara), arguments about the details of Pantisocracy – Southey was beginning to suggest there should be two classes of Pantisocrats, masters and servants, which appalled Coleridge – and pathetic references to Mary jostle for place. 'She WAS VERY lovely, Southey!'[114]

Pantisocracy now seemed to him to be an imposed exile from home and from Mary:

> And though in distant climes to roam
> A Wanderer from my native home
> I fain would woo a gentle Fair

> To soothe the aching sense of Care,
> Thy Image may not banish'd be –
> Still, Mary! still I sigh for thee![115]

With that insensitivity to the feelings of others which coexisted with his extreme sensitivity about his own feelings, he sent this poem not to Mary, but to Southey.

Having replied to George's reproaches with self-abasement and protestation, berating his own indolence but denying that he was a democrat, Coleridge went to London to see him in November 1794. He probably also hoped to see Mary once more. But she was now engaged to another man, and Coleridge had to accept that she was utterly lost to him. His acknowledgement of the fact did not, however, reconcile him to marriage with Sara. First he told Southey on 9 December that his engagement to her had resulted from his having 'mistaken the ebullience of *schematism* for affection'; then, more desperately, on 29 December, he wrote:

> Love makes all things pure and heavenly like itself: – but to marry a woman whom I do *not* love – to degrade her, whom I call my Wife, by making her the Instrument of low Desire – and on the removal of a desultory Appetite, to be perhaps not displeased with her Absence![116]

This was prophetic indeed. But Coleridge, in awe of Southey's rectitude, even while he chided him for it, added the fatal words, 'Mark you, Southey! – *I will do my Duty.*'

3

Bristol and Marriage 1795–1796

O fair is Love's first hope to gentle mind!
As Eve's first star thro' fleecy cloudlet peeping;
And sweeter than the gentle south-west wind,
O'er willowy meads, and shadow'd waters creeping,
And Ceres' golden fields; – the sultry hind
Meets it with brow uplift, and stays his reaping.
Coleridge 'First Advent of Love' (?1824)

Though Coleridge's state of mind at the end of December 1794 was painfully confused, he was, did he but know it, about to enter the happiest and most productive years of his life. In the very letters to Southey in which he prevaricated over Sara Fricker, he boldly criticized Southey's poetry, adopting a superior, even condescending tone towards the brother poet whom he already recognized as his inferior in versifying. He himself was writing better poetry than before. In November 1794 he read an English translation of Schiller's *Robbers*, a 'Shakespearean' play about the adventures of a noble rebel, Karl Moor.[1] Coleridge was immediately fired to tell Southey all about it:

> 'Tis past one o clock in the morning – I sate down at twelve o'clock to read the 'Robbers' of Schiller – I had read chill and trembling until I came to the part where Moor fires a pistol over the Robbers who are asleep – I could read no more – My God! Southey! Who is this Schiller? This Convulser of the Heart? Did he write his Tragedy amid the yelling of Fiends? – I should not like to [be] able to describe such Characters – I tremble like an Aspen Leaf – Upon my Soul, I write to you because I am frightened – I had better go to Bed. Why have we ever called Milton sublime?[2]

This is Coleridge at his most impressionable. 'He is so made that he can hear the crepitation of a leaf', as Virginia Woolf observed.[3] Alarming

himself by reading sublime Gothic tragedy in the small hours, with probably a dose of laudanum acting to make him even more open to exciting
sensations, he recapitulates his childhood experience of reading (especially
of the often frightening *Arabian Nights*), dreaming and imagining. Some of
his own best poetry was to be in the sublime Gothic vein; he would excite
himself into creating nightmare experiences in 'The Ancient Mariner' and
'Christabel', poems which *he* may be said to have conjured up as if 'amid the
yelling of Fiends'.

It was this Coleridge, the magician–poet of the dark recesses of human
experience, whose influence on the next generation was to be extraordinary. Mary Shelley's *Frankenstein* (1818), the culminating work of Romantic
Gothic narrative, was conceived after the young author, with her husband
and Byron, had indulged in a late-night reading of 'Christabel' during a
storm on the shores of Lake Geneva in June 1816. On that occasion
Shelley ran screaming from the room on hearing the lines describing the
disrobing of Geraldine read aloud.[4] And *Frankenstein* itself rings with echoes
– direct quotations, half-quotations, and near-quotations – of 'The Ancient
Mariner'. When Mary Shelley met Coleridge in London in January 1824,
she noted that his 'beautiful descriptions, metaphysical talk & subtle
distinctions' reminded her of Shelley. In the frequent depressions of her
later years, she quoted feelingly in her journal the lines from *The Ancient
Mariner*:

> Alone, alone, all, all alone,
> Alone on a wide wide sea.[5]

The reading of Schiller's play marked a beginning for Coleridge. It
crystallized the elements from which he was to create his best poetry. The
immediate poetic result was a fine sonnet addressed to the German author.
It conveys all the fear and excitement so breathlessly described in the letter
to Southey, but demonstrates too an impressive structural control over the
psychological material:

> Schiller! that hour I would have wish'd to die,
> If thro' the shuddering midnight I had sent
> From the dark dungeon of the Tower time-rent
> That fearful voice, a famish'd Father's cry –
> Lest in some after moment aught more mean
> Might stamp me mortal! A triumphant shout
> Black Horror scream'd, and all her *goblin* rout
> Diminish'd shrunk from the more withering scene!
> Ah! Bard tremendous in sublimity!
> Could I behold thee in thy loftier mood
> Wandering at eve with finely-frenzied eye
> Beneath some vast old tempest-swinging wood!
> Awhile with mute awe gazing I would brood:
> Then weep aloud in a wild ecstasy![6]

With its strong rhythms, its striking opening line, its confident use of apostrophe and exclamation, the sonnet leaves behind the Bowles-like sentiment of most of his poetry so far, even while it resorts to certain Gothic cliches about dungeons, towers, and 'black horror'. At the age of twenty-two, Coleridge comes of age as a poet.

Interestingly, he seems to have half-realized that he had just made a leap into poetic adulthood. In December 1794 he composed a sonnet addressed to Bowles, in which he wrote – note the past tense – 'My heart has thank'd thee, Bowles! for those soft Strains'.[7] Soft strains alone were not to be Coleridge's *forte*; the stamp of his genius was to be found rather in the 'finely-frenzied eye' of a Schiller, refashioned as the 'flashing eyes' of the figure of the poet in 'Kubla Khan'.

The sonnet to Bowles was published in the *Morning Chronicle* on 26 December 1794. Ten days earlier Coleridge had dined with Gray and Perry, the proprietors and editors of the paper, at this time the most influential of the anti-ministerial journals.[8] Coleridge now got to know, through Perry, and probably through George Dyer and Lamb too, several of London's leading radical writers and activists. He met Holcroft, just released from prison where he had been held with Thelwall, Tooke and Hardy. Holcroft, in turn, introduced him to Godwin, the most famous theorist of the radical movement.[9] As Hazlitt memorably recalled in *The Spirit of the Age* (1825), 'no work in our time gave such a blow to the philosophical mind of the country as the celebrated *Enquiry concerning Political Justice*.' 'Tom Paine was considered for the time as a Tom Fool to him; Paley an old woman; Edmund Burke a flashy sophist.'[10]

Coleridge was in his element in this circle. Agreeing with their radical political views, he found himself at odds with Godwin and Holcroft on religious questions. Before meeting Godwin, Coleridge was aware of his atheism, and told Southey, 'I set him at defiance.'[11] Now he entered into the lists in conversation with both adversaries. Of course Coleridge, with his astonishing eloquence, won the argument. Holcroft 'absolutely infests you with *Atheism*', he told Southey, but 'my great *coolness* and command of impressive Language certainly *did him over*'.[12]

His ultimate success with the more formidable Godwin was even more impressive. Though at this time the two men agreed to differ on religion, when they next met in London in the winter of 1799–1800 Coleridge, on Godwin's frank admission, converted him, if not to Christianity, at least to a form of 'theism'.[13] Meanwhile Coleridge, conscious of the intellectual debt of his and Southey's Pantisocracy scheme to Godwin's *Political Justice*, and impressed by Godwin's brave support of the victims of the State Trials, addressed a sonnet to him in the series 'Sonnets on Eminent Chracters' which he published in the *Morning Chronicle* in December 1794 and January 1795. He was perhaps right to dismiss this poem as '*miserably magazinish*', but one notices with interest that he uses provocatively religious language in his praise of the atheist Godwin:

> Nor will I not thy holy guidance bless,
> And hymn thee, GODWIN! with an ardent lay.[14]

In other words, even as he celebrates Godwin, his metaphors continue the argument on religion with him.

Other sonnets in this series are addressed to Coleridge's poetical and political heroes: Bowles, Southey, Priestley, Sheridan, the Polish patriot Kosciusko and Thomas Erskine. Sheridan is praised for speaking up in the House of Commons against the war with France; Erskine is memorialized as a lone spokesman for 'British Freedom' in his dual role as Whig orator and indefatigable defence lawyer at the trials of Tooke, Hardy and Thelwall.[15]

There are also two sonnets addressed to anti-heroes: Burke and Pitt. Burke is accused of apostasy – he had supported the American Revolution but not the French – and Pitt is blamed for the same *volte face*. Here Coleridge writes daringly, given the continuing suspension of Habeas Corpus and the Government's determination, despite the setback of the State Trial acquittals, to suppress opposition:

> Yon dark Scowler view,
> Who with proud words of dear-lov'd Freedom came –
> More blasting than the mildew from the South!
> And kiss'd his country with Iscariot mouth
> (Ah! foul apostate from his Father's fame!)
> Then fix'd her on the Cross of deep distress,
> And at safe distance marks the thirsty Lance
> Pierce her big side![16]

Coleridge undoubtedly courted prosecution for this attack, not least because of the emotive allusion to Britain as Christ betrayed by Judas-Pitt.

All this time Southey was anxiously awaiting Coleridge in Bath. But Coleridge was enjoying his London company and his connection with the *Morning Chronicle*, and he dreaded a meeting with Sara. 'Think you I wish to stay in Town?' he asked Southey indignantly on 29 December. 'I am all eagerness to leave it – and am resolved, whatever be the consequence, to be at Bath by Saturday', meaning 3 January 1795.[17] On 2 January he wrote about the impossibility of sitting on the outside of a coach for 'a Man who like me has no great Coat, is cold and rheumatismferous', not to mention almost penniless. Guilt and opium provide wings for a flight of giddy rhetoric:

> I will dash through the towns and helter skelter it into Bath in the Flying Waggon! Two Miles an hour! That's your Sort –! I shall be supplied with Bread and Cheese from Christ's Hospital and shall take a bottle of Gin for

myself and Tuom, the Waggoner! – Plenty of Oronoko Tobacco – smoke all
the Way – that's your Sort!
   Wrapped up in Hay – so warm! There are four or five Calves Inside –
Passengers like myself – I shall fraternize with them![18]

Southey and Robert Lovell walked to Marlborough the following
Wednesday to meet this comical waggon, 'but no S.T. Coleridge was therein!'
On Friday 9 January Southey wrote in exasperation to poor Sara Fricker
that he was 'kept in exercise by walking to meet the coaches . . . Why will he
ever fix a day if he cannot abide by it?'[19]
   Finally Southey came up to London to find his friend. He reported to
Edith Fricker on 12 January that he had arrived at the Salutation and Cat,
which, for all its cheap and cheerful attractions for Coleridge, struck the
more fastidious Southey as 'a most foul stye'. Coleridge had gone with
Lamb to the Unitarian Chapel; when he came back he objected to
Southey's recent modification of the Pantisocracy scheme, a plan to do
some modest farming in Wales preparatory to emigration. Coleridge's
counter-idea was to stay in London and earn money by writing for newspapers.[20] The friends were finding themselves further apart than they had
hoped, and both were miserable. However, for better or worse, Southey
extracted Coleridge from his niche in Newgate Street, and duly took him to
Bristol and Miss Fricker.
   Poor Sara Fricker. She had seen Coleridge for only two weeks or so the
previous summer, when he had arrived in Bristol 'brown as a berry' from
his walking tour with Hucks, looking 'plain, but eloquent and clever', as she
remembered much later. 'His clothes were worn out; his hair wanted
cutting.'[21] The pressures on her to like him were great. Southey was besot-
ted with him; her sisters Edith and Mary already had partners. She may have
come to regret that she did not do as her third sister Martha did when
proposed to by George Burnett at the height of the Pantisocratic excitement, namely refuse on the grounds that he only wanted 'a wife in a hurry',
not her in particular.[22] It was hardly Sara's fault if Coleridge did not know
his own mind.
   When Coleridge was finally brought into contact with Sara again in
mid-January 1795, he was pleasantly surprised. It was flattering to hear that
she had recently rejected two suitors, 'one of them of large Fortune',
against understandable family pressure to accept the man with the fortune.[23] Coleridge now seemed not unhappy at the prospect of marriage to
Sara.
   He was also busy. At Christmas 1794 he had begun in London a long
poem in blank verse 'on the Nativity'.[24] This was 'Religious Musings', his
first poem of any length and pretensions, at which he worked for another
year before publishing it in 1796 as the centrepiece of his first volume of
poems. He had also plunged straight into the political life of Bristol, and
was soon giving public lectures which stirred up the inhabitants of that
thriving city.

Bristol in the 1790s was an important sea port and trading centre, a city in which merchants could make fortunes, and one of those provincial centres where religious dissent and zeal for parliamentary reform were strong. One of the petitions presented to Parliament in 1785 arguing for the abolition of the slave trade had come from nearby Bridgwater.[25] At the same time, because of its importance as a port, Bristol had many sugar refineries, so that there was also fierce local opposition to the many bills put before Parliament, chiefly by William Wilberforce, during the 1790s. Coleridge contributed robustly to the debate with a bold lecture against the slave trade in June 1795.[26]

On his arrival in the city in January Coleridge was naturally introduced to prominent dissenters and radicals. Here, too, he found a publisher for his poetry. Joseph Cottle was a young bookseller with pretensions to be a poet himself and a spirit of generosity towards aspiring authors. As Southey wrote years later, 'It can rarely happen that a young author should meet with a bookseller as inexperienced and as ardent as himself.'[27] Cottle took on both Southey and Coleridge, advancing them small sums which he never expected to be paid back. In 1798 he brought out *Lyrical Ballads*, the genius of which went almost wholly unrecognized by critics and commentators at the time.

It is from Cottle that we learn most about Coleridge's life in Bristol, for the publisher rapidly fell under Coleridge's spell. 'I instantly descried his intellectual character', wrote Cottle later, 'exhibiting as he did, an eye, a brow, and a forehead, indicative of commanding genius'.[28] Cottle observed that in the Pantisocratic discussions which went on between Coleridge, Southey and George Burnett, Coleridge was 'the Mercury', who 'ingeniously parried every adverse argument' and often announced that he was about to write 'a quarto volume in defence of Pantisocracy'.[29]

Though Cottle allowed some sourness to enter into his retrospective account because he felt he had been unjustly left out of Coleridge's own biographical writings, particularly *Biographia Literaria*, and though he mangled dates and places and took unwarrantable editorial liberties with the many Coleridge letters in his possession, he is nevertheless the most important source for Coleridge's life at this time. We must treat his account with caution, but we cannot do without it.[30]

Coleridge and Southey were still arguing about the Welsh farming idea, but they agreed that a way of raising money for the American venture – not yet given up – was to give public lectures. Southey delivered a set of historical lectures in March and April 1795, and Coleridge gave three lectures on politics in February. He told Dyer later that month that he might have given a fourth but, he added rather proudly,

the opposition of the Aristocrats is so furious and determined, that I begin to fear, that the Good I do is not proportionate to the Evil I occasion – Mobs and Mayors, Blockheads and Brickbats, Placards and Press gangs have leagued in horrible Conspiracy against me – The Democrats are as sturdy in support of me – but their number is comparatively small –/ Two or three uncouth and unbrained Automata have threatened my Life – and in the last Lecture the Genus infirmum were scarcely restrained from attacking the house in which the 'damn'd Jacobine was jawing away'.[31]

Years later, when Coleridge had become more conservative and orthodox in religious and political matters, he attempted to give the impression that he had never been a 'Jacobin', or even a 'Democrat'. He had perhaps some excuse for fudging the issue, in that he had long been the victim of vicious periodical onslaughts on his politics, old and new, on his domestic life, and on his writings. Attacked up to about 1802 for his radicalism, he began soon afterwards to be the chief butt of younger radicals like Shelley and Hazlitt, who were merciless towards his defection from radical causes. In *The Spirit of the Age* Hazlitt declared that 'Liberty (the philosopher's and the poet's bride)' had fallen victim to 'the murderous practices of the hag Legitimacy'; Coleridge had 'stood at bay, and at last turned on the pivot of a subtle casuistry to the *unclean side*'. Hazlitt's only concession to the change in Coleridge's opinions from those early days was to grant that he had not moved as far to the right as either Wordsworth or Southey. He had not taken the King's shilling: 'his discursive reason would not let him trammel himself into a poet-laureate [Southey from 1813] or stamp-distributor [Wordsworth from 1813]'.[32]

Hence Coleridge's brushing aside of the Bristol period in *Biographia Literaria,* a work which displays a neurotic concern for his reputation; hence also his selective printing the following year in the 1818 *Friend* of one of the Bristol lectures, with the careful omission of the most radical passages and a preface containing a disingenuous retort to 'an infamous Libel in proof of the Author's former Jacobinism' (by Hazlitt).[33] Even as early as 1803 Coleridge was writing to his and Wordsworth's friends, Sir George and Lady Beaumont, half-denying that he was ever a flaming radical, half-admitting it, and pleading his youth and loneliness in extenuation. His self-analysis begins astutely, then runs into self-praise, self-criticism, and sometimes both, in extravagant measure. He tells his noble friends that

with an ebullient Fancy, a flowing Utterance, a light & dancing Heart, & a disposition to catch fire by the very rapidity of my own motion, & to speak vehemently from mere verbal associations, choosing sentences & sentiments for the very reason, that would have made me recoil with a dying away of the Heart & an unutterable Horror from the actions expressed in such sentences & sentiments – namely, because they were wild, & original, & vehement & fantastic! – I aided the Jacobins, by witty sarcasms & subtle reasonings & declamations full of genuine feeling against all Rulers & against all established Forms![34]

It is impossible not to hear the accents of pride in this piece of head-shaking over his reckless past. As Virginia Woolf so brilliantly remarked, Coleridge is a Micawber, but with a difference, for he 'knows that he is

Micawber': 'Dickens would need to be doubled with Henry James, to be trebled with Proust, in order to convey the complexity and the conflict of a Pecksniff who despises his own hypocrisy, of a Micawber who is humiliated by his own humiliation.'[35]

In fact, Coleridge's political lectures were very radical indeed. The first, 'A Moral and Political Lecture, by S. T. Coleridge, of Jesus College, Cambridge', was delivered in late January or early February 1795 in the Corn Market in Bristol, and published a few days later as a sixpenny pamphlet. It was a spirited, imaginative piece, stopping short of seditious libel (as well it might, with Habeas Corpus still suspended), but not pulling many punches in its attack on Pitt and his Government. Coleridge's trump card was his religious belief and his facility in quoting from Scripture in support of his political points. In the Advertisement to the lecture he cleverly announced that

> They, who in these days of jealousy and Party rage dare publicly explain the Principles of Freedom, must expect to have their Intentions misrepresented, and to be entitled like the Apostles of Jesus, 'stirrers up of the People and men accused of Sedition'.[36]

The lecture bristles with Biblical language, moral outrage about tyranny, and scornful puns on Pitt's name: 'In the principles, which this Apostate has, by his emissaries [i.e., spies and *agents provocateurs*], sown among a few blind zealots for Freedom, he has digged a pit into which he himself may perhaps be doomed to fall.' Against this 'bad man' are ranged 'that small but glorious band, whom we may truly distinguish by the name of thinking and disinterested Patriots', including 'the illustrious Triumvirate', Muir, Palmer and Margarot of the Edinburgh Trials. While Coleridge threatens the Government with the possibility of bloody revolt, he is careful to range himself on the side of those whose struggle is non-violent; those, like Godwin and Thelwall, who take up the pen in defence of liberty rather than the sword.[37] The difference between Coleridge and the other two lies in their disdain for religion of all kinds, as against his hatred of the rituals of the Church of England but embracing of Unitarianism, love of Christ, and reverence for the Bible.

Though Coleridge and Thelwall had not yet met, they were already aware of one another. It is likely that Coleridge was encouraged in his Bristol lecturing by the knowledge that Thelwall, recently released from Newgate, had courageously renewed the political lecturing for which he had been arrested the previous year. Thelwall's first lecture coincided almost exactly with Coleridge's; on 6 February 1795 he spoke in London 'Upon the Moral and Political Importance of the Liberty of Speech', the very topic Coleridge also chose. Thelwall's reputation was such that hundreds attended his lectures, some having to be turned away at the door.[38] Coleridge's audience was no doubt smaller, but according to Cottle it was appreciative. Many years later a Bristolian calling himself simply 'Q' recalled in the *Monthly Magazine* how Coleridge the lecturer had appeared in Bristol 'like a comet or meteor in our horizon'.[39]

Two more lectures followed in February. The texts are lost, but they were published in a slightly altered form as *Conciones ad Populum. Or Addresses to the People* in December 1795.[40] This pamphlet opens with 'A Letter from Liberty to her Dear Friend Famine'. Liberty, writing from 'Dover Cliff' (signifying that she is ready to flee Pitt's England), boldly addresses Famine, asking her to 'plead my cause', since all attempts to catch 'the ear of Majesty' or appeal to established Religion for justice or mercy have failed. In thus personifying Famine, Coleridge is not being unduly melodramatic. The winter of 1794–5 was exceptionally cold, resulting in a doubling of the death rate; the price of wheat was high; bread riots had broken out all over the country.[41] By September the philanthropic Tom Poole had begun to experiment with methods of making a cheaper loaf; he tried making bread out of wheat, barley, beans, and potatoes.[42]

Coleridge was risking prosecution with this outspoken attack on the King, Church and Government. One of the lectures was a sustained criticism of the war with France. Coleridge argued, as Fox did in Parliament, that it was not a 'just and necessary' war. Moreover, Pitt's answer to suggestions that he should negotiate a peace with France, namely that he could not honourably treat with men so stained with atrocities, is given short shrift by the young lecturer:

> Admire, I pray you, the cautious Delicacy of our Government! that will profess itself the Ally of the Immaculate only – of the MERCIFUL Catherine [Catherine the Great of Russia, known for her ruthlessness, particularly towards the Poles], the HONEST King of Prussia [Friedrich Wilhelm II, who had used subsidies, given by Britain to help him fight the French, to invade Poland], and that most CHRISTIAN Arch-pirate, the Dey of Algiers! [Britain condoned Algerian piracy][43]

This is strong stuff, as is Coleridge's direct assault on Pitt's speeches in the House of Commons – 'Mystery concealing Meanness, as steam-clouds invelope a dunghill' (an allusion to the famous Gillray cartoon of December 1791 of Pitt as a fungus growing on a dunghill).[44] Coleridge quotes Pitt's own speeches of 1781 attacking the 'iniquitous and unjust War' with America against him, ending magnificently with 'All this – O calumniated Judas Iscariot! all this WILLIAM PITT said!'[45] People starved, the Government introduced taxes, freedom of speech was stifled, crimping and bribery procured recruits for the army in its lunatic war against France. 'Over a recruiting place in this city I have seen pieces of Beef hung up to attract the half-famished Mechanic.'[46]

In May 1795 Pitt introduced a new tax to bring in revenue to finance the war, the tax on hair powder. Democrats and Liberals, Coleridge and Tom Poole included, took pleasure in responding to this; they simply stopped powdering.[47]

On 16 June Coleridge lectured against the slave trade. Drawing heavily on Thomas Clarkson's *Essay on the Impolicy of the African Slave Trade* (1788) and other works which he and Southey borrowed from Bristol Public Library, he put before his audience the ghastly details of the slaves' conditions both aboard the ships carrying them from Africa to the West Indies – 'fettered with leg-shackles & handcuffs, two and two' and so closely confined between decks that 'slaves who have been thrust down at night in health have been brought up dead in the morning' – and on their arrival to work on the sugar plantations. He quotes Sir Hans Sloane's account of a 'Gentleman' who '*thought fit* to roast his slave alive'.[48] And yet Pitt, who had once advocated abolition of the trade, would not support it now. Coleridge appealed to British citizens, in the name of 'the inspired Philanthropist of Galilee', to leave off buying sugar and rum. He ended the lecture provocatively:

> But I have heard another argument in favor of the Slave Trade, namely, that the Slaves are as well off as the Peasantry in England! Now this argument I have [seen] in publications on the Subject – and were I the attorney General, I should *certainly* have prosecuted the author for seditious & treasonable Writings. For I appeal to common sense whether to affirm that the Slaves are as well off as our Peasantry, be not the same as to assert that our Peasantry are as bad off as Negro Slaves – and whether if the Peasantry believed it there is a man amongst them who [would] not rebel? and be justified in Rebellion?[49]

By the time Coleridge published *Conciones ad Populum* on 3 December 1795, two notorious bills brought forward by Pitt and his cousin, the Leader of the House of Lords, Lord Grenville, in November were on the point of becoming law. Known as the Gagging Acts, they severely restricted press freedom and freedom of speech by extending the meaning of treason far beyond actual plotting against the King's life, and made it as difficult as possible for meetings of over fifty people to take place. Some clauses were directed specifically at Thelwall, who soon found it impossible to hire rooms in which to lecture.[50] Coleridge himself was extremely lucky not to be prosecuted under the Acts. It was foolish of him to claim in *The Friend* in June 1809, 'I may safely defy my worst enemy to shew, in any of my few writings, the least bias to Irreligion, Immorality, or Jacobinism.'[51] As Southey retorted to this piece of Pecksniffism, if Coleridge was not a Jacobin in 1795, 'I wonder who the Devil was. I am sure I was.'[52]

Coleridge even tackled the two bills head-on in a lecture given at the Pelican Inn, Bristol, on 26 November 1795, shortly before they became law. Pitt's excuse for bringing in the bills was that unrest was rife following a mass meeting in Islington on 26 October calling for an end to war and demanding universal suffrage and annual parliaments. Though the meeting had not been riotous, it was followed three days later by an attack on George III's carriage as he was on his way to open Parliament. Coleridge in his lecture asked the same rhetorical questions which Fox and Sheridan were putting in Parliament:

> Where, when, & by whom have factious & seditious speeches been made, and the public Peace endangered –. In various parts of the Kingdom, and especially within this last year, heavy grievances have called together numberless meetings –. Which of these have been disorderly riotous![53]

So draconian were the proposed measures that they made anyone liable to prosecution who did not accept that 'the established Government & constitution is perfect – that therefore all Censure is Calumny – all pretended exposure of Abuses misrepresentation & falsehood'.[54]

Coleridge worked up and expanded this lecture into a pamphlet, *The Plot Discovered*, which was published early in December, as the bills were about to be passed (see plate 4).[55] It was certainly seditious under the terms of the law, passed on 18 December, its subtitle being 'An Address to the People, against Ministerial Treason'. Coleridge shows himself an able polemicist. The pamphlet begins with a quotation from a remark by the Bishop of Rochester in the House of Lords that 'the mass of the people have nothing to do with the laws, but to obey them!' Capitalizing on his provocative title accusing the *Government* of treason against the sovereign *people*, he immediately takes the moral – and Christian – high ground:

> Ere yet this foul treason against the majesty of man, ere yet this blasphemy against the goodness of God be registered among our statutes, I enter my protest! Ere yet our laws as well as our religion be muffled up in mysteries, as a CHRISTIAN I protest against this worse than Pagan darkness! Ere yet the sword descends, the two-edged sword that is now waving over the head of Freedom, as a BRITON, I protest against slavery! Ere yet it be made legal for Ministers to act with vigour beyond law, as a CHILD OF PEACE I protest against civil war![56]

One injustice singled out by Coleridge is that to Thelwall. Another is the censorship of plays. He notes that Schiller's *Robbers* has now been suppressed 'by that thing yclept a Lord Chamberlain'. Pitt himself is nothing but a Caligula wishing to 'behead' the whole state.[57]

Coleridge's lectures were praised for their courage in a contemporary Bristol publication called *The Observer*:

> Undaunted by the storms of popular prejudice, unswayed by magisterial influence, he spoke in public what none had the courage in this City to do before – he told Men that they have Rights.[58]

According to Cottle, Coleridge was a good lecturer, well able to cope with the odd heckler. When a group of 'gentlemen of the opposite party' hissed him, Coleridge apparently replied coolly, 'I am not at all surprised, when the red hot prejudices of aristocrats are suddenly plunged into the cool water of reason, that they should go off with a hiss!'[59] This was a clever reply, notwithstanding the inappropriate description of his own rhetoric as 'cool', and it served to silence the objectors.

The Observer also had something to say about Coleridge's appearance. His person was 'slovenly; a clean appearance is as good a criterion whereby to know a scholar as a person of mean appearance'. Southey was held up as a contrary example of the compatibility of scholarliness and clean linen. Mr Coleridge, the critic went on, would 'do well to appear with cleaner stockings in public' and his hair would benefit from being combed.[60] Coleridge might have echoed what Samuel Johnson, another notorious sloven, said of Christopher Smart, namely that 'he did not love clean linen; and I have no passion for it'.[61]

He must have put on a clean shirt to sit for his portrait to Peter Vandyke, a descendant of the great Van Dyke. The painter had settled in Bristol and, fortunately for us, painted Coleridge in 1795, when he was full of activity and excitement (see cover illustration). Cottle says 'a better likeness was never taken'.[62] In it, Coleridge looks rather younger than his twenty-two years. The visual portrait is matched remarkably well by one of Coleridge's frank verbal self-portraits, delivered a year later in a letter to Thelwall. 'As to me', he wrote in November 1796, 'my face, unless when animated by immediate eloquence, expresses great Sloth, & great, indeed almost ideotic, good nature. 'Tis a mere carcase of a face: fat, flabby, & expressive chiefly of inexpression.' Nevertheless, 'I am told that my eyes, eyebrows, & forehead are physiognomically good –; but of this the Deponent knoweth not'.[63]

Cottle records that Coleridge, when expressing his gratitude for the loans and advances offered at this time, used to regret, 'with even pungency of feeling, that he had no friend in the world, to whom, in a time of extremity, he could apply "for a guinea"'. The generous publisher, though well aware of the strain of humbug in Coleridge, which emerged regularly when money was at stake, notes with amazement: 'He appeared like a being dropt from the clouds, without tie or connexion on earth; and during the years in which I knew him, he never once visited (that I could learn) any one of his relations, nor exchanged a letter with them.' Coleridge presumably omitted to explain how he had disappointed his brothers by running away, degreeless, from Cambridge after they had baled him out of the army, for Cottle remarks how astonished he was 'that such a man should, apparently, be abandoned'.[64]

No letters between the brothers survive from Coleridge's time in Bristol. He certainly felt abandoned, however much the feeling was complicated by guilt. The more he recognized his share of the blame in the breakdown of relations with his family, the more vehement was his denunciation of them, as is seen in his contorted letter to the Beaumonts in 1803, with its denials, retractions, and yet proud defiance about his radical years in Bristol:

My relations, & the Churchmen & 'Aristocrats', to use the phrase of the
Day [Coleridge is mindful of the status of Sir George and Lady
Beaumont] . . . abhorred my person, I abhorred their actions: they set up the
long howl of Hydrophoby at my principles, & I repayed their Hatred & Terror
by the bitterness of Contempt. Who then remained to listen to me? to be kind
to me? to be my friends – to look at me with kindness, to shake my hand with
kindness, to open the door, & spread the hospitable board, & to let me feel
that I was a man well-loved.

The familiar cry for love was met, says Coleridge reproachfully, by others.
'These offices of Love the Democrats only performed to me.'[65]

It is interesting that Coleridge should have felt, both in 1795 and on
looking back in 1803, that a man of twenty-two naturally needed, and
deserved, financial as well as moral support from others. This is the more
striking given the fact that it was the custom in the Coleridge family for the
young men to leave home and become independent at relatively early ages.
Part of Coleridge, as a matter of fact, never came to believe that he ought
to be self-supporting, though another part was acutely critical of his inability ever to become so in a life lasting nearly sixty-two years.

Bristol's Democrats did come to his aid. In May and June 1795 he
delivered 'Six Lectures on Revealed Religion', in which he preached Unitarianism and radical politics together, as Priestley had done a few years
earlier. These lectures were financed by Cottle and his brothers Amos and
Robert and their father, with support from Mr Morgan, a wine shipper, the
Revd John Prior Estlin, a Unitarian minister, and probably Josiah Wade, a
wealthy Bristol tradesman.[66]

The topic of the lectures was religion and its perversions into
Anglicanism on the one hand – attacked for its trinitarianism and
'mysteries', as well as its close connection with the Tory Government
through the bishops in the House of Lords – and impious atheism on the
other. Coleridge, a confirmed Unitarian at this time, is keen to attack
orthodoxy but equally keen to show his abhorrence of atheism, so often
associated in the public mind with the radical movement. This was the
more important because of the notoriety of Godwin and Thelwall in this
respect.

In order to establish Unitarianism as the golden mean between these two
extremes, to claim for it an equal foundation in reason and in revelation,
Coleridge resorts to an elaborate allegory. In Bunyanesque manner he
opens the first lecture, given about 19 May 1795 at the Assembly
Coffeehouse on the Quay at Bristol, with an account of a vision supposed to
have taken place on 'a vast Plain, which I immediately knew to be the Valley
of Life'. He sees 'a great number of men in Black Robes' (Church of
England clergymen) who are 'collecting with scrupulous care' tithes for the
church. The visionary enters the 'Temple of *Religion*', where he is immediately relieved of his money. He is led by a priest into a 'large and gloomy
pile'. The building is almost totally dark and full of riddling inscriptions, or
'mysteries' (the articles of faith of the Church of England). Discovering

that this is the Temple not of Religion but of Superstition, he makes his escape.

Spenser, Milton and Bunyan lie behind this tale. The visionary sees a woman in white (true religion) who takes him to an 'eminence', as Adam is taken by the Archangel Michael in book XI of *Paradise Lost*, from which he views the valley below. Topically enough, she gives him an 'optic glass', a favourite instrument for travellers and artists to view landscapes with. The glass, representing faith or revelation, assists him, 'without contradicting' his natural vision (i.e., reason), to view the valley. What he sees, thus guided but not brainwashed, is 'a vast and dusky Cave', the counterpart of the Temple of Superstition. Here sits a whore (atheism) accompanied by 'the Monster Blasphemy'.[67]

Coleridge, having thus dramatically established his median position between the two extremes, proceeds during this lecture and those following it to proselytize for the Unitarian faith. One topic on which he touches rather airily, in view of his later deep and distressed concern with it, is the origin of evil. Here, influenced by Priestley and by David Hartley's philosophical optimism as expressed in his work, *Observations on Man*, first published in 1749 and reissued in 1791 in an edition which Coleridge read, he accepts the 'total Benevolence' of God.[68] 'Instead of evil, a disputable word, let us use Pain', says Coleridge. By a rather weak chain of reasoning he arrives at the view that 'Pain is intended as a stimulus to Man in order that he may remove moral Evil'. The example given is a toothache, which Coleridge says is the result of 'uncleanliness or scorbutic Diseases' which in turn are 'immediately or remotely the Effect of Moral Evil'.[69] It is likely that he is here suppressing both his own experience of physical pain and his strong sense of sinfulness in order to serve an attractive theory.

In the fifth lecture Coleridge vigorously attacks belief in the Trinity: 'it is the mysterious cookery of the Orthodox'.[70] For him, the true Christian is not concerned with dogmatic mysteries like redemption and Christ's atonement for others' sins, but rather with living a good life in imitation of the good man Christ. The Church of England and Roman Catholicism are lumped together in the Temple of Superstition. Ten years on he had reversed his position. 'Unitarianism', runs a notebook entry of 12 February 1805, 'in all its Forms is Idolatry', 'the Religion of a man, whose Reason would make him an Atheist but whose Heart and Common sense will not permit him to be so'.[71] Even later he returned to the opening allegory of these Unitarian lectures, using it again, but with significant alterations, in an article in the *Courier* in 1811. This time not the Church of England, but Roman Catholicism alone occupies the Temple of Superstition, and Anglicanism has replaced Unitarianism as the true religion.[72]

When Coleridge began lecturing in February 1795, he and Southey were happily sharing lodgings and making plans. 'Coleridge is writing at the same table', Southey told Grosvenor Bedford on 8 February: 'our names are written in the book of destiny, on the same page'.[73] They were indeed, but the future was not to be quite what either of the eager fiancés, lecturers and Pantisocrats expected.

During the spring of 1795 they helped one another with material for their lectures, briefly planned to co-found a new journal, to be called, not very excitingly, the *Provincial Magazine*, which would be 'the vehicle of all our poetry'. This plan fell through at an early stage. But America was still 'the place to which our ultimate views tend', though Southey now thought it would be 'years' before they could afford to go.[74] By May Southey was complaining of feeling 'languid'; he told Bedford he was avoiding company, unlike Coleridge, who was revelling in it. On 27 May Southey was anticipating being 'dragged into a party of pleasure to-morrow for two days'. With a vehemence of phrase which was characteristic of him, he swore that 'an hour's hanging would be luxury compared with these detestable schemes'.[75]

The particular scheme may have been a walking excursion he made with Coleridge, Edith and Sara Fricker, and Cottle, to Tintern Abbey. Cottle tells the story at length in his memoirs. Southey was apparently angry with Coleridge for failing to give a scheduled lecture the night before. A dispute arose, with each female siding with her fiancé and Cottle mediating. The party got lost and argued about which direction to take.[76] We can infer that Southey was beginning to find Coleridge an unreliable, if still inspiriting, companion. He may already have privately given up the idea of America.

In August something occurred which caused Southey to abandon Pantisocracy and his radical principles altogether. His uncle, Herbert Hill, wrote urging him to become a clergyman and offering to help him find a parish.[77] To Coleridge's amazement the prudent Southey did not immediately reject the idea. Coleridge gave him a moral lecture. He would perjure himself if he entered the Church: 'You disapprove of an Establishment altogether – you believe it iniquitous – a mother of Crimes! – It is impossible that *you* could uphold it by assuming the badge of Affiliation!'[78]

Southey did not take long to decide that Coleridge was right. But he proved more receptive to his uncle's next proposal, namely that he should accompany him to Lisbon for a few months, then return to England to train as a lawyer. This was not as bad as becoming a clergyman, but it put an end to all hopes of America and Pantisocracy, and to Coleridge it felt like a betrayal. No letters between the two friends survive between August and November. Coleridge had found that his admired friend was capable of despicable worldliness. His first great adult friendship suffered a serious breach.

Not until 13 November did Coleridge finally express his opinion. This was the eve of Southey's wedding, which was to take place secretly before his departure, without Edith, to Portugal. In an extremely long letter Coleridge held up an unflattering mirror to his former friend, prefacing it with the announcement, 'You are *lost* to *me*, because you are lost to Virtue . . . As this will probably be the last time I shall have occasion to address you, I will glance thro' the History of our connection, and regularly retrace your Conduct and my own.'

Coleridge runs through the story of their meeting, their plans, their desire to build a society not based on selfish principles or personal property. Southey, in suggesting the Welsh farming plan, had begun to think less communally and more individually: 'it was "I and I" and "will and will" – sentences of gloomy and self-centering Resolve.' Southey had also become 'cold and gloomy' in his manners, and Coleridge had begun to dread that he was 'meditating a Separation'. Worse followed:

> Remember when we went to Ashton on the Strawberry Party. Your conversation with George Burnet[t] on the day following he detailed to me. It scorched my throat. Your private resources were to remain your individual property, and every thing to be separate except on five or six acres. In short, we were to commence Partners in a petty Farming Trade. This was the Mouse of which the Mountain Pantisocracy was at last safely delivered![79]

Southey had been happy enough at the idea of sharing property and income while none of the friends *had* either property or income. But at this time his old schoolfriend C. W. Williams Wynn promised him an annuity of £160 when he came of age, which would be at the end of 1796, and Southey began to think differently on the matter.[80]

Southey had to endure not only this reasonably justified criticism of his falling off from the Pantisocratic ideal, but, much worse, Coleridge's characteristic personal twisting of the knife. These things would have been less terrible if it had not become 'such a deep-rooted Habit of my Soul' to think 'with almost superstitious Veneration of you'. Coleridge paints the scene in the lodgings at College Street when Southey had been offered the position in the Church by his uncle: 'You went to Bed. George sat half-petrified – gaping at the pigmy Virtue of his supposed Giant. I performed the Office of still-struggling Friendship by writing you my free Sentiments concerning the enormous Guilt of that which your Uncle's doughty Sophistry recommended.'[81]

Coleridge acknowledges that Southey's behaviour has severely put to the test the philosophical optimism he had adopted and lectured on, which required him to believe that 'however wickedly you might act, God would make it ULTIMATELY the best'. This philosophy Southey himself had named – 'not unwittily' – Panglossian after Dr Pangloss in Voltaire's *Candide*, who could view even the terrible Lisbon earthquake as part of God's benevolent plan, all being for the best in the best of all possible worlds. Well, Coleridge writes now, in that way of his which combines righteousness with witty insult: 'Heaven forbid, that I should not now have faith, that however foul your Stream may run here, yet that it will filtrate & become pure in it's subterraneous Passage to the Ocean of Universal Redemption.'[82]

Nor can Coleridge resist the temptation to taunt Southey with the contrast between them. He, Coleridge, now newly married to Sara and with a responsibility to care for her, as well as her mother and younger brother, will struggle hard 'by my own exertions' to keep a family. And Southey? 'O Selfish, money-loving Man! what Principle have you not given up? . . . O God! that *such a mind* should fall in love with that low, dirty, gutter-grubbing Trull, WORLDLY PRUDENCE!!'[83] With a passing piece of nastiness about how in collaborating on their lectures, whatever the *quantity* of material each supplied to the other, 'all the *Tug* of Brain was mine', Coleridge ends this long harangue with the lament: 'You have left a large Void in my Heart – I know no man big enough to fill it.' Then follows a glimpse of self-knowledge: 'I did not only venerate you for your own Virtues, I prized you as the Sheet Anchor of mine!'[84]

Coleridge had lost his sheet anchor and his partner in Pantisocracy; he had gained a wife (see plate 5).

It is difficult to get a clear view of Coleridge's relationship with Sara Fricker in the months leading up to their marriage on 4 October 1795. Sara later destroyed most of his letters to her,[85] and she is scarcely mentioned in his surviving letters of the time. We know, of course, that he returned from London to honour his engagement with the greatest reluctance, but that he was pleasantly surprised when he met her again on his return to Bristol. Despite Southey's defection from their communal plans, which caused an awkward rift between Sara and her sister Edith, Coleridge did not on this occasion run away from his responsibilities.

During his engagement to Sara he wrote a few short poems. They are mostly conventional enough addresses to 'My Sara', but two, the poem later known as 'The Eolian Harp', composed on 20 August 1795 at Clevedon, and 'Lines Written at Shurton Bars, near Bridgewater, September 1795', are interesting. Both express anticipation of the delights of marriage.

In August Coleridge found a cottage at Clevedon, overlooking the Bristol Channel. This was to be his first married home, and on a pre-nuptial visit with Sara he wrote 'The Eolian Harp', the first of that fine group of poems which became known as the 'Conversation Poems'. It opens quietly yet dramatically, setting the scene for speaker, addressee and reader:

> My pensive Sara! thy soft cheek reclined
> Thus on mine arm, most soothing sweet it is
> To sit beside our Cot, our Cot o'ergrown
> With white-flower'd Jasmin, and the broad-leav'd Myrtle,
> (Meet emblems they of Innocence and Love!)
> And watch the clouds, that late were rich with light,
> Slow saddening round, and mark the star of eve
> Serenely brilliant (such should Wisdom be)
> Shine opposite! How exquisite the scents
> Snatch'd from yon bean-field! and the world *so* hush'd!

The stilly murmur of the distant Sea
Tells us of silence.[86]

This shows an exact eye for natural detail combined with a sharp ear for
rhythms both conversational and yet heightened into poetic form: 'that late
were rich with light', 'the scents/Snatch'd from yon bean-field!' 'Innocence and Love' denote sexual love not yet fulfilled, a happiness deferred
till marriage. Coleridge clearly appreciates the courting period for its licensed desire, its guiltlessness, and its ideal nature; a love not yet consum-
mated is one not yet spoilt or disappointing. His only sexual experiences so
far were guilty; in the poem he relishes the pleasure of the moment outside
the cottage in which he will have guiltless sexual experience. Clement
Carlyon, one of his companions in Germany in 1799, remembered
Coleridge discoursing, 'with considerable animation', on 'the endearments
of virtuous love'. He had experienced, he told Carlyon, 'no happiness at all
to be compared with his state of mind during the blissful period which
intervened between consent and love'.[87]

In 'Lines Written at Shurton Bars', a less accomplished poem, he even
dares to anticipate metaphorically the soon-to-be-enjoyed sexual congress
with Sara:

> How oft my Love! with shapings sweet
> I paint the moment, we shall meet!
>   With eager speed I dart –
> I seize you in the vacant air,
> And fancy, with a husband's care
> I press you to my heart!
>
> 'Tis said, in Summer's evening hour
> Flashes the golden-colour'd flower
>   A fair electric flame:
> And so shall flash my love-charg'd eye
> When all the heart's big ecstasy
> Shoots rapid through the frame![88]

Coleridge may have been afraid of the coming consummation, not to
mention learning to live with a real woman, rather than the image of a
pure, ideal, but conveniently unavailable one he had fashioned of Mary
Evans and was to create of Sara Hutchinson. ('If life is a lesson, he never
learnt it', said E. M. Forster pithily of Coleridge.[89]) He gave away perhaps
more than he intended, or understood, when he said in conversation in
1830 that it was 'the perfection of woman to be *characterless*'.[90]

Maybe Coleridge could not have remained in love with any woman –
surely his hopeless love for Sara Hutchinson lasted so long precisely because it *was* hopeless and therefore never put to the test – any more than he
could keep a male friend without quarrelling with him. There is more than
a grain of truth in John Bowring's remark in an excellent review of

Coleridge's poems in 1830. On the evidence of the poetry, says Bowring, Coleridge 'knows nothing of the passion of love, but by observation and reflection'. 'We look in vain for the peculiar and genuine language of that mightiest of passions.'[91] Coleridge's best poetry is concerned rather with the exploration by means of natural or supernatural analogies of the individual psyche in a state of fear or guilt or dejection.

Nevertheless, Coleridge could feel some happiness at the thought of marrying Sara. There is a displacement of sexual desire in 'The Eolian Harp' on to the cottage, the flowers, even the harp itself, which he fancies as a woman being wooed:

> And that simplest Lute,
> Placed length-ways in the clasping casement, hark!
> How by the desultory breeze caress'd,
> Like some coy maid half yielding to her lover,
> It pours such sweet upbraidings, as must needs
> Tempt to repeat the wrong![92]

In another displacement Coleridge attributes to Sara, 'O belovéd Woman', his self-reproof at the flirtation with pantheism in the middle of the poem:

> Or what if all of animated nature
> Be but Organic Harps diversely fram'd,
> That tremble into thought, as o'er them sweeps
> Plastic and vast, one intellectual breeze,
> At once the Soul of each, and God of all?

'The Eolian Harp' is, however, only incidentally a love poem to Sara. Primarily it is a beautifully modulated mental excursion, a musing on life, love and religion, with the Aeolian Harp as its central and multi-functional symbol. The harp, an instrument played on by the wind and a favourite plaything of Romantic writers, who saw it as a metaphor for poetic inspiration,[93] is a perfect example of a poetic symbol as Coleridge influentially defined the term in *The Statesman's Manual* in 1816: 'It always partakes of the Reality which it renders intelligible; and while it enunciates the whole, abides itself as a living part in that Unity, of which it is the representative.'[94]

Coleridge and Sara were married on Sunday 4 October 1795 in 'poor Chatterton's Church', St Mary Redcliffe, Bristol (see plate 6).[95] Josiah Wade and Martha Fricker were the witnesses. Southey and Edith did not attend. Cottle was asked at the last minute to procure various household items for the honeymoon cottage at Clevedon. These included a kettle, a brush and pan, a cheese toaster, coffee, raisins, currants, cinnamon, ginger, rice (but no sugar and no rum).[96]

Coleridge wrote delightedly to Poole that he was married, 'united to the woman, whom I love best of all created Beings', and that he was busily gathering together his poems for a collection to be published by Cottle. His good spirits and high hopes are evident:

> Cottle has entered into an engagement to give me a guinea & a half for every hundred Lines of Poetry, I write – which will be perfectly sufficient for my maintenance, I only amusing myself on Mornings – and all my prose works he is eager to purchase.[97]

Poole's reply was warm and would-be poetic:

> May you both long, long be happy, and may the lowering morning of your days [Coleridge's unhappy childhood] precede a meridian serenely bright and cloudless, leading in due time, naturally, to the soft close of a tranquil evening . . .
>
> I cannot tell you, my dear friend, for such I am sure I may call you, how much I am interested in everything which concerns you. The world is all before you; your road seems yet to choose. Providence has been pleased, if I may so express myself, to drop you on this globe as a meteor from the clouds, the track of which is undetermined. But you have now, by marrying, in some sense fixed yourself. You have created a rallying point. It is the threshold of your life.[98]

Poole was as smitten by Coleridge as others had been, and his overflowing expressions of admiration qualified him to fill the place in Coleridge's affections just vacated by Southey. But even Poole, though happy to be an enabler of another's genius, could not resist setting out an agenda for Coleridge. 'Your friends augur higher things [than mere magazine writing]', he wrote, 'and don't, don't disappoint us'. '*Original* works of genius are your forte.' Such confidence was naturally pleasing to Coleridge, who came to rely on Poole's generous support. However, Poole was no more destined to remain his one best friend than Southey, for in September 1795 a momentous meeting took place in Bristol between Coleridge and Wordsworth.

It was Wordsworth's lot, like Coleridge's, to be at odds with his family and financially insecure yet determined not to compromise his gifts as a writer and his principles as a radical by taking up a profession. He, too, was an ardent Democrat. He was planning a radical magazine with his friend William Mathews, a venture which, like Coleridge's and Southey's *Provincial Magazine*, never got off the ground. His future was uncertain, even as to where he and his sister Dorothy would settle. But Wordsworth, though less immediately charming and brilliant in company than Coleridge, also inspired others with confidence in his genius. His friend Raisley Calvert left him £900 on his early death in January 1795. And John and Azariah Pinney, sons of a wealthy Bristol merchant and – unfortunately – sugar plantationist, John Pretor Pinney, offered him the free use of a house in Dorset owned by their father, Racedown Lodge.[99]

While in Bristol preparing to take up this offer in September 1795,

Wordsworth was introduced, possibly in Pinney's house, to Southey and Coleridge.[100] Though Wordsworth had published 'An Evening Walk' and 'Descriptive Sketches' in 1793, is was undoubtedly Southey and Coleridge, authors of *The Fall of Robespierre* and bold lecturers in Bristol, who had the greater reputation. Coleridge did not record the meeting. Wordsworth told Mathews that 'Coleridge was at Bristol part of the time I was there. I saw but little of him. I wished indeed to have seen more – his talent appears to me very great.'[101]

We know that Coleridge was acquainted by this time with 'An Evening Walk', for in his September 1795 poem, 'Lines Written at Shurton Bars', he pays Wordsworth the compliment of quoting him:

> I mark the glow-worm as I pass,
> Move with 'green radiance' through the grass,
> An emerald of light.[102]

Wordsworth's poem is a descriptive poetic landscape in the vein of Thomson, a kind of verbal equivalent of a Claude painting, with a closely observed landscape leading the eye/ear to a human group. Wordsworth imagines a homeless woman whose soldier husband is absent; she drags her children along 'this weary way':

> Oft has she taught them on her lap to play
> Delighted, with the glow-worms' harmless ray
> Toss'd light from hand to hand; while on the ground
> Small circles of green radiance gleam around.[103]

Thus began, with a brief meeting and the echoing of a poetic phrase, the most momentous relationship in the lives of both men, and one which determined the course that English poetry would take. These consequences were, however, deferred for another eighteen months or so, for Wordsworth left Bristol to take up residence at Racedown, and Coleridge married and settled in Clevedon.

The Clevedon cottage, though picturesque, turned out to be impractical, being too far from Bristol for Coleridge to walk there and back in a day to visit the library, consult Cottle about his collection of poems, and publish his *Conciones ad Populum.* Nor did domestic bliss at first tempt him away from politics. On 17 November he attended a meeting in Bristol Guildhall called to send a message to George III, congratulating him on surviving the attempt on his life while on the way to open Parliament. Coleridge and other Democrats, including Dr Thomas Beddoes, who in April 1793 had left his post as Chemical Reader at Oxford after agitating against slavery and in favour of the French Revolutionary Government, rose to vote for an amendment to the message.[104] This called on the King 'to remove the present heavy Calamities and Distresses of the People, by restoring to them the Blessings of Peace'.[105]

According to the report in the London evening paper, the *Star*, Coleridge 'began the most elegant, the most pathetic, and the most sublime Address that was ever heard, perhaps, within the walls of that building'. This was high praise indeed, considering that Edmund Burke had spoken in the Guildhall when MP for Bristol. Typically, Coleridge fastened on the paradox, also a prominent feature of his long poem, 'Religious Musings', that the war with France was being defended in Parliament on the absurd grounds that 'the way to procure peace was by the sword'.[106]

The day after the meeting Beddoes published a pamphlet, 'A Word in Defence of the Bill of Rights Against Gagging Bills', in which he suggested a second meeting of Bristol citizens to frame a petition expressing disapproval of the two bills. At that meeting, on 20 November, as Azariah Pinney reported to Wordsworth, 'the whole was carried with greatest decorum and propriety':

> Dr. Beddoes is no Orator, but spoke to the purpose – Coleridge voted that the Petition might be carried into the House by Mr. Fox, and Mr. Sheridan, but willingly acceded to Beddoes's opposition, who thought it would command greater attention by being presented by our Members [one of whom, Lord Sheffield, a Tory, reluctantly presented it to Parliament].[107]

Such activities, though invigorating, did nothing to bring Coleridge an income. He thought of schoolteaching, even of returning to Cambridge to 'finish my great work of Imitations in 2 vols'.[108] Instead, he settled on the idea of publishing a periodical to respond to the dangers to civil liberty he believed Pitt's Government to be fostering. To be called *The Watchman*, it was to be financed by subscription. The title may have been suggested by a speech of Thomas Erskine, the admired Whig politician and defence lawyer in the State Trials, delivered in December 1795. Erskine had called on every friend of freedom to act as 'a species of watchman on the outworks of the Constitution'.[109] The phrase exactly describes Coleridge's sense of himself at this time.

On 9 January 1796 Coleridge set off on a tour of the provinces in search of subscribers. During the month he was away from Bristol he reported to his chief subscriber, Josiah Wade, on his successes and failures with the radical and dissenting circles of Birmingham, Derby, Nottingham, Sheffield, Manchester and Lichfield. Continuing the close connection between his Unitarianism and his Democratic politics, he gave several lay sermons in Unitarian chapels in these cities, describing them to Wade as '*preciously peppered with politics*'.[110]

Because it was important to him to preach voluntarily, without payment, and thus distinguish himself from Church of England clergymen, he refused on most occasions to preach in priestly black, preferring 'a blue coat and white waistcoat, that not a rag of the woman of Babylon might be seen on me'.[111] The reference is to the whore of Babylon in Revelation, long associated by Protestants with the Church of Rome, but here used with deliberate emphasis to mean the Church of England. To his regret, as he told Wade, he allowed himself at Birmingham to be '*overpersuaded*' by the Revd John Edwards to preach in black.[112] According to Cottle, the portrait taken of Coleridge by Robert Hancock at this time shows him in the very blue coat and white waistcoat in which he most liked to preach (see plate 7).[113]

At Derby he met, and discussed religion with, Erasmus Darwin, the famous physician, democrat and atheist. 'Dr. Darwin possesses, perhaps, a greater range of knowledge than any other man in Europe', said Coleridge, 'and is the most inventive of philosophical men', except when arguing against religion, when Coleridge thought him disgracefully full of cliche.[114] Coleridge's letters to Wade are lively, often cheerful, sometimes comic, as when he describes a fellow traveller in a coach who was endowed with

> a huge projection, which might be called a Belly with the same propriety that you might name Mount Atlas a Molehill – Heavens! that a man should be unconscionable enough to enter a stage-coach, who would want elbow-room if he were walking on Salisbury Plain![115]

Though as always Coleridge thrived on getting about and meeting people, impressing strangers with his eloquence and reporting wittily on his adventures in letters home, he also showed some anxiety on this provincial tour. Subscriptions were not always easy to raise; he had heard from his wife that she was ill, fearing a miscarriage of her first pregnancy; and he himself was soon taking laudanum daily to relieve feverish symptoms and undoubtedly also to gain temporary oblivion from his family and financial worries. From Lichfield he wrote to Wade, about 10 February, just before cutting short his tour to return home to Sara, expressing for the first time since the fevered Cambridge days a sense of guilt, anxiety and loss of direction: 'My past life seems to me like a dream, a feverish dream! all one gloomy huddle of strange actions, and dim-discovered motives! Friend-ships lost by indolence, and happiness murdered by mismanaged sensibility!'[116]

This is the first recorded use of that euphemistic phrase, 'mismanaged sensibility', in Coleridge's writings. Over the next few years of tremendous activity and achievement he must have felt he could dispel these glooms at will. But as De Quincey chillingly noted, comparing opium-induced dreams to childish fancies about summoning phantoms: 'I can tell them to go, and they go; but sometimes they come, when I don't tell them to come.'[117]

When he returned in mid-February, it was not to the cottage in Clevedon. Sara was now living with her mother on Redcliffe Hill, Bristol. The cottage was given up as too far from the city. Coleridge commemorated once more the jasmine and the myrtle, as he had done in 'The Eolian Harp'. This time, however, the poem, 'Reflections on Having Left a Place of Retirement', was valedictory. As befitted the self-named 'Watchman', Coleridge bids farewell to the 'Valley of Seclusion', claiming,

> I was constrain'd to quit you. Was it right,
> While my unnumber'd brethren toil'd and bled,
> That I should dream away the trusted hours
> On rose-leaf beds, pampering the coward heart
> With feelings all too delicate for use?[118]

The first number of *The Watchman* appeared on Tuesday 1 March 1796, preceded by a Prospectus bearing the motto, adapted from John 8.32, 'That All may know the TRUTH;/ And that the TRUTH may make us FREE!' As Coleridge described it, his object was to bring out a provincial newspaper which was not a ministerial organ (four of the five Bristol daily papers were pro-Pitt); to agitate against enforcement of the two Gagging Acts; and to support the 'Patriotic Societies' in calling for 'a Right of Suffrage general and frequent'.[119] The paper was published every eighth day to avoid the stamp tax which would have had to be paid for a weekly paper conveying large amounts of news, and cost fourpence as against the four-and-a-half pence charged for London newspapers.

Consisting in part of digests from the London opposition papers, the *Morning Chronicle, Star* and *Morning Post*, especially their reporting of proceedings in Parliament, the paper also included editorial essays by Coleridge, reviews of recent works such as Beddoes's *Letter to Pitt on the Means of Relieving the Present Scarcity and Preventing the Diseases that Arise from Meagre Food*, and several poems, most of them by Coleridge himself. Pitt's taxes, particularly the very newspaper tax *The Watchman* set out to dodge, were attacked in the first number:

> In the debate concerning an additional duty on newspapers, Mr. Pitt asserted that they were fit objects of taxation, as being *mere luxuries*. A *mere luxury* for the proprietors to be informed concerning the measures of the directors! a *mere luxury* for the principals to know what their agents are doing.[120]

Coleridge's tone is both reasonable and sarcastic. His attacks on Pitt, on the war, and on individual cases of poverty and injustice in the ten numbers he published are sustained, but noticeably less flamboyant in their language than his lectures of the previous year had been. He went a little wrong in the second number, on 9 March, when he attacked fast-days – a special one having been set by the Church for that very day. Though his subscribers at Bristol and elsewhere were mainly dissenters and therefore frowned on fast-days as priest-led, many were offended by the jocularity of the tone. Sounding almost like Swift in his *Modest Proposal* (1729) for fattening the children of the poor to feed them to the rich, he wrote:

> It is ridiculous to enjoin fasting on the poor (they are Pythagoreans, and already eat neither fish, flesh, or fowl at any time), and it is the crimes of the poor and labouring classes that have brought down the Judgement of Heaven

on the nation. This is *probable* a priori from their being incalculably the greater number, and it is *proved* by the absurd and dangerous consequences of the contrary supposition: for if our public calamities were to be attributed to the wickedness of the rich and powerful, it would more than insinuate doubts of the incorruptness of our House of Commons, and the justice and the necessity of the present war – for by the rich and powerful chiefly was the present war begun and supported, and in every country, directly or indirectly, the rich and powerful hold the reins of Government.

As to the pretence of the rich to call eating 'salt fish, egg sauce, and parsnips' a fast when the poor 'can afford to eat nothing but bread and cheese on Christmas days', Coleridge affects to find it baffling.[121]

The tone of this was too bantering for some of his subscribers. 'The Essay on Fasting has not promoted my work', he confessed to the Revd John Edwards.[122] In *Biographia Literaria*, in which he treated the whole Bristol period of his life with uneasy (and unnecessary) sarcasm, he claimed with a flourish that the fast-day essay had lost him 'near five hundred of my subscribers at one blow'. This was an exaggeration, as was his self-exculpatory statement that he only began *The Watchman* because he was 'persuaded by sundry Philanthropists and Anti-polemists to set on foot a periodical work' which would promote their views.[123] In a way peculiar to him, Coleridge here qualifies a positive noun, 'Philanthropists', with a faintly derogatory adjective, 'sundry', in order to distance himself from a venture in which he had been whole-heartedly engaged at the time and for which he had no reason in 1817 to apologize.

The Watchman is a highly readable miscellany, ably balancing material borrowed from other newspapers with original writing. Among the poems he reprinted was the probably libellous sonnet, addressed to Pitt as Judas, first published in the *Morning Chronicle* in December 1794. He also included an extract from 'Religious Musings', his long poem still in progress. The paper came to an end on 13 May, largely because of lack of funds, and perhaps also because Coleridge felt he had now had his say on contemporary political affairs. He took his leave of his readers, commending to them his old friend Benjamin Flower's *Cambridge Intelligencer* and the new liberal *Monthly Magazine*. As for himself: 'I have endeavoured to do well. And it must be attributed to defect of ability, not of inclination or effort, if the words of the Prophet be altogether applicable to me, '*O Watchman! thou hast watched in vain!*'[124]

Lack of money became an acute problem in the spring of 1796. Coleridge found himself responsible not only for his pregnant wife, but also for Mrs Fricker and her son George, and for George Burnett too – 'five mouths opening & shutting as I pull the string!' as he told Edwards in March.[125] Burnett was supposed to be helping him with *The Watchman*, but his work was unreliable.[126] He was an unfortunate man, an opium addict, dependent on others, particularly Coleridge, and a self-confessed relic of the great

Pantisocracy scheme. In 1803, poor and drifting in London, he applied to Poole for money, harking back pathetically: 'The enchantment of Pantisocracy threw a gorgeous light over the objects of life; but it soon disappeared, and has left *me* in the darkness of ruin.' Burnett died in Marylebone Workhouse in 1811, aged thirty-five.[127]

By May Coleridge was deep in family troubles. He poured out a description to Poole. Sara's mother was thought to be dying (though in fact she lived on, more or less an invalid, until October 1809[128]); his brother-in-law, Robert Lovell, had just died of 'a putrid fever', leaving a distraught and poor widow with an infant; Sara 'asks about baby-linen & anticipates the funeral expences of her poor Mother'. Meanwhile Coleridge, on whose shoulders all this burden fell, was struggling with the last number of his paper:

> It is not pleasant, Thomas Poole! to have worked 14 weeks for nothing – *for nothing* – nay – to have given the Public in addition to that toil five and 40 pounds! . . .
> O Watch Man! thou hast watched in vain – said the Prophet Ezekiel, when, I suppose, he was taking a prophetic glimpse of my sorrow-sallowed Cheeks.[129]

He obviously expected no financial gain from his first volume of poetry, *Poems on Various Subjects*, which Cottle brought out in the middle of the *Watchman* run, on 16 April, though Cottle did give him thirty guineas for the copyright.[130] But he did hope for critical approval, if not of the assorted sonnets, 'Epistles', and 'Effusions' (including the poem later better known as 'The Eolian Harp'), then at least of the long poem which concludes the miscellaneous little volume, 'Religious Musings'. This poem, begun at Christmas 1794 when he was in London avoiding Southey and Sara, he finished in March 1796. On it, he told Poole. 'I pin all my poetical credit'.[131]

The publication of this volume also provided an excuse to open a correspondence with Thelwall, whose career fascinated him. Thelwall had published his Newgate poems in 1795, and had attempted to continue lecturing in the aftermath of the Gagging Acts. He succeeded for a time by the simple expedient of lecturing ostensibly on Roman history, but with an obvious message for the present day, to which he drew attention in his bullish Prospectus.[132] Thelwall happened also to have published a collection of poetry in 1787, called, like Coleridge's, *Poems on Various Subjects*.

Coleridge now courted his acquaintance by appealing to his experience and judgement, except on the question of religion. He also established a pattern of acting as his own severe critic:

> I beg your acceptance of my Poems – you will find much to blame in them – much effeminacy of sentiment, much faulty glitter of expression. I build all my poetic pretentions on the Religious Musings – which you will read with a

POET'S Eye, with the same unprejudicedness, I wish, I could add, the same pleasure, with which the atheistic Poem of Lucretius. A Necessitarian, I cannot possibly disesteem a man for his religious or anti-religious Opinions – and as an *Optimist,* I feel diminished concern.[133]

Coleridge was keen to try his powers on Thelwall. If 'Religious Musings' did not convert the atheist, his next step would be to try what personal acquaintance and Coleridge's great face-to-face influence could do.

'Religious Musings', subtitled 'A Desultory Poem, Written on the Christmas Eve of 1794', is a kind of poetical miscellany, mirroring in its four hundred or so lines Coleridge's preoccupations in religion and politics over the fifteen months of its fragmented composition. In parts it is little more than poeticized opinion, a blank verse, iambic pentameter run-through of ideas familiar from his lectures and letters. Pitt's Government, the slave trade ('loud-laughing TRADE/ More hideous packs his bales of living anguish'); the war and the defences of it in Parliament which turn God into 'Accomplice Deity'; property; a startling verbal picture of 'th'imbrothelled Atheist'; and the Church of England, boldly described as 'mitred Atheism' – these are the chief targets for the poet's rhetoric and rhythm of scorn.[134] 'Musings' is hardly an appropriate description of the sustained tone of righteous horror in the poem.

The poet, echoing Milton in 'On the Morning of Christ's Nativity', introduces himself as a modern prophet treading in the footsteps of St John of Revelation. Much of the language, particularly that describing the after-math of the French Revolution, is borrowed directly from Revelation to express Coleridge's view that earthquake, falling stars and a whirlwind of destruction will be followed by a New Heaven and New Earth. This is a conventional use of revelatory rhetoric for the interpretation of contemporary political events, and it accords with the philosophical opti-mism he mentioned in his letter to Thelwall, though that had been sorely tried by Southey's behaviour and by Sara's sufferings when she thought she was miscarrying their child. Coleridge had witten to the Revd John Edwards in March that 'the pangs which the Woman suffers seem inexplicable in the system of optimism.'[135]

But the poem does establish a positive set of ideals to do battle with the wrongs described in the blood-stained hyperbole of Revolutionary and Revelatory rhetoric. First, there is Christ himself, whose birth is celebrated in the opening lines:

> This is the time, when most divine to hear,
> As with a Cherub's 'loud uplifted' trump
> The voice of Adoration my thrill'd heart
> Rouses! And with the rushing noise of wings
> Transports my spirit to the favor'd fields
> Of Bethlehem![136]

Here Coleridge sets up a deliberate echo of Milton's poem of 1629, which opens:

> This is the Month, and this the happy morn,
> Wherein the son of Heav'n's eternal King,
> Of wedded Maid, and Virgin Mother born,
> Our great redemption from above did bring.

Coleridge's Unitarianism renders his description of Christ rather more emphatically human than this – 'despiséd Galilean!' 'Man of Woes!' 'the oppressed Good Man' – though by one of those interesting quirks of history Milton's own views on the Trinity and the Atonement are now known to have been much less orthodox than he was able comfortably to express. He was, in fact, an Arian, or Unitarian, a fact which became publicly known later in Coleridge's lifetime, when his Latin treatise, *De Doctrina Christiana*, came to light in the Record Office in 1823 and was published, in English, by Cambridge University Press in 1825. Coleridge himself described Milton in a conversation of 1833 as 'a high Arian in his mature life'.[137]

From Christ Coleridge moves on to 'the elect', an enlightened band of great souls who have carried/are carrying/will carry the cause of universal good through the history of the world. Coleridge's heroes make up this group: Milton, Newton, Benjamin Franklin – the 'Patriot Sage' who 'called the red lightnings from the o'er-rushing cloud' (i.e., proved that lightning was electric), as well as playing his part in the achievement of American independence. Coleridge puts his faith in 'heavenly Science' to alleviate poverty and sickness.[138] The young visionary ends this heterogeneous, overwritten, yet nevertheless impressive poem on a quieter note, full of modest optimism amid natural scenery:

> I discipline my young noviciate thought
> In ministeries of heart-stirring song,
> And aye on Meditation's heaven-ward wing
> Soaring aloft I breathe the imperial air
> Of Love, omnific, omnipresent Love,
> Whose day-spring rises glorious in my soul
> As the great Sun, when he his influence
> Sheds on the frost-bound waters – the glad stream
> Flows to the ray and warbles as it flows.

Poems on Various Subjects was politely received by reviewers. As Coleridge told John Prior Estlin, 'The Monthly has *cataracted* panegyric on my poems; the Critical has *cascaded* it; and the Analytical has *dribbled* it with very tolerable civility.'[139] Such criticisms as there were only confirmed Coleridge's own view of the redundancy of metaphor, compound epithets, bombast and extravagance which disfigured his early poems. He cheerfully admitted these blemishes in the preface to the new edition Cottle published in 1797, announcing that he had 'pruned the double-epithets with no unsparing hand'.[140]

After *The Watchman* and *Poems*, Coleridge was still casting around for a source of regular income. He toyed with the idea of swallowing his scruples about hired priests and becoming a Unitarian minister. Or perhaps he could get a London bookseller to advance him money to translate 'all the works of Schiller' ('I am studying German'), in which case he and his family could live at Jena for a while. He would meet Schiller there, and study the works of 'Semler & Michaelis, the German Theologians, & of Kant, the great german Metaphysician'. Then on his return he could open a school and teach his pupils universal knowledge.

What made him think that he would make money out of translations? And did he really imagine he was suited to running a school? Or was he perhaps angling for a rescue from these possibilities, put forward as feasible plans for earning 'bread and cheese' but not likely to strike sensible people as such? The correspondent who received the letter of 5 May in which he described these solutions to his desperate financial situation was the eminently sensible, admiring and generous Tom Poole.[141]

Poole responded immediately with an offer of help he had been contemplating since the end of March. He and 'seven or eight' friends of Coleridge, with Estlin as treasurer, pledged to give him a small annuity – £35 or £40 – as a 'trifling mark of their esteem, gratitude, and admiration' for 'the extraordinary marks of sublime genius' with which they recognized Coleridge to be endowed.[142] Coleridge was grateful for this help, and flattered by the sentiments, but of course he still had to find a proper source of income.

In July 1796 James Perry of the *Morning Chronicle* asked Coleridge, through Beddoes, to come to London and write regularly for his paper. Coleridge accepted at first, but drew back, being unwilling to take his family to live in London.[143] Another plan, to move to Darley, near Derby, to teach the children of a Mrs Evans for £150 a year, looked more attractive, but by early August Mrs Evans had been prevailed upon by her relations not to hire him, though she did invite him and Sara for a visit, presenting them with £95 and 'all her baby clothes' when they left.[144]

At this time too Coleridge paid a brief visit – without Sara – to Ottery to be reconciled with his family. He told Estlin, probably exaggerating, that his mother received him 'with transport', his brother George 'with joy & tenderness', and his other brothers 'with affectionate civility'.[145] We can guess at his motive for going. He probably felt he might need to call on his brothers for help; Sara might have to rely on them in the event of his dying unexpectedly. He was soon to become a father, and all his activities during the summer of 1796 were aimed at finding ways of supporting himself and his dependants.

He finally found what looked like the perfect solution. Charles Lloyd, the unstable, poetically-inclined son of a rich Quaker family Coleridge had met in Birmingham, attached himself to Coleridge. A plan soon formed for him to reside with the Coleridges and pay Coleridge £80 a year for board and lodging and for private tutoring. Together with the £35 or so from Poole and his friends, this would make a sufficient, though by no means wealthy, annual income. Coleridge was in Birmingham gaining the approval of Lloyd's father when he received a letter saying that Sara had delivered herself of a son on Monday 19 September. She had thought the baby was not due for another three weeks.[146] Coleridge hurried home, rather insensitively but of necessity taking Charles Lloyd with him.

Coleridge confessed in a letter to Poole, and also in a sonnet written on the subject, that he felt no thrill on first seeing his child – to be called David Hartley Coleridge in honour of one of Coleridge's saints – but when he 'saw it at the bosom of it's Mother; on her arm; and her eye tearful & watching it's little features, then I was thrilled & melted, & gave it the Kiss of a FATHER'.[147] The sonnet describes the same moment, addressing Sara in perhaps the warmest words that survive from their relationship:

> I seem'd to see an angel-form appear –
> 'Twas even thine, belovéd woman mild!
> So for the mother's sake the child was dear,
> And dearer was the mother for the child.[148]

Sara is to us a largely invisible character during the first year of her marriage. Coleridge mentions her only fleetingly in letters; his plans, decisions, changes of mind take her into account, of course, as a dependant, but not, it seems, as a partner to be consulted. No doubt Coleridge's view of womankind as best when 'characterless' and Sara's own lack of interest in matters poetical, political and intellectual played their part in this state of affairs. From now on we hear more of Sara, much of it negative, but in the autumn of 1796, with the birth of Hartley, as the boy was always called, and the promise of an income of about £120, Coleridge seemed ready to begin a more settled life. He had made an auspicious beginning as a lecturer, journalist and poet. He had good friends in Bristol, useful connections in London and in other cities, and had taken up correspondence with three congenial men: Thelwall, Lamb (after a gap since their snug evenings in the Salutation and Cat), and Wordsworth.

4

Nether Stowey and 'Kubla Khan'
1796–1797

Five miles meandering with a mazy motion
Through wood and dale the sacred river ran.

'Kubla Khan' (1797)

Charles Lamb made his appearance once more in Coleridge's life in May 1796. There seems to have been no contact between the two friends since Coleridge had been plucked from the Salutation and Cat more than a year earlier. Now Lamb assured Coleridge in a letter of 27 May that he had paid off a debt Coleridge owed the pub's landlord: 'I was flush of money, & am so still to all the purposes of a single life, so give yourself no further concern about it.' He sent Coleridge news of their old schoolfellows, Robert Allen, now married to a widow with money, and Valentine Le Grice, 'gone to make puns in Cornwall' as tutor to the family of another widow.

Lamb explained why he had not written for so long: 'The six weeks that finished last year & began this your very humble servant spent very agreeably in a *mad house at Hoxton* –. I am got somewhat rational now, & *dont bite any one*. But *mad* I was . . .'[1] Moreover, somewhat unsettlingly, 'my head ran on you in my madness as much almost as on another Person, who I am inclined to think was the more immediate cause of my temporary frenzy', namely a young woman with whom he was unhappily in love.[2]

For the next few years Coleridge was to be Lamb's chief correspondent; Lamb relied heavily on his friend for consolation and support in his troubled life. The extreme sensitivity of both men led to misunderstandings and quarrels, though no permanent breach occurred between them. Lamb offered Coleridge, in return for spiritual support, a true, though not uncritical, admiration of his poetry. Thus he responded with lively enthusiasm to *The Watchman* and *Poems* of 1796. 'I have read all your Rel. Musings with uninterrupted feelings of profound admiration. You may safely rest your fame on it', he wrote gratifyingly. He had objections, but he managed to put them with a lightness of touch which rendered them inoffensive to the author. 'If there be any thing in ['Religious Musings'] approaching to tumidity', he thought, 'it is the Gigantic hyperbole by which you describe the Evils of existing Society. Snakes Lions hyenas & behemoths, is carrying your resentment beyond bounds.'[3]

Of the break with Southey, who had returned to Bristol from Portugal in May, he wrote reasonably, 'Between you two there should be peace, tho' I must say I have borne him no good will since he spirited you away from among *us*.'[4] Lamb even tried, though diffidently, to attract Coleridge back to London, 'the only fostering soil for *Genius*'. 'God love you, Coleridge, and prosper you thro' life, tho' mine will be loss, if your lot is cast at Bristol or at Nottingham [as a Unitarian minister] or any where but *London*.'[5]

Lamb soon had need of Coleridge's love and support. The hereditary insanity which had recently visited him also afflicted his beloved sister Mary. Lamb wrote to Coleridge on 27 September 1796:

> My dearest friend –
>   White or some of my friends or the public papers by this time may have informed you of the terrible calamities that have fallen on our family. I will only give you the outlines. My poor dear dearest sister in a fit of insanity has been the death of her own mother. I was at hand only time enough to snatch the knife out of her grasp. She is at present in a mad house, from whence I fear she must be moved to an hospital. God has preserved to me my senses, – I eat and drink and sleep, and have my judgment I believe very sound. My poor father was slightly wounded, and I am left to take care of him and my aunt.[6]

Lamb's aunt was melancholy and religious, and his father elderly and confused. Lamb supported them by his work as a clerk at the East India Company, and heroic efforts were required of him at home. Coleridge was the one correspondent he was able to confide in, as he did on 1 December:

> I am starving at the India house, near 7 oClock without my dinner, & so it has been & will be almost all the *week* –. I get home at night oe'r wearied, quite faint – & then to *Cards* with my father, who will not let me enjoy a meal in peace . . .
>   I am got home at last, & after repeated games at Cribbage have got my father's leave to write awhile: with difficulty got it, for when I expostulated about playing any more, he very aptly replied, 'if you wont play with me, you might as well not come home at all!' The argument was unanswerable, & I set to afresh.[7]

Small wonder that Lamb appealed to his friend for 'as religious a letter as possible' in these dreadful circumstances. Coleridge obliged immediately.[8] He bolstered Lamb's religious faith – Lamb being a Unitarian like himself – and tried to set the horror in the context of his philosophical optimism:

> Your poor father is, I hope, almost senseless of the calamity; the unconscious instrument of Divine Providence knows it not, and your mother is in heaven. It is sweet to be roused from a frightful dream by the song of birds and the gladsome rays of the morning. Ah, how infinitely more sweet to be awakened from the blackness and amazement of a sudden horror by the glories of God manifest and the hallelujahs of angels.[9]

Coleridge invited Lamb to visit him, which he finally did in the summer of 1797.

Lamb's dreadful troubles during the autumn of 1796 did not prevent him from taking a sympathetic and astute interest in his friend's affairs. Hearing about Coleridge's various plans and fits and starts, he wrote in October:

> I grieve from my very soul to observe you in your plans of life, veering about from this hope to the other, & settling no where. Is it an untoward fatality (speaking humanly) that does this for you?, a stubborn irresistible concurrence of events? or lies the fault, as I fear it does, in your *own* mind? You seem to be taking up splendid schemes of fortune only to lay them down again, & your fortunes are an ignis fatuus [will o' the wisp] that has been conducting you, in thought, from Lancaster Court, Strand [offices of the *Morning Chronicle*], to somewhere near Matlock, then jumping across to Dr. Somebody's whose sons' tutor you were likely to be, & would to God, the dancing demon *may* conduct you at last in peace & comfort to the 'life & labors of a cottager'.[10]

The allusion is to Coleridge's latest plan, to take 'a cottage and half a dozen acres of land in an enchanting Situation about eight miles from Bridgewater'. Coleridge explained his reasons to Charles Lloyd's father, whose £80 a year was the means of making it possible for him to retire thus to the country. He was anxious that his children 'should be bred up from earliest infancy in the simplicity of peasants, their food, dress, and habits completely rustic'. (Lamb wrote humorously in January 1797 on this point with regard to Coleridge's plans for Hartley: 'You dont mean to make an actual plowman of him?!'[11]) Warming to the subject, Coleridge continued, 'if I live in cities, my children . . . will necessarily become acquainted with politicians and politics – a set of men and a kind of study which I deem highly unfavourable to all Christian graces'. Though we must allow for a certain amount of posturing to impress Mr Lloyd, it was indeed the case that when Coleridge left Bristol for the country he began to withdraw from the public politics he had been pursuing in the city for the past two years. 'I have accordingly snapped my squeaking baby-trumpet of sedition, and have hung up its fragments in the chamber of Penitences', he concluded, using a metaphorical phrase he liked enough to employ it again in 1798 when writing a letter of appeasement to his brother George.[12]

It was to be a different cottage, a small house in Nether Stowey at the bottom of Tom Poole's garden, that Coleridge finally moved on the last day of the year.[13] Tiny, dark, and damp, facing straight on to the street, with a gutter running past the front door, an infestation of mice, and the smell of Poole's nearby tannery all too prevalent, the cottage nevertheless represented true happiness to Coleridge. The garden was connected by a jasmine-covered arbour to Poole's larger one, and Poole's spacious library was at Coleridge's disposal. As he wrote in the volume of his 1796 *Poems* which he gave to Poole: 'I love to shut my eyes, and bring before my imagination that Arbour, in which I have repeated so many of these compositions to you. Dear Arbour! An Elysium to which I have often passed by your Cerberus, and Tartarean tan-pits!'[14] In July 1797, during his most idyllic summer, Coleridge ensured that Poole's arbour would have permanent fame when he wrote the exquisite poem 'This Lime-Tree Bower My Prison'.

The cottage must have seemed all the more attractive to an increasingly desperate Coleridge when it looked, in December 1796, as if Poole was regretting his invitation to him to come and be his close neighbour. Much though Poole admired, even adored, Coleridge, he is likely to have been taken aback by an excitable letter of 5 November, in which Coleridge described having been 'seized with an intolerable pain from my right temple to the tip of my right shoulder'. 'I was nearly frantic – and ran about the House naked, endeavouring by every means to excite sensations in different parts of my body, & so to weaken the enemy by creating a division.' The pain returned several times the next day, and Coleridge 'took between 60 and 70 drops of Laudanum, and *sopped* the Cerberus just as his mouth began to open':

> But *this morning* he returned in full force, & his Name is Legion! – Giant-fiend of an hundred hands! with a shower of arrowy Death-pangs he transpierced me, & then he became a Wolf & lay gnawing my bones. – I am not mad, most noble Festus! – but in sober sadness I have suffered this day more bodily pain than I had before a conception of –.[15]

Coleridge wrote again two days later, apologizing for his '*flighty* letter', written 'under the immediate inspiration [note the word] of Laudanum', but insisted on the accuracy of the description none the less.[16] Poole may have felt that the man who could suffer such physical and mental agonies as these, and describe them so graphically, was indeed a dangerous one to bring almost into his own home. Not only Coleridge, but his frail houseguest, Charles Lloyd, was ill at this time. On 15 November Coleridge told Poole that he had been nursing Lloyd through alarming epileptic fits and nightmares, and had called in Dr Beddoes.[17]

It is therefore not to be wondered at that Poole had second thoughts, especially as his family and friends were predisposed to think Coleridge a dangerous Jacobin. But when Coleridge realized that Poole was hesitating, raising objections to the cottage and suggesting an alternative residence at Acton, he unleashed a letter of extraordinary force, by turns desperate, accusing, cajoling and pathetic, yet kept under control by a sharpness of wit and an astute moral appeal to Poole to act on all his protestations of love by taking the Nether Stowey cottage for him forthwith. Some extracts from this long letter of 13 December give an idea of the versatility of Coleridge's persuasive powers:

> O my God! my God! when am I to find rest! Disappointment follows disappointment; and Hope seems given to me merely to prevent my becoming callous to Misery! – Now I know not where to turn myself.

Then comes an analysis of Poole's objections, undertaken point by point with the acuity of one of Shakespeare's argumentative clowns:

> I find three reasons assigned for my not settling at Stowey. The first, the distance from my friends, & the Press. This I answered in the former letter – As to my friends, what can they do for me – & as to the Press, even if Cottle had not promised, to correct it for me, yet I might as well be 50 miles from it, as 12, for any purpose of correcting the Printer's copy [of the second edition of *Poems*]. – Secondly, the Expence of moving. Well, but I must move to Acton: and what will the difference be? – Perhaps, three guineas. – Ought a Friend to have advised another Friend to live at a distance from him, and as a reason to urge that the latter would save three guineas by it? – I would give three guineas, that you had not assigned this Reason. – Thirdly , the wretchedness of that Cottage, which alone we can get. – But surely, in the house, which I saw, *two* rooms may be found, which by a little green List, and a carpet, and a slight alteration in the fireplace, may be made to exclude the cold: and this is all, we want.[18]

Coleridge moves from the satiric to the pathetic vein:

> Surely, surely, my friend! something has occurred which you have not mentioned to me. Your Mother has manifested a strong dislike to our living near you – or some thing or other . . . Mrs Coleridge has observed the workings of my face, while I have been writing; and is intreating to know what is the matter – I dread to shew her your Letter – I dread it. My God! my God! what if she should dare to think, that my most beloved Friend is grown cold towards me!

Poole had mentioned something about a ghost. Coleridge snorts:

> Ghosts indeed! I should be haunted with Ghosts enough – the Ghosts of Otway & Chatterton, & the phantasms of a Wife broken-hearted, & a hunger-bitten Baby! O Thomas Poole! O Thomas Poole! if you did but know what a Father & Husband must feel, who toils with his brain for uncertain bread![19]

What friend could refuse the appeal contained in such a letter? Poole was certainly not the man to do so.

Poole was not the only friend Coleridge bombarded with letters at this time. He was still writing letters of close friendship to Lamb, and though these are lost, we can tell what they were like from Lamb's replies. Lamb, disappointed that Coleridge had opted for a country cottage rather than London and the joys of 'pipes, tobacco, Egghot, welch Rabbits, metaphysics, & *Poetry*' at the Salutation and Cat, wrote in that comic, sweetly sour way of his, 'Is it a farm you have got? & what does your worship know about farming?'[20]

Lamb also encouraged Coleridge to keep writing poetry, exhorting him to 'cultivate simplicity', or at least 'banish elaborateness'. Like so many of Coleridge's friends, he perceived Coleridge's powers but felt obliged to lecture him on the proper use of them: 'Coleridge, I want you to write an Epic poem. Nothing short of it can satisfy the vast capacity of true poetic genius.'[21] It is a pity Coleridge's reply to this exhortation is lost. Epic seemed to him, as to Lamb, the highest form of poetic achievement – his notebook for 1796 contains a title for a projected poem, 'The Origin of Evil, an Epic Poem'.[22] In due course he would play the role towards Wordsworth which Lamb now adopted towards him, encouraging him in his great epic venture, 'The Recluse'.

Coleridge and Wordsworth appear to have corresponded briefly during 1796, though neither side of the correspondence survives. In May Coleridge had reported to Thelwall that Wordsworth had read and approved of 'Religious Musings' – 'and this man is a Republican & at least a *Semi*-atheist', he assured Thelwall.[23] He had read, through Cottle, the manuscript of Wordsworth's poem 'Guilt and Sorrow; or Incidents upon Salisbury Plain', marking it with pieces of paper for Wordsworth's special attention. He described Wordsworth to Thelwall, prematurely but presciently, as 'a very dear friend of mine, who is in my opinion the best poet of the age'.[24]

It was inevitable that Wordsworth and Coleridge should become friends, now that Wordsworth had come to live in the West Country and since the two men both published their poetry with Cottle. But Coleridge was also actively cultivating Thelwall at this time, eagerly beginning a correspondence with this man whom he had admired from afar, and whose atheism he took it upon himself to combat. In a way, Thelwall did duty here for Godwin, whose influential theory of society Coleridge was keen to attack for its lack of religion and, as Coleridge thought, morality. In *The Watchman* he had addressed Thelwall as 'Good Citizen ——— ... You are not a PATRIOT! You have studied Mr. Godwin's Essay on Political Justice; but to think filial affection folly, gratitude a crime, marriage injustice, and the promiscuous intercourse of the sexes right and wise, may class you among the despisers of vulgar prejudices, but cannot increase the probability that you are a PATRIOT.'[25]

In a letter of 13 May 1796 Coleridge quoted these words and justified them to Thelwall. He took the particular example of marriage, of which Godwin was known to disapprove as coercive (though in March 1797 he broke his own rule to marry Mary Wollstonecraft before she gave birth to his child): 'What more do we mean by *Marriage* than that state in which it would be criminal to tempt to, or permit, an act of inconstancy? But if criminal at *one moment*, criminal always: in other words, *Marriage is indissoluble.*'[26] He was never to swerve from this view, though temptation and guilt would come to torture him. Coleridge seems to have known that Thelwall was happily married and would not take offence at this. His letter continued with gossip about Godwin and something he had heard about the sexual activities of the Edinburgh martyr Joseph Gerrald.[27] Thelwall was invited to visit the West Country.

Throughout 1796 Coleridge was defining and refining his religious and philosophical opinions, and he used his correspondence with an intelligent antagonist like Thelwall to help him do this. Presumably he chose Thelwall rather than Godwin for this purpose because he had met, and not much liked, Godwin, and because he wanted to be free to attack Godwin's influential writings in a book – 'a six shilling Octavo' – he was contemplating.[28]

Though anxious not to equate atheism and immorality in a crude way, Coleridge did feel strongly that religious faith was a necessary bulwark against sinful actions. This was a view he held ever more strongly as he got older. In a very late notebook, in 1833, he commented on having long ago warned Thelwall, 'that wrong-headed but good-hearted man', about the danger of bringing his children up as atheists. 'Prepare your mind', he remembers telling Thelwall, for one or other of your children to 'become a profligate, & be shot, or shoot himself, be hung or hang himself', and for another to 'turn out an ultra Calvinistic Fanatic, eg Revd. Sidney Thelwall'. 'Alas!', the entry concludes, in 'Citizen Thelwall's' case, 'how has the Prediction been verified!'[29]

Aware that many '*professed Christians*' act immorally, he insisted to Thelwall in 1796 that even they would allow that 'they were acting contrary to Christianity', whereas 'an atheistic bad Man manufactures his system of principles with an eye to his peculiar propensities'.[30] (Coleridge makes no mention of the possibility of the existence of an atheistic *good* man.) At bottom, whatever theory Coleridge embraced or nearly embraced at any time, be it Hartleian optimism, Spinozan pantheism, Kantian stoicism or Christian orthodoxy, his own psychological and emotional experiences told him – and this was surely the chief motive for his eventual return to the orthodox fold – that human beings were all too capable of sin and needed help beyond the human to resist it. Even in such a cheerful poem as 'The Eolian Harp' he had dramatized a mental toying with pantheism and engineered a return to faith in a personal God who 'with his saving mercies healéd me,/ A sinful and most miserable man'.

He continued in his efforts to convert Thelwall by letter, wooing him with some lively self-criticism along the way. To Thelwall he gave his famous self-portrait: fat and flabby face, 'sensual thick lips', awkward walk, 'the *Whole man* indicates *indolence capable of energies*'. He claimed to have read 'almost every thing', to be 'a library-cormorant', and recognized his tendency to become 'impassioned' in conversation, to argue with an eagerness 'which is often mistaken for personal asperity – for I am ever so swallowed up in the *thing*, that I perfectly forget my *opponent*'.[31]

Thelwall puzzled Coleridge because he seemed to be an exception to Coleridge's belief that lack of faith must 'lead to Sensuality', there being no hope, or fear, of an afterlife in which 'we shall continue to enjoy or suffer the consequences & natural effects of the Habits we have formed here, whether good or evil'. Coleridge, perhaps because of his desire to dissociate himself from atheism, had moved from Hartleian necessitarianism to Berkleian idealism, according to which material things depend for their existence on being perceived by a mind, in the first instance the mind of God. To Thelwall he merely throws out the sentence, 'I am a Berkleian.'[32]

In *Biographia Literaria* he struggled to explain how and why he had abandoned Hartley's theory of ideas as derived from sense experience in favour of a reasoned, if qualified, idealism, made up of his reading of, among others, Plato, the neo-Platonists, Bishop Berkeley, and Kant. Philosophies which start with sense experience and build up to ideas are likely to end, as Hume's did (though not Hartley's) in atheism, since it is not only difficult to make the leap from the particular to the general, but even harder to make the further leap to the necessary religious ideas of God and immortality. 'In Hartley's scheme', says Coleridge in *Biographia Literaria*, 'the soul is present only to be pinched or *stroked*'. 'The existence of an infinite spirit, of an intelligent and holy will, must on this system be mere articulated motions of the air.'[33] As he summed it up in 1832, after years of study, 'the pith of my system is to make the Senses out of the Mind – not the mind from the Senses'.[34]

There is much talk of 'brotherly kindness' in Coleridge's letters to Thelwall. With Southey back in Bristol, Coleridge's own stock of that commodity was being tested. It was Southey who took the first step towards a reconciliation at the end of September, prompted perhaps by the recent birth of Hartley and Edith's desire to visit her sister. Southey sent Coleridge a slip of paper with a sentence from Schiller's play *Fiesko*: 'Fiesco! Fiesco! thou leavest a void in my bosom, which the human race, thrice told, will never fill up.'[35] Coleridge was slow to thaw, though urged by Lamb, who told him he and Southey had been very foolish 'to fall out like two boarding-school misses'.[36] On 27 December Coleridge thanked Southey rather grandly for his copy of Southey's new edition of poetry: 'I thank you, Robert Southey! for your poems; and by way of return present you with a collection of (what appear to me) the faults.' He proceeded to a merciless denunciation of certain lines, some of which 'appear to drag excrementally' and others to be 'very *beautiful*; but (pardon my obtuseness) have they any *meaning?*'[37]

Southey seems to have swallowed these insults in the name of reconciliation, and the quarrel was patched up. But Coleridge would never again feel the original warmth towards his brother-in-law, as he hastened to tell his new friend Thelwall:

> Between ourselves, the *Enthusiasm* of Friendship is not with S. & me. We quarreled – & the quarrel lasted for a twelvemonth – We are now reconciled; but the cause of the difference was solemn – & 'the blasted oak puts not forth it's buds anew' – we are *acquaintances* – & feel *kindliness* towards each other; but I do not *esteem*, or LOVE Southey, as I must esteem & love the man whom I dared to call by the holy name of FRIEND![38]

Coleridge probably thought of the move to Nether Stowey with Sara and baby Hartley as a home-grown realization of Pantisocracy, albeit without the larger community but with Poole as a new 'sheet anchor' in comforting proximity, and with the prospect of congenial friends like Lamb and Thelwall coming from the crowded city on extended visits. He told Cottle on 6 January 1797 that the family was well settled in; Sara 'likes Stowey, & loves Thomas Poole, & his Mother, who love her'. To Estlin he wrote that he was 'already an expert Gardener' (in January!). And Thelwall was treated to an idyllic picture of home life at Nether Stowey: 'We are *very* happy – & my little David Hartley grows a sweet boy – & has his health – he laughs at us till he makes us weep for very fondness. – You would smile to see my eye rolling up to the ceiling in a Lyric fury, and on my knee a *Diaper* pinned, to warm.'[39]

Coleridge's enjoyment of domestic life, his unabashed pleasure in taking a lively part in bringing up infants, is of a piece with the Pantisocratic ideals. He and Wordsworth were really quite unusual in their expressions of doting fatherhood. Both observed their children minutely, taking an interest in every aspect of their development and education in the spirit of the educational philosophies of Rousseau and Hartley. (In 1795 Wordsworth and Dorothy had taken on the upbringing of the two-year-old son of Basil Montagu, whose wife had died soon after his birth. Dorothy described their experiments in liberal education of the child in several letters.[40]) They were passionately concerned not to bring up their children oppressively. A country upbringing, miscellaneous rather than censored reading, minimal punishment, and open-minded teaching were the goals they set themselves as fathers and teachers.

As befitted the poet–philosopher–gardener he prided himself on being, Coleridge filled his notebooks with lists of works he meant to write alongside homely recipes for ginger wine and beef stew. One literary list has among its items the old Cambridge plan for 'Imitations of the Modern Latin Poets', the epic poem on the origin of evil, 'Strictures on Godwin, Paley &c &c', 'Poems', 'A Liturgy On the different Sects of Religion & Infidelity', and 'A Tragedy'. Immediately following is a recipe wittily couched in democratic terms (except for the inclusion of the essential, but politically incorrect, ingredient sugar):

Six Gallons of Water –
Twelve pounds of Sugar
Half a pound of Ginger
Eighteen Lemons.

Ginger to be sliced – Lemons to be peeled – The Sugar & Water to be boiled together, & the scum – viz – the Monarchical part must go to the Pot . . . then let the Sum total be put in the Barrel with Three Spoonfuls of Yeast – let it work three Days (Sundays Excepted –) . . . Close up the Barrel – Nota Bene: you may do it legally the habeas corpus act being suspended – let it remain a fortnight – then bottle it.[41]

Thus settled, Coleridge busied himself during the spring with the second edition of his verse. *Poems* of 1797 is an even more heterogeneous volume than its predecessor the year before. Several poems are retained, though the sonnets to eminent political heroes (confusingly entitled 'Effusions' in 1796) are omitted. 'Religious Musings' still crowns the volume, but there follow almost a hundred pages of poems by Lamb and Lloyd, with a few more of Coleridge's added as an afterthought, 'reprieved from immediate oblivion', as he cheerfully puts it in a note.[42] A pious preface claims to have responded to criticisms of the previous edition by 'taming the swell and glitter both of thought and diction'.[43] An examination of the contents hardly bears out the claim, since the chief new poem in the volume is the 'Ode on the Departing Year', first published in Flower's *Cambridge Intelligencer* on 31 December 1796. Commemorating in scornful rhetoric the death of the wicked Catherine of Russia, it prophesies in revelatory tones similar to those of 'Religous Musings' the downfall of Britain – 'O Albion! O my mother Isle!' – as a result of her alliances with tyrants and her continued war against France.[44]

Only a few sonnets and 'The Eolian Harp', still known under the title 'Composed at Clevedon, Somersetshire', display Coleridge's gift for simplicity rising, as if effortlessly, to sublimity. There is, too, a fine dedicatory poem to his brother George, made possible by the reconciliation of the previous summer, and, according to Cottle, suggested by him: 'I then pressed him to dedicate his Poems to one of his relatives, his brother George, of whom he occasionally spoke with peculiar kindness.'[45] Lamb, too, had urged him to 'cultivate the filial feelings' towards his family.[46]

The dedicatory poem, dated 26 May 1797, dramatizes Coleridge's feelings about himself in relation to the other Coleridges. It begins with a picture of George's 'blesséd lot', his having passed through 'the stir/ And turmoil of the world' to settle into a happy, secure, domestic life. Coleridge then contrasts his own history:

To me the Eternal Wisdom hath dispens'd
A different fortune and more different mind –
Me from the spot where first I sprang to light

> Too soon transplanted, ere my soul had fix'd
> Its first domestic loves; and hence through life
> Chasing chance-started friendships.

He details these friendships, with himself always passive to their influence. Some have been like the leaves of a tree which begin by sheltering him from the rain but end by depositing 'the collected shower' on his head when ruffled by a sudden breeze. Others have tempted him 'to slumber in their shade', only to poison him with venom like the 'false and fair-foliag'd Manchineel', an attractive West Indian tree with poisonous sap and incidentally the subject of a lecture from his headmaster at Christ's Hospital, who prohibited the use of the metaphor by his pupils as too cliched.[47] Now, the poet rejoices, he has found 'permanent shelter' with 'one Friend' (Poole), who is the oak tree under which Coleridge has 'rais'd a lowly shed'. The sustained metaphor of trees giving shelter is cleverly managed; it comes naturally to Coleridge to think of himself as needing protection.

Coleridge pulls off the considerable trick in this poem of showing gratitude and reverence towards George as his first protector –

> Thee, who didst watch my boyhood and my youth;
> Didst trace my wanderings with a father's eye –

while at the same time representing himself as friendless and unwelcome in his childhood home –

> My soul is sad, that I have roam'd through life
> Still most a stranger, most with naked heart
> At mine own home and birth-place.

Perhaps it is not surprising that George responded to the criticism and not the praise. Coleridge noted on a copy of the edition, 'If this volume should ever be delivered according to its direction, *i.e.* to Posterity, let it be known that the Reverend George Coleridge was displeased and thought his character endangered by the Dedication.'[48] Ironically, one of the few reviewers who noticed *Poems* of 1797 singled out the dedicatory poem as giving 'a favourable idea of the brother to whom he offers the produce of his talents'.[49] Southey, too, spending the summer in Hampshire, where Cottle visited him in July with a copy of Coleridge's poems, thought the dedication to George 'one of the most beautiful poems I ever read'.[50]

In 1797 Coleridge's mind was running rather a lot on his early life. In February he began his series of autobiographical letters to his neighbour Poole, declaring, 'To me the task will be a useful one; it will renew and deepen *my* reflections on the past.' As for Poole, he would be enabled to 'behold with no unforgiving or impatient eye those weaknesses and defects in my character, which so many untoward circumstances have concurred to plant there'.[51] He would also learn about Coleridge's steady movement away from the philosophical materialism of Priestley and Hartley – 'experimentalists' who 'contemplate nothing but *parts*' – towards a more elevated, ideal view of the world in its wholeness, a movement Coleridge saw as an inevitable result of his father's acquainting him at an early age with the largeness of the universe.[52]

Coleridge was kept busy not only with seeing his poems through the press, but also with lines he was contributing to Southey's epic poem, *Joan of Arc*. Some of these were finally included in the obscure and fragmentary poem, 'The Destiny of Nations', which was not published in its entirety until 1817. Lamb frankly criticized the lines he read in February 1797: 'You are not going, I hope, to annex to that most splendid ornament of Southey's poem [Joan herself] all this cock & a bull story of Joan the Publican's daughter of Neufchatel.'[53] Coleridge duly dropped the idea of including a version of his lines in his own volume of 1797.

The chief, perhaps only, interest of the poem, or rather set of fragments strung together, is that it displays Coleridge's reading at this time of books which yielded much finer fruit in 'The Ancient Mariner', begun later the same year. He talks here of 'the Greenland Wizard', of 'untravelled realms of Ocean's bed', of the Spirit of Good' and her counterpart the malignant spirit, 'a nameless female', referring the reader in a note to Crantz's *History of Greenland*. It is worth quoting a few lines to show how far Coleridge travelled poetically between this merely descriptive treatment of legend and the brilliant enactment of myth in 'The Ancient Mariner':

> Or if the Greenland Wizard in strange trance
> Pierces the untravelled realms of Ocean's bed
> Over the abysm, even to that uttermost cave
> By mis-shaped prodigies beleaguered, such
> As Earth ne'er bred, nor Air, nor the upper Sea:
> Where dwells the Fury Form, whose unheard name
> With eager eye, pale cheek, suspended breath,
> And lips half-opening with the dread of sound,
> Unsleeping Silence guards, worn out with fear
> Lest haply 'scaping on some treacherous blast
> The fateful word let slip the Elements
> And frenzy Nature.[54]

In February Coleridge sat down to review Matthew Lewis's sensational Gothic novel, *The Monk*, for the *Critical Review*, to which he and Southey had been asked to contribute, probably through George Dyer. Coleridge's article, while praising the skilful handling of the plot and the 'variety and impressiveness of the incidents', is severe on both the aesthetic and the moral aspects of the work. 'Figures that shock the imagination, and narratives that mangle the feelings, rarely discover *genius*, and always betray a low and vulgar *taste*.' The 'most painful impression' left on his mind by reading Lewis's novel of monkish lust and murder 'was that of great acquirements and splendid genius employed to furnish a *mormo* [imaginary terror] for children, a poison for youth, and a provocative for the debauchee'. But Coleridge's attitude is not merely that of the offended moralist. He makes an important point – and one which is surely shared by most readers of *The Monk* – that 'the merit of the novelist is in proportion (not simply to the effect, but) to the *pleasurable* effect which he produces . . . Situations of torment, and images of naked horror, are easily conceived; and a writer in whose works they abound, deserves our gratitude almost equally with him who should drag us by way of sport through a military hospital, or force us to sit at the dissecting-table of a natural philosopher.'[55]

In February, too, Sheridan, manager of the Drury Lane Theatre, asked Coleridge through a friend if he would 'write a tragedy on some popular subject'. Coleridge replied that he was 'gratified and somewhat elated by the proposal'; it jogged him into starting on a tragedy.[56] He sat down to begin *Osorio*, with Shakespeare and Schiller as his chief models and the tragic actors Kemble and Mrs Siddons in mind for the leading parts. Interestingly, he told Bowles that the plan for the play was 'romantic & wild & somewhat terrible', adding, 'but indeed I am almost weary of the Terrible', as well he might be after reading *The Monk*.[57]

Though busy with all these projects, Coleridge still had problems – financial ones, of course, but also domestic ones due to Lloyd's alarming fits and, we may assume, the strain of having this unstable young man sharing such a small house with him and Sara and Hartley. Though Coleridge did not complain of Lloyd's behaviour at this time, he probably found it tiresome, as Southey certainly did when Lloyd arrived in August 1797 as an unexpected guest at the house in Hampshire he and Edith had taken for the summer.[58] Lloyd disloyally told tales of Coleridge's unfriendly remarks about Southey, who responded by avoiding a planned visit to Nether Stowey.[59]

Though partially reconciled, Coleridge and Southey still felt cool towards one another. They were hardly together at all during 1797. In March Southey was in London; he spent the whole summer in Hampshire; when he returned to Bath in September he avoided meeting Coleridge. In short, it is significant that Southey was not on the scene during the months in which Coleridge became intimate with Wordsworth.

In early April 1797 Coleridge wrote to Cottle that he 'felt a depression too dreadful to be described'.[60] This was presumably the cause of his epistolary neglect of Lamb, who remonstrated on 7 April, 'your last letter was dated the 19th February; in it you promised to write again the next day.'[61] On 15 April Lamb wrote again, holding up Lloyd as a sad example – 'he has, by his own confession, kept a letter of mine *unopen'd 3 weeks!*'[62] Coleridge did not write to Lamb until about 11 June, when the latter replied gratefully: 'I stared with wild wonderment to see thy well-known hand again. It revived many a pleasing recollection of an epistolary intercourse, of late strangely suspended, once the pride of my life.'[63]

In the meantime Coleridge had begun his momentous friendship with Wordsworth. In April 1797 Wordsworth was in Bristol; on his way back to Racedown he visited Coleridge at Nether Stowey. Coleridge told Cottle that his depression had been lifted by the visit: 'Wordsworth's conversation, &c roused me somewhat.'[64] He was working once more on his tragedy. Conversations with Wordsworth had naturally included a discussion of Southey's merits as a poet. As Coleridge reported to Cottle, Wordsworth thought Southey wrote '*too much at his ease*', and Coleridge added that he relied too much on '*story* and *event*', to the neglect of 'those *lofty imaginings*, that are peculiar to, and definitive of, the poet'. If this sounds like a premature description of Wordsworth's great poetic enterprise, the beginning of which still lay two years in the future, so also does Coleridge's immediately following reference to Milton and his extravagant declaration, 'I should not think of devoting less than 20 years to an Epic Poem.'[65]

Though Coleridge's financial position was still precarious, he had by now made a name for himself, particularly in Bristol; his first volume of poems had sold out; his second was due out in a few weeks; and he had been commissioned to write for the London theatre. Wordsworth was at this time in a rather worse plight. He, too, had money problems, despite the legacy from Calvert, much of which he had lent to friends who could not pay him back. Though Wordsworth was confident of his powers as a poet – none more so – he had as yet published very little poetry, and he had no reputation as a journalist or lecturer. His name was not yet one to conjure with.[66]

The great friendship which was just beginning was of enormous importance to both men and for the course their poetry took. It crystallized the elements already existing in both into an extraordinary mutual, yet also markedly separate, effort which resulted in *Lyrical Ballads* in the first instance and the *Prelude* and *Biographia Literaria* in the longer term. No literary partnership, except perhaps that between Goethe and Schiller begun a couple of years earlier (and also issuing forth in a joint collection of ballads in 1798), is so famous in literary history. The personal relationship suffered a collapse in time, but their admiration of one another's genius never diminished. Coleridge, much the less confident of the two, saw his sense of his own worth as a poet decrease before Wordsworth, but the fact remains that in the spring and early summer of 1797 their coming together was a marvellously fruitful event for both.

On 5 June 1797 Coleridge arrived on his first visit to Wordsworth and Dorothy at Racedown, carrying with him two and a half acts of *Osorio*. Such was the impression his arrival made that Wordsworth remembered nearly fifty years later that Coleridge 'did not keep to the high road, but leapt over a gate and bounded down the pathless field, by which he cut off an angle'.[67] His sister Dorothy commented excitedly at the time in a letter to Mary Hutchinson. Dorothy's portrait of Coleridge is both a detailed and natural description and a conscious perception of Coleridge as the ideal of the poet, the quintessential Romantic genius:

> You had a great loss in not seeing Coleridge. He is a wonderful man. His conversation teems with soul, mind, and spirit . . . At first I thought him very plain, that is, for about three minutes: he is pale and thin [odd that she should think so, when most accounts, including Coleridge's own, put him down as corpulent], has a wide mouth, thick lips, and not very good teeth, longish loose-growing half-curling rough black hair. But if you hear him speak for five minutes you think no more of them. His eye is large and full, not dark but grey; such an eye as would receive from a heavy soul the dullest expression; but it speaks every emotion of his animated mind; it has more of the 'poet's eye in a fine frenzy rolling' than I ever witnessed. He has fine dark eyebrows, and an overhanging forehead.[68]

There it is, right down to the passage from Act V of *A Midsummer Night's Dream* about the lunatic, the lover and the poet being of imagination all compact: the portrait of the artist as a young man.

As for Coleridge, he was soon writing about Wordsworth to Cottle and Estlin; he felt himself 'a *little man by his side*; & yet do not think myself the less man, than I formerly thought myself'. And, simply, 'Wordsworth is a great man.'[69] When Coleridge read aloud what he had written of *Osorio*, Wordsworth admired it, giving him 'great hopes'. Wordsworth, too, was writing a tragedy, which Coleridge found 'absolutely wonderful'.[70] This was *The Borderers*, a play not unlike *Osorio* in its echoes of Shakespeare, its touches of Gothic, and its central concern with human guilt. Coleridge told Cottle that there were in Wordsworth's play 'those *profound* touches of the human heart, which I find three or four times in 'The Robbers' of Schiller, & often in Shakespere'.[71]

Shakespeare and Schiller (and Godwin, too) are visible influences on *Osorio*, on which Coleridge worked during the two weeks he spent at Racedown. The plot turns on the relationship between a good and a corrupted brother and their love of the same woman. Coleridge sets the play in Spain in the reign of Philip II, deriving some of the complications of the plot from the persecution of the Moors by the Spanish Inquisition. There is cruelty, disguise, secrecy, a hidden cave, and a dungeon into which the good brother, Albert, is thrown. The heroine, Maria, who has remained faithful to Albert even though his brother Osorio has reported him dead and is courting her himself, like Isabella in *Measure for Measure* finally pleads for mercy for the man who has wronged her.[72] And Albert, a character who embodies the Godwinian ideal of an enlightened man, forgives his brother. Osorio himself, having originally plotted to have his brother murdered and having killed a noble Moorish chieftain in the course of the play, finally feels the bitterness of remorse:

> I have stood silent like a slave before thee,
> That I might taste the wormwood and the gall,

And satiate this self-accusing spirit
With bitterer agonies than death can give.[73]

Here are the bare, if melodramatic, beginnings of an exploration of the psychological death-in-life such as that experienced by the Ancient Mariner.

The play, though interesting for what it reveals of Coleridge's thinking about the individual and society, about justice and mercy, and about the growth of evil in a man not originally evil, fails as a drama. Sheridan duly turned it down, though he kept it for months without letting Coleridge know what he had decided. The action is too complicated, turning on a scene in which characters look at a picture which has been swapped with another, but which the audience cannot see; Coleridge explains the swap in a stage direction which it would be impossible for actors to make intelligible. Other illogicalities include the fact that Albert spends a long time on stage, disguised, in the presence of either his fiancée or his brother or both, yet neither of them recognizes his voice or his bearing. Too much is merely described, either in stage directions or in the speeches themselves. That Coleridge recognized this is clear from the preface to the play (not published, as the play was never performed):

> In this sketch of a tragedy, all is imperfect, and much obscure. Among other equally great defects (millstones round the slender neck of its merits) it presupposes a long story; and this long story, which yet is necessary to the complete understanding of the play, is not half told . . . Worse than all, the growth of Osorio's character is nowhere explained – and yet I had a most clear and psychologically accurate idea of the whole of it . . . A man who, from constitutional calmness of appetites, is seduced into pride and power, by these into misanthropism, or rather a contempt for mankind . . .
>
> In short, the thing is but an embryo . . . It furnished me with a most important lesson, namely, that to have conceived strongly, does not always imply the power of successful execution.[74]

Thus Coleridge anatomized his own effort. The 'embryo' developed, much later, into the drama *Remorse*, which had a successful run at Drury Lane in 1813. Meanwhile Coleridge salvaged two scenes from *Osorio* for publication in *Lyrical Ballads*, 'The Foster-Mother's Tale' and 'The Dungeon'. *Osorio*, like *The Borderers*, was neither staged nor published, despite the efforts of both authors to get them accepted in London. The two poets now came into continued close contact, for after his two weeks at Racedown, Coleridge brought Wordsworth and Dorothy back to Nether Stowey with him. By 14 July they had signed the lease for Alfoxden, a house only three miles from Nether Stowey, and immediately moved in, attracted by the magnet that was Coleridge.

'Wordsworth and his exquisite Sister are with me', wrote Coleridge to Cottle on 3 July. Having already told Cottle his opinion of Wordsworth, he concentrated now on describing Dorothy: 'Her manners are simple, ardent, impressive.' Moreover, 'her information various – her eye watchful in minutest observation of nature – and her taste a perfect electrometer'.[75] This was an astute portrait of the woman whose journals are such a barometer of what we now call 'Romantic' taste, with its detailed appreciation of natural phenomena – animals, flowers, skies, seasons – combined with a conscious simplicity of domestic life. Dorothy was an unusual woman, an outdoor enthusiast with a 'gypsy tan', as De Quincey noted, and, as he also observed, a tendency to express 'the irrepressible instincts of her temperament' and not to cultivate the usual feminine graces of manners and deportment.[76]

Dorothy and Wordsworth, having succumbed to Coleridge's charms, soon surrendered themselves to the delights of the countryside around Stowey. In a letter to Mary Hutchinson of 4 July, Dorothy drew the scenery which was to be such a fundamental element in Coleridge's poems of 1797: 'There is everything here; sea, woods wild as fancy ever painted, brooks clear and pebbly as in Cumberland, villages so romantic; and William and I, in a wander by ourselves, found out a sequestered waterfall in a dell formed by steep hills covered with full-grown timber trees.'[77] On this ramble brother and sister had seen Alfoxden and dreamt of 'happiness in a cottage' nearby; on hearing that the big house itself was to let at only £23 per annum, they had taken it, the 'principal inducement' being 'Coleridge's society'.[78]

Coleridge himself wrote excitedly to Southey that he had settled the Wordsworths in 'a gentleman's seat, with a park & woods, elegantly & completely *furnished* – with 9 *lodging rooms*, three parlours & a Hall – in a most beautiful & romantic situation by the sea side'. He could not resist informing Southey, the fallen idol, how wonderful Wordsworth was: 'Wordsworth is a very great man – the only man, to whom *at all times*, & in *all modes of excellence* I feel myself inferior – the only one, I mean, whom *I have yet met with* – for the London Literati appear to me very much like little Potatoes – i.e. *no great Things*! – a compost of Nullity & Dullity.'[79]

The contrast between the house taken by Wordsworth and Coleridge's own little cottage must have seemed all the greater – though Coleridge in his happiness did not complain of it – because Lamb had arrived on a visit on 7 July while the Wordsworths were still in residence with Coleridge. Lamb had written despondently on 24 June, 'I see nobody, and sit, and read or walk, alone, and hear nothing. I am quite lost to conversation from disuse.' Coleridge had once more urged him to visit, but Lamb hesitated: 'If I come to Stowey, what conversation can I furnish to compensate my friend for those stores of knowledge and of fancy, those delightful treasures of wisdom, which I know he will open to me?'[80] Five days later he wrote that he could visit '*next week*':

> May I, can I, shall I come so soon? . . . I long, I yearn, with all the longings of a child do I desire to see you, to come among you – to see the young

philosopher [Hartley, now nine months old] to thank Sara for her last year's invitation in person – to read your tragedy – to read over together our little book [*Poems* of 1797, not yet published] – to breathe fresh air – to revive in me vivid images of 'Salvation scenery.'[81]

Lamb stayed a week; he enjoyed meeting Sara, the Wordsworths and Tom Poole. He must have observed that Coleridge's attention was fully absorbed by Wordsworth, and that he was now breathing, intellectually and emotionally, country air with all the excitement he had once enjoyed with Lamb in the smoky, dingy room at the Salutation and Cat in Newgate Street. Still, Lamb was the chief subject and recipient of the beautiful poem 'This Lime-Tree Bower My Prison', which Coleridge wrote one evening in the jasmine arbour separating his and Poole's gardens. Coleridge explained the occasion of the poem to Southey, for whom he copied it. Sara had 'accidentally emptied a skillet of boiling milk on my foot, which confined me during the whole time of C. Lamb's stay'. While Wordsworth, Dorothy, and Lamb were out walking in the neighbourhood of Stowey, Coleridge composed the poem, 'with which I am pleased'.[82]

He had much to be pleased with. The poem perfects the 'plain style' he had adopted in 'The Eolian Harp'. It is certainly plain compared to 'Religious Musings' and his other declamatory poems, and yet the tone is versatile, modulating from the conversational to the dramatic, from the descriptive to the apostrophizing, and the story told is both simple and humanly complex. In fact, in ways familiar from his letter-writing, Coleridge *makes* the conversational and the chatty into something unusually arresting. The elements he appreciated in Cowper's long meditative, associative poem, *The Task* (1785) – 'the divine chit-chat' he had mentioned to Thelwall[83] – he here makes his own, outdoing even Cowper's modulations between lightheartedness and reflectiveness.

Both poets exploit the possibilities of blank verse for changes of tempo and tone. Both use the tradition of the 'prospect poem' to send the eye (and the inner eye) roving over a scene which is generalized and at the same time particular. Both contrast the country with London, which Cowper calls a 'crowded coop'. But Coleridge leaves behind the abstract rhetoric of Cowper and of his own earlier poems, the talk of 'sturdy swains' and 'labouring teams', of 'spacious meads' and 'woodland scenes'.[84] He writes with a fine particularity of description in the poem, enacting the process of discovering that because he cannot join his friends on the much-loved walk he had hoped to lead them on, he must conjure it from memory in his mind's eye, and finding that he gains an extra unexpected pleasure from the experience.

The first version of the poem, sent to Southey, is a mere fifty-six lines long. (Twenty lines were added for publication in 1800 in the *Annual Anthology*.) The original poem is in two paragraphs of roughly equal length:

Well – they are gone: and here must I remain,
Lam'd by the scathe of fire, lonely & faint,

This lime-tree bower my prison. They, meantime,
My friends, whom I may never meet again,
On springy heath, along the hill-top edge,
Wander delighted, and look down, perchance,
On that same rifted Dell, where many an Ash
Twists it's wild limbs beside the ferny rock,
Whose plumy ferns for ever nod and drip
Spray'd by the waterfall. But chiefly Thou,
My gentle-hearted CHARLES! thou, who hast pin'd
And hunger'd after Nature many a year
In the great City pent, winning thy way,
With sad yet bowed soul, thro' evil & pain
And strange calamity. – Ah slowly sink
Behind the western ridge; thou glorious Sun!
Shine in the slant beams of the sinking orb,
Ye purple Heath-flowers! Richlier burn, ye Clouds!
Live in the yellow Light, ye distant Groves!
And kindle, thou blue Ocean! So my friend
Struck with joy's deepest calm, and gazing round
On the wide view, may gaze till all doth seem
Less gross than bodily, a living Thing
That acts upon the mind, and with such hues
As cloathe the Almighty Spirit, when he makes
Spirits perceive His presence!

                              A Delight
Comes sudden on my heart, and I am glad
As I myself were there! Nor in this bower
Want I sweet sounds or pleasing shapes. I watch'd
The sunshine of each broad transparent Leaf
Broke by the shadows of the Leaf or Stem,
Which hung above it: and that Wall-nut Tree
Was richly ting'd: and a deep radiance lay
Full on the ancient ivy which usurps
Those fronting elms, and now with blackest mass
Makes their dark foliage gleam a lighter hue
Thro' the last twilight.– And tho' the rapid bat
Wheels silent by and not a swallow twitters,
Yet still the solitary humble-bee
Sings in the bean-flower. Henceforth, I shall know
That nature ne'er deserts the wise & pure,
No scene so narrow, but may well employ
Each faculty of sense, and keep the heart
Awake to Love & Beauty: and sometimes
'Tis well to be bereav'd of promis'd good
That we may lift the soul, & contemplate
With lively joys the joys, we cannot share.
My Sister & my Friends! when the last Rook
Beat it's straight path along the dusky air
Homewards, I bless'd it; deeming, it's black wing
Cross'd, like a speck, the blaze of setting day,

> While ye stood gazing; or when all was still,
> Flew creaking o'er your heads, & had a charm
> For you, my Sister & my Friends! to whom
> No sound is dissonant, which tells of Life![85]

The first paragraph sets out the circumstance: his friends have gone on a walk without him. His separation from them is expressed in the simple oppositions they/I and 'this lime-tree bower'/'that same rifted Dell'. The tone is resigned and talkative – 'Well – they are gone' – and yet a little petulant and self-dramatizing –

> Lam'd by the scathe of fire, lonely & faint.

(This line was omitted from the published version.) Thinking of where his friends might now be and how they might be reacting, he particularizes Lamb, the city-bound clerk who has had strange troubles. Sympathy with his friend leads him to apostrophize Nature, illogically but movingly adjuring the sunset to be even more glorious than usual for Lamb's sake. Here the poem strikes a religious note, but unobtrusively in honour of Lamb's quiet Unitarianism and perhaps also in expression of Coleridge's own half-mindedness towards the pantheistic love of nature he had briefly allowed himself to express in 'The Eolian Harp'.

A mental movement occurs, heralded by the break between paragraphs and enacted by the frequent enjambements suited to the motions of a mind in action. Instead of the separateness from his friends which informed the opening lines, the poet now speaks of a communal feeling. In following Lamb's course imaginatively, he has brought real pleasure to himself too. He can now turn back from 'there' to 'here' and enjoy 'this bower', no longer overdramatized as a prison. He details the beauty immediately surrounding him and draws, but gently, the moral of nature's beneficent effect through keeping the mind alive to beauty. Finally, the poet, by blessing the rook flying home and seeing it as a moving link between his friends there and himself here, can celebrate without resentment the pleasures he has conjured for them.

Coleridge may have gained encouragement from Wordsworth about the possibility of making poetry out of exact observation, endeavouring 'to look steadily at my subject', as Wordsworth termed it in the 1800 Preface to *Lyrical Ballads*, and so avoid 'falsehood of description'.[86] In return, Wordsworth paid Coleridge the compliment of echoing him in those lines of 'Tintern Abbey', composed a year later to complete the volume of *Lyrical Ballads*:

> Knowing that Nature never did betray
> The heart that loved her.

Coleridge himself built on the perception expressed here, that the mind's activity in contemplating nature can have a morally and spiritually beneficial effect on the owner of the mind, when he allowed the Ancient Mariner to watch water snakes playing in the sea and to 'bless them unawares'.

Lamb had no sooner returned to London than John Thelwall arrived as a guest of the Coleridges. Thelwall had been hounded and harassed as he attempted to give his lectures in London and elsewhere. The 'Gagging Acts' caused landlords to eject him from their public rooms rather than risk prosecution and loss of their licences, and in May 1797 he gave up the unequal struggle and began to think about finding a rural retreat. In 1798 he was enabled by the generosity of friends to settle on a farm in Wales, but first, attracted by the idea of meeting the man with whom he had been corresponding for several months, he accepted Coleridge's invitation to come to Nether Stowey.

The visit was a success. Coleridge reported to Josiah Wade that Thelwall was 'a very warm hearted honest man' and 'a great favorite with Sara'. Their disagreement about religion seemed only to make their mutual liking more piquant. Coleridge set about asking friends to look out for a cottage '*any where* 5 or 6 miles round Stowey' for Thelwall.[87] As for the latter, he was enchanted. He wrote to his wife on 18 July, the day after his arrival:

> Everything but my Stella and my babes are now banished from my mind by the enchanting retreat (the Academus of Stowey) from which I write this, and by the delightful society of Coleridge and of Wordsworth, the present occupier of Allfox Den. We have been having a delightful ramble to-day among the plantations, and along a wild, romantic dell in these grounds, through which a foaming, rushing, murmuring torrent of water winds its long artless course.[88]

Thelwall was seduced by the notion of himself, Coleridge and Wordsworth as a 'literary and political triumvirate', 'a most philosophical party', able to 'burst forth in poetical flights of enthusiasm' and to philosophize on the joys of a tranquil country life which 'the residents of cities can never know'.[89] The influence of Wordsworth and Coleridge, particularly Coleridge, is apparent in the poem he wrote in Bridgwater on his way to Bristol from Stowey on 27 July, 'Lines, written at Bridgewater, in Somersetshire, on the 17th of July, 1797; during a long excursion, in quest of a peaceful retreat'. The poem, a lengthy versified account of past 'storms and persecutions' and hopes of future peace, centres squarely on Nether Stowey and Coleridge as the focus for his future life and happiness:

> Ah! let me, far in some sequester'd dell,
> Build my low cot; most happy might it prove,
> My Samuel! near to thine, that I might oft
> Share thy sweet converse, best-belov'd of friends! –

Long-lov'd ere known: for kindred sympathies
Link'd, tho' far distant, our congenial souls.

Thelwall even revives the Pantisocratic utopia in lines which run on and
on, a breathless piece of argument arranged in iambic pentameters in this
example of a rather bad conversation poem:

Ah! 'twould be sweet, beneath the neighb'ring thatch,
In philosophic amity to dwell.
Inditing moral verse, or tale, or theme,
Gay or instructive; and it would be sweet,
With kindly interchange of mutual aid,
To delve our little garden plots, the while
Sweet converse flow'd, suspending oft the arm
And half-driven spade, while, eager, one propounds,
And listens one, weighing each pregnant word,
And pondering fit reply . . .

And so on for several more lines of close recapitulation of the Southey and
Coleridge plans for American harmony. Thelwall pictures

by our sides
Thy Sara, and my Susan, and, perchance,
Alfoxden's musing tenant, and the maid
Of ardent eye, who, with fraternal love,
Sweetens his solitude . . .

. . . O, it would be
A Golden Age reviv'd![90]

The little cottage, for all its dampness and crampedness and popularity
with mice, seemed to be the centre of a personal, poetic and philosophical
idyll during that summer of 1797. Cottle visited then, too, and remembered
the jasmine arbour with a table 'laden with delicious bread and cheese,
surmounted by a brown mug of the true Taunton ale' and pleasant
company sitting in 'our sylvan hall of splendour'. Coleridge was at his
happiest, especially when 'Mrs Coleridge approached, with her fine
Hartley', causing Coleridge's eyes to 'beam transcendental joy'.[91] Near the
end of his life Coleridge recalled sitting in the garden with Thelwall. 'I said
to him – "Citizen John! this is a fine place to talk treason in!" "Nay! Citizen
Samuel!" replied he, "it is a place to make a man forget that there is any
necessity for treason".'[92]
However, Thelwall did not in the end settle in Stowey, and fear of
treasonable talk was the chief cause. By 21 August Coleridge was writing to
put him off:

Very great odium T. Poole incurred by bringing *me* here – my peaceable
manners & known attachment to Christianity had almost worn it away – when

Wordsworth came & he likewise by T. Poole's agency settled here –/ You cannot conceive the tumult, calumnies, & apparatus of threatened persecutions which this event has occasioned round about us. If *you* too should come, I am afraid, that even riots & dangerous riots might be the consequence.[93]

Though this sounds suspiciously like a piece of Coleridgean 'specious argumentation' and exaggeration to evade difficulties, it was actually based on fact. In August 1797 Wordsworth and Coleridge were under surveillance by a government spy, later called by Coleridge in a pun on Spinoza, whose works he was reading and discussing with Thelwall at this time, 'Spy Nozy'.[94]

In February 1797 British fears of a French invasion, long stoked by Pitt's Government, had been briefly realized. A small expeditionary force landed near Fishguard on the Pembrokeshire coast. The soldiers were quickly overpowered and taken prisoner, so that their plan to attack Bristol came to nothing, but there was a frisson of alarm in the area and a renewed official suspicion of British radicals and friends of France. Wordsworth and Coleridge, accustomed to rambling near the coast with notebook and pencil in hand and known – especially Coleridge – for their radical views, came under scrutiny. A local informant gave the Duke of Portland at the Home Office an account of the recent arrival at Alfoxden of Wordsworth and Dorothy, who, probably because of their North Country accents and sunburnt appearance, were taken for foreigners:

On the 8th. inst. I took the liberty to acquaint your Grace with a very suspicious business concerning an emigrant family, who have contrived to get possession of a Mansion House at Alfoxton . . . the master of the house has no wife with him, but only a woman who passes for his sister – the man has Camp Stools, which he & his visitors carry with them when they go about the country upon their nocturnal or diurnal expeditions, & have also a Portfolio in which they enter their observations . . .[95]

A Home Office spy, James Walsh, was sent to Somerset to check on the story. Having previously been detailed to spy on Thelwall in London, he now learned that Thelwall himself had only recently left the 'mischiefous gang of disaffected Englishmen' gathered around Tom Poole, a 'Sett of Violent Democrats' including 'Coldridge', 'reckoned a Man of superior Ability' (another impressive testimony to Coleridge's reputation as a genius), and Wordsworth, described by a servant at Alfoxden as 'a Phylosopher'.[96] Nothing more happened, since the spy could not prove a French connection.

There must, however, have been some adverse gossip locally, for Poole exerted himself to assure the owner of Alfoxden, a Mrs St Albyn, that her tenant was not a dangerous radical. On 16 September he wrote to her dissociating Wordsworth, and by extension himself and Coleridge, from Thelwall's known political views:

By accident Mr Thelwall as he was travelling through the neighbourhood called at Stowey – the person he called on at Stowey took him to Allfoxen [sic] – no person at Stowey nor Mr Wordsworth knew of his coming – Mr Wordsworth had never spoken to him before nor indeed had any one of Stowey . . . Mr Wordsworth of all men alive is the last who will give any one cause to complain of his opinions his conduct or his disturbing the peace of any one.[97]

Poole's valiant efforts did not prevent Mrs St Albyn from refusing to renew Wordsworth's lease on Alfoxden beyond midsummer 1798, a quite understandable decision on her part which had a reverberating effect on the future movements of both the Wordsworths and Coleridge himself.

Meanwhile Wordsworth and Coleridge carried on with their nocturnal and diurnal ramblings, and Wordsworth and Dorothy continued to shock and puzzle local people with their relationship; in short, they devoted themselves to being what they were – Romantic poets. Thelwall, who would have liked to make a third, was, however, excluded.

Coleridge, Wordsworth and Dorothy rambled all summer among the 'combes' – valleys on the flank of a hill running to and from the coast – of the Quantock Hills and the Somerset and Devon coastlines. Sara Coleridge was too busy looking after Hartley to accompany them; in July she had a miscarriage, 'but in so very early a stage, that it occasioned but little pain, one day's indisposition and no confinement', as Coleridge told Wade.[98] Even as late as November 1797 Dorothy described one such walk to Mary Hutchinson:

From Porlock we kept close to the shore about four miles. Our road lay through wood, rising almost perpendicularly from the sea, with views of the opposite mountains of Wales: thence we came by twilight to Lynmouth, in Devonshire. The next morning we were guided to a valley at the top of one of these immense hills which open at each end to the sea, and is from its rocky appearance called the Valley of the Stones. We mounted a cliff at the end of the valley, and looked from it immediately on to the sea.[99]

On at least one occasion Coleridge walked alone in this isolated region on the north Somerset–Devon border. His solitary walk resulted in one of the most famous poems in the language. Many mysteries surround 'Kubla Khan', including the date of its composition. Unusually, no references to it survive in Coleridge's letters; nor do Coleridge's friends and correspondents discuss it in their surviving papers.[100] We do not even know, as we do with the unfinished and much discussed 'Christabel', why Coleridge chose not to publish 'Kubla Khan' until 1816. When he did, he accompanied it with the most famous, but probably not the most accurate, preface in literary history.

In 1816 Coleridge was in low spirits. He had published very little in recent years; he was constantly being criticized in the periodicals, by Hazlitt and others, for not doing more with his famous gifts; his confidence in himself, particularly as a poet, was at its lowest ebb. Knowing that whatever he published would be attacked, yet aware that despite the failure of his repeated efforts to finish 'Christabel', that poem had been admired (and borrowed from) in its unpublished form by Scott and Byron, the two most successful poets of the age, he ventured to send out 'Kubla Khan' with 'Christabel' in a slim volume with his painful poem descriptive of opium nightmares, 'The Pains of Sleep'. As protection against the scorn of critics, he subtitled 'Kubla Khan' 'A Fragment' – which, unlike 'Christabel', it may not have been – and appended to it a self-justificatory and self-deprecating preface: 'The following fragment is here published at the request of a poet of great and deserved celebrity [Byron], and, as far as the Author's own opinions are concerned, rather as a psychological curiosity, than on the ground of any supposed *poetic* merits.'[101]

This looks astonishing to us now; but Coleridge's fears were borne out by the reviews of the little 1816 volume. Most concentrated on 'Christabel', which was universally ridiculed. 'Kubla Khan' was either completely ignored or derided. Hazlitt typically announced at the end of his review in the *Examiner* that 'Kubla Khan' 'only shows that Mr Coleridge can write better *nonsense* than any man in England'.[102] Coleridge further complicated matters by describing (inventing?) the interruption of his 'reverie' by 'a person on business from Porlock' which made him forget most of the lines he had composed in his sleep.

The date Coleridge assigned to the poem's composition in this preface – summer 1797 – may be more accurate than many of his biographers and editors have taken it to be. In a notebook of 1810 he connected 'Kubla Khan' with a quarrel with Charles Lloyd which erupted in the spring of 1798, leading some scholars to accept that period as the time of the poem's composition.[103] But in 1934 an undated manuscript of 'Kubla Khan' came to light – the Crewe Manuscript – in which Coleridge specifies the place and date of composition in more detail than in the preface (and without reference to the person from Porlock): 'This fragment with a good deal more, not recoverable, composed in a sort of Reverie brought on by two grains of Opium, taken to check a dysentery, at a Farm House between Porlock & Linton, a quarter of a mile from Culbone Church, in the fall of the year, 1797.'[104]

The farmhouse has been identified as Ash Farm, above Culbone Combe, and early October 1797 seems the most likely date. On 14 October Coleridge wrote one of his 'flighty', opium-influenced letters to Thelwall. Its vocabulary and diction are similar to the poem's, as are those of the final act of *Osorio*, only recently written, from which Coleridge quotes to his friend some lines about 'the *fall of the year*' with its 'hanging Woods, most lovely in decay'. (Did Wordsworth hear an echo of this when he wrote in Book VI of *The Prelude*, on the crossing of the Alps, of 'the immeasurable height/ Of woods decaying, never to be decayed'?) In the letter Coleridge plays with the idea of oblivion:

I adopt the Brahman Creed, & say – It is better to sit than to stand, it is better to lie than to sit, it is better to sleep than to wake – but Death is the best of all! – I should much wish, like the Indian Vishna [Vishnu] to float about along an infinite ocean cradled in the flower of the Lotos, & wake once in a million years for a few minutes – just to know that I was going to sleep a million years more.[105]

The floating, the infinite ocean, the being in a state of enchantment and suspended animation, the thought of oneself as 'the only Being alive': all these have their echoes in 'Kubla Khan', with its 'caverns measureless to man', its 'lifeless ocean', 'the shadow of the dome of pleasure' floating 'midway on the waves', and the vision of the isolated poet with 'his flashing eyes, his floating hair'. And in the letter Coleridge also quotes a few lines – the religious ones – from 'This Lime-Tree Bower My Prison', a poem which has more in common with 'Kubla Khan' than might at first appear.

'Kubla Khan' is fifty-four lines long:

> In Xanadu did Kubla Khan
> A stately pleasure-dome decree:
> Where Alph, the sacred river, ran
> Through caverns measureless to man
>   Down to a sunless sea.
> So twice five miles of fertile ground
> With walls and towers were girdled round:
> And there were gardens bright with sinuous rills
> Where blossomed many an incense-bearing tree;
> And here were forests ancient as the hills,
> Enfolding sunny spots of greenery.
>
> But oh! that deep romantic chasm which slanted
> Down the green hill athwart a cedarn cover!
> A savage place! as holy and enchanted
> As e'er beneath a waning moon was haunted
> By woman wailing for her demon-lover!
> And from this chasm, with ceaseless turmoil seething,
> As if this earth in fast thick pants were breathing,
> A mighty fountain momently was forced:
> Amid whose swift half-intermitted burst
> Huge fragments vaulted like rebounding hail,
> Or chaffy grain beneath the thresher's flail:
> And 'mid these dancing rocks at once and ever
> It flung up momently the sacred river.
> Five miles meandering with a mazy motion
> Through wood and dale the sacred river ran,
> Then reached the caverns measureless to man,
> And sank in tumult to a lifeless ocean:
> And 'mid this tumult Kubla heard from far
> Ancestral voices prophesying war!

The shadow of the dome of pleasure
Floated midway on the waves;
Where was heard the mingled mèasure
From the fountain and the caves.
It was a miracle of rare device,
A sunny pleasure-dome with caves of ice!

A damsel with a dulcimer
In a vision once I saw:
It was an Abyssinian maid,
And on her dulcimer she played,
Singing of Mount Abora.
Could I revive within me
Her symphony and song,
To such a deep delight 'twould win me,
That with music loud and long,
I would build that dome in air,
That sunny dome! those caves of ice!
And all who heard should see them there,
And all should cry, Beware! Beware!
His flashing eyes, his floating hair!
Weave a circle round him thrice,
And close your eyes with holy dread,
For he on honey-dew hath fed,
And drunk the milk of Paradise.

                                                                    [see plate 8]

The differences between the two poems of this summer and autumn of
1797 seem at first sight more striking than their similarities. 'Kubla Khan'
is written chiefly in lines of four stressed syllables, though with many lines
of five stresses and some of three. The poem is rhymed, though in a
complex, irregular way.[106] This is in contrast to the regular five-stress blank
verse of 'This Lime-Tree Bower My Prison', with its many lines run on
rather than end-stopped, giving it a feeling of following the sense of spoken, or thought, sentences. 'Kubla Khan' is much more highly patterned.
Moreover, it does not seem to tell a story or follow a logical progression;
one thinks of the much-discussed break at line thirty-six before the introduction of the damsel with the dulcimer. It ends with a verbal evocation of
the inspired poet of Plato's *Ion*, who gets inspiration from the honey-
flowing fountains in the garden of the Muses, and who, being thus inspired
by the gods, is 'out of his mind and there is no reason in him'. The last lines
of 'Kubla Khan' allude also to the very passage in *A Midsummer Night's Dream*
which Dorothy Wordsworth had chosen to describe her first sight of
Coleridge:

            The poet's eye, in a fine frenzy rolling,
            Doth glance from heaven to earth, from earth to heaven;
            And as imagination bodies forth
            The form of things unknown, the poet's pen

Turns them to shapes, and gives to airy nothing
A local habitation and a name.

(Act V, scene i, lines 12–17)

Coleridge has conjured up an exotic eastern scene of paradise, describing in words the architectural 'miracle of rare device' which is Kubla Khan's palace. The poem embraces the visual beauty of the palace in its grounds; like the second line of the Shakespeare passage quoted above, there is repetition and a mirroring, two-way pull in the shadow of the dome of pleasure floating midway on the waves. It also embraces – and this is accentuated by an emphatic rhyme – the music of nature; the shadow of the dome of *pleasure* is rhymed with the mingled *measure* of the fountain. As in Shakespeare, the poet is the ultimate artist, rendering in verse the qualities of both the visual arts and music.

'Kubla Khan' is full of allusions to travel literature, not only to Samuel Purchas's *Pilgrimage* (1614), mentioned in the preface, and which also informed the setting of 'The Ancient Mariner', but also to Plato, Shakespeare, Milton (particularly the books of *Paradise Lost* set in Eden), the New Jerusalem in Revelation and a myriad more sources near or distant.[107] But it is also set in the very scenery which Coleridge had had to conjure up from memory in 'This Lime-Tree Bower My Prison', and of which Dorothy Wordsworth and Thelwall spoke in their letters, the landscape lying between his cottage and the Somerset coast. Here once more are the 'rifted dell', the 'ferny rock', the 'plumy ferns', and the waterfall of the conversation poem. Here also is the closest at hand of all the sources for the 'deep romantic chasm', the 'mighty fountain', and the 'dancing rocks' of 'Kubla Khan'.

So the visionary poem merges an actual English landscape with the exotic locations read about in books; it condenses settings real and imagined, present, past, and mythical, personal and public, into one extraordinary utterance. The poem may also express imaginatively Coleridge's experience of taking opium, at least as to its pleasurable effects, as is seen from a comparison of its vocabulary with that in the letter to George Coleridge in March 1798, with its 'spots of inchantment', fountains, flowers, and trees.[108]

It is hard to know where to lay the interpretative stress when contemplating 'Kubla Khan'. The psychology and mythology of its creation is a huge subject in itself; J. Livingston Lowes has shown in *The Road to Xanadu* that a whole book can be written identifying the manifold reading experiences of Coleridge the library cormorant which inform the language and allusions of one short poem. What the poem certainly is, however, is a celebration of artistic creation itself, with its view of the inspired poet. But it is more than that. With its hints of tyranny (Kubla Khan himself), war, and mourning (the woman wailing), it is a vision of a paradoxical paradise, one which contains opposites – a 'sunny dome' and 'caves of ice' – and the alarming figure of the poet singled out – is this a blessing or a curse? – for genius and inspiration. Its influence, direct and indirect, on subsequent poetry has been immense. Tennyson's 'Palace of Art' and Yeats's Byzantium poems, for example, would be unthinkable without 'Kubla Khan', perhaps the first great non-discursive poem.

The final paradox is that his wonderful paradisal poem should have had as an inseparable element in its composition the serpent opium. At the height of youth, love, friendship, happiness and poetic power in his Somersetshire idyll, Coleridge produced this pleasurable object out of an experience in which pain, physical and psychological, merged with the heightened pleasure resulting – but only temporarily – from taking opium.

After the heady summer of visits, friendships and poetic activity, Coleridge approached the winter of 1797, as he had the previous one, in a state of hesitation between different plans. He wanted to get *Osorio* staged and published, telling Southey, to whom he read the tragedy on a visit to Bath in the autumn, that he hoped to earn £500 or £600 from it and would sink the sum partly in 'an annuity for Mrs Coleridge's life', and partly in a plan to go to Germany to study medicine. Southey's opinion was that he should continue to write for the stage, for, 'little industrious as his habits are, he may well produce a play yearly'.[109]

By December *Osorio* had been rejected (as had *The Borderers*), and no more was heard about writing plays. But the plan to go to Germany was not dropped, though it was not clear how it would be financed. In November Coleridge told Cottle that he was 'translating the Oberon of Wieland', and asked Cottle to send him a German grammar. His method was to translate as a means of learning the language. He was also, he mentioned in passing, at work on a ballad, of which he had written 'about 300 lines'.[110] This, with Dorothy's comment in a letter of 20 November that 'William and Coleridge' had on a recent walk to the coast 'employed themselves in laying the plan of a ballad, to be published with some pieces of William's', is the first casual reference to the origin of 'The Ancient Mariner' and the *Lyrical Ballads* of which it would form part.[111]

Coleridge still had no regular source of income, though at midsummer Poole and his friends had given him twenty guineas from the fund they had collected, five of which Coleridge asked to be sent to his mother-in-law at Bristol. 'I hope & trust', he wrote to Estlin on 9 June, 'that this will be the last year, that I can conscientiously accept of those contributions, which in my present lot & conscious of my present occupations, I feel no pain in doing'.[112] In fact, it turned out that this *was* the last year in which Coleridge was helped by Poole and his friends. But the change which occurred in his prospects was not in the end from accepting the help of admiring friends to earning a decent income from regular employment.

At first it looked as if Coleridge would have to find a proper job. More than once he was on the point of taking up a Unitarian ministry as a desperate last resort. Estlin had mentioned an opening at Norwich, but

Coleridge balked at the idea of 'performing or receiving the Lord's supper', and he still had his old scruples about preaching for hire.[113]

It was a meeting between Coleridge and Tom Wedgwood in September 1797 which was to produce the change in Coleridge's fortunes which finally enabled him to give up all thoughts of becoming a minister, a schoolmaster or a full-time journalist. In the middle of September Tom and John Wedgwood, sons of the famous Staffordshire potter, Josiah Wedgwood, who had died in 1795 leaving his three sons wealthy, paid a visit to Wordsworth at Alfoxden. Of the brothers John, the eldest, was a banker who lived at Cote House near Bristol, Josiah had succeeded his father as manager of the potteries, and Tom, chronically ill with an intestinal disease and so unfit for regular work, was a gifted but unhappy visionary, full of radical schemes for educating children, an enthusiastic metaphysician, soon to be the inventor with Humphry Davy of a method of producing 'photographs' by using nitrate of silver, and an experimenter with medicines and drugs.[114] Given his situation and character, Tom was bound to be attracted to Coleridge, whom he met at Alfoxden, and Coleridge to him. And so it proved.

Tom Wedgwood settled with his brother John at Cote House in order to benefit from Dr Beddoes's experimental treatment of his ailments. Beddoes was planning his famous Pneumatic Institution at Clifton, Bristol, where he could put into practice his theories about the beneficial effects of gases, or 'factitious airs', in treating disorders of a respiratory nature.[115] Beddoes was one of a group of radically-minded scientists and philanthropists which included Erasmus Darwin and other members of the group calling itself the Lunar Society, based in and around the rapidly industrializing Midlands.

So called because it met regularly at the full moon, the society included Darwin, Priestley until his emigration, James Watt of steam engine fame and his son, also James, Maria Edgeworth's father, and the Wedgwoods.[116] Many of the group intermarried. Beddoes himself was married to Maria Edgeworth's sister, and Tom Wedgwood's sister was the wife of Dr Robert Darwin, son of Erasmus and father of the more famous Charles (who in turn married a Wedgwood cousin, Emma, daughter of the younger Josiah Wedgwood). A certain notoriety attended this large circle of talented men and women, partly because of their 'French' politics and partly because of the stories which circulated about the disreputable nature of some of their experiments. The Pneumatic Institution was finally opened early in 1799 with financial help from this group, the most magnificent gift being Tom Wedgwood's donation of £1,000.[117]

When Coleridge, who already knew Beddoes from the *Watchman* days, met Tom Wedgwood, the latter had already given generously to impoverished men of talent. The mathematician and inventor John Leslie, who had travelled abroad with Tom in 1796, had an annuity to help him with his work; another beneficiary was James, later Sir James, Mackintosh, who in 1798 married Josiah Wedgwood's sister-in-law.[118] Mackintosh was most famous for his reply to Burke's *Reflections on the Revolution in France*, an enthusiastic pamphlet called *Vindiciae Gallicae* (1791). He had several things in common with Coleridge, particularly a much remarked-on conversational gift, and a growing addiction to opium.

In November 1797 Mackintosh heard of Coleridge's talents from the Wedgwoods and wrote from London offering to procure work for him on the *Morning Post*, owned since 1795 by his brother-in-law Daniel Stuart.[119] Coleridge accepted, and received a guinea a week for the next five months for contributions in prose and verse to Stuart's anti-war, anti-ministerial paper.[120] One of his first contributions, on 26 December, was 'The Visions of the Maid of Orleans. A Fragment', consisting of 148 lines from his abandoned verses on Joan of Arc, later known as 'The Destiny of Nations'.[121]

But a guinea a week would not provide bread and cheese for the inhabitants of the cottage at Nether Stowey. On 23 December Tom and Josiah Wedgwood sent Coleridge a draft for £100 with the accompanying note by Josiah:

> Dear Sir
>   My Brother Thomas & myself had separately determined that it would be right to enable you to defer entering into an engagement, we understand you are about to form from the most urgent of motives. We therefore request, that you will accept the inclosed Draft with the same simplicity with which it is offered to you.[122]

The 'engagement' was an offer, sent to Coleridge through Estlin, of the vacant Unitarian ministry at Shrewsbury. The chronology of events is complicated, but it seems that Coleridge and the Wedgwoods knew that the vacancy had arisen and that Coleridge was likely to be asked to fill it, hence their counter-offer. They wanted to save Coleridge for poetry, philosophy and science. On 27 December he wrote accepting their £100, saying it would bring him 'the tranquillity & leisure of independence for the next two years'.[123] The next day he received a firm offer of the Shrewsbury pulpit. From a sense of obligation to Estlin for his efforts on his behalf, and weighing, too, the benefits of a long-term, secure salary against the one-off gift of £100, Coleridge at last, on 5 January 1798, wrote a long letter to Josiah Wedgwood. He returned the £100 with a detailed explanation of his motives, hoping, childlike, that the Wedgwoods would 'be pleased with my conduct'. He repeated his gratitude, but pointed out that though their £100 would have given him security for two years, his obligations to his wife and family (Sara being pregnant with Berkeley, who was born on 14 May 1798), and to Mrs Fricker, whom he supported with £20 a year, were such as to require him to think beyond the short term.[124]

Coleridge appears to have used this letter to Wedgwood to argue *himself* into final acceptance of the Shrewsbury post. To the objection that he would have to smother intellectual doubts, he replied that all he would be required to believe was that 'Jesus Christ was the Messiah – in all other points I may play off my intellect *ad libitum*'. But the most pressing reason to accept the position was to ensure 'a regular income sufficient to free me from all anxiety respecting my absolute wants'. He would receive, he told Wedgwood, £120 a year and 'a good house, valued at £30 a year'. There would be the bonus of living in fine countryside – 'no mean ingredient in the composition of a poet's happiness' – and having leisure to write. He finished the letter with a shame-faced reference to the 'enlightened Selfishness' which motivated him in choosing Shrewsbury, and a comment which might be construed as an appeal to the Wedgwoods to make a better offer:

> It is chilling to go among *strangers* – & I leave a lovely country, and one friend [Poole] so eminently near to my affections that his society has almost been consolidated with my ideas of happiness. However I shall go to Shrewsbury, remain a little while amongst the congregation: if no new argument arise against the ministerial office, and if old ones assume no new strength, there I shall *certainly* pitch my *tents*, & *probably* shall build up my permanent Dwelling.[125]

In defence of Coleridge's undoubted emotional blackmail in this letter it may be said that in January 1798 he was once more financially desperate, owing money to Cottle's printer Biggs, to his shoemaker, his coal merchant, and the chandler, as well as a quarter's rent, the maid's wages, and Mrs Fricker's quarterly five guineas.[126]

This was the uneasy state of Coleridge's affairs – and his mind was in no less uneasy a condition – when he set off to do some preliminary preaching at Shrewsbury, where he arrived on 13 January 1798. Having preached twice on Sunday 14 January, he received a letter from the Wedgwoods, written on 10 January and sent to Stowey, where Poole opened it and forwarded a copy with a letter of his own urging his friend to accept the surely not wholly unexpected new offer contained in it. Tom Wedgwood wrote that he and Josiah were 'possessed of a considerable superfluity of fortune', which they desired to 'convert into a fund of beneficence', and they considered Coleridge a suitable recipient, given what they knew of his situation, his prospects, his character, and his abilities. Josiah, the business partner, wrote to offer 'an annuity for life of £150 to be regularly paid by us, no condition whatsoever being attached to it'.[127]

Poole, in his accompanying letter, extravagantly addressed to 'my dearly beloved', urged Coleridge to accept the annuity as more suited to his 'peculiar character' than the pulpit. 'Religion, if you please, may be, as it will be, the basis of your moral writings – it may shine in your lighter productions, inspire and purify your poetry'. Coleridge was to be, in short, a recipient of patronage of a new kind: instead of being the paid servant of a royal or noble family, obliged to write to order, or at least to be mindful of the expediency of writing celebrations of his patrons, he was to use his recognized gifts for the good of mankind, in whatever kind of writing he chose, and the Wedgwoods waived all rights to direct his efforts.

Though Poole may well have been right in thinking Coleridge unsuited to the ministry, he was overly sanguine about the probable effect on Coleridge's psyche of receiving this money, without conditions attached, for life. 'You are not shackled', he wrote. 'Your independence of mind is *part of the bond.*'[128] Perhaps, but Coleridge was so constituted that the very freedom afforded him became a burden under which he buckled. As Southey later put it, 'with a strong sense of duty he has neglected it in every relation of life'.[129] By exaggerating in his own mind the obligation laid upon him – taking it to mean no less than that he should enlighten mankind on every subject of inquiry – Coleridge so embroiled himself as to render himself incapable of repaying the Wedgwoods' generosity on a smaller, more reasonable scale by work with which they and everyone else would have been perfectly satisfied. But we have the easy wisdom of hindsight. To the Wedgwoods and Poole, and to Coleridge himself in January 1798, this seemed to be a solution made in heaven.

By 16 January the die was cast. Coleridge wrote first to Estlin to exculpate himself from the charge he feared would be made that he was avoiding his duty to become a minister, adducing David Hartley as a model of the religious man with a vocation to benefit mankind, but *not* from the pulpit.[130] The next day Coleridge, still in Shrewsbury, wrote to Josiah Wedgwood accepting the annuity, and also to Poole, who he knew would be delighted.

Two days before, on Sunday 14 January, he had preached at Shrewsbury. By one of those delightful quirks of history whereby a moment which might have been lost to posterity is gloriously saved for it, an eager member of the congregation which so nearly became Coleridge's was none other than the nineteen-year-old William Hazlitt. Hazlitt, whose father was Unitarian minister in Wem, ten miles from Shrewsbury, described the event in his famous essay, 'My First Acquaintance with Poets', in 1823.[131] By this time Hazlitt had written frequently about Coleridge, usually in savage terms. Indeed Coleridge considered him, with some reason, to be his arch enemy. Yet, as Lamb saw, 'a kind of respect shines thro' the disrespect that to those who know the rare compound (that is the subject of it) almost balances the reproof'.[132]

In his recollection of hearing Coleridge preach Hazlitt allows that respect to show in full. He even becomes confessional about his own unhappiness at the time (he was at odds with his father over his future career): 'My heart, shut up in the prison-house of this rude clay, has never found, nor will it ever find, a heart to speak to; but that my understanding also did not remain dumb and brutish, or at length found a language to express itself, I owe to Coleridge.'[133]

Then he launches into one of his finest paragraphs:

> It was in January, 1798, that I rose one morning before daylight, to walk ten miles in the mud, and went to hear this celebrated person preach. Never, the

longest day I have to live, shall I have such another walk as this cold, raw, comfortless one, in the winter of the year 1798. *Il y a des impressions que ni le tems ni les circonstances peuvent effacer. Dusse-je vivre des siècles entiers, le doux tems de ma jeunesse ne peut renaître pour moi, ni s'effacer jamais dans ma mémoire.* When I got there, the organ was playing the 100th psalm, and, when it was done, Mr. Coleridge rose and gave out his text, 'And he went up into the mountains to pray, HIMSELF, ALONE.' As he gave out his text, his voice 'rose like a steam of rich distilled perfumes', and when he came to the two last words, which he pronounced loud, deep, and distinct, it seemed to me, who was then young, as if the sounds had echoed from the bottom of the human heart, and as if that prayer might have floated in solemn silence through the universe. The idea of St. John came into mind, 'of one crying in the wilderness, who had his loins girt about, and whose food was locusts and wild honey'. The preacher then launched into his subject, like an eagle dallying with the wind. The sermon was upon peace and war; upon church and state – not their alliance, but their separation – on the spirit of the world and the spirit of Christianity, not as the same, but as opposed to one another. He talked of those who had 'inscribed the cross of Christ on banners dripping with human gore'. He made a poetical and pastoral excursion, – and to shew the fatal effects of war, drew a striking contrast between the simple shepherd boy, driving his team afield, or sitting under the hawthorn, piping to his flock, 'as though he should never be old', and the same poor country-lad, crimped, kidnapped, brought into town, made drunk at an alehouse, turned into a wretched drummer-boy, with his hair sticking on end with powder and pomatum, a long cue at his back, and tricked out in the loathsome finery of the profession of blood.

'Such were the notes our once-lov'd poet sung'.

And for myself, I could not have been more delighted if I had heard the music of the spheres. Poetry and Philosophy had met together. Truth and Genius had embraced, under the eye and with the sanction of Religion. This was even beyond my hopes. I returned home well satisfied. The sun that was still labouring pale and wan through the sky, obscured by thick mists, seemed an emblem of the *good cause*; and the cold dank drops of dew that hung half melted on the beard of the thistle, had something genial and refreshing in them; for there was a spirit of hope and youth in all nature, that turned every thing into good.[134]

It is interesting to hear from Hazlitt that Coleridge was still peppering his sermons with radical, anti-war politics, and to notice that in the verbal portrait of the boy soldier he described a younger, lower class version of himself as Silas Tomkyn Comberbache. It is significant, too, that Hazlitt knew of Coleridge's reputation in 1798 as a poet, though of course he draws on his knowledge of the poetry Coleridge had not yet written or published. While writing his essay Hazlitt may have had half-consciously in his mind, when he compared the speaker to St John 'crying in the wilderness' and living on locusts and wild honey, that other image of the inspired poet of 'Kubla Khan', who has fed on honey dew and drunk the milk of Paradise. This image, in turn, is redolent of the very passage from the Gospel of St Matthew that Hazlitt quotes, as well as from Plato's *Ion*.

In short, Hazlitt gives a portrait of Coleridge before he had dwindled, in Hazlitt's astute if exaggerated view, into conversation, indolence and humbuggery. He is caught in a brief romanticized moment: radical, poetic, sincere, eloquent, magical, perfect.

5

The Ancient Mariner 1798

It is an ancyent Marinere,
And he stoppeth one of three.
'By thy long grey beard and thy glittering eye,
Now wherefore stoppest me?'

'The Rime of the Ancyent Marinere' (1798)

Coleridge's writings in the *Morning Post* early in 1798 were as radical as anything he had done, despite his having chosen to retreat from Bristol and public life. 'On Peace', an article which appeared on 2 January, attacked Pitt's proposed new taxes to raise revenue for the continuing war with France. On 8 January his poem 'Fire, Famine, and Slaughter: A War Eclogue' appeared. It is chiefly remarkable for its success in closely echoing the witches' speeches in *Macbeth* without actually quoting from them at any point.[1]

Coleridge practises in this minor poem what we might call the Shakespearean Gothic mode, which also informs 'The Ancient Mariner', on which he was at work at this time, and 'Christabel', begun a few months later. The rhymed tetrameters, the high level of repetition, and the incantatory quality of the rhythm, are its main features, along with its bold allusion to Pitt as the devil for whom the wicked sisters Fire, Famine, and Slaughter are working. The refrain, in answer to the repeated question, 'And who sent you?' runs 'Four letters form his name'. The three then cry out together:

> He let us loose, and cried Halloo!
> How shall we yield him honour due?[2]

The Gothic was something on which Coleridge's mind was running rather a lot at this time. On 23 January he told Wordsworth that he had just read 'Monk' Lewis's play, *The Castle Spectre*, which he described succinctly as 'Schiller Lewisized – i.e. a flat, flabby, unimaginative Bombast oddly sprinkled with colloquialisms'.[3] Lewis's success with his play at Drury Lane was galling for Wordsworth and Coleridge, with their rejected tragedies. Both mentioned it prominently in letters at this time. *The Castle Spectre* was said to have earned an astonishing £18,000 during its London run.[4] Coleridge noted in his letter that Lewis had included in his drama 'a pretty little Ballad-song', which Coleridge compared to the old ballad of 'Sir Cauline', from which he himself may have taken the name Christabel.[5] In 'Sir Cauline', published in Percy's *Reliques of Ancient English Poetry*, the 'fair Christabelle' is the king's daughter whom Sir Cauline loves and serves.

For all Coleridge's awareness of the excesses of Lewis's works, he was as interested as Lewis himself in the ballad genre, in Shakespearean–Schillerian tragedy, and, more generally, in the German poetry of the movement known as 'Sturm und Drang' (Storm and Stress), to which Schiller's *Robbers* belonged. Percy's *Reliques* was influential not only on Coleridge and Wordsworth and their generation in Britain, but also in Germany, where imitations of English and Scottish ballads were common. Indeed, Gottfried August Bürger's *Lenore*, published in 1774, was a German version of the Scottish ballad 'Sweet William's Ghost' which travelled back to Britain in 1796–7 in the form of no fewer than five translations, one of them, 'William and Helen', by Walter Scott.[6]

As Coleridge himself pointed out in a review of Charles Robert Maturin's Gothic drama, *Bertram*, in 1816, 'the so-called German drama is *English* in its *origin, English* in its *materials*, and *English* by re-adoption'. He named Horace Walpole's *Castle of Otranto* (1765) and Edward Young's *Night Thoughts* (1742–5) as obvious examples of English works which had influenced the younger generation of German authors, whose works in turn affected English writers and audiences in the 1790s and beyond.[7]

It was Coleridge who, for all his scornful remarks about the 'ruined castles, the dungeons, the trap-doors, the skeletons, the flesh-and-blood ghosts, and the perpetual moonshine' of the popular literature of both England and Germany,[8] represented in his own work the 'Gothic' at its aesthetic and psychological best. The spring of 1798 saw him writing several poems containing Gothic elements. Interestingly, they took a variety of poetic forms: conversation poems such as 'Frost at Midnight' and 'The Nightingale'; ballads of magic and guilt like 'The Ancient Mariner', the fragmentary 'Three Graves' and 'Ballad of the Dark Ladie'; and public odes and versified sermons such as 'France: An Ode' and 'Fears in Solitude'. And there is a scrap of verse introducing the prose fragment on the theme of guilt and exile, 'The Wanderings of Cain', which began as a collaborative venture with Wordsworth.

The idea for *Lyrical Ballads* itself was actually rather a late one. Not until the end of May 1798 did Wordsworth and Coleridge discuss with Cottle a joint publication of their poems.[9] But they had been walking and talking since Wordsworth's arrival in the area the previous summer, and in the winter of 1797–8 an attempt at collaboration had been made, a mode of composition more to Coleridge's taste than to Wordsworth's. In 1828 Coleridge told the story of how he had suggested 'The Wanderings of Cain', a prose work to be written in 'three books or cantos' on the model of Salomon Gessner's *Der Tod Abels* (*The Death of Abel*, 1758). Wordsworth undertook to write the first canto, Coleridge the second, and whoever finished first was to set about the third:

> Almost thirty years have passed by; yet at this moment I cannot without something more than a smile moot the question which of the two things was the more impracticable, for a mind so eminently original [as Wordsworth's] to compose another man's thoughts and fancies, or for a taste so austerely pure and simple to imitate the Death of Abel? Methinks I see his grand and noble countenance as at the moment when having despatched my own portion of the task at full-finger speed, I hastened to him with my manuscript – that look of humorous despondency fixed on his almost blank sheet of paper, and then its silent mock-piteous admission of failure struggling with the sense of the exceeding ridiculousness of the whole scheme – which broke up in a laugh: and the Ancient Mariner was written instead.[10]

What was left of 'The Wanderings of Cain', consisting of eighteen lines of verse and just over four pages of prose, remained unpublished until 1828. It has certain affinities with both 'Kubla Khan' and 'The Ancient Mariner'. The setting combines the Biblical scene on the Euphrates with its 'cedars, palms, pines' with the landscape of the Valley of the Rocks near Linton on the Devon–Somerset coast, where Wordsworth and Coleridge loved to ramble. Hazlitt, whom Coleridge had invited to Stowey while staying in Shrewsbury in January, spent three weeks as his guest in late May and early June 1798. Coleridge took him on all their favourite walks, including one to the Valley of the Rocks, which Hazlitt described as 'bedded among precipices overhanging the sea, with rocky caverns beneath, into which the waves dash, and where the sea-gull forever wheels its screaming flight'. Coleridge told Hazlitt that he and Wordsworth were to have 'made this place the scene of a prose-tale' on the death of Abel, but that 'they had relinquished the design'.[11]

The few lines of poetry which survive from this plan are close to 'Kubla Khan' both metrically and in terms of the atmosphere they create, suggestive of the pictorial:

> Encinctured with a twine of leaves,
> That leafy twine his only dress!
> A lovely boy was plucking fruits,
> By moonlight, in a wilderness.
> The moon was bright, the air was free,
> And fruits and flowers together grew
> On many a shrub and many a tree:

And all put on a gentle hue,
Hanging in the shadowy air
Like a picture rich and rare.

The prose fragment deals with Cain, bowed down with guilt after killing his brother, and wandering in the moonlight led by his child Enos. The landscape corresponds to the barrenness of his spirit: 'There was no spring, no summer, no autumn: and the winter's snow, that would have been lovely, fell not on these hot rocks and scorching sands.' Cain is parched, as are the mariners after the killing of the albatross, and like the Ancient Mariner himself, Cain has a dreadful look: 'his countenance told in a strange and terrible language of agonies that had been, and were, and were still to continue to be'.[12] The guilty man wishes to die; his punishment is that he cannot, but must ever be, as Genesis has it, 'a fugitive and a wanderer on the earth', bearing a mark put on him by God explicitly to stop others from killing him.[13]

'The Ancient Mariner' is Coleridge's consummate poetic expression of the problem of human guilt. The shooting of the albatross was suggested by Wordsworth, who had been reading George Shelvocke's *A Voyage Round the World, by the way of the Great South Sea* (1726); it was Wordsworth, too, who thought of the lines describing the Mariner's appearance as 'long and lank and brown/ As is the ribbed sea sand', and who suggested the navigation of the ship by the dead men.[14]

Coleridge made the Mariner's action the centre of his nightmare vision. Not the least part of the mystery and horror evoked in the poem is the fact that the Mariner shoots the bird for no reason; at least no reason is offered. In the very letter in March 1798 in which Coleridge shares with his brother George the 'paradisal' experience that opium gives in relieving pain – 'a spot of enchantment' in 'the very heart of a waste of Sands' – he also writes about guilt and sin:

I believe most stedfastly in original Sin; that from our mothers' wombs our understandings are darkened; and even where our understandings are in the Light, that our organization is depraved, & our volitions imperfect; and we sometimes see the good without *wishing* to attain it, and oftener *wish* it without the energy that wills & performs.[15]

This describes the human condition as Coleridge understood it; it also indirectly describes his particular experience of the undesirable effects of taking opium, especially the paralysis of the will. It is hardly surprising that Coleridge soon came to associate himself with his own creation, the Mariner.

In 'The Ancient Mariner', as in many traditional ballads, the natural and the supernatural appear to merge. Strange though the setting is, it is based on true accounts. The crossing of the Equator, the movements of the sun and moon, the ice, 'mast-high', which 'came floating by,/ As green as emerald', all these are described in various travel accounts of sea voyages to the southern hemisphere.[16] As for the metre and rhyme, these share with the traditional ballad a pattern of four-line stanzas, each line having four stressed syllables, and with the second and fourth lines rhyming. To this traditional form Coleridge adds a remarkable amount of internal rhyming in the first and third lines, thus giving a sense of frequent, even compulsive, rhyming over all:

> Listen, Stranger! Mist and Snow,
> And it grew wond'rous cauld:
> And Ice mast-high came floating by
> As green as Emerauld.
>
> And thro' the drifts the snowy clifts
> Did send a dismal sheen;
> Ne shapes of men ne beasts we ken –
> The Ice was all between.
>
> The Ice was here, the Ice was there,
> The Ice was all around:
> It crack'd and growl'd, and roar'd and howl'd –
> Like noises in a swound.[17]

Coleridge also varies the number of lines in a stanza, sometimes extending these to five or even six. In such cases the verse is imitative of the emotion or experience it expresses, as in the following verses:

> I clos'd my lids and kept them close,
> Till the balls like pulses beat;
> For the sky and the sea, and the sea and the sky
> Lay like a load on my weary eye,
> And the dead were at my feet.
>
> [...]
>
> The sun right up above the mast
> Had fix'd her to the ocean:
> But in a minute she 'gan stir
> With a short uneasy motion –
> Backwards and forwards half her length
> With a short uneasy motion.[18]

In these and similar cases the effect is to enhance the strangeness of the experience and at the same time to render it 'real' by suggesting so feelingly what the experience was *like*. Another method by which Coleridge brings the nightmare experience close to us while emphasizing its unusualness is his use of simile. As a rule, poets seek to describe something unfamiliar by comparing it to something familiar, as when Milton writes of Satan preparing to tempt Eve in Book IX of *Paradise Lost*:

> As one who long in populous City pent,
> Where Houses thick and Sewers annoy the Air,

> Forth issuing on a Summer's Morn to breathe
> Among the pleasant Villages and Farms
> Adjoin'd, from each thing met conceives delight,
> The smell of Grain, or tedded Grass, or Kine,
> Or Dairy, each rural sight, each rural sound;
> If chance with Nymphlike step fair Virgin pass,
> What pleasing seem'd, for her now pleases more,
> She most, and in her look sums all Delight.
> Such Pleasure took the Serpent to behold
> This flowery Plat, the sweet recess of *Eve*
> Thus early, thus alone.[19]

Throughout *Paradise Lost* Milton uses similes to describe Satan and his actions, since we do not know what Satan is 'like'. In 'The Ancient Mariner' Coleridge reverses the process. In order to tell us what the Mariner's unfamiliar experience was like, he resorts time and again to comparisons with something else *even less familiar*. For example:

> Ne dim ne red, like God's own head,
> The glorious Sun uprist:
> Then all averr'd, I had kill'd the Bird
> That brought the fog and mist.
> 'Twas right, said they, such birds to slay
> That bring the fog and mist.
>
> [. . .]
>
> About, about, in reel and rout
> The Death-fires danc'd at night;
> The water, like a witch's oils,
> Burnt green and blue and white.[20]

We do not know what God's head or witches' oils look like, but at a certain level we have been led to think that we have been made familiar with the Mariner's experience through their being invoked, because we are accustomed to having similes appeal to that which we can readily recognize.

A particularly interesting example of this use of simile is Coleridge's imagining what it is like to be becalmed. By a process of inversion he calls up the idea of a painted ship, the copy of a real one, to describe the unnatural state of the Mariner's ship when it is becalmed:

> Day after day, day after day,
> We stuck, ne breath ne motion,
> As idle as a painted Ship
> Upon a painted Ocean.
>
> [. . .]
>
> The very deeps did rot: O Christ!
> That ever this should be!

> Yea, slimy things did crawl with legs
> Upon the slimy Sea.[21]

Coleridge had never been on any ocean, let alone experienced being stuck in this way. Leigh Hunt thought Coleridge had 'touched upon that matter with the hand of a master' when he himself experienced a becalming in the Bay of Biscay in 1822. 'A calm', he wrote later in his *Autobiography*, 'is not repose: it is a very unresting and unpleasant thing'. The sea, 'heaving in huge oily-looking fields' and 'foul with putrid substances', made the crew and passengers shudder to think what it would be like 'if the calm continued a month'.[22]

Coleridge's wide reading and his extreme sensitivity and suggestiveness have combined with extraordinary metrical subtlety in this poem to render the Mariner's physical and psychological torture vivid to the reader. He draws on his own knowledge of nightmare fears, familiar since childhood and extended by his opium experiences; on literature from the traditional ballad to the dark moments in Shakespeare and Milton; on travel accounts; and possibly too on Fletcher Christian's supposed statement at his trial for mutiny in 1792 that he was 'in Hell' after setting Captain Bligh adrift from the Bounty.[23]

Just as the Mariner shoots the albatross without conscious motive, so he commits a restorative act equally without premeditation. In the midst of his isolation he sees water snakes, appreciates their colourful beauty, and blesses them:

> O happy living things! no tongue
> Their beauty might declare:
> A spring of love gusht from my heart,
> And I bless'd them unaware!
> Sure my kind saint took pity on me,
> And I bless'd them unaware.
>
> The self-same moment I could pray;
> And from my neck so free
> The Albatross fell off, and sank
> Like lead into the sea.[24]

Here is a mysterious – and frightening, because not able to be willed – version of the loving movement Coleridge makes towards Lamb in 'This Lime-Tree Bower My Prison'. The Mariner momentarily thinks of some creatures outside himself. As in the conversation poem, the traveller returns, but the curse of the Mariner is not yet expiated. A more sinister type of the already potentially sinister figure of the inspired poet at the end of 'Kubla Khan', he is compelled from time to time to compel a stranger to listen to his story. The protagonist remains, Cain-like, essentially separate; he is not fully reintegrated into a community of friends, as is the mental traveller of 'This Lime-Tree Bower My Prison'.

The reader is left puzzled, in two minds, believing with the Mariner that he has done 'an hellish thing' in killing the albatross, but aghast at the terrible form his punishment takes. The simple moral preached at the end seems disproportionate to the experience at the heart of the poem:

> He prayeth best who loveth best,
> All things both great and small:
> For the dear God, who loveth us,
> He made and loveth all.[25]

In 1832 Coleridge remembered that the minor poet Mrs Barbauld told him the poem 'had no moral', to which he had replied that, on the contrary, it had too much moral, 'and that too openly obtruded on the reader'. He went on to make a comparison with a story from the *Arabian Nights*, that collection of stories in which callous humour and arbitrary punishments abound and which had made part of his precocious, anxious childhood:

> It ought to have had no more moral than the story of the merchant sitting down to eat dates by the side of a well, and throwing the shells aside, and the Genii starting up and saying he must kill the merchant, because a date shell had put out the eye of the Genii's son.[26]

On this point Coleridge himself shifted his position at different times. For the second edition of *Lyrical Ballads* in 1800 he added to the brief 'Argument' preceding the poem the words 'how the Ancient Mariner cruelly and in contempt of the laws of hospitality killed a Seabird and how he was followed by many and strange Judgements'. In 1798 the Argument had said nothing judgemental, reading merely:

> How a Ship having passed the Line was driven by storms to the cold Country towards the South Pole; and how from thence she made her course to the tropical Latitude of the Great Pacific Ocean; and of the strange things that befell; and in what manner the Ancyent Marinere came back to his own Country.

For the 1817 publication of the poem in *Sibylline Leaves* Coleridge added a marginal prose gloss in the style of one of his favourite seventeenth-century authors, Jeremy Taylor, a kind of middle style between the 'medievalizing' language in the poem – suiting a journey presumed to have been made after Columbus' voyage of discovery of 1492 but before Magellan's in 1519 – and Coleridge's own, albeit balladesque, language of 1800. This gloss further points the moral, being, unlike the poem itself, unequivocal about the albatross proving 'a bird of good omen' and describing the shooting as a crime which is in due course avenged. Though the original poem of course embraces these meanings, it is frighteningly unsure about causes and effects. While it is undoubtedly an imaginative exploration of guilt, it is not to be reduced to a mere tale of sin and retribution, as Coleridge again hinted in later life. In 1830 he said that the 'moral sentiment' at the end was too apparent 'in a work of such pure imagination'.[27]

Another remark of Coleridge's is worth noting in this context. He referred to a set of engravings of the Mariner by the painter David Scott (published with the poem in 1837, after Coleridge's death), saying it was 'an enormous blunder' to represent the Mariner as an old man while aboard ship. 'He was in my mind the everlasting Jew – had told this story ten thousand times since the voyage which was in early youth and fifty years before'.[28] This aligns the Mariner with Cain, and also fits with our impression on reading this poem of 'pure imagination' that its language is both of a particular time – the late fifteenth century – and timeless. Along with the use of simile, the paradoxically particular yet generalized diction enhances the effect of making the unfamiliar seem familiar to the reader, of procuring, as Coleridge said in perhaps his single most famous remark about poetry, 'that willing suspension of disbelief for the moment, which constitutes poetic faith'.[29]

The originality of Coleridge's poem can hardly be overstated. As Leslie Stephen noticed, part of the secret of the poem's magnificence is the 'ease' with which Coleridge moves in a world of mystical machinery, of Polar Spirits, benevolent and malignant. Stephen quotes from 'Il Penseroso', where Milton invokes 'the spirit of Plato' to raise

> . . . those demons that are found
> In fire, air, flood, and underground,
> Whose powers have a true consent
> With planet and with element

and concludes:

> If such a man [i.e., one who moves easily in the spirit world] fell asleep in his 'high lonely tower', his dreams would present to him in sensuous imagery the very world in which the strange history of the 'Ancient Mariner' was transacted. It is a world in which both animated things, and stones, and brooks, and clouds, and plants are moved by spiritual agency; in which, as he would put it, the veil of the senses is nothing but a symbolism everywhere telling of unseen and supernatural forces.

Compare this, says Stephen, to the poetry of Pope, or even of Gray, Goldsmith and Cowper, 'poetry which is the direct utterance of a string of moral, political, or religious reflections', and you see what is meant by the phrase 'a literary revolution'.[30] Though sweeping and overly dismissive of eighteenth-century poetry, Stephen's comment is valuable. Anyone seeking to understand the idea of a 'Romantic revolution' in poetry could do worse than start with 'The Ancient Mariner'.

Coleridge finished 'The Ancient Mariner' in late March 1798, taking it to Alfoxden on the 23rd to read to Wordsworth and Dorothy.[31] At this time he and Wordsworth, though often together and even writing at the same table, as Coleridge and Southey had done two years earlier, were still contemplating separate publications. Wordsworth was writing 'The Ruined Cottage', which was eventually published in 1814 as part of *The Excursion*, and Coleridge was negotiating with Cottle for a third edition of his *Poems*. Lamb's and Lloyd's poems were not to be included this time, for they – particularly Lloyd – had taken offence at some satirical sonnets Coleridge had published in the *Monthly Magazine* in November 1797. Coleridge told Cottle that the three mock sonnets, by 'Nehemiah Higginbottom', were intended to ridicule his own poetry, as well as Lamb's and Lloyd's, parodying their 'affectation of unaffectedness' and 'puny pathos'.[32]

No doubt Coleridge thought that if he could take his own ridicule in good part, his friends ought to be able to do so too. But Lloyd was sensitive, Lamb hardly less so, and even Southey assumed that the sonnet 'To Simplicity' (beginning 'O! I do love thee, meek *Simplicity*!') was a satire on *his* poetry. The joke backfired badly, for not only did Lloyd ask Cottle to remove his poems from the projected new edition – not much of a loss – but he also brought out, with Cottle as publisher, his novel *Edmund Oliver* (1798), in which the 'hero' bears a suspicious resemblance to Coleridge.

Edmund Oliver is a weak young man who, as Coleridge pointed out in an aggrieved letter to Lamb, undergoes a set of adventures very like his own, namely a 'love-fit, debaucheries, leaving college, & going into the army'.[33] Lloyd explains in the preface that Oliver is 'a character of excessive sensibility, and impetuous desires'; he also announces that 'the incidents relative to the Army were given me by an intimate friend', presumably Southey, with whom Lloyd had been staying in the autumn of 1797, when the novel was begun.[34] When Oliver sinks into debt, he runs away, gets drunk, and exclaims, 'I have some laudanum in my pocket. I will quell these mortal upbraidings! – I cannot endure them!'[35]

There is even some evidence that Lloyd wove the recent story of the Wedgwood annuity into his novel, which was published in April 1798. A rich philanthropist, Charles Maurice, offers to share his wealth with Oliver so that the latter can become 'a benefactor to your species'. The latter responds with tears, then

> he evidently struggled with himself – he measured the room in long strides – he was much agitated – however in a few minutes he turned towards me and with an inexpressible look exclaimed – 'I yield – I yield – I could call myself thy debtor, but I will not.'[36]

Though Lloyd's novel is not otherwise notable for its humour, this sounds like a sly dig at Coleridge's way of accepting financial help. Others noticed Coleridge's manner too, and disliked it. One of these was Tom Wedgwood's sister, Kitty, who protested in 1803 when preparing for a visit by Coleridge to Cote House that he showed 'too great a parade of superior feeling' and had, in her opinion, too willingly 'consented to be so much obliged towards you'.[37] Hazlitt, who was with Coleridge in Shropshire when the Wedgwoods' letter arrived offering the annuity, recalled somewhat spitefully that, for all his agonizing about what to do, he 'seemed to make up his mind to close with the proposal in the act of tying on one of his shoes'.[38]

Coleridge realized that he had been foolish to publish his parodies, as he confessed to Cottle, though he also complained to Lamb of Lloyd's 'heated mind'.[39] In 1802 he published an epigram which showed that he was still smarting at Lloyd's blabbing of personal secrets, 'To One who Published in Print what had been Entrusted to Him by my Fireside':

> Two things hast thou made known to half the nation,
> My secrets and my want of penetration:
> For O! far more than all which thou hast penn'd
> It shames me to have call'd a wretch, like thee, my friend![40]

In March 1798 an event occurred which moved Coleridge further from the Jacobinism of a few years before and closer to support of the British establishment, though he continued to be anti-Pitt for another two years or so. France invaded Switzerland, thus proving right those who had claimed that the post-Revolutionary Government was pursuing an aggressive, rather than a defensive, foreign policy. Coleridge soon went into print with his poem 'The Recantation: An Ode', later known as 'France: An Ode'. It was published in the *Morning Post* on 16 April 1798, with an introduction by the editor, Daniel Stuart, who signalled that the paper, too, had changed its view of France: 'The following excellent Ode will be in unison with the feelings of every friend to Liberty and foe to Oppression; of all who, admiring the French Revolution, detest and deplore the conduct of France towards Switzerland.'[41]

The Ode rehearses Coleridge's poetic history as a lover of liberty, and portrays France as treacherous and changeable. At the time of the French Revolution –

> When France in wrath her giant-limbs upreared –

he had supported her against 'the Monarchs' of Europe who had wished to suppress liberty in France as they already did at home. He had sung of Britain's shame in joining various alliances against France with tyrants like Catherine the Great. When the Revolution had turned into the Terror, he had thought of it as a necessary temporary storm, like that in Revelation (and 'Religious Musings'), before the rising of a bright new day. Now France had let him down by becoming tyrannical and oppressive of that 'peaceful country' Switzerland, and he dissociates himself from his earlier support.

When in April there was a general fear that France would once more attempt an invasion of Britain, perhaps through Ireland, which was now in a state of rebellion, Coleridge wrote another poem, 'Fears in Solitude', expressing, though rather more vaguely, his changed view. In this poem, which Coleridge characterized shrewdly as 'a sort of middle thing between Poetry and Oratory – sermoni propriora',[42] he still writes from an anti-Pitt, even anti-war, point of view, but aligns himself with his countrymen – 'O Britons! O my brethren!' – against 'the vengeful enemy'. His retirement to the country and his status as a family man are used to express a wish for peace. Showing signs of his closeness to Wordsworth, he praises the country life, 'God in nature', and his own particular spot of native land:

> And now, belovéd Stowey! I behold
> Thy church-tower, and, methinks, the four huge elms
> Clustering, which mark the mansion of my friend;
> And close behind them, hidden from my view,
> Is my own lowly cottage, where my babe
> And my babe's mother dwell in peace! With light
> And quickened footsteps thitherward I tend,
> Remembering thee, O green and silent dell!
> And grateful, that by nature's quietness
> And solitary musings, all my heart
> Is softened, and made worthy to indulge
> Love, and the thoughts that yearn for human kind.[43]

The man who wrote these lines on 20 April 1798 ought to have been settling down to the quiet family life described here, secure financially thanks to the Wedgwoods, and secure emotionally with his wife, baby, neighbour Poole and friends Wordsworth and Dorothy; writing poetry, publishing occasional prose and verse in the *Morning Post*, and pursuing his philosophical studies so that he could fulfil Tom Wedgwood's hopes that he would benefit mankind with his thoughts on religion, philosophy and education. He was to be another Hartley or Priestley in this respect.

It was not to be. He who wrote so feelingly about Nether Stowey would spend only another few months there as a permanent resident. The fond father of the infant Hartley would be chronically unfit to fulfil a father's role towards him. The praiser of domestic rootedness would embark on a life of wandering undertaken apart from his family. But in the spring of 1798 Coleridge did not know how it would be. On the contrary, he and Wordsworth now entered with gusto into plans for a joint publication of their poems.

In February 1798 Coleridge had written one of his most delightful conversation poems, 'Frost at Midnight', turning his thoughts of present, past and future on the tradition known to him from childhood, but also borrowed from Cowper's *Task*, that a film of soot in the grate portends the arrival of a stranger:

The frost performs its secret ministry,
Unhelped by any wind. The owlet's cry
Came loud – and hark, again! loud as before.
The inmates of my cottage, all at rest,
Have left me to that solitude, which suits
Abstruser musings: save that at my side
My cradled infant slumbers peacefully.
'Tis calm indeed! so calm, that it disturbs
And vexes meditation with its strange
And extreme silentness. Sea, hill, and wood,
With all the numberless goings-on of life,
Inaudible as dreams! the thin blue flame
Lies on my low burnt fire, and quivers not;
Only that film, which fluttered on the grate,
Still flutters there, the sole unquiet thing.
Methinks, its motion in this hush of nature
Gives it dim sympathies with me who live.[44]

The domestic scene is rendered in quiet language, and yet it has something mysterious about it – the adjective is redundant in the phrase 'extreme silentness' and a mystery (though a natural one) is created by the simile 'numberless goings-on of life,/ *Inaudible* as dreams' (my italics). This prepares for the mental toying with the fanciful idea of the film in the grate:

But O! how oft,
How oft, at school, with most believing mind,
Presageful, have I gazed upon the bars,
To watch that fluttering *stranger*! and as oft
With unclosed lids, already had I dreamt
Of my sweet birth-place . . .

Memory breeds memory in this way in an enactment of Hartleian association, until the poet turns to his sleeping baby:

Dear Babe, that sleepest cradled by my side,
Whose gentle breathings, heard in this deep calm,
Fill up the interspersèd vacancies
And momentary pauses of the thought!
My babe so beautiful! it thrills my heart
With tender gladness, thus to look at thee,
And think that thou shalt learn far other lore,
And in far other scenes!

The comparing and contrasting faculty leads him back to his own (deprived) childhood, then on once again in anticipation of a better one for Hartley:

> For I was reared
> In the great city, pent 'mid cloisters dim,
> And saw nought lovely but the sky and stars.
> But thou, my babe! shalt wander like a breeze
> By lakes and sandy shores, beneath the crags
> Of ancient mountain, and beneath the clouds,
> Which image in their bulk both lakes and shores
> And mountain crags: so shalt thou see and hear
> The lovely shapes and sounds intelligible
> Of that eternal language, which thy God
> Utters, who from eternity doth teach
> Himself in all, and all things in himself.[45]

The repetition of lakes, shores and mountain crags imitates the action of the clouds in reflecting these features. It is a local, natural equivalent of the mirror image of the shadow of the dome of pleasure in 'Kubla Khan'. The poem ends on a quiet note of blessing for the child in his close connection with beautiful nature. The frost has performed a miracle by inducing Coleridge to see his child in terms recalled from a superstition of his own childhood. The mental journey outwards and back ends in lifted spirits and resolution. A kind of natural magic has been performed by Coleridge. 'Frost at Midnight' enacts a mental process comparable to that in Wordsworth's 'Tintern Abbey', written in July 1798 to complete the *Lyrical Ballads* volume.

Oddly, 'Frost at Midnight' does not seem to have been considered for inclusion in the collection. Instead, Coleridge arranged for Joseph Johnson, the radical Unitarian publisher and friend of Godwin and Mary Wollstonecraft, to publish a quarto pamphlet containing 'Frost at Midnight', 'Fears in Solitude', and 'France: An Ode'. He visited Johnson in London in September 1798, on his way to Germany.[46] (A few months later Johnson was in prison, found guilty of selling in his bookshop in St Paul's Churchyard a 'seditious pamphlet' by Gilbert Wakefield.[47])

Another conversation poem, written in April 1798, was included in *Lyrical Ballads*. This was 'The Nightingale', a poem which makes the nightingale's song a starting-point for a loosely-structured mental wandering addressed to Wordsworth and Dorothy, 'My Friend, and my Friend's sister'. It sets out from Milton's famous line in 'Il Penseroso' describing the nightingale as 'most musical, most melancholy'. Coleridge quotes the line and uses it to correct the poetic tradition about nightingales having a sad note because in classical legend Philomel was raped, had her tongue cut out to stop her telling of the rape, and was turned into a nightingale. No, says Coleridge, 'In Nature there is nothing melancholy'. Rather 'some night-wandering man whose heart was pierced/ With the remembrance of a grievous wrong' interpreted the song as melancholy because he 'filled all things with himself' – a fine phrase for what Ruskin later called the pathetic fallacy.

However, the night setting and the sad tradition, though drawn upon in order that the poet may question the latter, allow him to indulge none the less in some fanciful, quietly Gothic descriptions of a wild grove with 'tangling underwood', and a 'gentle Maid' living 'hard by a castle' who 'glides through the pathways'. The associational element is looser than in 'This Lime-Tree Bower My Prison' or 'Frost at Midnight'. Coleridge lets the bird's song interrupt him and call him back to himself – as Keats famously did in his Coleridge-inspired 'Ode to a Nightingale' – and he ends the poem with a reference to his child Hartley. Echoing a notebook entry about Hartley crying and being taken outside, whereupon 'the Moon caught his eye – he ceased crying immediately – & his eyes & the tears in them, how they glittered in the Moonlight!'[48] he writes:

> I hurried with him to our orchard-plot,
> And he beholds the moon, and, hushed at once,
> Suspends his sobs, and laughs most silently,
> While his fair eyes, that swam with undropped tears,
> Did glitter in the yellow moon-beam! Well! –
> It is a father's tale: But if that Heaven
> Should give me life, his childhood shall grow up
> Familiar with these songs, that with the night
> He may associate joy.[49]

Coleridge sent the poem to Wordsworth on 10 May with a humorously self-deprecating accompanying note which begins:

> In stale blank verse a subject stale
> I send *per post* my *Nightingale*;
> And like an honest bard, dear Wordsworth,
> You'll tell me what you think, my Bird's worth.[50]

Bantering though this is, and however beautiful the final lines about Hartley are, 'The Nightingale' is as a whole a less successful poem than the other conversation poems. It has rather a blank at the centre, just where the others pivot on a significant controlling idea.[51]

On 14 May 1798 Berkeley Coleridge was born. Like his older brother he was named after a philosopher for whom Coleridge had a particular respect at the time. (When parodying and guying the Romantic poets in his comic Gothic novel, *Nightmare Abbey*, 1818, Thomas Love Peacock embraced this peculiarity of Coleridge's in the naming of his children; Peacock's Mr Flosky calls his eldest son 'Emanuel Kant Flosky'.[52])

A plan had existed at least since March for the Coleridges and the Wordsworths to visit Germany for a prolonged stay. The idea seems to have arisen with a view to the two poets learning German, which Coleridge had already begun, and studying science at one of the German universities so that they would come back able to pass on their knowledge either as teachers or as writers. For Wordsworth the plan represented an immediate solution to a difficulty; since September 1797 he had known that the lease on Alfoxden would not be renewed after midsummer 1798. Living costs were cheaper in Germany. The 'delightful scheme', described by Wordsworth to his friend James Losh on 11 March, was to spend two years, from midsummer, abroad.[53] In June Dorothy was explaining to a friend that they would settle first in a small town or village, where rents were low, then move to a university town for about a year, so that Wordsworth and Coleridge could study.[54]

When Southey heard about the plan, he took a sour but not uncommonsensical view of it: 'Coleridge I hear is going to Germany: a wilder and more ridiculous scheme was never undertaken than this – to go with a wife and two infants merely to learn a language which may be learnt by his own fireside!'[55] In the end, because of Coleridge's uncertainty about how the family could live there and even more because of the unsettled state of Germany itself during the Napoleonic wars, Sara and the children remained behind in Nether Stowey with Poole as their protector.[56] In a momentous decision undertaken rather casually, Coleridge went alone with the Wordsworths.

Meanwhile Cottle offered to publish a collection of poems by the two friends. Coleridge was keen for the volume to appear anonymously. 'Wordsworth's name is nothing – to a large number of persons mine *stinks*', he told Cottle on 28 May. He also reported that Wordsworth did not want to publish his own poems separately. 'He deems that they would want variety &c &c – if this apply in his case, it applies with tenfold force to mine.'[57] This was a curious judgement, since Wordsworth's contributions ranged from sad stories of poverty, displacement and bereavement in the rural England of the war period, such as 'The Female Vagrant' and 'The Thorn', to cautionary tales involving the poet–speaker, such as 'Simon Lee', 'Anecdote for Fathers', and 'We Are Seven', to the comic-pathetic 'Idiot Boy', to poems expressing the spirit of place, of which the finest – not added until the last minute – was to be 'Lines written a few miles above Tintern Abbey'.

As for Coleridge's recent output, since it included poems as diverse, and as good, as 'This Lime-Tree Bower My Prison', 'Kubla Khan', 'Frost at Midnight', and 'The Ancient Mariner', his comment to Cottle seems at least as odd with regard to his own work. But Coleridge was not the best judge of his own poetry. Also, unlike Wordsworth who was always reluctant to publish but when he did took great care with the presentation and defence of his poems, Coleridge had a fatal carelessness about going before the poetry-reading public. A reading of his prefaces and footnotes to all the editions of his poetry – 1796, 1797, 1803, 1816, 1817, 1828, 1829 and 1834 – leaves one astonished at his apparently offhand attitude towards his work.

In 1796 he talks of the 'disadvantages' of a miscellany of occasional poems such as his; in 1797 he claims to have improved the reprinted poems in response to criticism, but adds at the last minute some he had announced he was consigning to oblivion. He sends forth 'Christabel', 'Kubla Khan', and 'The Pains of Sleep' in 1816 with an extraordinary *mea culpa* about his indolence and apologies for the fragmentariness of all three poems, though only 'Christabel' is obviously unfinished. *Sibylline Leaves* in 1817 uses its title and a most unhappy preface to indicate the worthlessness of the contents. And from 1828 to 1834 he simply reprints the prefaces of 1796 and 1797. 'Reflections on Having Left a Place of Retirement' was first published in the *Monthly Magazine* as 'Reflections on entering into active life. A poem which affects not to be Poetry'.[58] And so on. Coleridge seems to have been pathologically incapable of sending forth his works to stand or fall by their own merits. It was as if he had to equip them with crutches which he then used, perversely, to knock the feet from under them.

Lyrical Ballads was, in fact, a rather heterogeneous collection. The title suggests that the poems inside will be ballads having something in common with those in Percy's *Reliques* and the new fashion for atmospheric ballads such as Bürger's *Lenore*, but with a 'lyrical' element allowing for expressions of personal sentiment of opinion, which is usually absent from traditional ballads.[59] The title thus conveys something of the paradoxical and complex nature of the works included in the volume, but it does not prepare the reader for poems so different from each other as, say, 'The Ancient Mariner', 'The Nightingale', 'The Thorn', and 'Tintern Abbey'.

Indeed, from what little we know of the two authors' intentions at the time (as distinct from what both said retrospectively, Wordsworth in his prefaces to the enlarged editions of 1800 and 1802 and Coleridge in *Biographia Literaria*), it seems that the original idea *was* for a volume of ballads, which might be expected to succeed, given the current taste for the genre. Coleridge produced 'The Ancient Mariner' with this in mind, and started 'Christabel'.

But Wordsworth, though productive in his chosen mode of illustrative tales of country people suffering and enduring at a time of great change and danger from industrialization and war and the havoc they played with ordinary lives, was also writing another kind of poetry altogether. As he told James Tobin in March 1798, he had composed '1300 lines of a poem in which I contrive to convey most of the knowledge of which I am possessed'. This was the projected long poem, 'The Recluse'. 'My object', he continued, 'is to give pictures of Nature, Man, and Society. Indeed I know not any thing which will not come within the scope of my plan.'[60] Both *The Excursion*, published in 1814, and *The Prelude*, which did not appear until after his death in 1850, were part of this larger plan.

Coleridge, too, was writing successfully in this more meditative mode. 'Frost at Midnight' and 'Tintern Abbey' belong to the same poetic kind and express similar responses to natural surroundings and their effect on the individual mind that drinks them in. In March 1798 Coleridge wrote to his brother George about his poetic plans in phrases so appropriate to the poems Wordsworth was increasingly to write that they must surely have stemmed from the poets' daily conversations at this time. In poetry, he told George, he aimed 'to elevate the imagination & set the affections in right time by the beauty of the inanimate impregnated, as with a living soul, by the presence of Life . . . I love fields & woods & mountains with almost a visionary fondness – and because I have found benevolence & quietness growing within me as that fondness has increased, therefore I should wish to be the means of implanting it in others.'[61] This, sounding to later ears so exactly like a description of Wordsworth's poetry, confirms what Wordsworth later spoke of as 'the most unreserved intercourse' between the two men.[62]

Of the ballads both poets were writing, Wordsworth's were much more numerous and much shorter than 'The Ancient Mariner', the only one Coleridge finished. 'The Three Graves' was a joint effort which failed and was left incomplete. Coleridge's 'Ballad of the Dark Ladie' also went nowhere. 'Christabel' got stuck at Part I. When they came to collect their offerings for Cottle in the summer of 1798, they intended to use the two extracts from *Osorio*, the ballads, and those tales of Wordsworth's which had affinities with the traditional ballad form. Coleridge was probably hoping to finish 'Christabel' for inclusion. 'Tintern Abbey' was added at the last minute, being written as late as July during a short walking tour Wordsworth took while seeing the volume through the press in Bristol. Had they originally envisaged the inclusion of such a poem, surely Coleridge's 'Frost at Midnight' and 'This Lime-Tree Bower My Prison', not yet published, would have found a place too.

A brief Advertisement was added to introduce the volume. It talked insistently of 'the author' as a single identity. The poems were 'to be considered as experiments', chiefly using 'the language of conversation in the middle and lower classes of society' and avoiding 'the gaudiness and inane phraseology of many modern writers'. They contained 'a natural delineation of human passions, human characters, and human incident'. Though sufficiently vague to cover some of the different kinds of poem in the collection, this description hardly fits 'The Ancient Mariner', the most ballad-like of all and the one chosen to open the volume. As if anticipating this objection, the Advertisement adds: 'The Rime of the Ancyent Marinere was professedly written in imitation of the *style*, as well as the spirit of the elder poets; but with a few exceptions, the Author believes that the language adopted in it has been equally intelligible for these three last centuries.'[63]

Coleridge's famous story in *Biographia Literaria* of the origins of, and principles behind, *Lyrical Ballads* must be seen as a retrospective rationalization of a collection which came together somewhat haphazardly. Yet it is a brilliant description of the kinds of poetry to be found there; nor is there any reason to disbelieve his account of the volume arising out of the two poets' discussions about poetry during 1797–8:

During the first year that Mr Wordsworth and I were neighbours, our conversations turned frequently on the two cardinal points of poetry, the power of exciting the sympathy of the reader by a faithful adherence to the truth of nature, and the power of giving the interest of novelty by the modifying colours of the imagination.

In formulating this idea, Coleridge says, the poets took their cue from nature itself, noticing the 'sudden charm' arising from 'accidents of light and shade', 'moon-light or sun-set diffused over a known and familiar landscape'. It occurred to them 'that a series of poems might be composed of two sorts':

> In the one, the incidents and agents were to be, in part at least, supernatural; and the excellence aimed at was to consist in the interesting of the affections by the dramatic truth of such emotions, as would naturally accompany such situations, supposing them real. And real in *this* sense they have been to every human being who, from whatever source of delusion, has at any time believed himself under supernatural agency.

This is a perfect description of the effect achieved by 'The Ancient Mariner', just as Coleridge's subsequent definition of the other type of poem is a fine account of Wordsworth's contributions:

> For the second class, subjects were to be chosen from ordinary life; the characters and incidents were to be such, as will be found in every village and its vicinity, where there is a meditative and feeling mind to seek after them, or to notice them, when they present themselves.

There follows in *Biographia Literaria* one of the most famous paragraphs in all literary history. The passage belongs equally to the particular account of the origin of *Lyrical Ballads* and to the larger history of critical thinking about poetry. It is entirely appropriate that Coleridge, in recalling the aims of that most extraordinary volume, should *at the same time* give voice to what is recognized as a central statement of Romantic criticism, one which was echoed by Keats in his letters and by Shelley in his 'Defence of Poetry':

> In this idea originated the plan of the 'Lyrical Ballads'; in which it was agreed, that my endeavours should be directed to persons and characters supernatural, or at least romantic; yet so as to transfer from our inward nature a human interest and a semblance of truth sufficient to procure for these shadows of imagination that willing suspension of disbelief for the moment, which constitutes poetic faith. Mr. Wordsworth, on the other hand, was to propose to himself as his object, to give the charm of novelty to things of every day, and to excite a feeling analogous to the supernatural, by awakening the mind's attention from the lethargy of custom, and directing it to the loveliness and the wonders of the world before us; an inexhaustible treasure, but for which in consequence of the film of familiarity and selfish solicitude

we have eyes, yet see not, ears that hear not, and hearts that neither feel nor understand.[64]

In the 1805 version of *The Prelude*, Wordsworth looked back at the extra-ordinary year stretching from midsummer 1797 to midsummer 1798, during which he and Coleridge were constantly together and, stimulated by one another's company, wrote such fine poetry. As is characteristic of his method in *The Prelude*, he condenses the year into one marvellous summer:

> That summer when on Quantock's grassy hills
> Far ranging, and among the sylvan coombs,
> Thou in delicious words, with happy heart,
> Didst speak the vision of that ancient man,
> The bright-eyed Mariner, and rueful woes
> Didst utter of the Lady Christabel;
> [. . .]
> When thou dost to that summer turn thy thoughts,
> And hast before thee all which then we were,
> To thee, in memory of that happiness,
> It will be known – by thee ar least, my friend,
> Felt – that the history of a poet's mind
> Is labour not unworthy of regard:
> To thee the work shall justify itself.[65]

The story of the unfinished 'Christabel', alluded to here, is a long, complicated, and largely melancholy one. It will be told in a later chapter. Suffice it to note here that the first part was written at Nether Stowey during this *annus mirabilis*, and that it was intended as an experimental ballad in a new metre, with a Gothic, mysterious and sinister setting and story. It concerns curses, spells and metaphorphoses of a malevolent kind, thus belonging as much to the literature of nightmare as 'The Ancient Mariner'. Its unfinished state, Coleridge's efforts to complete it, his promises and disappointments, its beauties and its absurdities, all became something of a *cause célèbre* in the first two decades of the nineteenth century. It was to be, like 'Kubla Khan', a literary historical phenomenon.

So also, of course, was *Lyrical Ballads* itself. Cottle, having given it to the world in September 1798, gave up his publishing business, selling the print run of 500 copies 'at a loss' to 'Mr Arch, a London bookseller'. A year later Cottle sold all his copyrights to Longman and Rees. Longman reckoned the worth of *Lyrical Ballads* 'as nothing' and so Cottle asked for the copyright back, in order to return it to Wordsworth. Cottle may be allowed his moment of self-congratulation when in his memoirs he recalls 'the most remarkable instance on record, of a volume of Poems remaining for so long a time, almost totally neglected, and afterwards acquiring, and that almost rapidly, so much deserved popularity'.[66]

Wordsworth and Coleridge did not wait to see how their anonymous volume would be received. Coleridge had told Cottle that his name 'stank' in certain quarters. This was certainly true. Even as he embarked for Germany, the conservative *Gentleman's Magazine* saw fit to abuse him as a 'democrat', and to gossip about his past. In a review of an anonymous publication, *Literary Memoirs of Living Authors of Great Britain* (1798), which had a sympathetic entry on Coleridge, the *Gentleman's Magazine* sneered:

> Squire Coleridge was educated at Christ's Hospital, and sent thence to Jesus college, whence this worthy gentleman and splendid genius ran away, nobody knew why, nor whither he was gone; in consequence of which, the master and fellows had ordered him to be written off the books . . . And the next news heard of him was, that he was become as exalted a democrat as Mr. Thelwall or Mr. Horne Tooke. Let the memoir-writer, who mourns over his 'disappointed hope and distressful adversity', say *who* is the cause of it.[67]

In the very months during which Coleridge was revising his political radicalism in response to events, his name was being put before the public as a Jacobin not only in the *Gentleman's Magazine* but also in the extremely successful *Anti-Jacobin; or, Weekly Examiner*, written by the young Tory wits George Canning, a member of Pitt's Cabinet, George Ellis and John Hookham Frere. Beginning in November 1797 and running for eight months, the magazine lashed out at literary as well as political figures of the left. Godwin, Thelwall, Tooke and Priestley were attacked; Erasmus Darwin's poetry was parodied, as were Southey's democratic verses. In the last number, on 9 July 1798, Canning wrote a poem which addresses the radicals, including Coleridge and Southey and their friends:

> And ye five other wandering Bards that move
> In sweet accord of harmony and love,
> C——dge, and S——th–y, L——d, and L—be and Co.,
> Tune all your mystic harps to praise LEPAUX![68]

(Lepaux was a minor French revolutionary.)

Later in July this part of the poem was reprinted with an accompanying cartoon by James Gillray, entitled 'The New Morality', showing Paine, Holcroft, Godwin, Priestley, Thelwall, Tooke and others as various animal and human types, with Lamb and Lloyd as a frog and a toad, and Coleridge and Southey as asses flourishing volumes of 'Sapphics' and 'Dactylics'.[69]

The irony was that Coleridge, at least, was moving away from radicalism, while Lamb and Lloyd had never been political agitators but were attacked for their known association with Coleridge and Southey. As Southey said of 'The New Morality', 'I know not what poor Lamb has done to be croaking there.'[70] There was further irony in the fact that these four poets, so unceremoniously lumped together in the *Anti-Jacobin* attacks as boon companions, were actually in a state of mutual coolness. Coleridge and Southey had never fully recovered their friendship since the Pantisocracy *débâcle*; Lloyd and Coleridge were bitter towards one another, and Lamb, too, was upset by something Lloyd reported Coleridge to have said about him. He wrote to Southey on 28 July: 'Samuel Taylor Coleridge, to the eternal regret of his native Devonshire, emigrates to Westphalia – "poor Lamb" (these were his last words) "if he wants any *knowledge*, he may apply to me".'[71]

Lamb had already written to Coleridge a satirical letter addressed to 'Learned Sir, my Friend', and sending a set of 'Theological Propositions' for Coleridge to unravel. These include the questions 'Whether God loves a lying Angel better than a true Man?' and 'Whether the higher order of Seraphim Illuminati ever sneer?' He signs off, 'wishing Learned Sir, that you may see Schiller' and 'eat fat hams of Westphalia, I remain Your friend and docile Pupil to instruct, Charles Lamb'.[72] The correspondence between Lamb and Coleridge was thus broken off for two years. Though the friends subsequently became fully reconciled, this rupture was for Coleridge something of a repetition of that with Southey in 1795 and a foretaste of worse breaches to come.

Having 'darted into Wales' with Wordsworth and Dorothy in August to visit Thelwall on his farm, Coleridge set off for Germany in the middle of September, just as *Lyrical Ballads* was published. On the 15th he wrote to Poole from Yarmouth that he was 'on the point of leaving my native country for the first time'. He promised to write alternately to Poole and to Sara, 'twice every week' during an intended absence of about four months, after which he might 'fetch over' his family to join him.[73]

6

To Germany and Back 1798–1800

If I had but two little wings
And were a little feathery bird,
To you I'd fly, my dear!
But thoughts like these are idle things,
And I stay here.

Coleridge, 'Something Childish, but
Very Natural, written in Germany' (23 April 1799)

On Sunday 16 September 1798, at eleven o'clock, Coleridge set sail from Yarmouth. He was accompanied by Wordsworth, Dorothy and a Stowey friend, John Chester, whom Hazlitt described as 'one of those who were attracted to Coleridge's discourse as flies are to honey, or bees in swarming-time to the sound of a brass pan'. He remembered that Chester, on the walking expedition to the Somerset coast which Hazlitt had also joined, kept up 'a sort of trot by the side of Coleridge, like a running footman by a state coach, that he might not lose a syllable or sound that fell from Coleridge's lips'. With wry humour, Hazlitt commented further that Chester 'followed Coleridge into Germany, where the Kantian philosophers were puzzled how to bring him under any of their categories'.[1]

As a matter of fact, though by the time Hazlitt wrote this Coleridge was famous for his interpretations of, and borrowings from, Kant's philosophy, he did not, as far as we know, pay much attention to it until after his return from Germany. In May 1796, when he first mooted the idea of a German trip in a letter to Poole, he had mentioned a desire to study the works of 'the great german Metaphysician', but he was also under the impression – common in England, where apart from some essays by Coleridge's Bristol acquaintance, Thomas Beddoes, Kant's *Critiques* were known only through a poor French translation[2] – that the Kantian philosophy was 'most unintelligible'.[3] His chief aims on setting out in 1798 were to become proficient in the language, to study natural sciences at a university, and to gather materials for a projected life of Lessing. All these things he did, as his letters and notebooks show, though the work on Lessing was never written, despite Coleridge's lively interest in the German author and his copious note-taking during his time in Germany.[4]

Coleridge wrote to Poole the day before he left England – 'a country which, God Almighty knows, is dear to me above all things for the love I bear to you'. Perhaps aware that Poole was resentful of his new friendship with Wordsworth, as were the Wedgwoods, Southey and Lamb, all of whom commented sourly on it, he insisted fulsomely that 'of many friends, whom I love and esteem, my head & heart have ever chosen you as the Friend – as the one being, in whom is involved the full & whole meaning of the sacred Title'.[5]

The letters Coleridge would send alternately to Poole and to Sara were to be copied by Poole's assistant Thomas Ward and parts of them preserved for publication, rather in the way Mary Wollstonecraft had published her *Letters Written during a Short Residence in Sweden, Norway, and Denmark* (1796). Coleridge's travel letters were not, however, published until 1809, when he included pastiches of those to Poole and Sara as 'Satyrane's Letters' in *The Friend*.

Coleridge's German letters are among the best he wrote. At last some of his correspondence with his wife is preserved. His letters to her, and hers to him, make it clear that there was still some warmth in their relationship, though this had diminished by the time Coleridge finally, belatedly, returned home. At first, however, Coleridge sets out to interest and amuse Sara by describing fashions in dress and domestic customs, as well as sending expressions of love and longing to her and the children. The first letter opens romantically. In the spirit of the conversation poems, Coleridge uses his absence to suggest presence through a feature of nature: 'Over what place does the Moon hang to your eye, my dearest Sara? To me it hangs over the left bank of the Elbe; and a long trembling road of moonlight reaches from thence up to the stern of our Vessel, & there it ends.'[6]

Expressions of excitement, curiosity, homesickness and high spirits, with gushes of love and warmth, tumble out of him. 'When we lost sight of land, the moment that we quite lost sight of it, & the heavens all round me rested upon the waters', he writes, 'my dear Babies came upon me like a flash of lightning – I saw their faces so distinctly!' He boasts about his unexpected lack of seasickness. Chester, Wordsworth, and, worst of all, Dorothy, were ill the whole way, 'vomiting, & groaning, unspeakably! and I neither sick nor giddy, but gay as a lark'. He describes watching the sea at night – 'a beautiful white cloud of foam' with 'detachments' of foam darting away from the ship's side 'with their galaxies of stars looking like a Tartar troop over a wilderness!'[7]

In his next letter, Coleridge gives a comic account of his fellow shipmates, especially an irrepressible Dane who 'declaimed like a Member of the Corresponding Society about the Rights of Man', all the while sending his mulatto servant boy on repeated errands for sugar and brandy; he notices a 'single solitary wild duck' swimming on the waves; he describes himself spending half the night on deck wrapped in a greatcoat he had bought in London for twenty-eight shillings, rather than go down to the stinking cabins full of vomiting passengers.[8]

As so often before, when Coleridge set out on an adventure, seeing new places and meeting new people, he was initially invigorated by the experience. Once more, he struck people as extraordinary. First there was the comic Dane on board ship who took him for a 'Docteur Teology' because of his black dress, but accepted Coleridge's description of himself as '*un Philosophe*', and was soon exclaiming 'O my Heafen! You are a God!'[9]. Then there was the widowed pastor in Ratzeburg with whom Coleridge settled as a lodger. Like a Rousseau or a young Werther, the twenty-six-year-old poet–philosopher won the hearts of all he met. 'The Gentry and Nobility here [in Ratzeburg] pay me almost an adulatory attention', he reported to Sara on 20 October.[10]

Part of his attraction, he conceded, was the fact of his being English. Not only was English literature in vogue, especially Shakespeare, ballads and the eighteenth-century literature of sentiment, but fear and hatred of France's aggressive policies, and appreciation of Britain's position as a country at war with her, led to a veritable 'madness for the English'. Coleridge noticed that the shops, cafés and hotels often 'write English over their doors' and that commodities ranging from playing cards to sticking plaster proclaimed themselves English as a selling feature. The Germans at Ratzeburg celebrated Nelson's victory in the Battle of the Nile (fought on 1 August) as deliriously as the English themselves:

> At the Concert, when I entered, the Band played 'Britannia! rule the waves' – and at the dinner which was given in honor of Nelson's Victory, 21 guns were fired by order of the military Governour, and between each Firing the Military Band played an English Tune – I never saw such enthusiasm, or heard such tumultuous shouting, as when the Governour gave as a toast, 'The Great Nation'. – By this name they always designate England, in opposition to the same title self-assumed by France.[11]

Meanwhile, Poole was writing to Coleridge to tell him of the celebrations in Somerset in early October, when the coaches arrived covered with laurels and streaming with ribbons, and 'we illuminated at Stowey'. 'The resplendent victory', wrote Poole the democrat but also, like Coleridge, the true patriotic Briton, 'has, I imagine, lit up the world from the north to the southern pole'.[12] Though Poole and Coleridge were still antagonistic towards Pitt's anti-democratic measures at home, their support for France had quite disappeared in the last months. Coleridge noticed that the same was true of democrats and erstwhile French enthusiasts in Germany. Many had been democrats, he told Poole, 'but like me, have *published* Abjurations of the French – among which number are Klopstock, Goethe (the author of the Sorrows of Werter), Wieland, Schiller, & Kotzebu[e]'.[13]

In the few days after their arrival, while they were still in Hamburg, Wordsworth and Coleridge had called on the ageing poet Klopstock, author of a German *Paradise Lost, Der Messias,* which was held in great esteem in Germany. Coleridge reported the meeting, at which, since neither he nor Wordsworth could yet speak German, Wordsworth and Klopstock communicated in French, a language Coleridge, somewhat surprisingly, did not know. Thus Coleridge was reduced to the role of amused spectator, except when he ventured a few sentences in Latin. He and Wordsworth found Klopstock's pretensions absurd, his anger at being considered a mere imitator of Milton embarrassing, and his dress and demeanour pathetic. Coleridge regretted that 'the Father of German Poetry' wore a powdered wig, observing, as was natural in a romantic poet who had given up powder as a political gesture:

> It is an honor to Poets & Great Men that you think of them as parts of Nature; and any thing of Trick & Fashion wounds you in them as much as when you see Yews clipped into miserable peacocks. – The Author of the Messiah should have worn his own Grey Hair. – Powder and the Periwig were to the Eye what *Mr* Milton would be to the Ear.[14]

Wordsworth and Coleridge planned at first to take the long journey to Weimar, where Goethe, Wieland and Herder were, with Schiller in nearby Jena. It would have been a curious and perhaps significant encounter if the four greatest poets of the age, Wordsworth, Coleridge, Goethe and Schiller, had indeed become acquainted. But expense was a worry, and travelling was difficult because of the war, so Coleridge and Chester decided on Ratzeburg instead, while Wordsworth and Dorothy, thinking even Ratzeburg too expensive, went to Goslar in the Hartz Mountains, where provisions and lodgings were cheaper.[15]

The separation so soon after their arrival in Germany is perhaps surprising, but it does not appear to have been the result of any coolness or quarrel. The friends corresponded regularly between Goslar and Ratzeburg, and Coleridge often expressed his longing to be with Wordsworth and Dorothy.

But at home Coleridge's friends were exultant. Lamb, still smarting from the affront he thought he had suffered, wrote gleefully to Southey, who was also semi-estranged from Coleridge and suspicious of Coleridge's adoration of Wordsworth: 'I hear that the Two Noble Englishmen have parted no sooner than they set foot on german Earth, but I have not heard the reason – Possibly to give Moralists an handle to exclaim "Ah! me! what things are perfect?"'[16]

Sara Coleridge, who had been left out of the excited ramblings around Nether Stowey and who, unlike Dorothy, had little interest in the poetic experiments of Wordsworth and Coleridge, while she did, again unlike Dorothy, have two children to look after, was likewise relieved at the separation. Poole, too, congratulated Coleridge. 'The Wordsworths have left you – so there is an end of our fears about amalgamation, etc.', he wrote with characteristic tactlessness.[17] Josiah Wedgwood was also pleased. 'I hope that Wordsworth & he will continue separated', he told Poole in February 1799. 'I am persuaded Coleridge will derive great benefit from living thrown into mixed society.'[18]

Both Poole and Wedgwood welcomed the separation because they wanted Coleridge to become thoroughly Germanized and not keep exclusively in Wordsworth's company, as, given his idolatry of Wordsworth, he might have been tempted to do. Poole's letters to Coleridge were full of advice to 'attend *wholly* to those things which are better attained in Germany than elsewhere'. He even warned his friend to 'beware of being too much with Chester', a companion much less to Coleridge's taste than Wordsworth. 'Speak nothing but German. Live with Germans. Read in German. Think in German', lectured Poole, venturing to criticize the beloved but wayward genius:

> Make a strict arrangement of your time and chain yourself down to it. This may not be advisable for the generality, but I am persuaded it would counteract a *disease* of your mind – which is an active subtilty of imagination ever suggesting reasons to push off whatever excites a moment of languor or *ennui*. This many of your friends falsely call irresolution. No one has more resolution than you; no one sooner sees the side of a question on which the balance of argument turns. But then that same habit of giving free scope to the activity of your imagination, makes it death to you to chain the mind long to any particular object.[19]

To this astute characterization Coleridge replied docilely enough, confessing that the disease of his mind was that it 'wastes itself in the contemplations of the many things which it might do!' He planned to overcome the danger by sticking at his work on Lessing. Referring obliquely to opium, he assured Poole that 'the Journey to Germany has certainly *done me good* – my habits are less irregular; & my *mind* more in my own *power*!'[20]

Nevertheless, he missed the Wordsworths almost as much as he did his family at home. Letters from England were excruciatingly slow in arriving, and Coleridge became frantic with worry about his children's health. He kept himself busy with experimental hexameters, which he sent to Wordsworth. Some lines in this metre – a metre much more common (and successful) in German than in English – express his longing for his friend's companionship while also exploiting the amusing, even ludicrous, aspects of the long, galloping lines. Their reference to his being 'feverish and wakeful' and his remark that 'there was a great deal more, which I have forgotten', suggest recourse to opium:

William, my teacher, my friend! dear William and dear Dorothea!
Smooth out the folds of my letter, and place it on desk or on table;
Place it on table or desk; and your right hands loosely half-closing,
Gently sustain them in air, and extending the digit didactic,
Rest it a moment on each of the forks of the five-forkéd left hand,
Twice on the breadth of the thumb, and once on the tip of each finger;
Read with a nod of the head in a humouring recitativo;
And, as I live, you will see my hexameters hopping before you.
This is a galloping measure; a hop, and a trot, and a gallop!
[. . .]
William, my head and my heart! dear Poet that feelest and thinkest!
Dorothy, eager of soul, my most affectionate sister!
Many a mile, O! many a wearisome mile are ye distant,
Long, long, comfortless roads, with no one eye that doth know us.
[. . .]
William, my head and my heart! dear William and dear Dorothea!
You have all in each other; but I am lonely, and want you![21]

Here is the first expression of that destructive jealousy Coleridge was to feel for the rest of his life of Wordsworth's happiness in his personal relations.

The contrast between the activities of the two poets could not have been more marked, and this, too, was prophetic of the future. While Coleridge played with metrical experiments – his notebooks are full of examples from Greek, Latin and German verse, with notes about what is permissible in English and what not[22] – Wordsworth was occupied in a quite different way. With what Coleridge called his '*unseeking* manners', he avoided company, beavering away in Goslar, with Dorothy by his side, 'not very much at the German',[23] but rather at producing marvellous poetry in English. Homesickness in his case bore fruit in the form of exquisite poems relating to his own childhood in the Lake District.

Coleridge must have been astonished, perhaps even mortified, to receive Wordsworth's letter of mid-December containing 'two or three little Rhyme poems, which I hope will amuse you'. These were the first versions of the 'Lucy' poems, 'She dwelt among the untrodden ways' and 'Strange fits of passion I have known'. In the same letter follow, in Dorothy's hand, the wonderful lines about skating, describing 'William's boyish pleasures' in response to Coleridge's raptures about skating on the lake at Ratzeburg. Also here are the lines about boat-stealing and about nutting in the Lakes, 'whither', Dorothy admitted, 'we wish to decoy you' after the German visit.[24] All these verses, on scenes fetched up from Wordsworth's youth, were in due course incorporated in *The Prelude*. His productivity in this, his most characteristic mode of writing, discovered finally while in a kind of exile in Germany, is breathtaking.

Coleridge had already responded, on 10 December, to the verses known as 'There was a Boy', which Wordsworth had also sent him. Of the lines –

> that uncertain heaven received
> Into the bosom of the steady lake –

he declared rapturously that he would have recognized them anywhere. 'And had I met these lines running wild in the deserts of Arabia, I should have instantly screamed out "Wordsworth!"'[25] Small wonder that Wordsworth addressed *The Prelude* to this friend who so brilliantly appreciated his genius.

Coleridge's feelings about home were strong too. He fretted about not receiving letters, telling Sara about the 'burthen and Sickness of heart, which I experience every post day'.[26] 'The Day-Dream, From an Emigrant to his Absent Wife' may have been written on one of those occasions when he was waiting for post, anxious about his family, a prey to morbid fears, and seeking relief in opium:

> If thou wert here, these Tears were Tears of Light!
> – But from as sweet a Day-dream did I start
> As ever made these Eyes grow idly bright;
> And tho' I weep yet still about the *heart*
> A dear & playful Tenderness doth linger
> Touching my Heart as with a Baby's finger.
> [. . .]
> Across my chest there liv'd a weight so warm
> As if some bird had taken shelter there,
> And lo! upon the Couch a Woman's Form!
> Thine Sara! thine! O Joy, if thine it were!
> I gaz'd with anxious hope, and fear'd to stir it –
> [A deeper] Trance ne'er wrapt a yearning Spirit!
>
> And now when I seem'd *sure* my Love to see,
> Her very Self in her own quiet Home,
> There came an elfish Laugh, and waken'd me!
> 'Twas Hartley, who behind my chair had clomb,
> And with his bright Eyes at my face was peeping –
> I bless'd him – try'd to laugh – and fell a weeping.[27]

As it turned out, Coleridge's anxiety about his children was not ill-founded. On 1 November 1798 Sara wrote him a letter which he received a month later. For the first time, we have both sides of the correspondence between husband and wife. Sara writes:

My dear Samuel
I received your welcome letter from Hamburgh and, since that, two containing the journal (which gave us all a great deal of pleasure) and should have answered the first but I was at that time struggling under the most severe trial that I had ever had to undergo and when you have heard my account of it I am sure you will pity me.

About three weeks after you left Stowey, Mrs R. Poole proposed to inoculate her child and sent round to the inhabitants . . . on Saturday her child was inoculated and ours and several others . . . my dear baby [Berkeley] on the eighth day began to droop, on the ninth he was very ill and on the tenth the pustles began to appear in the skin by hundreds.

He lay upon my lap like a dead child, burning like fire and all over he was as red as scarlet; after I had counted about two hundred I could almost see them coming out and every one that appeared after that, seemed to me a little ugly messenger come to bid me prepare for his death! . . . What I felt is impossible to write – I had no husband to comfort me and share my grief – perhaps the boy would die, and he far away! All the responsibility of the infant's life was upon me, and it was a weight that dragged me to the earth! He was blind – his nose was clogged that he could not suck and his dear gums and tongue were covered and he was so hoarse that he could not cry; but he made a *horrid noise in his throat* which when I dozed for a minute I always heard in my dreams . . . In the midst of all this, to fill my bitter cup the fuller, I was seized with a pain in my eye; it in a few hours became quite closed – my face and neck swollen, my head swimming; in short, I had caught a most violent cold in sitting up at night and sometimes lying on the ground in the smokey parlour . . .

You will easily believe, my dear Samuel, that I have been at great expences during this trying time: two nurses, one for the night and the other for the day . . . [28]

If this seems a long litany of woe, showing little imagination about what the recipient would feel on reading it, especially since – though Sara could not know this – it was the first letter Coleridge received in the two months he had been in Germany, there is no doubt that Sara had reason enough to be miserable. As she said in her next letter, on 13 December, 'It seems cruel to vex you, after so many inquietudes, but I must either write to you my griefs, or not write at all for alas! my Samuel,

> There's nae gude luck about the house
> Sen my gude Mon's awa'.'[29]

In his reply Coleridge attempted self-restraint. He did not chide Sara for her complaining, yet he fell short of entering fully into her agony about Berkeley. He dwelt on his own sorrow at hearing about Berkeley's danger, and went on to match Sara's swollen eye with one of his own:

God, the Infinite, be praised that my Babes are alive. His mercy will forgive me that late and all too slowly I raised up my heart in thanksgiving. – At first and for a time, I wept as passionately as if they had been dead . . . I had long expected, I had passionately expected, a letter; I received it, and my frame trembled – I saw your hand, and all feelings of mind and body crowded together – had the news been chearful & only, 'We are as you left us' – I must have wept, to have delivered myself of the stress and tumult of my animal sensibility – But when I read the danger and the agony – My dear Sara! – my love! my wife! – God bless you & preserve us – I am well; but a stye, or something of that kind, has come upon & enormously swelled my eye-lids, so that it is painful and improper for me to read or write! . . .

1 Church of Ottery St Mary. (By permission of Tom Mayberry)

2 George Coleridge, by J. Keenan.
(By permission of Lord Coleridge)

3 Christ's Hospital from the Cloisters. (Copyright British Museum)

THE

PLOT DISCOVERED;

OR

An ADDRESS

TO THE

PEOPLE,

AGAINST

MINISTERIAL TREASON.

~~~~~~~~~~

By S. T. COLERIDGE.

~~~~~~~~~~

BRISTOL, 1795.

Odi profanum vulgus, et arceo —
Favete linguis &: *Hor:*

I hate the Mob — avaunt the Vulgar —

4 Title-page of Coleridge, *The Plot Discovered*, 1795.
(By permission of The British Library)

5 Sara Coleridge, 1809, by Matilda Betham. (Hulton Deutsch Collection Ltd, by kind permission of Mrs A. H. B. Coleridge)

6 St Mary Redcliffe, Bristol. (Somerset Archaeological and Natural History Society)

7 Coleridge, 1796, by Robert Hancock. (National Portrait Gallery)

8 Crewe Manuscript of 'Kubla Khan'.
(By permission of The British Library)

In a vision once I saw:
It was an Abyssinian Maid,
And on her Dulcimer she play'd
Singing of Mount Amara.
Could I revive within me
Her Symphony & Song,
To such a deep Delight 'twould win me,
That with Music loud and long
I would build that Dome in Air,
That sunny Dome! those Caves of Ice!
And all, who heard, should see them there,
And all should cry, Beware! Beware!
His flashing Eyes! his floating Hair!
Weave a circle round him thrice,
And close your Eyes in holy Dread
For He on Honey-dew hath fed
And drank the Milk of Paradise.——

This fragment with a good deal more, not
recoverable, composed, in a sort of Reverie brought
on by two grains of Opium, taken to check a
dysentery, at a Farm House between Porlock &
Linton, a quarter of a mile from Culbone Church,
in the fall of the year, 1797.

S. T. Coleridge

9 *Two Men Contemplating the Moon*, 1819, by Caspar David Friedrich. (Gemäldegalerie Neue Meister, Dresden)

10 *Rydal Waterfall*, 1795, by Joseph Wright of Derby. (Derby Museums and Art Gallery)

I received your letter Friday, November [30th]. – I cannot well account for
the slowness – O my babies! – absence makes it painful to be a Father! –
My Wife, believe and know that I pant to be home & with you.[30]

Much, much worse was to follow. Poole instructed Sara to spare
Coleridge the details of Berkeley's illness. He himself wrote cheerfully on
22 November about the baby having been 'well peppered with the small-
pox, but never in any danger'. Yet vaccination for smallpox was an extremely recent innovation, Edward Jenner having first inoculated a patient
with the cowpox virus in 1796, and it was therefore, as Sara showed in her
first letter to Coleridge, a matter of doubt and difficulty to decide whether
to vaccinate or not. Poole hurries off the subject, eager to continue his
exhortation of Coleridge: 'Your progress in the German language amazes
us. Proceed, proceed. Make yourself, I charge you, completely master of it.'
He reminds his friend that Daniel Stuart of the *Morning Post* is expecting a
promised contribution on German literature for his paper: 'Why have you
not sent it?'[31]

But Sara could not help dwelling on her worries. On 13 December she
told Coleridge that she was aware how much her account of Berkeley's
sufferings would hurt him, but promised that 'the instant that I have a
glimpse of comfort I will sit down to impart it to you, and make you a
partaker of my pleasures as well as my sorrows'. She was thoughtful enough
to mention a letter from Edith reporting that Southey had bought 'a very
beautiful poem of yours in London, "Fears in Solitude"', though it is
noticeable that she sounds as if she herself is not acquainted with her
husband's poem.[32]

In subsequent letters to Sara and Poole, Coleridge expressed his anxiety
about Berkeley, to be answered cheerily by Poole on 24 January 1799
that the baby had improved. Poole fibbed grandly: 'When Berkeley had
the small-pox, and gave his mother trouble, I assure you she and all of us
rejoiced you were not at home.' 'Let, my dear Col., nothing trouble you.'[33]
Thus while Sara poured out her worries and craved her husband's
sympathy and support in this crisis, Poole downplayed her troubles and
bade Coleridge dismiss them from his mind. The plain truth is that
Coleridge could enter only too fervently into these anxieties, but less with
reference to his wife than with reference to himself. Thus he simul-
taneously, and disastrously, fell short of fellow feeling and was prostrated by
excess of it.

On 11 February Sara wrote, not to Coleridge, as she had been instructed
to spare him, but to Poole himself with the news of Berkeley's death the
previous day of convulsions. She and Hartley now moved in with Southey
and Edith, and Southey took charge of the funeral arrangements. Even in
the midst of her own grief she could imagine what Coleridge's would be
when he heard, and she assured Poole that in her letters to him she would
'pass over all disagreeable subjects with the greatest care, for I well know
their violent effect on him'. Yet she longed to have his consolation too.[34]

Poor Sara, to have a husband absent and so sensitive that he must not be allowed to share her grief over the loss of their child. As Lamb was later to say, Coleridge 'ought not to have a wife or children; he should have a sort of diocesan care of the world, no parish duty'.[35]

Letters were taking about a month to arrive at their destination, as northern Europe, as well as being affected by war, was in this last year of the century in the grip of the coldest winter of that century. Ice on the Elbe held up ships. Coleridge wrote to Sara on 10 March, describing his coach journey from Ratzeburg to Göttingen, where he was now enrolled as a student at the University. Part of the journey took place on the night of Thursday 7 February, the very coldest for a hundred years. Unaware of the calamity at Nether Stowey, he talked of picturing Sara and 'the little ones' and of how he 'languished after home'.[36]

Meanwhile Poole at first insisted that Coleridge should not be told. For all that he had assured Coleridge when urging him to accept the Wedgwood annuity the previous year that he would be under no obligation or bond, it is clear that he and Josiah Wedgwood put their plans for Coleridge's education before a consideration of his and his wife's feelings. Poole told Wedgwood:

> I have advised [Sara] not to inform Coleridge of [Berkeley's] death. For he indulges in such tumultuous feelings upon every possible occasion where his wife and children are concerned, and his untired imagination is so active in conjuring up every possible scene of distress which could have occurred to them, that I am persuaded the knowledge of this event would either hurry him home, or at least prevent for a long time his exerting himself to any advantage.[37]

Poole then decided that Coleridge would have to be told the bad news after all, and he was determined to be the one to do it. On 15 March he wrote, talking blunderingly of infants not being endowed with reason and declaring that 'sensible men' should not mourn their passing too much. Sara, he assured Coleridge, though feeling 'as a mother', '*never forgot herself*. . . She is now perfectly well, and does not make herself miserable by recalling the engaging, though, remember, mere instinctive attractions of an infant a few months old. Heaven and Earth! I have myself within the last month experienced disappointments more weighty than the death of ten infants.' And the bachelor Poole goes on to record matters of local business.[38]

Sara herself wrote a letter postmarked 25 March, giving details of Berkeley's illness and death, and telling Coleridge that 'it is a suffering beyond your conception! You will feel, and lament the death of your child, but you will only recollect him a baby of 14 weeks'. She, his mother, had fed and loved him and watched over him day and night for nine months. 'I have seen him twice on the brink of the grave but he has returned, and recovered and smiled upon me like an angel – and now I am lamenting that he is gone!' She longs for Coleridge's return, and will be disappointed if he does not come home by May. Hartley 'talks of his Father every day' and wants him to come home. 'O God! I hope you never more will quit it!'

Grief-stricken as she is, she tries to find cheerful news to tell Coleridge, or at least news that will interest him. She talks of Lloyd and Southey and their writing, and, less sensitively, of how *Lyrical Ballads* 'are not esteemed' much in Bristol. Inevitably she circles back to her own unenviable position, complaining, 'I am very sore on the subject of absent husbands just at this time'. Poor Sara also explains how her hair 'during my long confinement was utterly spoiled. I have had it all cut off close to my head, and I believe I must get some false hair untill my own is grown, only I am affriad [sic] you will not like it.'[39] When Sara destroyed most of her correspondence with Coleridge after his death, she spared this letter, noting in the margin, 'No secrets herein. I will not burn it for the sake of my sweet Berkeley.'

Sara hoped, but did not expect, that Coleridge would pack up and come home immediately. Urged by Poole, she accepted that he must be allowed some time to complete a course of study at Göttingen and so bring home the learning he had gone to Germany to get. In a joint letter with Poole on 8–15 May, she follows meekly, but not without protest. Her part of the letter begins: 'My dearest Love, I cannot speak of your delay with the same degree of coolness as our friend does. I experienced a most bitter disappointment. I am however fully satisfied with your reasons.' Once she starts lamenting, however, she cannot help going on. When he comes back, she writes, they must leave 'this horrible place'. 'The house is so hateful to me' now, 'for oh! I am so tired of this cruel absence – my dear, dear Samuel, do not lose a moment of time in finishing your book – for I feel like a poor deserted thing'.[40]

Such pleading, utterly natural in the circumstances in which Sara found herself, was enough to make Coleridge delay, rather than hasten, his homecoming.

He did not, in fact, return until late July. His response to trouble was once more to seek to avoid it, or at least put off facing it. The reply he sent on 8 April to Sara's letter breaking the news of the baby's death, though loving in its way, fails to console. He discourses about God's purpose in the death of babies, declares himself discontented with Priestley's doctrine, which 'denies the future existence of Infants', and affirms his lasting belief in God's goodness. He even calls up a remnant of the philosophical optimism of a few years before, hoping that Berkeley's death may 'in many and various ways be good for us'. We get a glimpse of some past problems between them: 'When in Moments of fretfulness and Imbecillity I am disposed to anger or reproach, it will, I trust, be always a restoring thought – "We have wept over the same little one – & with whom am I angry? – with her who so patiently and unweariedly sustained my poor and sickly Infant through his long Pains."' He hopes to be home in '10 or 11 weeks' and is hopeful that he will 'repay myself by the work which I am writing, to such an amount, that I shall have spent out of my income only 50 pounds at the end of August'.[41]

The work was, of course, the life of Lessing, on which, as his copious notes show, he was working hard. He relished the similarities between Lessing's career and his own: 'He was intended for a Clergyman by his Parents – but a Lessing will seldom be what his Parents intend him to be.'[42] He had noticed a portrait of Lessing in the house in Hamburg of Klopstock's brother, commenting that 'his eyes were uncommonly like mine – if any thing, rather larger & more prominent'.[43]

His plan was now to interweave the life of this man of learning, literature and liberal theology with a larger project, no less than a history of German literature from its beginnings to the present day.[44] He told Sara on 23 April that he was reading and transcribing 'from 8 to 10 hours every day'. Irritated by her calls for him to return home as soon as possible, he insisted on the importance of this work: 'So large a work with so great a variety of information from sources so scattered, & so little known even in Germany, will, of course, establish my character for industry & erudition, certainly; & I would fain hope, for reflection & genius.'[45]

On his return to England he was to find that the recent vogue for German literature, its ballads, its Gothic novels and its sentimental plays, had been rudely curtailed by the successful *Anti-Jacobin* attacks and by the general perception that German literature was 'Jacobin'. Canning and Frere, as well as parodying Coleridge's and especially Southey's democratic verses, had written a spoof play, 'The Rovers; or, the Double Arrangement', set, as it happens, in the University of Göttingen and ridiculing Goethe's drama of sentiment, *Stella*.[46] But Coleridge could not know that there would be this reduced interest in German literature.

A mixture of motives kept him in Germany. He did want to collect more materials; he did intend to write his works on Lessing and German literature. He was also aware that he had spent all his Wedgwood allowance, so that 'if I return now, we shall be embarrassed & in debt', as he told Sara on 23 April.[47] Moreover, he feared returning to a grieving and possibly resentful Sara, as well as to Poole and the Wedgwoods, who would be eager to know what he had achieved in the way of scholarship and publishable writings. He had failed to send essays to Daniel Stuart for the *Morning Post*.

Nursing his guilty conscience he told Sara irritatedly that 'had I followed my impulses, I should have packed up & gone with Wordsworth & his Sister', who had recently passed through Göttingen on their way home. They were still unconversant with German, but were happy in one another's company and carried luggage augmented by many pages of English poetry on which Wordsworth would continue to work on his return and which would gradually grow into *The Prelude*. Coleridge would have had to return empty-handed, and he simply avoided doing so.

It was nearly three more months before he did return, with no more to show for his ten months in Germany than a mass of unsorted notes and a bad conscience. Years later, in an anguished letter of 1814 to his friend John Morgan who had taken him into his home to try and cure his opium addiction, Coleridge wrote astutely of his terrible incapacity to do what he saw clearly enough to be the right thing. He was referring to the 'complete derangement' of his volition caused by 'the accursed Poison' opium. Though in 1799 he was not yet fully aware of the horrors of addiction, his behaviour already conformed to the pattern he described with such painful clarity in 1814: 'The worst was, that in *exact proportion* to the *importance* and *urgency* of any Duty was it, as of a fatal necessity, sure to be neglected . . . In exact proportion, as I *loved* any person or persons more than others, & would have sacrificed my Life for them, were *they* sure to be the most barbarously mistreated by silence, absence, or breach of promise.'[48]

Undoubtedly Coleridge read widely in Germany, making himself even more learned and attending the natural history lectures of the famous Professor J. F. Blumenbach and the divinity lectures of J. G. Eichhorn. The latter was sceptical of the truth of scripture, reading the Bible as fiction where its accounts did not accord with reason. He was an important member of the influential German school of Biblical criticism which, in the spirit of Kant's critical philosophy, 'assumed a disbelief of any religious point, and then considered the grounds of such disbelief', in the words of Clement Carlyon, a fellow student of Coleridge's at Göttingen.[49] Another Englishman in Göttingen, one Parry, wrote home telling his family that Christianity was 'at a very low ebb' there. Eichhorn, though a good man, seemed bent on 'destroying the evidences on which we ground our belief'. Against him Coleridge was 'an able vindicator of those important truths'. 'His fervour is particularly agreeable when contrasted with the chilling speculations of the German Philosophers.'[50] Many years later Coleridge would fill his notebooks with theological analysis and speculation, in which he often alluded to Eichhorn, frequently disagreeing with him but always respecting his intelligence and humanity.

Both Carlyon and Parry remarked that Coleridge was much liked despite his 'many peculiarities'. He was a particular favourite of the Blumenbach family, who were 'astonished' and 'delighted' by his conversation. He 'dashed on', said Carlyon, 'with fluent diction, but with the very worst German accent imaginable, through the thick and thin of his subject'.[51]

On 6 May Coleridge wrote despondently (and guiltily) to Poole, confessing that he laid the blame for Berkeley's death on his absence from home – '*not intellectually*; but I have a strange sort of sensation, as if while I was present, none could die whom I intensely loved'. 'My dear Poole!', he added, 'don't let little Hartley die before I come home'. He mentioned that when the Wordsworths had visited Göttingen on their way to England, they had declared their wish to have him move to the Lake District, where they had decided to settle. An experienced Coleridge-watcher can see Coleridge putting this proposal to Poole, who would of course be the chief loser if it were acted on, and observe that his very protestations about not wishing to go are a kind of evidence of the strength of the magnetic attraction Wordsworth exercised on him:

> I told him, that independent of the expence of removing, & the impropriety of taking Mrs Coleridge to a place where she would have no acquaintance, two insurmountable objections, the Library [of Sir Frederick Vane, to be put at Wordsworth's disposal] was no inducement, for I wanted old books chiefly, such as could be procured any where better than in a Gentleman's new fashionable Collection/– Finally, I told him plainly, that *you* had been the man in whom *first* and in whom alone, I had felt an *anchor*.[52]

The insurmountable objections would in due course be surmounted.

Coleridge appended a note for Sara to this rather anguished and disingenuous letter. Astonishingly, it said that on the following Saturday he was going on a walking tour to 'the famous Hartz Mountains – about 20 english miles' from Göttingen, 'to see the mines & other curiosities'.[53] He accordingly set off on 11 May with the two Parry brothers, Charles and Frederick, Carlyon, Chester, Charles Bellas Greenough (later President of the Royal Geological Society), and a son of Professor Blumenbach. He sent his travel journal to Sara, no doubt hoping to publish it on his return. The landscape is described in minute detail, but Coleridge confesses that he is 'not a good Hand at description. – I see what I write/ but alas! I cannot write what I see.'[54]

The main aim of the tour was to climb the Brocken, the highest mountain in the region and the 'seat of innumerable Superstitions . . . On the first day of May all the Witches dance here at midnight/ & those who go may see their own Ghosts walking up & down with a little Billet on the Back, giving the Names of those who wished them there: for "I wish you on Top of the Brocken" is a common Curse throughout the whole Empire.' Goethe famously set his witches' scene in *Faust*, the 'Walpurgisnacht', on the Brocken. Coleridge and his companions, climbing it on Whit Sunday, 12 May, missed seeing the famous natural–supernatural phenomenon known as the Brocken Spectre. Carlyon recorded that they went at the wrong time of day to experience this trick of the light by which, around dawn, travellers often saw a huge shadow of themselves.[55]

Coleridge wrote some verses for the album (Stammbuch) held at the inn at Elbingerode, where the travellers were staying. He told Sara they possessed not a grain of merit 'as Poetry'. They do indeed have a rather tired and dutiful ring, reviving only when he ceases to describe the Brocken and imagines being in England:

> I stood on Brocken's sovran height & saw
> Woods crowding upon woods, hills over hills,
> A *surging* Scene and only limited

By the blue Distance.
[. . .]
O 'dear dear' England, how my longing Eye
Turn'd Westward, shaping in the steady Clouds
Thy sands & high white Cliffs! Sweet Native Isle,
This Heart was proud, yea, mine Eyes swam with Tears
To think of Thee; & all the goodly view
From sov'ran Brocken, woods and woody Hills,
Floated away, like a departing Dream,
Feeble and dim.[56]

And yet Coleridge enjoyed his adventure, happy to be at the centre of attention. Carlyon, not one of Coleridge's natural admirers, remembered his 'vehemence of manner and wonderful flow of words and ideas', which seemed comically at odds with his shabby dress. In spite of his indifference to clothes, he struck Carlyon as vain, 'fixing his prominent eyes upon himself (as he was wont to do, whenever there was a mirror in the room), with a singularly coxcombical expression of countenance'. He kept up a running conversation, or monologue, on Burke and the sublime, on Eichhorn, on Pitt and Fox, still attacking the former and defending the latter, and he recited passages from 'Fears in Solitude' and from the unfinished 'Christabel'. He appears not to have told his companions about the death of his child. On the contrary, he was playful, comical and 'in good spirits'.[57] He behaved, in short, like any bachelor student released from the lecture room and without responsibilities.

Back in Göttingen on 21 May, he wrote to Josiah Wedgwood claiming to have had 'six huge *Letters*' lying by his side addressed to Wedgwood 'for these three months', waiting for a Mr Hamilton to take them to England. He now gives the account he feels is required of his achievements since leaving home:

What have I done in Germany? – I have learnt the language, both high & low German/ I can read both, & speak the former so fluently, that it must be a *torture* for a German to be in my company – that is, I have words enough & phrases enough, & I arrange them tolerably; but my pronunciation is hideous . . . I have attended the lectures on Physiology, Anatomy, & Natural History with regularity, & have endeavoured to understand these subjects . . . I have read & made collections for an history of the Belles Lettres in Germany before the time of Lessing . . . I shall have bought 30 pounds worth of books (chiefly metaphysics/ & with a view to the one work, to which I hope to dedicate in silence the prime of my life) – but I believe & indeed doubt not, that before Christmas I shall have repayed myself; but before that time I shall have been under the necessity of requesting your permission, that I may during the year *anticipate* for 40 or fifty pound.[58]

It is striking that Coleridge no longer seems to think of himself as a poet. Even giving due allowance to the fact that he is here writing to Wedgwood, who has invested in him in the hope that he will benefit mankind by work of an educative, moral, religious or philosophical kind, it is true that in Germany he managed only a few poetic translations, experiments with metre and occasional lines such as those written in the Elbingerode album.

When Wordsworth arrived in England in May 1799 he immediately set about inquiring of Cottle and others how many copies of *Lyrical Ballads* had been sold, and what the critical response had been. He soon learned that sales had been slow and reviews disappointing. Worse, he formed the impression – only half justified by the actual criticisms of the collection – that 'The Ancyent Mariner has upon the whole been an injury to the volume, I mean that the old words and the strangeness of it have deterred readers from going on'. With that firm self-interestedness which caused Coleridge's friends to regret the latter's emotional dependence on him, Wordsworth told Cottle on 24 June that 'if the volume should come to a second Edition I [note the pronoun] would put in its place some little things which would be more likely to suit the common taste'.[59]

In fact the reviews were mixed. None was wholly admiring, but the harshest criticism was divided between 'The Ancient Mariner' and Wordsworth's more daring ballads, particularly 'The Thorn' and 'The Idiot Boy'. Charles Burney in the *Monthly Review* (June 1799) confessed that he could not regard the poems 'as *poetry*'; in common with other reviewers, he talked vaguely about the 'genius' of the author. All the reviewers assumed, as they were intended to, that the poems were the work of one hand; one, the reviewer in the *British Critic*, named the author as 'Mr Coleridge'. The writer of the article in the *Critical Review* (October 1798) was scornful of 'The Idiot Boy' for the 'worthlessness of its design', and lamented that the author should have 'condescended to write such pieces' as 'The Last of the Flock' and most of the ballads.[60]

The author of this harsh review, who also had unkind things to say of 'The Ancient Mariner', was none other than Southey. In a letter to his friend Wynn he spoke slightingly of the volume, though much less aggressively than in his review. 'The Ancient Mariner' was 'nonsense', 'The Nightingale' 'tolerable', 'Tintern Abbey' the best poem in the volume, and 'The Idiot Boy' 'sadly dilated'.[61] Wordsworth was furious at Southey's denigration of his poems in the *Critical Review* article. Resorting naturally to the single personal pronoun, he exploded to Cottle:

> Southey's review I have seen. He knew that I published those poems for money and money alone. He knew that money was of importance to me. If he could not conscientiously have spoken differently of the volume, he ought to have declined the task of reviewing it.
> The bulk of the poems he has described as destitute of merit. Am I recompensed for this by vague praises of my talents?[62]

If Wordsworth felt thus let down by Southey, how much more distressed would Coleridge feel when he read Southey's denunciation of 'The Ancient Mariner' as 'a Dutch attempt at German sublimity', with many stanzas which are 'laboriously beautiful' but 'absurd or unintelligible'? As with Wordsworth, Southey offers a sop to Coleridge's pride by announcing that 'genius has here been employed in producing a poem of little merit'.[63] Perhaps Coleridge was partly prepared for Southey's hostile reaction by Sara's tactless remark in her letter about the poor reception of *Lyrical Ballads* in Bristol. Since she was living with Southey at that time, just after the death of Berkeley, she no doubt formed this view in conversation with her brother-in-law. To Poole she also declared in March 1799, with that curious lack of warmth that characterized her attitude to Coleridge's writings, 'the Lyrical Ballads are laughed at and disliked by all with very few excepted'.[64]

Still, it was unfortunate that Southey and other reviewers fixed on 'The Ancient Mariner' as an example of a 'German' or 'unintelligible' poem. The writer in the *Analytical Review* thought it had 'more of the extravagance of a mad german poet, than of the simplicity of our ancient ballad writers', and Burney in the *Monthly Review* called it 'the strangest story of a cock and a bull that we ever saw on paper'.[65] Oddly enough, a favourable comment came – but alas, not publicly – from Francis Jeffrey, who as editor of the prestigious *Edinburgh Review* from 1802 would be the chief scourge of Coleridge, Wordsworth and Southey, and whom Coleridge later held mainly responsible for his disrepute as a writer. Jeffrey wrote in a letter of March 1799 that he had been 'enchanted with a little volume of poems, lately published, called "Lyrical Ballads" . . . In the 'Rime of the Ancient Mariner', with which it begins, there is more true poetical horror and more new images than in all the German ballads and tragedies, that have been holding our hair on end for these last three years. I take this to be some of Coleridge's doings, though I am no infallible discoverer of styles.'[66]

This is a most suggestive description of the poem as a piece of superior Gothic with claims to originality in its imagery; but Coleridge had to wait until 'The Ancient Mariner' was republished in *Sibylline Leaves* in 1817 for an intelligent *public* response. It was his misfortune to publish the poem first just when the vogue for 'Schauerromantik' – horror stories, often originally in German – was waning and its more ludicrous exponents and imitators were being ridiculed in the periodicals, led by the *Anti-Jacobin*. Coleridge's feelings about the reception of his poem are unknown; we can imagine that he was hurt, but probably more by Southey's harshness and Wordsworth's refusal to defend the poem than by the anonymous reviewers in the journals.

A robust defence *was* forthcoming, but as with Jeffrey's remark Coleridge was fated not to know of it. Lamb, still estranged from his old friend, chided Southey in a letter of 8 November 1798. What a pity he did not go into print with his opinion, surely one of the most astute of all the responses during Coleridge's lifetime:

> I am sorry you are so sparing of praise to the 'Ancient Marinere'; – so far from calling it, as you do, with some wit, but more severity, 'A Dutch Attempt', &c.,

I call it a right English attempt, and a successful one, to dethrone German sublimity. You have selected a passage fertile in unmeaning miracles, but have passed by fifty passages as miraculous as the miracles they celebrate. I never so deeply felt the pathetic as in that part,

> A spring of love gush'd from my heart,
> And I bless'd them unaware –

It stung me into high pleasure through sufferings . . . But you allow some elaborate beauties – you should have extracted 'em. 'The Ancient Marinere' plays more tricks with the mind than that last poem, which is yet one of the finest written [i.e. 'Tintern Abbey'].[67]

That Southey should have been so unsympathetic towards 'The Ancient Mariner' is the more unfortunate because he himself wrote a sea-faring ballad at the very time he was reviewing *Lyrical Ballads*, and his ballad shows unmistakable signs of direct influence from 'The Ancient Mariner'. His short ballad entitled 'The Sailor who had served in the Slave Trade' was sent in a letter of October 1798 to his brother Tom, telling him that about six weeks before 'a friend of Cottle's found a sailor thus praying in a cowhouse & held a conversation with him of which the exact substance is in the ballad'. It is the confession to a stranger of a sailor who on a voyage in a slave vessel had, on the orders of the captain, flogged a female slave until she died and was thrown overboard. Apart from the similarity of the setting and the confession to a stranger, taken from a real episode by Southey, there are some verbal and rhythmical echoes of Coleridge's poem. Compare the following pairs of examples from the two poems, first Coleridge's then Southey's:

> And I had done an hellish thing
> And it would work 'em woe

and

> Oh I have done a wicked thing
> It haunts me night & day.

Again:

> O let me be awake, my God!
> Or let me sleep alway!

and

> But when O Christ – O blessed God –
> Shall I have rest again.[68]

The imitation is a pale one. There is no mystery about the source of guilt, and no extraordinary imagery, no sense of a universe turned upside down, as in the greater poem. But it is an imitation none the less by a man who publicly dismissed his model in a few carelessly unkind words.

Coleridge appears not to have upbraided Southey for his criticism. On the contrary, one of the first things he did on arriving home from Germany towards the end of July 1799 was to write to Southey offering to bury the hatchet. No doubt Sara had urged him to do so out of gratitude for Southey's support after Berkeley's death. Coleridge and his wife were not happy. He felt guilty about having stayed away so long – and in truth he had not hurried back, even after his jaunt to the Brocken – and so probably took a high moral tone with her. Sara was probably petulant and complaining. She may have begun to hold Southey up as a model husband, as she was certainly to do later. This was the pattern of their relationship for the future.

Domestic discord is more than hinted at even in his approach to Southey: 'If *you* knew, that domestic affliction was hard upon me, and that my own health was declining, would you not have shootings within you of an affection, which ('tho' fall'n, tho' chang'd') has played too important a part in the events of our lives & the formation of our characters, ever to be *forgotten?*'[69] Southey was not immediately mollified; it took a further letter from Coleridge, proof that Lloyd had been making trouble, and an endorsement from Poole of Coleridge's assurance that he had never spoken hostilely about Southey in Poole's presence, before Southey agreed to a full reconciliation.[70]

Thereupon, Southey and Edith visited Stowey for a fortnight, after which both families set out for Devon on a visit to Coleridge's relations, where Sara was at last introduced to her in-laws. As might be expected, those two 'upright-downright' men, Southey and George Coleridge, took to one another at once. Southey liked George's 'equalness and kindness of character' and held interesting conversations with him 'upon the tendency of Christianity'. Of Edward Coleridge, the least clever of the brothers, he reported that he 'seldom talks much to the purpose'; and of Coleridge's mother he gives a brief but telling glimpse: 'We were all a good deal amused by the old lady. She could not hear what was going on, but, seeing Samuel arguing with his brothers, took it for granted that he must have been wrong, and cried out, "Ah, if your poor father had been alive, he'd soon have convinced you!"'[71]

Coleridge himself was naturally less amused and delighted by the visit. When writing to Poole, he does not mention his mother, and is lukewarm about his brothers: 'I have three Brothers/ that is to say, Relations by Gore – two are Parsons and one is a Colonel – George & the Colonel good men as times go – very good men; but alas! we have neither Tastes nor Feelings in common. This I wisely learnt from their Conversation; & I did not suffer them to learn it from *mine.*' Thus Coleridge, ever the youngest brother at odds with his elders. He still, despite having tempered his radicalism, found the Ottery circle 'Bigots, unalphabeted in the first Feelings of Liberality'.[72]

Southey and Coleridge were, as the former reported to Charles Danvers, once more sitting 'at the same table'. Something of the old Coleridgean magic was at work again, for the brothers-in-law now planned a joint epic poem on Mahomet (never finished), collaborated on a satirical poem, 'The Devil's Thoughts', and were soon contemplating going abroad together. Southey confessed to Danvers that 'in one point of view Coleridge and I are bad companions for each other. Without being talkative I am conversational, and the hours slip away, and the ink dries upon the pen in my hand.'[73] Coleridge's company was unsettling for the self-disciplined Southey, but winning enough to make him crave more of it.

'The Devil's Thoughts', published by Daniel Stuart in the *Morning Post* on 6 September, is a comic ballad satirizing the current state of England. It recaptures something of the radical daring of its two authors when they were last together in Bristol, lecturing on politics in 1795. The devil walks out one day, pleased to observe his disciples about their daily business: a lawyer, an apothecary, a rich bookseller, a turnkey and a minister in Parliament. The poem caused the number of the *Morning Post* containing it to be sold out and reprinted, and it spawned many imitations, including Shelley's 'The Devil's Walk (1812) and Byron's 'The Devil's Drive' (1813).[74] Southey himself later reprinted the poem, now confusingly called 'The Devil's Walk', with an Advertisement describing the casual origin of the poem. It had been composed 'one morning before breakfast', the idea having struck Southey while he was shaving. Coleridge was shown the lines, to which he immediately added some of his own.[75]

The poem has some striking images, including an allusion to Satan in *Paradise Lost*:

> He went into a rich bookseller' shop,
> Quoth he! we are both of one college!
> For I sate myself, like a cormorant once
> Upon the tree of knowledge.

Pitt's continuing war and his raising of taxes to pay for it are attacked, as is also the slowness of Parliament to abolish the slave trade (an achievement not managed for another eight years):

> Old Nicholas grinn'd and swish'd his tail
> For joy and admiration;
> And he thought of his daughter, Victory,
> And his darling babe, Taxation.
>
> He saw a Turnkey in a trice
> Hand-cuff a troublesome blade,
> 'Nimbly', quoth he, 'the fingers move
> If a man is but us'd to his trade.'

> He saw the same Turnkey unfettering a man,
> With but little expedition,
> And he laugh'd for he thought of the long debates
> On the Slave-trade abolition.[76]

'Mahomet', or 'Mohammed', was to be 'a great hexameter work', Southey being fond of the metre, for which he was briskly parodied in the *Anti-Jacobin*, and Coleridge having experimented with it in Germany.[77] The latter recast Psalm 46 in hexameters, sending his version in a letter to George:

> God is our strength and our Refuge: therefore will we not tremble,
> Tho' the Earth be removed; and tho' the perpetual Mountains
> Sink in the Swell of the Ocean! God is our Strength & our Refuge.[78]

He also translated F. L. Stolberg's *Hymne an die Erde* (*Hymn to the Earth*) in the same metre, which he acknowledged to be a difficult one to sustain in English.[79]

Coleridge managed only fourteen lines of 'Mahomet'. These lines suggest the epic scope of the subject and also hold the clue to the impossibility of producing – even with the help of the more prolific Southey, who composed 109 lines – a whole long poem in this relentless metre. Southey told his friend William Taylor, one of the many translators of Bürger's *Lenore*, that he and Coleridge meant 'to march an army of hexameters into the country'.[80] The metaphor is apt. Coleridge's lines thunder mercilessly and unvaryingly:

> Utter the song, O my soul! the flight and return of Mohammed,
> Prophet and priest, who scatter'd abroad both evil and blessing,
> Huge wasteful empires founded and hallow'd slow persecution,
> Soul-withering, but crush'd the blasphemous rites of the Pagan
> And idolatrous Christians. – For veiling the Gospel of Jesus,
> They, the best corrupting, had made it worse than the vilest.
> Wherefore Heaven decreed th'enthusiastic warrior of Mecca,
> Choosing good from iniquity rather than evil from goodness.[81]

From this it is abundantly clear that the poets had chosen a protagonist who shared characteristics with their Robespierre and Coleridge's Osorio, and perhaps also Kubla Khan: flawed greatness, perverted goodness, misuse of power. It is also a mercy that they did not finish the work.

While toying thus with hexameters on Mohammed, the two friends were also experiencing what Southey described as 'the atmosphere of Mohammed's Paradise'. They were active participants in experiments taking place at Beddoes's Pneumatic Institution, which had finally been opened in Clifton in 1799. Southey had written to Wynn in March that the young man who managed it 'possesses the most miraculous talents I ever met with or heard of, and will I think do more for medicine than any person who has ever gone before him'.[82]

This prodigy was the twenty-year-old Humphry Davy, whom Beddoes had engaged in October 1798 to help him in the use of gases in curing a variety of ailments presented by his patients. Davy was a brilliant scientist, and an intrepid, not to say reckless, experimenter, who always tried out his new combinations of gases on himself. He nearly killed himself in an experiment with carbon monoxide. Cottle recalled him acting as if he had several lives and could afford to lose one or two: 'He has been known sometimes to breathe a deadly gas, with his finger on his pulse, to determine how much could be borne, before a serious declension occurred in the vital action.'[83]

In April 1799 Davy succeeded in discovering what Southey called 'the wonder-working gaseous oxyd of azote', otherwise known as nitrous oxide or, more familiarly, laughing gas. Southey, the Wedgwoods, George Burnett, and of course Coleridge queued up to join the experiments with this pleasurable gas, all in the name of medical science – for indeed the gas had a use as an anaesthetic – and at the same time for the novelty and thrill of it. Southey reported to William Taylor that the gas produced in him 'an involuntary and idiotic laughter, highly pleasurable and ridiculous'. Hence his summoning up of the notion of 'Mohammed's Paradise' in connection with it.[84]

Coleridge, already a great tinkerer with medicines and an inveterate observer of his own physiological and psychological states, reported his experience of taking nitrous oxide for Davy's official record of the experiments, *Researches, Chemical and Philosophical; chiefly concerning Nitrous Oxide*, published by Joseph Johnson in 1800. He did so in a suitably scientific and restrained manner:

> The first time I inspired the nitrous oxide, I felt an highly pleasurable sensation of warmth over my whole frame, resembling that which I remember once to have experienced after returning from a walk in the snow into a warm room. The only motion which I felt inclined to make, was that of laughing at those who were looking at me. My eyes felt distended, and towards the last, my heart beat as if it were leaping up and down. On removing the mouthpiece the whole sensation went off almost instantly.[85]

Davy himself described his own response to the gas in less restrained terms, giving, perhaps, an insight into the sort of experience Coleridge had when under the influence of opium, a drug which Davy also took freely:

> I felt a sense of tangible extension highly pleasurable in every limb; my visible impressions were dazzling and apparently magnified, I heard distinctly every sound in the room and was perfectly aware of my situation. By degrees as the pleasurable sensations increased, I lost all connection with external things; trains of vivid visible images rapidly passed through my mind and were

connected with words in such a manner, as to produce perceptions perfectly novel. I existed in a world of newly connected and newly modified ideas. I theorised; I imagined that I made discoveries. When I was awakened from this semi-delirious trance . . . I endeavoured to recall the ideas, they were feeble and indistinct; one collection of terms, however, presented itself: and with the most intense belief and prophetic manner, I exclaimed to Dr. Kinglake, '*Nothing exists but in thoughts! – the universe is composed of impressions, ideas, pleasures and pains!*' About three minutes and a half only, had elapsed during this experiment, though the time as measured by the relative vividness of the recollected ideas, appeared to me much longer.[86]

This account has its parallel in Coleridge's 1816 preface to 'Kubla Khan'. Indeed, Davy and Coleridge were in many ways kindred spirits. Davy, though primarily a scientist, was also a poet, an inveterate jotter of miscellanea in notebooks, an experimenter with drugs, and given to drug-assisted dreams and visions. The two men were attracted to one another. In 1802 Coleridge attended Davy's famous chemical lectures at the Royal Institution in London. When he and Tom Wedgwood wanted to try Indian hemp to relieve their ailments, they turned to Davy to supply it.[87] The laughing gas experiments offered an excuse to alter and enhance one's states of consciousness, but they had a serious side too, being efforts to find ways of alleviating human misery and pain. Such upright and non-addictive citizens as Southey and Josiah Wedgwood took part as well as the more susceptible Coleridge and Tom Wedgwood.

In September 1799 Coleridge was adding mercury to his medical store, having been prescribed it as a precaution against 'the Itch' (scabies), which Hartley was thought to have caught, to Sara's embarrassment, during their stay at Ottery St Mary.[88] Coleridge, who was irritated by Sara's 'hypersuperlative' reaction, recounted to Southey the three-year-old Hartley's response to being covered in brimstone to cure his condition: 'Moses [Hartley's nickname] received the Catholic Sacrament of Unction for the first time last night –/ He was very merry during the performance, singing or chanting – I be a funny Fellow, And my name is Brimstonello.'[89]

Another high-spirited letter to Southey tells of Sara's preventive measures:

For you must know that our apothecary persuaded me & Sara to wear Mercurial Girdles, as Preventives – accordingly Sara arrayed herself with this Cest of the Caledonian Venus, and I eke/– On the first day I walked myself into a perspiration, and O Christus Jesus! – how I stunk! . . . I walked, one Magnum Mercurii Excrementum, cursed with the faculty of Self-sentience . . . the next day a fit of the Rheumatism laid hold of me from the small of my back down to the Calves of my Legs, shooting thro' me like hot arrows headed with adders' Teeth. Since my Rheumatic Fever at School I have suffered nothing like it! – of course, I threw off my girdle – for such damned Twitches! I would rather have old Scratch himself, whom all the Brimstone in Hell can't cure, than endure them![90]

Coleridge also tells Southey that he is 'not in a poetical Mood', but is working on at the Lessing and the history of German literature. He asks Southey to borrow Herder's work on the history of the human race from the German enthusiast William Taylor; and he describes himself as 'sunk in Spinoza', the great pantheist philosopher whom Lessing was among the first to rescue from neglect. Other embryonic plans are to write a school book and take in a couple of pupils.[91] And he begins to mention his intention of finishing 'Christabel', which Southey wanted to publish in the *Annual Anthology* he was editing.[92]

But Coleridge was too unsettled to stick at any one thing. Undoubtedly he was dosing himself to relieve his rheumatism; his letters jump from topic to topic, from plan to plan. He hints at the criticism of Sara which was to become a constant theme: 'The Wife of a man of Genius who sympathizes effectively with her Husband in his habits & feelings is a rara avis [rare bird] with me.'[93] He was short of money again, and feeling restless once more. He told Southey he and Sara might visit Bristol soon; then he would perhaps go to London to chase up some travelling chests which had not yet finished their journey from Germany to Stowey.[94]

Once more Coleridge was undecided about his future, A move to London became likely when Daniel Stuart offered him regular employment on the *Morning Post* in November.[95] Such a move would bring a much needed income and interesting society, but London was not attractive as a permanent place to bring up Hartley. The Bristol circle was more congenial since the reconciliation with Southey and with Davy, Beddoes and the Wedgwoods there. Sara and Poole wanted to keep him in or near Stowey, but it was agreed that the cottage would have to be given up, so damp was it. 'Our little Hovel is almost afloat', Coleridge told Southey on 30 September.[96] Meanwhile, Wordsworth beckoned him towards the Lakes. He and Dorothy, having spent the summer with their friends the Hutchinsons at Sockburn in Yorkshire, were now about to start looking for a house to rent in the Lake District of their youth. They would prove a stronger attraction than those at London, Bristol or Stowey.

Coleridge and Sara may have quarrelled in October. At any rate, he now made a series of moves about which she knew nothing, and he did not write to her until December. Their marriage was not in a healthy state, nor had it been since Coleridge's prolonged absence in Germany and reluctant, discordant homecoming. While she and Hartley spent some time with friends near Watchet, twelve miles from Stowey, he went to Bristol. From there he continued, on 22 October, not to London in search of his chests as she expected, but, with Cottle as a companion, on a visit to Wordsworth at the Hutchinsons' farm in Sockburn. It was a fateful visit in two respects. Firstly, Wordsworth took him on a tour of the Lakes intended to attract him to that part of the country. Secondly, he now met Sara

Hutchinson, who was to become 'Asra', the idealized and beloved object of all his future emotional energies, the Sara who sympathized with him as his wife did not.

Coleridge and Cottle stayed overnight at Sockburn on 26 October, then set off with Wordsworth the next day to the Lakes, Coleridge having written in his notebook about his reception by the Hutchinsons, the brothers Thomas and George and the sisters Mary, Sara and Joanna: 'Few moments in life so interesting as those of an affectionate reception from those who have heard of you yet are strangers to your person.'[97] He was the more alive to their hospitality because of his late coolness with his wife.

The tour of the Lakes, described in his notebooks, took them first to Greta Bridge on 29 October, where Cottle left them to return to Bristol. 'Poor dear Cottle', wrote Coleridge to Dorothy, with the condescension of one who, for all his susceptibility to rheumatism and fevers, was always remarkably robust and energetic on walking tours, 'his timidity is indeed not greater than is easily explicable from his lameness & sedentary STATIONERY occupations; but it is extreme.'[98] The next day they were joined at Temple Sowerby by Wordsworth's brother John, and pushed on to Haweswater, Windermere, Hawkshead (where Wordsworth had been at school), Rydal and Grasmere. Wordsworth told Dorothy gleefully that they walked to 'the upper Water fall at Rydal & saw it through the gloom, & it was very magnificent' (see plate 10). Coleridge, he said, was 'much struck with Grasmere', and he himself had found a small house there for rent, which he was considering taking.[99] This was Dove Cottage, into which the Wordsworths moved on 20 December 1799.

Coleridge recorded his impressions of the tour in his notebook. One entry reads: 'Ghost of a mountain – the forms seizing my Body as I passed & became realities – I, a Ghost, till I had reconquered my substance.' His mind was still on Spinoza, the unity of whose philosophy of God in all things was attractive to him, not least as he viewed the grandeur of the Lake scenery in the company of his revered friend: 'If I begin a poem on Spinoza, thus it should begin/ I would make a pilgrimage to the burning sands of Arabia, or &c &c to find the Man who could explain to me there can be *one*ness, there being infinite Perceptions – yet there must be a *one*ness, not an intense Union, but an Absolute Unity.'[100]

He wrote, guiltily, to Southey from Keswick on 10 November apologizing for his long silence and saying in explanation of his sudden journey, 'I was called up to the North by alarming accounts of Wordsworth's Health/ which, thank God! are but little more than alarms.' He told Southey he had been invited by Stuart to write regularly for the *Morning Post*, and thought the income would 'enable me & Sara to reside in London for the next four or five months'.[101]

But it was a different Sara who was filling his thoughts. On 18 November he left Wordsworth and returned to Sockburn alone. Here he entered in his notebook the single phrase 'the long Entrancement of a True-love's

Kiss'. In October 1803, at a time of deep trouble, he added to his memories
of his stay in November 1799 with the Hutchinsons a passage in Latin
describing his guilty flirtation with the other Sara:

> et Sarae manum a tergo longum in tempus prensebam, and tunc temporis,
> tunc primum, amor me levi spiculo, venenato, eheu! & insanabili . . . [there
> follow seven lines heavily obliterated]

These lines may be translated:

> and pressed Sara's hand a long time behind her back, and then, then for
> the first time, love pricked me with its light arrow, poisoned alas! and
> hopeless.[102]

It was Sara Hutchinson's fate to be Asra, the ideal and unattainable
woman. As a close friend of Wordsworth and Dorothy and from October
1802, when Wordsworth married Mary Hutchinson, their sister-in-law
and frequent house-guest, she belonged to that magic circle which, though
it welcomed Coleridge into its midst – too much so for the liking of
Sara Coleridge, Poole and others – seemed to him to represent everything
that he was not and did not possess. Sara Hutchinson never married.
She was generous with her time, acting as amanuensis to both Wordsworth
and Coleridge, and she suffered from Coleridge's hopeless and sometimes
importunate feelings towards her. According to Coleridge's daughter
Sara, who understandably felt some resentment of this woman who seemed
a chief reason for her father's estrangement from her mother, she
had 'fine, long, light brown hair, I think her only beauty, except a fair skin,
for her features were plain and contracted, her figure dumpy, and devoid
of grace and dignity'. She was 'a plump woman, of little more that five
feet'.[103]

By 27 November Coleridge was in London, following up Stuart's offer
but still not writing to his wife. He gave Stuart a ballad, which was published
in the *Morning Post* on 21 December. 'The Ballad of the Dark Ladie' hints
at guilt, self-pity and hopeless love. The poet tells 'a Tale of Love and Woe'
to his beloved Genevieve, who

> listen'd with a flitting blush,
> With downcast eyes and modest grace:
> For well she knew, I could not choose
> But look upon her face.

The speaker, in telling the story of a knight's love for the dark lady, is really
addressing his own love for Genevieve:

> I told her how he pin'd , and ah!
> The deep, the low, the pleading tone,
> With which I sang another's love,
> Interpreted my own!

Unable to finish (or explain) the story of the knight's madness and death, he turns to the woman he wishes to woo by means of his song:

> She wept with pity and delight –
> She blush'd with love and maiden shame,
> And like the murmurs of a dream,
> I heard her breathe my name.

Softened by the story, Genevieve 'half-inclos'd me with her arms', and the poet claims a happy ending:

> And so I won my Genevieve,
> My bright and beaut'ous bride.

But, as if Coleridge cannot bear the guilt of such a wished for, but for him illicit, love, he has his speaker return immediately to the 'woeful tale of love' it is his duty to sing.[104] Coleridge published a slightly shorter version of the poem, with the new title 'Love', in the second edition of *Lyrical Ballads.*

Now at last he wrote to his wife, summoning her to bring Hartley to London, where they were to live 'for the next four months'.[105] He tried to persuade Southey to come to London too, to lodge with him at Buckingham Street, off the Strand, confident that the brothers-in-law could easily earn £150 each by journalism and book writing before April. But Southey's health was poor, and by April 1800 he was in Lisbon once more, having tried in his turn to entice Coleridge to go abroad with him.[106] On 19 December Coleridge confessed that he had 'scarce poetic Enthusiasm enough to finish Christabel',[107] which is all too credible given the lack of energy noticeable in 'The Ballad of the Dark Ladie', for all its superficial resemblance in metre to 'The Ancient Mariner'.

Just at this time, when he had in spirit separated from his wife after the meeting with Sara Hutchinson, a scurrilous publication came to his attention. This was *Beauties of the Anti-Jacobin* (1799), a selection of prose and poetry from Canning's and Frere's highly successful *Anti-Jacobin; or Weekly Examiner* of the previous year. Their poem 'The New Morality', with its swipe at Coleridge, Southey, Lloyd and Lamb, was reprinted and a note appended about Coleridge's early career. Perhaps borrowing from the gossip printed in the *Gentleman's Magazine* the year before, the author of this note wrote of Coleridge's 'avowed deism' at Cambridge and his comic enlisting in the army of the man he called 'despot' Pitt. The note finishes: 'He has since married, had children, and has now quitted the country, become a citizen of the world, left his little ones fatherless, and his wife destitute.'[108]

Coleridge was annoyed enough to consider prosecution for libel; in *The Friend* (1809) and in *Biographia Literaria* he complained publicly about his treatment at the hands of the compilers of these so-called *Beauties.*[109]

Though he always professed not to like living in London, Coleridge soon settled down, as he had done before, to a life of hard work and frequent socializing. At last he responded to Stuart's repeated requests to write regular pieces on contemporary affairs – in effect what we now call leaders – for the *Morning Post*. Coleridge had neglected to send anything for the paper from Germany; in February 1799 Stuart had written somewhat forlornly to Mrs Coleridge: 'Have you heard lately from Mr Coleridge? Do you think I have any reason to hope for Communications from him?'[110] Since his return from Germany Coleridge had sent Stuart a few poems, including his 'Lines Written in the Album at Elbingerode' and one or two poems translated or 'imitated' from poems by Lessing and Stolberg.[111]

Stuart needed an eloquent writer who could pursue his anti-Pitt, anti-war policy while showing independence of Jacobinism. Both he and Coleridge had hopes that Napoleon, who had returned from Egypt in October 1799 and effected a *coup d'état* in November, would lead the French to a less aggressive system of government.[112] Accordingly, Coleridge's articles in the paper for January and February 1800 attacked Pitt as ferociously as ever and showed a high degree of optimism about Napoleon's desire for peace. Peace was also the theme of his poem 'A Christmas Carol', which appeared in the paper on 25 December 1799. The Virgin Mary's poverty, maternity and peace-lovingness are stressed, as she denounces war as 'a ruffian, all with guilt defiled,/ That from the agéd father tears his child!'[113]

In February 1800 Coleridge began to visit the House of Commons as a parliamentary reporter. He gave an account of this work in a high-spirited letter to Josiah Wedgwood, in which he describes attending a debate until 3 a.m., then coming home and writing till 8 a.m. 'We Newspaper scribes are true Galley-Slaves', yet 'it is not unflattering to a man's Vanity to reflect that what he writes at 12 at night will before 12 hours is over have perhaps 5 or 6000 Readers!'[114] Coleridge was obviously enjoying himself and doing his job well, though Stuart later claimed that he had been occasionally unreliable with copy. An unseemly controversy broke out between Stuart and Coleridge's nephew and son-in-law Henry Nelson Coleridge in 1838, after the latter had published remarks by Coleridge boasting that he had raised the circulation of the *Morning Post* single-handedly by his contributions between 1800 and 1803, when Stuart sold the paper.[115] The details of the row need not concern us. Coleridge exaggerated his achievements and failed to comment on Stuart's continuing generosity to him, and Stuart was stung in turn into underestimating Coleridge. At the time there is no doubt that Coleridge wrote a great many articles of a high standard and that Stuart was so pleased with them that he offered Coleridge more money and an editorial role.[116] But Coleridge, who had never intended to spend more than the winter months in London, and who had the life of Lessing on his mind and conscience, declined, withdrawing from the *Morning Post* and from London in March 1800.

One of his last contributions for the time being was a majestic 'character' of Pitt, an essay which was hard-hitting but philosophical, delving into Pitt's precocious childhood in search of explanations for his merits and short-comings as a man and politician. This piece is most interesting for the way in which Coleridge, consciously or not, sees Pitt as a kind of antipathetic other self. Like Coleridge Pitt was 'far beyond his fellows, both at school and at college'. His vanity was formed early by his being shown off as a declaimer in childhood. 'He was always full grown' intellectually. Love of praise and power was the key to his character. In some respects, however, he seems to resemble Coleridge's respected opposite, Southey, more than Coleridge himself:

> At college he was a severe student . . . That revelry and that debauchery, which are so often fatal to the powers of intellect, would probably have been serviceable to him; they would have given him a closer communion with realities . . .
> The influencer of his country and of his species was a young man, the creature of another's [i.e., his father's] predetermination, sheltered and weather-fended from all the elements of experience; a young man, whose feet had never wandered; whose very eye had never turned to the right or to the left; whose whole track had been as curveless as the motion of a fascinated reptile![117]

Thus Coleridge, as earlier with Southey, manages a stately insult through the enumeration of those characteristics of a man which might by a more simple-minded observer be thought matter for praise.

Finally, Coleridge sums up the man's shortcomings in terms both polite and pointed, referring obliquely to Pitt's heavy drinking and possible homosexuality:

> He has patronised no science, he has raised no man of genius from obscurity, he counts no one prime work of God among his friends. From the same source he has no attachment to female society, no fondness for children, no perceptions of beauty in natural scenery; but he is fond of convivial indul-gences, of that stimulation, which, keeping up the glow of self-importance and the sense of internal power, gives feelings without the mediation of ideas.[118]

Socially, Coleridge was himself at the centre of a convivial London group which included Lamb, with whom he now became reconciled and who was once more enchanted with his old friend. 'The rogue has given me potions to make me love him', Lamb confessed, echoing Falstaff in *Henry IV* Part One.[119] More surprisingly, Coleridge now became friendly with his old adversary Godwin, taking Sara and Hartley to have Christmas dinner in the Godwin household at Somers Town and noticing how oppressed Godwin's children appeared. These were three-year-old Mary, daughter of Mary Wollstonecraft, who had died soon after giving birth to her in 1797, and Fanny, the five-year-old daughter of Mary Wollstonecraft's affair with Gilbert Imlay. Coleridge wrote to Southey on 24 December:

To morrow Sara & I dine at Mister Gobwin's as Hartley calls him – who gave the philosopher such a Rap on the shins with a ninepin that Gobwin in huge pain *lectured* Sara on his boisterousness. I was not at home. Est modus in rebus. ['There is a medium in all things' (Horace)] Moshes [Hartley] is somewhat too rough & noisy/ but the cadaverous Silence of Godwin's Children is to me quite catacomb-ish: & thinking of Mary Wolstencroft I was oppressed by it the day Davy & I dined there.[120]

Coleridge introduced Godwin to Lamb, who joked about expecting the roof to 'fall and crush the Atheist' but was pleasantly surprised to find him 'a well behaved decent man' without horns or claws.[121] Godwin had just published his philosophical Gothic novel *St Leon*, which Coleridge praised and criticized in conversation with him. Godwin took the critical points to heart and set about revising the work.[122] For his part, Coleridge noted that Godwin had earned £400 for the novel, which had sold out immediately, and was soon suggesting to Southey that together they (Coleridge and Southey) 'might easily *toss up* a novel', adding extravagantly, 'As sure as Ink flows in my Pen, by help of an amanuensis, I could write a volume a week'.[123]

If Coleridge was pleasantly stimulated by Godwin's company, holding out enticing visions of getting together a group, a pantisocracy of intellects to include Godwin, Wordsworth, Davy and Coleridge himself,[124] Godwin was even more significantly affected by Coleridge's friendship. It was at this time, he later recalled, that he renounced atheism for a kind of theism which consisted 'in a reverent and soothing contemplation of all that is beautiful, grand, or mysterious in the system of the universe' without feeling the need to analyse and define it. 'Into this train of thinking,' he concluded, 'I was first led by the conversations of S. T. Coleridge.'[125]

Coleridge's religious thinking was at this time as fluid as Godwin's note suggests. Though in a rare letter to his old Unitarian friend in Bristol, John Prior Estlin, he used the phrase 'We Dissenters', he would in 1800 no longer have defined himself as a Unitarian.[126] Some time in the autumn of 1799 he had entered into his notebook a brief but suggestive description of his dissent from that faith. He had begun to feel that the rationalism of the Unitarian creed, which he had once valued in opposition to the 'superstition' of established religion, was after all cold and comfortless. The entry reads: 'Socinianism Moonlight – Methodism &c a Stove! O for some Sun that shall unite Light & Warmth.'[127] But he had not yet returned to the Church of England fold. If he was anything in particular, he was a Spinozist, attracted by the monism of Spinoza's belief in the unity of matter and spirit, of God and Nature.[128]

It is probable that he talked about Spinoza with Humphry Davy, who had come to London in December 1799 to publish his *Researches* on nitrous oxide, and whom Coleridge was keen to include in his dreams of a colony of intellectual brothers. They met often, and Coleridge told Davy in an excited letter of 1 January 1800 that he had defended Davy against Godwin, who had talked of his 'degrading his vast Talents to Chemistry':

> Why, quoth I, how, Godwin! can you thus talk of a science, of which neither you nor I understand an iota? &c &c – & I defended Chemistry as knowingly at least as Godwin attacked it – affirmed that it united the opposite advantages of immaterializing the mind without destroying the definiteness of the Ideas – nay even while it gave clearness to them – And eke that being necessarily performed with the passion of Hope, it was poetical – & we both agreed (for G. as well as I thinks himself a Poet) that *the Poet* is the Greatest possible character – &c &c. Modest Creatures! – ... You, & I, & Godwin, & Shakespere, & Milton, with what an athanasiophagous Grin we shall march together – *we poets*: Down with all the rest of the World! – By the word athanasiophagous I mean devouring Immortality by anticipation – 'Tis a sweet Word!

Coleridge ends this piece of rhapsodic fancy with a request that Davy, his fellow experimenter with drugs, will 'take my nonsense like a pinch of snuff – sneeze it off, it clears the head'.[129]

Davy filled his notebooks at this time with notes for a projected poem, 'The Spinozist'. He and Coleridge may also have planned a joint 'philosophic epic' on the subject of Moses. It was to be in six books of blank verse, dealing with the (Wordsworthian) theme of Nature, Man and Society. Though there are no surviving references to the plan in Coleridge's writings, Davy's notebook gives a detailed sketch of its intended course from man in a primitive state of society to man in a highly civilized state, as in the Egypt of the Pyramids, through stages of degeneracy and vice to the departure of the Israelites across the desert and the enunciation of Mosaic law.[130] Coleridge thought Davy an 'extraordinary young man', though he told Tom Wedgwood that he knew 'one whom I feel to be the superior', namely Wordsworth.[131]

His thoughts were frequently with Wordsworth in the early months of 1800. When his four months in London were coming to their end, he was much exercised about where to settle next. Coleridge knew that his other friends would not approve if he followed Wordsworth to the Lakes, and he knew, as he had written to Poole from Germany, that it would be unkind to take Sara so far away from her family and friends in the Bristol area. He told Southey in February that he would probably return to Stowey.[132] Stung by a reproach from Poole that he had treated him with 'unmerited silence', he wrote asking his kind friend to look out for a suitable house with a garden and a study somewhere in the neighbourhood of Stowey.[133]

Complaints about Sara began to creep into his letters to his friends. Poole was told that he did not know where to settle, 'for that situation which suits my wife does not suit me, and what suits me does not suit my wife'.[134] Southey and Josiah Wedgwood received letters with postscripts in Latin bewailing his and Sara's incompatibility. He expresses his envy of Southey's happiness with Edith, while Sara, though an excellent mother and a woman of the 'purest mind', does not constitute that 'greatest gift of God', a perfectly suited wife. 'Her everyday disposition, and her sympathies in minor details, are at complete variance with my studies, my temperament, and alas! my weaknesses – therefore we cannot be completely happy.'[135]

Despite this domestic unhappiness, Coleridge knew by the end of January that Sara was pregnant, and it therefore became pressing that they should be settled *somewhere* by July.[136] They were. By the end of June Coleridge had allowed himself to be drawn to Grasmere, where he and Sara stayed with Wordsworth and Dorothy until they moved into a house of their own in nearby Keswick a month later.

But in March Coleridge was still talking of finding a house in Stowey and telling Poole that he wished he could get Wordsworth to take Alfoxden again (if the owner would let him), 'but he will never quit the North of England'.[137] His plan at this time was to let Sara and Hartley return to Stowey, which they did on 2 March, while he stayed on in London, at Lamb's house in Pentonville, prior to setting out on another visit to Wordsworth. The publisher Longman had promised him £100 for an account of his 'Tour in the North of England'.[138]

Coleridge had earlier entered into an arrangement with Longman to translate the three parts of Schiller's historical drama *Wallenstein*. This work he began in February, telling Poole he was labouring 'with my pen in my hand 14 hours every day'.[139] He carried on the work with some gusto while staying with Lamb during March. The days were spent translating in 'a dressing-gown (value, fivepence), in which you used to sit and look like a conjuror', as Lamb recalled in August, and the evenings drinking rather too much with Lamb and Godwin.[140]

Longman paid Coleridge £50 for the translating work, and he managed to complete the two main parts of the trilogy, *The Piccolomini* and *The Death of Wallenstein*. Schiller had written these in 'very polish'd Blank Verse', as he told Southey,[141] but the introductory piece, *Wallenstein's Camp*, was in 'Knittelverse', rhyming couplets of four stresses with a varying number of syllables, as suited its idiomatic, folksy rendering of the speech of Wallenstein's rough soldiers during the Thirty Years War. Coleridge admired Schiller almost as much as he did Lessing, and though he complained about 'these cursed Plays', he was referring to Longman's pressing him for the translation – 'Mr Longman is kept in constant dread that some rival Translation may pop out before mine'[142] – rather than to the merit of the plays themselves.

Lamb was delighted to have Coleridge with him. 'I am living in a continuous feast', he told his friend Manning on 17 March. 'Coleridge has been with me now for nigh three weeks, and the more I see of him in the quotidian undress and relaxation of his mind, the more cause I see to love him'. For Lamb, the longer the work on Schiller lasted, the better: 'He is engaged in Translations, which I hope will keep him this month to come.'[143]

But by 5 April Lamb was reporting disconsolately that Coleridge had 'left us, to go into the North, on a visit to his God, Wordsworth'.[144] Poole, too, saw that Coleridge was likely to settle with Wordsworth and not return to Stowey. 'You charge me with prostration in regard to Wordsworth', Coleridge wrote indignantly to Poole. 'Have I affirmed anything miraculous of W.? Is it impossible that a greater poet than any since Milton may appear in our days?' And, ominously, 'my faculties appear to myself dwindling.'[145] A week later, on 6 April, he arrived at Grasmere. Within the month he had found a suitable house to which to take the pregnant Sara and Hartley. In his pocket he kept 'a little of [the other] Sara's Hair'.[146]

7

Greta Hall 1800–1802

He dwells upon a small hill by the side of Keswick, in a comfortable house, quite enveloped on all sides by a net of mountains: great floundering bears & monsters they seem'd, all couchant & asleep. We got in in the evening, travelling in a Post Chaise from Penrith, in the midst of a gorgeous sun shine, which transmuted all the mountains into colours, purple, &c.&c. We thought we had got into Fairy Land . . . Glorious creatures, fine old fellows, Skiddaw &c. I never shall forget ye, how ye lay about that night, like an intrenchment, gone to bed as it seemed for the night, but promising that ye were to be seen in the morning. Coleridge had got a blazing fire in his study, which is a large antique ill-shaped room, with an old fashioned organ, never play'd upon, big enough for a church. Shelves of scattered folios, an Eolian Harp, & an old sofa, half bed &c. And all looking out upon the last fading view of Skiddaw & his broad-breasted brethren: What a night!

Lamb to Manning, 24 September 1802

On 24 July 1800 the Coleridges, having spent three weeks at Grasmere, moved into the front part of a large house, Greta Hall, on a hill just outside Keswick. The owner, a Mr Jackson, and his housekeeper Mrs Wilson lived in the other half. Dorothy had been in negotiation with Mr Jackson on Coleridge's behalf since June.[1] Coleridge's landlord was a carrier who had been successful enough to become comfortably off and who possessed a library of 'nearly 500 volumes of our most esteemed modern Writers', as Coleridge told Josiah Wedgwood.[2]

The Coleridges had wonderful views on all sides; from his study Coleridge could see two lakes, Keswick and Bassenthwaite, the river Greta, and 'the most fantastic mountains, that ever Earthquakes made in sport; as fantastic, as if Nature had *laughed* herself into the convulsion, in which they were made' (see plate 11).[3] He and Sara and Hartley went on 'heavenly walks'; Coleridge thought nothing of walking the thirteen miles across

Helvellyn to the Wordsworths at Grasmere, a journey he made several times during the summer and autumn.[4]

Hartley, now nearly four, enchanted his father with his joyful response to his surroundings. He was 'a spirit that dances on an aspin leaf – the air, which yonder sallow-faced & yawning Tourist is breathing, is to my Babe a perpetual Nitrous Oxide', wrote Coleridge, appropriately, to Davy.[5] Coleridge observed his child closely and dotingly, and experimented unashamedly with the boy's sensibilities. One day 'I sent him naked into a shallow of the river Greta; he trembled with the novelty, yet you cannot conceive his raptures', he told James Tobin.[6] Hartley's doings and sayings are recorded with increasing frequency in Coleridge's letters and notebooks. 'He is a very extraordinary creature', he told Poole, and 'if he live, will I doubt not prove a great Genius'.[7]

This was not simply a father's partiality speaking. The Wordsworths and Southey were also entranced by Hartley's precociousness. Wordsworth addressed him in a poem of 1802, 'To H. C. Six Years Old' (published in 1807), which described him as a 'faery voyager' and 'exquisitely wild'.[8] Southey told Coleridge in 1803 that the boy kept him 'in perpetual Wonderment – his Thoughts are so truly his own'.[9]

The summer of 1800 was almost an idyllic one. Even Sara, who had been reluctant to move three hundred miles from her mother and sisters – the removal from their society was for Coleridge a blessed relief[10] – settled in happily. She wrote to George Coleridge's wife on 10 September, only four days before the birth of the baby (called Derwent after the nearby river), describing Greta Hall as 'a large and very convenient house furnished with every article of comfort', for which they were to pay 'a very moderate rent'.[11] That, at least, must have pleased her more than living in the tiny damp cottage in Nether Stowey or rented rooms in London.

As for Coleridge, he was now settled near his greatest friend. Despite having been ill on first arriving, he rambled about the Lakes with great energy; he was forever stalking across the hills to visit Wordsworth to walk and talk. Dorothy's journal gives glimpses of the ideal life of the busy bachelor poet living in harmony with his usefully domestic but also aesthetically sensitive sister. The entry for 22 August is typical: 'A very fine morning. Wm was composing all the morning. I shelled peas, gathered beans, and worked in the garden till ½ past 12 then walked with William in the wood. The Gleams of sunshine and the stirring trees and gleaming boughs, cheerful lake, most delightful.'[12] Coleridge was often with them, sharing in their rural idyll.

Yet all was not well with him. He was oppressively aware that he should be getting on with the life of Lessing to prove to the Wedgwoods and Poole that his German residence had not been in vain. Longman had been promised an account of the German tour as well as the North of England one. Another publisher, Richard Phillips, had given him an advance for some other work; and he owed Stuart articles and poems for the *Morning Post*.[13] Instead of settling to any of these uncongenial tasks, he spent his time out of doors. When he did sit down in his study, it was to help prepare Wordsworth's second, enlarged edition of *Lyrical Ballads* for the press. For some months Wordsworth had been working on this edition, the first having unexpectedly sold out by June 1800.[14] Coleridge accepted that the new edition, in two volumes, should be published in Wordsworth's name only, since though Coleridge's original contributions were kept in the collection, they now amounted to an even smaller proportion of the whole than they had done in the one-volume edition of 1798.

Wordsworth had originally intended replacing 'The Ancient Mariner' with new poems of his own, but in the end he did include it, in a slightly revised form. No doubt in response to the adverse criticism of its archaisms, Coleridge modernized the spellings. 'Ancyent Marinere' became 'Ancient Mariner', 'cauld' became 'cold', 'emerauld' became 'emerald', and so on. Coleridge also omitted a few merely descriptive or repetitive stanzas. He retitled the poem 'The Ancient Mariner. A Poet's Reverie', a change which Lamb, for one, regretted. Sticking to his original view that the poem was a brilliant one, he lectured Wordsworth:

> I am sorry that Coleridge has christened his Ancient Marinere 'a poet's Reverie' – it is as bad as Bottom the Weaver's declaration that *he is* not a Lion but only the scenical representation of a Lion. What new idea is gained by this Title, but one subversive of all credit, which the Tale should force upon us, of its truth? – For me, I was never so affected with any human Tale. After first reading it, I was totally possessed with it for many days.[15]

Lamb also took Wordsworth to task for the note he now appended to the poem, protesting, 'I am hurt and vexed that you should think it necessary, with a prose apology, to open the eyes of dead men that cannot see.'[16] Wordsworth omitted the note in subsequent editions, perhaps in recognition of the justice of Lamb's comment, perhaps in realization of the feelings his note must have aroused in Coleridge himself. But it did appear in the 1800 edition, where Wordsworth told the reading public that Coleridge had wished the poem to be suppressed from 'a consciousness of the defects of the Poem, and from a knowledge that many persons had been much displeased with it'.

In Coleridge's surviving letters and notebooks there is nothing to support or deny this assertion. It seems likely enough that in one of his moments of self-abasement he expressed himself in this way, perhaps in the (vain) hope that Wordsworth would counter with a defence of the poem. Years later, in 1818, he complained that both Wordsworth and Dorothy had given only 'cold praise and effective discouragement', being, as he noted with some acerbity, 'abundantly anxious to acquit their judgements of any blindness to the very numerous defects' of both 'The Ancient Mariner' and 'Christabel'.[17]

Wordsworth, so strong in his faith in his own work, despite the cold-to-lukewarm reception it regularly received from critics, no doubt could not see why Coleridge was not more robust in his confidence in *his*. He probably found Coleridge unreliable as well as self-deprecating. At bottom, however, was the fact that Coleridge's supernatural ballads were not really to Wordsworth's taste. His note continued with a brief enumeration of the 'great defects' of his friend's poem, namely that 'the principal person has no distinct character', that 'he does not act, but is continually acted upon', that the events have 'no necessary connection' with each other, and that 'the imagery is somewhat too laboriously accumulated'.[18] Apart from the last, these objections refer to the poem's *strengths*; Wordsworth's criticisms could only be upheld if Coleridge's object had been to write a poem entirely without mystery and the quality of nightmare; in short, if Coleridge had been intending an utterly different kind of poem from the one he actually wrote.

As well as making minor alterations to this maligned poem, Coleridge was also engaged in a painful attempt to finish 'Christabel' for inclusion in the new edition. Dorothy noted several visits by Coleridge in August and September, when he read 'Christabel' aloud. On 4 October she wrote: 'Exceedingly delighted with the 2nd part of Christabel'. The entry on the 5 October begins: 'Coleridge read a 2nd time Christabel – we had increasing pleasure.' But the notebook for the following day reads: 'Determined not to print Christabel with the LB.'[19]

It is not clear how the decision was arrived at, but the stark fact was that Coleridge was unable to finish the poem. He confessed to Tobin on 17 September that he was having difficulties: 'Every line [of Part II] has been produced by me with labor-pangs.' His depression is evident in the words which follow: 'I abandon Poetry altogether – I leave the higher & deeper Kinds to Wordsworth, the delightful, popular & simply dignified to Southey.'[20] He must have gone on trying for some time, for Wordsworth actually included a reference to 'the long and beautiful Poem of Christabel' in his Preface, already with the printers Biggs and Cottle, and had to cancel this during October. By 9 October Coleridge was rationalizing – and fictionalizing – the fate of 'Christabel' to Davy, who was in Bristol helping to see *Lyrical Ballads* through the press. Davy was told that the poem 'was running up to 1300 lines' and was 'so much admired by Wordsworth, that he thought it indelicate to print two Volumes with *his* name in which so much of another man's was included'. Then, more realistically: 'The poem was in direct opposition to the very purpose for which the Lyrical Ballads were published – viz – an experiment to see how far those passions, which alone give any value to extraordinary Incidents, were capable of interesting, in & for themselves, in the incidents of common Life.'[21]

This, together with the glaring fact that the poem was still unfinished (and had probably never reached 1300 lines, since when it was finally published in 1816, still unfinished, it numbered fewer than 700 lines), is likely to have been the true reason for its exclusion in 1800. Wordsworth's Preface, discussed with Coleridge, who described it in 1802 as 'half a child of my own brain'[22] though he later still distanced himself from the ideas expressed in it, makes it clear that this principle of finding charm and interest in common incidents lies behind his poetry. Coleridge's complementary mode, to make the strange and uncanny seem credible, had no place in Wordsworth's explanation of his poetic principles.[23] This was even more the case now, since the new poems for the second volume included the Lucy poems, 'There Was a Boy', 'Nutting', several verses described as 'pastorals', and the fine poem Wordsworth set about writing – as he had before written 'Tintern Abbey' – to replace the unforthcoming 'Christabel'. This was 'Michael', composed with some difficulty between October and December, a moving and dignified pastoral poem which made a fitting end to the second volume.

Coleridge just could not find, or create, the conditions under which he could finish 'Christabel'. 'I tried & tried, & nothing would come of it', he confessed in a moment of plain, unvarnished truth-telling in an otherwise complicated and contradictory account to Josiah Wedgwood on 1 November.[24] A notebook entry for 30 October speaks eloquently of his problem: 'He knew not what to do – something, he felt, must be done – he rose, drew his writing-desk suddenly before him – sate down, took the pen – & found that he knew not what to do.'[25]

Wordsworth, too, saw the problem clearly enough. Surely Coleridge is the subject of a fragment he wrote at this time:

> Deep read in experience perhaps he is nice,
> On himself is so fond of bestowing advice
> And of puzzling at what may befall,
> So intent upon baking his bread without leaven
> And of giving to earth the perfection of heaven,
> That he thinks and does nothing at all.[26]

It was in Volume II of *Lyrical Ballads* that Wordsworth included 'A Character, in the antithetical Manner', which Coleridge recognized as a 'true sketch' of himself.[27] In addition to the 'weight' and 'levity' and the 'bustle and sluggishness' Wordsworth discerns in his friend's face there is the following telling paradox:

> There's indifference, alike when he fails and succeeds,
> And attention full ten times as much as there needs.[28]

Here Wordsworth encapsulates Coleridge's characteristic oscillation between expressions of throwaway carelessness about his work and desperately oversensitive responses to setbacks and criticisms.

With the delay over 'Christabel' and with Wordsworth still finishing 'Michael' in December, the second edition of *Lyrical Ballads* was not published by Longman until January 1801, though it bears the date 1800. Coleridge, who had shared with Dorothy the task of transcribing Wordsworth's poems for the printer, now dictated letters to various celebrated men who were to receive copies. These included the Opposition leader Fox and the anti-slavery campaigner Wilberforce. Coleridge was generous with his time and unstinting in his praise for this work which was such a monument to his friend's genius and steady application. He felt himself, by comparison, a failure. 'As to Poetry', he told Thelwall on 17 December, 'I have altogether abandoned it, being convinced that I never had the essentials of poetic Genius, & that I mistook a strong desire for original power.'[29] Two days later he wrote to Francis Wrangham, comparing Wordsworth and himself: 'He is a great, a true Poet – I am only a kind of a Metaphysician.'[30]

The idyll that was Wordsworth's and that Coleridge had hoped to share thus proved, for Coleridge, illusory. It was perhaps inevitable that he would be depressed rather than stimulated by constant companionship with a poet who was so much more happily constituted, and situated, than he. The contrast was soon exacerbated for Coleridge by the arrival of the unattainable Sara Hutchinson on a prolonged stay in November 1800, and two years later by Wordsworth's marriage to her sister Mary.

Meanwhile, Coleridge had had a chance encounter which he recorded in a letter to a now rather neglected Poole in August 1800, and which has a certain poignancy when we latecomers read Coleridge's simple account:

> I was standing on the very top of Skiddaw, by a little Shed of Slate-stones on which I had scribbled with a bit of slate my name among the other names – a lean expressive-faced Man came up the Hill, stood beside me, a little while, then running over the names, exclaimed, *Coleridge!* I lay my life, that is the *Poet Coleridge.*[31]

The poet was not yet dead in him, despite his protestations, but it is true that he was from now on seldom able to sustain an imaginative utterance in verse.

The unfinished poem 'Christabel' presents the student of Coleridge with several problems. Questions arise about how it would have ended and about its metre, which Coleridge claimed was experimental and new. Though not published until 1816, the poem was known to, and admired by, a number of Coleridge's acquaintances from Carlyon and others who heard him declaim Part I in the Hartz Mountains in 1799 to his many readings of the two parts in literary circles in the Lakes and later in London between 1800 and 1816. Several manuscripts in different hands survive;[32] and the two most successful poets of the age, Scott and Byron, heard it read from a manuscript and imitated it in poems of their own which *preceded* the original in their date of publication.[33]

We have therefore a case of a poem existing in slightly variant forms which were, in a sense, public property before publication. (*The Prelude* is, of course, a greater example of the same phenomenon.) 'Christabel' is a nightmare narrative with a Gothic setting, a supernatural aspect, and an unsolved mystery. Thus far it has affinities with 'The Ancient Mariner'. But there are striking differences too. The mystery in 'Christabel' is whether the Lady Geraldine, who casts a spell on the heroine, is herself the innocent victim of an evil enchantment or a kind of incarnation of evil. What there is of the poem raises the question, but does not answer it.

In Part I Geraldine, whom Christabel finds in a wood by moonlight, says she has been abducted by 'five warriors' and has 'lain entranced' in some versions, or 'lain in fits' in others. She is invited into Christabel's father's castle, with repeated crossing of thresholds: 'they crossed the moat', 'over the threshold of the gate', 'they crossed the court', 'they passed the hall'. Once over the final threshold and inside Christabel's chamber, the strange lady engages in a muttered verbal tussle with the spirit of Christabel's dead mother. 'Off, wandering mother! Peak and pine!' says Geraldine in an echo of one of Macbeth's witches, as she puts a malignant spell on Christabel, who thereafter is unable to warn her father about this dangerous guest.

Christabel has been initiated into guilt and needs to be saved. The question remains unanswered as to how this would have happened. Coleridge would presumably have had to decide not only whether Geraldine was evil in herself or under another's spell, but also how her influence was to be negated.[34] At some point after 1816 he apparently told Gillman that in the continuation which he went on promising in every edition from 1816 on, except the last in 1834, Geraldine was to have been defeated by the return of Christabel's absent lover.[35]

We can make a guess about why Coleridge found it impossible to finish the poem. At its centre is the heroine's initiation into what seems like sexual guilt. She acts hospitably and is violated by Geraldine. Famously, Christabel gets into bed and watches Geraldine undress. There follows the well-known stanza which caused Shelley to scream and which influenced Keats in the dream scenes of both 'Lamia' and 'The Eve of St Agnes':

> Beneath the lamp the lady bowed,
> And slowly rolled her eyes around;
> Then drawing in her breath aloud,
> Like one that shuddered, she unbound
> The cincture from beneath her breast:
> Her silken robe, and inner vest,
> Dropt to her feet, and full in view,
> Behold! her bosom and half her side –
> [Are lean and old and foul of hue]
> A sight to dream of, not to tell!
> O shield her! Shield sweet Christabel![36]

The line in brackets appears only in certain manuscript versions, one of which Hazlitt saw and gleefully restored (slightly misquoting it) in his review of the poem in 1816. He used its omission from the published version to suggest both the strong sexual element in the poem and Coleridge's timidity in handling it: 'There is something disgusting at the bottom of his subject, which is but ill glossed over.'[37] Of the many parodies of 'Christabel', that by William Maginn in *Blackwood's Magazine* in 1819 picks up this something, boldly making Geraldine a man in disguise. The bewildered Christabel finds herself pregnant, and Maginn asks cheekily:

> Pale Christabel, who could divine
> That its sire was the Ladie Geraldine?[38]

This is all good, if not clean, fun. It also gets to the heart of 'Christabel' as a poem which gives expression to sexual guilt and compulsion.

Coleridge was a prey to guilty nightmares of emotional and sexual desires. Such experiences lie behind the pseudo-sexual attraction-cum-repulsion in 'Christabel' which Hazlitt was the first to spot. The Gothic setting with its melodramatic and potentially comic elements – the owls, the crowing cock, the castle clock, the mastiff bitch, the midnight excursion, the ghost of Christabel's mother – is used by Coleridge much as the Gothic novelists used such trappings, as a distancing device to render the sexual and the sinful acceptable subjects.

But for Coleridge such subjects were not, in fact, acceptable. He disliked the 'pernicious' obsession with lust in Lewis's *Monk*, the 'libidinous minuteness' with which the monk's temptations are described.[39] This does not mean, of course, that he was not interested in such temptations. On the contrary, he was fascinated, but felt guilty about expressing sexual guilt, even metaphorically. In 1802 he wrote vehemently of his horror at such 'misery-making Writings' as Lewis's: 'My head turns giddy, my heart sickens, at the very thought of seeing such books in the hands of a child of mine.'[40]

It is likely that Coleridge was frightened at his own excursion in 'Christabel' into this territory, and that after his meeting with Sara Hutchinson it became more impossible than ever for him to handle it in the poem. When he wrote Part I, he had not yet seen Sara. The undressing of Geraldine was perhaps a combination of the imagination of illicit pleasure and a memory from his brothel-visiting days in London as a student. Now he knew and loved Sara, with whom no consummation was possible except in the guilt-ridden imaginings confided to his notebooks. Restoring Christabel by means of a returning legitimate lover was perhaps too simple and happy a solution, given the tangled nature of his own feelings.

In November 1800, while staying at Grasmere, where Sara also was, he recorded a sexual nightmare: 'A most frightful Dream of a Woman whose features were blended with darkness catching hold of my right eye & attempting to pull it out – I caught hold of her arm fast – a horrid feel – Wordsworth cried out aloud to me hearing my scream – heard his cry &

thought it cruel he did not come/ but did not wake till his cry was repeated a third time.'[41]

'Christabel' is of a piece with such horrible dreams. This should be borne in mind when we feel inclined to wonder if an element of humour does not pervade the poem. Not only is it an easy target for parody; it skirts comedy itself. This has mainly to do with its metre and rhyme scheme. In his preface of 1816 Coleridge declared, handing his critics a stick to beat him with, that the metre was 'founded on a new principle, that of counting in each line the accents, not the syllables'. Thus, though the number of syllables in a line might vary between seven and twelve, there were four stressed syllables in every line. (One hostile critic, probably Thomas Moore, writing in the *Edinburgh Review*, set out to prove, without much difficulty, that several lines did not conform to this 'principle' at all.[42])

The problem is that such a verse form lends itself more readily to comic than to tragic themes. The opening lines of 'Christabel' allow a sense that the poem is somehow ironic, even self-parodying:

> 'Tis the middle of the night by the castle clock
> And the owls have awakened the crowing cock;
> Tu-whit! – Tu-whoo!
> And hark, again! the crowing cock,
> How drowsily it crew.

This daring experiment in combining an insistent, chiming stress with irregularity in the number of unstressed syllables draws attention to itself in a sometimes unfortunate way. Coleridge adapted the form from German verses, usually comic, by such writers as Stolberg, Voss, Gessner and Ramler, minor poets whose experiments with counting stresses rather than syllables he had copied into his notebooks in Germany. The first part of *Wallenstein*, which he did not translate, is written in this 'Knittelvers', as are some of Schiller's satirical verses, with which Coleridge was familiar.[43] Goethe's *Faust*, Part I (1808), also uses the verse form for its comic or irreverent scenes.

The astonishing thing is that while 'Christabel' was mocked when it was published, it was so much admired by Walter Scott that he imitated the metre in his *Lay of the Last Minstrel* (1805), though he was, cannily, much less bold in varying the number of syllables per line. *His* poem sold 15,000 copies and was in general favourably reviewed.[44] Yet a reading of Scott's poem can only send one back to Coleridge's with an enhanced sense of that poem's superiority in everything except completeness of narrative. The relationship between the two poems, and indeed between the two poets, is an interesting and instructive one.

One of the many visitors to Grasmere during the autumn of 1800, when Coleridge was struggling to finish Part II for *Lyrical Ballads*, was Scott's friend Dr John Stoddart, who heard Coleridge read the poem aloud and to whom Coleridge gave a manuscript copy. Stoddart wrote to Scott just after the visit, telling him that Coleridge was 'engaged on a poetical Romance called Christabel, of very high merit'.[45] Some time in 1802 Stoddart read the poem to Scott, and the following year the latter told Wordsworth and Dorothy, who were on a visit to Scotland, that he knew much of it by heart. He gave Wordsworth the impression that he had already started his own poem when he heard 'Christabel' and was 'delighted to meet with so happy a specimen of the same kind of irregular metre which he had adopted'.[46] Even if there is some truth in this, there is no doubt that he borrowed a single line from Coleridge for the very first canto of his *Lay*. Coleridge's line

> Jesu Maria, shield her well!

chosen to rhyme with Christabel, becomes in Scott's poem

> Jesu Maria, shield us well!

Much later, in the 1830 collected edition of his works, Scott confessed to the borrowing, making 'the acknowledgement due from the pupil to his master', but in such a way as still to suggest more of coincidence than of literary theft. Like the car thief who displaces the blame from himself to the owner who left his vehicle unlocked, Scott dares to chide Coleridge for not taking enough care of his own property. He does so with all the skill of the amiable advocate he was:

> Were I ever to take the unbecoming freedom of censuring a man of Mr Coleridge's extraordinary talents, it would be on account of the caprice and indolence with which he has thrown from him, as if in mere wantonness, those unfinished scraps of poetry, which, like the Torso of antiquity, defy the skill of his poetical brethren to complete them.[47]

Scott was right, of course, and Coleridge could have learned from his example. No Coleridgean can afford to become righteously angry on the subject of Scott's petty plagiarisms. What we can do is marvel at how Scott, by prefacing and packaging and pleasantly confessing while still retaining his dignity, succeeded in deflecting the kind of criticism that Coleridge, with his inexpert shuffling in such matters, brought down in abundance on his own head.

The Lay of the Last Minstrel is a simple, though lengthy, story of medieval knights and ladies, full of descriptions of battles, castles, journeys, and a family feud which ends happily. Gothic and balladesque like 'Christabel', it has neither the latter's complexity nor its uneasiness. Lest the reader find the metre ludicrous, as well he might on encountering lines like

> Be it scroll, or be it book,
> Into it, Knight, thou must not look
> (Canto I, stanza xxii)

and

> 'Yes! I am come of high degree,
> For I am the heir of bold Buccleuch'
> (Canto III, stanza xix)

Scott writes a preparatory word disarming criticism. In his brief introduction he tells us the poem is 'put into the mouth of an ancient Minstrel' singing of 'customs and manners which anciently prevailed on the Borders of England and Scotland', to whom, the inference seems to be, we must attribute any puerility we might find in the poem.[48]

We may conclude that Scott owed his success with the reading public to the simplicity and facility of his work. It is strong on story and local colour. It is less difficult than Coleridge's, or Wordsworth's, poetry. But that the critics in the literary magazines should have preferred the *Lay* to 'The Ancient Mariner' and the *Lyrical Ballads* is more mysterious. Politics may have played a part in this, for Scott was humanely Tory, dealing amusedly with a romantic past, while Wordsworth's poems were democratic in their insistence on demanding sympathy for the lives of the poor and the dispossessed. Coleridge's poem was perhaps too original, too *sui generis*, to gain immediate approval. Then, too, Scott's self-presentation may have helped him. Even Wordsworth, though confident about his powers, was not much better than Coleridge in sending his work out into the world well armed against hostile criticism.

That other consummate seeker of literary success, Byron, also wrote a poem containing an echo of 'Christabel'. In a note to his poem 'The Siege of Corinth', published in 1816, a few months before 'Christabel', he described how he had heard 'that wild and singularly original and beautiful poem' of Coleridge's read out to him (by none other than Scott) and might have 'unintentionally' borrowed from it. Taking a leaf out of Scott's book, he too adopts a tone of amiable superiority towards Coleridge, hoping that 'he will not longer delay the publication of "Christabel"'.[49] By way of making amends, Byron used his influence with his publisher John Murray to enable Coleridge to publish his poem later the same year.[50] 'Christabel' appeared to a chorus of adverse criticism none the less.

One work which Coleridge did finish during the course of 1800 was his translation of the two main parts of *Wallenstein*. Though he complained about the drudgery of translating, and told Godwin that the original was 'prolix & crowded & dragging', he also allowed that the German trilogy was 'quite a model for its judicious management of the *Sequence* of Scenes'.[51] And at least he stuck at it, so that Longman was able to publish *The Piccolomini* in April and *The Death of Wallenstein* in June 1800. Coleridge was translating, not from the published version of Schiller's work, but from a manuscript copy, Schiller having authorized an English version through John Bell, an English publisher who transferred the transaction to Longman.[52]

As was so often the way with Coleridge's works, his rendering of *Wallenstein* later came to be regarded as a model of poetic translation. Indeed, it became a commonplace in the 1820s and 1830s for English critics to claim the translation's superiority to the original, and for English translators of other German works to refer to it as a model of achievement, balanced perfectly between a free and a literal rendering.[53] Unfortunately, however, the work had no success on its appearance in 1800. Reviews were lukewarm and sales poor.

Longman apparently lost £250, of which £50 was Coleridge's payment for the labour. As Coleridge ruefully told William Sotheby in 1802, this was 'poor pay, Heaven knows! for a thick Octavo volume of blank Verse – & yet I am sure, that Longman never thinks of me but Wallenstein & the Ghosts of his departed Guineas dance an ugly Waltz round my Idea.'[54]

A rather snide reference to him as a 'partizan of the German theatre' by John Ferriar in the *Monthly Review* had Coleridge reaching for his pen and writing to the editor on 18 November 1800 saying that 'the mere circumstance of translating a manuscript play is not even evidence that I admired that one play, much less that I am a general admirer of the plays in that language'.[55] This was over-sensitive, though it is true that his translation suffered from the general turning against German drama as absurd or, worse, Jacobinical. Ironically, Wordsworth himself contributed to this view by a dismissive phrase in the 1800 Preface to *Lyrical Ballads* about 'sickly and stupid German Tragedies'. Yet one cannot help feeling that if Coleridge had been bolder and more calculating, he could have made a case in his preface to the translation for giving fair attention to this fine historical drama of Schiller's.

He did mention in his preface to *The Death of Wallenstein* that the plays were comparable to Shakespeare's history plays, but his phrasing was half-hearted: 'Few, I trust, would be rash or ignorant enough to compare Schiller with Shakspeare yet, merely as illustration, I would say that we should proceed to the perusal of Wallenstein, not from Lear or Othello, but from Richard the Second, or the three parts of Henry the Sixth.'[56] Timid as the claim was, it was picked up by the reviewers, who sneered at any suggestion that the work of a German author could be compared to even the least mature works of Shakespeare. They ignored Coleridge's rather interesting remark in the Preface that 'translation of poetry into poetry is difficult, because the Translator must give a brilliancy to his language without that warmth of original conception, from which such brilliancy would follow of its own accord'.

In fact Coleridge's translation is a masterpiece of the genre. He is helped by the fact that Schiller had Shakespeare as his chief model, and Coleridge, in translating into blank verse, naturally wrote in his Shakespearean vein, often rendering Schiller's echoes of *Julius Caesar*, say, or *Macbeth* in directly Shakespearean phrase.[57] The subject of the trilogy was congenial to Coleridge, who found in the rise, success, and fall of the great military leader in the Thirty Years War a type like Robespierre, a strong man whose love of power and weakness for believing astrological forecasts contribute to his downfall. Coleridge's verse, though falling short of Shakespeare's metrical ease and energy, is usually very good, while conveying a faithful sense of Schiller's original. Here, for example, are some lines from Act V, scene ii of *The Death of Wallenstein* at a point when Wallenstein's world is crumbling around him and he attempts optimism:

> Who now persists in calling Fortune false?
> To me she has proved faithful, with fond love
> Took me form out the common ranks of men,
> And like a mother goddess, with strong arm
> Carried me swiftly up the steps of life.
> Nothing is common in my destiny,
> Nor in the furrows of my hand. Who dares
> Interpret then my life for me as 'twere
> One of the undistinguishable many?
> True in this present moment I appear
> Fallen low indeed; but I shall rise again.
> The high flood will soon follow on this ebb;
> The fountain of my fortune, which now stops
> Repressed and bound by some malicious star,
> Will soon in joy play forth from all its pipes.[58]

Late in life, with his reputation at last established, Coleridge was able to be generous in his praise of *Wallenstein* as a fine example of 'the diffused drama of history, in which alone [Schiller] had ample scope for his varied powers', and as 'the greatest of his works – not unlike Shakespeare's historical plays – a species by itself'.[59] He had already written some astute comments on a manuscript of his translation, praising the portrayal of the likeable Max Piccolomini and describing *Wallenstein* as 'far above anything since the dramatists of Elizabeth & James the first'. But measured against Shakespeare, Schiller was found wanting; he could not manage tragi-comedy, in which 'none but Shakespere has succeeded', and his low characters talk in a ludicrously high style.[60] This latter fault Coleridge characterized brilliantly in conversation with Henry Crabb Robinson in 1812 as 'a sort of ventriloquism in poetry',[61] a defect not avoided in his own early dramatic efforts, *The Fall of Robespierre* and *Osorio*.

Of course, the lack of success of Coleridge's translation served to deepen his gloom during the autumn and winter of 1800. There had been a fear that the baby Derwent – 'Why will he give his children such Heathenish names?' wondered Southey; 'did he dip him in the river and baptize him in the name of the Stream God?' [62] – might die. He was indeed baptized in a hurry on 27 September. Coleridge noted that 'the child hour after hour made a noise exactly like the Creaking of a door which is being shut very slowly to prevent its creaking'.[63]

On 10 October the first snow fell on Skiddaw, and around that date Coleridge 'climbed Carrock – descended just over the last house in Swinside & almost broke my neck'.[64] Though he was delighted with the scenery, he was soon unable to keep up his frequent strenuous pedestrian visits to Grasmere. On 14 November Dorothy Wordsworth wrote in her journal that two letters had come from Coleridge – 'very ill'. On 4 December he was suffering from boils; on the 20th he visited the Wordsworths, but was 'rheumatic, feverish' in the incessant rain.[65]

The cold, damp climate of the Lakes in winter affected Coleridge seriously. His first letter of 1801, written to Poole on 6 January, contains a litany of physical ailments: the old rheumatic fever, a swollen testicle, swollen eyelids, boils behind the ears, '& heaven knows what!'[66] It was probably now that he began to take his opium in the form of the Kendal Black Drop, a preparation made exclusively in the Lake District and known as a cure-all locally.[67] Poor Poole was treated to a sombre account of his pain, his falling behind with publishing ventures, and the consequent shortage of money.

A few days later Humphry Davy received a more winning description of his problems. The two letters provide an interesting example of how Coleridge adapted his style according to the recipient. He was eager to cultivate Davy's friendship (of Poole's he was assured) and to impress a fellow genius with his chemical and medical knowledge. He was also accustomed to talking frankly to Davy on the subject of opium and other drugs:

My dear Davy

> With legs astraddle & bebolster'd back,
> Alack! alack!

I received your letter just in time to break up some speculations on the Hernia Humoralis, degenerating into Sarcocele, 'in which (after a long paragraph of Horrors) the Patient is at last carried off in great misery.' – From the week that Stoddart left me to the present I have been harrassed by a succession of Indispositions, inflamed eyes, swoln eyelids, boils behind my ear, &c &c – Somewhat more than 3 weeks ago I walked to Grasmere, & was wet thro' – I changed immediately – but still the next day I was taken ill, & by the Lettre de cachet of a Rheumatic Fever sentenced me to the Bed-bastille – the Fever left me, and on the Friday before last I was well enough to be conveyed home in a chaise – but immediately took to my bed again – a most excruciating pain on the least motion, but not without motion, playing Robespierre & Marat in my left Hip & the small of my back – but alas! worse than all, my left Testicle swelled . . . a Fluid had collected between the Epididymus & the Body of the Testicle (*how* learned a Misfortune of this kind makes one) – Fomentations & fumigations of Vinegar having no effect, I applied Sal ammoniac dissolved in verjuice, & to considerable purpose; but the smart was followed by such a frantic & intolerable *Itching* over the whole surface of the Scrotum, that I am convinced it is the identical Torment which the Damned suffer in Hell, & that Jesus, the good-natured one of the Trinity, had it built of Brimstone, in a pang of pity for the poor Devils.[68]

A few weeks later he felt better and more cheerful, hoping, as he told Poole, that he would soon be looking back on his illness as 'only a Storehouse of wild Dreams for Poems, or intellectual Facts for metaphysical Speculation'. Davy, he added, 'in the kindness of his heart calls me a Poet-philosopher'. The clouds of self-doubt are briefly lifted: 'I feel, that I have power within me.'[69] Despite the disappointment over 'Christabel' (which he scarcely mentions in letters now), Coleridge had managed some moments of poetic inspiration in recent months. The fruits can best be described as examples of the 'Wordsworthian' Coleridge, though the influence between 1800 and 1802 can by no means be described as flowing in one direction only.

A poem of Coleridge's had appeared in the *Morning Post* in October 1800 entitled 'The Voice from the Side of Etna; or, The Mad Monk. An Ode, in Mrs Ratcliffe's [i.e., Mrs Radcliffe's] Manner'. Though not a very striking whole, the poem contains a second verse which is startlingly similar to lines in Wordsworth's 'Immortality Ode', begun nearly two years later in March 1802. The lines in 'The Mad Monk' run:

> There was a time when earth, and sea, and skies,
> The bright green vale, and forest's dark recess,
> With all things, lay before mine eyes
> In steady loveliness:
> But now I feel, on earth's uneasy scene,
> Such motions as will never cease;–
> I only ask for peace;
> If I must live to know that such a time has been!

The opening stanza of Wordsworth's 'Ode: Intimations of Immortality from Recollections of Early Childhood', published in 1807, reads:

> There was a time, when meadow, grove, and stream,
> The earth, and every common sight,
> To me did seem
> Apparelled in celestial light,
> The glory and the freshness of a dream.
> It is not now as it hath been of yore;–
> Turn whereso'er I may,
> By night or day,
> The things which I have seen I now can see no more.[70]

There is some doubt as to whether Coleridge, or Wordsworth, or both, or Coleridge imitating Wordsworth, wrote 'The Mad Monk'.[71] What emerges from these years when they were near neighbours is a sense of collaboration oddly more complete than that which took place in Somerset and which culminated in the publication of the first edition of *Lyrical Ballads*. The difference may be located in the fact – a melancholy one for Coleridge – that whereas in 1797–8 the friendship and the talk about poetry had spawned poems by each poet which were characteristic of his distinctive genius, their proximity now produced poems which were characteristically Wordsworthian.

Coleridge's special genius scarcely surfaced, though it would do so once more in his great poem 'Dejection: An Ode' (1802), a poetic reply to Wordsworth's 'Resolution and Independence'. In that poem of despair expressed, indulged, and partially triumphed over, Coleridge remembered a phrase he first used in the almost-hopeful letter to Poole of 1 February 1801, when he had got over his illness. He referred there to 'this Night Wind that pipes its thin doleful climbing sinking Notes like a child that has lost its way and is crying aloud, half in grief and half in the hope to be heard by its Mother'.[72]

Though applied to the wind and based on a sound actually heard, the comparison cannot but ring in our ears as a displaced expression of Coleridge's mood, not to mention as a reference to that momentous event from his own childhood, his night out of doors in Ottery after running away from his mother.

The strong suggestion of a submerged personal reference in the letter to Poole is reinforced by some remarks which immediately follow on the recent death of 'poor dear Mrs Robinson'. This was the poet and former actress, 'Perdita' Robinson, so called because she had taken the heroine's role in *The Winter's Tale*, attracting the Prince Regent, whose mistress she became, before transferring her favours to Charles James Fox. Coleridge had met her in London and liked her. They both contributed verses to the *Morning Post*, exchanging compliments in prose and verse in the pages of the paper.[73]

She published in October 1800 verses entitled 'Mrs Robinson to the Poet Coleridge', in which she describes the scene of the unpublished 'Kubla Khan', which Coleridge must have read to her in London during the winter of 1799–1800:

> Rapt in the visionary theme!
> Spirit Divine! with thee I'll wander
> [. . .]
> I'll mark thy 'sunny dome', and view
> Thy 'caves of ice', thy fields of dew![74]

In his letter to Poole, mentioning her death, Coleridge finds in her a female version of himself in terms of her marriage: 'O Poole! that that Woman had but been married to a noble Being, what a noble Being she herself would have been. Latterly, she felt this with a poignant anguish. – Well!'[75]

One other circumstance linked Coleridge to Mrs Robinson: the claim to have composed poetry in an opium-induced dream. Mrs Robinson's *Memoirs* were published by her daughter in 1801. They include a detailed description of the composition of her poem 'The Maniac' (1791), dictated to her daughter after she had, 'by order of her physician', swallowed nearly eighty drops of laudanum and fallen asleep. Apparently she had no recollection the next day of having dictated the poem, though she knew she had dreamt of a harmless lunatic she had met.[76] Coleridge, with his close interest in her unhappy life, probably read these memoirs. Perhaps he remembered the story of the poem's origin when he told, in the 1816 preface to 'Kubla Khan', his own tale of the origin of that poem in a dream.

Tom Poole knew that with Coleridge's move to the Lakes, he had been pushed aside by Wordsworth, and he resented it. 'What reason is there', he wrote in November 1800, 'why you cannot write to me with as much pleasure as heretofore?'[77] He received in return more gloomy accounts of Coleridge's health. Poole was the victim partly of Coleridge's tendency to have at any time one best friend to the near exclusion of others, partly of his close connection with the Wedgwoods – towards whom Coleridge felt guilty, with the albatross of the annuity round his neck – and partly of his propensity to lecture Coleridge on his duty. For example, he told Coleridge in January 1801 not to 'tumble about on precipices, nor expose yourself to stormy wet weather, nor remain with wet feet and wet clothes'. Nor could he refrain from complaining: 'I bitterly regret your leaving Stowey. I fancy if you had continued here this [i.e., Coleridge's illness] would not have happened.'[78] After another year in Keswick Coleridge would be bound to agree that his health simply could not stand up to the northern climate. But Poole's reproaches were hardly calculated to please him. This was a relationship which no longer held the attraction for Coleridge which it once had.

He continued, however, to woo the more interesting Davy. On 3 February 1801 he wrote asking for advice on reading books on chemistry, saying that during his illness he had been meditating on 'the Relation of Thoughts to things, in the language of Hume, of Ideas to Impressions'.[79] Soon he was able to report to Poole, for relaying to the Wedgwoods, that he was about to write some letters describing and criticizing the philosophy of Locke and of Descartes, with references to Leibnitz and Kant, whose works he was reading, 'such a purus putus Metaphysicus am I become'.[80]

At the same time he was recounting to Dorothy examples of 'Hartley's Metaphysics', i.e., his child's, not David Hartley's, whose associationism he was even then abandoning under the influence of Kant. Little Hartley, aged four-and-a-half, engaged in curious conversations with his father: 'He pointed out without difficulty that there might be five Hartleys, Real Hartley, Shadow Hartley, Picture Hartley, Looking Glass Hartley, and Echo Hartley/ and as to the difference between his Shadow & the Reflection in the looking Glass, he said, the Shadow was black, and he could not see his *eyes* in it.'[81]

Coleridge now set about writing what are known as his 'metaphysical letters' to Josiah Wedgwood, representing at last some return on the latter's investment in him. There were four letters in all, written during February 1801, though the fourth may not have been sent, since Wedgwood unfortunately showed little interest in the first three. He wrote to Poole at the end of March, 'as to metaphysics I know little about them, and my head is at present so full of various affairs that I have not even read the letters Coleridge has written on those subjects, as I have honestly told him'. Even Tom Wedgwood, who was more interested in philosophical questions than his practical brother, was not able to respond, being 'not well enough to pursue his own speculations or to attend to those of others'.[82]

Coleridge's interest in philosophy had begun when he was at school, though in his young adulthood his reading and thinking had run into religious and political channels rather than leading him to purely epistemological questions about what we can know and how. He had accepted Hartley's theory of association, which itself followed upon the empiricism of Locke's *Essay Concerning Human Understanding* (1690) and Hume's *Treatise of Human Nature* (1739–40). All these thinkers started with sense experience and proceeded to argue from that to ideas, in contrast to the rationalist or idealist school of Descartes and Leibnitz, who began with ideas and argued from these to individual sense data.

But increasingly Coleridge came to feel that the empirical method was too limiting on the powers of the mind: indeed Hume had found that he could not *prove* the operation of cause and effect, though he was content to accept that we act *as if* we were sure of their operation. Coleridge became dissatisfied with the materialist, mechanical basis of associationism. In *Biographia Literaria*, in which he attempted to chart his intellectual odyssey in the realm of metaphysics, he wrote of 'the process by which Hume degraded the notion of cause and effect into a blind product of delusion and habit, into the mere sensation of proceeding life (*nisus vitalis*) associated with the images of memory.' In this system, 'every fundamental idea in ethics or theology' is 'degraded'.[83]

In Hartley's scheme, he wrote memorably in *Biographia*, 'the soul is present only to be pinched or *stroked*', and 'the sum total of moral and intellectual intercourse' is 'reduced to extension, motion, degrees of velocity and those diminished copies of configurative motion which form what we call notions, and notions of notions'.[84] Inasmuch as Coleridge sought a unified system of thought which would take proper account of metaphysics, ethics and religion, he could not rest satisfied with empiricism, which led to scepticism in all these spheres.

'The pith of my system', he said simply in 1832, 'is to make the senses out of the mind – not the mind out of the senses, as Locke did'.[85] It was in 1801 that he went through his mental revolution in this respect, and he did so particularly through his reading of Kant, who sought to answer Hume's scepticism without reverting to the 'dogmatic' assertions of the rationalist philosophers about innate ideas. In a moment of unadorned honesty in *Biographia*, he declared that Kant's works 'took possession of me as with a giant's hand', at once 'invigorating and disciplining my understanding'.[86]

Kant, in his three great works, *The Critique of Pure Reason* (1781, revised 1787), *The Critique of Practical Reason* (1788), and *The Critique of Judgement*

(1790), tackled the problems of knowledge, ethics and aesthetics respectively. His self-appointed task was to accept as a starting-point Hume's scepticism about our claims to knowledge of abstract ideas such as God and immortality, but to find a way of going beyond that scepticism. This he did by proposing a 'transcendental' mode of knowledge; we begin with sense experience but apply pre-existing categories of perception to such experience rather than being passive and mechanical recipients of it – 'lazy lookers-on on an external world', as Coleridge put it.[87] In *Biographia Literaria* Coleridge offered a succinct paraphrase of Kant's argument: 'We learn all things indeed by occasion of experience; but the very facts so learnt force us inward on the antecedents, that must be pre-supposed in order to render experience itself possible.'[88]

By this means Kant, and Coleridge following him, frees the will and reason from the slavery of being wholly dependent on material presented first to the senses. Even in his child Hartley, Coleridge observed at this time the *activity* of the mind. His notebook for 17 March 1801 reads:

> Hartley looking out of my study window fixed his eyes steadily & for some time on the opposite prospect, & then said – Will yon Mountains *always* be? – I shewed him the whole magnificent Prospect in a Looking Glass, and held it up, so that the whole was like a Canopy or Ceiling over his head, & he struggled to express himself concerning the difference between the thing & the Image almost with convulsive Effort. – I never before saw such an Abstract of *Thinking* as a pure act & energy, of *Thinking* as distinguished from *Thoughts*.[89]

The four philosophical letters written for Josiah Wedgwood, and copied for Poole, in February 1801 are disappointing as arguments. In that way of his which was to cause so much trouble for him in future in his published works, he failed to state his aims clearly or to give due credit in the proper place to Kant's importance and influence. As was to happen in *Biographia Literaria* and *Aids to Reflection*, he mentioned Kant's name at the margins, in passing, or in a throwaway fashion, rather than declaring his indebtedness. Part of the problem was that Coleridge was reading not only Kant but also other German philosophers, and he was re-reading Leibnitz, Plato and the seventeeth-century Neo-Platonists, as well as a host of English and French thinkers from Malebranche to Lord Monboddo.[90]

As Hazlitt was to point out, Coleridge knew *too much*, read too many authors, with the result that he intruded them in his arguments to the detriment of clarity and sometimes with the effect of obscuring specific intellectual debts. Already in these letters, impressive though they are in their scope and range of reference, and important as indices of the way Coleridge's mind was working and moving, we can see the paradox caught by Hazlitt in an essay in 1820. If Hazlitt is excessively waspish, there is nevertheless fundamental truth in what he says:

The man of perhaps the greatest ability now living is the one who has not only done the least, but who is actually incapable of ever doing any thing worthy of him – unless he had a hundred hands to write with, and a hundred mouths to utter *all that it hath entered into his heart to conceive* [my italics], and centuries before him to embody the endless volume of his waking dreams.[91]

Even Coleridge's devoted daughter Sara, when editing *Biographia Literaria* in 1845, complained gently that she wished her father 'would just have read more *common-place-ishly*, and not quoted from such a number of out-of-the-way books, which not five persons in England but himself, would ever look into'.[92]

The letters to Wedgwood are cluttered with names and quotations; Coleridge vehemently claims to show that Locke owed more than had previously been thought to the system of Descartes. He laboriously extricates himself from his old adherence to empiricism. Kant is not mentioned specifically, though typically Coleridge writes in a follow-up letter of 16 March to Poole that he plans to propose to Longman 'a work on the originality & merits of Locke, Hobbes, & Hume/ which work I mean as a *Pioneer* to my greater work, and as exhibiting a proof that I have not formed opinions without an attentive Perusal of the works of my Predecessors from Aristotle to Kant.'[93]

Coleridge's illness persisted during the spring of 1801. Not only was he disappointed that Josiah Wedgwood had not replied to his philosophical letters,[94] but he allowed Wordsworth to convince him that his hard reading and brainwork had undermined his health still more.[95] To Godwin he wrote fancifully that he had been 'chasing down metaphysical Game' until he found himself 'unaware at the Root of Pure Mathematics – and up that tall smooth Tree, whose few poor Branches are all at its very summit, I am climbing by pure adhesive strength of arms and thighs – still slipping down, still renewing my ascent'. Though proud of these mental activities and his energy in pursuing them despite ill health, he acknowledged that

The Poet is dead in me – my imagination (or rather the somewhat that had been imaginative) lies, like the Cold Snuff on the circular Rim of a Brass Candlestick, without even a stink of Tallow to remind you that it was once cloathed & mitred with Flame. That is past by! – I was once a Volume of Gold Leaf, rising & riding on every breath of Fancy – but I have beaten myself back into weight & density, & now I sink in quicksilver, yea, remain squat and square on the earth amid the hurricane, that makes Oaks and Straws join in one Dance, fifty yards high in the Element.[96]

Not for the last time did Coleridge here express imaginatively his sorrow at what he conceived was the loss of imaginative power.

Once more, as in his letters to Thelwall and Wrangham in December 1800, he associated his sense of failure as a poet directly with his perception of Wordsworth's success. 'Have you seen the second Volume of the Lyrical

Ballads', he asks Godwin, referring to the new poems, all by Wordsworth. Then: 'If I die, and the Booksellers give you any thing for my Life, be sure to say – "Wordsworth descended on him, like the Γνῶθι σεαυτον [Know thyself] from Heaven; by shewing to him what true Poetry was, he made him know, that he himself was no Poet."'[97]

Death was on his mind. He told several correspondents, including Thelwall, to whom he wrote in April 1801, that he was 'going down to the Grave', and he now frequently mentioned that he might be forced to go abroad to recover his health.[98] His notebooks tell of laudanum and, though he did not yet make the connection, of the painful bouts of constipation which were one of the symptoms of his addiction.[99] Southey, expected soon from Portugal, was told in May that Coleridge doubted if he could spend another winter 'in this Country'.[100]

At the same time, domestic discord worsened. The notebooks are full of allusions to his wife's coldness, both sexual and emotional: 'Nothing affects her with pain or pleasure as it is but only as other people will *say it is* – nay by an habitual absence of *reality* in her affections I have had an hundred instances that the being beloved, or the not being beloved, is a thing indifferent; but the *notion* of not being beloved – that wounds her pride deeply.'[101] And he sent to Southey twenty-two lines of verse expressing his guilt at sometimes speaking too sharply to his beloved Hartley, beginning

> A little child, a limber Elf
> Singing, dancing to itself;
> A fiery thing with red round cheeks,
> That always *finds*, and never *seeks* –
> Doth make a Vision to the Sight,
> Which fills a Father's Eyes with Light!
> And Pleasures flow in so thick & fast
> Upon his Heart, that he at last
> Must needs express his Love's Excess
> In Words of Wrong and Bitterness.[102]

These lines were published, somewhat oddly, as the conclusion to Part II of 'Christabel'.

Coleridge's growing dissatisfaction with his marriage was exacerbated by his once more coming into contact with Sara Hutchinson in July 1801. He spent some weeks as the guest of her brother George near Durham, where she was acting as housekeeper. The ostensible purpose of the visit was to use the library of Durham Cathedral to read the works of Duns Scotus,[103] but undoubtedly Sara was the chief attraction. On his return home he made notebook entries full of references to his 'infinitely beloved Darling'.[104] His letters to friends described his increasing incompatibility with his wife.[105]

Plans to escape from the North for the sake of his health merged with the need he felt to get away from Sara. In November he wrote joyfully of the ceremony of the five-year-old Hartley's passage from petticoats to breeches – 'he ran to & fro in a sort of dance to the Jingle of the Load of Money, that had been put in his breeches pocket' – then modulated his tone from fatherly pride to pathos: 'If my wife loved me, and I my wife, half as well as we both love our children, I should be the happiest of men alive – but this is not – will not be!'[106]

A few months earlier Dorothy had reported to Mary Hutchinson, to whom Wordsworth was soon to become engaged,[107] on a visit she had paid to Greta Hall during April, when Coleridge was confined to bed with gout. The Wordsworths were as fearful as he that he might die: 'We both trembled, and till we entered the door I durst hardly speak. He was sitting in the parlour, and looked dreadfully pale and weak. He was very, very unwell . . . ill all over, back and stomach and limbs and so weak that he changed colour whenever he exerted himself at all.' She and Wordsworth were to have Hartley – 'dear little fellow!' – for some time at Grasmere, where he would attend school. And Dorothy commented on the obvious marital unhappiness at Greta Hall: 'Mrs C. is in excellent health. She is indeed a bad nurse for C., but she has several great merits. She is much very much to be pitied, for when one party is ill matched the other necessarily must be so too. She would have made a very good wife to many another man, but for Coleridge!! Her radical fault is want of sensibility and what can such a woman be to Coleridge?'[108]

The Wordsworths naturally sympathized more with Coleridge than with Sara. They made genuine but not always helpful efforts for their friend, and undoubtedly exacerbated rather than soothed the dyspathy between husband and wife. Southey commented harshly in 1807, when he heard that Coleridge was on the brink of separating from his wife:

It is from his idolatry of that family that this has begun – they have always humoured him in all his follies, listened to his complaints of his wife, and when he has complained of his itch, helped him to scratch, instead of covering him with brimstone ointment, and shutting him up by himself. Wordsworth and his sister who pride themselves upon having no selfishness, are of all human beings whom I have ever known the most intensely selfish. The one thing to which W. would sacrifice all others is his own reputation, concerning which his anxiety is perfectly childish – like a woman of her beauty: and so he can get Coleridge to talk his own writings over with him, and criticise them, and (without amending them) teach him how to do it – to be in fact the very rain and air and sunshine of his intellect, he thinks C. is very well employed and his arrangement a very good one.[109]

Since illness, opium and marital unhappiness combined to make 1801 a year in which he published nothing but a few articles and verses in the *Morning Post*, lack of money was a further problem. Wordsworth made clumsy efforts to help by approaching Poole in July asking for £50 to send Coleridge to the Azores for his health. Poole, whom Coleridge was treating unkindly, was offended, as he made clear in a letter to Coleridge in which, however, he offered to lend £20.[110] Coleridge's reply shows him turning on the rack of embarrassment, self-pity, pride and self-righteousness. To Poole's suggestion that he apply to his brothers for help he wrote, frankly enough, 'What claims have I on my family? A name & nothing but a name': 'My family – I have wholly neglected them – I do not love them – their ways are not my ways, nor their thoughts my thoughts – I have no recollections of childhood connected with them, none but painful thoughts in my after years – at present, I think of them habitually as commonplace rich men, bigots from ignorance, and ignorant from bigotry.'[111]

The end of the unhappy year 1801 saw Coleridge not in the Azores but in London, desperately earning money once more by writing for Stuart. 1801 had been an eventful year for public affairs. Pitt had resigned in February, ostensibly over the still-raging question of Catholic disabilities, but really because he wanted nothing to do with the lengthy peace negotiations with France which began in October 1801, culminating in the short-lived Peace of Amiens in March of the following year. On 4 December 1801 Coleridge's 'Ode to Tranquillity' appeared in the *Morning Post*. It is a rather lofty piece of verse rhetoric in which the poet congratulates himself on having withdrawn from the hurly-burly of politics. In his prose articles for Stuart, Coleridge expressed suspicion of Pitt's successor, Henry Addington, whose administration showed little sign of lifting Pitt's suspension of Habeas Corpus or repealing his Seditious Meetings Act.[112]

Coleridge spent the last days of 1801 and the first two weeks of 1802 visiting Poole, with whom he returned to London on 21 January. London had its usual effect on Coleridge's spirits. Though he complained that it did not suit him, he once more settled into the social round of old friends, including Godwin, who had just married his second wife, Mrs Clairmont. He confessed to Godwin, with one of those flashes of self-knowledge memorably expressed, that he was 'a Starling self-incaged' whose 'whole Note is, Tomorrow, & tomorrow, & tomorrow'.[113]

He also saw Humphry Davy, who had been appointed Professor of Chemistry at the Royal Institution and was taking educated London by storm with his lectures on chemistry, complete with experiments. Coleridge attended several of them, making copious notes and remarking mischievously, 'if all aristocrats here, how easily Davy might poison them all'.[114] The cartoonist Gillray produced an irreverent caricature of Davy carrying out experiments suggestive of much bubbling and stinking (see plate 12). One of Coleridge's notes describes such a moment: 'Strength of Feeling connected with vividness of Idea – Davy at the Lectures. Jan.28, 1802/ gave a spark with the Electric machine – I felt nothing – he then gave a very vivid spark with the Leyden Phial – & I distinctly felt the shock.'[115]

By 24 February Coleridge was contemplating returning to his family. He told his wife to expect him on 7 March.[116] But once again he did not go straight home. He had been talking 'unwisely', as Southey noted, to his

London friends about a separation.[117] But he did not set one in train. What he did do was visit the Hutchinsons again, with the inevitable result that when he did finally return to Keswick in late March, he was full of guilt and anger and passion and frustration, though the birth of his daughter Sara in December 1802 is proof of a resumption of sexual relations between him and his wife shortly after his return. His notebooks record his feelings for Sara Hutchinson and his plans to write poems about her:

> Can see nothing extraordinary in her – a Poem noting all the virtues of the mild & retired kind . . .
> Poem on this night on Helvellin/ William & Dorothy & Mary/ – Sara & I – . . .
> Poem on the length of our acquaintance/ all the hours that I have been thinking of her &c.[118]

The first entry seems to be an echo of a remark made about Sara, possibly by Coleridge's unfortunate wife, who increasingly had to hear him extol the other Sara's virtues. Not all these poems came into existence. But one extraordinary poem *was* written on the subject, namely 'Dejection: an Ode'.

The poem went through several drafts before being published in the *Morning Post* on 4 October 1802, the day of Wordsworth's wedding and the seventh anniversary of Coleridge's own. (Was it coincidence that Wordsworth chose this date? And did Coleridge deliberately arrange matters so that the poem expressing his hopelessness should appear precisely then?) The first draft, entitled simply 'A Letter to —' and sent to Sara Hutchinson, was written on Sunday 4 April. This date, too, was significant, for it was the day on which Wordsworth left Keswick to propose to Mary Hutchinson, having spent the previous evening talking to Coleridge about it. As Coleridge remembered in a distressed notebook entry of 1808, 'in my bed I – then ill – continued talking with [Wordsworth] the whole night till the Dawn of the Day, urging him to conclude on marrying [Mary]'.[119]

The verse letter to Sara is poignant and astonishing. Here is the familiar Coleridge of the letters: self-pitying, guilty, accusatory, questioning, self-torturing, demanding, proud and generous by turns. Some extracts will indicate the gamut of emotions to which expression is given. They tend to give the lie to his fear that his poetic power has vanished, though that fear is one of the contributory sources of his dejection. The opening stanza has the fine conversational yet heightened tone familiar from the poems of 1797–8:

> Well! if the Bard was weatherwise, who made
> The grand old Ballad of Sir Patrick Spence,
> This Night, so tranquil now, will not go hence
> Unrous'd by winds, that ply a busier trade
> Than that, which moulds yon clouds in lazy flakes,

Or the dull sobbing Draft, that drones & rakes
Upon the Strings of this Eolian Lute,
        Which better far were mute.
For, lo! the New Moon, winter-bright!
And overspread with phantom Light
(With swimming phantom Light o'erspread
But rimm'd & circled with a silver Thread)
I see the Old Moon in her Lap, foretelling
The coming-on of Rain & squally Blast –
O! Sara! that the Gust ev'n now were swelling,
And the slant Night-shower driving loud & fast!

There follow the lines that J. S. Mill was famously to quote in his *Autobi-ography* (1873) as 'exactly' describing his case during a mental crisis he suffered in 1826:

A Grief without a pang, void, dark, & drear,
A stifling, drowsy, unimpassion'd Grief
That finds no natural Outlet, no Relief
        In word, or sigh, or tear –[120]

In such a disheartened mood, now alas become habitual with him, he can no longer thrill to the delights of nature or respond imaginatively to them:

O dearest Sara! in this heartless Mood
All this long Eve, so balmy & serene,
Have I been gazing on the western Sky
And it's peculiar Tint of Yellow Green –
And still I gaze – & with how blank an eye!
And those thin Clouds above, in flakes & bars,
That give away their Motion to the Stars;
Those Stars, that glide behind them, or between,
Now sparkling, now bedimm'd, but always seen;
Yon crescent Moon, as fix'd as if it grew
In it's own cloudless, starless Lake of Blue –
A boat becalm'd! dear William's Sky Canoe!
– I see them all, so excellently fair!
I see, not feel, how beautiful they are.

'William', is, of course, Wordsworth, whose poetry (*Peter Bell* is referred to here) is a reproach to him in this respect. For Wordsworth could turn even depression into something positive, by that precious faculty of *letting himself be comforted* by influences from without, particularly moments, how-ever apparently trivial, of outdoor experience. As he had put it in 'Expostu-lation and Reply' in 1798:

The eye it cannot chuse but see,
We cannot bid the ear be still;

Our bodies feel, where'er they be,
Against, or with our will.

Nor less I deem that there are powers,
Which of themselves our minds impress,
That we can feed this mind of ours,
In a wise passiveness.[121]

For Coleridge, however – and his experience is likely to strike a chord with more readers than does Wordsworth's characteristic finding of a gain to counteract loss, however magnificently expressed – dejection colours everything, refusing external aid. This psychological state paralyses him as a poet:

My genial Spirits fail –
And what can these avail
To lift the smoth'ring Weight from off my Breast?
It were a vain Endeavor,
Tho' I should gaze for ever
On that Green Light which lingers in the West!
I may not hope from outward Forms to win
The Passion & the Life whose Fountains are within!

Here Coleridge's poetic expression of psychological experience agrees with the direction in which his philosophical studies had lately taken him with reference to the *activity* of the mind in perception. But the agreement is hardly cheering, since the unhappy mind is not cajolable, even amidst the beautiful scenery of the Lakes, to which Coleridge had moved with such hopes:

These Mountains, too, these Vales, these Woods, these Lakes,
Scenes full of Beauty & of Loftiness
Where all my Life I fondly hop'd to live –
I were sunk low indeed, did they *no* solace give;
But oft I seem to feel, & evermore I fear,
They are not to me the things, which once they were.

This verse is in direct unhappy dialogue with the first stanza of Wordsworth's 'Immortality Ode', already quoted, with its final line:

The things which I have seen I now can see no more.

Coleridge's echo seems deliberate. Wordsworth had begun his Ode on 27 March 1802, only a week before Coleridge wrote his.[122]

The chief cause of Coleridge's despair was his marital unhappiness and his love – which he knew was oppressive and distressing to its object – for Sara Hutchinson.[123] In passages which he wisely omitted from the published version in the *Morning Post* he complains of

> those habitual Ills
> That wear out Life, when two unequal Minds
> Meet in one House, & two discordant Wills.

And, worst of all, the joy he takes in his children is made painful to the point of his indulging guilty wishes:

> My little Children are a Joy, a Love,
> A good Gift from above!
> But what is Bliss, that still calls up a Woe,
> And makes it doubly keen
> Compelling me to *feel*, as well as KNOW,
> What a most blessed Lot mine might have been.
> Those little Angel Children (woe is me!)
> There have been hours, when feeling how they bind
> And pluck out the Wing-feathers of my Mind,
> Turning my Error to Necessity,
> I have half-wish'd, they never had been born!
> *That* seldom! But sad Thoughts they always bring,
> And like the Poet's Philomel, I sing
> My Love-song, with my breast against a Thorn.

Somehow, out of this misery, the poet/lover/correspondent pulls some hope, though not for himself. In a moving reprise, but in a minor key, of the ending of 'This Lime-Tree Bower My Prison', with its expression of joy in Lamb's joy, Coleridge celebrates Sara and wishes for her a happiness he no longer hopes for in his own life:

> JOY, Sara! is the Spirit & the Power,
> That wedding Nature to us gives in Dower
> A new Earth & new Heaven
> Undreamt of by the Sensual & the Proud!
> Joy is that strong Voice, Joy that luminous Cloud –
> We, we ourselves rejoice!
> [. . .]
> O dear! O Innocent! O full of Love!
> A very Friend! A Sister of my Choice –
> O dear, as Light & Impulse from above!
> Thus may'st thou ever, evermore rejoice![124]

This moving poem is more taut in its shorter published version, when it appeared as 'Dejection: An Ode, written April 4, 1802' above the signature 'ΕΣΤΗΣΕ', which he had begun to use in his newspaper articles, telling a new friend, William Sotheby, in September 1802 that this Greek form of his initials, STC, signified 'He hath stood'.[125] But the original verse letter to Sara is perhaps the more touching, especially when read in its place in the sequence of Coleridge's extant letters. The next surviving letter was written a month later to Poole, and gives no more than a hint of his sufferings. It even attempts, though in a gloomy way, to look forward with optimism. Fresh from reading the poem to Sara we become aware of Coleridge's effort at self-control:

My dear Poole
    I were sunk low indeed, if I had neglected to write to you from any lack of affection / I have written to no human being – which I mention, not as an excuse, but as preventive of any aggravation of my fault. I have neither been very well, nor very happy; but I have been far from idle / and I can venture to promise you that by the end of the year I shall have disburthened myself of all my metaphysics, &c – & that the next year I shall, if I am alive & in possession of my present faculties, devote to a long poem.

As for his wife, she is 'indisposed, & I have too much reason to suspect that she is breeding again / an event, which was to have been deprecated'.[126]

Poole had received a portrait of Coleridge done in Germany by an unknown artist. He admired it, though feeling that it *wants character'*, being '*Mr. Coleridge* and not *Coleridge*. You are in the drawing-room, and not in the vales of Quantock, or on the top of Skiddaw.'[127] Poole's remark was apropos. After several months of chronic illness and serious expectation that he might die, Coleridge undertook during the summer of 1802 walking feats of a strenuousness that might defeat the healthiest individual. Dorothy commented often on this oddity of Coleridge's. On 10 June he appeared at Grasmere, coming over Grisdale Hawes 'with a wallet of books – he had had a furious wind to struggle with, and had been attacked by a vicious cow, luckily without horns, so he was no worse – he had been ill the day before – but he looked and *was* well – strong he must have been for he brought a load over those Fells that I would not have carried to Ambleside for five shillings.'[128]

    Then, on 1 August, Coleridge set off alone on a nine-day fell walk around the Lake District which took him to the top of Scafell, the second highest peak in England. This walk, recorded minutely in his notebooks, which he rewrote as travel letters to Sara Hutchinson, was bravely undertaken. It was not common, even for locals, to do such difficult walking and climbing without a guide or companion.[129] For a man of uncertain health it was astonishing. But Coleridge relished both the grandeur of the scenery and the physical challenge of the excursion. He cheerfully described his setting out to Sara Hutchinson:

On Sunday Augt. 1st – ½ after 12 I had a Shirt, cravat, 2 pair of Stockings, a little paper & half a dozen Pens, a German Book (Voss's Poems) & a little Tea & Sugar, with my Night Cap, packed up in my natty green oil-skin, neatly squared, and put into my *net* Knapsack / and the Knap-sack on my back & the Besom stick in my hand, which for want of a better, and in spite of Mrs C. & Mary, who both raised their voices against it, especially as I left the Besom scattered on the Kitchen Floor, off I sallied.[130]

When faced with a difficult descent he took the kind of risk 'not of the least criminal kind for a man who has children': 'When I find it convenient to descend from a mountain, I am too confident & too indolent to look round about & wind about 'till I find a track or other symptom of safety; but I wander on, & where it is first *possible* to descend, there I go – relying upon fortune for how far down this possibility will continue.' Describing one such perilous descent by a series of drops from rock to rock, he recalls feeling 'overawed' when finally resting on a dangerously narrow ledge. 'I lay in a state of almost prophetic Trance & Delight – & blessed God aloud, for the powers of Reason & the Will, which remaining no Danger can overpower us!'

It is interesting to find him here putting his recently acquired philosophical system to the test in an extreme situation; interesting, too, is his immediately contrasting this daylight faith in Reason and the Will with his nightmare terrors and guilt-ridden suspension of willpower:

> God, I exclaimed aloud – how calm, how blessed am I now / I know not how to proceed, how to return/ but I am calm & fearless & confident / if this Reality were a Dream, if I were asleep, what agonies had I suffered! what screams! – When the Reason & the Will are away, what remains to us but Darkness & Dimness & a bewildering Shame, and Pain that is utterly Lord over us, or fantastic Pleasure, that draws the Soul along swimming through the air in many shapes, even as a Flight of Starlings in a Wind.[131]

This reflection on his experience is as eloquent in its way as the poetic utterance of such nightmare paralysis in 'The Ancient Mariner'. It helps, too, to explain the emotional urgency which Coleridge brought to his philosophical studies, his need to find a resting-place which would accommodate his sense of sinfulness and his belief in the higher human faculties which combat sin as well as satisfying him intellectually. In a notebook entry following his description of his solitary journey, he expresses his dissatisfaction with Unitarianism – too rational and optimistic for a man with his weight of guilt – and with Methodism – too irrational for one with his powers of reasoning – in terms of light versus heat.[132]

He was edging back towards Anglicanism, as he told his brother George in June and July in two letters clearly intended to repair relations.[133] Coleridge's motives in writing to George at this time, after long neglect, are not hard to infer. He was ill and thought he might die; Sara was pregnant and would need help in the event of his death. He wanted to plant a seed in George's mind for this eventuality, and he was keen to indicate his new-found orthodoxy to his clergyman brother.

Coleridge's walk was, of course, an escape from home, where he and Sara were getting on worse than ever. On 20 October, the day before his thirtieth birthday – though he thought it *was* his birthday – he confided to Tom Wedgwood that marital relations had reached crisis point in the summer when 'after a violent quarrel I was taken suddenly ill with spasms in my stomach – I expected to die – Mrs C. was, of course, shocked & frightened beyond measure' and promised to improve her behaviour. That his own demeanour might also be faulty he acknowledged, but somehow managed to blame Sara for that too:

> If any woman wanted an exact & copious Recipe, 'How to make a Husband compleatly miserable', I could furnish her with one – with a Probatum est, tacked to it. – Ill tempered Speeches sent after me when I went out of the House, ill-tempered Speeches on my return, my friends received with freezing looks, the least opposition or contradiction occasioning screams of passion, & the sentiments, which I held most base, ostentatiously avowed – all this added to the utter negation of all, which a Husband expects from a Wife – especially, living in retirement – & the consciousness, that I was myself growing a worse man / O dear Sir! no one can tell what I have suffered.[134]

Though he reported to Wedgwood that things had improved between them, it is clear that the relationship was already, before the birth of their last child, a broken one. However irritable Mrs Coleridge was, she had to take terrible, even hypocritical, criticism from her clever husband. His guilt about his feelings for Sara Hutchinson took the practical form of pressing her merits on his wife and taking offence at her jealousy, not only of the other Sara, but of the whole Wordsworth circle, from which she was so firmly excluded. When he left the Lakes for a stay with Tom Wedgwood in Wales in November 1802, he wrote her a letter expressing self-pity and self-righteousness wrought to a quite extraordinary pitch.

After showing due concern for her health – she was eight months pregnant and had fainted on one occasion – he begins complaining. Her fretfulness about his visiting Sara Hutchinson on his way south 'immediately disordered my Heart, and Bowels'. She cannot '*enter into* a state of Health so utterly different from your own natural Constitution', and this is one of the causes which 'render the marriage of unequal & unlike Understandings & Dispositions so exceedingly miserable'. In a sentence understandably inked out by someone – perhaps the very daughter who was about to be born when he wrote it, or her husband and cousin Henry Nelson Coleridge – he continues, 'I often say inly – in the words of Christ – Father forgive her! she knows not what she does.' Then he justifies his love for the other Sara, announcing grandly that 'no human Being can have a right to be jealous' in this respect. Mrs Coleridge is to accept that he is her superior 'in sex, acquirements, and in the quantity and quality of natural endowments whether of Feeling, or of Intellect'. Therefore he has a right to demand that she should 'to a certain degree love, & act kindly to those whom I deem worthy of my Love'.[135]

He had, of course, gone through tortures of jealousy himself at the time of Wordsworth's wedding. The night before, on 3 October, he had one of his Christ's Hospital dreams, in which 'boys & nurses' daughters' 'peeped' at him and 'a frightful pale woman' wanted to kiss him and give him 'a shameful Disease'.[136] This time Wordsworth and Mary Hutchinson featured too, as did Dorothy, who was herself suffering agonies of jealousy over giving up her beloved brother to another woman. She wore the wedding ring that night, and when she gave it to Wordsworth in the morning, 'he slipped it again on to my finger and blessed me fervently', after which she retired to her room rather than attend the ceremony.[137]

Wordsworth and Dorothy had taken advantage of the peace to go over to France at the end of July to see Annette Vallon and her child Caroline, whose father Wordsworth was. The secret of his affair with Annette in 1791–2 during a post-Revolutionary trip to France was staunchly kept by the next generation of Wordsworth's family, and by Coleridge, who seems to have been told it at this time.[138]

While Wordsworth was away Coleridge ruminated on the questions raised by the 1800 Preface to *Lyrical Ballads* and elucidated his own views in letters to Southey and to William Sotheby, a writer and translator with whom he now became friendly. He told Sotheby that he and Wordsworth had discussed how '*metre itself* implies a *passion*, i.e. a state of excitement in the Poet's mind, & is expected in that of the Reader', and that Wordsworth had dealt with the question 'in some sort' in the Preface. But 'we have had lately some little controversy on this subject – & we begin to suspect, that there is, somewhere or other, a *radical* Difference in our opinions'.[139] He told Southey the same, adding that he would 'endeavor to go to the Bottom' of the question and lay down 'some plain, & perspicuous, tho' not superficial, Canons of Criticism respecting Poetry'.[140]

This he was to do, though not until 1817 with the publication of *Biographia Literaria*. But some of the chief points made in that work appear first in these letters of 1802, most notably the distinction between the Fancy, 'or aggregating Faculty of the mind', and the Imagination, 'or the *modifying*, and *co-adunating* Faculty', a distinction closely related to his philosophical reading and his formulating of active mental faculties in the wake of reading Kant.[141]

Meanwhile, he was not writing much at all, though he claimed to be about to write a book on criticism, as well as to be almost ready for the press with 'a Volume on the Prose writings of Hall, Milton, & Taylor' – this to Tom Wedgwood with the annuity weighing heavily on his conscience.[142] He also claimed to be meditating 'a heroic poem on the Siege of Jerusalem by Titus', and he lied to Sotheby about having completed a translation of a poem by Salomon Gessner.[143] One poem he did translate (freely) from the German of Friederika Brun was 'Hymn Before Sun-Rise, in the Vale of Chamouni', which was published in the *Morning Post* on 11 September. Perversely, he fibbed to Sotheby that this was an original composition, 'involuntarily poured forth' after his ascent of Scafell and transferred 'in the Spirit' to the Vale of Chamounix.[144]

The only writing he did in the autumn of 1802 was for the *Morning Post*. There he wrote two 'Letters to Mr Fox', remonstrating with that statesman for visiting Napoleon in Paris during the uneasy peace.[145] (Poole was also in Paris, and wrote to Coleridge in August of Fox's being 'treated with great attention' there.[146]) Both he and Daniel Stuart were now less critical of the British Government than they had been two years before, and this was reflected in Stuart's reprinting in October of Coleridge's anti-French poems of 1798, 'France: An Ode' and part of 'Fears in Solitude', with the careful omission from the former of the lines attacking Pitt's ministry.[147] Coleridge also contributed in November two articles on a celebrated local case of impersonation and bigamy. Entitled 'The Keswick Impostor', the articles told the story of James Hatfield, who was revealed to have married a local beauty, Mary Robinson, under an assumed name. Wordsworth's interest in the plight of the unfortunate Mary found expression in the 'Maid of Buttermere' lines in *The Prelude*.[148]

Following his desire to escape from Sara and the worst of the winter weather in the Lakes, Coleridge travelled to London in November, with a half-formed plan to accompany Tom Wedgwood, also desperately ill, through France to Italy. Over the next few weeks the friends' plans chopped and changed. By mid-November they were in Wales together, trying out medicines and contemplating 'Naples, or Madeira, or Teneriffe'.[149] Coleridge's letters from Wales show signs of having been written under the influence of opium, so 'flighty' are they. From Crescelly in Pembrokeshire he instructs Sara that if the baby she is expecting is a boy he should be called Crescelly, if a girl Gretha. Perhaps he was joking here, but he certainly was not when he (cruelly) told Sara to have none other than Sara Hutchinson with her during the birth and lying-in.[150] Sara Coleridge, as the child was actually named, was born on 23 December 1802. As in 1796 when Hartley was born, Coleridge was on his way home but missed the birth; as before, he brought a friend with him, this time Tom Wedgwood.

The birth of this child did not reconcile him to home and Mrs Coleridge. From now on he would spend only short periods in Keswick. His health, his opium-taking, his misery about the two Saras, and his underlying restlessness of spirit, a kind of refusal at some level to grow up and take responsibility, all combined to make him feel about Greta Hall as the protagonist of his and Wordsworth's unfinished ballad 'The Three Graves' felt:

> He loved no other place, and yet
> Home was no home to him.[151]

The year 1802 had seen depths of despair, attempts at reconciliation, but no lasting change. How could there be? If the first thirty years of Coleridge's life could be called, Wilhelm Meister-like, his years of apprenticeship, the next thirty can be seen with equal appropriateness as his years of wandering.[152]

Part Two

1803–1834

8

In Search of Health:
To Malta and Back 1803–1806

Friend, Lover, Husband, Sister, Brother!
Dear names close in upon each other!
Alas! poor Fancy's bitter-sweet –
Our names, and but our names can meet.

Coleridge, 'An Exile' (1805)

In spite of the hope Coleridge had cherished when he moved to the Lakes in 1800 of increased health, happiness and progress as a writer, three years later his health seemed broken, so much so that he made a will and took out an insurance policy on his life. Though he went on deluding himself that he was not a slave to opium, he had become addicted. From his addiction stemmed many of his physical symptoms – fever, constipation, breathing difficulties – not to mention the psychological terrors of his increasingly frequent nightmares and the moral weight he carried at not being able to fulfil his obligations as a husband, father, friend and man of genius possessed of an annuity. He was caught in a vicious circle of guilt, escape from responsibility, intensified guilt, further escape, and so on for ever, it seemed.

If Coleridge had died at thirty, as he feared he might, he would have left behind not only a considerable body of writing but also memories planted in many minds of a marvellous genius, partly fulfilled but cut off while still full of promise. The world would have had 'The Ancient Mariner' and as much of 'Kubla Khan' and 'Christabel' as was ever written, the conversation poems and 'Dejection', the translation of *Wallenstein*, the Bristol political and religious lectures, *The Watchman*, and the articles and poems in the *Morning Post*. His biography would have contained the Christ's Hospital, Cambridge, Pantisocracy, Bristol, Nether Stowey and Keswick years. Someone would have collected his extraordinary letters; friends and acquaintances like Wordsworth, Southey, Poole, Cottle, Hazlitt, Godwin and Lamb would have paid moving tribute to his genius and personal magnetism. He would have been looked on as his younger contemporaries Byron, Shelley and Keats, all of whom died young, came to be looked on: as a writer of extraordinary talent tragically cut off. He would have been known as the great Romantic poet of mystery, magic, genial transformations of a psychological and symbolic kind; the archetypal poet of fine frenzy and rolling eye; the seer of visions of both hell and paradise.

But Coleridge lived another thirty or so years. The poems he wrote after 'Dejection' would hardly, with a few important exceptions, add to the reputation he was belatedly to enjoy for the poetry written before 1803. But a large dimension of his ultimate achievement was yet to come. Coleridge the philosophical thinker, the religious writer, the representative Romantic critic (both in theory and in practice), the first and best critic of Wordsworth, the increasingly conservative yet forward-looking analyst of British institutions, the opinion-former of a whole succeeding generation, the 'seminal mind' of the nineteenth century which J. S. Mill first identified as such – this Coleridge lived and worked and was an influence in the second half of his life. This is a thread we must be sure to keep a firm hold of as we follow him through to 1834.

Emotionally and psychologically, this means watching him sink into depths of despair unplumbed even in 'Dejection'. Intellectually, it is a hard task, for his thought was difficult, complex and influenced by a multitude of sources; which of us can claim to have read and understood a fraction of what he read and understood? Often enough, moreover, he wrote obscurely, even obfuscatingly. And for the student of Coleridge the man, there must be an honest confrontation of the fact that his peculiarities, so often charming, amusing, excusable in youth, are repellent in a man of middle and old age. We are less inclined to make allowances for his deceitfulness, boasting, self-pity, unfulfilled (and unfulfillable) promises, and tendency to deflect blame and criticism, returning it to its originator, whether his wife, Southey, Wordsworth, the periodical critics, or anyone else, at compound interest.

And yet the man continued to exercise his power over old friends who knew him at his worst, and he continued to fascinate new acquaintances. De Quincey, Henry Crabb Robinson and Byron were yet to come under his spell. Even Southey, who knew from experience how difficult a relationship with Coleridge could be, and who was on the receiving end of more complaints from Coleridge about Mrs Coleridge – his own wife's sister – than anyone else, could still succumb to the magic. In 1803, though he had acquired through his friend Wynn an appointment as secretary to a Government official, Southey was still searching for a home for himself, Edith, and their baby Margaret, known as 'the Passionate Pearl'. Coleridge enticed Southey to Keswick to share Greta Hall, the more eagerly because he himself intended to leave for an extended stay on the continent. 'I shall certainly be absent – even if I live – two years', he told Southey in February 1803. In the same letter he talked of taking out an insurance policy of

£1,000 with the Equitable Society, if they would accept him. 'I fear', he added, 'I must *rouge* a little.'¹

Southey resisted for a while; in February 1803 he told his Norwich friend William Taylor, translator of *Lenore*, who had inquired about Coleridge's proposed life of Lessing: 'I am grieved that you never met Coleridge: all other men whom I have ever known are mere children to him, and yet all is palsied by a total want of moral strength. He will leave nothing behind him to justify the opinion of his friends to the world; yet many of his scattered poems are such, that a man of feeling will see that the author was capable of executing the greatest works.'² (Did he include 'The Ancient Mariner', that 'Dutch attempt at German sublimity' in this estimate?) Southey, who was much in Coleridge's company at this time in London and Bristol, firmly believed Coleridge was going to die. 'It vexes and grieves me to the heart, that when he goes, as go he will, nobody will believe what a mind goes with him, – how infinitely and ten thousand-thousand-fold the mightiest of his generation', he told William Taylor.³

As it turned out, Southey did make his home with his wife and her sister Sara at Greta Hall. In September 1803 the baby Margaret died, and Edith wanted to be with her sister. The Southeys moved in, and sooner rather than later Southey found himself responsible not only for his own family, but also for Coleridge's.

Coleridge spent the spring of 1803 toing and froing between Bristol, where he stayed with Southey, Nether Stowey, where he was Poole's guest, and Gunville, Josiah Wedgwood's house in Dorset, where he and Tom Wedgwood apparently experimented with some 'Bang' which Poole's friend Samuel Purkis had obtained from Sir Joseph Banks, President of the Royal Society, and indeed with a whole variety of drugs. Coleridge looked forward to trying them out, as he told Tom on 17 February: 'We will have a fair Trial of *Bang* – Do bring down some of the Hyoscyamine Pills – & I will give a fair Trial of opium, Hensbane, & Nepenthe. Bye the bye, I always considered Homer's account of the *Nepenthe* as a *Banging* lie.'⁴

Coleridge was still planning to go abroad with Tom Wedgwood, who was becoming desperate about his illness – a 'thickening of the Gut', Coleridge called it when asking Purkis for the Indian hemp⁵ – and indeed he died just over two years later. But they were undecided about when and where to go. By March it looked likely that the war with France would resume after a year's peace, and the continent became once more closed and dangerous to travellers. Coleridge and Wedgwood would not have been good travelling companions for one another, since both were believed to be dying. In the end Wedgwood went to France with another friend, the artist T. R. Underwood, on 25 March. When war was resumed on 16 May, Wedgwood managed to get back home in the nick of time, but Underwood was detained at Napoleon's command and held in France for the next two years.⁶

One person who was not charmed by Coleridge's presence was Wedgwood's sister Kitty, who distrusted what she thought 'too great a parade of superior feeling' on his part, and who believed he was being 'very negligent' of his wife and children.[7] Lamb's friend John Rickman, Secretary to the Speaker of the House of Commons and originator of the first population census in 1801, who met Coleridge in London in March, was also resistant to Coleridge's attractions. He told Southey that he did not like Coleridge's 'habit of assentation' and delight in talking in company. 'I understand', he wrote, 'he is terribly pestered with invitations to go to parties, as a singer does, to amuse the guests by his talent; a hateful task I should think: I would rather not talk finely, than talk to such a purpose.'[8] The rather bizarre combination of child prodigy and valetudinarian in a man of thirty repelled Rickman.

Lamb, however, was still enamoured of his old friend, who stayed with him in London in early April. Coleridge was helpful when Mary Lamb had a fit of insanity – 'she *smiled* in an ominous way', said Coleridge – and had to be taken to a private madhouse at Hoxton. 'Charles is cut to the heart', Coleridge told his wife on 4 April.[9] By May Coleridge was back in Keswick after an absence of four months, having caught flu in the mail coach on the way.[10] While in London, he had succeeded in insuring his life and had negotiated with Longman for a new edition of his poems, which Lamb was seeing through the press.

This edition offers a striking example of the extreme apparent carelessness with which he treated his own works. It was simply a reissue of *Poems* of 1797 with the order of the poems slightly changed. Not only did Coleridge not think, as far as we know, of including 'Kubla Khan' or 'Christabel', he did not even add any of the poems which had appeared in pamphlet form or in the *Morning Post* – 'This Lime-Tree Bower My Prison', 'Frost at Midnight', 'Fears in Solitude', 'France: An Ode', or 'Dejection'. Nor did he take the opportunity of writing a preface voicing his recent thoughts about poetry, as expressed in letters to Southey and Sotheby. He simply reprinted the brief and unconfident prefaces of 1796 and 1797.

In a flash of self-knowledge Coleridge told Poole in October 1803 that he laid 'too many Eggs in the hot Sands with Ostrich Carelessness & Ostrich oblivion'. He was speaking mainly of his conversation, but his remark was prophetic in relation to his poetry too: 'And tho' many [eggs] are luckily trod on & smashed; as many crawl forth into Life, some to furnish Feathers for the Caps of others, and more alas! to plume the Shafts in the Quivers of my Enemies and of them "that lie in wait against my Soul".'[11]

Little is heard now of the great metaphysical work he intended to write, though he told Godwin in June that he was 'ready to go to the Press, with a work which I consider as introductory to a *System*'. He went on to detail the contents of this work, which would cover Aristotelian logic, the history of logic in general, Platonic logic, the work of Bacon, Descartes, Condillac and many more.[12] Nothing of the sort appeared at this time. Nor did Southey's plan to compile a 'Bibliotheca Britannica', a history of English literature, for which he earmarked Coleridge to do 'the schoolmen', come to anything. Coleridge entered into the idea with gusto, but his conception was 'too gigantic' for Southey, including as it did a 'complete history of all Welsh, Saxon, and Erse books that are not translations', in preparation for which he and Southey would first learn Welsh and Erse![13] Small wonder the plan fell through.

While he dreamed and planned in this ambitious way, he actually settled down to very little. Two articles on 'The Men and the Times' appeared in the *Morning Post* in July and August 1803, just as Stuart was on the point of selling the paper to an interest which may have included the Prime Minister Addington and the Prince Regent.[14] In the second of these articles Coleridge replied directly to Fox's long speech in Parliament denouncing England's resumption of war with France. Fox had argued that Napoleon's aggressive activities in Europe were no threat to Britain, despite his failed attempt to make Britain give up Malta: 'And all this for what? For Malta! Malta! plain, bare, naked Malta, unconnected with any other interests.' To this Coleridge replied that even if it was wrong to go to war over Malta, the war could be shown to be 'just and necessary from other sufficient and honourable causes', though these seem to have been no more than Britain's sense of 'insult' at France's potential expansion of empire.[15]

Coleridge's attitude towards war, and towards the Conservative administration, had changed considerably since the days of lofty rhetorical attack on Pitt and his ministry of 'Hyenas' in 1798.[16] He himself would become closely associated with British Government interests in Malta when he took up an invitation from John Stoddart, who went to Malta that summer as King's Advocate.[17]

Meanwhile, however, he was planning a walking tour of Scotland with Wordsworth and Dorothy. As usual with Coleridge, ill health did not stop him from undertaking long journeys on foot; he felt much worse when he sat at home thinking about work and doing none, swallowing opium, and quarrelling with Sara. Before he left on 15 August, he acted as godfather to Wordsworth's first child, John, on 17 July, and played host to Hazlitt, who visited the Lakes in July and painted portraits – now lost or destroyed – of Wordsworth, Coleridge, and six-year-old Hartley.[18]

Coleridge wrote interestingly of the young man who had made an idol of him on hearing him preach at Shrewsbury five years before. Hazlitt's manners were repellent – 'brow-hanging, shoe-contemplative, *strange*' – but his opinions original. 'He sends well-headed & well-feathered Thoughts straight forwards to the mark with a Twang of the Bow-string.' Hazlitt would do this all too brilliantly in his essay on Coleridge himself in *The Spirit of the Age* (1825). What Coleridge also notes in his description of Hazlitt is that he is 'addicted to women, as objects of sexual Indulgence.'[19] Indeed one underlying reason for Hazlitt's later venomousness towards Coleridge was Coleridge's knowledge of an incident of sexual harassment which had Hazlitt hurrying away from this visit to the Lakes, after being saved by Wordsworth and Coleridge from being attacked by a local girl's outraged friends and family.[20]

On 13 August Coleridge sent a copy of Wordsworth's 'Resolution and Independence' and a version of 'Dejection' to his new acquaintances Sir George and Lady Beaumont, who were visiting the Lakes. Sir George was a landscape painter and patron of the arts, and later founder of the National Gallery. He admired Wordsworth and Coleridge, and a mutually flattering correspondence began between the poets and the aristocrat. Coleridge was careful to mention his new noble friend in one of his rare letters to his brother George in October.[21] He was moving ever further away from his youthful democratic politics, becoming something of a Tory, just as he was on his way back from Unitarianism to the Church of England.

On 15 August Coleridge, Wordsworth, and Dorothy set off for Scotland 'in an Irish-Car and one horse', as Sara Coleridge reported to Southey. 'W. is to drive all the way, for poor Samuel is too weak to undertake the fatigue of driving.'[22] The journey was not a success, not so much because of Coleridge's health, for despite feeling dreadful he proved once more a doughty pedestrian, but because he and Wordsworth did not get on. In a repetition of the trip to Germany, Coleridge soon parted from the other two and set off alone from Arrochar to Glencoe, where he enjoyed the extreme solitude – 'for 18 miles there are but 2 Habitations!' – and eventually walked barefoot like the poor people in Scotland, having burnt his shoes when drying them at a fire.[23] Undaunted, he set out for Fort William, then Inverness, before turning south to Perth and Edinburgh.

At Perth he heard of the death of little Margaret Southey and wrote in sympathy to Southey, who was now in Keswick. He also sent a poem he had composed in all the misery of illness, opium and jealousy of Wordsworth, later known as 'The Pains of Sleep' and published with 'Kubla Khan' and 'Christabel' in 1816. He prefaced it with a description of the terrible juxtaposition of his daytime health and energy and his nightly agonies: 'I have walked 263 miles in eight Days – so I must have strength somewhere / but my spirits are dreadful, owing entirely to the Horrors of every night – I truly dread sleep / it is no shadow with me, but substantial Misery foot-thick, that makes me sit by my bedside of a morning, & *cry* –.' The poem itself is short, simple, and terrible. It begins:

> When on my bed my limbs I lay,
> It hath not been my use to pray
> With moving Lips or bended Knees;
> But silently, by slow degrees,
> My spirit I to Love compose,
> In humble trust my eyelids close,
> With reverential Resignation,
> No Wish conceiv'd, no Thought exprest,
> Only a *Sense* of Supplication,
> A *Sense* o'er all my soul imprest
> That I am weak, yet not unblest:

> Since *round* me, *in* me, every where,
> Eternal Strength & Goodness are! –

In the second verse comes the horror:

> But yesternight I pray'd aloud
> In Anguish & in Agony,
> Awaking from the fiendish Crowd
> Of Shapes & Thoughts that tortur'd me!
> Desire with Loathing strangely mixt,
> On wild or hateful Objects fixt:
> Pangs of Revenge, the powerless Will,
> Still baffled, & consuming still,
> Sense of intolerable Wrong,
> And men whom I despis'd made strong
> Vain-glorious Threats, unmanly Vaunting,
> Bad men my boasts & fury taunting
> Rage, sensual Passion, mad'ning Brawl,
> And Shame, and Terror over all!
> Deeds to be hid that were not hid,
> Which, all confus'd I might not know,
> Whether I suffer'd or I did:
> For all was Horror, Guilt & Woe,
> My own and others, still the same,
> Life-stifling Fear, soul-stifling Shame!

Here is sexual guilt – 'Desire with Loathing strangely mixt' – and the paralysis of willpower induced by opium which adds immeasurably to the dreamer's experience of being acted upon rather than acting. The poem ends on a painful balance of self-loathing and self-pity:

> Such Punishments, I thought, were due,
> To Natures, deepliest stain'd with Sin,
> Still to be stirring up anew
> The self-created Hell within;
> The Horror of their Crimes to view,
> To know, & loathe, yet wish & do!
> With such let Fiends make mockery –
> But I – O wherefore this on *me?*
> Frail is my Soul, yea, strengthless wholly,
> Unequal, restless, melancholy;
> But free from Hate, & sensual Folly!
> To live belov'd is all I need,
> And whom I love, I love indeed.[24]

His fellow-feeling with Southey made him hurry on to Edinburgh, which he described as 'a wonderful city' – 'what alternation of Height & Depth! – a city looked at in the polish'd back of a Brobdignag [sic] Spoon, held lengthways – so enormously *stretched-up* are the Houses!' He meant to visit

Walter Scott at Lasswade, just outside the city, but was too ill and too anxious to hurry back to Keswick to comfort Southey. Wordsworth and Dorothy did visit Scott, hearing him read out 'The Lay of the Last Minstrel' and immediately noticing the influence of 'Christabel' on it.[25]

By mid-September Coleridge was back in Keswick, having composed an epitaph for himself at Edinburgh, when in one of his nightly nightmares he dreamt he was dying:

> Here sleeps at length poor Col, & without Screaming,
> Who died, as he had always liv'd, a dreaming:
> Shot dead, while sleeping, by the Gout within,
> Alone, and all unknown, at E'nbro' in an Inn.[26]

The coolness with Wordsworth which had begun in Scotland in August continued on Coleridge's return. He told Poole in October (no doubt aware that Poole would be a willing listener to complaints about Wordsworth) that he now saw 'very little' of Wordsworth. The latter's indolence 'keeps him at home', and Coleridge's health does not allow him to walk over to Grasmere as before. Resentment at Wordsworth's domestic happiness, with a loving wife, sister, and sister-in-law (Sara Hutchinson) dancing attendance on him, makes him bitter. He moralizes about Wordsworth's 'self-involution': 'I saw him more & more benetted in hypochondriacal Fancies, living wholly among *Devotees* – having every the minutest Thing, almost his very Eating & Drinking, done for him by his Sister, or Wife – & I trembled, lest a Film should rise, and thicken on his moral Eye.'[27] Unbecoming as Coleridge's righteous tone may be, he was not alone in noticing how Wordsworth's family circumstances served to intensify his egotism. Henry Crabb Robinson thought he 'never saw a man so happy in *three wives* as Mr Wordsworth is', reported Mary Lamb in 1816 to one of them, Sara Hutchinson.[28]

Nor were relations with Mrs Coleridge much better than before. Though Coleridge was glad to have Southey in his household, the Fricker sisters, all of them inclined to irritability, were a source of misery to him. Filling his notebook on 19 October, a day of fasting decreed by the Government to express the general fear of a French invasion, and two days before his thirty-first birthday, he noted 'a day of Storm/ at dinner an explosion of Temper from the Sisters'. He also expressed his depression – always deepened around his birthday – at having 'done nothing' since his last birthday: 'O for God's sake, let me whip & spur, so that Christmas may not pass without some thing having been done /– at all events to finish The Men & the Times, & to collect them all & all my Newspaper Essays into one Volume/ to collect all my poems, finishing the Vision of the Maid of Orleans, & the Dark Ladie, & make a second Volume/ & to finish Christabel.'[29] For once, the list was a relatively modest one, not obviously beyond his capabilities, though he could not, of course, guarantee the return of *poetic* inspiration. Still, none of it was done.

Coleridge's gradual return to religious orthodoxy was marked by the fact that in November 1803 he had all three children christened, an occasion on which Derwent, aged three, 'slapped the parson's face', as he later remembered.[30] He also wrote in self-consciously extreme terms to the Beaumonts – whom he was keen to cultivate – about his having 'aided the Jacobins' once, before changing his political convictions over the last few years. Extraordinarily, he associated himself with Robert Emmet, an Irish patriot who was executed on 20 September 1803 for leading an uprising during which Lord Kilwarden was murdered. What a seething broth of mixed motives lies behind his melodramatic remarks about this 'poor young Enthusiast' of twenty-four whom he pities as he does his former self. What a strange, yet transparent, way he has of ingratiating himself with a member of the aristocracy:

> My honored Friends! as I live, I scarcely know what I have been writing; but the very circumstance of writing to *you*, added to the recollection of the unwise & unchristian feelings, with which at poor Emmet's Age *I* contemplated all persons of *your* rank in Society, & *that* recollection confronted with my present Feelings towards you – it has agitated me, dear Friends! and I have written, my Heart at a full Gallop adown Hill.[31]

Coleridge still wanted to get away from Keswick, if possible to go abroad, though that was now rendered difficult by the renewal of war. Wordsworth was busy enrolling in the Grasmere Volunteers, as the whole country made preparations for a possible invasion.[32] Coleridge talked patriotically and belligerently in a letter to Poole on 3 October of repelling a French invasion, of acting as 'Men, Christians, Englishmen – down goes the Corsican Miscreant, & Europe may have peace'.[33]

He also reported to Poole on his children, with whom he was now spending longer – nearly three uninterrupted months – than he ever would again. Hartley was still 'an utter Visionary! like the Moon among thin Clouds, he moves in a circle of Light of his own making'. Derwent was 'a fat large lovely Boy', and ten-month-old Sara a fine baby with 'large blue eyes – & she smiles, as if she were basking in a sunshine, as mild as moonlight, of her own quiet Happiness'. As for the women in the house, Mrs Southey 'I hope, is breeding', and the widowed Mrs Lovell is a confirmed hypochondriac. Together they are 'a large, a very large Bolus!' [i.e., pill].[34]

Keeping up his custom of addressing a pre-Christmas letter to Thelwall, he told him on 25 November that he would soon set out for either Malta or Madeira. He asked Thelwall, who was at Kendal, to buy for him 'an Ounce of crude opium, & 9 ounces of Laudanum, the Latter put in a stout bottle & so packed up as that it may travel a few hundred miles with safety'.[35] He obviously expected to be away for a long time, for his thoughts circled round his beloved children. He gave a Bristol acquaintance, Matthew Coates, a picture of Hartley – 'considered as a Genius by Wordsworth, & Southey' – and of Derwent, fat and greedy. Coleridge shows how good, and progressive, a father he might have been if he had himself been more stable and more permanently at home. Of Hartley he says that he is 'very backward in his Book-learning', but 'we have never been anxious about it, taking it for granted that loving me & seeing how I love books, he would come to it of his own accord. And so it has proved. For in the last month he has made more progress than in all his former life.'[36] Poor Hartley, so doted on and making his youthful appearance in fine poems by both Wordsworth and Coleridge, would fall victim to weaknesses inherited from his father, exacerbated by Coleridge's gigantic, brooding absence for large parts of his childhood. Little Sara would see even less of her father, meeting him almost as a stranger in 1823, at the age of twenty.

By 20 December Coleridge was with the Wordsworths at Grasmere, intending to go straight on to London, '& thence to Ottery' to try to borrow money from his brothers for his foreign journey.[37] In fact he did not leave Grasmere until 14 January, as Dorothy explained to her friend Catherine Clarkson: 'Day after day he was detained by sickness, or bad weather, or both, (for when the weather was damp or wet he never failed to be very ill) and yesterday he left us in indifferent health, though on a fine sunny morning.'[38] Before he left, Wordsworth read to him 'the second Part [Book] of his divine Self-biography [*The Prelude*]'.[39] Coleridge was so affected by this that he asked Wordsworth and Dorothy to copy out all of Wordsworth's poems for him to take abroad with him. And, anticipating his sustained appreciative criticism of Wordsworth's poetry in *Biographia Literaria*, as well as his remarks there on Shakespeare and Milton, he wrote to a London acquaintance, Richard Sharp, on 15 January 1804:

> Wordsworth is a Poet, a most original Poet – he no more resembles Milton than Milton resembles Shakespere – no more resembles Shakespere than Shakespere resembles Milton – he is himself: and I dare affirm that he will hereafter be admitted as the first & greatest philosophical Poet – the only man who has effected a compleat and constant synthesis of Thought & Feeling and combined them with Poetic Forms, with the music of pleasurable passion and with Imagination or the *modifying* Power in that highest sense of the word in which I have ventured to oppose it to Fancy, or the *aggregating* power – in that sense in which it is a dim Analogue of Creation, not all that we can *believe* but all that we can *conceive* of the creation.[40]

Once in London at the end of January, Coleridge took up again with his usual acquaintances. He lodged in Westminster with Poole, who was staying in London while he helped compile statistics on the poor for John Rickman, and saw Lamb, Davy and Godwin socially. On one occasion he drank too much punch and quarrelled with Godwin over Southey, whom Godwin accused of egotism. Coleridge 'thundered and lightened' at him 'with a vengeance, for more than an hour & a half', then apologized the next day, though he enjoyed telling Wordsworth and Southey how he had trounced the 'philosophicide'.[41]

Sir James Mackintosh, who had helped him get employment on the *Morning Post* in 1798, now offered to find him a job in India, where he was about to take up the post of Recorder of Bombay.[42] But Coleridge hated Mackintosh. He had attended Mackintosh's philosophical lectures in London early in 1801 and found them hackneyed and strained – 'the Steam of an Excrement' – and was now very scathing about this offer, finding an apt allusion in *Tristram Shandy*: 'I have called on Sir James Mackintosh who offered me his endeavors to procure me a place under him in India – of which endeavors he could not for a moment doubt the success – and assured me – *on his Honor* – *on his Soul*!!! (N.B. HIS Honor!!) (N.B. *his* Soul!!) that he was sincere. – Lillibullero – whoo! whoo! whoo! – Good Morning, Sir James.'[43]

Mackintosh was not the only *alter ego* Coleridge attacked in this forceful way; in February he met his old fellow Pantisocrat George Burnett, and reported that his eyes looked 'thoroughly those of an Opium-chewer'. A year earlier he had gone further in a letter to Southey: 'For myself, I have no heart to spare for a Coxcomb mad with vanity & stupified with opium.' And 'I grieve sincerely that there should be such helpless self-tormenting Tormentors.'[44]

A few political articles about the war and Addington's administration, probably by Coleridge, appeared in Daniel Stuart's new evening paper, the *Courier*, in February and March 1804, followed in April by a short dramatic poem satirizing the recent coalition of former enemies Pitt, Fox, Grey and Grenville. In a parody of the witches in *Macbeth*, the refrain runs:

> Double, double toil and trouble,
> Coalition Cauldron bubble.[45]

By 12 March Coleridge had settled on Malta and Sicily as his destinations. Rickman arranged a passage for him on the merchant brig *Speedwell*, due to leave from Portsmouth at the end of March. He borrowed £100 from Sotheby, with Wordsworth standing as security.[46] His acquaintance from his year in Germany, George Bellas Greenough, let him read his 'Journal of his Sights, Doings, and Done-untos in Sicily', and Humphry Davy, too, inspired him with a desire to see Mount Etna.[47] Davy wrote him a warm letter of farewell, expressing his gratitude for Coleridge's conversation and correspondence:

In whatever part of the World you are, you will often live with me, not as a fleeting idea but as a *recollection* possessed of creative energy, as an *Imagination* winged with fire inspiriting and rejoicing. –
You must not live much longer without giving to *all men* the *proof of power*, which those who know you feel in admiration . . . you are to be the historian of the Philosophy of feeling – do not in any way dissipate your noble nature / Do not give up your birth-right. –
May you soon recover perfect health; the health of strength and happiness! May you soon return to us confirmed in all the powers essential to the exertion of *genius* – You were born for your Country and your native land must be the scene of your activity. I shall expect the time when *your spirit*

bursting through the clouds of ill health will appear to *all men* not as an uncertain and brilliant *flame* but as a fair and permanent *light*, fixed though constantly in motion, as a sun which gives its fire not only to its attendant *Planets*; but which sends *beams* from all its *parts* into all worlds . . .[48]

So wrote the inspired chemist to the man he recognized as a kindred spirit.

Davy's were not the only kind words sent to Coleridge on the eve of his departure. Heartfelt letters went in both directions between Coleridge and many friends – Lamb, Southey, the Wordsworths, Sotheby, Stuart (but not Poole, who Coleridge complained had cooled towards him[49]). All of them believed he might not live. The Beaumonts offered money, declaring that they had 'gained from you and Wordsworth' advantages which 'more than a million times repay the trifling attentions we had it in our power to shew you both'.[50] Sir George commissioned a portrait of Coleridge from the painter James Northcote (see plate 13). Coleridge was ill, and probably sat only once, on 25 March.[51] The portrait shows Coleridge staring, melancholy, fat-faced, nearly hopeless; it is complemented by a notebook entry he made probably on the very day of the sitting: 'N. B. Opium always in the day-time increases the puffing Asthma, eye closing, & startlings.'[52]

To Sara Hutchinson Coleridge wrote on 10 March, sending a curious pen portrait of one of his favourite seventeenth-century authors, Sir Thomas Browne, and referring particularly to *Urn Burial*, Browne's famous essay on funeral rites. Coleridge may well have been conscious that he was describing a man with whom he himself had close affinities:

> A feeling Heart conjoined with a mind of active curiosity –: the natural & becoming egotism of a man, who loving other men as himself, gains the habit & the privilege of talking about himself as familiarly as about other men. Fond of the Curious, and a Hunter of Oddities & Strangenesses, while he conceived himself with quaint & humorous Gravity a useful enquirer into physical Truth & fundamental Science, he loved to contemplate & discuss his own Thoughts & Feelings, because *they* too were *curiosities.*[53]

His wife received a letter written from Portsmouth on 1 April, telling her that he was waiting for the arrival of the *Speedwell*, which would be accompanied by a man-of-war as convoy. He addressed her, summoning up as much warmth as he could, as 'the attentive and excellent Mother of my children'.[54]

Sara's brother-in-law and protector, the severe Southey, allowed himself a rare expression of strong feeling, though not to the departing Coleridge himself. He described to a female friend his emotion at Coleridge's leaving, perhaps never to return, and his description contains an astute analysis of his own and Coleridge's different temperaments:

> Coleridge is gone for Malta, and his departure affects me more than I let be seen. Let what will trouble me, I bear a calm face; and if the Boiling Well

could be drawn (which, however it heaves and is agitated below, presents a smooth, undisturbed surface), that should be my emblem. It is now almost ten years since he and I first met, in my rooms at Oxford, which meeting decided the destiny of both; and now, when, after so many ups and downs, I am, for a time, settled under his roof, he is driven abroad in search of health. Ill he is, certainly and sorely ill; yet I believe if his mind was as well regulated as mine, the body would be quite as manageable. I am perpetually pained and mortified by thinking what he ought to be, for mine is an eye of microscopic discernment to the faults of my friends; but the tidings of his death would come upon me more like a stroke of lightning than any evil I have ever yet endured; almost it would make me superstitious, for we were two ships that left port in company.[55]

As for the Wordsworths, they wrote that their hearts were 'full of you'. Wordsworth had now completed five books of *The Prelude*, and Dorothy wrote simply that 'William has begun another Part of the Poem addressed to you', her habitual description of the poem which was only given its final title after Wordsworth's death in 1850.[56] She added that Wordsworth had written 'some very affecting Lines', namely the fine paragraph in Book VI outlining Coleridge's history as a city schoolboy progressing towards the same profession of poet by a different route from Wordsworth himself. The section opens with an apt expression of wishes for the voyage to Malta, in which Wordsworth plays on the name of Coleridge's ship:

> Far art thou wandered now in search of health,
> And milder breezes – melancholy lot –
> But thou art with us, with us in the past,
> The present, with us in the times to come.
> There is no grief, no sorrow, no despair,
> No languor, no dejection, no dismay,
> No absence scarcely can there be, for those
> Who love as we do. Speed thee well! divide
> Thy pleasure with us; thy returning strength,
> Receive it daily as a joy of ours;
> Share with us thy fresh spirits, whether gift
> Of gales Etesian or of loving thoughts.[57]

The letters of Dorothy and Wordsworth were to be haunted for the next two years, as were those of Lamb and his sister, by anxiety and hope about Coleridge's health. He was setting off ill, depressed and alone on a journey which held many hazards, not least the state of war which made a military convoy a necessary protection for the *Speedwell*, which finally set sail with a fair wind on 9 April 1804.

Monday, April 9th, really set sail. In weighing anchor the men grumbled aloud a sort of mutiny – not half our complement of men – Two pressed in the Downs/ one ran away at Portsmouth, a rascal of a one-armed Cook better gone than stay'd/ – now we are Captain, Mate, 2 boys, 4 men, 3 passengers, one Sheep, 3 pigs, several Ducks & Chicken, 1 Dog, a Cat & 2 Kittens. – Was sickish & feverish for a few Hours on Monday; but mended before dinner, eat [sic] a better dinner than my usual – and continued well . . . No Health or Happiness without Work . . . On Monday night we travelled like a Top Bough on a Larch Tree in a high wind/ pitching & rocking at anchor in a Breeze that would have carried us 9 or 10 knots an hour.

So began Coleridge's journal aboard ship. He was determined to start a new work routine, as he confided to his notebook the following day:

1.   Up – wash – ginger Tea hot.
2.   Italian till Breakfast time.
3   Breakfast
4   Write or transcribe my Journal.
5th   read the Theodicee & take notes for my Consolations.
6th   Then write my Letters on literary Detraction/ or a review of Wordsworth/ in short, *something, beginning with this.*
7th   between dinner & tea what I can/. Read some Italian if possible. After tea till bed time try to compose. God grant me fortitude & a perseverant Spirit of Industry! –[58]

But illness, homesickness and jealousy got in the way of his best resolutions. He confessed to 'sickly thoughts' about the Wordsworths, fancying Mary dead and Wordsworth marrying Sara Hutchinson, an event which interestingly reflects not only his own terrible fears that Sara might marry and his jealousy of Wordsworth's good luck with women, but also the way his imagination played with a taboo almost as severe as that of incest, namely the marriage to one's deceased wife's sister, which was prohibited by the Anglican Church.[59] His notebooks, during his absence from home, became more and more the repository of his hopeless feelings about Sara. She appears not only as 'Asra' but now also as 'Isulia', and his dreams of her were guilty ones, being 'Xst Hospitalized' in the 'forms & incidents'.[60]

Coleridge also referred to this long voyage more and more often in terms of 'The Ancient Mariner', minutely noticing phenomena of sea and sky and climate, and on one occasion describing a ship's boy 'running up to the Main Top with a large Leg of Mutton swung, Albatross-fashion about his neck'.[61] When he reprinted the poem in *Sibylline Leaves* (1817), certain minor changes drew on his observations on this voyage.[62] He also commented retrospectively on the mariner's killing of the albatross when he saw a hawk alighting on the ship and being shot at: 'Poor Hawk! O Strange Lust of Murder in Man! – It is not cruelty/ it is more non-feeling from non-thinking.'[63]

On 18 May, nearly six weeks after setting out, he arrived in Malta, having suffered terrible bouts of seasickness and agonizing constipation in the last days of the journey.[64] The approach to his destination made him record his hope and prayers for a new beginning. 'O dear God', he wrote, 'give me strength of Soul to make one thorough Trial.' His aim was to 'go through one month of unstimulated Nature' in spite of 'all horrors'. Coleridge now knew too well the pain and difficulty of withdrawal from opium as well as the horror of dependence on it. In this prayer he combined a flash of self-knowledge with an expression of religious orthodoxy. The man who knows himself sinful and in need of spiritual aid requires a stern but loving God to vouchsafe that aid: 'I am loving & kind-hearted & cannot do wrong with impunity, but o! I am very, very weak – from my infancy have been so – & I exist for the moment! – Have mercy on me, have mercy on me, Father & God! omnipresent, incomprehensible, who with undeviating Laws eternal yet carest for the falling of a feather from the Sparrow's Wing. – Sunday Midnight, May 13th, 1804.'[65]

Coleridge became Stoddart's guest, and now wrote to his wife giving an account of the journey, his sickness, and his first impressions of Valetta.[66] Because of the distance, and the extra difficulty caused by the war, he could not be sure when his letters would arrive or when he would receive letters from home. The process, as had been the case during his stay in Germany, took months, and Coleridge was often frantic for lack of news of his family, while Wordsworth, Southey and other friends at home anxiously asked one another if anything had been heard of their absent friend. The first letter to his wife did not reach her till the end of August, over three months after it was sent.[67]

Unfortunately Coleridge arrived unannounced at Stoddart's house. Mary Lamb wrote to Stoddart's sister Sarah, who was staying with her brother in Malta (and who was to marry Hazlitt in 1808, making a pair as unsuited as ever Coleridge and *his* Sara were) thanking her for her 'kind reception of the forlorn wanderer'.[68] But Coleridge did not find her welcome at all kind. She reminded him of his wife in her reaction to his sudden arrival when neither Stoddart nor his wife was at home. Though she knew he had come, she took more than an hour to come down and receive him – 'O ipsissima!' – and refused to send a servant 'to the next street to inform St[oddart] of my arrival'.[69]

After this inauspicious beginning, he was given a warm welcome by the Stoddarts. But something caused a cooling between them. Mrs Stoddart gave birth to a daughter less than a week after Coleridge's arrival, and the child died on 5 June, so that the presence of a house-guest, particularly one who was himself ill and probably demanding, must have been a trial. At any rate, Coleridge did not stay long in their household. By early July he had got to know Sir Alexander Ball, the Governor of Malta, whom he described enthusiastically as 'the abstract Idea of a wise & good Governor' and on whom he immediately exercised his charm. Much later, in 1834, he described Malta in 1804 as 'an Augean stable' and Sir Alexander as having 'all the inclination to be a Hercules'.[70]

Ball's task was a difficult one, and Coleridge admired his efforts, though he was not impressed by the other administrative officials he met in Malta, Naples and Sicily. He recalled in 1833 that as a young man he had thought that 'ministers and men in office must of course know much better than any private person could possibly do' about the details of administration. It was not until he went to Malta that he discovered 'the extreme shallowness and ignorance with which men of some note too were able to carry on the government of important departments of the Empire'.[71]

Coleridge moved into the Governor's Palace on 6 July in high hopes of getting a salaried secretarial post under Ball. Indeed he was already active in preparing dispatches to London, and was soon Private Secretary to Sir Alexander Ball, at £25 a month, rising to Public Secretary in January 1805 on the death of the previous incumbent, Alexander Macaulay.[72] Coleridge appears not to have recorded his feelings at having to send these reports to a British Government led once more by his old enemy William Pitt, who had ousted Addington in May 1804.[73]

The Malta notebooks record Coleridge's study of the Italian language, his conversations on current affairs with Ball, and his observations on the flora and fauna of the region. He does not seem to have been particularly interested in the architecture he found in Malta, or even in that of Sicily and Rome, which he was also to visit. Cottle later expressed his surprise at this relative lack of interest in the otherwise all-curious Coleridge: 'On his return from Italy, and after having resided for some time in *Rome*, I remember his describing to me the state of society; the characters of the Pope and Cardinals; the gorgeous ceremonies, with the superstitions of the people, but not one word did he utter concerning St. Peter's, the Vatican, or the numerous *antiquities* of the place.'[74]

Several of his letters, and some letters to him, never reached their destinations. On 4 August he wrote despairingly to Southey that he had received 'NO LETTERS, some evil chance having intercepted them or sent them to the Fleet off Toulon'.[75]

On 10 August Coleridge visited Sicily to prepare reports for Sir Alexander Ball and to see the sights as a privileged tourist. Prepared by his discussions with Davy and his reading of Greenough's journal, he climbed Mount Etna on 19 August. G. F. Leckie, the English consul in Sicily, took him to the opera and held parties at which Coleridge was guiltily aware that he talked too much and too indiscreetly.[76] He flirted with an opera singer, Cecilia Bertozzoli, whom he met at Leckie's. In 1808, looking back, he remembered that only a 'heavenly vision' of Sara Hutchinson's face, appearing as 'the guardian Angel of my Innocence and Peace of mind', had saved him from seducing, or being seduced by, the 'too fascinating Siren, against whose witcheries Ulysses' Wax would have proved but a Half-protection'.[77]

October 1804 was miserable, not just because of his guilty flirtation, but because it was the month of his unfortunate, and Wordsworth's fortunate, marriage, and of his birthday. His notebook entry once more speaks of his anguish at having passed another year, his thirty-second, without achieving anything. Worse, his efforts to do without opium had failed. 'Body & mind, habit of bedrugging the feelings, & bodily movements, & habit of dreaming without distinct or rememberable' – here the manuscript breaks off, four leaves having been torn out by Coleridge or one of his executors.[78] He noticed that poppies were grown for opium in Sicily, and that the island also abounded in Indian hemp plants.[79] He found it all too easy to acquire the drugs he had been hoping to do without.

At home, his friends waited for letters and feared bad news. In October 1804 Coleridge's kind landlord Mr Jackson sold Greta Hall to a Mr White who, according to Dorothy, 'brought his wife with him and a *Mistress* in Boy's Clothes'. Mr White gave the Southeys and Coleridges notice to quit at Whitsun 1805. Dorothy was sorry for 'poor Mrs Coleridge' and knew Coleridge would be 'heart-struck at the thought of no more returning to his old Books in their old Book-case looking to Skiddaw'.[80] The Wordsworths declared themselves ready to leave Dove Cottage, which was too small for them now that children were being born, and, more surprisingly, to leave even their beloved Lake District altogether, in order to move to 'any place' where Coleridge might choose to settle with his family on his return.[81]

Coleridge was indeed dashed to hear the news about Greta Hall, as he told Southey in February 1805, though by that time the threat had been lifted, as the sale to the odious Mr White had fallen through.[82] To Southey Coleridge also confessed to an act of morbidity which he was increasingly to indulge in. Having waited so long for letters from home, he was 'so agitated' by the receipt of some at last that he could not bring himself to open them for two or three days, 'half-dreaming that from there being no Letter from Mrs C., some one of the Children had died'.[83] Thus in order to avoid immediate pain, he kept himself in an agony of suspense. This supersensitivity about his family and friends was compatible in Coleridge with a strange coolness towards them which Southey noticed also in young Hartley, 'the oddest of all God's creatures'. 'In one part of his character', wrote Southey in January 1805, 'he seems to me strikingly to resemble his father, – in the affection he has for those who are present with him, and the little he cares about them when he is out of their sight.'[84]

Coleridge had returned to Malta from Sicily in November 1804, and by early 1805 subscribed himself, as he told Southey, 'Segretario Publico dell'Isole de Malta, Gozo, e delle loro dipendenze' (see plate 14). He now sealed his letters with a signet bearing the imprints 'ΕΣΤΗΣΕ' and 'STC'.[85] Though his letters seem mostly cheerful, the notebooks tell a story of daily, or rather nightly, despair. On 23 December 1804 he noted an excruciating bout of colic and blamed himself for a 'stupid drunken Letter to Southey' (now lost). He also expressed a brave wish that his notebooks should not be destroyed, but should stand as a monument to his shame and yet also to his claim to have his case viewed charitably: 'O friend! Truth! Truth! but yet Charity! I have never loved Evil for its own sake; no! nor ever sought pleasure for its own sake, but only as a means of escaping the pains that coiled round my mental powers, as a serpent around the body & wings of an Eagle! My sole sensuality was *not* to be in pain!'[86] A few days after writing this confession, Coleridge began the practice of using a secret cipher for entries to do with opium and Sara Hutchinson. The entry for 27

December, composed entirely of numbers, has been deciphered to read simply 'no night without its guilt of opium and spirit!'[87]

At this time, too, Coleridge anatomized his habits as a licensed talker, seeing both the advantages and the disadvantages of his extraordinary gift, and incidentally giving an example in the analysis of the very fault he is describing. He is one of those 'talkative fellows' who

> use five hundred more ideas, images, reasons &c than there is any need of to arrive at their object/ till the only object arrived at is that the mind's eye of the bye-stander is dazzled with colors succeeding so rapidly as to leave one vague impression that there has been a great Blaze of colours all about something. Now this is my case – & a grievous fault it is/ my illustrations swallow up my thesis – I feel too intensely the omnipresence of all in each, platonically speaking – or psychologically my brain-fibres, or the spiritual Light which abides in the brain marrow as visible Light appears to do in sundry rotten mackerel & other *smashy* matters, is of too general an affinity with all things/ and tho' it perceives the *difference* of things, yet is eternally pursuing the likenesses, or rather that which is common/ bring me two things that seem the very same, & then I am quick enough to shew the difference, even to hair-splitting – but to go on from circle to circle till I break against the shore of my Hearer's patience, or have my Concentricals dashed to nothing by a Snore – that is my ordinary mishap.[88]

None of those who complained of his endless talk – not even Carlyle in his famous image of being a passive bucket to be filled by the stream of Coleridge's eloquence – described it with greater acuity than this.

The Malta notebooks contain more painful self-analysis than Coleridge recorded at any other period of a life of habitual self-contemplation. He was among strangers, away from home, cut off from love and facing his own self-loathing. His rather virulent anti-Catholicism, which he discovered in observing the rituals and superstitions of the Maltese, made it impossible that he should make close friendships.[89] We have seen that he despised most of the British officials he met. The feelings he dared not express in letters found a place in the notebooks. On 11 January 1805 he went through his life, seeing dread as a thread running from his childhood on, so that

> perhaps all my faulty actions have been the consequence of some Dread of other on my mind/ from fear of Pain, or Shame, not from prospect of Pleasure/– so in my childhood & Boyhood the horror of being detected with a sorehead [sic]; afterwards imaginary fears of having the Itch in my Blood – / then a short-lived Fit of Fears from sex – then horror of DUNS, & a state of struggling with madness from an incapability of hoping that I should be able to marry Mary Evans . . . Then came that stormy time/ and for a few months America really inspired Hope, & I became an exalted Being – then came Rob. Southey's alienation/ my marriage – constant dread in my mind respecting Mrs Coleridge's Temper, &c – and finally stimulants in the fear & prevention

of violent Bowel-attacks from mental agitation/ then almost epileptic night-horrors in my sleep/ & since then every error I have committed, has been the immediate effect of the Dread of these bad most shocking Dreams – any thing to prevent them.[90]

The same entry describes how 'the least languor expressed in a Letter from S. H. drives me wild/ & it is most unfortunate that I so fearfully despondent should have concentered my soul thus on one almost as feeble in Hope as myself'. Unfortunate for Sara Hutchinson too. She could not give him hope, as he knew, but her attempts to write neutrally sank his spirits disproportionately.

In February 1805 Coleridge began to talk in letters of coming home in a month or so, if a convoy became available.[91] But he was now Public Secretary to Sir Alexander Ball until a permanent successor to Macaulay could be found, and with Nelson and Napoleon's fleet on a war footing in the Mediterranean Coleridge found himself quite busy in strategic Malta. He was still not writing poetry or his metaphysical work, though his notebooks are full of transcriptions of German and Italian poetry, and in February he copied down from memory several of Shakespeare's sonnets, particularly those on the theme of absence.[92] He also made entries on philosophy and religion, describing his path from Unitarianism, the religion of a man 'whose Reason would make him an Atheist but whose Heart and Common sense will not permit him to be so', through Spinozism to 'Plato and St. John/ No Christ, No God!'[93]

He needed to cling to his faith. March 1805 was not the month in which he set out for home, but rather the time when he reached new depths of dejection. He fantasized about being permitted to make love to Sara Hutchinson, and ended up begging to awake from the despair and guilt to which the fantasy gave rise.[94] Then on 31 March he met Lady Ball in her drawing-room and was told abruptly that Wordsworth's brother John, Captain of the *Earl of Abergavenny*, had gone down on 5 February near Portland Bill with his ship and about three hundred men.[95] Wordsworth and Dorothy were deeply affected by the loss of their favourite brother, and they knew that Coleridge would be too. Wordsworth told Sir George Beaumont that he 'trembled for the moment when he is to hear of my Brothers death, it will distress him to the heart, and his poor body cannot bear sorrow. He loved my Brother, and he knows how we at Grasmere loved him.'[96]

The bad news had indeed caused Coleridge to turn pale: 'I was nearly strangled.' He thought of the Wordsworths, and of Sara Hutchinson, who had apparently been near to engagement with John Wordsworth in 1800, an event which Coleridge had willed himself to face with unselfish pleasure.[97] He also associated John with himself, as a traveller submitting himself to the hazards of the sea:

O William, O Dorothy, Dorothy! – Mary – & you loved him so! – and o blessed Sara, you whom in my imagination at one time I so often connected with him,

by an effort of agonizing Virtue, willing it with cold sweat-drops on my Brow!
– How shall I ever visit Langdale/ O it will look like an hollow Vault – like a
Cenotaph . . . God forgive me! – I for myself despair of ever seeing my home.
They are expecting me – did they not even so expect him! –[98]

The Wordsworths, who were in any case expecting Coleridge to make his
way home soon, thought he would be the more in a hurry to return to
comfort them for the loss of John. But as in the case of Berkeley's death
while he was in Germany, he lingered on for several months in Malta. The
delay was, to be fair, not entirely the result of wilful neglect or inability to
face grief. He was obliged to fulfil his secretarial duties, and he could only
leave when a suitable convoy became available. He told Stuart on 1 May that
his heart was 'almost broken that I could not go home this Convoy' and that
he had resolved to return home overland by way of Naples, Ancona, Trieste
and Germany at the end of May, if possible.[99]

He was upset to learn that several of his letters home had been lost when
the ship taking them was captured by the French on 3 February.[100] As late
as 21 July he was writing to his wife of his improved health but dejected
spirits, telling her he had been hoping to get away for five months past, but
his replacement as Public Secretary had not arrived, and 'Sir Alexander's
Importunities always overpowered me'.[101] He did not know that his friend
and benefactor Tom Wedgwood had died on 10 July. Sara Coleridge wrote
to Josiah in October, saying she had not told Coleridge, 'knowing how
much mischief things of that nature occasion him – he kept his bed for a
fortnight after being suddenly told of the fate of his friend Captain John
Wordsworth'.[102]

During the summer Coleridge experienced upheavals both external and
internal. On 3 July he recorded an earthquake which 'shook my bed like a
strong arm'. Two weeks later he noted 'the generation of violent Anger, in
dreams, in consequence of any pain or distressful sensation in the bowels or
lower parts of the Stomach'.[103] He was driven to anger also by the 'noisiness'
of the Maltese, particularly during religious festivals. He was never more
John Bullish than in his comments on the Maltese celebration of Easter and
other religious occasions – 'the immense *Noise* & Jingle Jangle, as if to
frighten away the Daemon, Common-sense'. He remembered his own
dread of the Easter holiday at Christ's Hospital, and thought it might have
its origin even further back:

> It is a subject not unworthy of meditation to myself, what the reason is that
> these sounds & bustles of Holidays, Fairs, Easter-mondays, & Tuesdays, &
> Christmas Days, even when I was a Child & when I was at Christ-Hospital,
> always made me so heart-sinking, so melancholy? Is it, that from my Habits, or
> my want of money all the first two or three and 20 years of my Life I have been
> *alone* at such times? – that by poor Frank's dislike of me when a little Child I
> was even from Infancy forced to be by myself?[104]

Meanwhile Wordsworth was eagerly awaiting his return. 'The expectation of Coleridge not a little unhinges me', he confessed to Sir George Beaumont in October 1805. He had finished *The Prelude*, the poem addressed to Coleridge, in May, despite his grief.[105] He had hoped to read his poem to his brother; he longed for Coleridge to come home and hear it.

Coleridge was finally enabled to leave Malta by the arrival of the new Public Secretary in September. On the 23rd of that month he set off, planning to sail from Messina to Naples, then travel on to Rome and Venice, hoping to keep out of the clutches of the French, who had several of the northern states of Italy in their control.[106] Travel was slow, and Coleridge stopped to enjoy the hospitality of the consul in Sicily. By mid-October he was poised to leave Messina, but his proposed overland route through Italy was made impossible by new victories of Bonaparte.[107] None of his letters survive from this journey home, which would take months, not weeks, to complete.

On the night of 15 October, while still in Messina, he made the 'melancholy observation' that he now had a prominent abdomen.[108] (At the same time, back home, Dorothy Wordsworth was observing to Lady Beaumont that Mrs Coleridge was growing 'exceedingly fat'.[109]) His birthday, 21 October, brought more expressions of despair. It was also the day of the Battle of Trafalgar, at which Nelson died. Coleridge travelled, perhaps with British troops, to Naples, arriving on 20 November.[110] There he visited the classical sites, including Virgil's tomb outside the city.[111]

On Christmas Day 1805 Coleridge set out for Rome, leaving behind most of his books and manuscripts because of the hazards of journeying in such uncertain times.[112] He met several artists and their patron, the Prussian minister to the Vatican, Wilhelm von Humboldt. He also became acquainted with the German writer and translator of Shakespeare, Ludwig Tieck. Rome had more interesting society than Malta, and Coleridge dallied there for some time. On 1 January 1806 he noted that he had heard that the arrival of French troops was expected in four days. As a recent employee of the British Government he was in particular danger of arrest. He wrote simply 'To stay or not to stay?'[113] He stayed.

Washington Allston, an American painter, invited him to his house at Olevano Romano, thirty miles from Rome. Allston painted Coleridge and discussed art with him, remembering years later how he walked and talked with Coleridge in Rome (where Coleridge did take an interest in the architecture in his conversations with Allston):

> To no other man whom I have known, do I owe so much intellectually, as to
> Mr. Coleridge, with whom I became acquainted in Rome . . . He used to call
> Rome the *silent* city; but I never could think of it as such, while with him; for,
> meet him when, or where I would, the fountain of his mind was never dry, but
> like the far-reaching acqueducts that once supplied this mistress of the world,
> its living streams seemed specially to flow for every classic ruin over which we

wandered. And when I recall some of our walks under the pines of the Villa
Borghese, I am almost tempted to dream that I once listened to Plato, in the
groves of the Academy. It was there he taught me this golden rule: *never to
judge any work of art by its defects*; a rule as wise as benevolent; and one that while
it has spared me much pain, has widened my sphere of pleasure.[114]

Coleridge's notebooks show that his interest in architecture was aroused
by his keeping company with Allston. Though a self-confessedly
wretched artist, he drew a Roman arch in his notebook and entered some
brief notes on the 'true Ideal' in art, instancing Michaelangelo's 'despairing Woman at the bottom of the Last Judgment' in the Sistine Chapel.[115]
He also described appreciatively Allston's picture of Diana and her
Nymphs in the Chase, a landscape with figures in the style of Claude
Lorrain.[116]

On 18 May 1806 Coleridge finally left Rome in the company of an
English art student, Thomas Russell. He later claimed that Napoleon
had sent an order for his arrest, but it seems more likely that a general
order went out for the expulsion of British citizens from papal territory.[117]
In Florence he visited the Uffizi Gallery, but was 'dangerously ill', as he
told Allston in a letter of 17 June. 'This day at Noon we set off for Leghorn',
he added, though 'Heaven knows, whether Leghorn may not be
blockaded/ However we go thither & shall go to England in an American
ship.'[118]

At Leghorn on 7 June, while waiting to board a ship, Coleridge gave vent
to one of his morbid anxieties about his children: 'O my Children –
Whether, and which of you are dead, whether any, & which among you, are
alive, I know not/ and were a Letter to arrive this moment from Keswick I
fear, that I should be unable to open it, so deep and black is my Despair.'
Thoughts of suicide indicate the extremity to which he had come, dreading
the journey back, aware that his health was no better than when he had
set out more than two years before, that his opium habit remained
unconquered, and that – apart from amassing a formidable amount of
miscellaneous matter in his notebooks – he had written nothing:

> Even this moment I could commit Suicide but for you, my Darlings (of
> Wordsworths – of Sara Hutchinson/ that is *passed* – or of remembered
> thoughts to make a Hell of/) O me! now racked with pain, now fallen abroad
> & suffocated with a sense of intolerable Despair/ & no other Refuge than
> Poisons that degrade the Being, while they suspend the torment, and which
> suspend only to make the blow fall heavier.[119]

He had indeed become the type of his Ancient Mariner. The additions
to the poem which he made in 1817 may well have originated with his
double experience of a lengthy sea voyage and real inner despair. He had
been scarcely hopeful on the journey *to* Malta; he was much less so now that
he was coming home. New lines such as the following, personifying natural
phenomena into vengeful fiends, catch this mood:

And now the STORM-BLAST came, and he
Was tyrannous and strong:
He struck with his o'ertaking wings,
And chased us south along.

With sloping masts and dipping prow,
As who pursued with yell and blow
Still treads the shadow of his foe,
And forward bends his head,
The ship drove fast, loud roared the blast,
And southward aye we fled.[120]

On 23 June he and Russell sailed for home on the American ship the *Gosport*. As on the outward journey, so on the homeward one he suffered from constipation, the Captain having to use instruments and brute strength to remove an obstruction from his rectum.[121] He arrived, more dead than alive, on English soil on 17 August. Characteristically, he neither made straight for Keswick nor wrote to his wife. She had, of course, been one of the chief reasons for delaying his homecoming. He was edging towards a showdown with her about a separation, but could not face it. The Wordsworths, whose letters for more than a year had expressed hourly expectation of his return, anxiety about his health, and a strong desire to read him *The Prelude*, were disappointed, though not wholly surprised, that he neither wrote nor came to them.

Coleridge did write to Southey from London on 20 August, saying that he was ill, 'shirtless, & almost penniless', and was about to move in temporarily with the Lambs.[122] It is rather a mystery why he should have had no money, since he had received a salary at Malta and had lived as a guest of Sir Alexander Ball's. But then, it always *was* a mystery how Coleridge managed to be quite so desperate financially most of the time. Many of his belongings were lost *en route* – some of his political papers having been thrown overboard when the *Gosport* was boarded by a Spanish privateer – and others had been deliberately left behind at Malta or Sicily.[123] Some of his clothes and papers had been packed by mistake in his companion Russell's trunk.[124] Coleridge used this last accident as an excuse to delay going home.

He seems to have asked Mary Lamb to write to Wordsworth and Southey urging them to persuade his wife to agree to a separation. Mary wrote sheepishly to Dorothy on 29 August that she had received a letter from Mrs Coleridge 'telling me as joyful news, that her husband is arrived' [i.e., in England], 'and I feel it very wrong in me even in the remotest degree to do anything to prevent her seeing that husband – she and her husband being the only people who ought to be concerned in the affair'.[125]

Another London friend Coleridge looked up was Daniel Stuart, who was on holiday in Margate but lent him money and offered him the use of his house at Brompton. Coleridge accepted gratefully, confessing abjectly that he was in fear that Wordsworth would 'come up to town, after me', much as Southey had done so many years before.[126] It was a prescient fear. On 8 September Wordsworth wrote to Sir George Beaumont:

> What shall I say of Coleridge? or what can I say? My dear friend this is certain, that he is destined to be unhappy . . . In fact, he dare not go home, he recoils so much from the thought of domesticating with Mrs. Coleridge, with whom, though on many accounts he much respects her, he is so miserable that he dare not encounter it. What a deplorable thing! I have written to him to say that if he does not come down immediately I must insist upon seeing him somewhere. If he appoints London, I shall go. I believe if any thing good is to be done for him, it must be done by me.[127]

Coleridge shuttled between London and Margate, taking in a short visit to the Clarksons in Essex. He was negotiating to contribute to Stuart's *Courier*, though his only piece published at this time was a sonnet modelled on one by the Elizabethan poet, Fulke Greville, 'Farewell to Love', which appeared in the paper on 27 September. Its theme represents a stiffening of his resolve to renounce all thoughts of Sara Hutchinson as expressed in his notebook in Leghorn when on the brink of returning to England. The final couplet reads:

> O grief! – but farewell, Love! I will go play me
> With thoughts that please me less, and less betray me.[128]

This resolution notwithstanding, his route from London to the Lakes took him via Penrith, where he hoped to see Sara.

But this was not for some weeks yet. He finally addressed his wife on 16 September, half promising to go home in the next week or two, but saying he might have to stay in London to give a course of lectures at the Royal Institution, and using the confusion over his books and papers as an excuse. 'Be assured', he told her, 'I feel with deep tho' sad affection toward you', and he signed himself, 'your faithful, tho' long absent, Husband'.[129] Five more letters were sent off to her, explaining and excusing his delay. There was a tale – not necessarily invented, but transparently given more importance than was in common sense necessary – of some attar of roses and Roman pearls he had bought for her, which the captain of the *Gosport* had promised, but failed, to return to him. There was his lack of a clean shirt, and there was the ever-present fact of his ill health.[130]

In the midst of this time of bad faith, Coleridge found the energy to write to his wife's younger brother, George Fricker, explaining why he had rejected Unitarianism. In a nutshell, the cause was his 'sense of our fallen nature; and the incapability of man to heal himself'.[131] He also began to take note of the publication (in 1805) of Scott's *Lay of the Last Minstrel,* asking Sara if Southey had found any resemblance to 'Christabel' in it. 'I have not read the L. myself; but at least half a dozen (among others Davy, Lamb, Mrs Clarkson, Miss Smith) have mentioned it.'[132] What Sara

Coleridge, who was not the least bit interested in her husband's poetry, but *was* anxious to see him come home, made of this we can only guess.

At last Coleridge set off from London on 9 October, but he proceeded indirectly by way of a visit to the Clarksons at Bury St Edmunds, where he wrote about the 'difference between the Reason, and the Understanding', or 'Vernunft' and 'Verstand' (Kant's terms), and repeated his view that Unitarianism was like atheism and Spinozism – 'no Sun, no Light with vivifying Warmth, but a cold and dull moonshine, or rather starlight, which shews itself but shews nothing else'.[133] From Bury he paid a brief visit to Cambridge, the first since he had failed to return to complete his degree twelve years before. Everything looked the same, he thought, even the students. He met another miserable *alter ego* from his past, the classical scholar Richard Porson, well known for his erudition, his conversation, and his drunkenness. 'He took no notice of me', wrote Coleridge, commenting on 'his pitiable State, quite *muddled*'.[134]

Having missed Sara Hutchinson at Penrith, as she had set off for the Lakes herself, Coleridge finally arrived at Kendal on 26 October. He saw the Wordsworths and Sara Hutchinson before they departed to spend the winter as guests of the Beaumonts at Coleorton in Leicestershire. They were startled on first seeing him. Dorothy told Mrs Clarkson she had never felt 'such a shock'. 'We all felt exactly in the same way – as if he were different from what we have expected to see'. He had grown so fat that his eyes were lost in flesh, and he had a distressing way of not talking to them about anything except public affairs at Malta.[135]

The meeting with the Wordsworths seems to have given Coleridge the courage to go home to Keswick at last, with the now irrevocable intention of demanding a separation. His son Derwent later remembered the joyful bustle at home in preparation for the returning husband and father: 'My mother had taken my pillow for my father's bed, who required several. In her telling me this, I exclaimed – "Oh! by all means. I would lie on straw for my father", greatly to my mother's delight & amusement. How well does this speak for my mother. I was just then at the close of my sixth year.'[136]

No record of Coleridge's feelings on seeing his children once more has been preserved. He told the Wordsworths in November that he and Sara had '*determined* to part absolutely and finally'. He would keep Hartley and Derwent with him, but they would visit their mother often. He did not specify where he and the boys would live, but it seems that the Wordsworths expected it to be with them, first at the Beaumonts' country seat. To assuage his guilt at insisting on the separation – a serious matter for the whole family and a cause of social stigma for his wife – he complained to the Wordsworths of Sara's 'temper, and selfishness, her manifest dislike of me', and now also 'her self-encouraged admiration of Southey as a vindictive feeling in which she delights herself as satirizing me'.[137]

As Southey, who could not help representing in all his uprightness the type of the husband and father Sara would have liked for herself and her children, observed, the Wordsworths encouraged Coleridge's manifest injustice to his wife. Wordsworth was authorized by Sir George Beaumont to invite Coleridge and Hartley to Coleorton.[138] That Sara Coleridge was less than fully reconciled to the separation he thus facilitated is clear from an unsympathetic remark of Dorothy's in December: 'I say she has agreed to the separation; but in a letter which we have received to-night he tells us that she breaks out into outrageous passions, and urges continually that one argument (in fact the only one which has the least effect upon her mind), that this person, and that person, and everybody will talk.'[139]

Coleridge did turn up at Coleorton shortly before Christmas 1806. He brought only Hartley with him, reporting to his wife on Christmas Day that he had almost lost him during a break in the coach journey (see plate 15). The episode eerily recalls Coleridge's own precocious and precarious childhood:

> I was out 5 minutes seeking him in great alarm, & found him at the further end of a wet meadow, on the marge of a river. After dinner, fearful of losing our places by the window (of the long Coach) I ordered him to go into the Coach & sit in the place where he was before: and I would follow. In about 5 minutes I followed: no Hartley! – Halloing – in vain! – At length, where should I discover him! In the same meadow, only at a greater distance, & close down on the very edge of the Water. I was angry from downright Fright! And what, think you, was Cataphract's excuse! – 'It was a misunderstanding, Father! I thought, you see, that you bid me go to the very same place, in the meadow, where I was.'

Before finishing this Christmas letter to the wife he has just left for good, Coleridge adds a cruel remark about Hartley and Sara Hutchinson: 'All here [at Coleorton] love him most dearly: and your name sake [Sara Hutchinson] takes upon her all the duties of his Mother & darling Friend, with all the Mother's love & fondness. He is very fond of *her*.'[140]

9

Friendships and *The Friend* 1807–1810

O studious Poet, eloquent for truth!
Philosopher! contemning wealth and death,
Yet docile, childlike, full of Life and Love!
Here, rather than on monumental stone,
This record of thy worth the Friend inscribes,
Thoughtful, with quiet tears upon his cheek.
Coleridge, 'A Tombless Epitaph', *The Friend*, November 1809

Coleridge and Hartley remained at Coleorton with the Wordsworths until April 1807. Dorothy Wordsworth had been jubilant about their arrival the previous Christmas, full of hopes that, once away from his wife, Coleridge would flourish. With great naivety she told Lady Beaumont that she and Wordsworth would keep Coleridge from drinking brandy and 'taking stimulants'; 'if he is not inclined to manage himself, we can manage him'.[1] The Wordsworths would learn a painful lesson in this respect during the next two years, when they had Coleridge living with them for most of the time. Southey commented acidly to his brother Henry that Coleridge had taken 'Job' [Hartley] to Coleorton, where Wordsworth's own children had whooping cough: 'But as they [the Wordsworths] disregarded the danger of bringing Hartley into it for the sake of having [Coleridge's] company, so is he so pleased with theirs that he keeps him in it. If Hartley were to catch it and die of it – and poor fellow there cannot possibly be a worse subject for the disease, Coleridge would break his heart – and deserve to do it.'[2]

One of the first things Wordsworth did on having Coleridge with him was to read aloud the now finished poem addressed to his friend. Coleridge's response was all that Wordsworth could have hoped for. He expressed it in a poem which was first published in *Sibylline Leaves* in 1817, but was written 'for the greater part on the Night, on which he finished the

recitation of his Poem (in thirteen Books) concerning the growth and
history of his own Mind, Jan. 1807, Coleorton, near Ashby de la Zouch'.[3]
The poem's title was 'To William Wordsworth'. Its tone, appropriately for a
celebration of poetic success in his friend by one who feels himself a failure,
is Wordsworthian. It is a generous paraphrase of the themes of *The Prelude*
itself, giving back to Wordsworth as in a mirror the story of

> that prophetic Lay
> Wherein (high theme by thee first sung aright)
> Of the foundations and the building up
> Of thy own Spirit, thou hast lov'd to tell
> What may be told, to th'understanding mind
> Revealable; and what within the mind
> May rise enkindled.[4]

Accepting for the moment Wordsworth's own view of the give and take
between his mind and the stimuli offered by Nature, Coleridge describes
the 'currents self-determined, as might seem,/ Or by some inner Power'.
That phrase, 'as might seem', is highly characteristic of Wordsworth, and
Coleridge adopts it chameleon-like as the natural way to praise his friend's
achievement. Philosophically, it differs from his own view of poetic creation
as expressed in 'Dejection':

> I may not hope from outward forms to win
> The passion and the life, whose fountains are within.[5]

But it accords entirely with Wordsworth's experience as described throughout *The Prelude.*

Something of the mental journey of the conversation poems occurs, for
Coleridge follows the expression of the life-giving effect on him of hearing
Wordsworth's verse with a backward-looking excursion into the reasons
behind his being himself 'one cast forth', 'a wanderer with a worn-out
heart'. He rehearses his early hopes of poetic glory, but ends in an image of
hope, youth, genius and knowledge turned into 'flowers/ Strewed on my
corse'. Once more, however, as in the fine poems of ten years before, he
achieves a return from this low point. Turning closely on the flower metaphor, the poem raises itself from mourning to praise:

> That way no more! and ill beseems it me,
> Who came a welcomer in herald's guise,
> Singing of Glory, and Futurity,
> To wander back on such unhealthful road,
> Plucking the poisons of self-harm! And ill
> Such intertwine beseems triumphal wreaths
> Strew'd before thy advancing!

Coleridge ends his tribute with the thought that the effect of hearing this
work has been that 'when I rose, I found myself in prayer'. Though of

course the poem is an epitaph for the passing of his poetic genius, it shows, as Coleridge is aware, 'momentary stars' of imaginative energy on his part, in response to the sustained 'Orphic song' of Wordsworth.

It must have cost Coleridge an effort to write this poem. Jealousy of Wordsworth, anxiety about the future, the now familiar burdens of ill health, indolence, guilt and debt combined to make him otherwise unproductive. This poetic gesture towards Wordsworth is all the more remarkable because on 27 December 1806 Coleridge had imagined that he saw Wordsworth and Sara Hutchinson in bed together at an inn near Coleorton. His notebook entry reads:

The Epoch
Saturday, 27th December, 1806 – Queen's Head, Stringston, 1/2 a mile from Coleorton Church, 50 minutes after 10.[6]

It was a moment Coleridge returned to often in his notebooks. On 13 September 1807 he 'awakened from a dream of Tears, & anguish of involuntary Jealousy, $^1/_2$ past 2' and went over and over his memory of 'that Saturday Morning' and what it signified. What it signified was that he recognized that Sara Hutchinson did not love him, and morbidly added in his imagination to the perceived gulf between his and Wordsworth's luck: 'O cruel! is he not beloved, adored by two – & two such Beings –/ and must I not be beloved *near* him except as a Satellite? . . . W. is greater, better, manlier, more dear, by nature, to Woman, than I – I – miserable I!'[7] Given his masochistic feelings, it is nothing short of miraculous that he could compose his poetic tribute to Wordsworth only a few days after 'the epoch' of his sick imagination.

In a pleasing effort to be a good father of growing boys, Coleridge managed to write a helpful little poem for Hartley, now ten, and Derwent, aged six, to teach them English metre. In a letter to Derwent on 3 March he included a rhymed stanza illustrating trochees, spondees, dactyls, iambs and so on in lines such as the following:

IAMBICS march from short to long:
With a Leap / and a Bound the swift ANAPESTS throng![8]

He also began writing, but did not finish, a Greek grammar for his sons.[9]

Coleridge planned to bring Sara round to the separation by taking her and the children on a visit to his family at Ottery St Mary. To this end he wrote to George in April, professing his desire to 'pour my whole Heart into you' and even declaring himself willing to settle in Devon if he could be of use to George, perhaps in the running of the school. He told George of the plan to separate from Sara, giving as the reason her 'temper & general tone of feeling', which he had found 'wholly incompatible with even an endurable Life'. The descent on Ottery was intended to make the separation 'look *respectable* for her'.

But George disapproved. He clearly feared that he would be expected to have Hartley and Derwent at his school, and he may have thought that Coleridge would settle them and then make his escape. In any case, he and his mother and brothers, so orthodox, were aghast at the prospect of the separation (divorce being, of course, out of the question except on grounds of the wife's adultery). He replied instantly, putting Coleridge off. There was illness in his house; 'our poor aged mother' was infirm; Colonel James's wife, 'who has an hereditary nervousness and despondency', would be 'out of her senses at the very approach of a family in addition to her own'. As for the school, he was about to give it up, and Coleridge must not think of sending his boys there. Finally, he thoroughly disapproved of the step Coleridge was about to take, thinking that 'your situation is no way desperate if your mind does not make it so'. He adroitly suggested that as Coleridge was going first to friends in Bristol, and to Poole in Nether Stowey, he should seek help from Sara's own family and friends there.[10]

Coleridge did not open this letter for over two months. When he did, he was shocked and disappointed, and his wife dismayed that they had all travelled so far and waited so long – they spent nearly two months with Poole – in order not to go to Ottery after all.[11] Meanwhile, in a letter which would be comic if it were not so painful, Coleridge lectured the wayward Hartley on how to behave when he visited his Ottery relations. He should not 'pick at or snatch up any thing, eatable or not', or interrupt his elders, or be frantic and 'pout-mouthing'. And he should try, wrote Coleridge in all solemnity, to correct his 'habits of procrastination'.[12]

Coleridge had spent some of April and May in London; in June he was in Nether Stowey with Sara and the children, all of them guests of Poole. From here Coleridge wrote to Josiah Wedgwood, who had been disappointed at not hearing from Coleridge after his return from Malta. George Coleridge, who had Josiah's son as a pupil at Ottery, sought to soften his bitter feelings towards Coleridge, and Josiah accepted that the latter was ill and unhappy, but he felt wounded nevertheless.[13] He got no answer to his request that Coleridge put together material for a memoir of Tom, to be added to an edition of Tom's philosophical speculations which Sir James Mackintosh, another beneficiary of the Wedgwood wealth, was to produce. On 25 June Coleridge wrote sheepishly to Josiah, explaining that under 'a strange cowardice of Pain' he had not opened letters, and claiming to have 'drawn at full a portrait of my friend's mind & character' while at Malta. The paper was, however, among his as yet unrecovered manuscripts.[14] Poor Josiah was unlucky in his efforts to have a fitting memorial to his brother published. Neither Coleridge nor Mackintosh produced anything.

In Bristol Coleridge renewed his acquaintance with his old friends Wade and Cottle, and made a new acquaintance, Thomas De Quincey. The latter was a student at Oxford – like Coleridge he would leave university without taking a degree – a disciple of Wordsworth, to whom he had written enthusiastic letters while still a schoolboy and whom he had *almost* visited at

Grasmere, turning back at the last minute through shyness.[15] Like
Coleridge he had a fabulous memory and a great facility for learning; like
Coleridge, he had lost his father at a young age and had difficult relations
with his mother and with the brother just above him in age; like Coleridge
he had begun to take opium to relieve pain and would soon be a confirmed
'opium eater'.

De Quincey, who admired Coleridge almost as much as he did
Wordsworth, was visiting Bristol in August 1807 and, hearing that Coleridge
was nearby, set off to Stowey, armed with a letter of introduction from
Cottle, to meet 'this illustrious man'.[16] His memory of his first sight of
Coleridge, written soon after Coleridge's death in 1834, is worth quoting,
though like everything he wrote, it has an air of exaggeration and sensation-
alizing about it. (De Quincey was a desperate and unscrupulous filler of
journalistic copy all his adult life, as well as sharing with Coleridge the
addict's propensity to deceive himself and others.) Where Dorothy
Wordsworth had hit on the Shakespearean idea of the poet with his eye
rolling in a fine frenzy on first seeing Coleridge leap over the gate at
Racedown Lodge, De Quincey gives us – with hindsight, of course – the
thirty-four-year-old author of 'The Ancient Mariner' as a luminous
dreamer, this being the aspect of Coleridge which most attracted the
younger man:

> In height he might seem to be about five feet eight (he was, in reality, about
> an inch and a-half taller, but his figure was of an order which drowns the
> height); his person was broad and full, and tended even to corpulence; his
> complexion was fair, though not what painters technically style fair, because
> it was associated with black hair; his eyes were large, and soft in their ex-
> pression; and it was from the peculiar appearance of haze or dreaminess which
> mixed with their light that I recognized my object. This was Coleridge.[17]

Like Hazlitt, De Quincey became something of a thorn in Coleridge's
flesh. Both younger men responded strongly to similarities between
Coleridge's character and circumstances and their own, and both reacted
equally strongly against their admired but disappointing idol. De Quincey
would later embarrass Coleridge with his revelations about opium, addiction, and he would be first on the scene after Coleridge's death with claims
of plagiarism from the Germans, De Quincey himself being no mean
German scholar. Indeed, in the very same essay in which he described his
first meeting with Coleridge, published in *Tait's Magazine* only a month
after Coleridge's death, De Quincey exposed the fact that Coleridge had
given an unacknowledged '*verbatim* translation from Schelling' in a long
passage in *Biographia Literaria*. To his strictures he added memorably and
not altogether unjustly:

> Had, then, Coleridge any need to borrow from Schelling? Did he borrow *in
> forma pauperis* [out of poverty]? Not at all: there lay the wonder. He spun daily,
> and at all hours, for mere amusement of his own activities, and from the loom

of his own magical brain, theories more gorgeous by far, and supported by a pomp and luxury of images such as neither Schelling – no, nor any German that ever breathed, not John Paul – could have emulated in his dreams. With the riches of El Dorado lying about him, he would condescend to filch a handful of gold from any man whose purse he fancied, and in fact reproduced in a new form, applying itself to intellectual wealth, that maniacal propensity which is sometimes well known to attack enormous proprietors and millionaires for acts of petty larceny.[18]

In August 1807 De Quincey was content to meet Coleridge and, generously, to 'lend' him £300 anonymously through Cottle.[19] Humphry Davy was also exerting himself on Coleridge's behalf. He wrote to Poole from London saying that the managers of the Royal Institution were keen to engage Coleridge for a series of lectures. Would Poole persuade him to agree, for the benefit of the public and himself, 'to say nothing of the benefit his purse might receive'?[20] Coleridge was willing to lecture on 'the Principles of Poetry', he told Davy, beginning with Spenser and Shakespeare and going on to Milton, Dryden, Pope and modern poetry. He would offer 'the result of many years' continued reflection on the subjects of Taste, Imagination, Fancy, Passion, the source of our pleasures in the fine Arts in the *antithetical* balance-loving nature of man, & the connection of such Pleasures with moral excellence.'[21] Here is the germ of the idea of the poet so memorably described in *Biographia Literaria* as one who 'by that synthetic and magical power to which we have exclusively appropriated the name of imagination' achieves 'the balance or reconciliation of opposite or discordant qualities'.

Coleridge told Davy he would be in London by the end of September. Instead, he stayed in Bristol until late November, while Sara and the children, their expected visit to Ottery thwarted, returned to Keswick in October with the gallant De Quincey as their companion. The arrangement suited all parties: Coleridge was not obliged to take his family home, Sara had a protector on the journey, and De Quincey could at last visit the Lakes and formally introduced himself to Wordsworth. Coleridge's journey from Bristol to London was delayed, since he had fallen ill 'owing to sitting in wet clothes', as Sara Coleridge told Poole, and had 'passed three weeks at the house of a Mr. Morgan', whose wife & sister nursed him 'in the kindest manner'.[22]

This was John Morgan, whom Coleridge had first known in Bristol in 1795. This family, with its two sympathetic females, later took Coleridge into their London home, looking after him during the darkest days of his life. Already they offered a safety net, and Coleridge immediately began to compare Mrs Morgan and her sister Charlotte Brent to Mary Wordsworth and Sara Hutchinson. He did this not only in a private letter to Dorothy on 24 November, but also – to the annoyance of Southey and Sara Coleridge[23] – in a rather poor poem, 'To Two Sisters', which Stuart accepted for the *Courier*. It appeared there on 10 December, mawkishly rehearsing its author's hopelessness and expressing a desire for 'some abiding-place of love'.[24]

In his plight Coleridge had found another predominantly female family on which to depend emotionally. But when he first got to London, despite seeing old friends like Lamb and Godwin and living above the *Courier* office in the Strand, Coleridge was visited by diarrhoea and vomiting, and felt more than ever depressed and lonely. When he did start lecturing at the Royal Institution in January 1808, he was so ill and vulnerable that he had to postpone several lectures. De Quincey later dramatically represented him as lying sick and opium-drugged in bed while Albemarle Street was 'closed by a "lock" of carriages, filled with women of distinction', all bent on hearing Coleridge lecture but doomed to disappointment.[25]

Coleridge sank into torpor, writing to Mrs Morgan on 10 February 1808, 'O it is a sad thing to be at once ill and friendless', and complaining bitterly about a '*dancing, frisking*' letter he had received from his wife, whose response to his description of his illness, which he thought might be a kidney stone, was '*Lord! how often you are ill! You must be* MORE *careful about Colds!*' So angry was he that he told Mrs Morgan he would keep her letter, together with a previous one in which there was 'not one sentence' that did not contain a complaint (!), and 'bequeath them with some other curiosities to some married man who has an amiable wife (at least a woman with a woman's Heart) to make him bless himself!'[26] Having fixed on the Morgans as his confidants, he wrote again on 17 February, representing himself as homeless and unable to go to Keswick – 'the *sight* of that woman would destroy me' – and bursting out with reproaches against Southey, the resident dominant male in the Keswick household and therefore resented by Coleridge, who now scratched the old wound: 'I played the fool, and cut the throat of my Happiness, of my genius, of my utility, in compliment to the merest phantom of over-strained Honor! – O Southey! Southey! an unthinking man were you – and are – & will be.'[27]

In fact Coleridge was in such a state physically and mentally at this time that it was amazing that he gave any public lectures at all. He had reached a nadir of unreasoning suspicion and jealousy. While staying with Poole, for whom he had some time ago lost his old affection yet of whose hospitality he was glad in the summer of 1807, he wrote pettishly in his notebook: 'Mr T. Poole of Nether Stowey in the C. of Somerset deems it an intolerable Tax on any person to find a Guest Pen and Ink while in his House, and an unreasonable Expectation on any Guest who should demand the same.'[28]

On 13 September 1807, also at Poole's house, he recorded waking up from his dream of anguish at the memory of his vision in December 1806 of Wordsworth in bed with Sara Hutchinson.[29] And still his 'crazy tenement' of a body did not collapse altogether; nor would it for another twenty-seven years.[30]

As a result of Davy's overtures, Coleridge was commissioned to give a course of twenty-five lectures at the Royal Institution, beginning in January 1808.[31] He was to be paid £140, of which £60 would be given in advance, but this arrangement was changed because of Coleridge's illness during February and March, when the course was interrupted, and because Coleridge terminated the course in June, before he had completed it. He probably gave about twenty lectures, for which he seems to have received £100 in instalments. It is impossible to recover the full texts of the lectures, since Coleridge never published them and his notes are scattered and fragmentary. He gave large parts of the lectures extempore, sometimes charming his audiences with these performances, at other times irritating them with repetitions and unfulfilled promises. At later courses a deliberate attempt was made by Coleridge's admirers to have shorthand notes taken, but for 1808 we have only some rough notes by Coleridge and a few brief comments from two of his hearers, De Quincey and Henry Crabb Robinson, a clubbable lawyer and seeker out of great men, who fortunately kept copious diaries.

Coleridge's unpoetical brother, Colonel James, on being told that his brother was planning to lecture on modern poetry, wrote unceremoniously to his son John on 25 January, 'If he wants any abuse I can help him out.'[32] This was not exactly Coleridge's plan. He began by asking questions about 'taste in regard to Poetry, & whether it have any fixed Principle'. His notes suggest that he distinguished between the simple sensation of taste and the metaphorical sense of 'an intellectual perception of any object blended with a distinct consciousness of pain or pleasure conceived as resulting from that Object'.[33] Here he probably brought to bear the results of his wide reading in eighteenth-century works on taste and judgement by writers such as Blair, Beattie, Johnson and Burke, as well as his acquaintance with German works on aesthetics by Herder, Schiller, and the brothers Friedrich and August Wilhelm Schlegel. In his second lecture, delivered on 5 February 1808, Coleridge discussed Greek and pre-Shakespearean drama. The 'general purport', according to De Quincey, was to 'clear the ground for a just estimate of Shakespeare by separating what he had individually from what he had as a member of a particular nation in a particular age'.[34]

Then followed a gap of nearly two months. Coleridge was so ill, and wrote such hopeless letters to his friends, that Wordsworth went to London in late February to see him, intending to take him back to Grasmere. But Coleridge resumed his lecturing on 30 March, and Wordsworth returned home without him on 3 April, full of gloom about his friend's state of mind and body.[35] During April Coleridge had the strange experience of being approached by his first love, Mary Evans, now Mrs Todd, who had heard he was lecturing and wrote asking to see him. Coleridge visited her, reporting to Daniel Stuart that she represented 'a counterpart of the very worst parts of my own Fate', being unhappily married.[36]

In May Coleridge unwisely wrote a complaining letter to Wordsworth, now lost, in which, as he observed in a notebook, he accused Wordsworth of 'High Self-opinion pampered in a hot bed' of 'moral & intellectual sympathy'.[37] Wordsworth was angered enough to draft a long reply, which he may not have sent. He objected to Coleridge's giving 'by voice and pen to your most lawless thoughts, and to your wildest fancies, an external existence'. He also strongly denied looking over Sara Hutchinson's letters to Coleridge – 'she is 34 years of age and what have I to do with overlooking her letters!' – and described Coleridge's letter as having come from 'a man in a lamentably insane state of mind'.[38]

This was a fair enough observation, as some raving letters from Coleridge at this time to the Morgans, William Sotheby and his brother George testify.[39] In a notebook entry of 16 May Coleridge empathizes with the song of a bird which he assumes to be in a cage. He identifies it with those familiar themes of his poetry up to and including 'Dejection':

> O that sweet Bird! Where is it? – it is encaged somewhere out of Sight – but from my bedroom at the Courier office, from the windows of which I look out on the walls of the Lyceum, I hear it, early Dawn – often alas! then lulling me to late Sleep – again when I awake – & all day long. – It is in Prison – all its Instincts ungratified – yet it feels the Influence of Spring – & calls with unceasing Melody to the Loves, that dwell in Fields & Greenwood bowers –; unconscious perhaps that it cries in vain. – O are they the Songs of a happy enduring Day-dream? has the Bird Hope? Or does it abandon itself to the Joy of its Frame – a living Harp of Eolus? – O that I could do so![40]

Coleridge was increasingly using his notebooks as a source of comfort for his despair. 'Ah! dear Book!' he wrote at this time, 'sole confidant of a breaking Heart, whose social nature compels *some* Outlet'. The old vision of Wordsworth and Sara Hutchinson together returned to haunt him.[41] He was so low that he even shrank from the company of the Lambs. Mary told Catherine Clarkson later that year that 'Coleridge in a manner gave us up when he was in town, and we have now lost all traces of him'.[42]

None the less, he went on lecturing during April, May and June, getting on to Shakespeare and Milton, and perhaps beyond. On 3 May he gave an extra lecture on the education of children, in which he praised the 'Madras system' of Dr Andrew Bell, according to which teachers of large numbers of poor children in a school Bell had founded in Madras managed with the help of monitors or 'tuition by the scholars themselves'. The system was also in use in poor areas of London. Wordsworth, who also admired Bell, later sent his youngest son, Willy, to be educated at a school in London run on Bell's system.[43]

Coleridge leapt into the midst of a red-hot controversy by dispraising Bell's rival educationalist, Joseph Lancaster, who had also introduced a system of monitors.[44] Coleridge accused Lancaster of stealing his ideas from Bell, and objected in strong terms to Lancaster's advocacy of cruel punishments, referring to his own ignominious experiences at school. 'This part was delivered with fervour', according to Crabb Robinson, who gave his friend Mrs Clarkson a full account of the lecture.[45] Coleridge's contribution to the debate between the Bell and Lancaster schools – divided also along religious lines since Bell was an Anglican minister and had the patronage of the Establishment while Lancaster was a Quaker – led him into a nasty scene at a dinner after the lecture.[46] He was also censured by the Royal Institution for breaking its rule prohibiting attacks on living persons.

Another controversial area into which Coleridge stepped was that of political reviewing. In May 1808 he offered a review of his friend Thomas Clarkson's *History of the Abolition of the Slave Trade* to Francis Jeffrey of the *Edinburgh Review*. Jeffrey had long targeted Coleridge, with Wordsworth and Southey, as a member of the 'Lake School' of poetry, and as recently as April 1808 had introduced into an article on Crabbe's poetry a remark about 'the Wordsworths, and the Southeys and Coleridges, and all that misguided fraternity' with their 'fantastical oddity' and 'puling childishness'.[47]

In his usual strangely pugnacious yet submissive fashion when addressing people whom he perceived to be in some way powerful, Coleridge offered his review first with a reproach: 'Without knowing me you have been, perhaps rather unwarrantably, severe on my morals and Understanding'. Then came his request to be allowed to send his article on Clarkson, and finally he took to flattery: 'Be assured, that with the greatest respect for your Talents . . . and every kind thought respecting your motives, I am, dear Sir, Your ob. humb. Servt. S. T. Coleridge.'[48]

To this Pecksniffism Jeffrey replied with his own mixture of pleasantness and insult. If Coleridge did not subscribe any more to that 'school or sect of poets', he should have '*advertised out* of it'; nevertheless, Jeffrey would be 'extremely happy' to see Coleridge's comments and had 'little doubt that I shall be disposed to insert them in the next No. of the Review'.[49] On receiving Coleridge's piece, Jeffrey accepted it gladly, though he took the liberty of 'bringing down' Coleridge's 'too rapturous' style in places. He kept the praise for Clarkson's efforts, but added a disclaimer to Coleridge's praise of Pitt's zeal in the cause of abolition.

Coleridge had certainly changed his tune about Pitt since the days of *The Watchman* and the *Morning Post* articles and poems. Jeffrey argued, reasonably enough, that Pitt's ostensible support for abolition – finally achieved in 1807, the year after his death – had been brought into question by certain facts, particularly 'the constant defeat of the scheme during his administration contrasted with the easy and instant victory of his successors'. Jeffrey 'thought it fair to bring these facts under the notice of our readers – but the tone of the article you will find is not sensibly altered'.[50]

Coleridge's review, the only article he ever wrote for the Whig *Edinburgh Review*, appeared in July 1808. He complained to T. G. Street, the publisher of the *Courier*, that Jeffrey had 'shamefully mutilated' the piece by inserting a paragraph of 'nauseous' praise of Wilberforce as well as the attack on Pitt's sincerity which Jeffrey had led him to expect, and that he, Coleridge, had thereby been made to appear to contradict himself.[51] His complaint was justified. The article reads oddly, first praising Pitt, then questioning his motives. Jeffrey is every bit as vehement in his strictures on Pitt on page 367 of the article as Coleridge is in his praise on page 359, yet the essay appears to be the work of one hand. Towards Clarkson himself Coleridge is fair but

scarcely enthusiastic, finding his efforts humane but his account of the
history of those efforts not particularly interestingly told.[52]

Privately, Coleridge's view of Clarkson was that in his enthusiasm for
reform of the slave trade he had ill-advisedly thrown in his lot with
the agitators for the reform of Parliament, a group from whom Coleridge
himself had long since dissociated himself. He told Crabb Robinson in 1811
that Clarkson had been 'made vain from benevolence', and that he was a
'moral steam engine' or 'giant with one idea'.[53] But he remained on
friendly terms with Clarkson. As for Jeffrey, though Coleridge could not
resist taking him to task for introducing a 'blank contradiction' into the
article, he humbly acceded to Jeffrey's right 'to alter or omit ad libitum'.[54]

Having recovered from the worst of his illness, Coleridge left London in
early July 1808 to visit the Clarksons at Bury St Edmunds. At the beginning
of September he arrived in Grasmere, where the Wordsworths had moved
into a larger house, Allan Bank, handing over Dove Cottage to De Quincey,
who had now settled in the Lakes. The arrangement was that Coleridge
would live with the Wordsworths, and that Hartley and Derwent, now at
Ambleside School, would visit there every weekend.

Coleridge settled in happily. His detestation of his wife was much
softened by her generosity in agreeing to his having the boys at weekends
and in letting him take little Sara, now nearly six, back to Grasmere with
him for a visit. He reported to his wife that everyone at Allan Bank was
delighted with the child, thanked her for her 'kind behaviour', and even
signed himself 'your affectionate Husband'.[55]

Young Sara remembered this visit to Allan Bank with mingled pleasure
and pain. Her father's motive in taking her was, she later thought, 'a wish
to fasten my affections on him'. He told her fairy stories at night, and
sympathized – how could he not? – with her 'night-fears', insisting that she
be allowed a candle in her room at Keswick on her return home. But Sara
displeased him by not immediately taking to him (whom she had hardly
seen) and the Wordsworths. When her mother came to fetch her home,
she 'flew to her, and wished not to be separated from her any more'.
Coleridge was offended, the more so as the Wordsworth children were so
affectionate with him. 'My father reproached me', she recalled, 'and contrasted my coldness with the childish caresses of the little Wordsworths'.
She slunk away, hiding in the woods behind the house until John
Wordsworth came to find her.[56]

In spite of such moments of angry and jealous love, Coleridge was
happier and more energetic than he had been for months, if not years. He
sought medical advice about his opium habit, and was able to reduce the
dose temporarily. And he was planning a new literary venture, one which
did, despite delays and setbacks, come to something. He wrote with pal-
pable relief to several friends – Estlin, Davy, Poole – about his attempts to
regulate himself and about the energy he now found he had for hard work.
To Davy he wrote almost cheerfully in December 1808: 'My Health and

Spirits are improved beyond my boldest Hopes – A very painful Effort of
moral Courage has been remunerated by Tranquillity – by Ease from the
Sting of Self-disapprobation. I have done more for the last 10 weeks than I
had done for three years before.'[57]

The new venture was a periodical, to be called *The Friend*. Unlike *The
Watchman*, it was not to deal with current affairs or party politics, but, as
Coleridge explained to Stuart, among others, it would concern itself with
founding 'true PRINCIPLES, to oppose false PRINCIPLES in Legislation,
Philosophy, Morals, International Law'. Ominously for sales of the periodical, he affirmed that he did not intend to write 'for the multitude of men',
but rather for those who 'by Rank, or Fortune, or Official situation, or by
Talents & Habits of Reflection, are to influence the multitude'.[58] He would
later define this set, or class, of men as the clerisy.

The first essay, Coleridge told Sir George Beaumont, would be 'on the
Nature and the Importance of *Principles*': 'i.e. of the pure REASON, which
dictates unconditionally, in distinction from the prudential understanding,
which employing its mole Eyes in an impossible calculation of Consequences perverts and mutilates its own Being, untenanting the function
which it is incapable of occupying.'[59]

This, thought Coleridge does not say so, was his vehement way of interpreting Kant's distinction between Reason (Vernunft) and Understanding
(Verstand). He had explained two years before to Clarkson the difference
he saw between the two faculties:

> That Faculty of the Soul which apprehends and retains the mere notices of
> Experience, as for instance that such an object has a triangular figure, that it
> is of such or such magnitude, and of such and such color, and consistency,
> with the anticipation of meeting the same under the same circumstances, in
> other words all the mere φαινόμενα [phenomena] of our nature, we may call
> the Understanding. But all such notices, as are characterized by UNIVER-
> SALITY and NECESSITY, as that every Triangle *must* in all places and at all
> times have it's two sides greater than it's third – and which are evidently not
> the effect of any Experience, but the condition of all Experience, & that
> indeed without which Experience itself would be inconceivable, we may call
> Reason – and this class of knowledge was called by the Ancients Noούμενα
> [noumena] in distinction from the former, or φαινόμενα.[60]

It was characteristic of Coleridge that he should direct Clarkson to 'the
Ancients' for this distinction between phenomena and noumena, terms
which Kant applied respectively to the appearances of things which are
apprehended, through the senses, by our understanding, and the 'things-
in-themselves' (Dinge-an-sich), which are beyond our speculative
knowledge. It was also characteristic of him to go a step further than Kant
had gone and make a claim for our knowledge, through Reason, of univer-
sality and necessity, the very entities to which Hume had said we had no
access, a position from which Kant did not dissent. Coleridge's dealings
with Kant here cause a double confusion. In the first place he introduces

Kantian concepts without acknowledging them to be Kantian; in the second place he adapts them to his own purposes, which is in itself no crime, but the matter becomes decidedly difficult to sort out since he often presents his own deviations from Kant as expressly 'Kantian'.[61]

Though his friends had their doubts about whether Coleridge would ever get his *Friend* into print, they all rallied round. Clarkson got several Quakers to subscribe; perhaps they thought the periodical was a Quaker one, in view of its title.[62] Southey, Lamb, Wordsworth, Stuart, Poole and others wrote letters on its behalf. Allan Bank was a hive of activity, with Sara Hutchinson acting as Coleridge's amanuensis. The copy went, Wordsworth recalled, 'from her Pen to the Printer no transcript being taken'.[63]

De Quincey was staying there too, teaching the Wordsworth children and helping Wordsworth with his political pamphlet attacking the Convention of Cintra, the British agreement of a truce with Napoleon's army in Spain which Wordsworth – and Coleridge and Southey – thought a betrayal of the brave resistance of Spain and Portugal to Napoleon. Wordsworth spent months on his pamphlet, which swelled to book length, and which De Quincey, after much effort and confusion, finally saw through the press in London in the spring of 1809.[64] Dorothy wrote to Mrs Clarkson on 8 December 1808, describing the happy industry of the large household, with the adults working in pairs, Sara and Coleridge in the parlour, William and Mary in William's study, and Dorothy herself with De Quincey in the dining room.[65]

Coleridge got a printer in Kendal, William Pennington, to set up a 'Prospectus of The Friend, A Weekly Essay, By S. T. Coleridge', copies of which were sent to friends. At the same time he asked William Savage, printer to the Royal Institution, to print a thousand more in London. This was over-optimistic, for despite all his best efforts, the number of subscribers was a much lower, though creditable, 398.[66] In any case, Savage failed to set up the Prospectus, and after some haggling over terms Coleridge, on the advice of Daniel Stuart, dropped Savage, thereby inducing an unfortunate coolness between himself and Humphry Davy.[67]

There was much wavering over whether to call *The Friend* a newspaper and publish it weekly, which would render it liable to Stamp Duty, or to call it a pamphlet and publish it less often, and so evade the duty. In the end Coleridge opted for the first plan, selling his stamped paper for a shilling and printing it on one sheet of sixteen pages, in imitation of William Cobbett's influential *Weekly Political Register.* Though Coleridge had hoped it would appear on the first Saturday in January 1809, by February he had still not found a printer or written the first number. He eventually settled on John Brown, 'Printer & Stationer' of Penrith, thus necessitating some walking to and fro over 'our most perilous & difficult Alpine Pass' (the steep, and in winter often impassable, Kirkstone Pass), to oversee the printing.[68]

However, despite problems with paper and printing, and the inevitable money difficulties, Coleridge did get started. What is more, he produced his paper from June 1809 to March 1810, with only occasional contributions from others such as Wordsworth and Southey. These two were not enthusiastic, however. Southey wrote to Rickman in January 1809 that the Prospectus 'looks too much like what it intends to be, talks confidently to the public about what the public cares not a curse for, and has about it a sort of unmanly *humblification*'.[69] Jeffrey offered Coleridge some direct advice on receiving his copy of the Prospectus, saying bluntly, 'you should not seem so awfully impressed with the importance of your task', and advising him to 'labour to be plain and reasonable'.[70]

Such advice was lost on Coleridge. He did too much throat-clearing aloud, involving his readers in the minute processes of his arriving at certain points of view rather than giving them clear accounts of those opinions once they had been arrived at. The Prospectus, as Southey foresaw, was prophetic in this respect, especially in its self-conscious expression of pride and apology about his fitness for the task:

> You know, too, that at different Periods of my Life I have not only planned, but collected the Materials for, many Works on various and important Subjects: so many indeed, that the Number of my unrealized Schemes, and the Mass of my miscellaneous Fragments, have often furnished my Friends with a subject of Raillery, and sometimes of Regret and Reproof . . . this Want of Perseverance has been produced in the Main by an Over-activity of Thought, modified by a constitutional Indolence, which made it more pleasant to me to continue acquiring, than to reduce what I had acquired to a regular Form.[71]

Honest and astute though this confession of scholarly temptations is, it is not calculated to induce confidence in the reader.

The essays themselves are a miscellany of comments, arguments and anecdotes on the general topic of the need for principles in all spheres of human activity. Coleridge's learning is inevitably paraded, sometimes at great length and with breathtaking multiplicity of reference. He is as waywardly digressive as the narrator of *Tristram Shandy*, with some footnotes threatening to become longer than the essay to which they are annexed. In the second number, published on 8 June 1809, he ill-advisedly complains in one such footnote about having been labelled a Jacobin and the deserter of his family, and dredges up the old attack on him in the *Beauties of the Anti-Jacobin* of 1799.

What possessed him to do this, goodness knows. A man who had without doubt been, if not a Jacobin, then at least a radical, and a well-known one at that, now denies point-blank that his writings ever showed 'the least bias' towards Jacobinism. A man who was even now living separated from his wife, though of course not having 'left her destitute', refutes the charge of abandoning her made ten years before.[72] All the resentment and denial and drawing attention to matters he would have been wiser, and happier, to ignore is totally unnecessary, nobody having recently charged him with either Jacobinism or Wife-desertion. Southey was impatient with this folly, remembering how they were both Jacobins in their youth, 'in the common acceptation of the name'.[73] And Dorothy Wordsworth thought it beneath him to justify himself 'against the calumnies of the Anti-Jacobin Review' and foolish of him 'to bring to light a thing long forgotten'.[74]

However, Dorothy thought the first two numbers showed 'the power of thought and the originality of a great mind', even though lacking 'a happiness of manner'. Her estimate is fair. No one could read through all the numbers consecutively without fearing for his or her sanity or falling into boredom. But in the midst of some turgid overloaded passages and much unfortunate self-justification there lurk passages of luminous lucidity, all the more remarkable for their unpromising context and their appearing within an avowedly abstract view of their topic. An example comes in the fourth number, of 7 September 1809, during a lengthy argument about the desirability of press freedom. It is characteristic of Coleridge that he should not only carry on the discussion over several numbers, but even – as he does – finish a sentence in number four which he had begun in number three! But we may set against such craziness in the management of his material the strength of his argument and the appropriateness of his illustration in this passage, which takes its cue from Milton's famous argument against censorship in *Areopagitica* (1644):

> We have therefore abundant reason to conclude, that the Law of England has done well and wisely in proceeding on the principle so clearly worded by Milton: that Books should be as freely admitted into the world as any other Birth; and if it prove a monster, who denies but that it may justly be burnt and sunk into the sea. We have reason then, it appears, to rest satisfied with our Laws, which no more prevent a book from coming into the world unlicensed, lest it should prove a Libel, than a Traveller from passing unquestioned through our Turnpike gates, because it is possible he may be a Highwayman. Innocence is presumed in both cases.[75]

Coleridge is at his best when speculating suggestively about the psychological basis of experience. He speaks with empathetic understanding, for example, of Luther sitting in his study in the Wartburg, being 'plagued with temptations' of the 'Flesh and the Devil'. That what follows is a kind of self-portrait does not make it any the less valid as a hypothesis about Luther:

> It is evident from his Letters that he suffered under great irritability of his nervous System, the common effect of deranged Digestion in men of sedentary habits, who are at the same time intense thinkers: and this irritability added to, and revivifying the impressions made upon him in early life, and fostered by the theological Systems of his Manhood, is abundantly sufficient to explain all his apparitions and all his nightly combats with evil Spirits. I see nothing improbable in the supposition, that in one of those unconscious half sleeps, or rather those rapid alternations of sleeping with the half waking state, which is *the true witching-time,*

'the season
Wherein the spirits hold their wont to walk'

the fruitful matrix of Ghosts – I see nothing improbable, that in some one of those momentary Slumbers, into which the suspension of all Thought in the perplexity of intense thinking so often passes; Luther should have had a full view of the Room in which he was sitting, of his writing Table and all the Implements of Study, as they really existed, and at the same time a brain-image of the Devil, vivid enough to have acquired apparent *Outness*, and a distance regulated by the proportion of its distinctness to that of the objects really impressed on the outward senses.[76]

Still, the effect of such passages is undoubtedly dissipated by the tedious-ness of much of *The Friend*. Coleridge's most astutely malignant critic, Hazlitt, put the case against the work in an article of 1816, referring wittily to the Barmecide (i.e., imaginary) Feast in the *Arabian Nights*:

What is his *Friend* itself but an enormous title-page; the longest and most tiresome prospectus that ever was written; an endless preface to an imaginary work; a table of contents that fills the whole volume; a huge bill of fare of all possible subjects . . . One number consists of a grave-faced promise to per-form something impossible in the next; and the next is taken up with a long-faced apology for not having done it. Through the whole of this work, Mr. Coleridge appears in the character of the Unborn Doctor; the very Barmecide of knowledge; the Prince of preparatory authors!

'He never is – but always to be *wise*.'

He is the Dog in the Manger of literature, an intellectual Mar-Plot, who will neither let any body else come to a conclusion, nor come to one himself.[77]

The extraordinary thing about *The Friend* is that it is possible to smile and agree with Hazlitt while finding that, in places, Coleridge illuminates his subject brilliantly.

Coleridge was dispirited at the response of readers to the obscurity of *The Friend*. He tried to vary the fare with extracts of his own and Wordsworth's poetry, including the passage on skating from Book I of *The Prelude*, with 'Satyrane's Letters', pastiches of his letters from Germany to Sara and Poole, and even with a planted 'letter to the editor' from a new neighbour in the Lakes, John Wilson.[78] But this was not enough to satisfy his readers, as he found when he tried to call in their subscriptions in January 1810.[79]

Somehow he kept the paper going for two months more, but the wonder is that with his constitution and his lack of financial acumen, let alone the self-confessed 'involution and *entortillage* [twisting and turning]' of his style, he should have managed for as long as he did.[80] Even Southey accepted that, though 'grievously mismanaged', *The Friend* had been of some use, since 'we must be glad to get some part of what is in him out of him in any way'. He added that 'Satyrane' was Coleridge himself, 'though, if you are versed in Spenser, you will think the name wonderfully inappropriate'.[81] Sir Satyrane is the 'noble warlike knight', son of a satyr and a nymph, who rescues Una from the satyrs in Book I of *The Faerie Queene.* He is thought – and presumably this is why Coleridge chose the name – to represent Luther himself rescuing the true religion from Catholicism.

Southey's opinion was innocently echoed by Mrs Coleridge in August 1810, when she wrote, beginning kindly enough, to Poole:

> S. T. C. has been here the last four or five months [he spent the summer at Greta Hall], and I am sorry to add that in all that time he has not *appeared* to be employed in composition, although he has repeatedly assured me he was. The last No of the "Friend" lies on his Desk, the sight of which fills my heart with grief, and my Eyes with tears; but [I] am obliged to conceal my trouble as much as possible, as the slightest expression of regret never fails to excite resentment – Poor Man! – I have not the least doubt but he is the most unhappy of the two; and the reason is too obvious to need any explanation.

Then follows a complaint about her husband's mismanagement and inability to provide for his family, with Hartley reaching his fourteenth birthday in September 1810 and Derwent his tenth in the same month:

> Heaven knows, I am so bewildered about our affairs that I know not what to wish or what to *do* – these Lads too, H. in particular is fast approaching towards Manhood – what can he think is to become of them if he does not exert himself – these dear Boys are the source of much pleasure to me at present – heaven only knows how long it will last![82]

Though Coleridge's wayward conduct of the periodical form one number to the next and its unremitting complexity of argument constitute the main reasons for the failure of *The Friend* after ten months, its lack of direct political comment may also have been a factor. During its run the long war with France was the source of heated disagreement, inside and outside Parliament, with the Whigs advocating peace and the Tories favouring intensified aggression. The administration under the Duke of Portland inclined to appeasement, as was shown by the signing of the Convention of Cintra in August 1808. There was further controversy over the retreat of a British army unit under Sir John Moore to Corunna, where a defensive battle was fought against the French in December 1808.

The strong support of the *Edinburgh Review* for appeasement in an article published in October 1808 led to anger among the conservatives. Wordsworth wrote his pamphlet against the Convention, and Scott cancelled his subscription to the *Edinburgh*, becoming prominent in the setting up in 1809 of the rival *Quarterly Review*, a Tory periodical to which Southey also became a frequent contributor.

Coleridge added his weight to the political commentary in some articles entitled 'Letters on the Spaniards' in the *Courier* in December 1809 and

January 1810.[83] He told Samuel Purkis in October that he was about to write these articles, but added that he was not 'an Approver of the Courier' in every respect, thinking it probably 'a *venal* print'. This may be a hint at what would soon become widely known, namely that Stuart's partner and – with Stuart now semi-retired – managing editor of the *Courier*, T.G. Street, was in the pay of the Tory Government.[84] 'But', said Coleridge, 'it has manfully fought the good fight for Spain & against Peace-men'.

He also vented his disapproval in print of the duel fought in September 1809 between Canning and Castlereagh, which led to the downfall of the Portland Cabinet. 'What think you of two Cabinet Ministers *duelling* on *Cabinet* Measures?' he asked Purkis. 'Is it not wringing the Dregs for the last Drops of Degradation?'[85] But even his *Courier* articles are less party-political than philosophical, aiming to analyse recent events in Spain in terms of 'THE HISTORY OF PAST AGES' and what it suggests to us 'RESPECTING THE WAR OF A PEOPLE AGAINST ARMIES'.[86]

In *The Friend* Coleridge touched on political matters, but he did so in philosophical-historical terms, writing, over several numbers, essays 'On the Principles of Political Philosophy' and 'On the Errors of Party Spirit: or Extremes Meet' (September–October 1809). One wonders what his readers made of these essays with their lengthy preface quoting Spinoza on the need for deducing principles which square best with practice and their tortured, antithetical mode of reasoning, rich with digressions.

Coleridge realized relatively early on that he was not carrying his readers with him. As early as October 1809 he quaintly asked Southey to 'write a letter to The Friend in a lively style, chiefly urging, in a humorous manner, my Don Quixotism in expecting that the public will ever pretend to understand my lucubrations'.[87] Southey obliged, but instead of inserting his letter Coleridge promised in the eleventh number on 26 October to 'endeavour to correct' his fault of writing convolutedly in the fashion of his favourite seventeeth-century authors Hooker, Bacon and Jeremy Taylor.[88]

In October, too, he wrote to his brother George asking for a loan to buy paper for *The Friend*. George wrote back telling him that their mother was dying. Coleridge reported bitterly yet with relish to Southey that she was 'dying in great torture, death eating her piecemeal', and that she 'wishes to see me before her death': 'But tho' my Brother knows I am penniless, not an offer of a Bank note to enable me to set off. In truth, I know not what to do – for there is not a shilling in our whole House.'[89]

Coleridge did not visit his mother, who died on 4 November. Nor did he attend her funeral. His brother James commented on George's receiving no answer to his letters asking Coleridge to come to Devon: 'It is strange, passing strange, but such men there are. My brother Sam will be admirable, in my opinion, but neither respectable, nor venerable.'[90] As it happened, Coleridge's mother-in-law, Mrs Fricker, had died only a few days before his mother, as Southey announced in a letter of 26 October. Her death was 'a great blessing for herself & poor Martha', the unmarried sister who had looked after her mother during her long illness.[91] Coleridge makes no reference to either his unloved mother or his detested mother-in-law in surviving letters at this time.

Coleridge was in Keswick from early May 1810, having become once more friendly with his wife, at least as far as their children were concerned. 'What a quaint Brace of Doglets these Striplings of ours are!' he wrote to her in February; in April he declared that Hartley 'looks and behaves all that the fondest Parent could wish' and Derwent was 'a nice little fellow – and no Lackwit either'.[92] He even managed a jest at his own expense, telling Sara that De Quincey planned a visit to Keswick, 'tho' between ourselves, he is as great a *To-morrower* to the full as your poor Husband'. Coleridge himself stayed in Greta Hall from May till October.

None of Coleridge's letters from the summer of 1810 survives, but he filled his notebooks with matter intellectual and emotional. Many of the entries discuss religious questions; in June he was still arguing against Socinianism and elaborating the necessity of believing in the Trinity:

> God was manifested in the flesh – justified in the Spirit – seen of Angels – preached unto the Gentiles – believed on in the World – received up into Glory –
> With the above Creed no man can be a Heretic/ let his opinions be what they will on subordinate questions, as of the canonical Books, what & what not – the *origin* of the Gospels – the inspiration & what & whether.[93]

His return to Anglican orthodoxy was a matter of winning through by means of arguing with other faiths and philosophies. In 1809 he had expressed his dissatisfaction with Spinoza and Kant on the question of faith as a guarantor of morality. 'Is not *Sin*, or Guilt, the first thing that makes the idea of a God necessary', he asked, rather than merely the idea of divinity in the abstract? 'Therefore is not the incarnation a beautiful consequence of the το θεον [the divine] first revealing itself as ὁ Θεος [a God]?'[94] Spinoza's idea of God as substance leads to determinism in questions of practical morality: 'to think vices mere necessitated movements'. And Kant's belief in a stern moral law operating by means of the Categorical Imperative – according to which we will to do only what we could always and everywhere will others to do – leaves out the human propensity to err and to require forgiveness. Only a personal God can offer the latter.

Interestingly, Coleridge identified a paradox in Spinoza's life and work, namely that his 'Innocence and Virtue, guarded and matured into invincible Habit of Being by a Life of constant Meditation and intellectual pursuit', constituted the very conditions under which he could 'form & maintain a system subversive of all Virtue': 'He saw clearly the *folly* and *absurdity* of Wickedness, and felt so weakly & languidly the passions tempting to it, that he concluded nothing was wanting to a course of well-doing but clear conceptions and the fortitudo intellectualis/ while his very modesty, a prominent feature in his character, rendered him, as it did Hartley, less averse to the system of Necessity.'[95]

Coleridge's own case was, by contrast, one of a sinful man in need of a philosophy which gave proper weight to the difficulty of acting morally and the human need for God's forgiveness when actions fall short of the virtuous. His sense of his fallen self is at the bottom of his reasoning. In this connection, many notebook entries discuss his opium addiction and its moral enchaining of his spirit.[96] Others detail his love for Sara Hutchinson and his irritation at his wife. Sometimes his dislike of the latter leads him to describe her demeanour in terms of the anti-type of perfect wifehood:

> Among the ways & means of thoroughly alienating an husband forget not that of appearing unusually gloomy, sighing oft & deep, when he happens to have been out in company, & comes in unusual good spirits, full of what he has heard & seen – Likewise, always to look grave & perfectly indifferent when he is speaking, telling a joke, & especially, if every one else seems interested & pleased – Likewise, if he should relate any thing ridiculous or blame-worthy of another, to observe – I dare say, he is a very good man, and a good husband too – &c &c &c &c &c &c &c &c &c.[97]

Sometimes he gloomily, and childishly, consoles himself with the thought that 'so large a proportion of good, great, and learned Men have been made miserable (many even heart-broken) by ill-tempered wives', instancing Hooker, Milton and Priestley among others.[98]

As for Sara Hutchinson, he continued to pour out his love for her, but also showed jealousy and even criticism. The most extreme expression of his ultra-sensitivity occurs in a note of October 1808, where he describes the 'astonishing Effect of an unbecoming Cap on Sara' which was so painful to him that he went so far as to call her wearing it 'morally culpable'.[99] In 1810 he suffered paroxysms of jealousy about her. Her cousin, John Monkhouse, visited Grasmere in February and took her with him to Wales on 5 March. Coleridge subsequently dreamt that she was to marry him, and woke up ranting: 'O no! no! no! let me die tho' in the rack of the Stone [kidney stone] – only let me die before I suspect it, broad-awake! *Yet*, the too, too evident, the undeniable *joining* in the *conspiracy* with M [Wordsworth] and Δ [Dorothy] to deceive me, & her *cruel neglect* & *contemptuous Silence* ever *since!*'[100]

Though extreme to the point of derangement, such comments do have a basis in fact. Dorothy had written to Catherine Clarkson in April analysing the Coleridge–Sara relationship. Dorothy was glad Sara had gone to Wales because Coleridge, in the course of dictating copy of *The Friend* to her, had 'harassed and agitated her mind continually, and we saw that he was doing her health perpetual injury'. Of Coleridge's feelings for Sara Dorothy took a harsh view: 'His love for her is no more than a fanciful dream – otherwise he would prove it by a desire to make her happy. No! He likes to have her about him as his own, as one devoted to him, but when she stood in the way of other gratifications [presumably opium] it was all over.'

This would seem to agree with Coleridge's sense that Sara was avoiding him. In his unbalanced state he took it for a cruel conspiracy of all the

Wordsworths. If he had seen this letter of Dorothy's (which she twice tells her correspondent to burn), he would have been horrified, for he could not face seeing himself as others saw him. Dorothy paints a picture of a man in disarray, and one whom she has given up hope of 'managing':

> We have no hope of him – none that he will ever do anything more than he has already done. If he were not under our Roof, he would be just as much the slave of stimulants as ever; and his whole time and thoughts, (except when he is reading and he reads a great deal), are employed in deceiving himself, and seeking to deceive others . . . He lies in bed, always till after 12 o'clock, sometimes much later; and never walks out – Even the finest spring day does not tempt him to seek the fresh air; and this beautiful valley seems a blank to him . . . Sometimes he does not speak a word, and when he does talk it is always very much and upon subjects as far aloof from himself or his friends as possible. The boys come every week and he talks to them, especially to Hartley, but he never examines them in their books.[101]

As Southey was to say a few months later to his friend Bedford, 'O Grosvenor what a mind is here overthrown!'[102] The enthusiastic, nature-loving, mountain-climbing Coleridge of the early years in the Lakes, not to mention the happier times in Somerset, was gone for ever. His next journey to London would take him from the beloved Lakes for good.

Coleridge did not, of course, see Dorothy's letter. But in October 1810 he left Keswick in the company of Wordsworth's friend Basil Montagu, and on their arrival in London Montagu informed him how the Wordsworths felt about him. The effect was shattering to Coleridge, who was now so sensitive to criticism that it was inevitable that a careless word dropped by Montagu would have an effect far out of proportion to its severity. It is not perhaps a coincidence that Coleridge proved such a suggestive critic of Shakespeare's works, particularly the tragedies. His own mind was as near the end of its tether as that of any Hamlet or Lear or Othello.

He had spent the summer deluding himself, as his house-mate Southey saw clearly enough, that *The Friend* might yet carry on after having broken off on 15 March with the optimistic words 'To be concluded in the next Number'. Southey commented to Rickman in August:

> God help him! He has been in better health than usual, and excellent spirits, reading very hard and to no purpose – for nothing comes of it, except an accumulation of knowledge equal to that of any man living and a body of sound philosophy superior to what any man either of this or any former age has possessed – all which will perish with him. I do not know any other motive that he has for going to London, than that he becomes daily more and more uneasy at having done nothing for so long, and therefore flies away to avoid the sight of persons, who he knows must be grieved by his misconduct, tho they refrain from all remonstrance.[103]

Coleridge wrote a long letter to Wordsworth in early October, shortly before leaving for London. It was the last communication he was to have with Wordsworth for nearly two years, so mortified was he by Montagu's revelations on his arrival in London at the end of the month. Coleridge tells Wordsworth that he is reading Scott's latest poem, *The Lady of the Lake*. He unleashes a torrent of astute critical abuse:

> Merciful Apollo! – what an easy pace dost thou jog on with thy unspurred yet unpinioned Pegasus! – The movement of the Poem (which is written with exception of a multitude of Songs in regular 8 syllable Iambics) is between a sleeping Canter and a Marketwoman's trot – but it is endless – I seem never to have made any way – I never remember a narrative poem in which I felt the sense of Progress so languid.

After giving some examples, he continues:

> A man accustomed to cast words in metre and familiar with descriptive Poets & Tourists, himself a Picturesque Tourist, must be troubled with a mental Strangury, if he could not lift up his leg six times at six different Corners, and each time p— a canto. – I should imagine that even Scott's warmest admirers must acknowledge & complain of the number of prosaic lines – PROSE IN POLYSYLLABLES, surely the worst of all prose for chivalrous Poetry.

Unerringly, Coleridge picks out the faults of the poem, and also touches on the secret of Scott's phenomenal success with the public. (30,000 copies of *The Lady of the Lake* were sold.) The poem is written to a recipe: it is Gothic, fantastic, archaising, and – a remarkably strong feature of Scott's work – name-dropping.[104] Coleridge tells Wordsworth he has tried out a scheme 'which was to serve for all romances a priori – only varying the proportions':

> Now I say, it is time to make out the componant parts of the Scottish Minstrelsy – The first Business must be, a vast string of patronymics, and names of Mountains, Rivers, &c – the most commonplace imagery the Bard gars look almaist as good as new [i.e., makes look almost as good as new], by the introduction of Benvoirlich, Uam Var,
>
>
>
> on copse-wood gray
> That *waved & wept* on *Loch Achray*,
> And mingled with the pine trees blue
> On the bold Cliffs of Benvenue – . . .
>
>
> . . . Secondly, all the nomenclature of Gothic Architecture, of Heraldry, of Arms, of Hunting, & Falconry – these possess the same power of reviving the caput mortuum & rust of old imagery – besides, they are strung together, and some attention is paid to the sound of the words – for no one attempts to understand the meaning, which indeed would snap the charm . . . some pathetic moralizing on old times, or any thing else, for the head & tail pieces – with a *Bard* (that is absolutely necessary) and Songs of course.

Lastly, Coleridge comments that the poem is 'not without it's peccadilloes against the 8th Commandment', instancing two lines of Scott which closely echo Wordsworth's poem 'Ruth'.[105]

This extended criticism is interesting for a number of reasons. Coleridge knew it was widely thought that Scott had imitated 'Christabel' in *The Lay of the Last Minstrel.* Francis Jeffrey visited the Lakes in the summer of 1810 and apparently confirmed that Scott had privately acknowledged the debt.[106] Jeffrey may also have drawn Coleridge's attention to, or Coleridge may have read, an article in the new *Quarterly Review* in November 1809 in which the reviewer (who was anonymous, but was actually Scott himself) declared that Scott was the first to use what he calls 'irregular Pindaric measure', meaning the stanza structure and metre which he first met in, and imitated from, 'Christabel'. Further, Scott repeated his audacious self-praise under cover of anonymity in the *Edinburgh Annual Register,* of which he was the co-founder. In the number nominally for 1808 but actually published in July 1810 he discussed 'contemporary literature', puffing himself, his friend and fellow *Quarterly* reviewer, Southey, and Thomas Campbell, as well as minor poets among his acquaintances such as William Rose and Joanna Baillie.

Wordsworth, with whom Scott was on good personal terms, was given some meagre praise, and Coleridge was damned in the complimentary-insulting mode which Scott so often adopted when writing about him:

> With extensive learning, an unbounded vigour of imagination, and the most ready command of expression both in verse and prose – advantages which none of his predecessors enjoy in a greater, if any possess them in an equal degree; this author has been uniformly deficient in the perseverance and the sound sense which were necessary to turn his exquisite talents to their proper use. He has only produced in a complete state one or two small pieces, and every thing else, begun on a larger scale, has been flung aside and left unfinished. This is not all: although commanding the most beautiful poetical language, he has every now and then thought fit to exchange it for the gratuitous pleasure of introducing whole stanzas of quaint and vulgar doggerel.[107]

This is breathtaking coming from Scott.

We do not know for sure that Coleridge read these comments, or whether he knew Scott was the author of them. But in the summer of 1810 he not only read *The Lady of the Lake* but evidently intended to review it, as a notebook entry of 7 July makes clear.[108] No review by Coleridge appeared, perhaps because of his customary dilatoriness, perhaps because the natural place for such a review was the *Quarterly Review,* of which Scott and Southey were the chief reviewers. Southey, who was also contributing at Scott's request to the *Edinburgh Annual Register,* may have dissuaded Coleridge from attacking Scott; or Coleridge may have desisted because he knew that

Southey's latest poem, *The Curse of Kehama*, was to be reviewed in the *Quarterly* by Scott.[109] In short, Southey and Scott were helping one another in the matter of reviewing and being reviewed, and Coleridge would have caused trouble if he had published his opinion of *The Lady of the Lake*.

He therefore vented his criticism privately to Wordsworth, identifying Scott's borrowing from *Wordsworth*, and not himself – thus soliciting the proud author's immediate sympathy with his argument. But he also picked out features of Scott's verse – '8 syllable Iambics', 'Gothic Architecture', 'a *Bard* (that is absolutely necessary)' – which are present in 'Christabel'. This seems to be an indirect expression of Coleridge's outrage that Scott has succeeded with a mechanical imitation of his own poem. He may also be indicating, consciously or not, that these very aspects of 'Christabel', however unusual they may have been when he wrote the poem, belong inescapably to a degraded, *passé* genre, the Gothic, with which he himself had lost patience. Perhaps we can find one reason why he never finished that poem lurking beneath his indignation with Scott's poem.

In 1810 a further dimension was added to this odd Scott–Coleridge business. On 15 September Daniel Stuart's *Courier* carried an article entitled 'Some Imitations of Scott', meaning imitations *by* Scott. The writer places passages from *The Lay of the Last Minstrel* and *Marmion* alongside passages from Ossian, Pope, Southey, Spenser and others, to prove that Scott is 'guilty of imitation'. The article appeared over the signature 'STC', well known to be Coleridge's. It was *not* by Coleridge, as Southey hastened to assure Scott in a letter of 17 September.[110] Scott replied charmingly, if disingenuously given his own recent reviewing activities, that he was pleased to be relieved from 'the very painful feeling, that a man of Mr. Coleridge's high talents, which I had always been among the first to appreciate as they deserve', had attacked him.[111]

Coleridge got Stuart to enter a disclaimer in the paper on 20 September.[112] The perpetrator of this piece of troublemaking was suspected by Southey to be Edward Dubois, a classical scholar and minor wit, editor of the *Monthly Mirror*, in which a series of attacks on Coleridge himself appeared between June and September 1810, and writer of a comic 'sequel' to Godwin's novel *St. Leon*, entitled *St. Godwin: A Tale of the Sixteenth, Seventeenth and Eighteenth Century* (1800).[113]

These annoyances over Scott were, however, mere high jinks compared to the thunderclap Coleridge was to suffer on arriving in London with Montagu and his wife on 26 October. His notebook carries the first reference to Montagu's indiscreet repetition, and possible embroidering, of Wordsworth's warning to him about taking Coleridge into his house. Coleridge noted: 'W. authorized M. to tell me, he had no Hope of me! – O God! what good reason for saying *this*? . . . W. once – was unhappy, dissatisfied, full of craving, then what Love & Friendship, now all calm & attached – and what contempt of the moral comfort of others.' And again: 'Sunday Night [28 October 1810]. No Hope of me! absol. Nuisance! God's mercy is it a Dream!'[114]

Coleridge was so hurt that he immediately stopped writing to Wordsworth. The latter, however, was used to long periods of silence from his friend, and so for nearly a year suspected nothing, assuming that Coleridge was not in 'good health and spirits, else I think that either Mr Southey or myself would have heard from him'.[115] Many friends became involved, and the break was finally mended in spring 1812, when Wordsworth came to London to have it out with Coleridge, with Crabb Robinson acting as patient go-between.[116]

The affair became a *cause célèbre* in London and the Lakes. Much energy on both Wordsworth's and Coleridge's parts was needlessly wasted in self-defence and accusation. As Andrew Lang later commented coolly, 'Wordsworth made a mistake, Montagu was an ass, and Coleridge was too free in his lamentations.'[117] The person who suffered most was, of course, Coleridge. He never again felt the old warmth towards Wordsworth. It was the severest case of his setting up a friend to be worshipped and his correspondingly overwrought response to finding the feet of clay.

The quarrel was also the catalyst which plunged the already desperately unbalanced Coleridge into the worst psychological hell he had yet known, worse even than the Malta experience. With all the horror, dread, guilt, nightmare and excruciatingly painful illnesses he had already suffered and recorded in letters and journals, one might think that he could not sink lower. But he did.

10

Life-in-Death: London 1810–1814

Sad lot, to have no Hope!

Coleridge, 'The Visionary Hope', ?1810

Coleridge's intention in coming to London was to live with the Montagus and consult their doctor Anthony Carlisle. On hearing Montagu's account of Wordsworth's complaints about his habits, he took himself off to Hudson's Hotel in Covent Garden. He did consult Carlisle, but not for long, as he soon suspected him of discussing the case with others. Southey, already entirely sceptical about the genuineness of Coleridge's desire to be cured, received 'a dismal letter' from Carlisle confirming his own view that Coleridge's case was 'utterly hopeless'.[1] Fortunately for Coleridge, his friend John Morgan plucked him from his lonely, paranoid existence in the hotel and took him to his home in Hammersmith, where he and his wife and Charlotte Brent acted as his 'Saviours, Body and Soul'.[2] Morgan was to perform this good deed several times, for Coleridge often left Hammersmith for a hotel at times of greatest despondency.

On one such occasion Coleridge had installed himself in Brown's Coffee House off Fleet Street, from where he wrote to the Morgans, explaining that he planned to 'write a plain, honest, and full account of my state' to send to another doctor, John Abernethy. He had left the Morgans because he felt he had been 'depressing your spirits, and spite of myself gradually alienating your esteem & chilling your affection toward me'. Bravely, yet with a hint of a request to be saved once more from his self-imposed solitude, he announced his plan to visit the Morgans for a few days before entering

into my Lodgings & on my dread ordeal – as some kind-hearted Catholics have taught, that the Soul is carried slowly along close by the walls of Paradise on it's way to Purgatory, and permitted to breathe in some snatches of blissful

Airs, in order to strengthen it's endurance during it's fiery Trial by this foretaste of what awaits it at the conclusion & final goal-delivery.[3]

Not much is known about Coleridge's exact movements to and from Morgan's house between November 1810 and March 1811. But we do know that despite being near the end of his tether – as his notebook outpourings about the treachery of supposed friends show[4] – he dined out a lot with Lamb, Godwin and also with his new acquaintance Henry Crabb Robinson, whose diary becomes from now on a chief source for accounts of his conversation. Coleridge seems to have kept his desperation hidden from Lamb, who reported to Dorothy Wordsworth on 13 November that his friend seemed cheerful. He had 'powdered his head, and looks like Bacchus, Bacchus ever sleek and young. He is going to turn sober, but his clock has not struck yet, meantime he pours down goblet after goblet, the 2d to see where the 1st is gone, the 3d to see no harm happens to the second, a fourth to say there's another coming, and a 5th to say he's not sure he's the last.'[5]

There is something grotesque about this innocently cheerful account of a man in purgatory. It had the unfortunate effect of sticking in the Wordsworths' minds when they finally heard in May 1811 about the Montagu business and Coleridge's reaction to it, leaving the impression on them that he was merely pretending to be deeply wounded.[6] Crabb Robinson also told them that Coleridge was well and in good spirits. He had met Coleridge at various evening parties, and wrote to Dorothy on 23 December expressing his delight with 'your friend', who had fully lived up to his expectations, expectations which 'were never raised so before by the fame of any man'.[7]

Crabb Robinson, like so many before him, was captivated by Coleridge's learning and eloquence, Being himself a German scholar, he took special notice of Coleridge's remarks on German philosophers and poets. At a party at Lamb's on 15 November Coleridge spoke in praise of Kant, saying that his successors Fichte and Schelling would 'be found at last wrong where they have left their master', though Fichte was 'a great logician' and Schelling 'a great man'. Coleridge apparently talked of meeting Tieck in Rome, and discussed the relative merits of Goethe and Schiller, much preferring the latter and finding Goethe wanting in '*moral life*'.[8]

Robinson noticed, shrewdly enough, that Coleridge's view of *Hamlet* was similar to the famous discussion of the play in Goethe's *Wilhelm Meisters Lehrjahre* (*Wilhelm Meister's Apprenticeship*, 1795–6). Robinson does not suggest a borrowing here; and indeed there is no evidence that Coleridge knew *Wilhelm Meister* until after 1812.[9] At some time he translated the first verse of Mignon's Song from Book III, chapter 1 of the novel, but it is not known when.[10]

Coleridge's comments on *Hamlet*, soon to be elaborated in his lectures of 1811–12 and 1813, came straight from his own experience. It was in 1827 that, according to Henry Nelson Coleridge, he made the famous remark, 'I have a smack of Hamlet myself'.[11] All Coleridge's genial comments in lectures and conversations on Hamlet's introspection and paralysis are already hinted at in his conversation with Crabb Robinson in December 1810. They have the ring of truth in the light of his own painful feelings at that time. According to Robinson he said that Hamlet was

> one whose internal images (*ideal*) are so vivid, that all actual objects are faint & dead to him; hence his soliloquies on the nature of man, his disregard of life & hence his vacillations & convulsive energies. I remarked that it seemed to me unaccountable why Sh. did not make Hamlet destroy himself. C. said that S. meant to show that even such a character was forced to be the slave of chance – a salutary moral lesson. He remained to the last inept & immovable; not even the spirit of his father could rouse him to action.[12]

Coleridge also talked to Robinson about the distinction between Imagination and Fancy. 'Fancy is the arbitrary bringing together of things that lie remote & forming them into a Unity: the materials lie ready for the fancy which acts by a sort of juxtaposition.' On the other hand, 'Imagination under some excitement generates & produces a form of its own'.[13] Coleridge's antithetical mode of thinking is evident, as is his attraction to the distinctions in Kant between the mental faculties, in particular with respect to their tendency to active versus reactive agency.

In one respect Coleridge did disappoint Crabb Robinson, a committed political reformer. Coleridge apparently defended George III, who had been on the throne for fifty years. The first royal jubilee ever was held in October 1809, probably with the aim of distracting public attention from the war, the King's increasing madness, and various royal scandals.[14] The King's state of mind had been discussed in Parliament on 5 November 1810, with the result that in February 1811 his outrageous eldest son was declared Prince Regent. George III was, meanwhile, intransigent on the question of reform, particularly of the Catholic disabilities, and, as Robinson pointed out to Coleridge, had been 'an enemy to the Americans, & a friend to the Slave Trade'. Nevertheless, Coleridge now defended him on account of his staunch resistance to the French.

Coleridge was also strongly against giving the Irish equal civil rights with the British, 'because they would claim equal power'. 'The Catholic spirit', said Coleridge, drawing on his experience of the Maltese, 'is incorrigible. The priests wd. claim the tithes & require to have their religion established'.[15] He had moved far to the right of the position he had taken on such questions in his early journalism and lectures.

In 1811 he became once more closely involved with politics, for Stuart at last prevailed on him to repay his patience and regular 'loans' with some copy for the *Courier*. Between March and December 1811 Coleridge wrote a staggering ninety articles for Stuart. Though he was now conservative in his views, he was not, and never would be, a complete party man. But the *Courier* under Street's management was more or less a Government organ, and Coleridge came in for some unwelcome attention on account of his connection with the paper.

The pro-Reform party was always on the lookout for evidence of his turncoatism. A sharp comment in Leigh Hunt's radical paper, the *Examiner*, in November 1810 brought home to roost Coleridge's foolish denial in *The Friend* that he was ever a Jacobin. Neatly picking up a favourite phrase from Coleridge himself, the author announced:

> Extremes meet. Mr. Coleridge, once a republican and a follower of Tom Paine, is now a courtier and a follower of Spencer Percival. Not succeeding in persuading the public to read the crampt and courtly metaphysics of his lately deceased paper, the *Friend*, he now takes his revenge by writing against the popular judgment in the hireling daily prints. – But even here he is as harmless as ever; for what with the general distaste to such writings, and what with the difficulty of getting at Mr. Coleridge's meaning, he obtains but very few readers.[16]

More of this public bickering between newpapers was to come. Here was Coleridge, known to have been a bold speaker and writer against Pitt's Gagging Acts of 1795, now writing for a paper slavishly reproducing the Government's views, while the radical opposition fell foul, as Coleridge had once risked doing, of the restrictive libel laws. William Cobbett was even then writing his *Political Register* from Newgate, where he was serving two years for an article against excessive military flogging. Leigh Hunt and his brother John were tried (and acquitted) in February 1811 on a charge of libel in the *Examiner*.[17] The following year they became the celebrated convicted libellers of the Prince Regent, and the *Examiner*, too, was conducted from prison. The *Courier* attacked the earlier acquittal of the Hunt brothers in February 1811; Cobbett blamed Coleridge for the article, telling him to retire 'to your patrons and a bottle' and there 'pour out libations to the departed *Friend*'. Coleridge responded by denying authorship.[18]

Coleridge did begin in April 1811 to supply some pro-Government articles to the *Courier*. He wrote in favour of Perceval, which was controversial, and against Napoleon, which was not. Drawing on his experience in Malta, he discussed the current state of the European powers and the war against France being waged in the Mediterranean.[19]

On one occasion, in July 1811, Coleridge wrote a piece for the paper which was critical of the Government. In June a motion raised in Parliament against the reappointment of George III's second son, Frederick Augustus, Duke of York, as Commander in Chief of the Army was defeated by a Government majority of 296 to 47. Coleridge wrote deprecating the decision on the grounds that after the Duke's retirement the previous year, the efficiency and success of the Army had soared. Moreover, it was inappropriate to reinstate a man who had been found guilty of taking bribes from those seeking military promotion.[20] The story had an even more scandalous element than that alluded to by

Coleridge. It was the Duke's mistress, Mary Anne Clarke, who had influenced him to accept the bribes. A former lover of hers, the MP Colonel Wardle, had revealed the payments in the house of Commons in 1809. Mrs Clarke then privately printed the Duke's love letters to her, 'allowing' the Government to buy them up and suppress publication at the cost of £7,000 and a pension of £400 a year to her for life.[21]

Coleridge's article opposing the Duke's reinstatement was suppressed by Street, as Coleridge told Crabb Robinson, though a number of copies had been printed and had to be cancelled. 'This affair makes Coleridge feel uncomfortable', Robinson wrote in his diary. 'He would gladly exchange his situation for that of *The Times*, but I informed him that Walter [the editor] will not want him while Fraser remains with him'.[22] There was nothing for it but to go on writing for the *Courier* and facing attack from the liberals. An eight-line poem appeared in the paper on 20 March 1811. Called 'Epitaph on an Infant', it was signed, not 'STC', but 'Aphilos', signifying 'friendless'.

Since his arrival in London Coleridge had naturally stopped writing to Wordsworth. He seems also to have neglected his wife and Southey, and he was once more leaving letters sent to him unopened. As Southey told Grosvenor Bedford in January 1811:

> This practice of Coleridge's is of all his wretched practices that which I can least pardon. It is a sort of wilful outlawry; or excommunication of himself – he makes himself deaf and dumb to all who have any claims either of affection or duty upon him. Never I believe did any other man for the sake of sparing immediate pain to himself inflict so much upon all who were connected with him, and lay up so heavy and unendurable a burthen of self-condemnation.[23]

One of the letters Coleridge did not open was from Southey, outlining the contents of two letters to Coleridge from George Burnett, opium addict and erstwhile Pantisocrat, in which he described his poverty and despair and asked for Coleridge's help. The letters had been sent to Keswick and opened by Southey, who then wrote to Coleridge suggesting he should try to help Burnett to a situation and offering to contribute £20 'towards equipping him for it'. Coleridge had not opened the letter. In February 1811 Burnett died in a fire in the workhouse of Marylebone Infirmary.[24] The news of his death shocked Coleridge and upset Mary Lamb so much that she had to be taken to an asylum on 9 March.[25]

Coleridge's terrible habit with letters, as sure a sign of serious depression as his inability to get out of bed before midday, was well known to his friends. Lamb got round it on 8 March by addressing a letter to John Morgan. It opened with the words 'There – don't read any further, because the Letter is not intended for you but for Coleridge, who perhaps might not have opened it directed to him'.[26]

Towards the end of April Coleridge spent two days in Richmond at the house of John May, a friend of his brothers. There he met two of his nephews, sons of Colonel James. Henry Nelson Coleridge, who would become his son-in-law, was aged twelve, and his brother John Taylor Coleridge was twenty. The latter was the most brilliant of the Colonel's six sons. Having done well at Eton despite his tendency to get into debt and explain it away with the fatal fluency of his Uncle Samuel, John was now at Oxford, where he took a First in 1812, going on to be a lawyer and judge.[27] In June 1810 he had won the Chancellor's Latin Verse Prize, as Coleridge had won the Greek Ode Prize at Cambridge. His family were proud and delighted, giving John the attention his uncle would have loved to receive for *his* academic success.

The nephew gave the uncle his prize poem to read, and was promised a letter responding to it. 'I need hardly say', wrote John to his brother James, 'that I have not heard one word from him!' Nevertheless John was excited by the meeting. 'So delightful and astonishing a man I never met with'. Coleridge had 'made a conquest' of all the family and guests at Richmond, and had been 'affected distressingly' at the first sight of his nephews.[28] No doubt Coleridge felt a pang at meeting boys not very different in age from his own two sons, whom he had not seen since leaving Keswick the previous October.

A plan to publish a volume of his poems was discussed with Longman in May 1811. The collection was to include some poems from previous editions, with the addition of some newspaper poems and 'The Ancient Mariner' and his other contributions to *Lyrical Ballads*, since Wordsworth 'means in any future Edition of the Lyrical Ballads, now sold, to publish his own separately'. Coleridge received a small advance, but the volume was not published, Coleridge believing that, though he was desperate for money, Longman's was too much 'a Jew Bargain' for him to accept. 'Great as my affection may be for the Angels of Paternoster Row, that sit in the appropriate Shape of Cormorants on the Tree of Knowledge', he told Stuart, 'I am selfish enough to have a still greater for S.T.C. and his three little ones.'[29]

Coleridge passed the summer and autumn socializing with Godwin, Lamb, Crabb Robinson and Hazlitt, who, now married to Sarah Stoddart, was living near the Morgans in Hammersmith.[30] In October he was asked at a party to recite 'Christabel' from memory, but according to Robinson – who wrote this part of his diary in German – he was 'unable to recollect the words', being 'affected by liquor'.[31] The party took place at the house of John Dyer Collier in Hatton Garden, where Robinson lodged, being a colleague of Collier's son, John Payne Collier, on *The Times*.

Both Robinson and Collier junior were prominent in helping Coleridge to arrange a new set of lectures, which were given at the London Philosophical Society's rooms off Fleet Street between November 1811 and January 1812. Collier reported on them occasionally in the *Morning Chronicle*, and Robinson 'with difficulty' persuaded Walter to insert a paragraph in *The Times* announcing the lectures.[32] More importantly, partly through the good offices of Southey, who was determined that the texts of these lectures should not be lost like those of 1808, it was arranged that Payne Collier would take them down in shorthand.[33] Unfortunately Collier later became infamous as a literary forger, and some doubt was cast on the authenticity of the text he published in 1856, *Seven Lectures on Shakespeare and Milton. By the late S. T. Coleridge.* Though he did embellish the published text somewhat, his shorthand notes have survived, as well as longhand transcripts, and these have been recently published in the *Collected Works* of Coleridge as the best text recoverable.[34]

The first lecture was given on Monday 18 November 1811. The Prospectus announced that there would be an introductory lecture on 'False Criticism' and its causes, followed by 'a philosophic Analysis and Explanation of all the principal *Characters* of our great Dramatist', a critical comparison of Shakespeare with his contemporaries Beaumont and Fletcher, Jonson, Ford and Massinger, and finally some lectures on Milton. There would be fifteen lectures, delivered on Mondays and Thursdays. Tickets for the whole course cost two guineas, 'or 3 Guineas with the privilege of introducing a Lady'.[35] According to Robinson, who went to hear them all, attendance was good, and in addition to all Coleridge's London friends one or more of the lectures was heard by the poets Byron and Samuel Rogers, who were spotted by Robinson at the second last lecture on 20 January 1812.[36]

Coleridge began by asserting the need for critics to apply principles in their work, and he was soon attacking the present age as one of 'personality and political gossip, where insects as in Egypt were worshipped and valued in proportion to the venom of their sting'.[37] The particular target was undoubtedly the *Edinburgh Review,* as it had recently been Byron's in his satire *English Bards and Scotch Reviewers* (1809), written in revenge for the drubbing his first volume of poetry had received from the *Edinburgh.*

Collier was disappointed at the lack of 'brilliancy' of this first lecture, and Robinson thought there was 'too much apology, too much reference to what he had before written, too much promise of what was to come' – the besetting sin also of *The Friend.*[38] What the 'several Fashionables' whom the *Courier* reported to have attended thought of the lecture we can only guess. Attendance seems to have kept up well, as Sara Hutchinson heard from her cousin Tom Monkhouse early in December.[39] One contributory factor to the less than sparkling success of the very first lecture was the severe constipation Coleridge suffered from, which he described colourfully to Robinson: 'Truly for 8 days together the Trunk of my poor Body was or seemed to be a Trunk which Nature had first locked, and then thrown away the Key'. Though he joked about the problem, he left Robinson in no doubt about the severe pain he endured.[40]

Both Collier and Robinson were delighted with the second lecture of 21 November. Collier was ecstatic: 'I felt myself more humble if possible than the meanest worm before the Almighty, and blessed my stars that I could comprehend what he had the power to invent.'[41] Much of the lecture was to be repeated in *Biographia Literaria,* particularly his remarks about poetry both expressing and producing excitement, having as its immediate object the production of pleasure, and being characterized by parts fitting into a pleasurable and irreducible whole.[42] Coleridge also touched in this second lecture on the predominant view among eighteenth-century critics and editors that Shakespeare was 'a sort of lusus naturae', or sport of nature, far above other writers and yet irregular in the matter of dramatic rules and classical learning.[43]

Piecing together what we can from Collier's incomplete transcripts, Robinson's notes in his diary, the reports in newspapers, and the remarks of occasional attenders such as Lamb, Hazlitt and Lady Beaumont, we can see that the lectures had all the virtues and all the faults which might have been expected. As in his conversation, Coleridge often dazzled listeners with his wide knowledge and suggestive *aperçus*. But he sometimes alienated them by being obscure, by digressing excessively, by repeating his favourite observations – 'chewing the cud of his past lectures', as Robinson put it[44] – by allowing his thoughts to 'crowd each other to death', as he himself had noted wryly in a piece of self-analysis in a notebook of 1808.[45]

Though the lectures were advertised as being on Shakespeare and Milton, Coleridge stretched the patience of his audience by deferring discussion of these authors while he rode various hobby horses, including, as in 1808, that of the education debate between Bell and Lancaster. A typical movement of his mind, by no means illogical but not consonant with the stated purpose of the lectures, occurred in the transition from the fifth to the sixth lecture. Discussing *Love's Labour's Lost* towards the end of Lecture five, he quoted Berowne's speech in Act I, scene i:

> Why should I joy in any abortive birth?
> At Christmas I no more desire a rose
> Than wish a snow in May's new-fangl'd shows;
> But like of each thing that in season grows.

He then drew a moral from this, 'to be impressed on every parent in this wonder-loving age', namely that children should not be pushed into reason prematurely, but rather be enjoyed for their 'natural infantile prattle'. This led him to express his gratitude that in his own childhood he had been allowed to read what he liked rather than only 'improving' works.

In the following lecture, instead of returning to Shakespeare, he took up where he had left off on the subject of education, now attacking the system of punishment adopted by 'a man of great reputation' (Lancaster), who had been known to suspend boys from the ceiling in baskets to be derided by their schoolmates.[46] At this point Lamb apparently whispered to Robinson that it was 'a pity he did not leave this till he got to *Henry VI* and then he might say he could not help taking part against the Lancastrians'.[47]

In his seventh lecture, on 9 December 1811, Coleridge analysed *Romeo and Juliet*. His personal feelings on the subject of love, so vividly and pathetically expressed with regard to himself and the two Saras in the privacy of his notebooks, find public utterance in a masterly appreciation of the psychological astuteness shown by Shakespeare. Collier's report reads:

> Shakespeare had described this passion in various states & he had begun as was most natural with love in the young mind. Did he begin with making Romeo & Juliet in love at the first glimpse as a common and ordinary thinker would do? – No – he knew what he was about, he was to develope the whole passion and he takes it in its first elements: that sense of imperfection, that yearning to combine itself with something lovely. – Romeo became enamoured of the ideal he formed in his own mind & then as it were christened the first real being as that which he desired. He appeared to be in love with Rosaline, but in truth he was in love only with his own idea. He felt the necessity of being beloved which no noble mind can be without: Shakespeare then introduces Romeo to Juliet and makes it not only a violent but permanent love at first sight which had been so often ridiculed in Shakespeare.[48]

Crabb Robinson was reduced to despair by the eighth lecture. His comment to Mrs Clarkson on 13 December catches all Coleridge's power and all his paralysis, his immense superiority of intellect and his underdeveloped sense of propriety, of the necessity of keeping within limits. Of the eight lectures already given – half the course – Robinson says:

> As evidences of splendid talent, original thought, & rare powers of expression & fancy, they are all his *admirers* can wish; but as discharge of his undertaking, a fulfilment of his promise to the public, they give his *friends* great uneasiness. As you express it, 'an enchanter's spell seems to be upon him' which takes from him the power of treating upon the only subject his hearers are anxious he should consider, while it leaves him infinite ability to riot & run wild on a variety of moral and religious themes. In his [sixth] lecture, he was by advertisement to speak of Romeo & Juliet and Shakespeare's females –
> Unhappily some demon whispered the name of Lancaster in his ear: And we had in one Eveng – An attack on the poor Quaker – a defence of boarding-school flogging – a parallel between the ages of Eliz: & Chas, a defence of what is untruly called unpoetic language, an account of the different languages of Europe And a vindication of Shakespear against the imputation of grossness!!!

After returning to *Romeo and Juliet* in the seventh lecture, Coleridge had been derailed in the eighth on to a discussion of incest. Robinson continues:

> Romeo & Juliet were forgotten. And in the next lecture we are really to hear something of these lovers. Now this will be the 4th time that his hearers will have been invited expressly to hear of this play, There are to be only fifteen lectures in the whole (half have been delivered) And the course is to include Shakespear & Milton the modern poets, &c!!![49]

With his ninth lecture Coleridge dug a hole for himself from which all the efforts of his defenders and admirers, from his daughter Sara to the most recent editor of his Shakespeare lectures, R. A. Foakes, have been unable wholly to extract him. He borrowed wholesale for his discussion of ancient versus modern drama and his account of *The Tempest* from A. W. Schlegel's *Lectures on Dramatic Art and Literature* (*Vorlesungen über dramatische Kunst und Litteratur*), which had been delivered in Vienna in 1808 and published in three volumes in 1809–10.[50]

As early as 6 November 1811 Coleridge had told Crabb Robinson he was 'anxious to see Schlegel's Werke before the Lectures commence'.[51] During the course of the ninth lecture he informed his audience that he had been given the day before 'a Work by a German writer', of which he had had time to read only a small part, but 'what he has read he approved & he should praise the book much more highly were it not that in truth it would be praising himself, as the sentiments contained in it were so coincident with those Coleridge had expressed at the Royal Institution' in 1808, as Collier reported.[52]

Since no proper record of the 1808 lectures survives, the claim cannot be tested. That he and Schlegel – how characteristic of Coleridge to talk only of 'a German writer' – should have come to similar views about the particular virtues of Shakespeare as argued against the prejudices of, in Schlegel's case, the French drama and dramaturgy which had dominated German thinking in the eighteenth century, and in Coleridge's, the eighteenth-century criticism of Shakespeare in England, is far from incredible. Both had read and admired Lessing, the first to argue Shakespeare's merits against French neo-classicism, and Herder. Both were influenced by Kant's analysis of the imagination as a bridge-building faculty between the senses and the Reason in his *Critique of Judgement* (1790). Both knew Schiller's writings on classical versus modern literature.

The German Romantic theorists were themselves indebted to works on rhetoric by Blair, Ferguson and other British writers, and to Burke's work on the sublime and the beautiful, which Coleridge, of course, also knew. So widely read was Coleridge in the subject of aesthetics that he formed his own opinions in response to a very wide range of critical writing, English, German and classical. As De Quincey pointed out, no one was better placed than Coleridge to offer a theory of literature illustrated with examples from many languages. With his penchant for abstract metaphysics brought into harmony with his practical experience as a poet, he was bound to become the finest literary critic of his day.

And so he undoubtedly did. Yet because of his fumbling and fudging and desperate acts of bad faith, which were inevitably seen through, he undermined from the start his own position. Since he made a fuss, claiming precedence in inappropriate places and quite unnecessarily hiding his sources, he induced students of his work to 'track' him relentlessly through the bushes and briars of the thorniest of subjects, plagiarism. A. W. Schlegel undoubtedly has a claim on our attention; his remarks about classical and Shakespearean drama, and his discussion of what he and his fellow German critics defined as 'Romantic' literature – imaginative, possessing organic unity, free from rules yet obeying an inner law of creation, characterized by the use of symbols – are fine contributions to the literary debate. But so are Coleridge's, and not only where he and Schlegel 'coincide'. In discussions of individual Shakespeare plays, Coleridge has the edge over Schlegel, whose analyses, though illuminating, are more general and impressionistic than Coleridge's. It is for Coleridge that we might claim the title of the first great practical critic.[53]

That uncanny talent for being beforehand with his critics in analysing himself is apparent in an odd letter to an unknown correspondent written in December 1811, just before the offending ninth lecture was delivered. The addressee had raised the question of plagiarism, but not by Coleridge. Rather, it was Scott's use of 'Christabel' in *The Lay of the Last Minstrel* which seems to have been mentioned. Coleridge's reply is deceptively calm and generous. He defends Scott against the charge of deliberate theft, saying that his reading was so vast and various that any borrowing would have been subsumed into a mass of elements feeding into his poems, which 'are evidently the indigenous Products of his Mind & Habits'.

This is not merely very tolerant towards Scott; it formulates a defence of Coleridge himself. In the same letter he describes how a German, 'a Mr Bernard Krusve', had approached him after his seventh or eighth lecture to tell him of the similarity of his argument about *Romeo and Juliet* to that in Schlegel's lectures. Coleridge tells his correspondent that at this time he had no acquaintance with Schlegel's lectures, but on being given a copy by Krusve, he had read them and certainly saw the resemblance. This led to the vague avowal of a likeness in Lecture nine, in which he was actually paraphrasing or translating Schlegel without acknowledgement. To his correspondent he accounts for the similarity by the fact that he and Schlegel had 'studied deeply & perseverently the philosophy of Kant, the distinguishing feature of which is to treat every subject in reference to the operation of the mental Faculties, to which it specially appertains'. If only Coleridge had said so at the lecture! And if only he had either avoided paraphrasing Schlegel or frankly quoted and praised him. In his letter he sums up the complex question of originality rather finely: 'He who can catch the Spirit of an original, has it already'.[54]

In the remaining lectures Coleridge, recognizing the need to speed up and concentrate his material if he was to get through the whole of Shakespeare and have time for Milton too, carried on the discussion of Shakespeare's genius with rather less blatant reliance on Schlegel. As might be expected of an English critic of Shakespeare lecturing to an English audience, he often made his points in opposition to the criticism of Samuel Johnson in his *Preface to Shakespeare* (1765). Johnson was a *bête noire* of Coleridge's. Many a notebook entry shows him working out his ideas in reaction to Johnson. In a conversation with Southey on 7 July 1810 he expressed annoyance at the 'damnable rage of judging by the faults' of

Shakespeare, talking of the 'vile Johnsonian Antithesis of Black & White': 'One would suppose from Johnson's Preface that Sh. was a pie-bald Poet – & that he, the Critic, was standing by, in the worthy employment of counting & pointing out, black spots against white – hence: a black spot on his right ear, just half an inch in diameter – but just on his forehead there is a white spot, of the same size – & so on thro' the whole skin of the poor becritick'd Animal.'[55]

It is worth pointing out, however, that though Coleridge naturally formulated his own views partly in opposition to the greatest English critic of the previous age, he was in some respects quite close to Johnson. For when Johnson discusses Shakespeare's breaking of the dramatic rules governing unity of time, place and action as set out by Aristotle and refined or adapted by mainly French neo-classical critics, he is as strong in defence of Shakespeare as Coleridge could be. The difference lies in the precise vocabulary used and in the general intellectual and cultural context in which the two men wrote. Thus Johnson tackles the question of stage illusion with robust common sense:

> The objection arising from the impossibility of passing the first hour at Alexandria and the next at Rome supposes that when the play opens the spectator really imagines himself at Alexandria, and believes that his walk to the theatre has been a voyage to Egypt and that he lives in the days of Antony and Cleopatra. Surely he that imagines this may imagine more . . . Delusion, if delusion be admitted, has no certain limitation; if the spectator can be once persuaded that his old acquaintance are Alexander and Caesar, that a room illuminated with candles is the plain of Pharsalia, or the bank of Granicus, he is in a state of elevation above the reach of reason or of truth . . .
>
> The truth is that the spectators are always in their senses, and know from the first act to the last that the stage is only a stage, and that the players are only players.[56]

Schlegel, too, deals with the matter of stage illusion, describing theatrical illusion as 'a waking dream, to which we voluntarily surrender ourselves'.[57] And Coleridge in a set of 'Desultory Remarks on the Stage', probably written in preparation for the 1808 lectures, wrote of the purpose of stage presentations being 'to produce a sort of temporary Half-Faith, which the Spectator encourages in himself & supports by a voluntary contribution on his own part, because he knows that it is at all times in his power to see the thing as it really is'.[58] Both Coleridge and Schlegel knew Johnson's work, and both knew Herder's Shakespeare essay in *Von Deutscher Art und Kunst (Of German Art,* 1773), in which a similar point is made. Coleridge and Wordsworth annotated Richard Payne Knight's *Analytical Inquiry into the Principles of Taste* (third edition, 1806), which discusses the same subject.[59]

In other words, there was a wealth of literature in Britain and Germany in the latter half of the eighteenth century defending Shakespeare's breaking of the rules of dramatic unity. One can scarcely talk of originality or plagiarism here. It is a matter of a gradually changing intellectual climate, with later writers like Coleridge and Schlegel appealing less to common sense or logic as a sanction for their critical views and more to imaginative and emotional needs on the part of both author and readers or spectators. It is entirely characteristic both of Coleridge's habits and of the way ideas become current and find particular expression in the work of one among many writers that the most famous formula of all about illusion was made by Coleridge in *Biographia Literaria*, but not specifically in relation to Shakespeare or the stage. He transferred the idea from dramatic illusion to poetic illusion, applying it to the description of his own aim in writing 'The Ancient Mariner' for *Lyrical Ballads*, namely to 'procure for these shadows of imagination that willing suspension of disbelief for the moment, which constitutes poetic faith'.[60]

On 2 January 1812, in his twelfth lecture, Coleridge came to *Hamlet*, to which he responded with native critical astuteness and close personal identification:

> Yet with all this sense of duty, this resolution arising out of conviction nothing is done: this admirable & consistent character, deeply acquainted with his own feelings, painting them with such wonderful power & accuracy, and just as strongly convinced of the fitness of executing the solemn charge committed to him, still yields to the same retiring from all reality, which is the result of having what we express by the term a world within himself.
>   Such a mind as this is near akin to madness: Dryden has said
>
>   Great wit to madness, *nearly* is allied
>
> and he was right: for he means by wit that greatness of genius, which led Hamlet to the perfect knowledge of his own character, which with all strength of motive was so weak as to be unable to carry into effect his most obvious duty.[61]

Crabb Robinson's comment on this, when writing to Mrs Clarkson the day after the lecture, was 'Somebody said to me, this is a Satire on himself; No, said I it is an Elegy.'[62]

Collier appears not to have taken notes of the last five lectures, numbers thirteen to seventeen. According to Robinson's brief accounts, Coleridge took issue with Johnson in lectures thirteen and fourteen, arriving at Milton in lecture fifteen, though he was still vilifying Johnson, whom he called a 'fellow', thereby eliciting a hiss from the audience. Robinson noted that on this occasion (as long ago in Bristol) Coleridge turned the opposition to account. He 'happily apologized' for his remark by observing 'that it was in the nature of evil to beget evil, and that he had, therefore, in censuring Johnson fallen into the same fault himself'.[63]

The series was counted a success. For the last lecture, on 27 January, 'the room was crowded' and Coleridge showed himself brilliant in defence of Milton's treatment of God in *Paradise Lost*.[64] Coleridge was sufficiently encouraged by his success to begin thinking of another course almost as soon as this one had ended.[65]

A week or so after the lectures finished, Coleridge wrote to his wife to say that he was coming north on the Liverpool Mail.[66] He was eagerly expected at Keswick, not only by his family but also by a young poet, Percy Bysshe Shelley, who had been staying in lodgings in the town. Southey, on meeting Shelley, wrote to Grosvenor Bedford that it had been like meeting his own ghost:

> He is just what I was in 1794. His name is Shelley, son to the member from Shoreham: with 6000*l* a year entailed upon him, and as much more in his father's power to cut off. Beginning with romances of ghost and murder, and with poetry at Eton, he passed, at Oxford, into metaphysics; printed half-a-dozen pages which he entitled *The Necessity of Atheism*; sent one anonymously to Coplestone, in expectation, I suppose, of converting him; was expelled in consequence; married a girl of seventeen, after being turned out of doors by his father; and here they both are, in lodgings, living upon 200*l* a year, which her father allows them. He is come to the fittest physician in the world. At present he has got to the Pantheistic stage of philosophy, and, in the course of week, I expect he will be a Berkeleyan, for I have put him upon a course of Berkeley.[67]

Shelley was hoping to meet Coleridge, but left Keswick before Coleridge arrived in February 1812. Of the older generation of poets, Coleridge was the one Shelley revered most, buying copies of all his works. When living near Geneva in 1816, he wrote asking Thomas Love Peacock for news of the current literature of England, 'of which when I speak Coleridge is in my thoughts'.[68] Though Shelley did not meet the poet in 1812, he did see the other members of the Coleridge family at Greta Hall. He commented tersely on Mrs Southey as 'very stupid' and Mrs Coleridge as 'worse'.[69]

As had happened often before, Coleridge was so moved by seeing his children that he had a temporary surge of warmth towards his wife. He reported proudly to Morgan on 23 February that little Sara was 'a sweet-tempered, meek, blue-eyed Fairy', who, thanks to her mother's teaching, read 'French tolerably & Italian fluently' at the tender age of nine. The boys, too, pleased him. He had collected them from Mr Dawes's school at Ambleside on his way to Keswick and found Derwent 'the self-same fond small Samuel Taylor Coleridge as ever'. Hartley, more like his father in temperament, had 'turned pale & trembled all over' when he saw his father, then instantly asked him 'some questions about the connection of the Greek with the Latin'. To this letter Coleridge added the postcript in Latin, for Morgan's eyes only, about his wife's modesty and excellence as a mother, yet his feeling of horror at the thought of sexual congress with her, 'as though my wife were my very own sister'.[70]

Hartley had cause to turn pale once more when Coleridge set off with his boys for Keswick. As Mrs Coleridge told Poole later that year, Coleridge 'rode through Grasmere without stopping at Wordsworth's!' The children had not been told of the rift between their father and Wordsworth, and since Coleridge's absence had continued to visit at Grasmere, with their mother also having frequent and pleasant relations with the Wordsworths now that the volatile element in the two families' relationship – namely Coleridge – was removed from the scene. Sara told Poole how

> poor Hartley sat in speechless astonishment as the Chaise passed the turning to the Vicarage where W. lives, but he dared not hazard one remark and Derwent fixed his eyes full of tears upon his father, who turned his head away to conceal his own emotions – when they had an opportunity they both eagerly asked the meaning of this paradox, and H. turned as white, as lime, when I told him that Mr W. had a little vexed his father by something he had said to Mr Montagu – which through mistake had been misrepresented: these children in the habit of going weekly to Grasmere could not comprehend how these things were. – Numerous were the letters and messages I received from Miss W. to urge C. to write to her and not to leave the country without seeing them; but he would not go to *them* and *they* did not come to him, so after staying 6 weeks he returned to give his Lectures at Willis's rooms.[71]

For his part, Coleridge tortured himself about this non-reconciliation with Wordsworth, rehearsing the grounds of the break once more in a letter to Morgan and confessing that 'the Grasmere Business has kept me in a fever of agitation – and will end in complete alienation'.[72] By the middle of April 1812 he was back in London, never again to return to the Lake District to which he had been so lovingly lured by Wordsworth in 1800. Several ironies resound through the following passage of his wife's letter to Poole about the affair:

> When C. was here in Febry he was cheerful & good natured & full of fair promises – he talked of our settling finally in London, that is, when he had gone on for a year or so giving me, and all his friends satisfaction as to the possibility of making a livelihood by his writings so as to enable us to live in great credit there – I listened, I own, with incredulous ears, while he was building these 'airy castles' and calmly told him that I thought it was much better that I and the children should remain in the country until the Boys had finished their School-education and then, if he found himself in circumstances that would admit of it, I would cheerfully take leave of *dear Keswick*, and follow his amended fortunes; he agreed to this, & in the meantime, a regular correspondence *was* to be kept up between himself, and me, and the children; and *never more* was he to keep a letter of mine, or the Boys', or Southey's *un*opened – his promises, poor fellow, are like his Castles, – airy nothings![73]

Now that his feelings towards Wordsworth were soured, the Lake District was no longer attractive to Coleridge. As always with him, things were to get better if he moved somewhere – anywhere – else. It is, nevertheless, odd – and pathetic – to hear him proposing London as a permanent residence, considering his erstwhile love of the outdoors, his minute appreciation of nuances of climate and scenery, his tremendous physical energy and courage when walking or climbing. And it is odd, too, to read Sara's description of 'dear Keswick', for twelve years earlier she had been reluctant to leave friends in the West Country to go north at Coleridge's summons. Of course, she had a stable existence at Greta Hall with her sister and Southey; but she had also found that Wordsworth was a good friend to her and the children, even as he had become a lost friend to Coleridge. He 'has a most friendly regard' for Hartley, she told Poole, and was already thinking ahead to the time when provision would need to be made for Hartley to go to University.[74] None of the circle expected Coleridge himself to make plans for his son's future.

Once arrived back in London, Coleridge went to join the Morgans at Berners Street, where they had recently moved from Hammersmith. With help from the Beaumonts and other friends he began raising subscriptions for another set of lectures, on drama 'of the Greek, French, Italian, English, and Spanish Stage, chiefly with reference to the Works of Shakespeare', to be delivered in the fashionable Willis's Rooms in St James's.[75] As he was preparing for these, Wordsworth arrived in London to discuss the Montagu affair. Lamb became involved in attempts at reconciliation, as did Crabb Robinson, whose patient going between a pained and sensitive Coleridge, who often wept when discussing the affair, and a proud Wordsworth finally brought about a reconciliation.[76] Robinson noted a conversation with Lamb on 9 May in which Lamb pronounced Wordsworth 'cold'; Robinson's own feeling was that 'the *coolness* of such a man' was preferable to 'the heat of Coleridge'.[77]

To his brother Crabb Robinson wrote that he was pleased to have helped heal the breach between 'two *such men* as W. and C. (One I believe the greatest man now living in this Country. And the other a man of astonishing genius & talents tho' not harmoniously blended as in his happier friend to form a great & good man)'.[78] His remark is interesting as an indication that despite the fact that neither Wordsworth nor Coleridge earned anything much from their writings and that they were routinely ridiculed by the powerful quarterly reviews – Jeffrey was to open his famous review of *The Excursion* (1814) with the words 'This will never do' – an increasing number of their contemporaries now took it for granted, as Robinson did, that they were the two greatest poets of the age. And this notwithstanding the much greater popular success of Scott and, more recently, Byron, the first two cantos of *Childe Harold's Pilgrimage* having been published with *éclat* early in 1812. Not only Crabb Robinson, but Hazlitt (though a treacherous friend), De Quincey, John Wilson, and now Shelley, too, were as clear about the predominance of the two men as any later generation would be.

Many a letter had been exchanged on the subject of the quarrel over the last year or so among the Wordsworth and Coleridge circles, and it was a chief topic of literary gossip in London and beyond.[79] Dorothy feared that Coleridge would convince the London world that Wordsworth had wronged him; her friend Catherine Clarkson wrote to Crabb Robinson on

22 April 1812, raising the gossip to an even higher pitch of excitement. Very much taking Wordsworth's side, she expressed her fear of Coleridge's fabled conversational gift: 'I know so well the power of Coleridge's presence & the effect of his eloquence that something ought to be done by W – to counteract them. – It appears now that C– – has been living for the last month at an Inn in Penrith – The Morgans had written to Keswick to enquire after him . . . His picture was wanted for the exhibition. In short there was a complete hue & cry after him. Not a soul knew what had become of him.'[80]

The picture alluded to here seems to have been a drawing done by George Dawe, who also took a mask of Coleridge from which he modelled a bust for exhibition at the Royal Academy in April 1812 (see plate 16).[81] The drawing shows an overweight Coleridge casting his eye upwards with a quizzical, self-righteous glance. In the first letter he addressed to Wordsworth since leaving Grasmere nearly two years before, Coleridge exhibited some of that self-righteousness. Writing on 4 May, he reiterated the cause of the quarrel from his side, defended himself against the charge of trumpeting it all over London, spoke of his hurt, and responded to Wordsworth's 'sneer' about his wearing powder, as reported by Lamb late in 1810. He had resorted to powder, he said, because his hair was thinning and becoming grey in patches.

All in all, the letter is relatively restrained, and it contains two passages which must have warmed Wordsworth's cool heart. Firstly, Coleridge mentions having sent Lady Beaumont a copy of 'To William Wordsworth', the verses 'composed after your recitation of the great Poem at Coleorton'. Secondly, he finishes his long letter as follows: 'Whatever be the result of this long delayed explanation, I have loved you & your's too long & too deeply to have it in my power to cease to do so.'[82]

Wordsworth accepted the explanation and the homage, and the two men walked together to Hampstead as a sign of renewed friendship.[83] Wordsworth also attended some of Coleridge's lectures, which began, not on 12 May as advertised, but a week later because of the assassination of the Prime Minister, Spencer Perceval, in the House of Commons on 11 May. Coleridge was deeply shaken by the event and the evidence it gave of 'the atrocious sentiments universal among the Populace'. He told Southey that he had been to the *Courier* office to offer his services (the piece praising Percival in the paper on 14 May was possibly his), and on his way back had called in at 'a large Public House frequented about 1 o/clock by the lower Orders'. 'It was really shocking – nothing but exultation'.[84]

Nobody took shorthand notes of the new course of six lectures. Coleridge seems to have repeated much of the Schlegel material on ancient and modern drama before concentrating on Greek drama. Robinson thought the lectures 'very German'.[85] He had himself read Schlegel's lectures on Shakespeare in February 1812 and had commented on the first set of lectures that Coleridge 'did not disdain to borrow observations from Schlegel, though the coincidences between the two lectures are, for the greater part, coincidences merely and not the one caused by the other.'[86] Attendance fell off, and the course was not a financial success, though the experience did not deter Coleridge from beginning yet another set in November, once more on Shakespeare. Only a few notes, and a few remarks by Crabb Robinson, remain of these.

It seems likely that in the lectures begun in November Coleridge repeated material from the previous courses. This time, he may have used Schlegel more openly, for he took a copy of Schlegel's *Lectures* into the lecture room with him.[87] Following Schlegel, he distinguished between classical and Romantic art, characterizing the former as 'finite', 'statuesque', having as its elements 'Grace, Elegance, Proportion, Fancy, Dignity, Majesty, whatever is capable of being definitely conveyed by defined Forms or Thoughts'. By contrast, modern or Romantic art deals in 'the infinite, & indefinite as the vehicle of the Infinite', with 'Passions, the Obscure Hopes & Fears – the wandring thro' infinite – grander moral Feelings – more august conception of man as man – the Future rather than the Present – Sublimity' as its characteristic features, according to Coleridge's notes for the lecture.[88]

These distinctions are a commonplace in German Romantic criticism, occurring in the works of both A. W. and Friedrich Schlegel, and having their roots in Kant and Schiller. One can detect also a hint of Burke's distinction between the sublime (modern) and the beautiful (classical) and Coleridge's own sense of the difference between Fancy, operating mechanically, and Imagination, working by a kind of free will. This course was a success, with Coleridge receiving 'three rounds of applause on entering the lecture room' for his last lecture on 26 January 1813, as Robinson noted.[89]

On 9 November 1812 Josiah Wedgwood wrote a brief letter to Coleridge, explaining that he had 'for some time' been suffering business losses and could no longer pay his half of the £150 annuity. He would continue to pay Tom's half. In his reply, Coleridge squirmed on the hook of pride and humility, guilt and gratitude. If he had not lost 'more than £200 from the non-payment of the Subscriptions' to *The Friend*, he would have 'resigned my claims on your Bounty'; he felt nothing but gratitude, but he also feared he had been 'cruelly calumniated'. Wedgwood replied firmly and coolly that no-one had criticized Coleridge to him, but that he knew of 'circumstances of your habits which have given me pain'. He wished Coleridge well, but 'I cannot form a hope that we can again feel towards each other as we have done'.[90] The unspoken reproach is that Coleridge never stirred himself to write anything about Tom after the latter's death. Coleridge was only too aware of that nagging debt; he admitted to Daniel Stuart that he was relieved to have got rid of the accumulated weight of responsibility and guilt towards Josiah.[91]

As for the loss of the £75 per annum, this was less of a blow than it might have been, for Coleridge had just heard that his play *Remorse*, a reworking of *Osorio*, had been accepted for performance at Drury Lane.[92] Coleridge took a keen interest in rehearsals, which began in December 1812. In fact, he rather meanly used them as an excuse not to visit the Wordsworths, who were in despair following the death from measles of their six-year-old son Thomas. Thomas was the second of their children to die in 1812; in June three-year-old Catherine, the child commemorated in Wordsworth's marvellous sonnet 'Surprised by Joy', had died of convulsions. Coleridge, with such tender feelings towards the Wordsworth children, as well as his own, was too cowardly to go and comfort his friend. He wrote an awkward letter of condolence, holding out a half-promise that he would leave London after Christmas and go to 'live among you as long as I live', if his play was successful.[93]

Remorse ran for twenty nights, beginning on 23 January 1813, a successful run by the standards of the time. It earned Coleridge £400, more, as he wryly told Poole, 'than all my literary Labors put together'.[94] But he did not go to the Wordsworths, from a mixture of his usual inertia and paralysis of will where a duty showed itself, with a continuing soreness about Wordsworth, despite the reconciliation. By April 1813 Dorothy had given up hope of his coming north either to comfort them or to see about Hartley's future.[95]

Coleridge had good reason to feel pleased with his dramatic success. For once he was getting a decent financial return on his efforts. On Saturday 23 January, at the first performance of his play, he was noticed by the audience, whereupon he basked in unaccustomed adulation. 'They all turned their faces towards our Box, & gave a treble chear of Claps', he told his wife in a cheerful letter. He added piously that he mentioned this because 'it will please Southey to hear that there is a large number of Persons in London, who hail with enthusiasm any prospect of the Stage's being purified & rendered classical'.[96]

Coleridge's remark, though lacking in modesty, was apt. The state of the London theatres was hardly edifying or full of vitality. Only two theatres had royal patents (granted by Charles II) and could stage serious drama. Yet managements found it difficult, then as now, and without official subsidies, to square the ideal of presenting good drama with the practical necessity to fill the theatre. Shakespeare was, of course, by far the most represented dramatist. But of new drama, particularly tragedy, there was a dearth. In these circumstances it is not surprising that *Remorse*, being a tragedy and 'Shakespearean', was eagerly taken up by the Drury Lane management. The theatre had been owned by Sheridan, who had rejected *Osorio* in 1797. He had been ruined by the fire which had ravaged the theatre in February 1809 (though he was famously reported to have taken a stool and a glass of port to watch the fire, saying, 'May not a man have a drink by his own fireside?'). The rebuilt theatre opened in October 1812, now run by a Whig politician, Samuel Whitbread, and a five-man management committee which was later, in 1815–16, to include Byron.[97] The committee's aim was to produce drama of high quality. *Remorse* was one of the first productions in the new building.

Coleridge had revised the play in such a way as to make the complicated plot less opaque. A new opening scene contrives to fill the audience in on the hinterland of the action rather more adroitly than its counterpart in *Osorio*. The two brothers are renamed: Osorio becomes Ordonio, and the good brother Albert is now Alvar. Some of the lengthier speeches have been reduced, as have the impossible stage directions. The business with the pictures is made clearer, though at the cost of introducing some stagey contrivance. The scene takes place in 'a Hall of Armory, with an Altar at the back of the Stage'. In order that the audience as well as the heroine, now called Teresa, should see the picture, it appears in an illuminated picture of Alvar's assassination in a fire on the altar.[98]

The play remains difficult to follow, unrelieved by any moments of comedy, unaided by parallel actions, and, though Coleridge prided himself on the 'variety of metres', still sounds unvariedly ranting and rhetorical. The final speech of the play, delivered by the good brother Alvar, shows some strength in its metre but indulges in moral haranguing:

> In these strange dread events
> Just Heaven instructs us with an awful voice,
> That Conscience rules us e'en against our choice.
> Our inward Monitress to guide or warn,
> If listened to; but if repelled with scorn,
> At length as dire Remorse, she reappears,
> Works in our guilty hopes, and selfish fears!
> Still bids, Remember! and still cries, Too late!
> And while she scares us, goads us to our fate.[99]

Crabb Robinson, who loyally attended the first night, commented that the play was more poetic than dramatic, that Coleridge 'indulges before the public in those metaphysical and philosophical speculations which are becoming only in solitude and with select minds'. Both the hero and the villain are 'dreamers', and the action is improbable, the 'contrivance with the picture' clumsy, and the poetic diction too ornate, yet Robinson was surprised to find that the play was nevertheless received 'with great and almost unmixed applause'.[100]

The reviews, of which there were many, tended to agree with Robinson. Thomas Barnes, writing in Leigh Hunt's *Examiner*, praised Coleridge's 'poetic talents' and even his skill at managing dramatic effect, which Barnes suggests, not implausibly, that he may have learned from Schiller.[101] As a matter of fact, *Wallenstein* was in Coleridge's mind while he was revising his play during 1812. In August of that year he had discussed Schiller's play with Crabb Robinson, praising it but noticing Schiller's ventriloquism.[102] *Remorse* suffers from the same fault of using characters indiscriminately as authorial mouthpieces.

Coleridge even borrowed a line from his own translation of *Wallenstein* about an evil demon 'beating his black wings close above my head'.[103] Telling Southey on 9 February about the success of his drama, Coleridge made a defiant confession on this point: 'As to my Thefts from the Wallenstein, they were on compulsion from the necessity of Haste – & do not lie heavy on my Conscience, being partly thefts from myself, & because I gave Schiller 20 for one I have taken.'[104]

Remorse won praise from Coleridge's political enemy Leigh Hunt in an article on tragic actors in February 1815, in which he describes 'the exceeding barrenness which the stage has exhibited of late years'. Coleridge's play 'has been the only tragedy touched with real poetry for the last fifty years'.[105] Southey commented to his brother that it was 'full of rich poetry, and a bad play, both of which are to a certain degree against it', but that it was not surprising that it had been produced to good effect on the stage. He regretted that Sheridan had rejected the first version fifteen years before: 'Had it been acted then C. might have written fifteen better by this time for there is no man upon whom the applause of pit box and gallery would produce more effect. Better late than never, and the success is in seasonable time for his family.'[106]

Southey asked John Murray, publisher of the *Quarterly Review*, to be sure to include a review of *Remorse*. The notice which appeared in April 1814 was accordingly a friendly one, though coolly so (as well as rather late in the day), ending on an exhortation to Coleridge to seek 'a better application' of his talents.[107] The reviewer was John Taylor Coleridge, now pursuing his law studies in London.

No fewer than three editions of *Remorse* were published in 1813. Coleridge wrote a preface, as usual offering a hostage to fortune by revealing the unhappy history of the play in its earlier incarnation. He blamed Sheridan for having first encouraged him and then rejected *Osorio*, claiming Sheridan had poured scorn on it in 1806 before a 'large company at the house of a highly respectable Member of Parliament'. Coleridge now broadcast to *his* audience Sheridan's supposed quotation of a line of *Osorio* as

Drip! drip! drip! there's nothing here but dripping.

Coleridge resents this travesty, but since the original lines in his first play, spoken by Ferdinand in a cavern in Act IV, were

Drip! drip! drip! drip! – in such a place as this
It has nothing else to do but drip! drip! drip!
I wish it had not dripp'd upon my torch[108]

it was somewhat perverse of him to complain. It was also foolish to bring the subject up at all in connection with *Remorse*, from which Coleridge had wisely omitted the dripping speech.

Coleridge was always unable to judge the likely effect of his sayings and doings, a failing which became worse as he got older. Thus he went on writing querulous prefaces and washing his dirty linen in public. He also offended friends. Having told the Wordsworths that he would visit them when free from lecturing and attending the play, he went off instead in March 1813 for a short holiday on the Sussex coast. Mrs Clarkson's response on hearing this was to conclude that 'C. if he love any body but himself shews it by tormenting them'.[109]

Soon Coleridge was to be called upon to make an effort on behalf of his benefactors the Morgans. Though he was negligent about Hartley's future, leaving it to Southey and Wordsworth to arrange for funds to see him through university, he did manage to stir himself to help when John Morgan's business crashed in the autumn of 1813. The Berners Street house was let; Morgan fled to Ireland to avoid going to debtors' prison; Mrs Morgan and her sister went to friends in the country; and Coleridge rather surprisingly organized a rescue. He pawned his books, and some time in October 1813 set off to raise money in Bristol, where the Morgans had lived until 1808 and had many friends. Dorothy Wordsworth thought the Morgans were going to settle, with Coleridge, in Keswick, and viewed the prospect with nervousness. She foresaw 'nothing but jealousies and discomforts' if Coleridge returned to live so near his wife. To Sara Hutchinson she wrote, 'It is altogether a melancholy business – coming with them [the Morgans] and would not come to see his children! No plans laid for H[artley]!'[110]

Meanwhile Coleridge was in Bristol looking up all his old friends for loans for Morgan – Cottle, Wade, Estlin and Poole. He manfully gave eight of his literary lectures again in the city in which he had made his glorious début as a lecturer. The Bristol press reported them enthusiastically.[111] But under the unaccustomed effort and assumption of responsibility his health broke down. No letters survive between December 1813 and April 1814. In February poor Sara Coleridge wrote to Poole, hoping he might know where Coleridge was. She had not seen him for two years and had received only one letter from him in that time. She had hoped that he would come and see the children at Christmas, had hoped for a letter 'giving some direction about Hartley's studies'. But no word came.

Sara tells Poole of the death in Southey's house of her brother George, and of the recent honours done to Wordsworth and Southey, the former's appointment as Distributor of Stamps for Westmorland at £400 a year and with 'a secretary to do the drudgery', and Southey's elevation to the Poet Laureateship. Her understandable resentment of her husband's neglect combines with jealousy at his friends' and fellow poets' successes:

Coleridge has been very ill – but is better & intends coming soon – if he does not shortly *recollect* that he has a *wife & three children* in the *north* of England, who can *now, less than ever,* do without his pecuniary aid – I believe they must all travel *south* and join him & try their fortune together . . . if it were not for the protection that Southey's house affords me – I know not how we should [*all* have gone on] at this present writing – I remain however in *much trouble* yet thankful for the *blessings* remaining to me.[112]

Coleridge, still in Bristol, was living in torture. When he began writing to friends again in the spring of 1814 it was to recount his misery. To Morgan, now living near Bath, he wrote in May, 'I had been crucified, dead, and buried, descended into *Hell*, and am now, I humbly trust, rising again, tho' slowly and gradually', He rehearsed the whole case against himself:

> I used to think St. James's Text, 'He who offendeth in one point of the Law, offendeth in all', very harsh; but my own sad experience has taught me it's aweful, dreadful Truth. – What crime is there scarcely which has not been included or followed from the one guilt of taking opium? Not to speak of ingratitude to my maker for the wasted Talents; of ingratitude to so many friends who have loved me I know not why: of barbarous neglect of my family; excess of cruelty to Mary & Charlotte, when at Box, and both ill – (a vision of Hell to me when I think of it!) I have in this one dirty business of Laudanum an hundred times deceived, tricked, nay, actually & consciously LIED.[113]

He had once more contemplated suicide, but his old friend Josiah Wade had saved him by having someone 'sleep by my bed side, on a bed on the floor: so that I might never be altogether alone – O Good God! why do such good men love me!' Friendship and prayer were his two supports: 'Help, Help! – I believe! help thou my unbelief!'[114]

Another old friend, Cottle, tried to help too. He wrote a kindly meant letter of exhortation: 'In recalling what the expectations concerning you once were . . . my heart bleeds, to see how you are now fallen . . . renounce, from this moment opium and spirits, as your bane!'[115] Coleridge writhed at this pouring of 'oil of Vitriol' into 'the raw and festering Wound' of his conscience. Cottle received perhaps the most terrible expression of all Coleridge's insights into his condition: 'You bid me rouse myself – go, bid a man paralytic in both arms rub them briskly together, & that will cure him. Alas! (he would reply) that I cannot move my arms is my Complaint & my misery.'[116] The brilliantly imagined torture of the Ancient Mariner –

> I look'd to Heav'n, and try'd to pray;
> But or ever a prayer had gusht,
> A wicked whisper came and made
> My heart as dry as dust –

had become a reality. 'You have no conception', he told Cottle, 'of the dreadful Hell of my mind & conscience & body': 'You bid me, pray. O I do pray inwardly to be able to *pray*; but indeed to pray, to pray with the faith to which Blessing is promised, this is the reward of Faith, this is the Gift of God to the Elect.'[117] Never did Coleridge come closer to his despairing fellow poet William Cowper, obsessed to insanity with thoughts of his own damnation, which he expressed in his own ballad of a sea voyage, 'The Castaway' (1799). Small wonder that Coleridge's remaining written works, from *Biographia Literaria* to *On the Constitution of Church and State*, should have as a chief theme or destination the problems of belief and of sin.

Apologizing to Wade in June 1814 for abusing his love and hospitality by cheating to get opium beyond that prescribed to keep him sane, he expressed his wish that after his death 'a full and unqualified narration of my wretchedness, and of its guilty cause, may be made public, that at least some little good may be effected by the direful example!'[118] Cottle seized on this letter when publishing his *Early Recollections* in 1837, in which he printed Coleridge's 'letters from Hell' to himself. He drew down the wrath of the Coleridge family for doing so, but it is hard to blame him, though we could wish that he had been more accurate in his handling of these interesting and pathetic documents.

Somehow Coleridge climbed out of the pit. He gave more lectures in Bristol in April 1814, a set of six on Milton and Cervantes. No text of these survives. He also gave, on 26 April, the first of three political lectures on the rise of the French Revolution, the immediate impetus for these being the entry of the allies into Paris and the abdication of Napoleon at the end of March. But he had to close the lecture early and indefinitely postpone the other two because of illness.[119]

As he continued to leave letters unopened or at least unanswered, his friends in the Lakes were forced to take upon themselves the responsibility of arranging Hartley's future. It was a delicate business, not only because Wordsworth and Southey had to appeal to others for funds, but because they had not got Coleridge's permission to go ahead. This was not for want of trying. Direct appeals to Coleridge received no reply. Dorothy wrote to Wade, hoping he would pass the letter on. Hartley was now seventeen, and no time should be lost in finding out what Coleridge's views were. But she got no result.[120] In April 1814 Southey wrote to Cottle, discouraging him from settling an annuity on Coleridge, which Cottle was disposed to ask his friends to help him do. In Southey's view Coleridge would simply swallow the money in the form of opium: 'In the quantity which Coleridge takes it would consume more than the whole annuity which you propose to raise. A frightful consumption of spirits added to this – in this way bodily ailments are produced, and the wonder is he is still alive.'[121]

Far better, Southey thought, for money to be raised for the education of Coleridge's children. Southey, as ignorant as his contemporaries of the physical as well as the psychological aspect of drug dependency, had long ago lost patience with his brother-in-law. With unconscious irony he referred to Sara Coleridge's constitution – the very thing Coleridge had found it impossible to live with – which had enabled her to keep up her spirits in a situation in which 'any other woman would have broken her heart'.[122]

In October, while still waiting for a sign from Coleridge, Southey took the step of applying to Coleridge's brothers at Ottery for help with sending Hartley to college. Lady Beaumont promised £30 a year and the faithful and discarded Poole £10. The Ottery family agreed to help, though James took a dim view of the matter, writing to his son John that he would 'muster' with George 'at least £30' but adding: 'Southey seems to have behaved most kindly and generously whilst their *Mad* Father is at Bristol, or God knows where, living on the bounty of his friends. I expect that *that Stream* will dry up and then we must have a heavier blow! unless Opium or something removed him to another World. What a humbling lesson to all men is Samuel Coleridge.'[123]

Cottle and Basil Montagu also offered help, the latter perhaps as restitution for his part in the break with Wordsworth.[124] Finally the brilliant and eccentric Hartley was enabled to matriculate at Merton College, Oxford, in May 1815, being taken there by Wordsworth and Lamb. Southey, thanking Cottle for his unsolicited contribution of £5 a year, commented harshly on Hartley's father, who had left his family 'to chance and charity'.[125]

At about the same time Southey wrote to John Taylor Coleridge describing to him his cousin Hartley:

> Without being an ugly fellow, he is a marvellously odd one – he is very short, with remarkably strong features, some of the thickest and blackest eyebrows you ever saw, and a beard which a Turk might envy. His manners are almost as peculiar as his appearance, and having discovered that he is awkward by nature, he has formed an unhappy conclusion that art will never make him otherwise, and so resigns himself to his fate.

As to Hartley's character, Southey gives a picture of a boy not very different from Coleridge himself as a young man. His disposition 'is excellent, his principles thoroughly good, and he has instinctively a devotional feeling which I hope will keep them so'. The 'dangerous points of his character' are 'an overweening confidence in his own talents, and a perilous habit of finding out reasons for whatever he likes to do'. When it comes to learning, 'Hartley has Greek enough for a whole college'.[126] This was the quasi-fatherless boy who now began what it was hoped would be a brilliant university career.

While all this activity was proceeding on Hartley's account, Coleridge was dragging himself back into the land of the living, first among his Bristol friends, then, from December 1814 to April 1816, at Calne in Wiltshire, where he lived with the financially restored Morgans. He must have told Lamb about having descended into hell and risen again, for Lamb addressed him in August 1814 as 'Dear Resuscitate'.[127] He was having his portrait painted at this time by his old Rome acquaintance Washington Allston, whose art he much admired, though he still had a low opinion of his own face: 'The face *itself* is a FEEBLE, unmanly face (see plate 17).'[128] He feared that he had a venereal disease, contracted in his twenty-second year, since when he had 'never had any illicit connection'.[129]

Remarkably, the next three years were to be among the most productive of his life, certainly in comparison to any similar period since the journey to Malta. Why this was so is inevitably somewhat mysterious, for, though he was able more or less to regulate his opium doses, he was by no means free from his addiction, and still often weakened from his good intentions. The

Morgans were loyal friends and house-fellows, of course. And Coleridge did not want for projects and proposals from friends and publishers. But that had been the case for years, and for every publishing idea that came to something, many more remained at the glint-in-the-eye stage.

Perhaps things got better because they could not get worse. By the end of 1814 Coleridge had touched bottom, even for him, and risen again. The greatest pity is that he did not rise far enough to resume his long-neglected role as father to his children. But he did resurrect himself as a writer. Indeed, his future reputation as a critic and thinker was to depend on the work completed between 1815 and 1817.

11

Risen Again: *Biographia Literaria* 1814–1817

See, O World, see thy salvation!
Let the Heavens with praises ring.
Who would have a Throne above,
Let him hope, believe and love.
    Coleridge, 'Faith, Hope, and Charity, from the Italian of Guarini', 1815

The review of *Remorse* which appeared in 1814, written, though Coleridge did not know it, by his nephew, rankled with him. He complained to Stuart in September that in it he had been 'insolently reproved' for *'not publishing'*. Coleridge told Stuart that he was even then preparing a book to be called 'Christianity the one true Philosophy', to which he would add a preface consisting of 'fragments of *Auto*-biography'.[1] In the event, he began dictating to Morgan in 1815 during their quiet residence at Calne a work, *Biographia Literaria*, which was both autobiography and treatise on philosophy and religion – though not in the proportions outlined to Stuart – and which turned out to be Coleridge's most sustained work of literary criticism too.

But first, needing to earn money, he wrote to the publisher John Murray with a proposal to translate Goethe's *Faust*. Crabb Robinson had been asked by Murray to approach Coleridge, which he did through Lamb, for Coleridge was recognized as the man 'most likely to execute the work adequately'.[2] Coleridge expressed his willingness to undertake the task, if Murray would propose terms.[3]

Murray did propose terms – £100 – which caused Coleridge to write an aggressive-defensive letter about the 'humiliatingly low' offer. He re-hearsed, not very encouragingly for Murray, the failure of the *Wallenstein* translation to make money, claimed the exceeding difficulty of undertaking *Faust*, and ended, illogically, by accepting the terms.[4] Meanwhile Lamb, who had passed on the hint in the first place, wrote on 16 August counselling Coleridge to 'let it alone. How canst thou translate the language of cat-monkeys? qua-wa-peep-peep-peep whee-whee-sipt-sipt-sipt mal-wu-waaa – *fie* on such fantasies'.[5]

This is an exaggerated imitation of the speaking monkeys in the 'Witch's Kitchen' scene, about which Lamb had read in Madame de Staël's influential book, *De l'Allemagne*. This work had become a *cause célèbre* since its appearance in France in 1810. Napoleon had banned it because of its praise of German culture at the expense of French; consequently the author was lionized when she visited London in 1813. Her book was reprinted in London, and she was invited out all over the city as the noble victim of the Corsican tyrant. Southey had introduced Coleridge to her in October 1813, an occasion of which Madame de Staël, herself a fabled conversationalist, said, 'pour M. Coleridge, il est tout à fait *un monologue!*'[6]

Coleridge had offended Murray, who told him he was dropping the idea of a translation of *Faust*. This aroused the spirit of contradiction in Coleridge. He wrote back on 10 September 1814 declaring emphatically that he thought the play 'a work of genius'. His reasons are interesting, showing that he responded to the Gothic elements with excitement, but that his own experience of being criticized for his 'Dutch attempts at German sublimity' made him fear for the reputation of Goethe – and Goethe's translator – in England:

> The Scenes in the Cathedral and in the Prison must delight and affect all Readers not pre-determined to dislike. But the Scenes of Witchery and that astonishing Witch-Gallop up the Brocken will be denounced as *fantastic* and absurd [see plate 18]. Fantastic they are, and were meant to be; but I need not tell you, how many will detect the supposed fault for one, who can enter into the philosophy of that imaginative Superstition, which justifies it.[7]

The plan was dropped. This was a great pity, for Goethe's varied use of metre and rhyme and his bold shifts of tone from metaphysical scenes to scenes of natural sublimity, from love scenes to episodes of the comic grotesque, would have been a challenge to which Coleridge could have risen, given his own history of experimentation and success in different metres and registers. It is probable that he would have found some of the comic scenes too crude and the Prologue in Heaven too blasphemous for comfort. Yet Crabb Robinson, who had discussed *Faust* with Coleridge in August 1812, was surprised then to find that the Prologue in Heaven, in which Mephistopheles enters into a wager with God on the outcome of their struggle for Faust's soul, 'did not offend Coleridge as I thought it would, notwithstanding it is a parody of Job'.[8]

Coleridge was probably right in his instinct that the English public, or at least the reviewers, would cry out against the 'immorality' and 'irreverence' of *Faust*. Though Carlyle's stirring essays in hero worship of Goethe in the late 1820s and early 1830s encouraged a spate of translations of *Faust*, they all bowdlerized the text by softening or omitting some of the ruder language.[9] Even Shelley, who in 1821–2 translated two scenes, the Prologue in Heaven and the Walpurgisnacht scene, omitted some lines in his spirited rendering.[10] Byron urged Shelley to translate the whole play, but Shelley apparently replied that 'the translator of "Wallenstein" was the only person living who could venture to attempt it'.[11] When Coleridge met Shelley's friend Maria Gisborne in June 1820 he told her that he would like to translate *Faust*, but thought parts 'could not be endured in English and by the English'.[12]

Coleridge's later remarks on *Faust* are interesting. In the course of a long conversation in February 1833 with Henry Nelson Coleridge he claimed that he had drawn up a plan for a similar play 'before the Faust was published'. Though this may not be true, what he goes on to say he would have done constitutes, by its similarities with and its differences from Goethe's play, a valuable criticism of the German work. It is also a darkened allegory of his own experience.

Coleridge's Faust was to have been the thirteenth-century Scottish meta-physician and alchemist Michael Scott, the very hero chosen by Walter Scott for the minstrel's story in the *Lay of the Last Minstrel*. Michael Scott 'did not love knowledge for itself, for its own exceeding great reward, but in order to be powerful'. This is a 'poison-speck' infecting his mind from the start. He becomes disillusioned. Coleridge describes the plan as if he has actually written the work:

> Anon I began to tempt him. I made him dream, and gave him wine and passed women before him, whom he could not obtain. Is there no knowledge by which these pleasures may be commanded? *That* way lay witchcraft – and to witchcraft Michael turns with all his soul. He has many failures and some successes – he learns the chemistry of exciting drugs and exploding powders, and some of the properties of transmitted and reflected light; his appetite and curiosity are both stimulated, and his old craving for power and mental domination over others revives. Michael at last tries to raise the Devil, and the Devil comes at his call.

Coleridge's devil was to have been, like Goethe's Mephistopheles, 'the Universal Humorist, who should make all things vain and nothing worth by a perpetual collation of the great with the little in the presence of the infinite'. Like a more miserable and more reckless version of Coleridge himself, Michael hears the Devil whisper *'Try that* Michael!' 'The horror increases, and Michael feels that he is a slave and a condemned criminal.' In the end, as in Goethe's play, 'after subjecting Michael to every horror and agony, I make him triumphant, and pour Peace into his mind in the conviction of Redemption of Sinners through God's grace'.

Undoubtedly Michael Scott would have had more than a smack of Coleridge in him, whereas Goethe's Faust is a remarkably neutrally con-ceived figure. Coleridge calls him 'dull and meaningless', though he ad-mires the representation of Mephistopheles and Margaret (Gretchen), likes the natural-supernatural scene on the Brocken, and finds the songs beautiful. But, he adds in a fair criticism of the structure of *Faust*, 'there is no whole in Faust – the scenes are mere magic-lantern pictures'.[13] By the end of this interesting monologue Coleridge has climbed on to his high moral horse, claiming that one reason he did not translate the play was that he had 'debated with myself whether it became my moral character to render into English – and so far certainly lend my countenance to language – much of which I thought vulgar, licentious and most blasphemous'.[14]

And that was unfortunately that. Instead of translating *Faust*, Coleridge went on with his philosophical studies, filling notebooks and letters with passages from Fichte and Schelling, wrestling with questions of knowledge, will, freedom and morality. Time and again he acknowledges the 'righteous and gentle Spirit' Spinoza and his 'iron Chain of Logic', but dissents from Spinoza's pantheism as denying the doctrine of 'the Living God, having himself, and the originating Principle of all dependent Existence in his Will and Word'.[15] Spinoza's God is an object. The philosophies of Kant, Fichte and Shelling posit an active and reactive relationship between subject and object, an approach to which Coleridge was strongly drawn.

He even wrote a rare poem about this time on the subject. Called 'Human Life: On the Denial of Immortality' and published in *Sibylline Leaves* in 1817, it addresses the problem of pantheism:

> If the breath
> Be Life itself, and not its task and tent,
> If even a soul like Milton's can know death;
> O Man! thou vessel purposeless, unmeant,
> Yet drone-hive strange of phantom purposes!
> Surplus of Nature's dread activity,
> [. . .]
> Blank accident! nothing's anomaly![16]

Gone for ever for Coleridge was the sheer enjoyment of Nature for her own sake that he had expressed in the conversation poems. Without belief in a shaping, creating God behind Nature, a God who was also a guarantee of redemption and immortality for the erring but believing soul, human life for Coleridge would be not only 'blank' and 'purposeless', but a matter of irreversible despair.

On 1 March 1815 the Government introduced a Corn Bill prohibiting the importing of cheap wheat, and Coleridge found himself joining in a public protest in the market-place in Calne. He drew up a petition against the Bill, 'and afterwards mounted on the Butcher's Table made a butcherly sort of Speech of an hour long to a very ragged but not butcherly audience; for by their pale faces few of them seemed to have had more than a very occasional acquaintance with Butcher's Meat.'[17]

He himself was in distress, as he confessed to Cottle, and planned, unrealistically, to take in day pupils to make money. But he saw so many fellow creatures in a worse condition than his that he was forced, though not altering his conservative principles against 'the so called Parliamentary

Reformers' who agitated for the extension of the franchise, to 'join in pleading for Reform' to alleviate the misery of the poor.[18] Meanwhile, Napoleon had escaped from imprisonment on Elba and landed in France on 1 March. The long war was not over yet, and when it did end, after Wellington's victory at Waterloo in June 1815, the economic problems at home, and the clamour for reform, increased greatly with the return of soldiers to swell the ranks of the unenfranchised, the poor and the unemployed.

Waterloo itself was celebrated throughout Britain. A bonfire was lit on the very top of Skiddaw, where in the summer of 1800 Coleridge had scribbled his name and heard a stranger exclaim 'I lay my life, that is the *Poet Coleridge*'. Sara Coleridge reported on the Waterloo celebrations to Poole. The Wordsworths and Southey attended, but Sara herself was 'not equal to a walk of ten miles mountain road', and young Sara, now nearly thirteen, was thought to be 'much too delicate to be permitted such a thing'.[19] This child, who was to revere her father's memory, devoting herself to editing his unpublished works, had scarcely seen him. All the children, Mrs Coleridge told Poole in an earlier letter, were 'miserable if their father is mentioned for fear they should hear anything like blame attached to [him]'.[20]

Sara was bitter about her husband's long silence towards her and the children, especially as efforts had been made by so many others to get Hartley to Oxford, where he joined a cousin, William Hart Coleridge, only son of Coleridge's medical brother Luke, in May 1815. Hartley did begin, however, to see something of his father, for he spent his first long vacation at Calne. Southey made a gloomy prediction that Coleridge would 'unsettle his mind upon the most important subjects, and the end would be utter and irremediable ruin':

> For Coleridge, totally regardless of all consequences, will lead him into all the depths and mazes of metaphysics: he would root up from his mind, without intending it, all established principles . . . and [Hartley] would be thrown out from the only profession [i.e., that of clergyman and scholar] or way of life for which he is qualified . . . I know but too well, and Coleridge also knows, what an evil it is to be thus as it were cut adrift upon the sea of life; but experience is lost upon him.[21]

Hartley did get derailed, but not by Coleridge's metaphysics, which were not disruptive of religious orthodoxy, as Southey feared. Rather Hartley had inherited his father's brilliance and also his unstable, dependent temperament, which was in his case rendered further vulnerable by his having not a dead father, but one who was absent yet everywhere talked about.

Coleridge was desperately trying to pull himself together, to regulate his intake of opium with the help of Dr Brabant of nearby Devizes, and to earn some money. Sara Coleridge had complained to Poole in January 1815 that she did not know what she would do if he did not exert himself to pay some of her debts.[22] He wrote to Byron on 29 March asking him to use his influence to find a publisher for his poems, which he wanted to bring out in two volumes, preceded by a preface on the principles of criticism.[23] Byron replied promptly and deferentially, promising to do what he could and, being about to join the management committee of Drury Lane, encouraging Coleridge to write another tragedy. 'We have had nothing to mention in the same breath with *Remorse* for many years', he added gratifyingly.[24]

Byron was as good as his word. The plan to publish two volumes of poetry with a theoretical preface metamorphosed during the summer of 1815 into one volume of poetry, *Sibylline Leaves*, and two volumes of prose, *Biographia Literaria*. These were not in the end published by Byron's publisher, John Murray, but by the firm of Rest Fenner in 1817. But Murray, whom Coleridge could scarcely have approached directly after the fiasco over *Faust*, did agree, thanks to Byron, to bring out a slim volume in 1816, for which he gave Coleridge £80.[25] This was *Christabel; Kubla Khan, A Vision; The Pains of Sleep*, of which Sara Coleridge, no doubt echoing Southey, exclaimed: 'Oh! when will he ever give his friends anything but pain?'[26] The Greta Hall view was that he had been 'unwise' to publish his fragments, and it was borne out by reviews.

Poor Coleridge! Damned when he did not publish; damned when he did. But Sara was right to be nervous. As well as the famous 'person from Porlock' preface to 'Kubla Khan', he now wrote an awkward preface to 'Christabel', promising a third part and touching on the question of originality and plagiarism. Though his poem was the one sinned against in this respect, his own more recent reputation as a borrower from Schlegel disposed critics against him. Byron had urged him to finish 'Christabel', telling him in October 1815 that earlier in the year Scott had 'repeated to me a considerable portion' of the poem and that he, Byron, thought it 'the wildest & finest I ever heard in that kind of composition'. Byron showed himself as adept as Scott at deflecting criticism from his own borrowings, for he wrote again to Coleridge saying a passage in his 'Siege of Corinth' was unintentionally indebted to 'Christabel' and promising to append a note to that effect when it was published, as it was in 1816, shortly before Coleridge's poem finally appeared in print.[27]

Byron did more. He wrote to his friend Tom Moore telling him that Coleridge, 'a man of wonderful talent, and in distress', was about to publish. Since he had been 'worse used by the critics than ever we were', Byron asked Moore to 'promise me to review him favourably' in the *Edinburgh Review*. 'I do think he only wants a pioneer and a sparkle or two to explode most gloriously.'[28] Byron's generosity – he sent Coleridge a gift of £100 in February 1816[29] – was not matched by Moore. Of all the hostile reviews, many of which objected to the use of Byron's name in advertisements for the volume, the one in the *Edinburgh*, thought to be by Moore with possible tampering by Jeffrey, was the most damaging.[30] 'Forth steps Mr. Coleridge, like a giant refreshed with sleep', writes the reviewer, only to produce 'one of the most notable pieces of impertinence of which the press has lately been guilty'.[31] As Lamb was to tell Coleridge in 1824, with reference to the reception of his works in general, 'You are one of Fortune's *Ne'er-do-wells'*.[32]

In addition to critical scorn, 'Christabel' immediately attracted parodies. James Hogg, the Scottish poet known as 'The Ettrick Shepherd', cleverly called his parody in *The Poetic Mirror* (1816) 'Isabelle', so that he could echo Coleridge's rhymes. His version is mild and amusing, and Coleridge is not his only victim: Wordsworth, Byron, Southey, and Scott share the honour. A benign pastiche of the poem also appeared *before* Coleridge's original. Anna Vardill, a friend of Crabb Robinson to whom he had read from a manuscript of 'Christabel' in December 1814, produced her decidedly uninteresting poem 'Christobell, a Gothic Tale' in the *European Magazine* in April 1815.[33] Soon more damning parodies such as Maginn's in *Blackwood's Magazine* in 1819 began to appear.[34]

Though it was both unbecoming and counterproductive of Coleridge to complain publicly about his treatment at the hands of critics, he was, as Byron said, extremely badly served. Not only was the 'Christabel' volume derided, so also were the larger works Coleridge set about publishing in 1816–17. The biggest culprit was Hazlitt, who had once been so dazzled by Coleridge's genius. Over the next few years he reviewed all Coleridge's publications, sometimes twice over, and on one occasion he did so even before the work appeared, basing his review of *The Statesman's Manual* on the pre-publication prospectus.

It is an odd spectacle: the man now widely viewed as the second best literary critic of the period laying about him in the *Edinburgh Review* and the *Examiner* in witty ridicule of the best critic of the age. In October 1815 he even cheekily appropriated Coleridge's well-known signature 'Estese' (for STC), which he spelt 'Estesi', in a letter to the *Examiner* attacking Malthus's *Essay on Population*.[35]

Hazlitt's motivation was both political and personal. He was disillusioned by Coleridge's lapse into conservatism from his radical youth, and he had been made to look foolish on that occasion in the Lake District in 1803 when he had, in Wordsworth's words to Henry Crabb Robinson, 'narrowly escaped being ducked by the populace, and probably sent to prison for some gross attacks on women'.[36] Wordsworth and Coleridge had not kept the affair secret.

Coleridge was indignant at what he took to be ingratitude on Hazlitt's part, picturesquely claiming in a letter to Francis Wrangham that he had given Hazlitt 'the very shoes off my feet to enable him to escape over the mountains' in 1803, and repeating what Hazlitt was supposed to have said of him: 'Damn him! *I hate him*: FOR I am under obligations to him.'[37] Coleridge's circle frequently discussed the strange psychology of Hazlitt. According to Crabb Robinson, Lamb said that his articles, with their wonderful moments of astute praise for Coleridge immediately undermined by a cascade of abuse, were 'like saluting a man: "Sir, you are the greatest man I ever saw," and then pulling him by the nose'.[38]

Hazlitt's campaign was particularly unfortunate given the fact of Coleridge's distress in 1816 and the heroism of his efforts to rise above it. He was so hard up at this time that he asked William Sotheby to appeal to the Royal Literary Fund on his behalf, and was grateful to receive £30 in February 1816.[39] He also needed saving from his opium addiction, which was once more at a peak. He confessed to Byron in April that he had a 'daily habit of taking enormous doses of Laudanum'. In the same month he approached an apothecary-surgeon in Highgate, James Gillman, asking to be taken into his home as a paying guest for a month, so that his opium-taking could be medically supervised. He asked Gillman to refuse his requests for 'this detested Poison' and to outwit the attempts he knew he would make to evade constraint, knowing that he had 'the cunning of a specific madness'.[40]

On this basis Coleridge moved in with Gillman and his family, and stayed with them for the rest of his life. Though Gillman's patience and resolve were to help him enormously, Coleridge never conquered his addiction or the guilt associated with it. Indeed, within a few days of moving to Highgate, he was finding a way of getting laudanum without Gillman's knowledge. Of all people, John Murray was asked to send, with a packet of books, the contents of a package which 'a porter' would bring to Murray's office for the purpose.[41]

The move to Gillman's did not mean that he had fallen out with Morgan or Morgan with him. As Coleridge explained to Gillman, Morgan would continue to come to him 'as my literary Counsellor and Amanuensis at $\frac{1}{2}$ past 11 every morning & stay with me till $\frac{1}{2}$ past 3', for 'I now cannot compose without him'.[42] He had, however, had tiffs with the Morgan family, particularly the women. By November 1815 he was determined to leave their household, for, as he told his notebook – in Latin – 'his wife and his wife's sister exult too tyrannically in the scope of the women's domain'.[43] He also felt that he would be more likely to fulfil his 'penance' and his 'duty' outside their home, for he meant to 'devote my future Life to *Work*'.[44]

Morgan was hurt by Coleridge's move. Southey told Wordsworth in May 1817 that he was 'cut to the heart' by Coleridge's 'turning his back on him'.[45] He did, however, continue to help Coleridge with his writing after Coleridge's installation in Gillman's house in Highgate. Lamb also reported sharply on Coleridge's change of abode in a letter to Wordsworth, to whom Coleridge appears not to have written directly in the years following the reconciliation: 'He is at present under the medical care of a Mr *Gilman (Killman?)* a Highgate Apothecary, where he *plays at leaving off Laud —— m.* – I think his essentials not touched, he is very bad, but then he wonderfully picks up another day, and his face when he repeats his verses hath its ancient glory, an Arch angel a little damaged.'[46] This wonderful description, from a friend who mingled an unsentimental sharpness with his admiration, echoes Dorothy Wordsworth's equally astonished comments of fifteen years before, when she used to see Coleridge rise from what appeared almost his deathbed to walk over the roughest hills of the Lake District in the foulest weather.

Lamb's feelings towards his friend were strong, if subject to buffeting by Coleridge's behaviour. In the same letter to Wordsworth he spoke of the excitement of being within the 'whiff & wind' of his genius. A few months later he wrote again to Wordsworth about their friend, expressing admiration, puzzlement, and annoyance:

> I have seen Colerge. but once this 3 or 4 months, he is an odd person, when he first comes to town he is quite hot upon visiting, and then he turns off & absolutely never comes at all, but seems to forget there are anysuch people in the world. I made one attempt to visit him (a morning call) at Highgate, but there was something in him or his Apothecary which I found so unattractively-repulsing-from any temptation to call again, that I stay away as naturally as a Lover visits. The rogue gives you Love Powders, and then a strong horse drench to bring 'em off your stomach that they may'nt hurt you.[47]

Crabb Robinson, who had been with Lamb on that visit, on 14 July 1816, also complained that Gillman had come in during the visit 'very much with the air of a man who meant we should understand him to mean: "Gentlemen, it is time for you to go!"'[48] Such difficulties were ironed out in time, and Gillman became the last in a long line of faithful friends who took Coleridge on out of admiration for his genius as well as pity for his plight. When not outmanoevred by Coleridge, he managed to restrain his patient by allowing him severely reduced doses of opium.[49]

Coleridge had charmed Gillman, and part of the charm was his ability still to recite his poetry beautifully. Lamb noted in April that he repeated 'Kubla Khan' 'so enchantingly that it irradiates & brings heaven & Elysian bowers into my parlour while he sings or says it'.[50] Coleridge also recited 'Kubla Khan' to Byron in April 1816. Leigh Hunt remembered that Byron came away 'highly struck with his poem, and saying how wonderfully [Coleridge] talked'.[51]

Hazlitt's 'review' of the not yet published *Statesman's Manual* is extraordinary for the venom and the astuteness it shows. It is worth quoting from because it illustrates what Coleridge had to put up with – though not uniquely, of course, for Keats was soon to be particularly roughly handled by the *Quarterly Review* and *Blackwood's Magazine*. There is more than a grain of truth in Hazlitt's criticism of the congested nature of Coleridge's prose works. Hazlitt's preemptive criticism in the *Examiner* in September 1816 opens with a long paragraph of witty allusion and extravagant metaphor to describe Coleridge's work, known as a 'Lay Sermon': 'This Lay-Sermon puts us in mind of Mahomet's coffin, which was suspended between heaven and earth, or of the flying island at Laputa, which hovered over the head of Gulliver.' The attack ranges from scorn for Coleridge's prospectus, in which he 'merely haunts the public imagination with obscure noises' or announces 'his spiritual appearance for next week', to criticism of the

1809–10 *Friend* as no more than 'an enormous Title-page'. 'Mr Shandy would have settled the question at once: "You have little or no nose, Sir"', says Hazlitt in allusion to Coleridge's physiognomy and lack of willpower. Finally: 'Let him talk on for ever in this world and the next', but let him not write prose.[52]

When Hazlitt came in December 1816 to review *The Statesman's Manual* after publication, he did so twice, in the *Examiner* and in the *Edinburgh Review*. Once more he elaborated on Coleridge's faults, attacking both his digressive style and his political turning away from the ideals and practice of the French Revolution:'This trifling can only be compared to that of the impertinent barber of Baghdad, who being sent for to shave the prince, spent the whole morning in preparing his razors, took the height of the sun with an astrolabe, sung the song of Zimri, and danced the dance of Zamtout, and concluded by declining to perform the operation at all, because the day was unfavourable to its success.'[53]

Turning from the *Examiner* to the *Edinburgh*, Hazlitt writes with more restraint, but points out wittily enough that Coleridge's lay sermon, instead of attending to current political and social problems, takes refuge in abstraction: 'Our Lay-preacher, in order to qualify himself for the office of a guide to the blind, has not, of course, once thought of looking about for matters of fact, but very wisely draws a metaphysical bandage over his eyes, sits quietly down where he was, takes his nap, and talks in his sleep.'[54]

The Statesman's Manual is a rhapsodic piece of writing, the direction of which is not always clear, as Coleridge is aware, since he expresses his apprehension towards the end of the pamphlet that the foregoing pages 'may be thought to resemble the overflow of an earnest mind rather than an orderly premeditated composition'. The immediate impulse behind the work, of which Coleridge expected his readers to be aware, was the need to address social problems in a country which had recently concluded a war lasting nearly twenty-two years. In his view, Britain was required to contend with unemployment, distress and discontent, and to find a way forward politically without giving way to certain demands for reform of which he was suspicious. So much is clear. But Coleridge's way of setting about answering the question 'Whither Britain?' is eccentric. The full title of the pamphlet is

THE STATESMAN'S MANUAL;
or
THE BIBLE THE BEST GUIDE TO POLITICAL
SKILL AND FORESIGHT:
A Lay Sermon,
addressed to
THE HIGHER CLASSES OF SOCIETY,
WITH AN APPENDIX
containing
COMMENTS AND ESSAYS

connected with
THE STUDY OF THE INSPIRED WRITINGS[55]

It is quite consistent with Coleridge's recent thinking as seen in his notebooks and letters that he should refer any question to first principles and that he should look for these principles in the Bible. It is also understandable, biographically speaking, that he should appeal to Reason as 'the integral *spirit* of the regenerated man'.[56] Yet it is hardly what a contemporary reader concerned about political and economic problems would expect. Coleridge rides his hobby horses in places, as when he vehemently attacks Hume for his atheism and Joseph Lancaster once more for his system of education.[57] Perhaps the finest single insight in the work is a paragraph in which, in that brilliant way of his, he establishes memorably a distinction between two similar things. These are symbol and allegory:

> Now an Allegory is but a translation of abstract notions into a picture-language which is itself nothing but an abstraction from objects of the senses . . . On the other hand a Symbol . . . is characterized by a translucence of the Special in the Individual or of the General in the Especial or of the Universal in the General. Above all by the translucence of the Eternal through and in the Temporal. It always partakes of the Reality which it renders intelligible; and while it enunciates the whole, abides itself as a living part in that Unity, of which it is the representative.[58]

Coleridge followed up this pamphlet with another, *A Lay Sermon, addressed to the Higher and Middle Classes, on the Existing Distresses and Discontents*, published by Rest Fenner in March 1817. This took up the questions introduced in *The Statesman's Manual* and considered more directly the social and political conditions of post-Waterloo Britain. After Hazlitt's attack on its predecessor, Coleridge was less than hopeful about its probable reception. In his presentation copy to Southey he wrote in Latin that 'the butcher who hacked my first Lay Sermon to pieces with such malign ignorance in the Edingb. Rev. is that wretch Hazlitt, no man but a monster'. Hoping Southey would arrange a review in the *Quarterly*, he added somewhat pathetically: 'As regards this work, I beg you to help me, who was once your Coleridge; for you are able, and, likewise, have the will to do so.'[59]

He was out of luck. The *Lay Sermon* was not noticed in the *Quarterly*. Crabb Robinson struggled to be kind to it in the *Critical Review*, as he had done for its predecessor, though he had there mildly pointed out that Coleridge made a mistake in supposing that the higher classes would be willing or able to follow him in his abstract arguments, 'foreign equally to our language and philosophy'.[60] At least Hazlitt did not review it. The second pamphlet riskily opened with the 'Allegoric Vision' which had begun life as the stirring opening to his anti-Anglican religious lecture of 1795. Where before he had identified superstition with the Established Church, he now referred to Roman Catholicism as the false religion.[61]

Where before he had embraced Unitarianism, he now attacked it. And he argued against the 'false prophets', the middle-class reformers like William Cobbett who roused the underprivileged with 'vague and violent invective' and 'an ungoverned appetite for abuse and defamation'.[62]

Coleridge saw as well as the reformers that all was not well in British society, but his remedy was gradual reform achieved in unspecified ways and in a Christian spirit.[63] Coleridge had intended to write a third lay sermon 'addressed to the Laboring classes', but this, perhaps mercifully, did not appear.[64] Dorothy Wordsworth's comment on the first of the pamphlets was that it was 'ten times more obscure than the darkest parts of the Friend'.[65] In the same letter of March 1817 she alludes to the recent suspension of Habeas Corpus, one of a series of repressive measures taken by the Government in response to the bread riots of the preceding few months. Coleridge's sermon hardly strikes an appropriate note given the urgent problems of mass poverty and discontent and the Government's unsympathetic way of handling them. The pamphlet lacks the directness and energy of Coleridge's political writings of the 1790s.

Sara Hutchinson, whom Coleridge now mentioned much less frequently in his notebooks, wrote rather tartly to her cousin Tom Monkhouse that she had heard *The Statesman's Manual* was 'of all obscures the most obscure'.[66] As for Southey, who was himself embattled on all sides because of his anti-reform stance, he wrote that Coleridge in his *Lay Sermon* had made 'some excellent remarks' in his essay on 'the over-balance of the commercial spirit, that greediness of gain among all ranks to which I have more than once alluded in the Quarterly', adding: 'If Coleridge could but learn how to deliver his opinions in a way to make them read, and to separate that which would be profitable to all, from that which scarcely half a dozen men in England can understand (I certainly am not one of the number), he would be the most useful man of the age, as I verily believe him in acquirements and in powers of mind to be very far the greatest.'[67]

The reformers were active in these post-Waterloo years. William Hone, the radical bookseller, published three pamphlets in 1817 against the system of buying and selling parliamentary seats. The first of these, called *The Late John Wilkes's Catechism of a Ministerial Member*, is a witty piece, purporting to be a question-and-answer session between a minister and an applicant (named Lick Spittle) for the post of placeman or pensioner. Among the 'articles of belief' to which the applicant is obliged to swear are the following:

> I believe in GEORGE, the Regent Almighty, Maker of New Streets and Knights of the Bath;
>
> And in the present Ministry, his only choice, who were conceived of Toryism, brought forth of WILLIAM PITT, suffered loss of place under CHARLES JAMES FOX, were execrated, dead, and buried. In a few months they rose again from their minority; they re-ascended to the Treasury Benches, and sit at the right hand of a little man in a large wig; from whence

they *laugh* at the Petitions of the People, who pray for Reform, and that the
sweat of their brow may procure them Bread.[68]

Accompanied by Cruikshank's cartoons, these pamphlets made a laugh-
ing-stock of Lord Liverpool's Government, which promptly prosecuted
Hone for libel. Three times he was charged and three times acquitted. Even
Coleridge, who 'loathed' parodies on religion, wrote to the *Morning Chron-
icle* in January 1818 saying he 'exulted in Hone's acquittal and Lord
Ellenborough's deserved humiliation' – Ellenborough, being Lord Chief
Justice, had presided over two of the trials – because he loathed even more
the Government's repressive measures.[69]

Coleridge and Southey were themselves butts of the radicals at this time.
Southey, Poet Laureate and stalwart of the *Quarterly Review*, was discomfited
by the unauthorized printing of his republican play, *Wat Tyler*, written in
1794. He tried and failed to get an injunction from Chancery to stop
publication. In March 1817 William Smith, the Radical MP for Norwich,
read out passages in the House of Commons side by side with extracts from
recent articles by Southey in the *Quarterly*.[70] Coleridge leapt to his friend's
defence in two letters to the *Courier* on 17 and 18 March, in which he made
the not very convincing case that Southey was a 'deluded' youth of nineteen
when he wrote *Wat Tyler* and should not be held to account now. As
Dorothy Wordsworth said of this effort, 'of injudicious defenders he is
surely the Master Leader'.[71]

Coleridge was also a victim of the dredging up of youthful utterances.
Leigh Hunt reprinted in the *Examiner* in November 1816 the poem 'Fire,
Famine, and Slaughter'. Then in January 1817 Hazlitt went into print
against him again, though this time the result, intended to embarrass the
Anglican, conservative Coleridge of the *Lay Sermons*, was the first version of
his wonderful picture of Coleridge preaching in the Unitarian Chapel at
Shrewsbury in January 1798, when the young Hazlitt thought he was hearing 'the music of the spheres'.[72] Coleridge got little consolation from
reading thus about his younger self, but we are thankful to Hazlitt for
presenting such a lively and attractive view of his former idol.

In the midst of all this controversy Coleridge was ill and in financial
difficulties. In October 1817 Southey thought he would 'sooner or later' be
arrested for debt.[73] This did not happen, but his situation was precarious. In
September 1816 he told Dr Brabant that he 'longed for Death with an
intensity that I have never seen exprest but in the Book of Job'. He described how he had struggled out of bed to go and see his sister-in-law
Martha Fricker, who was thought to be dying. She was, he said, 'the only
one of the Brood that I had any regard for,' adding that 'the fine Ladies at
Keswick' had left her 'as a laborious Mantua-maker in London after having
tantalized her with a year's intercourse with Sirs, Lords, and Dukes at
Keswick'.[74] Harsh though this was towards his wife and her other sisters, it
was endorsed by Crabb Robinson, who saw them on a visit to Wordsworth
that September. On meeting the inmates of Greta Hall he commented that

he did not like any of the women. Sara Coleridge, in particular, he found 'a very unpleasant woman: she is not *handsome*, and her manners are obtrusive. She inquired about her husband with more *affectation* of feeling than real feeling.'[75] Robinson also mentioned that Derwent, now sixteen, was 'a hearty boy' but 'no scholar', and that Hartley, home from Oxford for the long vacation, was 'one of the strangest boys or young men I ever saw'.

With Hartley proceeding through Merton College, the family's attention now turned to Derwent. Once more Coleridge was a problem. Nothing could be done without his permission, but he was in no position to do anything beyond holding out vague hopes of help from friends in London. In July 1817 he told Poole that a friend had 'offered me all his interest with regard to Derwent, if he was sent to Cambridge'.[76] The friend was John Hookham Frere, Tory writer in the *Quarterly Review* and erstwhile scourge of the young Coleridge in the *Anti-Jacobin* of 1797–8. Though Frere did eventually contribute £300 towards seeing Derwent through St John's College, Cambridge, which he entered in May 1820, the offer did not come to anything immediately. Derwent, having left school in 1817, took up a tutorship in a family in Lancashire without his father's knowledge, holding the position until December 1819.[77]

Hartley, meanwhile, was spending part of the summer vacation of 1817 with his father. In a rare letter to Poole in July, sending him complimentary copies of *Biographia Literaria* and *Sibylline Leaves*, Coleridge referred to having had Hartley with him at Highgate for the last month. 'He is very much improved', wrote the incorrigible genius, 'and if I could see him more systematic in his studies and in the employment of his Time, I should have little to complain of in him or to wish for'. Coleridge asked Poole to invite Hartley to Nether Stowey for a few weeks, which Poole, having fond memories of the boy's magical early years, duly did.[78]

Indeed, Poole replied with all his old affection, saying there was no one he would rather see than Hartley, whose old nurse, Mrs Rich, would 'leap for joy' when she heard he was coming.[79] Hartley caused a stir at Stowey, becoming known as 'the Black Dwarf' because of his strange looks.[80] The Tory parson, William Holland, meeting him on 18 September, thought him 'an odd genius', 'scarce five foot high and broad shouldered, a short neck, jet black hair and eyebrows, wild eyes and a voice more peculiar still'. Holland noted that he was the son of 'a Mr Coleridge who distinguished himself some time ago as a writer'.[81]

The 'Mr Coleridge who distinguished himself some time ago as a writer' now published the prose work which would in the long term add mightily to his reputation, though it was once more his fate to be ridiculed at the time of publication. *Biographia Literaria* was finally published, after nearly two years' delay, in July 1817. The 'immethodical miscellany', as Coleridge described it in chapter four, is a most extraordinary document as regards its genesis, its publication, its contents and its reception.

The story of the composition and publication is extremely complicated.[82] Coleridge dictated the work to Morgan while staying in Calne during 1815, and in September of that year Morgan sent the manuscript to the Bristol printer and old school fellow of Coleridge, John Mathew Gutch, hoping meanwhile to find a London publisher. When Murray, through Byron's good offices, accepted the *Christabel* volume in the spring of 1816, Coleridge assumed he would publish his other works as well. There was also the question of Coleridge's play, *Zapolya*, rejected by both Covent Garden and Drury Lane but bought by Murray, and a revised edition of *The Friend*, in which Murray expressed cautious interest. However, his interest apparently cooled after the poor reception of the *Christabel* volume.

A further problem arose in May 1816 when Gutch told Coleridge the manuscript was too long for one volume and would comfortably make two. By July it was clear that Gutch had miscalculated and that a further 150 pages were required to fill the second volume. Much to the detriment of an already eccentrically conceived and structured work, Coleridge found himself in desperation adding at the end of the second volume the already warmed-over 'Satyrane's Letters' from Germany. He also added a bad-tempered review of C. R. Maturin's Gothic drama *Bertram*, accepted for performance at Drury Lane in 1816 just when *Zapolya* was turned down. Not only was this another republication – the criticism had appeared in five letters to the *Courier* in August and September 1816 – but it smacked of sour grapes and, worst of all, ran counter to Coleridge's emphasis in the early chapters of *Biographia* on the need for philosophical criticism, not nit-picking and nastiness of the sort indulged in by periodicals such as the *Edinburgh Review*. In the Conclusion, Coleridge injudiciously replied to critics – Hazlitt was particularly in his mind – of 'Christabel' and *The Statesman's Manual*. The work, thus filled out, was eventually published by the small London firm of Rest Fenner (which went bankrupt in 1819[83]).

For good or ill *Biographia Literaria* contained, apart from the appendages just described, an expression of all Coleridge's major concerns over more than fifteen years. In a loose and unusual way it is autobiographical, as the title suggests. There are anecdotes in the early chapters from Coleridge's schooldays, in which he remembers Boyer's robust criticisms of his school-boy verses, recalls his 'friendless wanderings on our *leave-days*', and, significantly in terms of his sense of his childhood self, represents himself as an orphan with 'scarce any connections in London'.[84] In chapter ten he digresses from his metaphysical discussion to give a comic but bitter account of his attempts to raise subscriptions for *The Friend*, and before that *The Watchman*, to which he adds his description of the 'Spy Nozy' episode in Somerset in 1797.[85]

His current preoccupation with the critical attacks on his own work led him to make a vigorous onslaught on the craft of reviewing, particularly as practised by the *Edinburgh Review*. Rather than bemoan his own case directly, he chose to discuss in chapter three the critical animus against

Southey. But this put him in a difficulty. Since he was not, as his notebooks amply demonstrate, enthusiastic about Southey's merits as a poet, he could hardly mount a vigorous defence of his friend's work.[86] As Hazlitt was quick to notice in his inevitable review of *Biographia*, in response to hostile criticisms of Southey's poetry 'Mr Coleridge answers, that he is an early riser and not a late sitter up'.[87] In other words Coleridge appeals to Southey's irreproachable domestic habits to refute literary and political accusations.

As we might expect, the autobiographical strain is not the chief one in the book. Coleridge could hardly have written with composure about his time in Cambridge and in the army, about his unhappy and now broken marriage and his all-consuming obsession, the opium addiction (let alone the unrequited passion for Sara Hutchinson or the jealousy of Wordsworth). He does refer to opium obliquely, rather unfortunately relating it to his habit of engaging in metaphysical studies. Echoing the lines in 'Dejection' about stealing from his own nature all the natural man, he confesses in chapter one to having 'sought a refuge from bodily pain and mismanaged sensibility in abstruse researches'.[88]

The express link between opium, procrastination, and the negatively described 'abstruse researches' is at odds with Coleridge's otherwise staunchly maintained sense of metaphysics as a vital activity, necessary to underpin a reasoned faith in God and an active moral and spiritual creed argued against the prevailing sceptical, materialist, Utilitarian philosophy which Coleridge traces in the philosophical chapters of *Biographia* to Locke, Hume, Hartley, and the French materialist school of Voltaire and Condillac.

Indeed, one of the two aims which we may identify as primary in *Biographia* is precisely the establishing of a principled, unified approach to the great questions of philosophy: how do we build up our knowledge? what are the limits of human knowledge? how do we relate knowledge to action in the moral sphere? what is the relation between the faculty of Reason and God's purposes? The final paragraph of *Biographia Literaria* sums up Coleridge's dearest wish to connect these questions and arrive at a Christian philosophy:

> O! that this my personal as well as my LITERARY LIFE might conclude! the unquenched desire, I mean, not without the consciousness of having earnestly endeavoured to kindle young minds, and to guard them against the temptations of Scorners, by shewing that the Scheme of Christianity, as taught in the Liturgy and Homilies of our Church, though not discoverable by human Reason, is yet in accordance with it; that link follows link by necessary consequence; that Religion passes out of the ken of Reason only where the eye of Reason has reached its own Horizon; and that Faith is but its continuation: even as the Day softens away into the sweet Twilight, and Twilight, hushed and breathless, steals into the Darkness. It is Night, sacred Night! the upraised Eye views only the starry Heaven which manifests itself alone: and the outward Beholding is fixed on the sparks twinkling in the aweful depth,

though Suns of other Worlds, only to preserve the Soul steady and collected in its pure *Act* of inward Adoration to the great I AM, and to the filial WORD that re-affirmeth it from Eternity to Eternity, whose choral Echo is the Universe.[89]

This rhapsodic ending contains the main lines of Coleridge's reasoning. With the help of Kant's critical philosophy he goes beyond the scepticism of Hume which stated that our knowledge is limited, that we have no faculty for knowing universal and necessary truths such as the existence of God, immortality and free will, that human knowledge is a matter of relative judgements based on observation and custom. Our knowledge in the speculative sphere is limited to what arises from experience, as Hume had said, but we apply categories of understanding to experience using faculties which exist independently of experience. And in the practical, or moral, sphere, we act *as if* we had full knowledge of God and free will, since faith takes over where speculative Reason is unable to proceed.

The difficult chapters five to twelve, in which Coleridge discusses these questions at length and with a multitude of scholarly references only possible in a man of the widest reading, are intellectual autobiography of a kind. They trace Coleridge's own path from acceptance of Hume's and Hartley's law of association to questioning and rejecting this 'reductive' law of a passive, reactive, limited mind with the help of Kant, Fichte and Schelling.

Coleridge's discussion is so full and sustained, if problematic, that it actually represents his *magnum opus* on the subject, though typically he regards it as merely preliminary to 'my *Logosophia*' in which 'I shall give (deo volente) the demonstrations and constructions of the Dynamic Philosophy scientifically arranged'.[90] *Biographia Literaria* was, taking due account of differences of genre and emphasis, to the never written 'Logosophia' what Wordsworth's *Prelude* was to the never completed 'Recluse'. In each case the writer had achieved in his 'preliminary' work the full expression of his aim in the great work-to-be. Of course, Coleridge suffered for his impossible promise. Hazlitt made much of it; so also did Shelley's friend Thomas Love Peacock in *Nightmare Abbey* (1818). Coleridge's *alter ego* Mr Flosky announces that he has written 'seven hundred pages of promise to elucidate' the philosophical distinction between Fancy and Imagination, 'which promise I shall keep as faithfully as the bank will its promise to pay'.[91]

Famously, *Biographia Literaria* itself contains the distinction between Fancy and Imagination. But before discussing this, the most celebrated section of the work, and the one which caused Victorian and early twentieth-century critics to claim for Coleridge the highest status as critic – with George Saintsbury exclaiming dramatically 'So, then, there abide these three, Aristotle, Longinus, and Coleridge'[92] – we must do Coleridge the justice to attend to the philosophical route by which he arrived at his distinction.

The Imagination as a faculty is educed in the course of the philosophical chapters; it is closely related in his scheme to Reason, just as Reason is closely related to Faith. Coleridge attempts nothing less than a whole metaphysics of mind, as his most influential mentor, Kant, had done. Kant had proceeded methodically and undistractedly, writing three separate but related works: *The Critique of Pure Reason* (1781, revised 1787), dealing with epistemology, or how and what we can know; *The Critique of Practical Reason* (1788), with its discussion of the existence of God and practical ethics; and *The Critique of Judgement* (1790), which concerns itself with matters of taste and judgement in the realm of aesthetics. Coleridge distils his reading of Kant, among others, into a much shorter discussion, and proceeds less methodically.

He also proceeds problematically. Partly because of the speed with which he needed to finish the book, partly because he was dictating to Morgan from memory and from his notebooks, partly because he simply knew too much, being acquainted with almost the whole of western philosophy from the Greeks to the later eighteenth century, and partly because of the strain of dishonesty which he denied – even to himself – Coleridge plagiarized for large portions of his discourse. Much has been written about his thefts, from De Quincey to the present day, and every attitude has been adopted towards the prisoner at the bar, from outright condemnation to eloquent pleas in mitigation. The most recent editors of *Biographia Literaria* offer a chart detailing the percentage of stolen matter in chapters five to nine, twelve and thirteen. They also distinguish between direct unacknowledged translation, close paraphrase, loose paraphrase, and summaries in Coleridge's own words.[93]

Suffice it to say that Coleridge's argument is indebted to the works of Kant, with which he had been familiar since 1801, of Johann Gebhard Ehrenreich Maas on the imagination, of Schelling and Fichte, of Schiller and other German philosophers and critics of the later eighteenth century. The worst offence is against Schelling who provides most of the very difficult argument about subject and object, mind and nature, and the mutual relationship between these pairs in chapters twelve and thirteen. It is hard to believe that Coleridge, even with his phenomenal memory, dictated these chapters to Morgan solely from his *memory* of reading Schelling. Many of the passages were written down in notebooks, and probably this was his main source. He may, as his daughter Sara suggested in her edition of *Biographia Literaria* in 1847, have been unaware of the full extent of his debts, since he was in the habit of copying out long passages both in the original language and in translation and not always identifying the source.[94]

For example, a notebook entry of September 1815 is a loose translation with some deviations – for Coleridge was always capable of being critical of his sources – of Schelling's *System des transscendentalen Idealismus* (1800). It makes no mention of Schelling's name. This entry forms the basis of the argument in chapter twelve of *Biographia*.[95] Coleridge *might* have forgotten the extent of the debt to Schelling in this entry, though it would surely be stretching credulity to claim that when he adapted it for inclusion in his work he had no inkling that the argument was not originally his own. In my view, he knew what he was doing, but with that peculiar facility, exacerbated by opium and need, for rationalizing his baser instincts and actions, he went ahead and tried to deceive. As with his acts of cunning in procuring opium behind the backs of his keepers, so here. Desperation made him do it; a false sense of his position made him think he would escape detection; and with part of himself he believed there was no crime to be confessed to. As De Quincey pointed out, he had no need to borrow, since his own brain was equal to the most complicated operations, but the indolence and paralysis to which he was prone caused him to steal.

A less complicated man, one either more or less honest, one less desperate and more confident, would have acknowledged his sources and hoped to gain a reputation as an interpreter of the best in German philosophy to his fellow countrymen. He would have reasoned that any philosopher necessarily depends on his predecessors for his own thinking. Did not the great Kant, 'the illustrious sage of Königsberg' himself, owe much to those who went before, particularly Hume, whose seemingly unanswerable scepticism roused him, as he said in *The Critique of Pure Reason*, to seek a way out of the *impasse*? And without Kant's three *Critiques* how could Fichte or Schelling have claimed their particular contribution? With one part of himself Coleridge knew that there was no such thing as a completely original idea; he excused Scott, after all, on this ground. On the other hand, he craved recognition for his own works, and could see no other way of seeking it than by claiming their originality. He was still, in this respect, the precocious boy for whom nothing less than astonished admiration for his genius would do.

In *Biographia Literaria* itself he airs the whole range of possible responses to the vexed question of originality and indebtedness. In chapter nine, already deep in his adaptation of German writers, Coleridge stops to pay full tribute to Kant, 'the founder of the Critical Philosophy', whose works 'took possession of me as with a giant's hand'. In the midst of paraphrasing Schelling in the same chapter he 'warns' his readers that 'an identity of thought' with Schelling need not be taken as proof of borrowing, for 'we have studied in the same school', namely that of Kant. Further, he says that he would be happy if he succeeded in 'rendering the system itself intelligible to my countrymen', and would willingly have all the honour attributed to Schelling. Finally, rather grandly, he claims to regard truth in any case as 'a divine ventriloquist: I care not from whose mouth the sounds are supposed to proceed, if only the words are audible and intelligible'.[96] Once again Coleridge preempts the arguments of both prosecuting and defence counsel, and of judge and jury as well.

As a matter of fact, as – to their credit – most commentators from Coleridge's contemporaries onwards acknowledged even as they shook

their heads, his distillation-cum-translation-cum-adaptation-cum-culmi-
nation of the German transcendental school of philosophy in *Biographia
Literaria* is a thing *sui generis*. This applies to the faults, the obscurity, the
nervousness shown in chapter thirteen – in which he invents a letter from
'a friend' complaining of the difficulty of the previous chapters – and a
clogged, over-allusive style. It also applies to the merits. Chief among these
is the intellectual mastery of abstruse material and an ability to illustrate
abstract ideas by means of telling examples and metaphors. One thinks
of his illustration, original as far as I know, of the notion expressed in
different ways by writers including Locke, Hobbes, Wolff, Tetens, Maas
and Fichte,[97] of the active–passive nature of thought and the role of the
imagination:

> Most of my readers will have observed a small water-insect on the surface of
> rivulets, which throws a cinque-spotted shadow fringed with prismatic colours
> on the sunny bottom of the brook; and will have noticed, how the little animal
> *wins* its way up against the stream, by alternate pulses of active and passive
> motion, now resisting the current, and now yielding to it in order to gather
> strength and a momentary *fulcrum* for a further propulsion. This in no unapt
> emblem of the mind's self-experience in the act of thinking. There are
> evidently two powers at work, which relatively to each other are active and
> passive; and this is not possible without an intermediate faculty, which is at
> once both active and passive. (In philosophical language, we must denomi-
> nate this intermediate faculty in all its degrees and determinations, the
> IMAGINATION.)[98]

The first volume of *Biographia Literaria* in effect rehearses Coleridge's
mental journey from adherence to Hume's and Hartley's idea of the mind
responding to external stimuli and building up knowledge by means of
associated ideas to rejection of the passive, mechanical nature of this system. 'The existence of an infinite spirit, of an intelligent and holy will, must
on this system be mere articulated motions of air', he says in chapter seven.
In Hartley's scheme 'the soul is present only to be pinched or *stroked*'; there
is no higher faculty independent of immediate sense experience.[99] But with
Kant's aid Coleridge goes beyond Hume and Hartley: 'We learn all things
indeed by *occasion* of experience; but the very facts so learnt force us inward
on the antecedents, that must be pre-supposed in order to render experience itself possible.'[100] Thus, following Kant, Coleridge establishes independence for the faculties of Reason and Imagination from the otherwise
operative law of association.

The results of this discussion are momentous in two ways. Firstly, as we
have seen, Reason is freed from slavery to the senses and can be linked to
religious faith in this respect. Secondly, the Imagination – topic of so much
discussion in Britain and Germany in the works of so many writers, including Locke, Hobbes, Hume, Hartley, Mark Akenside, Alexander Gerard,
Blair, Beattie, Lessing, Herder, Tetens, Maas, Kant, Schiller, Schelling and

the brothers Schlegel[101] – is also freed from mechanical reaction. It is given a near-divine status as an imitation of God's ['the great I AM'] activity in creating the world.

At the end of chapter thirteen Coleridge gives his definition of the Imagination. It is derived, as he promised it would be, from the preliminary argument about the relationship between the mind (I am) and the world or Nature (it is). Without a realization of this, the definition seems unnecessarily obscure. Yet even with all its obscurities on its head, this became the most famous definition of all, which proves, if nothing else, that Coleridge had a way with words, a genius for the culminating phrase, the memorable description. Of all the discussions of the nature and function of the imagination in what we now call the pre-Romantic and Romantic periods, Coleridge's is the one to which readers and critics look first. It is the representative Romantic definition.

Volume one of Biographia, then, ends as follows:

> The IMAGINATION then I consider either as primary, or secondary. The primary IMAGINATION I hold to be the living Power and prime Agent of all human Perception, and as a repetition in the finite mind of the eternal act of creation in the infinite I AM. The secondary I consider as an echo of the former, co-existing with the conscious will, yet still as identical with the primary in the *kind* of its agency, and differing only in *degree*, and in the *mode* of its operation. It dissolves, diffuses, dissipates, in order to re-create; or where this process is rendered impossible, yet still at all events it struggles to idealize and to unify. It is essentially *vital*, even as all objects (*as* objects) are essentially fixed and dead.
>
> FANCY, on the contrary, has no other counters to play with, but fixities and definites. The Fancy is indeed no other than a mode of Memory emancipated from the order of time and space; and blended with, and modified by the word CHOICE. But equally with the ordinary memory it must receive all its materials ready made from the law of association.[102]

The primary Imagination is the ordinary faculty of imagining, possessed by all as part of the mental make-up of the human species as created by God. The secondary Imagination is the artist's imagination, and its characteristic activity is unifying, active, harmonizing. It acts according to mental laws, but these are organic, growing from within, not mechanical or merely reactive to experience given to the senses, or limited, as memory is, by external factors.

This is both familiar and in a sense original. Ideas of organic unity, balancing of opposites, the imagination as a link between Reason and the senses, are common in German aesthetics from Kant on, and Kant himself had read many British writers on the subject of literary taste and judgement. The notion of the artist as a second God in creation was common currency in the eighteenth century. Much earlier Philip Sidney, in his *Apology for Poetry* (1595), had claimed memorably that while the world of Nature is 'brazen', 'the poets only deliver a golden' world, suggesting the power and freedom of the poet in the act of creation.

But there is also something unique to Coleridge in his formulation of the poet's activity in chapter thirteen and the subsequent chapters of *Biographia Literaria*. Only Schiller among his fellow labourers in the field was to the same extent a practising poet and a philosophical critic, and he tended in his essays, such as *Über die ästhetische Erziehung des Menschen (On the Aesthetic Education of Man*, 1795) and *Über naive und sentimentalische Dichtung (On Naive and Reflective Poetry*, 1795–6), to write generally and abstractly rather than concretely and suggestively.

Coleridge, by contrast, not only describes the poet's activity of bringing the whole soul into activity, reconciling opposite or discordant qualities, the familiar with the strange, and so on. He also gives examples. He is the first English critic to elucidate on a philosophical basis the 'principles of literary criticism'. Equally, he is the first critic to apply those principles 'to purposes of practical criticism', as he says in chapter fifteen.[103]

The term 'practical criticism', which has been taken up by the academy in this century, originates with Coleridge. I. A. Richards's famous work *Practical Criticism* (1929) has led the way with its protocols of his students' responses to literature at Cambridge. Richards, one of the most influential critics of the twentieth century, also wrote *Principles of Literary Criticism* (1924), which looks to Coleridge more than any other predecessor, ancient or modern, for insights into the workings of poetry. Coleridge, he says, has 'put his finger more nearly than anyone else upon the essential characteristic of poetic as of all valuable experience'.[104]

For if one main aim of *Biographia Literaria* was to establish, as Coleridge does in the first volume, the principles of literary criticism as educed from philosophy, the other was to *apply* those principles, which he does in the second volume. When setting out the principles he is often, as we have seen, unnecessarily obscure, digressive and anxious. But his procedure in actual criticism is rather more clear and logical.

Coleridge says very little about his own poetry in illustration of the principles he has educed. As we might expect, he looks to Shakespeare as the nearest embodiment of the poet 'described in *ideal* perfection'. Anxious to claim an original position in this respect, he exaggerated his differences from Johnson, whose Preface to Shakespeare he thought 'strangely over-rated, contradictory & most illogical'.[105] And he resented the suggestion that he owed his view of Shakespeare as expressed in his lectures to A. W. Schlegel.[106] *Biographia* adds extensively to our sense of Coleridge as critic of 'our myriad-minded Shakespeare' (chapter nineteen) already gleaned from what we know of the texts of his lectures. Though Johnson and Schlegel were both before him in refuting the charge that Shakespeare was an untutored genius and child of nature, Coleridge once more takes the palm for a fine cumulative statement of Shakespeare's merits. Having discussed in some detail *Venus and Adonis* and *The Rape of Lucrece*, he concludes:

Shakspeare, no mere child of nature; no automaton of genius; no passive vehicle of inspiration possessed by the spirit, not possessing it; first studied patiently, meditated deeply, understood minutely, till knowledge become habitual and intuitive wedded itself to his habitual feelings, and at length gave birth to that stupendous power, by which he stands alone, with no equal or second in his own class; to that power, which seated him on one of the two glory-smitten summits of the poetic mountain, with Milton as his compeer not rival. While the former darts himself forth, and passes into all the forms of human character and passion, the one Proteus of the fire and the flood; the other attracts all forms and things to himself, into the unity of his own IDEAL. All things and modes of action shape themselves anew in the being of MILTON; while SHAKSPEARE becomes all things, yet for ever remaining himself.[107]

It is striking that Coleridge illuminates Shakespeare's genius by contrasting it with Milton's, thus offering a suggestive criticism of both. Also significant is the quotation he chooses to illustrate and round off his remarks. It is taken from that other great genius (and another chief impetus for Coleridge in writing his work), Wordsworth. Coleridge finishes his fine chapter fifteen with four stirring lines from one of Wordsworth's patriotic sonnets, first published in 1803:

> We must be free or die, who speak the tongue,
> Which SHAKSPEARE spake; the faith and morals hold,
> Which MILTON held. In every thing we are sprung
> Of earth's first blood, have titles manifold![108]

From chapter seventeen on, *Biographia Literaria* consists chiefly of a sustained and brilliant discussion of Wordsworth's poetry. It is Coleridge's tribute to the man he thought the greatest living poet, able to achieve 'a union of deep and subtle thought with sensibility; a sympathy with man as man' by means of the 'blending and fusing' power of the imagination. Here is an example of Coleridge applying his definition in his fine critical discussion of one of the less well-known poems in *Lyrical Ballads*, 'The Mad Mother':

> I can not refrain from quoting two of the stanzas, both of them for their pathos, and the former for the fine transition in the two concluding lines of the stanza, so expressive of that deranged state, in which from the increased sensibility the sufferer's attention is abruptly drawn off by every trifle, and in the same instant plucked back again by the one despotic thought, and bringing home with it, by the blending, *fusing* power of Imagination and Passion, the alien object to which it had been so abruptly diverted, no longer an alien but an ally and an inmate:
>
> > Suck, little babe, oh suck again!
> > It cools my blood; it cools my brain:
> > Thy lips, I feel them, baby! they
> > Draw from my heart the pain away.
> > Oh! press me with thy little hand;

It loosens something at my chest;
About that tight and deadly band
I feel thy little fingers prest.
The breeze I see is in the tree!
It comes to cool my babe and me.

Thy father cares not for my breast,
'Tis thine, sweet baby, there to rest,
'Tis all thine own! – and if its hue
Be changed, that was so fair to view,
'Tis fair enough for thee, my dove!
My beauty, little child, is flown,
But thou wilt live with me in love,
And what if my poor cheek be brown?
'Tis well for me, thou can'st not see
How pale and wan it else would be.[109]

Coleridge's insight into the sympathetic imagination here echoes his remark in chapter four that Lear's words –

What! have his daughters brought him to this pass? –

exhibit mania, itself an example, though an excessive one, of the power of the imagination. And this in turn bears on notes prepared for his first lectures on Shakespeare in 1808, when he wrote: 'We find undoubted proof in [Shakespeare's] mind of Imagination or the power by which one image or feeling is made to modify many others, & by a sort of *fusion to force many into one* – that which after shewed itself in such might & energy in Lear, where the deep anguish of a Father spreads the feeling of Ingratitude & Cruelty over the very Elements of Heaven.'[110]

Time and again in *Biographia Literaria* Coleridge praises Wordsworth and illustrates his excellences with a range of examples. He also gives space to a discussion of Wordsworth's 'defects'. One of these is an occasional 'incongruity of style', as when Wordsworth 'sinks' from such lines as

They flash upon that inward eye,
Which is the bliss of solitude!

to the lines immediately following:

And then my heart with pleasure fills,
And dances with the *daffodils*.[111]

As Coleridge shows in the course of a long argument, he values Wordsworth's reflective or philosophical more than his pathetic verse, except where, as in 'The Mad Mother', the two kinds coincide. Another, opposite, defect is 'a species of ventriloquism, where two are represented as talking, while in truth one man only speaks'. This is essentially a criticism of the absence of the dramatic gift in Wordsworth, one which might well be illustrated – though Coleridge does not do so – by contrasting the successful figure of the Ancient Mariner with the less fully realized narrator of 'The Thorn'.[112]

Then, too, Coleridge finds in Wordsworth 'not seldom a *matter-of-factness* in certain poems', a too literal adherence to the 'minute presentation of objects, and their positions, as they appeared to the poet himself'.[113] Coleridge here puts his finger on a fault, doing so with a coinage of his own: 'matter-of-factness'. There is evidence of a mind working to the top of its bent in the fact that Coleridge coins nearly a dozen words in the course of *Biographia Literaria*. The editors of the *Collected Works* note the following: analogue, reliability (said of Southey's character), desynonymize, intensify, substrate, thoroughbred (as a noun), hypostasized, and potence.[114] As for Wordsworth's matter-of-factness, Coleridge gives full credit to the other side of that coin, praising 'the perfect truth to nature in his images and descriptions'. He rises to inspired metaphor here: 'Like the moisture or the polish on a pebble, genius neither distorts nor false-colours its objects; but on the contrary brings out many a vein and many a tint, which escape the eye of common observation, thus raising to the rank of gems, what had been often kicked away by the hurrying foot of the traveller on the dusty high road of custom.'[115]

The discussion of Wordsworth's merits and defects is conducted against the background of their long-standing, though weakened, friendship with its extraordinary collaboration in Somerset and the Lakes between 1797 and 1802. Coleridge wanted to establish the fact of the two complementary kinds of ballad in *Lyrical Ballads*, for in his prefaces of 1800 and 1802 Wordsworth had, naturally enough, described his own concerns with common language and rustic passions, calling forth an interest in the association of ideas 'in a state of excitement' and explaining that poetry is 'the spontaneous overflow of powerful feelings'.[116] Coleridge had been impressed by these prefaces, 'half a child' of his own brain, but had already adumbrated in letters of 1802 his differences with Wordsworth on the question of poetic language and the use of metre.[117]

Now in chapter fourteen of *Biographia Literaria* he gives an account of the plan for *Lyrical Ballads* as he remembered it. Wordsworth had aimed to throw charm over subjects from ordinary life by removing 'the film of familiarity' from them, a phrase echoed by Shelley in his 'Defence of Poetry', written in 1821.[118] Coleridge, conversely, had sought to render supernatural or extraordinary events believable by calling into being 'that willing suspension of disbelief for the moment, which constitutes poetic faith'.[119]

Undoubtedly the immediate spur to Coleridge to put down these thoughts at last was Wordsworth's 'Essay, Supplementary to the Preface', which he had recently published with his collected edition of *Poems* in 1815. The essay acted as a goad to Coleridge. In it Wordsworth touches on the idea of the imagination, but in a rather reductive way. He asserts that the word has been 'over-strained', 'forced to extend its services far beyond the point to which philosophy would have confined them'.[120] Coleridge, who had thought long and hard on the subject, was the man to give a new definition to the word, one which gloried in the extent of its 'services'. Wordsworth also gave offence by allowing to the Germans all the credit for seeing that Shakespeare was more than 'a wild irregular genius'.[121] Coleridge could not resist writing a defensive footnote to his own discussion of Shakespeare, claiming that he had aired the subject in his lectures in 1808, before Schlegel's lectures had been published.[122]

It is clear from a letter of July 1815 to Dr Brabant that a strong element in *Biographia* from the beginning was Coleridge's desire to argue with Wordsworth about language and to prove that his friend's practice seldom adhered to his theory about using 'the very language of men' in rustic life. 'I have no doubt', he told Brabant, 'that Wordsworth will be displeased'.[123] He expressed himself even more robustly to William Sotheby in January 1816: 'I anticipate that my Criticisms will not please or satisfy Wordsworth, or Wordsworth's Detractors [chiefly Jeffrey]; but I know, that a true philosophical Critique was wanting, & will be of more service to his just reputation than 20 idolators of his mannerisms.'[124]

Coleridge's unusually self-confident statement has been amply justified. *Biographia Literaria*, that compendium of genius and obscurity, the crowded offspring of the brain of a myriad-minded man, a book well-nigh impossible to read and yet impossible to do without, contains the finest single account of Wordsworth's poetry, some over-detailed negative criticism notwithstanding. And it does so in addition to being a treasure-house of insights into poetic genius, the psychology of both poet and reader – witness his remark in chapter fourteen about the reader being 'carried forward' by 'the pleasurable activity of mind excited by the attractions of the journey itself'[125] – and the characteristic genius of Shakespeare and Milton, as well as Wordsworth.

Wordsworth was not pleased. He wrote rather freezingly to R. P. Gillies in September 1817 that he had 'not read Mr. Coleridge's "Biographia", having contented myself with skimming parts of it'.[126] When Wordsworth visited London in December 1817, Henry Crabb Robinson discussed *Biographia Literaria* with him and found that 'Coleridge's book has given him no pleasure'. The praise of his poetry was 'too extravagant and the censure inconsiderate'. Robinson was reminded of something that Hazlitt had said about Wordsworth being unable to 'forgive a single censure mingled with however great a mass of eulogy'.[127]

A few weeks later Robinson, who usually expressed himself just this side of idolatry towards Wordsworth, related the conversation at a dinner party given by Tom Monkhouse, one of the now rare occasions when Wordsworth and Coleridge met:

I was for the first time in my life not pleased with Wordsworth, and Coleridge appeared to advantage in his presence. Coleridge spoke of painting in that style of mysticism which is now his habit of feeling. Wordsworth met this by dry, unfeeling contradiction. The manner of Coleridge towards Wordsworth was most respectful, but Wordsworth towards Coleridge was cold and scornful.[128]

At another party, this time at Lamb's house on 30 December, Robinson found 'a large party collected round the two poets, but Coleridge had the larger body'. From the two rival circles Robinson 'heard at one time Coleridge quoting Wordsworth's verses, and Wordsworth quoting – *not* Coleridge's, but his own'.[129] Such minor details throw into pathetic relief the loss of friendship between the two greatest literary geniuses of the age. It is worth remarking, however, that Wordsworth *did* read the criticisms of his work in *Biographia*; in subsequent editions of his poetry he made revisions to poems such as 'The Thorn' and the 'Immortality Ode' which are clearly responses to Coleridge's detailed objections to certain aspects of them.[130]

And what of the reviews of *Biographia*? Hazlitt, of course, took it to pieces in the *Edinburgh Review*. He went for the book's obvious weaknesses: its attack on himself and Jeffrey, its maladroit defence of Southey, its 'garrulous' accounts of Coleridge's youthful adventures, Coleridge's political turncoatism, and 'his mawkish spleen in fulsome eulogies of his own virtues'. As to the philosophical content, Hazlitt, who should have known better, scorns 'the great German oracle Kant', describing his system quite wrongheadedly as 'an enormous heap of dogmatical and hardened assumptions'.

Of Coleridge's own long metaphysical disquisition in the first volume he writes, less absurdly but still unfairly:

With Chap. IV begins the formidable ascent of that mountainous and barren ridge of clouds piled on precipices on clouds, from the top of which the author deludes us with a view of the Promised Land that divides the regions of Fancy from those of the Imagination, and extends through 200 pages with various inequalities and declensions to the end of the volume. The object of this long-winding metaphysical march, which resembles a patriarchal journey, is to point out and settle the true grounds of Mr. Wordsworth's claim to originality as a poet; which, if we rightly understand the deduction, turns out to be, that there is nothing peculiar about him; and that his poetry, in so far as it is good for anything at all, is just like any other good poetry.[131]

From Hazlitt, fellow critic and ex-admirer, comes not a word about Coleridge's fine exercises in practical criticism of Shakespeare and Milton, or about his fertility in creating memorable phrases to describe poetic activity. A footnote to Hazlitt's review contains a long self-justification by Jeffrey himself against Coleridge's charge in chapter three that after accepting his and Southey's hospitality at Keswick in 1810 Jeffrey continued to attack them at every opportunity in the *Edinburgh Review*. Crabb Robinson shrewdly summed up the Coleridge–Jeffrey controversy in his diary for 6 October 1817:

> I was interested by the review of Coleridge's Life written by Hazlitt, for which it is said he has received fifty guineas. Jeffrey had added a note with the initials of his name replying to the personalities in Coleridge's book. Jeffrey, of course, being a discreet and artful man, has the advantage over Coleridge in a personal dispute, who has so many infirmities of mind which lay him open to the attack of an adversary; but Jeffrey confesses enough to fix on himself the imputation of gross flattery and insincerity towards Coleridge. He says that he saw Coleridge liked compliments, and therefore gave them. He advised the publication of *Christabel* on the report of others, and then suffered Hazlitt to heap every species of obloquy on it in his review. [Robinson, like Coleridge, assumed that Hazlitt wrote that review, when it was most probably, as we have seen, Thomas Moore.][132]

Even worse than Hazlitt's review of *Biographia* – if that was possible – was John Wilson's in the new Edinburgh monthly, *Blackwood's Magazine*. Wilson makes the by now familiar criticism of Coleridge's convoluted and digressive prose. He drags up Jeffrey's old talk of 'the Lake School'; and he pays scant attention to the work in hand, except as it exhibits Coleridge's biography. There are unscrupulous remarks about 'the Metaphysical System of Kant, of which he knows less than nothing' – this from a man who accepted a politically motivated appointment as Professor of Moral Philosophy at Edinburgh University in 1820, relying on his friend De Quincey to provide material for lectures on a subject *he* knew nothing about. Finally, he picks up the gauntlet so rashly thrown down by Coleridge in connection with the old *Anti-Jacobin* attack on him for leaving his family destitute to go to Germany in 1798, and challenges Coleridge to deny that he has 'abandoned his wife and children'.[133] Coleridge considered prosecuting Wilson for libel, but was dissuaded by Robinson and others.[134] (By an odd coincidence Hazlitt prosecuted *Blackwood's* for libel in 1818 after an article by Wilson or J. G. Lockhart, or both, had attacked 'pimpled Hazlitt'.[135])

All in all, Coleridge received a predictably poor return from his contemporaries for his efforts and astonishing achievements in *Biographia Literaria*. Nevertheless, the book influenced his own ungrateful generation as well as those who came after. Shelley was one who appreciated it, as can be seen from his own 'Defence of Poetry'. Keats, in his suggestive, stream-of-consciousness letters of 1817 to 1819, echoed Coleridge, whose definition of 'negative faith' and 'willing suspension of disbelief' reappears in his own famous phrase, 'negative capability'. Keats talks in a letter of December 1817 to his brothers about Shakespeare's genius. Coleridge's comments about the 'Protean' Shakespeare, 'darting himself forth', are surely in his mind when he describes Shakespeare's quality of being 'capable of being in uncertainties, Mysteries, doubts, without any irritable reaching after fact &

reason', adding with significant if unconscious association, 'Coleridge, for instance, would let go by a fine isolated verisimilitude caught from the Penetralium of mystery, from being incapable of remaining content with half knowledge'.[136]

Maybe. But *Biographia Literaria* is rich in such fine verisimilitudes, in addition to being the most ambitious synthesis of philosophy, aesthetics and practical criticism in the language.

12

Highgate 1818–1821

Explaining metaphysics to the nation –
I wish he would explain his Explanation.

Byron, Dedication to Canto 1 of *Don Juan*, 1819

If *Biographia Literaria* was not a critical success on its appearance, neither was its companion volume of poetry, *Sibylline Leaves*. For this Coleridge was partly responsible. In the diffident preface he hints darkly at problems with the printer, and stresses the scattered and miscellaneous nature of the poems – hence the title – many of which had been published in newspapers. The volume is badly arranged, for which the printer must presumably take some blame. There is no index of titles. The poems, including several from the editions of 1796 and 1797, are printed in no apparent order. Coleridge's additions were not calculated to please, and were indeed picked out by the usual hostile reviewers. Among them are the marginal gloss now added to 'The Ancient Mariner'[1] and the 'Apologetic Preface' to 'Fire, Famine, and Slaughter'.

The gloss to Coleridge's great poem is at best a distraction from the ballad itself, at worst a misleading 'clarifying' device. It decides what the poem itself leaves in doubt, namely that the albatross is 'a bird of good omen' and that when the mariner is able to draw his eyes away from the curse of his dead shipmates, 'the curse is finally expiated'. The effect of the gloss is to Christianize and moralize where the poem exists in a kind of limbo with regard to Christianity and morality. The preface to 'Fire, Famine, and Slaughter' is one of Coleridge's long writhing defences of his youthful politics, half-upholding their sincerity, half-laughing at his former self, and somehow also claiming he had never really disapproved of Pitt, the familiar of the satanic witches in the poem. Needless to say, the reviewers seized on Coleridge's shuffling, while saying nothing incisive about the poems themselves.

Coleridge's play *Zapolya*, subtitled 'A Christmas Tale', rejected by the two legitimate theatres and bought for £50 by Murray, was actually published in November 1817 by Rest Fenner.[2] Byron, writing to Murray from Venice in October 1817, mentions Coleridge's attack in *Biographia Literaria* on Maturin's *Bertram* and the Drury Lane committee which accepted it, and complains of Coleridge's lack of gratitude and graciousness. *Zapolya*, says Byron, 'though poetical – did not appear at all practicable – and Bertram did – and hence this long tirade – which is the last Chapter of his vagabond life'.[3] Reviews of the published play were understandably lukewarm, consisting mainly of attempts to summarize the complicated yet strangely uninteresting plot concerning usurpation, restoration and reconciliation in Illyria. Coleridge made no more experiments in drama.

He was, however, engaged in further philosophical work. Still in need of money, he agreed to contribute to a new *Encyclopaedia Metropolitana* to be published by Rest Fenner. He wrote his 'Preliminary Treatise on Method', which appeared as volume one of the *Encyclopaedia* in January 1818, but 'so bewildered, so interpolated and topsy-turvied' by the printer that he was ashamed of it. Rest Fenner went bankrupt in March 1819, after only five parts of the *Encyclopaedia* had appeared.[4] Coleridge retrieved his tattered manuscript and published a revised version of it in the new 1818 edition of *The Friend*.

Before turning to the revision of his periodical he decided to lecture once more as a means of making money, since, despite his recent flurry of publications, he had earned very little from them, having been cheated, he thought, by the Revd Thomas Curtis of the firm of Rest Fenner.[5] The course was given at the rooms of the London Philosophical Society in Fleur-de-Luce Court, off Fleet Street, between 27 January and 13 March 1818. Coleridge gave fourteen lectures: three on early European history and literature, three on Shakespeare, three on Dante, Cervantes and Rabelais, and the rest on miscellaneous subjects including education (again), belief in witches and ghosts, the definition of the arts, and English prose style. No complete texts of these survive, though Coleridge's notebooks, Crabb Robinson's diaries, and notes taken by a young friend and disciple, Joseph Henry Green, give some idea of them.

Coleridge got Robinson and Lamb to drum up subscribers, and he managed to place advertisements and prospectuses in the *Courier*, *The Times*, and the *New Times*, edited by his old acquaintance in Malta, John Stoddart. Even the radical *Champion* announced the forthcoming lectures in a friendly manner. The editor was John Thelwall, another old acquaintance with whom Coleridge had long ago lost touch. Thelwall wrote that 'few men' were better qualified to lecture on European literature than Coleridge.[6]

The course was well attended and well received. Fortunately Coleridge did not see Sara Hutchinson's remark to her cousin Tom Monkhouse on 6 February about his lectures being 'both advertized & puffed' in the *Morning Chronicle* and declaring it was 'wonderful that the first Lecture was true to

11 *Derwent Water with Skiddaw in the Distance*, c.1795–6, by Joseph Wright of Derby. (Yale Center for British Art, Paul Mellon Collection)

12 Gillray cartoon of Davy's lecture at the Royal Institution, 1802.
(Copyright British Museum)

13 Coleridge, 1804, by James Northcote.
(Jesus College, Cambridge)

BANDO

Sua Eccellenza il Sig. Commissionario Regio prendendo in considerazione il vantaggio che dall'essere, e conservarsi in buono stato le Strade ne ridonda al Pubblico, la sua premura per l'ottenimento di sì importante scopo non gli permette di trascurare alcuno de'mezzi che possan farvelo pervenire.

Considerando quindi che le ruote de'Calessi, e de'Carri, tali quali si fanno attualmente, sono la cagion principale della deteriorazione e guasto delle Strade ordina, e comanda, che in avvenire simili ruote sien fatte sul modello da consegnarsi ai rispettivi Artefici, e senza che i chiodi risaltino sulle lamine di ferro, che contornan la loro circonferenza, sotto pena agli Artefici controventori di pagare, tante quante volte controverranno, la pena d'oncie venti da applicarsi per metà al fisco, e per l'altra metà al delatore.

Siccome poi spera Sua Eccellenza che la maggior parte dei Proprietarj de' Carri, e Calessi in vista del suo piacere, e del proprio lor comodo vorran riformare le ruote de' Carri, e Calessi loro spettanti, sebben già fatte, si ripromette fin da ora la soddisfazione di vedere trapeco introdotto generalmente un sistema da far le ruote, che nell'atto di risparmiare le Strade è pure di notabile vantaggio ai Proprietarj de' Calessi, e Carri, essendo molte facile a comprendere, che le grosse, e prominenti teste de' chiodi dando delle continue scosse ai Calessi, e Carri, ed alle Persone, o cose condotte, distruggon più presto il Calesse, o Carro istesso, ed in particolare le lamine di ferro, le quali ricevono immediatamente la scossa; scomodano chi è condotto; danneggiano le cose condotte; ed affaticano vieppiù l'animale poichè quelle prominenti teste [de'chiodi operano a guisa di tanti punti di resistenza, e di vetti opposte all'azione della forza movente.

Segreteria del Governo li 29 Gennajo 1805.

Samuel T. Coleridge Seg.º Pub.del Commiss.Regio.

G. N. Zammit Prosegretario.

Atti 31. Gennajo 1805. È stato lett. publicato, ed affisso nei luoghi soliti di q.ta quattro città e gloriana a vuono ti tronta in pregia ti moltissime persone. Sig.

11. Possibly the first proclamation signed by Coleridge in his official capacity as Public Secretary, Malta. 29 January 1805

14 Proclamation signed by Coleridge, Malta 1805. (National Library of Malta)

15 Hartley Coleridge aged 10, by Sir David Wilkie. (Hulton Deutsch)

16 Coleridge, 1811, by George Dawe. (Hulton Deutsch)

17 Coleridge, 1814, by Washington Allston.
(National Portrait Gallery)

FAUST AND MEPHISTOPHELES ASCEND THE BROCKEN.

18 *Faust and Mephistopheles Ascend the Brocken*, from Retzsch's *Outlines to Goethe's Faust*. (By permission of The British Library)

19 Coleridge, 1818, By Charles R. Leslie. (Hulton Deutsch, by kind permission of Mrs A. H. B. Coleridge)

20 Piranesi, prison drawing plate XIV. (Copyright British Museum)

21 Interior of Coleridge's room at Highgate, 1835, by George Scharf.
(Hulton Deutsch)

22 Coleridge, 1832, by Moses
Haughton. (The Governors
of Christ's Hospital)

the Prospectus'.[7] She and Coleridge had had a rare meeting in London in December 1817 at the Monkhouse dinner party at which Wordsworth had displeased Crabb Robinson by his coldness towards Coleridge. Sara herself seems to have felt no warmth for him now, and his own feelings for her were cooler. There is no mention in his notebooks of this meeting; indeed, he refers less and less to 'Asra'. But there is a sad note written on 25 February 1819, in which he bundles all his recent misfortunes together – Hazlitt's attacks, Curtis's cheating him over his works, and Sara's (long since) abandonment of him:

> Robb'd, jilted, slander'd, poor, without a hope,
> How can I chuse but be a Misanthrope?[8]

Before lecturing on Shakespeare again, Coleridge tried to preempt repetition of the old charge of plagiarism from Schlegel in letters he wrote to James Perry of the *Morning Chronicle* and William Mudford, now the editor of the *Courier*, asking for fair treatment.[9] But much of the material in these lectures was inevitably familiar to those who knew his previous courses and who had read his recent prose works.

At the same time as Coleridge was delivering his lectures, Hazlitt was giving a course on 'the English Poets' at the Surrey Institution. These were full of witty anecdote and personal allusions, of which by far the greatest number related to Coleridge, with whom Hazlitt was nothing short of obsessed. Certain critical remarks, such as that Shakespeare was 'nothing in himself' but 'all that others were, or that they could become', show Hazlitt to have been acquainted with, and influenced by, Coleridge's remarks in *Biographia Literaria*.[10] Moreover, when he reaches contemporary poets in his lectures, Hazlitt finishes the course with 'a few words of Mr. Coleridge'. These is the usual mixture of honey and bile: 'The Ancient Mariner' is 'his most remarkable performance', but it is 'high German'; his tragedies are poetic, but full of 'drawling sentiment and metaphysical jargon'. His prose works are 'dreary', yet in spite of everything, 'he is the only person I ever knew who answered to the idea of a man of genius. He is the only person from whom I ever learnt any thing . . . He was the first poet I ever knew. His genius at that time had angelic wings, and fed on manna. He talked on for ever; and yet you wished him to talk on for ever.'[11]

No one was more eloquent about the effect of Coleridge's presence than Hazlitt. For all that he here talks of his subject as though he were dead, Coleridge was still able to produce a remarkable effect, through his conversation and lecturing as well as through his writing, on those who met him for the first time. He was well aware of the dangers of thus putting his genius on show. A notebook entry of 1815 expresses his dilemma in this respect:

A is believed or talked of as a man of unusual Talent – People are anxious to meet him – if he says little or nothing, they wonder at the Report . . . But

> if . . . they put questions which cannot be answered but by a regression in principia – & then they complain of him as not conversing but lecturing – he is quite intolerable – might as well be hearing a sermon – in short, in answer to some objection A replies, Sir! this rests on the distinction between an Idea & an Image, & likewise its difference from a perfect Conception. – Pray, Sir! explain! Because he can not do, & therefore does not, as if they were talking of a game at whist – Lord! how long he talks![12]

Coleridge did submit to the inevitable in this respect; he became 'the Sage of Highgate'. His later years were spent receiving visitors who came expressly to hear him talk, in some cases, no doubt, with the intention of gaining publicity for themselves by retailing his oracular conversation in their articles and memoirs. Coleridge did, however, turn this state of affairs to serious account. Not only was Gillman an assiduous helper and disciple, but his fellow surgeon, J. H. Green, whom Coleridge met some time in 1817, willingly became Coleridge's 'bulldog', to borrow T. H. Huxley's description of his own role as proselytizer of Darwin's ideas. Green took notes at the lectures and laboured with Coleridge on a work on logic which remained in manuscript at Coleridge's death,[13] and on the great work Coleridge intended to write linking all branches of knowledge, philosophy and religion. After Coleridge's death Green devoted himself to trying to collect Coleridge's fragments. The result, *Spiritual Philosophy: founded on the Teaching of the late Samuel Taylor Coleridge*, was published after Green's own death, in 1865.[14] Green had studied anatomy in Germany, and was acquainted with German philosophy. He was therefore a man with whom Coleridge could discuss philosophy without having to act 'as if they were talking of a game at whist'.[15]

It was to Green that Coleridge communicated his differences from the systems of Kant and Schelling. Anticipating one of the important tenets of *Aids to Reflection*, he told Green in December 1817 that he could not agree with Kant's valuing of a dutiful motive over a naturally kind one in his system of ethics:

> I reject Kant's *stoic* principle, as false, unnatural, and even immoral, where in his Critik der Practischen Vernunft he treats the affections as indifferent (αδιαφορα) in ethics, and would persuade us that a man who disliking, and without feeling any Love for, Virtue yet *acted* virtuously, because and only because it was his *Duty*, is more worthy of our esteem, than the man whose *affections* were aidant to, and congruous with, his Conscience . . . But with these exceptions I reverence Immanuel Kant with my whole heart and soul; and believe him to be the only Philosopher, for *all men* who have the power of thinking.

Schelling, who had been such a strong influence on *Biographia Literaria*, was 'too ambitious, too eager to be the Grand Seignior of the allein selig-machende Philosophie [the only philosophy conducing to happiness], to be altogether a trust-worthy Philosopher'. Coleridge told Green that he regretted having adopted Schelling's system so wholeheartedly in *Biographia.*[16]

With Green, Coleridge set up a more or less regular 'series of conversations' about philosophy, science and religion, as he told his nephew William Hart Coleridge in April 1818.[17] It is one of the many ironies of Coleridge's life that he now became close to the clever sons of his brothers, though at this time he saw his own son Hartley only occasionally and his other children not at all. Nephews, of course, make fewer demands than one's own children, and are not such an unwelcome reminder of duties not fulfilled.

William Hart Coleridge, who had been kind to Hartley at Oxford, was now a clergyman living in London. He and his cousin, John Taylor Coleridge, attended some of their uncle's literary lectures. Coleridge's brother George heard about them and wrote to John in February 1818:

> You have been an Auditor at Coleridge's Lectures. I trust that you can continue the account that William gave of the first of them – that they are excellent. If he gets through them with credit and regularity I shall take it as a new era in his life, since he has for once performed what he promised. I should like to know what sort of a Balance sheet he is likely to make of it, for Fame at this part of his life is coming rather too late to fill his pocket. Poor Fellow! he has been walking in a vain shadow certainly . . . I pray that his latter day may be spent in a manner more consentaneous with reason and common-sense, and that Theology which has taken possession of his head may diffuse itself through his heart and actions.[18]

Another young man who came into his life at this time, and who within a few years became a surrogate son to him, was Thomas Allsop, a businessman who wrote admiringly to Coleridge after hearing his first lecture on 27 January. Coleridge was flattered, and wrote back warmly. Allsop was to be a less talented Boswell to Coleridge's Johnson, publishing in 1836 his useful *Letters, Conversations, and Recollections of S. T. Coleridge.* Others who sought Coleridge's company and serious conversation were Charles Augustus Tulk, a founder in 1810 of the Swedenborgian Society, to whom – appropriately – Coleridge wrote his most impenetrable letters illustrating his philosophical thinking,[19] and Hyman Hurwitz, a neighbour in Highgate who ran a Jewish academy. Two of Coleridge's rare poetic efforts at this time were translations from the Hebrew of occasional poems by Hurwitz. One was 'Israel's Lament', a dirge composed for the funeral of Princess Charlotte, who had died in childbirth in November 1817. The second was 'The Tears of a Grateful People', another dirge written on the occasion of George III's death in January 1820.

It is odd to read the following lines in the knowledge that they came from Coleridge's pen, even if it is only rendering the thoughts of Hurwitz:

> The Day-Star of our glory sets!
> Our King has breathed his latest breath!

> Each heart its wonted pulse forgets,
> As if it own'd the pow'r of death.
> [. . .]
> No age records a King so just,
> His virtues numerous as his days;
> The Lord Jehovah was his trust,
> And truth with mercy ruled his ways.[20]

Coleridge–Hurwitz seems here to be unofficially rivalling Southey, who as Poet Laureate had to mourn George III, which he did in *A Vision of Judgment* (1821), a poem overshadowed by Byron's parody of the same name. Less pious, if cruel, is Shelley's famous description of George III in his sonnet 'England in 1819', with its striking opening line –

> An old, mad, blind, despised, and dying king.

Henry Francis Cary, translator of Dante's *Divine Comedy*, was another new friend. The two men met at Littlehampton in October 1817 in a mirror image of some of Coleridge's earlier encounters with strangers. Cary was walking along the beach reciting Homer to his son when he was accosted by Coleridge, who had heard the Greek, with 'Sir, yours is a face I *should* know: I am Samuel Taylor Coleridge.'[21] It was to Cary that Coleridge gave his first impressions on reading Blake's *Songs of Innocence and Experience* (first published in 1795). He wrote amusedly in February 1818:

> I have this morning been reading a strange publication – viz. Poems with very wild and interesting pictures . . . printed and painted by the Author, W. Blake. He is a man of Genius – and I apprehend, a Swedenborgian – certainly, a mystic *emphatically*. You perhaps smile at *my* calling another Poet, a *Mystic*; but verily I am in the very mire of common-place common-sense compared with Mr Blake, apo- or rather ana-calyptic Poet, and Painter![22]

'I am writing as hard as I can put pen to Paper', Coleridge told Green on 30 April 1818, 'at the Spring Garden Coffee House in defence of the Bill for regulating the labor of the Children in Cotton Factories'.[23] Coleridge had read the *Courier*'s report of the debate in Parliament when Sir Robert Peel introduced the Bill, and wished to offer extra-parliamentary support. A letter to the editor on 31 March, signed 'Plato', was probably his. Playing devil's advocate, he declared Peel's proposed legislation for restricting child labour to twelve hours a day 'pregnant with fatal dangers to our most glorious Constitution':

> A renovated spirit of Luddism will infect these very children, whose present love and veneration for the machines, by which they are able to support their aged parents, can only be exceeded by the love and respect they bear towards their indulgent masters. But how fearfully will the scene be changed! Give them but the notion that they are under the protection of the laws, and instead of quietly piecing the yarn, and of cleaning the machinery during

dinner, their little hearts will be beating high for radical reform, annual Parliaments, and universal suffrage.[24]

Coleridge followed this with two pamphlets in which he scorned the Bill's opponents for seeming to believe that God had shown special favour towards the cotton factories by suspending the laws of nature in their case. In a rare example of strong, pithy prose, he answers the objectors to the Bill. Some have said that there should be no legislative interference with free labour. To this Coleridge replies that 'the *principle* of *all* constitutional law is to make the claims of each as much as possible compatible with the claims of all'. His answer to those who say that it can safely be left to factory owners themselves to reform from within is pungent: 'The age had been complimented with the epithets of enlightened, humane, etc., years before the abolition of the Slave Trade. And was that Trade abolished at last by the increasing humanity, the enlightened self-interest, of the slave owners?'[25] Coleridge had reason to be proud of these pamphlets, which were distributed in the House of Commons and may have helped the passage of the Bill.[26]

Something of the spark and sparkle that Coleridge could still muster was expressed by his oldest friend Lamb, who in dedicating the 1818 edition of his works to Coleridge inevitably recalled the Christ's Hospital days: 'The world has given you many a shrewd nip and gird since that time, but either my eyes are grown dimmer, or my old friend is the *same* who stood before me three and twenty years ago, his hair a little confessing the hand of time, but still shrouding the same capacious brain – his heart not altered, scarcely where it "alteration finds."'[27]

After the excitement of his leap into public controversy, Coleridge settled down to revising *The Friend* for his unsatisfactory publisher Rest Fenner. To the old edition of 1809–10 he added a dedication to the Gillmans, 'in testimony of high respect and grateful affection'. The original work had, of course, been written in the Wordsworth household, with the beloved Sara Hutchinson acting as amanuensis and Coleridge unconscious of the wound about to be inflicted on his great friendship with Wordsworth.

Coleridge added passages here and there to the existing essays and recast his 'Treatise on Method' with the title 'On the Grounds of Morals and Religion'.[28] In discussing the principles of method Coleridge genially gives Shakespeare's characters as an example of method personified:

> In all his various characters, we still feel ourselves communing with the same human nature, which is every where present as the vegetable sap in the branches, sprays, leaves, buds, blossoms, fruits, their shapes, tastes, and odours. Speaking of the effect, i.e. his works themselves, we may define the excellence of *their* method as consisting in that just proportion, that union and interpenetration of the universal and the particular, which must ever pervade all works of decided genius and true science. For Method implies a *progressive transition*, and it is the meaning of the word in the original language. The Greek Μεθοδος, is literally *a way*, or *path of Transit.*[29]

Coleridge himself could claim that there is method in the seeming madness, or at least digressiveness, of his argument, for eventually he comes to philosophical method by the simple process of claiming that 'from Shakspeare to Plato, from the philosophic poet to the poetic philosopher, the transition is easy'.[30] From Plato he moves to Aristotle, then to Francis Bacon, father of the empirical method in English philosophy. *The Friend* was published in three volumes in November 1818. It was not much noticed, though a friendly, if vague, review in the *Edinburgh Magazine* in 1821 described it as 'the only work published in modern times which breathes the same lofty and profound spirit of philosophy' as the great seventeenth-century writers Milton, Hooker and Jeremy Taylor.[31]

On 3 November 1818 Coleridge was introduced in a circumspect way to a portrait of his daughter, now nearly sixteen, by William Collins, father of the writer Wilkie Collins. Mrs Coleridge had told Poole about it and expressed anxiety about Coleridge's probable reaction to seeing a portrait of the daughter he had not seen since 1812. Sara had been painted as the 'Highland Girl' in Wordsworth's poem, and the picture was to be exhibited 'next Spring': 'Mr Collins is a great admirer of C. and means to show him this likeness of his daughter when he returns to Town; I fear poor Samuel will be made uncomfortable by seeing it, & then good Mr Collins will feel mortified, for he does not know him well enough to understand the extreme eccentricity of his character.'[32]

Coleridge's remark in a letter to Charlotte Brent after seeing the portrait was, 'It is the most beautiful Fancy-figure, I ever saw'. To Collins he wrote in December 1818 that the 'exquisite picture' had 'quite haunted my eye ever since'.[33] He was eventually given the picture, which hung on the wall of his room in Highgate until his death.[34]

In December 1818 Hartley Coleridge graduated. He took a second class degree which, as Southey remark ed, 'considering the defects of his school education, and that he had no assistance from his tutor (Merton being in that respect a miserable College) is as honourable for him, as a first class for one who has been regularly bred'.[35] Hartley himself wrote to his uncle George at Ottery, proud of his achievement but apologetic, and a little irked, that he had not done better. An echo of his father's rationalizing of disappointments is heard when he tells George that 'in my Sophocles I fail'd, chiefly from being put on in a misprinted passage – for the play was one I had studied with more than common attention'.[36]

Better news was to come. In April 1819 Hartley, whose brilliance was recognized at Oxford, was appointed to a Fellowship at Oriel College. Both parents, though severally, glowed with pride. Mrs Coleridge told Poole how delighted everyone was, including 'my kind friend Dorothy'. Hartley's old schoolmaster, Mr Dawes, gave the school a holiday in recognition of Hartley's achievement; Wordsworth's son William, a pupil of Dawes, reported that he had never seen his master in such a good humour – 'the boys all huzza'd and there was *such an uproar*'.[37]

Coleridge talked to friends of his 'Fatherly Pride' at Hartley's success, and boasted of his son's prowess 'as a Classic, a Logician, and a Theologian'.[38] Hartley, with all his eccentricity, had succeeded where his father and his uncle Southey had failed, or at least declined to succeed. Southey himself was reminded of his own student days soon after, for in June 1820 he was made an honorary LL.D at the University he had left twenty-five years before without taking his degree. As he told his wife, the visit to Oxford 'brought with it many melancholy thoughts', one of them being, we may imagine, the memory of being bowled over by a brilliant young 'Cantab' who helped to change his life.[39]

Coleridge's much increased activity now that he was established at the Gillmans' continued with his embarking in December 1818 on two sets of lectures at the Crown and Anchor Tavern on the Strand. He gave six on Shakespeare, starting with *The Tempest* and once more asserting his independence of Schlegel, a foolish move which was, of course, noticed by newspaper correspondents, one of whom – the writer in the *Morning Chronicle* – pointed out that some of Schlegel's remarks had been made even before his Vienna lectures of 1808.[40] Coleridge was sensitive enough on this sore point to enter a note on his copy of Shakespeare's works insisting on his independent discovery of Shakespeare's judgement being equal to his natural genius and alluding to Hazlitt's treachery towards him on the question.[41]

Poor Coleridge had to read a report in the *Champion* of his third lecture, on *Hamlet* (of which scant record survives), suggesting that he might have 'availed himself of the opinions of Hazlitt', who had published his *Characters of Shakespeare's Plays* in 1817, making no reference to Coleridge, though he wrote at length about the contribution to Shakespeare criticism of Johnson and Schlegel.[42] Of course an element of political distaste is in operation here, the *Champion* and Hazlitt being liberal and Coleridge a hopeless turncoat in their eyes.

The larger of the two courses of lectures given by Coleridge was philosophical. He gave fourteen lectures, beginning on 14 December 1818 and ending on 29 March 1819. This course was not well attended, perhaps because the natural audience for his lectures had already heard him lecture on literature, perhaps because the appetite for Coleridge's 'German' philosophy was small and kept that way by Hazlitt's sniping, Peacock's satire and Coleridge's own comparative failure to talk clearly on the subject. Hazlitt was lecturing at the same time as Coleridge, on 'English Comic Writers', and a kind of propaganda war was being carried on between the *Champion* and the *Courier* as to the relative merits of the rival lecturers.[43]

John Hookham Frere arranged and paid for shorthand notes to be taken of the philosophical lectures.[44] In the prospectus Coleridge says he will be addressing the questions all thinking men ask, such as 'What, and *for* what am I made? What *can* I, and what *ought* I to, make of myself? and in what relations do I stand to the world and to my fellow men?'[45] Coleridge spreads his net far and wide, beginning with philosophy 'from Thales and Pythagoras to the appearance of the Sophists', and ending with the present day.

The main thrust is that philosophy and religion are reconcilable, the second taking over where the first cannot go, namely into spiritual questions. In this respect Coleridge takes as his starting point the argument of the last paragraph of *Biographia Literaria.*

The importance of his effort in these lectures is that he wished to overcome the dualism which had dominated philosophy through the ages, with its separation and opposition of spirit and body, mind and matter. The problem was to avoid succumbing to the counter-attractions of monism, which seemed to lead inevitably, as with Spinoza and Schelling, to pantheism, in which God and the world are one. The answer was to describe a mutual relationship of opposites and their reconciliation, by Reason in the speculative sphere, by Imagination in the aesthetic, and by religious faith in the spiritual.

One of the most striking points Coleridge makes concerns the opposing methods of Plato and Aristotle, and the dependence of all subsequent philosophy on starting from either a Platonic or an Aristotelian viewpoint. 'The difference between Aristotle and Plato', he says in the fifth lecture, 'is that which will remain as long as we are men':

> Plato, with Pythagoras before him, had conceived that the phenomenon or outward appearance, all that we call thing or matter, is but as it were a language by which the invisible (that which is not the object of our senses) communicates its existence to our finite beings . . .
>
> Aristotle on the contrary, affirmed that all our knowledge had begun in experience, had begun through the senses, and that from the senses only we could take our notions of reality. The objects of the senses, therefore, he declared to be the true realities of nature; and with regard to those things which are invisible he resolved them into certain harmonies, into certain results, and so forth.[46]

This distinction, argued with such clarity by Coleridge, does not originate with him. Goethe made it in his *Farbenlehre* (*Theory of Colours*, 1808), which Coleridge read in Green's copy in January 1819, having read it once before, possibly in a copy brought to England by Ludwig Tieck, whom Coleridge met for the first time since Rome at Green's house in June 1817.[47]

Coleridge makes little mention in the lectures of Kant or Schelling. His letters to Green at this time show his dissatisfaction with both writers, but it is odd that he did not make more of them in his philosophical survey. Perhaps he was discouraged by the reputation of 'German mystic' which clung to him; probably he left himself too little time to go into modern philosophy in detail, having lectured at great length on ancient and early modern philosophy. Even Spinoza receives only a passing reference in lecture thirteen, and that refers mainly to his blameless and persecuted life. Kant is briefly praised for first examining the faculties critically before giving opinions on the results of using those faculties. Coleridge singles out, not the relative scepticism about our knowledge as expressed in the

Critique of Pure Reason, but the analysis of the will and the famous Categorical Imperative of the *Critique of Practical Reason*: 'thou shalt do to others as thou wouldst be done by: thou shalt act so that there shall be no contradiction in thy being'.[48]

The comments on Kant are clear and crisp, but they occupy less than two pages. Of Schelling he is almost totally dismissive, calling him 'this Roman Catholic pantheist', a sour allusion to Schelling's recent embracing of mystical theosophy under the influence of Catholic thinkers.[49]

Coleridge made little from his lectures. While continuing the philosophical course in February and March 1819, he commenced yet another short course, of seven lectures, on literature from Spenser and Shakespeare to Milton.[50] It was his final effort of the kind. He was exhausted, and so probably was his audience. Since 1808 he had delivered at least 120 lectures, of which almost half had been devoted to Shakespeare. His reputation as a critic of Shakespeare was slow in coming, partly because he did not publish the lectures, partly because of the unseemly skirmishing over Schlegel and precedence. His method, as we have seen, left much to be desired. He digressed, repeated material, and did not keep a strict timetable for his discussions of individual plays. Thus he talked at much greater length about some plays – notably *The Tempest, Romeo and Juliet*, and *Hamlet* – than about others.

As far as we know, he did not lecture on *Troilus and Cressida* or *Measure for Measure* at all. The reason for this was probably his dislike of these two plays. We know from marginal notes he made that he found *Troilus and Cressida* the hardest of all Shakespeare's plays to categorize and thought *Measure for Measure* 'the most painful' on account of the testing of Isabella, which was 'degrading to the character of woman'.[51] In conversation in 1827 he pronounced succinctly: 'Our feelings of justice are wounded in Angelo's escape [from punishment]. Isabella unamiable, and Claudio detestable.'[52]

Not until Henry Nelson Coleridge published some of the lecture notes in *Literary Remains* in 1836–9 did Coleridge's overall contribution to Shakespeare studies begin to be valued. He and subsequent editors grouped the scattered comments from lectures, notebooks, letters, *Biographia Literaria*, and other sources under the heading of individual plays.[53] Despite the miscellaneous nature of these collections, they confirm the view, first formed by the Victorians who read Henry Nelson Coleridge's collection, that Coleridge is our greatest Shakespeare critic.

A few examples may help to illustrate this claim, which can be upheld even against the strong claim to moments of fine criticism of Shakespeare in Keats's letters, Hazlitt's lectures and essays, and De Quincey in his startling essay 'On the Knocking at the Gate in *Macbeth*' (1823). Coleridge considers the art of exposition – an art in which he himself was woefully lacking as a dramatist – in a note on the opening scene of *Hamlet* which is brief but brilliant: 'The preparation *informative* of the audience, just as much as was precisely necessary – how gradual first, and with the uncertainty appertaining to a question, What, has *this* THING appeared *again* tonight? (even the word *again* has its credibilizing effect).'[54] 'Credibilizing' is yet another coinage for which the Oxford English Dictionary gives Coleridge credit.

As we have seen, he often associated himself as procrastinator with Hamlet, and this linking is at least as suggestive about the play as it is astute about his own psychology. For example:

> Endless reasoning and urging – perpetual solicitation of the mind to act, but as constant an escape from action – ceaseless reproaches of himself for his sloth, while the whole energy of his resolution passes away in those reproaches. This, too, not from cowardice, for he is made one of the bravest of his time – not from want of forethought or quickness of apprehension, for he sees through the very souls of all who surround him, but merely from that aversion to action which prevails among such as have a world within themselves.[55]

He also carries his reasoning about *Hamlet* into the area where philosophy and criticism meet, as in this comment of 1827:

> A Maxim is the conclusion upon observation of matters of fact. An Idea or Principle is prospective and carries knowledge within itself. Maxims all retrospective.
> Polonius a man of maxims; whilst descanting on matters of past experience, admirable; advising or projecting, a mere dotard. Hamlet as the man of ideas despises him.
> A man of maxims like Cyclops with one eye, but that eye placed in the back of his head.[56]

Some of Coleridge's most pregnant remarks were made about *Othello*. Perhaps his most famous phrase of all is his characterization of Iago's speeches as 'the motive-hunting of motiveless Malignity', which he scribbled on his edition of Shakespeare.[57] In conversation he talked of the great effects which follow the mere dropping of a handkerchief compared to Schiller's setting a whole town on fire in *The Robbers*.[58]

Such enlightened criticisms abound in Coleridge's writings, public and private. Together with his fine discussions of the character of Shakespeare's genius in *Biographia Literaria* they add up to philosophical-cum-practical criticism of the highest order.

Soon after he had finished his two sets of lectures in the spring of 1819 Coleridge met Keats. The latter told his brother and sister-in-law about the encounter in a breathless letter of 15 April:

> Last Sunday I took a Walk towards Highgate and in the lane that winds by the side of Lord Mansfield's Park I met Mr Green our Demonstrator at Guy's in conversation with Coleridge – I joined them, after enquiring by a look

whether it would be agreeable – I walked with him at his alderman-after dinner pace for near two miles I suppose. In those two Miles he broached a thousand things – let me see if I can give you a list – Nightingales, Poetry – on Poetical sensation – Metaphysics – Different genera and species of Dreams – Nightmare – a dream accompanied by a sense of touch – single and double touch – A dream related – First and second consciousness - the difference explained between will and Volition . . . Monsters – the Kraken – Mermaids . . . A Ghost story – Good morning – I heard his voice as he came towards me – I heard it as he moved away – I had heard it all the interval – if it may be called so. He was civil enough to ask me to call on him at Highgate.[59]

We can compare Keats's impression of Coleridge as alderman with a portrait painted by Charles R. Leslie the previous year. The Coleridge in the picture was forty-six; his hair was receding and greying, his figure stout, his look half-mournful, half-peaceful (see plate 19). For comparison we may read Sara Coleridge's description of herself in a letter to Poole in June 1819. She begins with Dorothy Wordsworth, who looked sixty – though she was only forty-eight – 'owing to her extreme leanness, and the loss of teeth'. By contrast, says Sara, '*I* am so *encreased* in size, that I could no more go down a dance, or climb a mountain, than I could fly over the Derwent'. Wordsworth, she notes, 'evidently prefers the nut-cracker nose & chin, to the full-moon phiz it must be confessed mine *does* somewhat resemble'.[60]

The matronly Sara's feelings towards her husband were benign now. She told Poole that she no longer regretted the separation, though 'I grieve on the children's account'. In her next letter, in September 1819, she reported that Coleridge was 'at Ramsgate with the family of those good people the Gilmans', adding that Mrs Gillman often wrote to her giving her news of her husband. Derwent was expecting to visit his father soon in preparation for his long delayed matriculation at Cambridge. In her frank way Sara gave Poole a sense of what life was like for her children, fatherless and yet tantalizingly aware of the great absent figure of Coleridge:

It would affect you much if you were to see the flush of hope & joy that spreads over the expressive countenance of poor Derwent at the idea of seeing his father next spring! He will be 19 years old; he was 11 when his father last beheld him! C. will be quite overpowered, and the boy too, I conjecture, at their meeting. Yesterday Hartley was 23 years old, some days older than his father was on the day of our marriage. I think H. is as excentric as his father *to the full* – may he be happier![61]

Coleridge was taking a rather more active interest in Derwent's future than he had done at a similar stage in Hartley's career – one of the many signs that he was leading a more regulated and less desperate life, thanks to the Gillmans' hospitality. He was also pleased to be able to arrange for Derwent's education through the help of London friends, bypassing Southey and Wordsworth, to whom he disliked being indebted for Hartley's support. He told Francis Wrangham in September 1819 that his children were 'unmingled blessings': 'DERWENT I am about to send to Cambridge, two or three of *my* connections (as distinguished from those in the North & from those of his own name in the South) having promised such a sum annually during his undergraduateship as with strict economy he *may* live on.'[62] His London friend John Hookham Frere was Derwent's chief benefactor.

On the whole, Coleridge was as settled and happy now as he had ever been since his marriage had gone sour and his addiction become confirmed nearly twenty years before. His notebooks are much less preoccupied with unrequited love and hopeless friendship, though there are still many entries relating to his physical ailments and his moral guilt about opium. The notebooks are full of theology, philosophy and science. He was following with interest the new craze of 'animal magnetism', a form of hypnotism, and the progress of knowledge about electricity. There are many notes on chemistry and mathematics – a subject he regretted having neglected until now[63] – and he was attempting to build up a 'Theory of Life'. Reading works by and about Mesmer, Schelling, Benjamin Franklin and others, he reinforced his philosophical-imaginative leaning towards the principle of the reconciliation of opposing forces: 'Thus then: Unity is manifested by Opposites. But it is equally true, that all true Opposites tend to Unity.'[64]

He could still be visited by distressing dreams. The old vision from December 1806 of Wordsworth and Sara Hutchinson in bed together, she with 'her most beautiful breast uncovered' (in Greek in the notebook) arose on the night of 4 May 1819. The following night Coleridge had another dream indicative of unresolved feelings of guilt towards friends, this time the Morgans, who had to some extent replaced the Wordsworths in his affections, and had subsequently been themselves displaced by the Gillmans:

> I have this morning had a fearful Dream in which I saw Mrs Morgan, threatening to publish all my letters to them, shewing how grateful I felt myself – and to abuse these over flying feelings of Gratitude to give confirmation to their scandalous Lies – Then poor J. J. Morgan himself, frightfully distorted with palsy, attempting with shaking and tottering limbs to assassinate me, first with a pen knife and then with a Razor.[65]

'Poor John Morgan' was in debt once more, was arrested some time in 1819, and died in late 1819 or early 1820.[66] Coleridge had reason to feel guilty. Morgan, who had been his saviour after the break with Wordsworth, and who had got *Biographia Literaria* out of him at a low time, was hurt at what he considered Coleridge's desertion of him. He even suggested that Gillman had a selfish motive in taking him on, that he was 'speculating upon him and hoping to ride upon his reputation'.[67] Though Henry James could not have seen this remark, unpublished in his time, it was precisely the motivation he chose to explore in his short story based on Coleridge's life at Highgate, *The Coxon Fund* (1894).

An irritation occurred with the publication of the first two Cantos of Byron's *Don Juan*, in which Coleridge's erstwhile admirer and supporter satirized him along with the other 'Lake Poets'. The Dedication – suppressed until 1833 because of its attack on Castlereagh and its sexual punning, mainly at Southey's expense – takes a swipe at Coleridge's metaphysics:

> Explaining metaphysics to the nation –
> I wish he would explain his Explanation.

Coleridge could not have seen this, but he did see Canto I, in which Byron expressed his poetic creed:

> Thou shalt believe in Milton, Dryden, Pope;
> Thou shalt not set up Wordsworth, Coleridge, Southey;
> Because the first is crazed beyond all hope,
> The second drunk, the third so quaint and mouthy.[68]

The euphemistic reference to his opium-taking stung Coleridge into a reply on 4 September 1819 which was highly characteristic of his tendency to swing between the extremes of excessive pride and excessive humility, this time balancing precariously on a heavy beam of satire:

> My Lord,
>   That I should be selected by you to share such immortality as Time may confer upon your Don Juan demands my acknowledgement, the quality of which is enlarged by the charge of inebriety you prefer against me.
>   Had you adorned me with indolence and irresolution the commendation had been just, but the more elegant acquirement of intemperance it were flattery to attribute to me.
>   This example of your Lordship's taste and knowledge would embolden me to esteem you as among the first of our great writers if you would condescend first to avoid a too servile flattery of your contemporaries, and next to obtain correct information on the habits of those you celebrate.
>   The sobriety of this letter is the unhappy proof of the extravagance of your praise.
>   I am / your Lordship's obedient sober servant, S. T. Coleridge.[69]

Byron's changed attitude towards Coleridge was in part a result of what he perceived to be Coleridge's shiftiness in dealing with Murray over the publication of his works in 1816–17, but more of his association in Byron's mind with Southey, who, Byron thought, had slandered him in conversation. Writing to Murray from his self-imposed exile in Venice in November 1818, he said of the first part of *Don Juan*, just sent off, that he had got back at 'Master Southey', who was supposed to have said that 'Shelley and I were in a league of Incest, etc., etc.' 'He is a burning liar! for the women to whom he alludes are not sisters' – Mary Shelley and Claire Clairmont – and 'there was no *promiscuous intercourse* whatever'. Further, 'I understand

Coleridge went about repeating Southey's lie with pleasure. I can believe it, for I had done him what is called a favour.'[70]

Byron had been misinformed. It was Brougham who circulated gossip about Byron and the Shelleys.[71] But a feud developed between him and Southey, and Coleridge was caught in the crossfire. When Canto III of *Don Juan* was published in 1821, it contained a saucy reference to Southey and Coleridge as brothers-in-law:

> All are not moralists, like Southey, when
> He prated to the world of 'Pantisocracy';
> Or Wordsworth unexcised, unhired, who then
> Season'd his pedlar poems with democracy;
> Or Coleridge, long before his flighty pen
> Let to the Morning Post its aristocracy;
> When he and Southey, following the same path,
> Espoused two partners (milliners of Bath).[72]

The reader was meant to understand by 'milliners' women of easy virtue (just as Byron used Regency slang in the suppressed Dedication in his pun on 'Bob' Southey and 'a dry bob', meaning sexual intercourse without ejaculation[73]). Coleridge appears not to have responded to this piece of rudeness, which Byron defended in a letter of 1822 to Murray: 'I hear that [Southey] says his wife was not a milliner at Bath. – Ask Luttrell – I have heard Nugent his friend say twenty times – that he knew both his & Coleridge's Sara at Bath – before they were married & that they were Milliners – or Dress-maker's apprentices. – There is no harm if they were that I know – nor did I mean it as any.'[74]

As Forster said, if life is a lesson, it is one Coleridge never learned. In 1819 he was naive and pompous enough to get embroiled with *Blackwood's Magazine*, familiarly known as 'Maga', the scandalous new Edinburgh monthly magazine set up in 1817 by the publisher Blackwood, with Wordsworth's neighbour John Wilson and a clever Oxford-educated lawyer, John Gibson Lockhart, as joint editors. James Hogg, the peasant poet known as the Ettrick Shepherd, was also a contributor, and the magazine specialized in scurrility and unaccountability, since no one person was identified as its editor. Wilson and Lockhart wrote alternate praise and satire on Wordsworth and Coleridge, with Wilson, as we have seen, going so far as to libel Coleridge in his nasty 'review' of *Biographia Literaria*. Wordsworth strong-mindedly banned the periodical from his house, though it found its way in nevertheless, since the women of the house had 'a great curiosity to see the Reviews &c of Wms Poems', as Sara Hutchinson confessed to her cousin Tom Monkhouse in July 1819.[75]

Coleridge, however, granted an interview in March 1819 with William Blackwood, the 'respectable' member of the editorial team, a Tory given to licensing attacks on the Whig *Edinburgh Review*, with which Coleridge was, of course, angry over his treatment at the hands of Jeffrey and Hazlitt.

Perhaps that was why he swallowed the bait offered by Blackwood, who flattered him by asking him to give, for publication, advice about the principles of periodical criticism. Coleridge had already aired the subject, petulantly, in *Biographia Literaria.* Now he had not the perspicuity or cynicism to see that he was being set up for a joke to be played on him.[76]

To William Mudford of the *Courier* Coleridge wrote in March 1819 that he might join *Blackwood's*, 'on the condition that the magazine is to be conducted henceforward first, pure from private slander and personal malignity; 2nd, on principles the direct opposite of those which have been hitherto supported by the Edingburgh Review'.[77] No doubt his motives were sincere and high-minded, though not unmixed with vanity. His judgement, however, was poor.

In a letter of 12 April to Blackwood he lectured the publisher on how to run the magazine, agreed to supply the equivalent of a leading article every month, and offered to be 'at all times prepared to give my best advice and opinion with regard to all other parts of the Magazine, to be, as it were, your London Editor or Curator'. Blackwood replied with a solemn promise to reform the 'too personal' tone of some of the early numbers.[78] There followed in June a letter from Lockhart, acting as editor, expressing his 'profound and sincere respect' for Coleridge's genius and asking for 'a Sketch of your views concerning the proper conduct of the Magazine'.[79] That very month 'Maga' carried Maginn's crude 'completion' of 'Christabel', but Coleridge was inclined to forgive Blackwood for 'the droll Christabelliad'.[80] Coleridge duly sent off the solicited essay in November.

Lockhart, the 'Scorpion' of *Blackwood's*, did not yet show his sting. Indeed, he had good reason genuinely to admire Coleridge, for he, too, was a German enthusiast who had spent the summer of 1817 in Weimar, translating on his return Friedrich Schlegel's *Geschichte der Alten und Neuen Literatur* (*Lectures on the History of Literature, Ancient and Modern*, 1818). While he was negotiating with Coleridge over the latter's contributions, he twice discussed his work. In July 1819 he published anonymously *Peter's Letters to his Kinsfolk*, in which 'Peter Morris' expresses his disapproval of the attack on *Biographia Literaria* in 'Maga', which he calls 'a sad offence'. 'If there be any man of grand and original genius alive at this moment in Europe', he says, 'such a man is Mr Coleridge'. This was gratifying indeed, though the praise is followed immediately, Hazlitt-fashion, by a concession to Coleridge's detractors, admitting his 'rambling discursive style' and his borrowings from German philosophy. Lockhart continues on a see-saw of high praise and mock-sorrowful criticism, with the praise predominating.[81]

Sharp Sara Hutchinson noted on reading these *Letters* that 'the praise and censure' were so extravagant that you 'see in a moment' that the author or authors 'have no principle at all'.[82] But Coleridge did not see it, or at least he turned a blind eye to the censure. He wrote to the unknown author in November 1819, elaborately describing his indifference to praise and contrasting himself in this respect with 'Atticus', for whom 'the admiration of his writings is not merely his gauge of men's *taste* – he reads it as an index of their *moral* character'. This was unfortunate, for it was clear that Coleridge had Wordsworth in mind, and when Lockhart printed the letter in *Blackwood's* in September 1820 without Coleridge's authorization, it caused the latter some embarrassment.[83]

Lockhart's second piece of praise was much less equivocal. In fact, it was the first truly positive, sympathetic, and intelligent review of Coleridge's works to be written by any critic in over twenty-five years. Marred, from Coleridge's point of view, by a mild reference to his eccentricity and the usual exhortation to Coleridge to overcome his indolence and publish more, the review was otherwise highly appreciative. Appearing in *Blackwood's* in October 1819, it gives proper attention to 'The Ancient Mariner', 'by far the most wonderful, the most original, and the most touching' of all Coleridge's poems. Lockhart quotes from it, inviting the reader to 'submit himself to the magic that is around him, and suffer his senses and his imagination to be blended together', a form of words which suggests that he knew chapter fourteen of *Biographia Literaria*. 'Christabel', too, is appreciated for its evocation of mystery and evil made more terrible by its being embodied in a woman of 'external beauty and great mildness of demeanour'.[84]

Finally, Lockhart praises Coleridge's 'wonderful translation, or rather improvement of the *Wallenstein*', an opinion which he repeated in 'Maga' in 1823, and which was taken up and echoed by other translators from German in the 1820s and 1830s.[85] No wonder Coleridge's heart was warmed by such appreciation. It is not too much to say that Lockhart set the tone for a marked change in critical attitudes to Coleridge's work.

Alas for Coleridge, his relations with Lockhart and 'Maga' were to deteriorate from this high point. His letter to 'Peter Morris' was printed in the magazine in September 1820 with a cheeky introduction by Peter himself admitting that the letter was meant to be private but saying he thought it so 'characteristic' of its author as to be worth publishing.[86] Coleridge was horrified. He told Lockhart in December 1820 that his sons had been 'vexed and distressed' on reading it, as they knew the reference to 'Atticus' would be recognized, and that would 'widen the breach or rather convert a coolness into a breach'.[87]

This was bad, for Coleridge was already extremely vulnerable at the end of 1820, as we shall see. But it was to get worse. John Scott, editor of the new *London Magazine*, recently set up to rival *Blackwood's*, seized on the latter's treatment of Coleridge, to which he may have been alerted by Lamb, one of his contributors. He turned the affair into a moral crusade, a war of words which ended, astonishingly, with the death of Scott in a duel fought with Lockhart's second, J. H. Christie, on 16 February 1821.[88]

Incredibly, Coleridge did not learn from this to shun *Blackwood's*. In October 1821 three letters of his to Blackwood were published, in which he long-windedly hovers on the brink of describing 'The Ideal of a Magazine', promising to do so 'in my next'.[89] Luckily for him, no such article followed, and Coleridge's foolish dealings with the pranksters of *Blackwood's* petered out. The one significant feature of these letters is that in one of them Coleridge described its 'characteristic plan and purposes' as 'Philosophical, Philological, and Aesthetic'. He added a footnote to the last word saying he wished he could find 'a more familiar word than aesthetic, for works of taste and criticism', but preferring it to 'belletristic'.[90] The word, so familiar to us now as a term for art and literature criticism, was probably first used in this sense in English by Coleridge here in *Blackwood's Magazine.* It had been used in Latin by the German writer Alexander Baumgarten in his *Aesthetica* (1750–8) and picked up by Kant to describe the experience of appreciating beauty in art. Once again Coleridge was the coiner or introducer of a new usage in English.[91]

When Coleridge finally met the chief *Blackwood's* culprit, Lockhart, in April 1825, that young wit had sobered down into the son-in-law of Walter Scott, and was soon to become the editor of the *Quarterly Review.*[92] *Blackwood's* itself settled down in the next generation to being an excellent miscellaneous magazine, well known for serializing new fiction, of which one example was the first work by the unknown George Eliot in 1857, *Scenes of Clerical Life.*

Meanwhile, Scott himself once more gave Coleridge cause for irritation. In chapter nine of *Ivanhoe* (1819) he quoted from 'The Knight's Tomb', an unpublished poem by Coleridge, introducing his (mis)remembered quotation with one of his damnings-with-faint-praise: 'To borrow lines from a contemporary poet, who has written but too little [this by now being an obvious allusion to Coleridge] –

> The knights are dust,
> And their good swords are rust,
> Their souls are with the saints, we trust.'

Though Coleridge did not mention this theft on first reading Scott's novel, he did give vent to his view of that work as 'a wretched Abortion' in a letter to Allsop of March 1820.[93]

The very day Coleridge wrote this letter Scott was raised to the baronetcy, an event which had Coleridge assuring Allsop a week later that he thought Scott 'a man of *very extraordinary* powers', whose works he usually read with 'pleasure and interest'.[94] Then his pen runs away with him and he gives, despite himself, an interesting view of the see-saw of good and bad in Scott's writings, not the less penetrating for being occasioned by personal annoyance and jealousy. There is, he says, in all that 'Ossianic Mock-Highland Motley Heroic' a good deal of *'false Effect,* & Stage trick', though 'the number of characters *so good* produced by one man & in so rapid a succession, must ever remain an illustrious phaenomenon in Literature', even if there are many borrowings from 'English & German Sources' in Scott's novels.

In a note in the margin of his copy of *Peveril of the Peak* (1823) Coleridge was to write, shrewdly, that 'the great felicity of Walter Scott is that his own intellect supplies the place of all intellect and all character in his heroes and heroines, and *representing* the intellect of his readers, supersedes all motive for its exertion, by never appearing alien, whether as above or below.'[95]

Coleridge's irritation at Scott's unacknowledged borrowings from himself, displaced in the letter to Allsop to unspecified 'English & German Sources', found direct expression in the margin of a manuscript copy of 'The Knight's Tomb' (not published until 1834), in which Coleridge assumes that his friend Frere 'must have repeated' the lines 'from memory to Sir W. Scott (for I had never committed them to paper)'.[96]

While all the business with Lockhart and *Blackwood's* was going on, Coleridge suffered the greatest shock and disappointment of his later life. In May 1820 Hartley was deprived of his fellowship at Oriel, or rather it was not renewed beyond his probationary year. He was charged with keeping irregular hours and frequently coming home late 'in a state of intoxication', as the Provost of Oriel, Edward Copleston, put it in a memorandum dated 15 June.[97] Hartley was unlucky. His behaviour was hardly unique at Oxford, but Oriel was a particularly strict college, and Hartley's eccentricities included an unfortunate social manner and an inherited tendency to procrastination and temporizing.

The story of his disgrace grew in the telling, and by the time his distant but doting father heard it from Gillman on 30 June, phrases such as 'sottishness, a love of low company, and general inattention to college rules' had become attached to Hartley.[98] Southey knew, but could not bring himself to write to Coleridge, though he told Mrs Coleridge in early July. She was utterly dashed by 'the worst news that ever reached my ears'.[99]

It was a disgrace which neither father nor mother nor the unhappy object of it could quickly or easily absorb. Coleridge sent Derwent to Oxford to talk to his brother, but when he got there, Hartley, like his father before him, had gone missing.[100] Poor Derwent, about to start his own university career at last, had only recently renewed his acquaintance with his father, visiting him at Highgate in April 1820 for the first time since March 1812, when he had been eleven years old.

Coleridge suffered 'strange & fearful Dreams' the night after hearing 'the sad news from Oriel'.[101] A miserable summer followed. He confided at once in Thomas Allsop, whom he considered as a son, telling him that the news had come 'sudden as a Peal of Thunder from a cloudless Sky'. He moved naturally from criticism of Hartley's destructive habits to defence of his own:

> I am convinced that [his drunkenness] is owing, *in great part*, to his habit almost constitutional (for it characterized his earliest Childhood) of eagerly *snatching* without knowing what he is doing, & whatever happens to be before him – bread, fruit, or Wine – pouring glass after glass, with a kind of St Vitus' nervousness – not exactly in the same way as my dear C.L [Lamb], but

similarly ... My Conscience indeed bears me witness, that from the time I quitted Cambridge no human Being was more indifferent to the pleasures of the Table than myself, or less needed any stimulation to my spirits: and that by a most unhappy Quackery after having been almost bed-rid for six months with swoln knees & other distressing symptoms of disordered digestive Functions, & thro' that most pernicious form of Ignorance, medical half-knowledge, I was *seduced* into the use of narcotics.[102]

And so on. The connection between father and son is as clear to Coleridge as it could be to anyone else. Writing to Derwent two days later he makes the same connection, but this time with a franker avowal of his own faults:

I wish that I dared believe that Hartley is bonâ fide on his road to Keswick – but the same Dread struck at once on Mr G's mind & on mine – that he is wandering on some wild scheme, in no dissimilar mood or chaos of thoughts and feelings to that which possessed his unhappy father at an earlier age during the month that ended in the Army-freak – & that he may even be scheming to take passage from Liverpool to America.[103]

Some time in August Hartley turned up in London, where he lodged with the Montagus in Bedford Square. He and Coleridge corresponded, chewing over the case, with Hartley rationalizing and justifying his behaviour, first confessing to unbecoming behaviour, then expressing outrage at the excessive charges against him. Coleridge did his best for his son. He wrote to the Provost of Oriel; he even visited him in Oxford in October. The college authorities acknowledged that they had been harsh, but did not back down. Hartley was officially deprived of his fellowship in October, but was offered £300 to avoid hardship. He and his father were offended and at first refused to accept, but by 1823 Hartley had been persuaded to take the money in order to pay his college debts and send the rest to his mother.[104]

The affair knocked Coleridge sideways. He came to depend more and more on his 'other' son, Allsop, the only one who did not, or might not, depend too heavily on him as a father.[105] Upset though he was, guilty and reproachful of others, especially of his wife, whom he accused of writing 'letter after letter to Derwent, about Hartley' by which she had 'completely overset him', the astonishing critical brain could still function. In the middle of this Hartley-obsessed letter of 8 August to Allsop, he made what is perhaps his single most apposite criticism of Wordsworth, dwelling on something problematic in his friend's work:

Wordsworth has remarked (in the 'Brothers', I believe)

The thought of Death sits light upon the man
That has been bred and dies among the Mountains.

But I fear, that this like some other few of W's *many* striking passages means less than it seems, or rather promises, to mean. Poets (especially if philosophizers too) are apt to represent the effect made on themselves as general – the Geese of Phoebus are all Swans, & Wordsworth's Shepherds & Estatesmen all Wordsworths, even (as in old Michael) in the *un*poetic traits of character. Whether mountains have any particular effect on the native inhabitants, by virtue of being mountains exclusively, & what that effect is, would be a difficult problem . . . I will not conceal from *you*, that this inferred dependency of the human soul on accidents of Birth-place & Abode together with the vague misty, rather than mystic, Confusion of God with the World & the accompanying Nature-worship, of which the asserted dependence forms a part, is the Trait in Wordsworth's poetic Works that I most dislike, as unhealthful, & denounce as contagious: while the odd occasional introduction of the popular, almost the vulgar, Religion in his later publications (the popping in, as Hartley says, of the old man with a beard) suggests the painful suspicion of worldly prudence . . . carried into *Religion*. At least, it conjures up to *my* fancy a sort of Janus-head of Spinoza and Dr Watts, or 'I and my Brother, the Dean'.[106]

The criticism that all Wordsworth's shepherds are versions of himself was one Coleridge had already made in *Biographia Literaria*. As to the supposed superiority of countrymen over town dwellers, Coleridge's remark on this goes to the heart of an unresolved philosophical problem in *The Prelude*. Is it true that country dwellers are more likely to grow up morally healthy than city dwellers? And if it is, what can be done for the disadvantaged many – increasing rapidly in the wake of the Industrial Revolution – who are unfortunate enough to have to live in cities?

As if Coleridge was not downhearted enough at the end of 1820, Hazlitt went into print once more in December, attacking him wittily in the *London Magazine*:

He is the man of all others to swim on empty bladders in a sea, without shore or soundings: to drive an empty stage-coach without passengers or lading, and arrive behind his time; to write marginal notes without a text; to look into a millstone to foster the rising genius of the age; to 'see merit in the chaos of its elements, and discern perfection in the great obscurity of nothing', as his most favourite author, Sir Thomas Brown[e], has it on another occasion.[107]

It was the end of a ghastly year, lightened only by the appearance of another article in the *London Magazine* which appeared in November 1820. This was Lamb's heartfelt account of Coleridge's time at Christ's Hospital as the '*inspired charity boy*' and budding genius holding spectators enthralled in the cloisters.[108]

Coleridge had been so preoccupied with Hartley that he had not had much time for comment on current affairs. The letter to the *Courier* of March 1818 about child labour in the cotton factories appears to have been the last political article he wrote. Rather surprisingly, he does not seem to have written, privately or publicly, about the chief event of 1819. This was Peterloo, so called because the cavalry was called in to charge a public meeting in St Peter's Fields in Manchester on 16 August in protest against the Corn Laws and in favour of electoral reform. Eleven were killed and 400 or so wounded at this meeting-turned-massacre –

A people starved and stabbed in the untilled field –

as Shelley described it in 'England in 1819'.

The crowd had turned out to hear Henry 'Orator' Hunt, a radical agitator who was one of the first to be prosecuted under the new legislation against sedition, the Six Acts, which were passed in December 1819.[109] In May 1820 Hunt and four others were sent to prison for violating the new Sedition Act. Coleridge's only extant comment, in conversation in 1823, was that the Government had been too slow in prosecuting 'Hunt and his associates'.[110]

1820 was a year of turmoil for the country, as well as for Coleridge personally. On 29 January George III finally died, to be succeeded by the unpopular George IV. He brought a problem with him, namely his refusal to allow his estranged wife, Queen Caroline, to share the throne. They had been separated for more than twenty years, and she had been persuaded to live abroad since 1813 on a generous pension. Rumours of sexual scandal surrounded her, but these were hardly worse than those which attached to the former Prince Regent himself. In the summer of 1820 Caroline came to Britain to claim her rights as Queen; meanwhile, George instituted divorce proceedings against her in the House of Lords on grounds of adultery.

The 'trial' began in August and lasted three months, with Henry Brougham, the brilliant Whig lawyer, defending Caroline. An enormous groundswell of public support for the injured Queen arose, resulting in meetings, pamphlets and ballads attacking the King's double standards. By November Lord Liverpool had abandoned the attempt to pass the bill through the Lords depriving her of her rights and prerogatives as Queen Consort.[111] It was a victory of a sort for the Queen, but the crisis rumbled on, with Caroline seeking entry to the coronation of George IV on 19 July 1821 and being refused. Finally, no doubt to the relief of all, she died suddenly on 7 August.[112]

Coleridge almost got publicly involved in the affair, but was wisely dissuaded by Gillman. His position was a complicated one. He sympathized with Caroline as the victim, but thought both parties morally unappealing. Crabb Robinson reported meeting him on 8 December 1820. 'I hope you are a Queenite', Coleridge apparently said, to which Robinson answered, 'No, only an anti-Kingite'. 'Aye', was the reply, 'that's all I mean.'[113] Coleridge's view was that divorce should not be an option for anyone, let alone for George IV, in whose case it would be pandering to 'an Individual's Lust and Hate'. The whole affair was degrading to the nation, a 'Live Puppet-shew of wicked Punch & his Wife', as he told Allsop in October 1820.[114]

It was at this time that Coleridge contemplated publishing an essay, 'Remarks Moral and Political', in the hope of 'giving some advice & warning to the Queen herself', and he approached the *Eclectic Review* with this in mind. Fortunately Gillman dissuaded him on the grounds that it would bring him notoriety and be injurious to Hartley and especially Derwent, just launched on his university career.[115] It would certainly have been a spectacle: an unhappily married man – widely known to be so and suspected in several quarters of having abandoned his wife and children – lecturing the King and Queen of England on how to conduct their broken marriage.

After Hartley's misfortune, Coleridge began to focus his fatherly anxiety on Derwent, exhorting him in May 1821 not to amass debts, remembering his own stupidity about money at Jesus, and expressing the hope that Derwent would leave Cambridge with 'an honorable character' and a 're-spectable Degree'.[116] Coleridge wished him to become a clergyman, as he now thought he himself ought to have done. 'WOULD I WERE! or *rather that I had been*' in orders, as he declared to Francis Wrangham.[117] Though steadier than Hartley, Derwent was to give his father some anxiety before settling down.

Hartley, meanwhile, lived with the Montagus in London, trying unsuc-cessfully to make a living out of writing for periodicals. He suffered from guilt feelings which caused him to run away from the Montagus for weeks at a time, installing himself in public houses, where he drank too much.[118] Thus he continued his uncannily close recapitulation of his father's young manhood.

No doubt at Coleridge's instigation Hartley wrote to one of his benefac-tors, Lady Beaumont, giving his version of the Oxford saga. He confessed to 'an unfortunate habit of Procrastination' and to drinking too much in 'one or two instances', but complained of 'a system of espionage' on the part of college scouts, porters and shoeblacks.[119] To Derwent, who was finding it hard to settle in at St John's, Cambridge, he assumed the role of mentor, adducing his own case as a warning. Like his father, he painted a picture of himself as victim, half-acknowledging his faults but unwilling to accept responsibility. Employing the passive mood, he told Derwent how, 'with few habits but those of negligence and self-indulgence, with principles honest indeed and charitable, but not ascetic', and 'with much vanity and much diffidence', with 'wavering hopes, uncertain spirits, and peculiar manners, *I was sent* [my emphasis] among men mostly irregular, in some instances vicious'.[120] It is the excuse once more of the grown child, dependent, as he thinks, on the will and whim of others.

As fate would have it, Coleridge himself was further taken back in memory to his own misspent youth by a rare visit to London of his older brother and surrogate father, George. Coleridge immediately resumed his old self-abasing, self-justifying tone towards George, who was staying in June 1821 with Luke's son, William Hart Coleridge. Writing to George, he compulsively ranged back over his past: the flight from Cambridge, his feelings of 'almost filial Reverence' for George, his regret at his 'apparent alienation from your affections'. Coleridge had visited George at Kensington and had been hoping for a return visit to Highgate, but George had put this off. Coleridge mingles hurt pride with his careful respect when he urges George to 'spare a few hours' for him and show the Gillmans the 'mark of respect' due to them as his kind hosts.[121]

The meeting between the brothers was the first, as Coleridge told Mrs Montagu, for twenty-three or twenty-four years.[122] It was also the last. The brothers did not see one another again before George's death in 1828.

13

Coleridge the Sage: *Aids to Reflection* 1821–1825

Yet well I ken the banks where amaranths blow,
Have traced the fount whence streams of nectar flow.
Coleridge, 'Work Without Hope', 1825

As he approached fifty, Coleridge found himself uncomfortably reliving his youth through his increasing involvement with the lives of his sons. He did not cope well with their problems and aberrations, once more revealing that extreme sensitivity which led to insensitive words and actions to those closest to him. But where he felt free of obligation, free to bestow love and support when he chose – i.e., outside the family circle – he showed tremendous kindness and patience. The chief example of this is the trouble he took in the frequent long letters he wrote to his chosen 'third son', Thomas Allsop.

Allsop was contemplating marriage in 1821, and Coleridge gave him his views on that 'state of deep and aweful interest'. Allsop, he said, must be sure that he had chosen 'a *Soul*-mate as well as a *House-* or a *Yoke-*Mate'. 'What then if instead of a Help-mate, we take an Obstacle, a daily Counteraction?'[1] When in March 1822 Allsop, newly married, complained that Mrs Gillman was snobbishly unwelcoming towards his wife, Coleridge assured him this was not so. As often in these letters to Allsop, he became confessional, remembering how he had ignored social barriers as a young man: 'And O! from 16 to 19 what hours of Paradise had Allen and I in escorting the Miss Evanses home on a Saturday, who were then at a Milliner's, whom we used to think, and who I believe really was, such a nice Lady.'[2] (An interesting reference, this, given Byron's recent allusion to the Fricker sisters in *Don Juan*, with its suggestion about the supposed licentiousness of milliners.)

In contrast to these soothing remarks to Allsop are Coleridge's stormy relations with Hartley and Derwent. In January 1822 reports of Derwent's socializing at Cambridge upset him, and he launched into accusing letters about the 'accursed Coxcombry' of 'extra-academic Society, Concerts, Balls – Dressing, and an hour and a half or two Hours not seldom devoted to so respectable a purpose'.[3] He could not resist lecturing Derwent: 'For God's sake, my dear Boy! for mine, for your Mother's, for dear little Sara's, do throw off these flappets and tag-points & appendages – Your business at present is to *learn*, to acquire, to *habituize* – not to teach – to *be*, not to *shew* – or rather to *become*.'[4]

Coleridge took offence when he heard that Derwent had complained of being obliged for his education to the generosity of others, not his father, and was agile in turning away this criticism of his own lack of financial independence:

> Suppose that a Bookseller had given me 300£ for my Lectures, instead of Mr Frere – would you think the sum more earned by me? Mr Southey received an annuity from his old School-fellow, Charles Wynne – which on Wynne's Marriage was commuted for a Pension – Had Southey used this for his Son's university education – would *Southey's* Son, think you, speak of himself as a mere poor child of charity, a dependent on the I know not what – and *contrast* his state with those, who are maintained by their Fathers?

Finally, with the remorseless logic of a man stung by the accusation of dependence, he accosts Derwent thus: 'If you are this mere Almsman, how preposterous must your present conduct be?'[5]

Hartley, meanwhile, was still giving cause for concern. John Taylor Coleridge invited him to dinner in December 1821 and noted that 'his condition seems a deplorable one – he said very unaffectedly that he by no means made it a practice regularly to dine, and always thought it a gain when he got a good dinner'. John encouraged Hartley to accept the £300 offered by Oriel in recompense for losing his fellowship, advice which Hartley eventually followed.[6] In May 1822 Coleridge was negotiating with Hartley's old schoolmaster at Ambleside, the Revd John Dawes, for Hartley to return there as a teacher. Coleridge was aware of the difficulties his son faced in trying to make a living out of occasional writing, something he himself had never quite managed.

In anatomizing Hartley, Coleridge once again anatomized himself. In the draft of his letter to Dawes he recalls Hartley's special childhood, how he was 'a spirit of Joy dancing on an aspen Leaf', as Wordsworth had put it in his poem addressed to Hartley when he was six years old. As for Hartley now, 'London he must not live in – the number of young men who will seek his company *to be amused*, his own want of pride, & the opportunity of living or imagining rather that he can live from hand to mouth by writing for Magazines &c – these are Ruin for him'.[7]

Hartley did join the staff of Ambleside School in November 1822. But he went reluctantly, knowing that Southey was determined not to have him in his household. Southey had written to Wordsworth in April in terms similar to those he habitually used about Coleridge himself: 'The scheme of sending him to be under his mother's eye is preposterous, even if it were possible. What authority can a mother exercise over a man of six and twenty – the very disease of whose nature is an impàtience of all ordinary observances, and of the restraints which he owes to himself as well as others!'[8] Hartley told Coleridge dejectedly that he could not bear the thought of going to Ambleside 'in the face of such unfavourable sentiments on the part of some'; he still hoped to 'make another trial of my talents in London'.[9]

But Hartley's behaviour in July 1822, when Derwent had typhus fever – caught in Cambridge, where an epidemic had broken out – and was thought to be in danger of his life, convinced Coleridge that he must be got out of London for good. Hartley went to ground while Coleridge and the Gillmans were nursing Derwent, which Coleridge thought heartless.[10] He also expressed himself strongly on the behaviour of his wife, who was terrified that Hartley would try to move in with her at Keswick against Southey's wishes. Coleridge, so alive to his own feelings of hurt and anxiety, failed to imagine what it was like for her, living for so long under Southey's roof and by his kindness. He exploded to Allsop: 'It will not be long, I trust, before Hartley may set off for the North – much against the Wish of his selfish *worretting* ever-complaining never-satisfied Mother. He might go to perdition body and soul, the trouble, embarrassment and anguish remaining on my shoulders, rather than be saved at the risk of any occasional annoyance to her, or of Mr Wordsworth's disapproabation.'[11]

In October 1822, writing to Allsop from Walmer, where he was on holiday with Mrs Gillman, he complained at length about the 'four griping and grasping Sorrows' he had experienced in his life. The first was when 'the Vision of a Happy Home sunk for ever, and it became impossible for me any longer even to *hope* for domestic happiness under the name of Husband'. The second was the quarrel with Wordsworth, 'when all the Superstructure raised by my idolatrous Fancy during an enthusiastic & self-sacrificing Friendship of 15 years' burst 'like a Bubble'. Of the third – the loss of Sara Hutchinson along with the loss of Wordsworth – he speaks more circumspectly. The fourth was Hartley's recent disgrace at Oxford, compounded by his 'desertion' of Derwent during his illness.[12] For the first time for many years, Coleridge almost raves in this letter, a sign that he was probably resorting to large doses of opium, even as he castigated others for their failures of will and action.

Though Coleridge published nothing between *The Friend* in 1818 and *Aids to Reflection*, which appeared in May 1825, he was going on with his reading and preparation on logic, philosophy and religion, with Green. In February 1822 he put an advertisement in the *Courier* proposing weekly classes for 'a small and select number of gentlemen, not younger than 19 or 20, for the purpose of assisting them in the formation of their minds, and the regulation of their studies'. Nothing came of this.[13]

A book was, however, taking shape in his mind. In January 1822 he tried out the idea on John Murray of a work about the early eighteenth-century nonconformist divine, Archbishop Leighton. Coleridge thought 'an interesting POCKET VOLUME' could be made of 'The Beauties of Archbishop Leighton selected and methodized' with a biographical and critical introduction. What he most valued in Leighton was the fact that he 'dissuades students and the generality of Christians from all attempts at explaining the Mysteries of Faith by *notional* and metaphysical speculations, and rather by a heavenly life and temper to obtain a closer view of these Truths, the full Sight and Knowledge of which it is in Heaven only that we shall possess.'[14] Murray showed enough interest to encourage Coleridge to go on with the work, which would eventually be *Aids to Reflection.* As before, however, he and Murray fell out over terms and arrangements, and the book was brought out by the firm of Taylor and Hessey.[15]

Strangely enough, Murray was the publisher early in 1822 of a work by Coleridge's daughter. Now nineteen, Sara was scholarly as well as beautiful – the Wordsworth circle commented frequently on her beauty and her brilliance – but rather cossetted by her mother and aunts because of her slight stature and nervous disposition.[16] She was to break down, mentally and physically, especially after the births of her children, from 1830 on. Incredible as it may seem, she resorted to opium in times of stress, becoming dependent on the drug.[17]

The book Sara published with Murray was a translation from the Latin of Martin Dobrizhoffer's *Account of the Abipones, an Equestrian People of Paraguay.* Derwent had begun the translation, at Southey's suggestion, before going to Cambridge. Sara offered to help, and on Derwent's giving up when Frere delivered the money to send him to university, she carried on alone, surprising her protective mother by her appetite for the task.[18] Of the many ironies surrounding this work as far as Coleridge was concerned, one was that the *Quarterly Review* noticed it favourably. Sara Hutchinson expressed the general view when she exclaimed that the translation was 'very well done' and that Sara was 'a wonderful little Creature – So laborious at her Books!'[19] No comment of Coleridge's survives from the time, though in a conversation in 1832 he spoke proudly of his daughter's achievement in rendering the book in 'pure mother English'.[20]

In January 1823 Sara arrived in Highgate with her mother on a long-awaited visit to the father she hardly knew. Having been preceded by the famous Collins portrait and now by her reputation for scholarship, she took literary London by storm. It was her first extended visit away from her Keswick home, a kind of coming out for the clever daughter of a clever father. She and her mother left Keswick in November 1822, proceeding southwards in leisurely fashion, staying on the way with the Beaumonts at Coleorton, with Derwent in Cambridge, and with the Clarksons at Playford in Essex. On 3 January they arrived at the Gillmans' house.

No record has survived of the feelings of the father, the mother, or the daughter on their reunion. In a letter to his friend the German business-man, Charles Aders, on the evening of their arrival, Coleridge merely announced that his daughter, 'a sweet and delightful Girl', was with him, '– & – Mrs Coleridge', a reference eloquent in its brevity.[21] Mrs Coleridge told Poole in March that the visit had given 'the greatest satisfaction to all parties'.[22] But these are hardly revealing remarks. More suggestive of the feelings and tensions aroused by the visit is Lamb's comment after 'the she Coleridges' had left London. 'Poor C.', he wrote, 'I wish he had a home to receive his daughter in. But he is as a stranger or a visitor in this world.'[23]

A meeting which took place at Gillman's house on 5 January was even more momentous for Sara than that with her father, and it turned out to be momentous for Coleridge too, or at least for his reputation. On that day Coleridge's nephews John Taylor and Henry Nelson Coleridge visited Highgate and met their cousin for the first time. Henry and Sara fell in love, and by the time she left London in early March they were already secretly engaged. Coleridge disapproved of the marriage of first cousins, as he revealed in conversation with Henry in June 1824,[24] and his brother the Colonel was no more enthusiastic about the engagement when he heard about it. But after waiting nearly six years while Henry established himself in his legal career, the cousins eventually married with the blessing of both fathers in 1829.

The advantage to Coleridge of this match was not only that it brought happiness to his daughter; it also meant that she became permanently resident in London; and it encouraged Henry in his admiration of his uncle turned father-in-law. Indeed, Henry became Coleridge's first editor and champion in the years immediately following Coleridge's death.

Even before the fateful meeting with Sara, Henry had performed some services for Coleridge. In the *Etonian* magazine in 1821 he wrote an article, 'On Coleridge's Poetry', under a pseudonym. There he talked of the 'power of language truly wonderful, more romantically splendid than Wordsworth's', and described 'The Ancient Mariner' as a work of 'perfect originality'.[25] What is striking about this eulogy is that it takes it for granted that Wordsworth and Coleridge are the chief poets of the age. Since Lockhart's praise of Coleridge in 1819 a high valuation of his poetry had become the norm. In October 1821, for example, Coleridge's political adversary Leigh Hunt wrote shrewdly about Coleridge's genius in a typically whimsical but sensitive piece in the *Examiner*. He noted that the young Coleridge had so made his mark at school that after he left Mr Boyer 'used to call him to mind as "that sensible fool, Coleridge"', and that he had 'bewitched' Hazlitt when preaching at Shrewsbury. Among the usual gossip about Coleridge's life Hunt makes some astute points. Of 'Kubla Khan', still much neglected by critics, he says, impressionistically yet catching the feeling of that elusive poem, that it is 'a voice and a vision, an everlasting tune in our mouths, a dream fit for Cambuscan and all his poets, a dance of pictures such as Giotto or Cimabue, revived and re-inspired, would have made for a Storie of Old Tartarie, a piece of the invisible world made visible by a sun at midnight and sliding before our eyes.

                    Beware, beware,
              His flashing eyes, his floating hair!'[26]

Coleridge's reputation was to rise and rise during the last decade of his
life, and Henry Nelson Coleridge was prominent in helping it to do so.
From December 1822, when he visited Highgate with his brother John for
the first time since meeting him in Richmond as a child, Henry kept
detailed notes of his uncle's fabled conversation, eventually publishing his
two volumes of *Table Talk* in 1835. On the day he met Sara he first noted
how 'lovely' and 'perfectly unaffected' she was, then went on to record
Coleridge's talk 'upon a thousand subjects'. These included, on this occasion, the suggestive remark about Schiller's and Shakespeare's relative
methods of producing dramatic effects by conflagration and handkerchief-
dropping respectively.[27] In the circumstances, it was heroic of Henry to pay
such close attention to Coleridge's words when presumably he had eyes
only for Sara.

John Taylor Coleridge, too, recorded a few of his uncle's conversations,
notably that on 9 January 1823, when Coleridge and Sara dined at his house
along with two clergymen, Thomas Rennell and William Lyall, whom
Coleridge apparently left standing in matters of theology, to John's astonishment and pride:

> I have heard him more brilliant, but he was very fine, and delighted both
> Rennell and Lyall very much . . . Nothing can be finer than the principles he
> lays down in morals and religion; the wonder, the painful wonder is that a
> man who can think and feel as he does – for I am convinced he feels as he
> speaks while he is speaking – should have acted and still act as he has done
> and does. His deep study of Scripture, too, is very astonishing; Rennell and
> Lyall were as children in his hands, not merely in the general views of
> theology, but in nice verbal criticism.[28]

From scripture the conversation turned to spirits and ghosts, a subject
on which Coleridge had lectured and in which he was particularly
interested both as a poet and as a religious thinker. The discussion sheds
light on his own nightmares and on his use of spectres in his poetry, as well
as indicating what we might call his believing scepticism about Biblical
accounts of miracles:

> We fell upon ghosts, and he exposed many of the stories metaphysically and
> physically. He seemed to think it impossible that you should really see with
> the bodily eye what was impalpable, unless it were a shadow; and what you
> fancied you saw with the bodily eye was in fact only an impression on the
> imagination; then you are seeing something 'out of your senses', and your
> testimony is full of uncertainty. He observed how uniformly in all the best
> attested stories of spectres the appearance might be accounted for from the
> disturbed state of the mind or body, as in Dion and Brutus . . . The man
> under delusion sees with the eye of the body and the eye of the imagination;
> if no one were present he would see the bed curtains with one and the spectre

with the other. If therefore a real person comes, he would see him as he would have seen anyone else in the same place, and he sees the spectre, they do not interfere with each other.[29]

Sara and Mrs Coleridge spent five weeks as guests of John Coleridge and his wife in Bloomsbury before leaving London on 5 March for a visit to the Ottery Coleridges. There Colonel James, not yet aware of his son's attachment to Sara, was enchanted by her and amused by Mrs Coleridge's chatter about the Southey and Wordsworth households: 'Sara is indeed a sweet creature, and she has attached herself to me, and indeed to us all . . . We get on with Mrs. Sam and let her run on about all the literary World . . . I shall not quiz her for the love I feel for her Daughter . . . I should think we might add £20 a year towards their support.'[30] What an irony that Mrs Coleridge, who appeared to Coleridge so deaf, blind, and dumb about his poetry, should have struck his unpoetical brother as a mine of information on 'all the literary World'.

Back in Highgate, Coleridge told Mrs Aders on 25 March that he had been ill 'during the whole of my dear Girl's stay in town' and had not been able to see her after she and her mother left Highgate for John's house in Bloomsbury.[31] Their visit had no doubt disturbed him, not least because his wife was an inevitable feature of it. He must have found it painful to be in her company. Moreover, it is not to be expected that he felt no pang of regret, remorse, and the ever-connected anger in the presence of his much admired daughter, in whose upbringing he had played no part.

Coleridge was fit enough on 4 April to attend a dinner given by Tom Monkhouse. Tom's cousin Sara Hutchinson was staying, with Wordsworth and Mary, with him in London. The stage was thus set for another of those meetings between the two poets which now took place only at long intervals and only in public. Crabb Robinson was there, of course, and so was Lamb, who duly dramatized the occasion:

> I dined in Parnassus, with Wordsworth, Coleridge, Rogers, and Tom Moore – half the Poetry of England constellated and clustered in Gloster Place! It was a delightful Eveng. Coleridge was in his finest vein of talk, had all the talk, and let 'em talk as evilly as they do of the envy of Poets, I am sure not one there but was content to be nothing but a listener. The Muses were dumb, while Apollo lectured on his and their fine Art.[32]

The very next evening several of the same people were gathered at a 'musical party and supper' given by Charles Aders.[33] At the end of the month Coleridge, who had not been able to visit his daughter for the five weeks of her stay at Bloomsbury, attended two dinner parties there in short succession. At the first, on 27 April, he reminisced to his nephews about the great men he had known in his youth. As so often, he set one person off against another. Thus Humphry Davy was a man whose thoughts 'were like the flower plucked wet with the dew; nay more, you could see them growing in the rich garden of his mind'. By contrast, Sir James Mackintosh's mind was 'a hortus siccus; full of specimens of every kind of plant, but dwarfed, ready cut and dried'.[34]

At John's party of 1 May Coleridge was once more 'in great force'. This time the other guests were none other than Colonel James and his wife. Henry was delighted to report the success of this meeting, the first between Coleridge and his older brother for many years. Coleridge was on his best behaviour, laughing diplomatically at his brother's Ottery anecdotes. 'He was looking remarkably well and rosy; and talked like a dragon', Henry told his brother Francis.[35] Though Coleridge and his brothers George and James would never see eye to eye, there is no doubt that they had recently softened their disapproval of him. This was partly, one supposes, because their sons were so full of praise for his learning and conversation, and because he was becoming less and less an object of public scorn.

Coleridge, even as his poetry began to be properly valued, now wrote only a few poems, but some of these are interesting. One was a playful response in May 1823 to the accusation of having plucked a flower from the garden of his Highgate neighbour Mrs Chisholm. Entitled 'The Reproof and Reply', it might stand as a metaphor for those more serious thefts of which he was often accused – namely intellectual ones:

> FIE, Mr. Coleridge! – and can this be you?
> Break two commandments? and in church-time too!
> [. . .]
> You, that knew better! In broad open day,
> Steal in, steal out, and steal our flowers away?

To this mock reproof the poet gives his mock reply:

> Thus, long-accustom'd on the twy-fork'd hill,
> To pluck both flower and floweret at my will;
> The garden's maze, like No-man's-land, I tread,
> Nor common law, nor statute in my head;
> For my own proper smell, sight, fancy, feeling,
> With autocratic hand at once repealing
> Five Acts of Parliament 'gainst private stealing!
> [. . .]
> For Chisholm speaks, 'Poor youth! he's but a waif!
> The spoons all right? the hen and chickens safe?
> Well, well, he shall not forfeit our regards –
> The Eighth Commandment was not made for Bards!'[36]

The idea of Coleridge treading, in terms of his wide reading, 'the garden's maze, like No-man's-land' and taking what suits him, is an alluring one.

Another poem, of which he copied a first draft into his notebook in September 1823, is less cheerful. 'Youth and Age' looks back to his hopeful youth:

> VERSE, a breeze mid blossoms straying,
> Where Hope clung feeding, like a bee –
> Both were mine! Life went a-maying
>   With Nature, Hope, and Poesy,
>   When I was young!
>
> When I was young? – Ah, woful When!
> Ah! for the change 'twixt Now and Then!
> This breathing house not built with hands,
> This body that does me grievous wrong,
> O'er aery cliffs and glittering sands,
> How lightly then it flashed along: –
> [. . .]
> Nought cared this body for wind or weather
> When Youth and I lived in't together.

The natural habitat of the young Coleridge had been out of doors. What a contrast with the grey-haired, corpulent, sickly Coleridge in his study at Highgate:

> Ere I was old? Ah woful Ere,
> Which tells me, Youth's no longer here!
> [. . .]
> I see these locks in silvery slips,
> This drooping gait, this altered size . . .

Highly conventional and lighthearted though the contrast is, it contains an acute awareness of Coleridge's special lot, the lot of the homeless man, at best a tolerated guest in another's house, not the contented patriarch in the manner of, say, Southey:

> Dew-drops are the gems of morning,
> But the tears of mournful eve!
> Where no hope is, life's a warning
> That only serves to make us grieve,
>   When we are old:
> That only serves to make us grieve
> With oft and tedious taking-leave,
> Like some poor nigh-related guest,
> That may not rudely be dismist;
> Yet hath outstay'd his welcome while,
> And tells the jest without the smile.[37]

In complete contrast to this quietly despairing poem is Coleridge's political squib about the activities of some members of the pro-Government party. John Stoddart was now editor of the right-wing *New Times*, and was widely known by radicals as 'Jack Snipe' and 'Dr. Slop' because of his slavishly pro-Government line. In 1820 he and the Duke of Wellington, among others, had formed the 'Bridge Street Committee', or Constitutional Association, which agitated for vigorous prosecution of all anti-Government, anti-Church, or anti-King writings. William Hone, three times prosecuted for libel and religious parodies in 1819, had been let off by the Attorney General Robert Gifford, but the radical bookseller Richard Carlile was less lucky; he sat in prison from 1819 to 1825 for selling libellous works. Coleridge shows in a notebook poem that he has no time for the prosecutors and persecutors:

> Jack Snipe
> Eats Tripe:
> It is therefore credible
> That Tripe is edible.
> And therefore, perforce,
> It follows of course
> That the Devil will gripe
> All who do not eat Tripe.
>
> And as Nic is too slow
> To fetch 'em below;
> And Gifford, the attorney
> Won't quicken their journey;
> The Bridge-Street Committee
> That colleague without pity,
> To imprison or hang
> Carlile and his gang
> Is the pride of the City,
> And 'tis Association
> That, alone, saves the Nation
> From Death and Damnation.[38]

The social excitements of 1823 kept Coleridge from completing any written work. But the book that would confirm his reputation as a thinker was, in fact, nearly complete. In August, after giving up hope that Murray would publish his book on Leighton, he turned to Taylor and Hessey, offering them 'Aids to Reflection: or Beauties and Characteristics of Archbishop Leighton, extracted from his various Writings, and arranged on a principle of connection under three Heads, of 1. Philosophical and Miscellaneous. 2. Moral and Prudential. 3. Spiritual – with a Life of Leighton & a critique on his writings and opinions – with Notes throughout by the Editor.'[39]

By February 1824 Coleridge was telling a young Dublin correspondent John Anster (later a translator of *Faust*) that 'a little volume will soon appear under the title of *Aids to Reflection*, which was at first intended only for a Selection of Passages from Leighton's Works', but had now 'become an original work almost'. It was with this work that he set up as a teacher of young men, and it contained the results of his conversations and studies with Green, who in 1824 became Professor of Anatomy at the Royal College of Surgeons. Coleridge told Anster that he intended the book for 'young men of ordinary education who are sincerely searching after moral and religious Truth but are perplexed by the common prejudice, that Faith in the peculiar Tenets of Christianity demands a Sacrifice of the Reason and is at enmity with Common-Sense'.[40]

Coleridge talks here as if the volume was already printing, when in fact publication did not take place for another year. Lamb supplies a clue to the delay, as well as once more putting his finger on the strange mixture of merits and faults in his marvellous friend. 'Coleridge's book is good part printed', he told Bernard Barton at the end of January 1824, 'but sticks a little for *more copy*'. And: 'It bears an unsaleable Title, Extracts from Bishop Leighton, but I am confident there will be plenty of good notes in it, more of Bishop Coleridge than Leighton, I hope, for what is Leighton?'[41]

Coleridge now saw himself primarily as a teacher, a leader of young men to moral and spiritual truths. He would have liked best of all to teach his own sons, and he had, in fact, tutored a willing Hartley during his Oxford vacation. But Hartley had disappointed him, and Derwent showed no sign of wanting his guidance, so he focused on younger admirers like Anster, who had first written to him in 1821 asking him to deliver a course of lectures in Dublin.[42] He also began to tutor Gillman's son James at this time. His most cheerful and informative letters are to these young men, surrogate sons, to whom he also complained – treacherously – about Hartley and Derwent. His letter to Anster in February 1824 describing the aims of *Aids to Reflection* contained a round-up of his news. While he and Mrs Gillman were in Ramsgate in the autumn of 1823, Gillman had moved house to No.3, The Grove, Highgate, the house in which Coleridge spent the rest of his life. The Royal Society of Literature was about to make him one of ten Royal Associates, for which he would receive 100 guineas a year in return for reading an annual essay.[43]

As for his children, Hartley was 'healthy, happy, industrious and universally beloved' at Ambleside, and Sara was 'every thing (save that her Health is delicate) that the fondest & most ambitious Parent could pray for'. 'The young men, & some of their elders, talk in raptures of her Beauty.'[44] But Derwent was a disappointment. He had passed through Highgate recently 'on his way to Plymouth, having accepted of the third Master's Place at a Public School recently instituted':

> He is well in body, and even improved in person; but alas! he has compleatly idled away his three years in talking and vanity, acquired no real knowledge of any kind but (of course, I write confidentially to you as a Son) has come back an avowed Atheist . . . I found however that he had been converted by young Austin & Macauley to this brutish Anti-Faith, & was so incapable of defining any one term, he made use of, and the arguments were so silly & so vaguely apprehended by him, that clearly perceiving that Vanity, aided by a sterile fluency . . . is at the bottom of it, I was more mortified by the shallowness than frightened by the wickedness & profligacy of his Creed: if only the same Vanity will but permit him to hold his tongue. – Still his Failure at

Cambridge, having merely taken an οι πολλοι Degree [i.e., a pass, not an honours, degree], & his Presumption, cannot but have been a heavy affliction to me.[45]

After this contentious meeting with his father, Derwent was in no hurry to repeat the experience; he simply kept out of Coleridge's way.

Hartley, somewhat restored in his father's favour, did his best to rehabilitate his brother. He tried to soothe Coleridge in a letter of 12 March 1824, declaring his confidence that Derwent's avowal of atheism was temporary and would give way to the stronger influence of his early life over the recent excitements at Cambridge in the company of such friends as those Coleridge privately called his 'Perverters', Charles Austin and Thomas Babington Macaulay.[46]

In April Wordsworth came on his usual spring visit to London, and the poets dined together again at the Monkhouses'. Wordsworth had translated the first three books of the *Aeneid*, and gave the manuscript to Coleridge for comment. This indicates that relations between them had thawed recently, though Wordsworth may well have regretted asking for Coleridge's criticisms when he saw them. Coleridge's remarks were devastating, though mixed, as always, with expressions of reverence and praise. The nub of his long note on the translation is contained in the following passage, in which he did not spare Wordsworth's feelings:

> Since Milton I know of no Poet, with so many *felicities* & unforgettable Lines & Stanzas as you – And to read therefore page after page without a single *brilliant* note, depresses me – & I grow peevish with you for having wasted your time on a work *so* much below you, and that you cannot *stoop & take*. Finally, my conviction is: that you undertook an IMPOSSIBILITY: and that there is no medium between a prose Version, and one on the avowed principle of *Compensation* in the widest sense – i.e. manner, genius, total effect.[47]

In relatively few words Coleridge here gives his view of the principles of poetic translation – that if rendered in verse it must not attempt to be literal, as Wordsworth's had – as well as reaffirming his opinion of the originality of Wordsworth's special genius. Perhaps because of this discouragement Wordsworth dropped the translation; he even echoed Coleridge's words about 'compensation' being necessary in verse translations in a letter of 1832.[48] Hartley Coleridge, ever the son of his father, also saw part of the translation, and commented, 'between Wordsworth's republican Austerity, and the courtly pomp of Virgil, the contrast is so wide, that I doubt, whether the more perfect correctness of sense, can atone in a translation for such disparity of mode'.[49]

In complete contrast to these commanding critical remarks of Coleridge are some slips of letters which survived his urgent instructions to '*destroy this instantly*'. These were clandestine notes written during 1824 to the Highgate chemist Thomas Henry Dunn about settling the bills for supplies of opium which Coleridge was getting surreptitiously, beyond the regulated amounts allowed him by Gillman. In one, dated 10 March, Coleridge urges Dunn in a postscript, 'I entreat you, be careful not to have any note delivered to me unless I am alone and passing your door.'[50]

Dunn was Coleridge's version of the 'celestial druggist' of De Quincey's recent *Confessions of an English Opium-Eater*, published first in the *London Magazine* in 1821, then as a book in 1822. In the section called 'The Pleasures of Opium' De Quincey rhapsodizes, though with heavy proleptic irony leading forward to the hell of opium addiction, about the 'Paradise of Opium-eaters', namely a chemist's shop in Oxford Street, where the drug is dispensed by 'an immortal druggist', the 'unconscious minister of celestial pleasures'.[51]

Coleridge could never have joked in this way about his addiction. In a note written in April 1826 giving the history of his recourse to opium he exclaimed: 'Oh! with what unutterable sorrow did I read the "Confessions of an Opium-eater", in which the writer with morbid vanity, makes a boast of what was my misfortune, for he had been faithfully and with an agony of zeal warned of the gulf, and yet wilfully struck into the current! – Heaven be merciful to him!'[52] Fortunately he was spared seeing De Quincey's enlarged version of 1856, in which he annoyed Coleridge's descendants by unseemly bickering about Coleridge's excuses for taking opium.

Though De Quincey does not in this first edition of *Confessions* refer to Coleridge by name, he drops a very large hint in a footnote on the fourth page about 'one celebrated man of the present day' who has 'greatly exceeded me in quantity'.[53] He also gives an uncomfortably astute analysis of the effect of taking laudanum on a personality such as Coleridge's and his own, half-quoting from Coleridge as he does so. In the section called 'The Pains of Opium' he unconsciously echoes Coleridge's own sad response to Cottle's chivvying in 1814, describing in detail the paralysis of will induced by opium addiction. The victim wishes as much as ever to do his duty, writes De Quincey, 'but his intellectual apprehension of what is possible infinitely outruns his power, not of execution only, but even of power to attempt'. He 'curses the spells which chain him down from motion: – he would lay down his life if he might but get up and walk; but he is powerless as an infant, and cannot even attempt to rise'.[54]

Describing in lush yet painful detail the nature of his dreams with their vast extension of time and space, De Quincey quotes from the darker moments of 'Kubla Khan':

> I seemed every night to descend, not metaphorically, but literally to descend, into chasms and sunless abysses, depths below depths, from which it seemed hopeless that I could ever reascend.[55]

De Quincey also recalls an occasion when he was in Coleridge's company:

> Many years ago, when I was looking over Piranesi's *Antiquities of Rome*, Mr. Coleridge, who was standing by, described to me a set of plates by that artist,

called his *Dreams*, and which record the scenery of his own visions during the delirium of a fever. Some of them (I describe only from memory of Mr. Coleridge's account) represented vast Gothic halls: on the floor of which stood all sorts of engines and machinery, wheels, cables, pulleys, levers, catapults, &c. expressive of enormous power put forth, and resistance over-come. Creeping along the sides of the walls, you perceived a staircase; and upon it, groping his way upwards, was Piranesi himself: follow the stairs a little further, and you perceive it come to a sudden abrupt termination, without any balustrade, and allowing no step onwards to him who had reached the extremity, except into the depths below.

The eye looks upward and sees another staircase with Piranesi on it, and so on 'until the unfinished stairs and Piranesi are lost in the upper gloom of the hall' (see plate 20). 'With the same power of endless growth and self-reproduction did my architecture proceed in dreams.'[56]

Coleridge's interest in Piranesi's 'astounding Engravings from Rome and the Campus Martius' dates back at least to 1808, when he sent Sara Hutchinson a packet of books and some 'Piranesi Folios'.[57] There is evidence in the notebooks that he, like De Quincey, associated Piranesi's drawings with his own nightmares. In September 1824 he mentions Piranesi next to a note written in Greek in which some guilty, distressful dream is reported.[58] His feelings towards De Quincey himself were guilty, for in August 1821 the latter, on the point of being arrested for debt, had written to him asking for the return of the 'loan' of £300 in 1807. Coleridge squirmed, recounted his own financial misfortunes, and ended on a note of self-righteousness not likely to be consoling to the desperate De Quincey: 'Dear De Quincey! I conjure you to feel convinced that were it in my power – let what would come the next week – to raise the money, you should not have received this melancholy History as an answer – Were you to see me at this moment, you would know with what anguish & sickness of soul I subscribe myself your *obliged* & grateful S. T. Coleridge.'[59]

In 1824 Coleridge also harboured guilty and irritated feelings towards the Gillmans. Perhaps they discovered, or suspected, his dealings with Dunn the chemist. Whatever the reason, Coleridge left them at the end of March to stay with Allsop and his wife. Mrs Gillman wrote apologizing for her 'cool behavior' and her impatience with his faults, and saying her husband was 'much hurt about your Book not being out' – suggesting that Coleridge was procrastinating about finishing *Aids to Reflection*.[60] Gillman came a day or two later, and, as Coleridge told Green in the tell-tale voice of the helpless child, 'fetched me home in a Coach on Wednesday Night'.[61] Relations remained ruffled for some months. In February 1825 Coleridge complained to Allsop about Mrs Gillman's 'restless and *interrogatory* anxieties' and her 'fidget-watching', particularly over the finishing of his book.[62]

This uneasy spell with Mrs Gillman makes a piece of gossip repeated by Lamb at this time even more of a mockery than Lamb himself thought it. On 29 November 1824, when Coleridge was again on holiday in Ramsgate with Mrs Gillman, Lamb told Crabb Robinson 'a little scandal' to 'divert' him which he had heard at a dinner party with F. W. Franklin, a schoolfellow of his and Coleridge's at Christ's Hospital:

> After dinner we talked of C., and F. who is a mighty good fellow in the main, but hath his cassock prejudices, inveighed against the moral character of C. I endeavoured to enlighten him on the subject, till having driven him out of some of his holds, he stopt my mouth at once by appealing to me whether it was not very well known that C. 'at that very moment was living in a state of open a ——— y with Mrs. ****** at Highgate? Nothing I could say serious or bantering after that could remove the deep inrooted conviction of the whole company assembled that such was the case! . . . Such it is if Ladies will go gadding about with other people's husbands at watering places.[63]

Lamb was also an amused bystander in the relationship between Coleridge and yet another young disciple, the charismatic Scottish preacher and friend of Thomas Carlyle, Edward Irving. Coleridge had gone in July 1823 to the Caledonian Church in Hatton Garden to hear this 'Idol of the World of Fashion, the Revd. Mr Irving, the super-Ciceronian, ultra-Demosthenic Pulpiteer of the Scotch Chapel'.[64] Irving became a regular visitor to Highgate, where he flattered Coleridge by echoing his views. Lamb thought him a charlatan, and told Leigh Hunt in 1825 how Irving had embarrassed Coleridge by dedicating a book to him in the most fulsome terms.[65] Coleridge was soon distancing himself from Irving, who became increasingly eccentric, until his 'speaking in tongues' with his congregation caused his ejection in 1832 for heresy.[66]

On 21 February 1825 Coleridge drafted in his notebook a poem composed on 'this premature warm and sunny day, antedating Spring', which he says was called forth 'in the manner of G. HERBERT'.[67] What follows is Coleridge's last really fine poem, 'Work Without Hope'. The Herbert poem in his mind was 'Praise', in particular the last few lines:

> O raise me then! Poore Bees, that work all day,
> > Sting my delay,
> Who have a work, as well as they,
> And much, much more.

Herbert's series of poems, *The Temple*, to which this belongs, had fallen from favour since its publication in 1633. Indeed, it was Coleridge's attention to Herbert in chapter nineteen of *Biographia Literaria* which heralded an increase in attention to him and the other metaphysical poets in the later nineteenth century.

Coleridge's poem, taking up from the end of 'Praise', with its moralizing about bees' work and his own idleness, was published in the *Bijou* in 1828. Though in the notebook the poem consists of fourteen lines followed by a break and then several more lines, many of them cancelled, the published version is of fourteen lines only, and looks like an inverted sonnet, with six lines of exposition preceding eight lines of elaboration. The opening lines observe the natural scene and express the speaker's regret, as yet unexplained, that he is somehow apart from it. For the second part of the poem a new tone is adopted; fanciful, heightened, mythical, nostalgic for a past when he had experienced not only hope but also the success of the poet wearing the laurel wreath and sucking the nectar of poetic inspiration. The last lines explain the loss.

Recapitulating the concerns of 'Dejection', Coleridge describes his idleness as a direct, unwanted consequence of his having no hope. With its links to the ecstasy of 'Kubla Khan' and the mourning for the loss of joy and inspiration in 'Dejection' and 'To William Wordsworth', this fine poem contains within it the paradox of success-and-failure:

> All Nature seems at work. Slugs leave their lair –
> The bees are stirring – birds are on the wing –
> And Winter slumbering in the open air,
> Wears on his smiling face a dream of Spring!
> And I the while, the sole unbusy thing,
> Nor honey make, nor pair, nor build, nor sing.
>
> Yet well I ken the banks where amaranths blow,
> Have traced the fount whence streams of nectar flow.
> Bloom, O ye amaranths! bloom for whom ye may,
> For me ye bloom not! Glide, rich streams, away!
> With lips unbrightened, wreathless brow I stroll:
> And would you learn the spells that drowse my soul?
> Work without Hope draws nectar in a sieve,
> And Hope without an object cannot live.[68]

Once more Coleridge steps forward as the great poet of an extreme psychological state, and though that state is an unhappy one, the poem, with its rich imagery and finely modulated tone – personal, confessional, domestic, drawing the reader in, yet capable of heightened rapture – is not a completely depressing or negative thing, since it glows with poetic life.

In contrast to this is his little versification of his sense of friendlessness in the public sphere, 'A Character', also composed in 1825. Written in doggerel couplets, it dramatizes his situation as a man forever being vilified for abandoning his earlier ideals. Coleridge the victim is to the fore:

> A bird, who for his other sins
> Had liv'd among the Jacobins;
> Though like a kitten amid rats,
> Or callow tit in nest of bats,
> He much abhorr'd all democrats.
> [. . .]
> Alas, poor Bird! and ill-bestarr'd –
> Or rather let us say, poor Bard!

[. . .]
Ah! silly Bard, unfed, untended,
His lamp but glimmer'd in its socket;
He lived unhonour'd and unfriended
With scarce a penny in his pocket, –
Nay – tho' he hid it from the many –
With scarce a pocket for his penny![69]

This piece of self-pity with a pinch of wit may have been called forth by the recent appearance of two books. The first was Hazlitt's *Spirit of the Age*, published in January 1825. In this extraordinary collection of pen portraits of his contemporaries Hazlitt had summed up all his admiration for, and all his objections to, Coleridge in a stylistic *tour de force*. As it happens, Hazlitt's own career had recently been at least as precarious and ludicrous as he delighted in pointing out Coleridge's was. His marriage to Sarah Stoddart, entered into without enthusiasm on his part, came to an abrupt and public end in 1822, when he and his wife obtained a divorce in Edinburgh, Scottish law allowing what English law would not. Hazlitt had lived apart from his wife at least since 1819, and had fallen in love with the daughter of his landlord, one Sarah Walker. After divorcing his wife, he hurried back to London to marry her, only to find that she had taken another lover. Distraught, he set about publishing his letters to her and to his friend and confidant Peter George Patmore in the rather crazy *Liber Amoris* (1823). In February 1823 he had been arrested for debt. By 1824 he was married to a Mrs Bridgwater, who left him the following year.[70] His life was in disarray, but his mind was as sharp as ever, and adversity had not made him kinder towards others.

His is a fine, cruel essay. Coleridge the 'most impressive talker of his age' but the writer of 'abortive prose'; the 'idol' of his schoolfellows who had fabulous reading at his command but who successively changed his allegiance and philosophical enthusiasm from Hartley to Priestley to Bishop Berkeley to Kant; the boy who 'sang for joy' when the Bastille fell but ended up a middle-aged praiser of Legitimacy; the owner of a mind which 'keeps open house, and entertains all comers' and the author of that 'work of genius' 'The Ancient Mariner' – Hazlitt's own prose falls over itself in order to render the rich and varied, but flawed, career of Coleridge.[71]

The other book which annoyed Coleridge was Thomas Medwin's *Conversations of Lord Byron*, a gossipy memoir rushed out soon after Byron's death in 1824. Medwin records Byron's having said of Coleridge: 'If he had never gone to Germany, nor spoilt his fine genius by the transcendental philosophy and German metaphysics, nor taken to write lay sermons, he would have made the greatest poet of the day . . . Coleridge might have been any thing: as it is, he is a thing "that dreams are made of".'[72]

Add this to Hazlitt's offhand remark that Coleridge 'wandered into Germany and lost himself in the labyrinths of the Hartz Forest and of the Kantean philosophy' and to the constant sniping of reviewers on this topic, and one can understand Coleridge's complaint to his nephew John in April

1825 about the damage done to his reputation: 'The prejudices excited against me by Jeffrey, combining with the mistaken notion of my German Metaphysics to which (I am told) some passages in some biographical Gossip-book about Lord Byron have given fresh currency, have rendered my authority with the TRADE worse than nothing.'

This reputation as a borrower of the obscurest of German philosophical ideas was given further expression in a work of that other Germanophile and plucker of flowers in others' gardens, Scott, as Coleridge complained to his nephew: 'A High German Transcendentalist I must be content to remain – and a young American Painter, Lesly . . . to whom I have been in the habit for ten years and more of shewing as cordial regards as I could to a near relation, has, I find, introduced a portrait of me in a picture from Sir W. Scott's Antiquary as Dr Dusterswevil, or whatever the name is.'[73] The artist was C. R. Leslie, who had done a portrait of Coleridge in 1818; his sketch of the German fraudster in *The Antiquary* does bear a passing rememblance to Coleridge.

Coleridge was particularly nervous at the time of writing his April letter to his nephew, who had been since December 1824 the editor of the *Quarterly Review*. *Aids to Reflection* was to be published the following month, and Coleridge anticipated another rough ride in the periodicals. He summed up his woes to Daniel Stuart in July 1825. Jeffrey of the *Edinburgh* 'has openly avowed his determination to "*cut up*" (I use his own phrase) whatever I shall publish'. As for the *Quarterly*, the previous editor, William Gifford, 'disliked me – & would never mention a book of mine – And now my own Nephew will not, I suppose, dare do it for fear of the charge of partiality'.[74] To another nephew, Edward, now teaching at Eton, he complained in November of the same set of circumstances, quoting Lamb's comment that he was 'one of Fortune's *Ne'er-do-wells*'.[75]

Coleridge usually claimed, however disingenuously, not to care much about the reception of his books. But he cared very much, and did not try to hide the fact, about the reception of *Aids to Reflection*. He believed that this work, the culmination of over twenty years of reading and thinking on philosophical and religious subjects, would be his most important contribution to knowledge. He meant it also to assist the debate on the moral condition of England at a time of change and uncertainty after the end of the long war with France, when reform measures were constantly being put before Parliament. He hoped his book would be of genuine use as a moral guide for young men, while at the same time securing his own reputation as something more than a dreamer and talker.

And so it did, though not immediately. When it finally appeared at the end of May 1825, the work was much changed from the original plan. Gone was the proposed biographical introduction on Leighton, perhaps because another work on Leighton was published, with 'a brief sketch of his life', by a W. Wilson in 1824.[76] Leighton, though still prominent, now shared Coleridge's attention with other religious thinkers such as Hooker, Richard

Baxter and Jeremy Taylor. German philosophy, particularly the work of Kant, Schelling and Tenemann, and the critique of the Gospel of St John by Coleridge's old Göttingen professor, J. G. Eichhorn, also form an important part of the intellectual context of the book.

Coleridge mingled his own accumulated opinions on the subjects of faith, reason and conscience with Leighton's, so that it was not always easy to see at a glance which of the 'Aphorisms' presented in the work are wholly Leighton's and which Coleridge's or a tapestry from himself and other thinkers.[77] Coleridge was aware of the problem, which he tried to solve by using the term 'Editor' not only for his own copious footnotes to Leighton, but also for those aphorisms which were wholly or partly his own.

On the face of it, a work by Coleridge commenting on Leighton commenting on St Peter's First Epistle does not sound promising for the education of the intelligent but general reader for whom Coleridge intended it. In fact, though the work is clumsily arranged and does in places exhibit Coleridge's labyrinthine mode of argument, it has a surprising freshness and clarity much of the time. This is in part due to the aphoristic nature of the enterprise, for which we have to thank Leighton, whose method rubbed off on Coleridge. Some of the Leighton–Coleridge sayings which were most influential on later thinkers are pithy and memorable. An example is 'Moral and Religious Aphorisms XXIV and XXV', the first by Leighton and the second by Coleridge, with their robust defence of the right to, and usefulness of, religious doubt:

APHORISM XXIV
WORTHY TO BE FRAMED AND HUNG UP IN THE LIBRARY OF
EVERY THEOLOGICAL STUDENT

Where there is a great deal of smoke, and no clear flame, it argues much moisture in the matter, yet it witnesseth certainly that there is fire there; and therefore dubious questioning is a much better evidence, than that senseless deadness which most take for believing. Men that know nothing in sciences, have no doubts. He never truly believed, who was not made first sensible and convinced of unbelief.

Never be afraid to doubt, if only you have the disposition to believe, and doubt in order that you may end in believing the Truth. I [Coleridge speaks here] will venture to add in my own name and from my own conviction the following:

APHORISM XXV

He, who begins by loving Christianity better than Truth, will proceed by loving his own Sect or Church better than Christianity, and end in loving himself better than all.[78]

The generation following Coleridge, facing a double onslaught on traditional religious belief from the Higher Biblical Criticism of Eichhorn's successors, Strauss and Feuerbach, and the evolutionary doctrine of Darwin, could seize on this positive creed of 'honest doubt' as a rudder to steer them through stormy waters. Tennyson's *In Memoriam* and Arnold's 'Dover

Beach' are only the best known expressions of that generation's difficulties and consolations in this respect. John Stuart Mill, in his appreciative essay on Coleridge in the *London and Westminster Review* in 1840, quoted Coleridge's Aphorism XXV with approval as part of his own plea for philosophical tolerance.[79]

One factor in the ultimate success of the work is undoubtedly the admirably clear introduction Coleridge provides. The opening sentence is a model one: 'An Author has three points to settle: to what sort his Work belongs, for what Description of Readers it is intended, and the specific end or object, which it is to answer.' He answers the questions briskly. The work is '*didactic*', intended to instruct; it is written for all those who 'wish for aid in disciplining their minds to habits of reflection' and who are interested in his position, 'namely, that the CHRISTIAN FAITH (*in which I include every article of belief and doctrine professed by the first Reformers in common*) IS THE PERFECTION OF HUMAN INTELLIGENCE'.[80]

More specifically, the book is intended 'for the studious Young at the close of their education or on their first entrance into the duties of manhood and the rights of self-government'. Anticipating his famous definition of a new class of men, the clerisy, in *On the Constitution of Church and State*, he says he means especially those whose chosen profession is the ministry, but also those other educated youths who 'have dedicated their future lives to the cultivation of their Race, as Pastors, Preachers, Missionaries, or Instructors of Youth'.

Here Coleridge seems to be including, quite simply, people like himself or Wordsworth or Southey, along with others outside the Church hierarchy such as scientists – the late Thomas Beddoes and Humphry Davy – and philanthropists like the Wedgwoods and Thomas Poole. Though he was against the coming extension of the franchise, he recognized that education must be widened, and he hoped that all political, social, and educational expansion would have a moral and spiritual basis such as that offered in the pages of his book.

As to the contents of his argument, he draws attention in his introduction to 'the value of the Science of Words, their use and abuse'. He himself coins some sixty new words or usages in the course of this work, from 'actualization' to 'bi-sexual' (for Adam at the Creation), to 'selfless' (of sterile female ants which look after the young in the nest).[81] A further aim, close to his heart, is to 'substantiate and set forth at large the momentous distinction between REASON and Understanding'. Here Coleridge's study of Kant, in particular, bears fruit in his characterization of the previous age, the eighteenth century, as materialist, mechanist, empirical, while the present age, by contrast and reaction, is – or *ought* to be – spiritual. He personifies the two mental faculties he is keen to distinguish:

Whatever is achievable by the UNDERSTANDING for the purposes of worldly interest, private or public, has in the present age been pursued with an activity and a success beyond all former experience, and to an extent which equally demands my admiration and excites my wonder. But likewise it is, and long has been, my conviction, that in no age since the first dawning of Science and Philosophy in this Island have the Truths, Interests, and Studies that especially belong to the REASON, contemplative or practical, sunk into such utter neglect, not to say contempt, as during the last century. It is therefore one main Object of this Volume to establish the position, that whoever transfers to the understanding the primacy due to the Reason, loses the one and spoils the other.[82]

Finally, he aims to show that the mysteries of religion 'are Reason, Reason in its highest form of Self-affirmation'.[83] His method is to follow Kant's distinction between 'speculative Reason' – the faculty which operates in the sphere of knowledge and which falls short of full cognition of necessary and universal truths, being limited to acting on the facts of experience – and 'practical Reason', which operates in the moral and spiritual sphere, where it has access to postulates of moral action and, for Coleridge if not so clearly for Kant, to spiritual truths. Understanding contrasts with both forms of Reason. It is a faculty entirely dependent on 'the objects of our senses'.[84]

Coleridge's intention here is perhaps clearer than his reasoning. He wants to avoid Kant's stoicism and the gulf still remaining in the Kantian system between the *moral* imperatives of Reason and the *spiritual* affirmations of religious faith. Crabb Robinson summed it up in May 1826: *Aids to Reflection* 'exhibits the best adaptation of Kantian principles to English religious sentiment'.[85] And Mill described the 'Germano-Coleridgean' doctrine of the work as a reaction to British empiricism, being ontological, conservative, and religious in opposition to Bentham's mechanistic and empirical philosophy.[86]

Aids to Reflection was ignored, as Coleridge had foreseen, by the *Quarterly Review*. The *Edinburgh* carried no review, not even a hostile one. The *British Critic* took it seriously, but the writer was grudging, making objections to the 'mystical notions of the critical [i.e., Kantian] philosophy' which he thought he saw 'intruding upon the Christian doctrines'.[87] In January 1826 Southey told Lockhart, who had just taken over the editorship of the *Quarterly* from John Taylor Coleridge, that he 'understood that Heraud had written a paper upon the *Aids to Reflection* by S.T.C. which was very ably written – but over laboured and too much like the book itself'.[88] A review by J. A. Heraud, a self-confessed disciple of Coleridge, appeared in *Fraser's Magazine* in 1832, addressing the second edition of *Aids to Reflection* (1831). It is striking in its rapture and respect for 'the venerable author', 'that profound thinker, writer, and speaker', S. T. Coleridge.

A sea change had occurred by this time in the public perception of Coleridge's work. *Aids to Reflection* was the chief marker and initiator of the change. Heraud addressed Coleridge in extravagant terms in his review: 'O how much is owing to thee by the greatest and brightest minds which now shine down upon the republic of letters . . . accept the small tribute of gratitude which we are now about to offer at the shrine of philosophic genius.'[89]

Fulsome and extreme though this is, it is a tone which would have been unthinkable in reviews of Coleridge ten, twenty or thirty years before. Heraud was by no means the only young man who now looked on Coleridge as his spiritual guide. Green, Gillman, Allsop and Tulk had attached themselves to him some years before. But Coleridge's wider fame as the Sage of Highgate who welcomed all comers and gave generously – some said too much so – of his wisdom began in earnest with *Aids to Reflection*.

Interestingly, given his flight from Cambridge as a young man, it was there that his influence was strongest. Julius Hare and his brother Augustus compiled their imitative work *Guesses at Truth* (1827) there. Other Cambridge men associated in the 1830s with the Broad Church Movement of the Church of England, which attempted to liberalize and re-spiritualize an over-worldly and much attacked institution, took their cue from Coleridge. Among them were John Sterling, Richard Chevenix Trench, William Bodham Donne, and Tennyson's friend Arthur Hallam.[90]

The reception of Coleridge's late work, and *Aids to Reflection* in particular, in America was remarkable too. James Marsh, President of the University of Vermont, brought out an American edition in 1829 with a long complimentary introduction. Coleridge quickly became a guru in American universities, as Marsh told Henry Nelson Coleridge in 1840.[91]

By 1842, when Frederick Denison Maurice brought out the second edition of his book, *The Kingdom of Christ*, he could write in his dedication addressed to Derwent Coleridge that in Coleridge's work, particularly *Aids to Reflection*, one could read 'the history of his mind, and therein the history of our time'.[92] Coleridge would have been delighted with the remark.

14

Progress and Permanence 1826–1829

The certainty that struck Hope dead,
Hath left Contentment in her stead . . .

Coleridge, 'The Improvisatore', 1827

Education was much on Coleridge's mind in the mid-1820s, as it was on many minds, particularly in London. In 1825 Thomas Campbell, Henry Brougham, and other liberals, with Bentham's financial and philosophical support, came together to found a university in London. Associated with the general movement for reform, the group met to establish an institution for the capital which would be, unlike Oxford and Cambridge, open to non-Anglicans and which would carry its religious tolerance into the fields of study too: modern languages and the sciences would be taught as well as the traditional subjects of classics, law and mathematics. There would be no school of divinity. The Universities of Edinburgh, Bonn, and Virginia served as models for 'the Metropolitan University', or 'the Cockney College', as it was soon dubbed in the public prints.[1] The University of London, later to be renamed University College London, opened in 1828.

On hearing in May 1825 that the scheme was afoot, Coleridge sounded out friends like Allsop and Green about the desirability of his entering the fray with a set of lectures on 'the Histories of Universities generally', 'the meaning of the term, University, and the true & only adequate Scheme of a University' with 'a plan of approximating to the Ideal'.[2] A week later he had given up the idea, 'lest I should be supposed to advocate' the particular scheme being proposed.[3] He had presumably taken fright at the radical and dissenting nature of the promoters and the proposed institution, which was soon nicknamed 'the godless institution of Gower Street'.[4] It was left to John Henry Newman to write the book Coleridge here envisaged as lectures, with his *Idea of a University Defined and Illustrated* (1873).

Still on the subject of education, Coleridge proposed to Hessey in May 1825 a set of six 'disquisitions' on faith, the Eucharist, the philosophy of prayer, the Hebrew Prophets, the Church, and the use of the scriptures. Not all of these were written, though the fifth became his next, and last, book, *On the Constitution of Church and State* (1830). The sixth, though first published by Henry Nelson Coleridge in 1840 as *Confessions of an Inquiring Spirit,* was written and sent to Hessey at this time. Coleridge explained his title on the opening page as linked with '*The Confessions of a Fair Saint* in Mr. Carlyle's recent translation of the *Wilhelm Meister,* which might, I think, have been better rendered literally, *The Confessions of a Beautiful Soul*'.[5]

Coleridge had met Carlyle in June 1824, when the latter accompanied his friend Irving on a visit to Highgate. On that occasion Carlyle presented Coleridge with a copy of his translation of Goethe's novel, and he soon gave a pungent rendering of the meeting in a letter to his brother John. Noticing Coleridge's physical demeanour and interpreting it, as Hazlitt did, as symbolic of his psychology, Carlyle described Coleridge, 'the Kantean metaphysician and quondam Lake poet', as follows:

> Figure a fat flabby incurvated personage, at once short, rotund and relaxed, with a watery mouth, a snuffy nose, a pair of strange brown timid yet earnest looking eyes, a high tapering brow, and a great bush of grey hair – you will have some faint idea of Coleridge. He is a kind, good soul, full of religion and affection, and poetry and animal magnetism. His cardinal sin is that he wants *will*; he has no resolution, he shrinks from pain or labour in any of its shapes. His very attitude bespeaks this: he never straightens his knee joints, he stoops with his fat ill shapen shoulders, and in walking he does not tread but shovel and slide – my father would call it *skluiffing*.[6]

It was a description he would later work up into the famous chapter on Coleridge in his *Life of John Sterling* (1851), in which he anatomized Coleridge's talk with its accumulation of 'formidable apparatus, logical swim-bladders, transcendental life-preservers and other precautionary vehicular gear, for setting out'. Carlyle, Germanist though he was, had little enthusiasm for what he rather too carelessly called, mimicking Coleridge's adenoidal speech, 'the hazy infinitude of Kantean transcendentalism, with its "sum-m-mjects" and "om-m-mjects"'.[7]

Like Hazlitt and De Quincey before him, Carlyle owed much to the man he ridiculed. Like them, he was irritated by certain beliefs, as well as mannerisms, of his mentor. In Carlyle's case it was Coleridge's championing of the Church of England – 'this dead English Church', as he called it here,[8] or the old clothes 'gone sorrowfully out-at-elbows', as he memorably described it in *Sartor Resartus* (1836). In characterizing his friend Sterling in a letter to Ralph Waldo Emerson in 1837, Carlyle paid a back-handed tribute to Coleridge's influence in the later 1820s. Sterling, he wrote, again with a sartorial metaphor, is one, and the best of a small class extant here, who nigh drowning in a black wreck of Infidelity (lighted up by some glare of Radicalism only, now growing *dim* too) and about to perish, saved themselves into Coleridgean Shovel hattedness, – or determination to *preach*, to preach peace; were it only the spent *echo* of a peace once preached. He is still only about thirty; young; and I think will shed the shovel-hat [the broad-brimmed hat of Anglican dignitaries] yet perhaps.[9]

Actually, Carlyle was unfair to castigate Coleridge for desiring the continuation of the Church of England in its idealess, worldly state. Coleridge agreed with Carlyle as to the diagnosis of the patient, but wanted to proffer a cure rather than sing and dance on the patient's grave. Indeed, Coleridge suggested to Hessey in May 1825 a publication supplementary to *Aids to Reflection* which would address the need to respiritualize the Church from within. Its title might be, he suggested, 'The grey-headed Passenger: or Conversations on Ship-board during a voyage to the Mediterranean, supplemental of the AIDS TO Reflection by S. T. Coleridge'.

Coleridge would be that traveller, and would converse with 'a young Clergyman, newly ordained who had subscribed to the 39 Articles', but who did not want to trouble his conscience about them. This young man would have a 'very compendious, convenient and portable faith', consisting largely of a desire to advocate honesty as the best policy and stick to 'the *morality* of the Gospel', ignoring matters of doctrine. In the course of philosophical discussions on the voyage, he would come to see the hollowness of his creed and to embrace the need to seek 'the first principles of all living & effective truth in the constitution and constituent faculties of the Mind itself'.[10]

This work, which would have fulfilled seriously Coleridge's mock portrait of the figure he cut on his very first voyage – to Germany in 1798 – when he was taken for a clergyman and announced himself a philosopher, was not written, though some of its ideas were included in *On the Constitution of Church and State*.

Coleridge had fallen easily during the last few years into the role of wise counsellor and elder statesman to his younger colleagues and followers. He was anxious about his nephew John's handling of the *Quarterly Review*, which he had hoped John would refuse to edit. Now that John *was* the editor, Coleridge was keen to offer advice. He disliked the unpleasant cut and thrust of reviewing, and was relieved when John gave up the job in November 1825 after less than a year in charge.[11]

Another nephew became close to Coleridge in the 1820s. This was Edward, to whom Coleridge turned for help with the education of the Gillmans' second son, Henry, whom he had been tutoring as he did James. Edward Coleridge was about to take up a teaching post at Eton in 1825, and Coleridge asked him for advice on coaching Henry for entrance there.[12] During the summer of 1825 Mrs Gillman ate, drank, woke, slept, thought and dreamed 'nothing but Henry Gillman & Eton College', as Coleridge told Edward. Coleridge himself accompanied Henry – as he had not done his own sons under similar circumstances – to Eton for his entrance examination at the end of July. Henry was accepted.[13]

By October poor Henry had got into trouble, and Coleridge left Ramsgate, where he was spending his annual holiday with Mrs Gillman, to go to Eton and sort things out. There had been talk of Henry's 'personal uncleanliness & "the act of *indecency*"' which shocked Mrs Gillman but brought out the best in Coleridge.[14] He busied himself, writing letters to Edward at Eton and to Gillman in Highgate, soothing the distraught mother, and visiting the unhappy Henry at Eton. From there he wrote as tactfully as possible to Gillman about Henry's weakness, his liking for floggings, and his inability to withstand temptation or 'repel Seduction' by other boys.[15] Coleridge's strength on this occasion does him credit; he may well have identified with the weak, easily led, homesick boy, having nightmarish memories of his own time at school. It was nevertheless decided that Henry should stay at Eton.

While all this was going on, Coleridge had no contact with his own sons. He did not know Derwent's address in December 1825, or whether he was about to take orders. Derwent was, in fact, about to do just that. When Coleridge found out that he was staying with a clergyman in Devon, he wrote accusingly: 'I go on from month to month as if I had no Sons in the world, never hearing *of* you or Hartley without a compounded or biforked Sting of grief and shame that I never hear *from* you.'[16] One wonders if Coleridge protected himself from drawing the obvious connection between his sons' neglect of him and his own behaviour throughout his life, first towards his brothers, then towards his wife and children.

Relations with Derwent, once re-established, improved when he reported to his father that he was returning to Cambridge to prepare himself for ordination before going to teach at Helston Grammar School in Cornwall.[17] But almost immediately Derwent struck another blow, announcing that he wanted to marry a Plymouth girl, Mary Pridham, which he eventually did in December 1827. Coleridge and his wife agreed in opposing the match, and on the same grounds – though they naturally expressed themselves in characteristically different ways. Mrs Coleridge was blunt, telling Derwent in January 1826, 'I hope no child of mine will marry without a good certainty of supporting a family. I have known so many difficulties myself that I have reason to warn my children!'[18] Coleridge's response was wordy and righteous, but just as heartfelt:

The most heart-withering Sorrow that can betide a high, honorable, morally sensitive and affectionate-natured Man, (a guilty conscience excepted) is: to have placed himself incautiously in such a relation to a Young Woman as neither to have it in his power to discontinue his attentions without dishonor & remorse, nor to continue them without inward repugnance, and a future *life* of Discomfort, of vain Heart-yearnings and remediless Heart-wastings distinctly before his eyes – as the alternative! – Either Misery of Remorse, or Misery of Regret![19]

Derwent settled down to his teaching and his curacy, and put off marrying until he was more secure. But Hartley, who never wrote to his father, was in a calamitous state. He was not happy in his teaching job. 'Great boys are the least agreeable animals in creation', he told his cousin John in February 1825. He often had nightmares about trying to discipline them.[20] In 1831 he told his mother that he had 'an instinctive terror of big boys, perhaps derived from the persecution I suffered from them when a little one'. Whenever he was unwell or feverish, he would have dreams peopled by boys 'hooting, pelting, spitting at me – stopping my ways – setting all sorts of hideous scornful faces at me – oppressing me with indescribable horrors, to which waking life has no parallel'.[21]

Despite these horrors, so similar to those of the father from whom he was alienated, Hartley stayed in the school. He was much loved by everyone in the neighbourhood of Ambleside. But by October 1825 the school had failed and Hartley was suddenly unemployed. He was given work on *Blackwood's Magazine* by John Wilson, and he also wrote for such minor organs of trivia as the *Gem*, the *Literary Souvenir*, and the *Winter's Wreath*.[22] As Hartley himself told Derwent wrily in 1826, he had written a 'bad, mainly silly, conceited, and impertinent' article for 'Maga', 'but it is fit for the company it is going into'.[23]

Hartley could no more make a living out of the magazine business in the Lakes than he had been able to do in London. He drank, despaired, and disappeared for stretches of time. In March 1826 he had 'one pupil from Ireland at £100 per annum', according to Dorothy Wordsworth, but by December he had been 'on his wanderings nearly a month', and his mother was 'in sad spirits' about him.[24] Mrs Coleridge herself told Poole disconsolately in August 1826 that Hartley was 'a sad loiterer in the land'. She had 'no hope that he will ever maintain himself wholly'.[25]

Hartley was Coleridge's Nemesis. He never wrote to, or saw, his father again, having last seen him in London in 1822. He was, as he noted in his journal, a self-destroyer. Not only did he never see his father, but after his sister Sara's marriage in 1829 he did not see her again either. Derwent visited him only twice, in 1843 and 1846, when Hartley was ill. He made shift as he could, with occasional handouts from his family and the Wordsworths and through the kindness of the local farmers, but his life was blighted. A notebook extract reads: 'I am far from all my kindred – not friendless indeed – but loveless and confined to a spot beautiful indeed – and dear – but where I am not what I might be elsewhere – where much that was dearest to me has been taken away – where I want a motive to strengthen my will – and worse than all – where I daily know myself my own heart's enemy.'[26]

It was a sad life for such a talented young man, who had given so much pleasure to family and friends in his delightful childhood. As Coleridge saw, his beloved son had uncannily fulfilled the prophetic fears expressed by Wordsworth in his poem of 1802, 'To H. C. Six Years Old':

> O blessèd vision! happy child!
> Thou art so exquisitely wild,
> I think of thee with many fears
> For what may be thy lot in future years.

In a note to Gillman in 1825 Colerige had fetched up a reminiscence from Hartley's boyhood. Quoting from his own poem, 'The Nightingale', he recalled an episode when Hartley was 'scarcely five years old': 'On some one asking him, if Anny Sealy (a little girl, he went to school with) was an Acquaintance of his, he replied very fervently, pressing his right hand on his heart – No! She is an *In*quaintance. "Well! 'tis a Father's tale!" – & the recollection soothes your old Friend & *In*quaintance S. T. Coleridge.'[27]

A poem written by Coleridge in his last decade – possibly about this time – seems to tell the story of the loss of Hartley. Entitled 'The Pang More Sharp than All', and not published until 1834, it begins with an unnamed 'he' who has 'flitted from his secret nest'. As if remembering the way Hartley had whirled in the wind as a child, he writes

> Like a loose blossom on a gusty night
> He flitted from me . . .

And:

> Ah! he is gone, and yet will not depart! –
> Is with me still, yet I from him exiled!
> For still there lives within my secret heart
> The magic image of the magic Child.[28]

Like father, like son. The magic possessed by both could easily turn into a curse. In November 1825 Coleridge had confided in his notebook his sense of his own combination of childlike innocence and deep guilt:

> Poor – embarrassed – sick – unpatronized, unread – But (replied the soft consoling Friend) *innocent.* – I felt only as one that recoils – & sinful dust and ashes that I am – groaning under self-reproached inproaches! – *I* innocent? – Be thankful still! (repeated the same so sweet Voice) you are an *innocent* man – Again I draw back but as a little child from a *kind* Stranger, but without letting go of the Stranger's hand/ . . . Ah but even in boyhood there was a cold hollow spot, an aching in that heart, when I said my prayers – that prevented my entire union with God that I could not *give up,* or that would not give *me* up – as if a snake had wreathed around my heart, and at this one spot its Mouth touched at & inbreathed a weak incapability of willing it away –/ – Never did I more sadly & sinkingly prostrate myself in sense of my worthlessness – and yet, after all, it was a *comfort* to me –/ My innocency was a comfort.[29]

If out of such tortured feelings he had as a young man produced 'The Ancient Mariner' and 'Christabel', in his later life this sensitivity to such extremes of guilt and innocence led him on his long odyssey into the philosophy of the Christian faith, the subject that concerned him more than any other from now until his death. As he put it in a notebook argument with Schleiermacher's *Discourses on Religion (Über die Religion, Reden an die Gebildeten unter ihren Verächtern*, 1799) early in 1826: 'I want, I need, a Redeemer.'[30] Being, as Keats had seen, incapable of remaining content with half-knowledge, he had to argue philosophically about his need.

Despite his anxieties about Derwent and Hartley, Coleridge was relatively cheerful early in 1826. Though he often talked in letters about his own death, he expressed himself calmly, even amusingly, about the prospect. He joked to Derwent on 11 January: 'We must all die of somewhat and ought, as the Irish Franciscan in a discourse of Final Causes observed – Let us all thank God and adore his wisdom and goodness in putting Death at the end of Life & thereby giving us all time for repentance.'[31]

The cause of this relaxed attitude is not far to seek. He felt that with the publication of *Aids to Reflection* he had at last achieved something worthwhile, and he was heartened by the admiring reception of the work among discerning men like Frere and the Spanish writer Blanco White, who 'procured an introduction to me from Sir George & Lady Beaumont' and showed a 'highly gratifying acquaintance with the book'.[32] He was able to tell Daniel Stuart in April 1826 that he had some confidence in personal salvation, particularly through 'the efficacy of Prayer', something about which he had previously despaired.[33]

The notebooks during 1826 show him undertaking a critical reading of the Gospels, grappling with the arguments of Herder, Eichhorn, and other writers of what had become known as the Higher Criticism since Eichhorn gave that name to his studies of the Bible. Eichhorn's purpose was to apply to the Old and New Testament texts the same historical and linguistic criteria he would to any other ancient document. He argued that there was an original document on which the three synoptic gospels were founded, to which the three writers of these had added material from other sources. Coleridge saw that such arguments, as well as the writings of Hume and others against miracles, would tend to undermine traditional belief in the truth of scripture. He himself, as his comments in *The Statesman's Manual* in 1816 on symbolism and allegory in relation to the Bible had shown, was – unlike so many of his contemporaries – not upset by such studies. In February 1826 he noted:

> The original sin of the German School is the comparing of this or that extraordinary narrative in the Gospel with some other analogous fact in recent or profane History – instead of taking the complexus of the New Testament Story & seeking for an analogy to *this*, in any other series of events allowed not to be miraculous. *In imagination* they snap each single Hair, with ease; but in reality, the generous Steed would have kicked their Brains out at the first kick – as foul Play. – No! – You must try your strength on the whole Tail.[34]

His aim, in the face of the controversy surrounding such critical under-mining of Biblical texts, was to help prepare the minds of theological students 'by shewing that whatever the final result might be, the truth of Christianity stood on foundations of Adamant', and having convinced them of this, to 'emancipate the believer from the Spirit of fear'.[35]

Nevertheless, he respected Eichhorn, whose works he discussed at length in his notebooks. Among the 'numerous services' rendered by his old German professor was, he thought, 'the confutation of the common notion of Mark's Gospel being an Abridgement of Matthew'.[36] By contrast, his attitude to Herder, who had suggested that the gospel accounts of the death, resurrection, and ascension of Christ were recastings of ancient Jewish stories, was much less reverential. Herder was 'a paltry Juggler, a tricksy gaudy Sophist, a rain-bow in the Steam of a Dunghill', he wrote succinctly in March 1826.[37] The confidence with which Coleridge carried on the debate with these German writers, albeit in the privacy of his notebook, is striking.

And yet, for all his improved sense of himself and his achievements, Coleridge was still a prey to vivid dreams and nightmares. On 26 April, only a week after writing his contented letter to Stuart, he suffered 'one of my most grievous and alarming Dreams'. With death much on his mind, since he had been ill with severe influenza a few weeks before, he had a kind of premonition that he would 'imitate my dear Father in this as faithfully as Nature imitates or repeats him in me in so many other points – viz. that I shall die in sleep'. He recalled his night at an inn in Edinburgh in 1803, when he had thought he was dying and composed his own epitaph about 'poor Col'. 'I remember, I awoke from the stimulus of pure vanity from the admiration of my own fortitude, coolness, and calmness in bearing my death so heroically – as to be able to compose my own Epitaph.'[38]

Swedenborg's work on heaven and hell had supplied the matter for some of his dreams, as had Piranesi's drawings of prisons. To Swedenborg 'I am indebted for imagining myself always in Hell, i.e. imagining all the wild Chambers, Ruins, Prisons, Bridewells, to be in Hell.' No one, he thought, had explained dreams adequately; 'this is the very nakedness thro' the scant & ragged Breeches of the modern Hartleio-Lockean Metaphysics, with its Impressions, Ideas, and Sensations, and its Jack of all Trades, Association'. The difference between Coleridge's account here and his earlier jottings about dreams is that he ends this one on a positive note of consolation: 'It is time to be saying my prayers, and to intreat protection "from the Spirits of Darkness" – a phrase in one of Jer. Taylor's fine Prayers, which I am always *inclined* to retain – tho' the fear of praying what I do not fully believe makes me alter it into – Afflictions of Sleep.'[39] Like his Ancient Mariner, he has been so far released from torment at least as to be able to pray.

On 8 February 1826 Coleridge wrote to his nephew Edward commenting on the recent financial crisis which had brought Walter Scott's publisher, Constable & Co, and the firm in which he was a partner, Ballantyne & Co, to ruin. Scott had borrowed so much to enlarge and decorate his house and estate at Abbotsford that he now owed over £110,000.⁴⁰ Coleridge was unsympathetic: Scott had been induced by 'Lust of Gain' to publish 'wretched trash' for the last three years or so.⁴¹ (He would nobly write a mass of worse trash over the next few years in order to clear his debt.) The crash led to Constable's accounts being opened to scrutiny, making it necessary for Scott to admit publicly what many, including Coleridge, knew, that he was the 'Great Unknown' of the Waverley novels.⁴²

In his letter to Edward he also mentioned the work just published by Edward's brother Henry Nelson Coleridge, *Six Months in the West Indies in 1825*. Late in 1824, Henry had gone to Barbados with his cousin, William Hart Coleridge, now Bishop of Barbados, returning in December 1825. His book was thought so flippant by the Ottery Coleridges that his father ordered it to be withdrawn.⁴³ Coleridge began reading it in February 1826, and regretted 'an imitation of Southey' in 'the frequent obtrusion of offensive images, Sweating &c; and again a little too much & too often of eating'. This quaint objection led to a severe comment on Southey's coarseness with regard to physical appetites other than sex – 'while he keeps clean of *one* outlet, he does not care what filth comes out of the other Orifices'.⁴⁴

Even Hartley, who, unlike his father, knew of his sister's secret engagement to Henry, disapproved of the book's 'vulgarity', and rather disapproved of Henry as a future husband for his beloved sister. He thought Henry insensitive, and told Derwent that 'our Sariola will require delicacy in a husband'.⁴⁵ Hartley also disliked Henry's tolerance of the slave system, a view shared by Coleridge. In June he noted in his journal that his 'harum-scarum nephew Henry' had argued that slavery was 'not abhorrent from the Christian Religion'. For Coleridge there was only one position to take on slavery, and it was the one he had always taken, namely that it was incompatible with either Christianity or morality.⁴⁶

It was through reading Henry's book that Coleridge finally became aware, some time before the end of July, of his long engagement to Sara. Henry had somewhat recklessly written in the book that he loved 'a cousin'. Poor Coleridge told his nephew Edward on 27 July that when he read this passage, he complained innocently to Mrs Gillman that people might think Sara was meant by it. Mrs Gillman, who had been let into the secret (known also to the Wordsworths and the Southeys) gently told him about the engagement.⁴⁷

Coleridge's reaction was interesting. He had already told Henry in conversation in 1824 – did Henry raise the question deliberately? – that he was inclined to disapprove of the marriage of first cousins, though he accepted the Church's tolerance of it. Still, though he would not have approved if asked his opinion, he accepted the *fait accompli*, 'for the man and the father are too strong in my soul, for me not to shrink from the thought of my only Daughter – & *such* a daughter – condemned to a miserable Heart-wasting'.⁴⁸

Coleridge's acquiescence and his unexpected ability to absorb the news without becoming ill or hysterical are remarkable. Perhaps his relative peace of mind about himself stretched to cover this shock; perhaps a father's greater indulgence towards daughters than towards sons came into play. Moreover, Sara, alone of his children, had not disappointed him, but had more than lived up to his expectations. Then, too, she was the child most like him in nervous constitution. He may have known that she had often been ill over the past two years (i.e., the time of her engagement). If so, understanding that psychological as well as physical causes were present, he would have feared making her worse by expressing his disapproval. So he accepted the engagement, and looked forward to seeing her in a few weeks, for she was due to come south to see him and also to renew acquaintance with the fiancé from whom she had been apart for nearly two years.

But Sara did not come. She and her mother set out from Keswick in July, shortly after the death of Southey's thirteen-year-old daughter Isabel, the fourth of Southey's children to die. Upset by this death, and only recently recovered from eye problems, Sara got as far as Kendal but, according to her mother, was 'so weak from repeated sleepless nights, that it was impossible to proceed – and I brought her back.' Mrs Coleridge was in a dilemma. Sara was growing 'daily thinner' and looked 'almost as white as this paper', she told Poole in August, yet if she was kept at home all winter brooding about not being able to make the journey, she might grow even worse. So another effort was to be made to get her to London, not least because Mrs Coleridge thought that Coleridge himself might not outlast the winter, for 'after 50 an ailing man may soon be carried off', as she put it, rather dispassionately, to Poole.[49]

Mrs Coleridge's fussing over her increasingly neurotic daughter is understandable; the Southeys and Wordsworths, too, were always talking about her delicate health. But Sara Hutchinson took a more robust view. She told Edward Quillinan about the failed journey to the not very desirable fiancé:

> Unluckily her mother accompanied her to Kendal & there persuaded her she was not fit for the journey, dosed her with Laudanum to make her sleep at a time when she could not have been expected to sleep if she had had the feeling of a stone . . . Now Sara is in despair – Her Father disappointed – Her Lover too (but why does he not fetch her?) . . . O how I do pity her! & hope that if she gets rid of her Mother that she may turn out something useful before she ceases to be ornamental. I am sorry to tell you (but it is a secret) that she is engaged to one of her Cousins – he who has written the conceited work about West India and who is very delicate in constitution – having had an affection of the spine – without fortune but what he can make by his wits & the Law.[50]

Coleridge was indeed disappointed. He, too, thought now that he might not see her before his death and wrote morbidly in his notebook on 30 July about his bodily languor and low spirits and his anxiety about his sinfulness, particularly as related to opium, 'a poison destructive of life' which has 'become necessary to life'.[51] Thoughts of his daughter had led to thoughts of his own death, and these in turn brought him close to religious despair about the mismanagement of his life. No wonder his letters and notebooks went on arguing about, and seeking arguments for, salvation: every arrival at peace, faith and certainty could so easily be undermined that a constant renewal of effort was needed. Sara did manage to begin what was to be a year-long visit to her father and her fiancé in the middle of September 1826.

Mrs Coleridge, writing to Poole in August 1826 about the postponement of Sara's visit to London, also announced the astonishing news that Southey had been made an MP during his absence on a journey to Holland. A certain Lord Radnor, an admirer or Southey's increasingly conservative writings, had used his 'interest' to have Southey put in as the member for Downton. Southey immediately decided to step down, but not out of disapproval of rotten or pocket borough patronage. Rather, as he said, though he was gratified by the gesture, 'a seat in Parliament is neither consistent with my circumstances, inclinations, habits, or pursuits in life'.[52]

No comment by Coleridge is recorded. Though not friendly to reform agitation, he had retained a greater tolerance of its promoters and their ideals than his old friend and erstwhile fellow Jacobin. When the Catholic Question became pressing again during the next two years, Coleridge was less hostile than Southey, saying in March 1827 that he would vote for civil rights for Catholics on the strict understanding that 'at no time and under no circumstances could a branch of the Romish Hierarchy as at present constituted become an estate of the Realm'.[53] In the last year of his life he even dreamed of bringing about – 'were I young, had I the bodily strength & animal spirits of early manhood with my present powers & convictions' – a 'Union between the *Protestant* and the now *papal* but still *Catholic* Church'.[54]

Young Sara spent some time at Highgate before going to stay with John Taylor Coleridge in Torrington Square, then with Edward and his wife at Eton. Henry, once more visiting Coleridge regularly, resumed his note-taking of his uncle's conversation, broken off when he had gone to Barbados. He now urged his fiancée to do so too, especially as 'he talks to you on plainer subjects'.[55] In October 1826 Coleridge went on his usual two-month visit with Mrs Gillman to Ramsgate, where once again bad news from Eton arrived. This time Henry Gillman was sent down for unspecified wrongdoing.

The affair brought about a coolness between Coleridge and his favourite nephew and confidant, Edward, who was Henry's tutor. Coleridge thought he could have done more. He told Edward of Mrs Gillman's distress, asking for sympathy with her strong ambition for her son. Interestingly, he makes one of his very few references to his own mother, and this time not an unkind one, reminding Edward 'how much our family (with the single exception of myself occasioned by my Father's sudden Death) owe to your Grandmother's maternal ambition'.[56] The comment in brackets might act as a succinct summing up of the psychic damage caused to Coleridge by his father's death and his mother's abandoning him.

Coleridge rallied the Gillmans and set about finding another school for Henry. The Free Grammar School at Shrewsbury was decided on. Its headmaster was a Samuel Butler, whom Coleridge had known at Cambridge. Indeed, Coleridge mused on the series of coincidences which surrounded Henry Gillman's education. Butler, Coleridge and Dr Keate, headmaster of Eton and father-in-law of Edward Coleridge, had been declared equal in the University Craven Scholarship in 1793. The scholarship had gone to Butler, as the youngest.[57]

The upheaval inevitably affected Coleridge's health, especially as he now heard from Mrs Coleridge about Hartley's wretched state. He complained to Mrs Aders in December of his depressed spirits and an 'erysepalatous inflammation of my left leg'.[58] He told another correspondent, William Worship, that 'poor dear dear Hartley' was the object of 'every one's love & admiration' and 'every one's sorrow and compassion'.[59] But at least Derwent seemed to be settling down. In October 1826 he was ordained deacon and began serving as a curate in Cornwall under yet another cousin, the Revd James Coleridge, eldest son of the Colonel. Coleridge now accepted Derwent's engagement to Mary Pridham, addressing her as 'dear tho' unseen' in a short poem of October 1827, shortly before her marriage.[60]

Coleridge wrote several short poems in 1826–7, none of them very good. One, 'The Two Founts', written for Mrs Aders in June 1826 when she had been ill, was published in the *Annual Register* for 1827 and reprinted in 1828 in another of the many literary annuals which sprang up in the 1820s, the *Bijou*, where Crabb Robinson read it along with 'The Wanderings of Cain', 'Youth and Age', 'A Day Dream', and the fine 'Work Without Hope'.[61] Another, 'Duty Surviving Self-Love', subtitled 'The Only Sure Friend of Declining Life', was kept for the 1828 edition of Coleridge's *Poetical Works*. It was presumably too gloomy to be suitable for the Christmas publications. An eight-line piece which did appear in one of these, the *Literary Magnet* of January 1827, sings simply of the joys of Christmas Day for 'him who hath a happy home' and the contrasting misery

> To him who walks alone through Life,
> The desolate in heart.[62]

Coleridge published these bits and pieces for the odd sums of money he could raise by them. With one son needing financial support and the other two children hoping to marry, he was acutely aware that he had nothing to give in the usual way of paternal support and settlement. That is why he was so dashed when his hopes of getting a sinecure of £200 a year from the

Prime Minister, Lord Liverpool, met a series of rebuffs. His friend Frere had extracted a promise from Liverpool in 1826, but before the honour could be conferred Liverpool suffered a paralytic stroke, in February 1827, from which he never recovered. Canning, who took over as Prime Minister, was apparently not interested in Coleridge's claim; the place went to someone else; and in any case Canning himself died in August 1827.[63]

Coleridge was bitter about his ill luck, which he put down partly to coincidence and partly to 'the Spirit of Calumny from the North and from the South', which he believed was blackening his name. He understood by 'the North' the Wordsworths, Southeys, and particulary his wife, as he revealed in a petulant outburst to Henry Nelson Coleridge in May 1827. In addition to the misfortune of the sinecure was the fact that Sir George Beaumont, who died in February, had left an annuity of £100 each to Wordsworth and Southey, and to *Mrs* Coleridge, but nothing to him. His harsh remark was: 'Poor Mrs C. – her hundred pound is but a poor compensation for the injurious influences on her children & herself, to which she has so long unthinkingly lent her aid in her rash and God knows! most unjust speeches & the impressions made & permitted to be made even on my own children!' He was even ruder about Lady Beaumont, whom he likened to Helen of Troy, though not in beauty:

> A bitch and a Mare set Old Troy Bells a knelling:
> The Mare was of Wood and the Bitch was call'd Helen![64]

Coleridge managed to hide his anger and jealousy in the presence of his beloved daughter, if not in this bad-tempered letter to her fiancé, for Mrs Coleridge heard from Sara that Coleridge, on hearing of the settlements, had 'expressed no sentiment but sorrow for the loss of his esteemed friend!'[65] He was sorry, too, that he was unable to raise 'a few thousand pounds', no less, to help Derwent (who had been ordained in July) and Mary consolidate their 'schemes' – probably to set up a school.[66]

In July 1827 Coleridge mused on a plan to publish with Alaric Watts, editor of the *Literary Souvenir,* an edition of Shakespeare's works with critical notes, prefaces, and analyses, 'comprizing the results of five and twenty Years' Study'.[67] Unfortunately, the project got no further, though a glance at Coleridge's *Table Talk* from the summer of 1827 shows he was thinking suggestively about Shakespeare.[68] These dinner-table comments on *Measure for Measure, Othello,* and *Hamlet* have become well known, thanks to Henry Nelson Coleridge, but a complete annotated edition of the plays would have been a wonderful consolidation of such scattered discussions.

On 12 January 1828 George Coleridge, whom Coleridge had 'lov'd as a brother' and 'as a son rever'd' ('To the Rev. George Coleridge', 1797), died at Ottery aged sixty-three. Something of Coleridge's mingled grief, guilt, and – guilt's corollary – the desire to exculpate himself, is expressed in his letter to his nephew, George May Coleridge, on 14 January: 'Before God have I sinned – and I have not hidden my offences before him – but he too knows, that the belief of my Brother's alienation and the grief that I was a stranger in the house of my second father has been the secret wound that to this hour never closed or healed up.'[69]

It had been a difficult relationship, cool and wary when not downright stormy, and if George had been somewhat unbending in his conventionality, Coleridge had certainly tested his generosity and patience to the limit. In a notebook written on 13 January, when he had first heard that George was dying, he poured out his feelings of gratitude for George's help until 'my Cambridge eccentric movements with my connection with the Unitarians and Liberals of Bristol, & imprudent marriage produced a Breach'. A kind of reconciliation had occurred in 1799, when Coleridge took Sara and little Hartley on a visit to Ottery, but 'the intense difference' between the brothers in 'character, habits, aims and ends, *constituted* an alienation'. Coleridge sums up the reminiscence with the old telling complaint of the orphan and the youngest brother: 'It was the Will of Providence, that I should pursue my pilgrimage *alone.*'[70]

Coleridge's natural tendency to introspection, sharpened by George's death, was exercised again in February 1828 when he read about himself in Leigh Hunt's *Lord Byron and Some of His Contemporaries*. Hunt describes Coleridge's appearance as 'sluggish and solid'. With his white hair and habitual black clothes and his 'very tranquil demeanour', Coleridge's appearance, says Hunt in his potboiler, 'is gentlemanly and begins to be reverend'. Hunt in his trivializing yet astute way resolves all Coleridge's metaphysical acumen into his bodily fatness: 'He is very metaphysical and very corporeal; and he does nothing.'[71]

It is the usual criticism, given authority by Hunt's casual carefulness to let it be known that he has a personal acquaintance with Coleridge. 'I heard him the other day under the grove at Highgate', he writes, 'repeat one of his melodious lamentations, as he walked up and down, his voice undulating in a stream of music, and his regrets of youth sparkling with visions ever young'. Hunt's is the first of a veritable rash of memoirs of the great man's later years by those who trod the path to Highgate on Thursday evenings for the sake of Coleridge's conversation. Not malicious, it is archly critical, presenting a picture of a rather tame – or tamed – creature, elderly in demeanour though not yet sixty, a figure to be indulged in his mild eccentricities. Hunt ends his pen portrait with a description of Coleridge in his famous attic study and garden (see plate 21):

> His room looks upon a delicious prospect of wood and meadow, with coloured gardens under the window, like an embroidery to a mantle. I thought, when I first saw it, that he had taken up his dwelling-place like an abbot. Here he cultivates his flowers, and has a set of birds for his pensioners, who come to breakfast with him. He may be seen taking his daily stroll up and down, with his black coat and white locks, and a book in his hand; and is a great acquaintance of the little children.[72]

One might have expected Coleridge to be offended by this somewhat diminishing sketch, but he was amused instead, even half-agreeing with Hunt's 'physiognomic Decision respecting my Sensuality'. Not to be out-done, Coleridge proceeds further with the idea in a letter to Henry Nelson Coleridge:

> The peccatum originale [original sin] with me might be, with friendly tender-ness, expressed by the Excess of *Power* with Deficiency of *Strength* – Facility, Infirmity, mental Cowardice of whatever might force my attention to myself &c &c.– I hope, I do not scribble such notes of Egoism often enough to tempt you to add Vanity & Self-worship to the vices of your affectionate Friend S. T. C.[73]

All in all, though he was still in anguish about opium and his life's great mistakes, Coleridge was able to be more accepting of his lot as the years went on. In a piece written for S. C. Hall's *Amulet* for 1828, 'The Improvisatore', he tackled the painful subject of marital unhappiness, but lightly, ending with some cheering lines for the disappointed husband:

> Though heart be lonesome, Hope laid low,
> Yet, Lady! deem him not unblest:
> The certainty that struck Hope dead,
> Hath left Contentment in her stead:
> And that is next to Best![74]

When Lady Beaumont urged him in May 1828 to try writing poetry once more in order not to 'throw away that precious gift you have received', he scribbled in the margin of her letter:

> Alas! how can I? – Is the power extinct? No! No! As in a still Summer Noon, when the lulled Air at irregular intervals wakes up with a startled *Hush*-st, that seems to re-demand the silence which it breaks, or heaves a long profound Sigh in it's Sleep, and an Aeolian Harp has been left in the chink of the not quite shut Casement – even so – how often! – scarce a week of my Life shuffles by, that does not at some moment feel the spur of the old genial impulse – even so do there fall on my inward Ear swells, and broken snatches of sweet Melody, reminding me that I still have that within me which is both Harp and Breeze. But in the same moment awakes the Sense of *Change without* – Life *unendeared*. The tenderest Strings no longer thrill'd.[75]

'Both Harp and Breeze'. Coleridge catches in the single phrase the sense of his critical philosophy as expressed in *Biographia Literaria*: the poet is both a receptacle for inspiration and an active, creative intelligence.

Once more Coleridge bewails the loss of imaginative power as a result of the loss of joy and reciprocated love. A slight poem, 'Love's Burial-Place', deals with the problem comically:

> Here lies a Love that once was mine,

But took a chill, as I divine,
And died at length of a Decline.[76]

This verse was published, with the title 'The Alienated Mistress', in the edition of his *Poetical Works* brought out by William Pickering, publisher of the *Bijou*, in three volumes in the summer of 1828.

This was the most complete edition of the poems yet. Most were now reprinted, though 'The Pains of Sleep' was omitted. Volume three contained the now acclaimed translation of *Wallenstein*, reprinted for the first time since 1800, as well as *Remorse* and *Zapolya*. The old prefaces of 1796 and 1797 were retained, now more unsuited than ever to the enlarged contents. As so often before, Coleridge allowed his poetry to go forth in more or less haphazard order and with inappropriate apparatus.

Matters were slightly improved in 1829, when Pickering reissued the edition with its many misprints corrected. This edition was rewarded with an excellent favourable review by John Bowring in the *Westminster Review*, radical organ though it was. Bowring saw the psychological astuteness of 'Christabel', with its representation of the involuntary fascination with something we dread. He praised the perfect melodiousness of 'Kubla Khan' and the 'graphic power' of 'The Ancient Mariner', commending Coleridge's ability in that poem to make the supernatural 'serve to unfold and illustrate what is natural, and the wildest and boldest creations of imagination develop the essential principles of humanity'. In this Coleridge is, says Bowring, like Shakespeare, a 'master of the magic art'.[77]

In April 1828 Coleridge was visited by his brother James, now reconciled to becoming in due course father-in-law to Coleridge's daughter,[78] and in the same month he dined with his old rival Scott and the visiting 'American Sir Walter', James Fenimore Cooper.[79] On 22 April at William Sotheby's house they gathered for dinner. Cooper described the two literary lions, Coleridge giving an 'exhibition' more extraordinary than anything Cooper had ever witnessed, 'not a discourse, but a dissertation', which he continued for more than an hour 'almost without interruption'. As for Scott, he sat, according to Cooper, 'immoveable as a statue, with his little grey eyes looking inward and outward, and evidently considering the whole as an exhibition', while he occasionally muttered 'Eloquent!' 'Wonderful!' 'Very extraordinary!'[80]

Scott himself, though silent at the table, was eloquent in his journal that night: 'Lockhart and I dined with Sotheby where we met a large dining party the orator of which was that extraordinary man Coleridge. After eating a hearty dinner during which he spoke not a word he began a most learnd harangue on the Samo-thracian misteries . . . Zounds', concluded Scott, echoing the bastard in Act II, scene i of *King John*, 'I was never so bethumped with words.'[81]

Wordsworth was spending his customary few weeks in London, and once more he and Coleridge met socially. Crabb Robinson recorded a breakfast at Aders's house on 18 June when Coleridge was 'as usual, very eloquent', particularly at Southey's expense. He accused his old friend of time-serving, 'suffering himself to be flattered into servility by that one-testicled fellow Peel'.[82] Though Coleridge and Southey were both nervous of political reform, Southey had, in Coleridge's opinion, become extreme in his views, which he regularly expressed in the *Quarterly Review* and in conversation. He, too, was in London that spring, and according to Robinson he only just restrained himself from an outburst on the Catholic Question on 28 May by remembering that he was dining at the table of a Catholic, Edward Quillinan.[83]

The Duke of Wellington had formed a new ministry in January 1828 on the condition, laid down by George IV, that Catholic relief was not to be granted. Peel was Home Secretary. When the Irish Catholic Daniel O'Connell was elected MP for County Clare later in 1828, the Government realized Catholic Emancipation was inevitable. Peel became a reluctant advocate and the Act was finally passed in April 1829 in the teeth of much opposition from the King downwards.[84] Southey was so angry about it that poor Mrs Coleridge had 'the greatest dread of that subject' at Greta Hall, as she told Poole in July 1829.[85] Southey wrote gloomily to Walter Savage Landor, predicting a struggle for Catholic domination in Ireland and a war 'upon a religious ground, not upon a civil pretext'.[86]

Coleridge's last published work, *On the Constitution of Church and State*, was to address itself specifically to the controversial measure, as is indicated by its subtitle, 'with Aids towards a right Judgment on the Late Catholic Bill'.

Another subject of discussion at Aders's breakfast party in June was Wordsworth's plan to spend a few weeks travelling in Belgium, Holland and the Rhineland with his daughter Dora (who was eventually, after much opposition from Wordsworth, to marry Edward Quillinan[87]). Relations with Coleridge were now relaxed enough – which means that Coleridge felt more cordial towards Wordsworth – for him to be included in the tour at the last minute. The 'two Poets and their amiable Daughter', as Dora put it, set off on 21 June.[88] She reported to Quillinan that the three travellers were getting on 'delightfully' together, despite Coleridge's falling ill at Liège towards the end of June.[89]

They spent some time with Mrs Aders at her summer home at Godesberg on the Rhine. She told her husband in London, who in turn told Crabb Robinson, that she was 'delighted with Wordsworth but still claims our old affectionate friend Coleridge as "her" Poet'.[90] Coleridge had eclipsed Wordsworth in Brussels too. A resident Englishman, T. C. Grattan, re-corded meeting the poets on 25 June during their stop there. Coleridge looked like 'an itinerant preacher'. His face was 'extremely handsome, its expression placid and benevolent', and his talk a 'wonderful attraction'. Wordsworth, by contrast, 'did not talk well', and looked more like a 'mountain farmer' than a poet.[91]

On 8 July 'a party of Bonn lions' was invited by Mrs Aders to meet her poets.[92] These included the distinguished historian Niebuhr and the foppish A. W. Schlegel who, according to Mrs Aders, 'abused England though thick & thin', which he would hardly have got away with if Coleridge had not been ill and only intermittently present on the occasion.[93] Coleridge seems not to have noted his impression of Schlegel, though a third party, the Englishman Julian Charles Young, observed that the two men flattered one another, Coleridge praising Schlegel's translation of Shakespeare (but not his criticism?) and Schlegel, 'twitching his brown scratch wig' and looking in the mirror, admiring Coleridge's *Wallenstein* in return.[94]

Though the tour appears to have been a success, and though Wordsworth and Dora gave no hint of tensions, a single entry in Coleridge's notebook suggests his old resentment of Wordsworth was still alive under his peaceful outward demeanour. It bursts into vitriolic life in an outraged comment written in German – a sure sign that Coleridge meant it for his own eyes only. The passage, dated 14 July, complains that from Bruges to Godesberg to Bingen and back he had 'never on earth known such hard, rigid, continual, in all points despotic Egotism'. Wordsworth is not named, but only he can be in mind, for Coleridge continues with comments about his commonplace talk and his 'coarse concern about money', concluding: 'In short, all the failings which characterised him in early manhood have grown astonishingly – the grandiose gigantic flowers of his philosophical and poetic genius are faded and withered.'[95]

By 6 August the travellers had arrived back in London. Coleridge cheerfully told Frederic Mansel Reynolds, editor of the *Keepsake*, that he was disposed to write some poems for him now that he had returned from his three-week tour, which 'the Poet, mihi magnus Apollo! and his fair Daughter have by pure force of attraction carried me on, o'er Ditch and Dell, River and Plain, not to speak of German Mountains and Dutch Steeples and Rhenish Towers'.[96]

Though he experienced difficulties with the rival editors of the annual magazines, they were proving useful providers of small sums of ready money for stray poems. Even Wordsworth succumbed, against his better judgement, to the temptation to place single poems with them, though he had read Hartley Coleridge 'some lectures on the subject', as Sara Coleridge noted in February 1828. 'He says [Hartley] must not write in Albums, and waste his powers in this manner.' Both Wordsworth and Coleridge found the editors occasionally unscrupulous in their use of material, but put up with this for the sake of the money.[97]

Coleridge's cheerfulness extended to some rowdy drunken parties at F. M. Reynolds's house during August 1828, though he paid for his excesses in headaches and 'a true Hell of Dreams' which made him think once more that he would die in his sleep like his father.[98] He owed Thomas Dunn money for the opium he was procuring behind Gillman's back – another reason for selling his poems to the magazines. It seems that Mrs Gillman discovered his alternative source of supply at this time; according to Dunn's apprentice, Seymour Porter, she went to Dunn's shop to ask him to stop supplying Coleridge. To this, apparently, Dunn replied that without it Coleridge would die.[99]

In October 1828, his birthday month, Coleridge's letters more frequently complained of his ill health and guilty conscience. He told Stuart on 14 October of his 'indescribable depression of Spirits' and 'a smart attack of erysipelas in both legs', rather shamefacedly reminding Stuart that he was about to set off for Ramsgate as usual. Stuart had been in the habit of sending him £30 a year for his holiday; on this occasion he sent £20.[100]

More money needed raising in December 1828, when Coleridge found that John Morgan's widow and her sister were in severe distress. He applied to S. C. Hall of the *Amulet* for £20 which he thought owing to him for the unauthorized publication of extracts from 'Over the Brocken', three of his 1799 letters from Germany.[101] In January 1829 he offered Thomas Hurst a 'reconstruction' of *Aids to Reflection*, the original being now out of print. This revised edition was finally published by Hurst, Chance & Co in 1831. And he secured £30 from Pickering for the new edition of his poems.[102] He also set about completing *On the Constitution of Church and State*. This flurry of activity was motivated by his desire to help two women who had once saved him, and also by a sense of urgency about his state of health. He wanted to get his thoughts on the Church of England, at such a difficult time for British institutions, into the public arena.

Perhaps he also hoped to spare some money for his beloved daughter, whose marriage to Henry was fixed first for August 1829, then, after a panic about Henry's health and prospective legal income, for 3 September. The wedding was almost postponed indefinitely because Henry's appointment as Secretary to the newly founded King's College London (set up by the Duke of Wellington and various bishops as an orthodox rival to the 'godless institution of Gower Street') fell through because of lack of funds.[103] Henry persuaded his family that his prospects were nevertheless good enough to let him marry now, after an engagement of five and a half years.

The long-suffering Sara was a guest of the Wordsworths between April and June, while her mother worried about her poor health and the precarious finances of the couple and about Sara's future as a barrister's wife in London, which she imagined would be one of 'utter loneliness' after the 'bustling' family life at Greta Hall. The change would affect Mrs Coleridge too; she was to follow her daughter from the Lakes home she had come to love. She told Poole in July that she was going first on a long visit to Derwent and his wife in Cornwall, but 'where I shall finally settle I know not, yet'.[104] Even Southey was moved and distressed by the prospect of losing his niece and sister-in-law. 'Next to a funeral', he wrote, 'methinks [marriage] the most melancholy of domestic events, where it compleatly takes away the member of a family'.[105]

Mrs Coleridge's chief worry was, of course, Hartley, who wrote a mock-cheerful, dreadfully miserable letter to his mother on hearing that the wedding was to take place. Referring to Derwent's baby son, 'little Dervy' (born in October 1828), he told her that he would love to see his nephew, but hoped that he bore no resemblance 'either in body, soul, mind, spirit, nose, eyes, mouth, or aught else that enters into the composition of that drug of the creation, Man' to his 'sole paternal uncle':

> Uncle! I can scarcely recognise myself under the title. To be sure, it is just the thing for an old Batchelor – and such was I foredoomed to be – e'er the voice of the first halleluyah of the new-created Angels broke in on the eternal silence. My Brother gets a wife – well – my Sister is to have a Husband – well – I remain alone, bare and barren and blasted, ill-omen'd and unsightly as Wordsworth's melancholy thorn on the bleak hill-top. So hath it been ordain'd, and it is well.

Hartley refers in his letter to the recent death, on 14 July 1829, of Lady Beaumont, one of those who had helped finance his studies at Oxford. Sounding once more like a pale version of his father, he declared that he wished she might have lived 'to see that she had not bestowed her bounty on an object utterly worthless and ingrate'. (Lady Beaumont left Coleridge £50 in her will, which he intended to send to his wife 'to lay out, as she thinks needful, for dear Hartley'.[106]) Hartley ends his miserable letter to his mother on a note of promise: 'I will be present at the celebration – if I walk all night, and all night again.'[107] But Hartley did not attend Sara's wedding.

Neither did Coleridge. No one seems to have expected his presence. His wife knew from Poole, who had visited Highgate earlier in the year, and from Mrs Gillman, that he was ill.[108] The ceremony was more a Wordsworth and Southey family affair than a Coleridge one. John Wordsworth conducted the service at Crosthwaite Church in Keswick; Dora Wordsworth and Southey's three daughters were among the bridesmaids; Southey, acting for the last time in lieu of the absent father, gave the bride away.[109] Southey told Grosvenor Bedford that all would have been satisfactory if the health of the bridegroom had been better, 'but where there is a weak constitution on one side, and a decidedly bad one on the other, the degree of consanguineity seems to give the children, if any there should be, a worse chance than they would have if the parents were strangers in blood'.[110] (Henry was to die in his mid-forties. Of seven pregnancies only two children of the marriage, Herbert and Edith, survived infancy, and Herbert died at thirty.[111])

Hartley did turn up at Rydal Mount a few days *after* the wedding, managing to miss both Sara and his mother, who was staying with the Wordsworths. She was distressed at having to leave the Lakes a few days later without having seen him.[112] Mrs Coleridge took her journey south, sorry to be leaving 'a beloved residence of 29 years duration' and friends who included the Wordsworths she had once so disliked and resented. She left Grasmere for Cornwall on 28 September.[113]

In Highgate Coleridge, suffering tortures of sciatic pain, 'as if four and twenty Rats "all in a row" from the right Hip to the Ancle Bone were gnawing away at me'[114], marked the date of Sara's wedding by inscribing his copy of Sotheby's polyglot version of Virgil's *Georgics* to her, saying that after his death he wanted Sotheby's magnificent gift to him to go to 'my beloved and loveworthy child, Sara Coleridge', and that if she should have a daughter it should be passed on to her in honour of her mother's 'unusual attainments in ancient and modern Languages' coexisting with 'a mind, character and demeanour so perfectly feminine'.[115] He felt some resistance to the wedding still; he chose the day before, 2 September, to dictate his will, leaving everything to his wife, and after her death to Sara, 'she being either single or (which God forefend!) an unprovided Widow'.[116]

These were not very cheerful thoughts on the eve of a wedding. But then Coleridge associated no happiness with the married state, and in any case his own thoughts were more about death. He would have liked to make provision for his children, particularly Hartley, with whom he was no longer in contact, but who was much on his mind. Accordingly, he devoted a paragraph of his will, which was finalized on 17 September, to Hartley. It is a strange document, for Coleridge had, of course, neither property nor money to leave, but only books, manuscripts – his intellectual property, as it were – and good wishes. These he bequeathed gladly to his family. As for Hartley:

> The sole regret I now feel at the scantiness of my means arises out of my inability to make such present provision for my dear Hartley, my first-born, as might set his feelings at ease, and his mind at liberty from the depressing anxieties of the To-day . . . knowing, that it is with him, as it ever has been with myself, that his Powers and the ability and disposition to exert them are greatest, when the motives from without are least or of least urgency.[117]

Other friends were remembered in ways appropriate to Coleridge's feelings towards them. Six gold mourning rings were to be made, with a lock of his hair, to be given to 'my oldest Friend, & ever-beloved Schoolfellow Charles Lamb', Basil Montagu, Tom Poole, Josiah Wade, Wade's son Launcelot, and – for old times' sake – Sara Hutchinson. As for Southey and Wordsworth, once best friends, Coleridge remarks in an equipoise of respect and malice: 'To Robert Southey, & to William Wordsworth, my children have a debt of Gratitude & reverential affection on their own account: and the sentiments, I have left on record in my Literary Life & in my Poems, and which are the convictions of the present moment, supersede the necessity of any other memorial of my Regard and Respect'.[118]

These former friends, once adored and still admired for their gifts, occupied a painful place in Coleridge's feelings. We have seen how he exploded on the German trip with Wordsworth the previous summer. A notebook entry of about May 1829 spits venom, probably again about Wordsworth, who had 'branded' him 'in the cruellest and most obtrusive manner for a step (my Separation from the Wife who had never been my Wife, i.e. who had never either loved me, or (from the hour we left the Altar at which I stood like cold marble weeping frost) professed to love me) to which, so help me God his own opinion & judgement had mainly determined me!'[119] Outbursts like these occur periodically in notebooks otherwise devoted to Biblical commentary, investigations into faith, and repeated prayer for God's mercy on the 'miserable sinner S. T. Coleridge'.

In December 1829 *On the Constitution of Church and State* was published by Hurst, Chance & Co with a cover date of 1830. It contained the fruits of Coleridge's thinking for the past thirty years about the Church of England and its relation to the State. He had given up, around 1801, his youthful views, influenced by his democratic and Unitarian sympathies and expressed vehemently in the sermon Hazlitt heard at Shrewsbury, in favour of the *separation* of Church and State.[120] Now Coleridge was all for conserving the relationship.

Work on the book had begun in 1825, when he wished to respond to the increasing agitation in the form of publications and the near passing of a Bill for Catholic relief brought before Parliament by Francis Burdett in 1825. Though Coleridge shared something of Southey's fear of Irish separation from the Union as a result of emancipation, he took a more liberal view both before and after the passing of the Act in April 1829. In the short second part of *Church and State* he addressed the Act itself, declaring that he would 'zealously vote for the admission of Lay Catholics, not only to both houses of the Legislature, but to all other offices below the Crown', on condition that, as he had said to Henry Nelson Coleridge in March 1827, the Roman Catholic priesthood never be recognised as an 'Estate of the realm'.[121] By this he meant that the Roman Catholic clergy should not enjoy any part of the national wealth set aside for the National Church.

But the main part of his work is concerned with the principles underlying the idea of a state and of a national church. Though this is the shortest of Coleridge's prose works, and the least freighted with obscure and myriad references, it does share with his other works the disadvantages of a lengthy sentence structure and a not altogether transparent structure as a whole. Fortunately for the reader, he adds at the end of chapter twelve a 'brief recapitulation' of the argument so far. Here can be found the kernel of his discussion elsewhere in the book, which is sometimes confusing in its mingling of *historical* information and analysis about the background to the formation of the Church of England with *philosophical* discussion of ideas and principles.

First, Coleridge insists on the importance of grasping the idea of a state before discussing its practical embodiment at any one time or place, 'State' being in this sense 'synonimous with a *constituted* Realm, Kingdom, Commonwealth, or Nation, *i.e.* where the integral parts, classes, or orders are so balanced, or interdependent, as to constitute, more or less, a moral unit, an organic whole'. Making up the 'organic whole' of the state, so understood, are the embodiments of two opposing but reconcilable principles, Permanence and Progression. The landed classes represent permanence, or tradition, as understood in terms of land and inherited wealth; the 'mercantile, or commercial, the manufacturing, the distributive and the professional' classes represent progression, as understood by economic, social, and political change or reform.[122] For Coleridge, the clue to stable and measured progress lies in the due balance of these two interests.

At one point, in chapter ten, Coleridge sounds almost radical, and certainly liberal, in his disapproval of too great a power lying with the landed interest. The example which he gives of the unacceptable holding up of progress by the reactionary party is taken from his own experience. It concerns Humphry Davy, who had died in May 1829. Coleridge writes of 'my illustrious (alas! I must add, I fear, my *late*) friend', and his commission twenty years before from the Royal Society to analyse 'an East Indian import, known by the name of cutch, and Terra Japonica'. Davy found it to consist almost entirely of tannin, and the discovery could have led to the benefit of the tanning trade and a reduction in the price of English leather. But no increase in the import of cutch occurred, for

> it was *generally understood*, that the Tanners had not been the only persons, whose attention had been drawn to the qualities of the article, and the consequences of its importation; and that a very intelligible hint had been given to persons of known influence in Leadenhall-street, that in case of any such importation being allowed, the East-India Company must not expect any support from the *Landed Interest* in parliament, at the next renewal, or motion for the renewal of their Charter.[123]

Coleridge could, of course, have chosen other, more prominent, examples of one interest acting against another – the vexed question of the Corn Laws, say – but it is likely that he chose tanning because he had recently heard of his old friend Davy's death, and because it permitted him to add a personal tribute to his even greater – though sadly neglected – friend, the faithful Tom Poole. A footnote paints a loving portrait of the tanner of Nether Stowey, and in a way goes over Coleridge's own past life in the process. Poole appears as a type of the universal man:

> A man whom I have seen now in his harvest field, or the market, now in a committee-room, with the Rickmans and Ricardos of the age; at another time with Davy, Woolaston, and the Wedgewoods; now with Wordsworth, Southey, and other friends not unheard of in the republic of letters; now in the drawing-rooms of the rich and noble, and now presiding at the annual dinner of a Village Benefit Society; and in each seeming to be in the very place he was intended for, and taking the part to which his tastes, talents, and attainments, gave him an admitted right.[124]

It is a moving tribute, almost an apology for Coleridge's ingratitude to Poole, to which Mrs Coleridge, in a rare reference to one of her husband's works, delightedly drew Poole's attention.[125]

One of the means by which the reconciliation of opposite principles and interests was to be achieved was through the activity of another class, which Coleridge called the clerisy. Famously, he coined the word (from the

German 'Clerisei', meaning body of scholars), and the class he had in mind was a sort of elaboration of his idea of himself. It included theologians, but also 'sages' and professors of 'all the so called liberal arts and sciences, the possession and application of which constitute the civilization of a country, as well as the Theological'.[126]

In the following generation, when so many educated men found they were unable to become clergymen because of doubts about Biblical texts or miracles or subscription to the 39 Articles, Coleridge's idea of the clerisy as a class not exclusively of clergymen was seized on with alacrity. Dr Arnold of Rugby was the great embodiment of the type; his son Matthew Arnold's *Culture and Anarchy* (1869) is predicated on it. John Sterling, the brothers Hare, Gladstone, as well as F. D. Maurice, who *was* a clergyman – these and more recorded their debt to Coleridge as a thinker, particularly the Coleridge of *Church and State*.[127] Sterling told his friend J. C. Hare in 1836, 'To Coleridge I owe *education*': 'He taught me to believe that an empirical philosophy is none, that Faith is the highest Reason, that all criticism, whether of literature, laws, or manners, is blind, without the power of discerning the organic unity of the object.'[128]

Carlyle, who in his *Life of Sterling* gave his unflattering portrait of Coleridge in full monologue, ought also to be counted amongst those who learned from Coleridge. His influential essays and his wild, satirical *Sartor Resartus* are close in concept to the Coleridge of *Church and State*, and even at times in tone. For Coleridge allows himself some satire against philosophical radicalism of the Bentham school. Though in favour of measured reform, he disliked the atheistic or at least dissenting cast of many of the current reformers. If the landed interest was a danger to balanced progress, so also, in Coleridge's view, was the headlong, destructive reform interest of the Broughams and Benthams, intellectual heirs of Hartley's mechanistic philosophy. In chapter seven he lists some of the dangers of letting this kind of reformer get his way:

> DR. HOLOFERNES, in a lecture on metaphysics, delivered at one of the Mechanics' Institutions, explodes *all* ideas but those of sensation; and his friend, DEPUTY COSTARD, has no *idea* of a better flavored haunch of venison, than he dined off at the London Tavern Last week . . .
> Talents without genius: a swarm of clever, well-informed men: an anarchy of minds, a despotism of maxims.[129]

It is a deliberate caricature of this, the 'golden age' of the (mechanical) understanding, in which progress is too often taken to mean economic improvement and manufacturing inventions in isolation from the spiritual and the moral.

These were precisely Carlyle's points too. But he included in his list of demons the Church of England itself, with its complacent, privileged, unthinking clergy. Coleridge, because he wished to promote the *idea* of a progressive but permanent Church, did not turn his attentions to actual abuses within the unreformed system. Nevertheless, his book was a starting-point for those in the next generation who wished to reform the institution from within, as well as those, like Carlyle, who preferred to remain outside.

Privately, Coleridge confessed that he felt a vocation to lead the Church to a more spiritual existence. There were moments when he seemed to hear himself 'called to the perilous Heraldry – when the Spirit of Luther has pointed to a Trumpet. Truth! *the* Truth! the *Whole* Truth! so only can a People be made *free*'. The Church of England was '*idealess*', but, 'as Leighton finely observes – the cold & the darkness are often greatest just before the Break of Dawn'.[130]

15

Last Years: *Church and State*
1830–1834

O, lift one thought in prayer for S. T. C.
That he who many a year with toil of breath
Found death in life, may here find life in death!

Coleridge, 'Epitaph', 1833

Coleridge's book on Church and State received immediate critical attention. A second edition, with clarifying chapter headings, was published in
spring 1830. Coleridge sent a copy to Poole, and worried to Henry Nelson
Coleridge and H. F. Cary about 'the Obscurity felt generally in my prose
writings'.[1] But in July 1831 a long, appreciative review appeared in the
Eclectic Review. The writer described Coleridge's habits of thought as 'strikingly desultory' and yet 'truly philosophical'. Coleridge 'never closes with
his subject, never comes to close quarters, but brings the artillery of his
learning and eloquence to bear upon large masses'. His 'varied and extensive erudition' are praised, as is the 'wisdom of much that he propounds'.[2]

It is Hazlitt's old argument repeated, but the tone is one of acceptance
and respect. If you want to benefit from the undoubted wisdom of
Coleridge, it seems to say, you must put up with his idiosyncratic, round-
about way of expressing it.

From now on the tone of reviews of Coleridge's works would become
increasingly positive. In 1835, even the *Edinburgh Review* carried a positive
article – alas, too late for Coleridge to savour – when Herman Merivale,
assessing Henry Nelson Coleridge's edition of *Table Talk*, acknowledged the
independence of his views on the English Church and on religious faith.
Merivale declares that Coleridge, 'who has had such an extensive influence
over the minds, especially of youthful and enthusiastic thinkers', enter-
tained more temperate views than most of his disciples on these subjects.
For example, he was 'liberal, even to daring, in discussion and interpretation' of Biblical texts, combining a mind 'deeply submissive to the myster-

ies of religion' with 'a most fearless spirit of research' and a scepticism about the genuineness of certain parts of scripture.[3]

Actually, Coleridge's table talk was even more liberal than Merivale could have known, since Henry's transcriptions of his conversation were submitted to the Coleridge family, led by John Taylor Coleridge, who censored some of the religious and political matter, including a robust remark of 6 June 1830 about the wrath of the orthodox which Coleridge thought would descend upon him if he were too directly to 'doubt the authenticity of the Book of Daniel or suggest that Inspiration did not mean verbal Dictation'. Coleridge followed up this point with a reminiscence, also omitted by Henry:

> I well remember, when only nine years old, listening with intense eagerness to the story of Jael murdering Sisera as read in Church, and to the war song of Deborah – the most sublime composition in the world – and when the words 'Blessed shall Jael be &c' were read, putting down my head between my hands and knees, and murmuring from my soul as even now I do – 'Cursed shall Jael be above women &c'.[4]

Some of Coleridge's critical comments, however, escaped the family censorship, and Henry's edition of *Table Talk*, together with *On the Constitution of Church and State*, allowed him to be read as the liberal-conservative thinker he was. In March 1832 he talked at length about the distinction between divine inspiration and divine dictation, which had been 'grievously confounded':

> Balaam and his Ass were the passive organs of Dictation; but no one, I believe, will venture to call either of those worthies inspired. It is my profound conviction that St Paul and St John were divinely inspired, but I totally disbelieve the dictation of any one word, sentence or argument throughout their writings. Observe, there was Revelation . . . but is it not a mere matter of the senses that John and Paul each dealt with those revelations – expounded them – insisted on them just exactly according to his own natural strength of intellect – habits of reasoning – moral and even physical temperament? Understand the matter so – and all difficulty vanishes; you read without fear lest your faith meet with some shock from a passage here and there which you cannot reconcile with immediate dictation by the Holy Spirit of God without an absurd violence offered to the text. You read the Bible as the best of all books – but still as a book, and make use of all the means and appliances which learning and skill under the blessing of God can afford towards rightly apprehending the genuine sense of it, not solicitous to find out doctrine in mere epistolary familiarity or facts in an allusion to national traditions.[5]

This view, informed by Coleridge's reading of Eichhorn, among others, came before the public in its fullest form in 1840, when Henry edited *Confessions of an Inquiring Spirit*, consisting of essays originally intended for inclusion in *Aids to Reflection*.[6]

Coleridge was also more critical in his conversation than in his work on *Church and State* of the Anglican Church as it was, rather than as it ought to be. On 8 September 1830 he accused the institution of being 'positively cursed and rotted and blighted with – Prudence', and of clinging too closely 'to Court and State instead of cultivating the People'. Even the Church of Rome was in this respect 'wiser'.[7]

His view about the need to believe in all the 39 Articles was surprisingly relaxed too. He reminded his company on 8 October 1830 (in a conversation *not* included by Henry), that the Church of England 'binds you by one of her own Articles [Article 19] to believe that she is *fallible* – and that all Churches have erred'. He concludes that a clergyman 'may conscientiously reject in [his] mind the Athanasian creed as manifestly heretical and uncharitable, and still remain a faithful Church Minister'.[8]

During 1830 Coleridge was more than once so ill that he thought death was imminent. In May he suffered an attack in his sleep and was found on the floor, 'pulseless and senseless', by a servant. As he comically recounted the episode to Blackwood:

> Before I had opened my eyes, I merely found that my medical friends and Mrs Gillman were flustering over me: my first words were, 'What a mystery we are! What a problem is presented in the strange contrast between the imperishability of our thoughts and the perishable fugacious nature of our consciousness', when I heard the voice of my friend exclaiming, 'Thank God! however, there is nothing of apoplexy in this seizure'.[9]

Coleridge soon recovered, for when Lamb saw him a few days later he thought him 'looking, and especially speaking, strong'.[10] Lamb's opinion is borne out by the extraordinary volume of conversation recorded by Henry in the summer of 1830. He and Sara moved in June into a house in Hampstead, just across the Heath from Coleridge. On 8 June he told his father the Colonel that Coleridge had 'quite come round, I think, & is very lively & entertaining in his conversation'. No doubt thinking of John Bowring's appreciation of Coleridge's poetry in the *Westminster Review* in January 1830, he continued:

> His influence is undoubtedly very extensive, & his popularity slowly but constantly increasing. No public critic *now* denies his genius & the pre-eminence of his works – at least his poems. In this last point Tory and Radical seem to agree. For a long time past I have been in the habit of noting down the remarkable things he says in conversation; I have 50 quarto pages of such memorabilia, & they would even now make one of the most interesting *Table Talks* that ever was published . . . the Johnsoniana seem to me poor stuff in comparison.[11]

The rehabilitation of the madcap younger brother in the eyes of the Colonel thus continued apace, thanks to the eager efforts of the enthralled younger generation of Coleridges.

What Henry says here is nothing less than the truth. Some of Coleridge's best table talk occurred between May and September 1830. As well as discussing freely the subjects dealt with in *Church and State*, Coleridge talked about literature and about current affairs. 1830 was a year of political change. Not only was Reform coming ever nearer, but with the death of the unlamented George IV in June 1830 and the accession of William IV, an election was called, with the Tories once more taking power. However, they were weakened by internal dissension about the recent Catholic Emancipation and by William IV's refusal to allow the topic of reform to be raised in the King's Speech to Parliament. This speech led to rioting and rick-burning; Wellington had to stand down, and Earl Grey came in with a Whig administration committed to parliamentary reform.

As if to underline symbolically the end of an era, William Huskisson, Tory MP and recent Colonial Secretary, was run over and killed on 15 September by George Stephenson's *Rocket* as he attended the opening of the Liverpool–Manchester railway. Coleridge was among those who saw the accident as having a significance beyond that of personal tragedy. 'So far as we know', he said on 19 September, 'he is the last of our Statesmen'.[12]

As for the passing of George IV, Coleridge, anticipating that long expected event, commented in April that George was a worse blackguard than any of the thieves and beggars swarming in the notorious slums of St Giles's, and that he had been deservedly unloved by the people.[13] Though he was wary of reform, Coleridge was withering about Wellington, whom he accused of trying to command the country in the same way as he had commanded 'a highly disciplined army'. And Peel, by his *volte face* on the Catholic Question, had 'ruined himself for ever by his glaring inconsistency'.[14]

On parliamentary reform Coleridge's position was cautious and conservative, but he was critical of the abuses and injustices of the status quo, and inclined to welcome a principled, gradual reform of institutions from within. His was the stance adopted by many liberal thinkers of the next generation: Matthew Arnold, for instance, or George Eliot, who called herself a radical conservative on questions of social and political reform. Her comment in an essay of 1856 on the German social historian Wilhelm Heinrich von Riehl gives metaphorical expression to the idea propounded by Coleridge in *Church and State* of the need to balance Permanence and Progression: '[Riehl] is as far as possible from the folly of supposing that the sun will go backward on the dial, because we put the hands of our clock backward; he only contends against the opposite folly of decreeing that it shall be mid-day, while in fact the sun is only just touching the mountain-tops, and all along the valley men are stumbling in the twilight'.[15]

Coleridge may have been declining bodily but he was, as Dorothy Wordsworth reported in November 1830, 'as vigorous as ever in mind'.[16] He made some brilliant remarks in his *Table Talk* in May on Shakespeare and Milton, building on the distinction he had made in *Biographia Literaria*:

Shakspeare is the Spinozistic Deity, an omnipresent creativeness. Milton is Prescience; he stands ab extra, and drives a fiery coach and four, making the horses feel the iron curb which holds them. Shakspeare's poetry is characterless; that is, it does not reflect the individual Shakspeare; but John Milton himself is in every line of the Paradise Lost. Shakspeare's rhymed verses are excessively condensed; epigrams with the point every where; but in his blank verse, he is diffused with a linked sweetness long drawn out.

[. . .]

No man can understand Shakspeare's superiority fully, until he has ascertained by comparison all that which he possessed in common with several other great dramatists of his age, and then calculated the surplus which is entirely Shakspeare's own.

[. . .]

Shakspeare's rhythm is so perfect that you may be sure you don't understand the real force of the line, if it does not run well as you read it. The necessary pause after every hemistich or imperfect line is always equal to the time that would have been taken up in reading the complete verse.[17]

These comments have that feature common to all great criticism: they carry immediate conviction, even half-recognition for the reader, seeming to put in just the right words opinions we would like to think we already held, but had not precisely formulated.

All this time that Coleridge was scintillating in conversation, he was suffering physically and even fearing senility. In January 1830 he caught himself playing whist at an evening party 'exactly as I have often observed very old Persons play, in the decay of their Faculties', and expressed a hope that Green or Gillman would tell him if they saw signs of encroaching 'senile Idiocy'.[18]

On 19 September he was drawn to discuss some of his contemporaries. The occasion was the death the previous day of his old enemy Hazlitt. Coleridge strove to be fair, in spite of his resentment at his treatment: 'I certainly always did say there was something original and powerful about Hazlitt at a time that Poole and Wordsworth were quite incredulous about it. I still think there was by Nature, but the Devil that was in him – the brutal savagery of mind – prevented any development.'[19]

Coleridge had already learned from Lamb at the end of August that Hazlitt was 'sick even to death, and alas! in almost utter destitution', with only Lamb of his former friends still visiting and trying to help.[20] On 18 September, the date of Hazlitt's death, Coleridge adapted an old epigram of his (originally entitled 'Epitaph on a Bad Man' and printed in the *Morning Post* in September 1801) to suit Hazlitt. Its harshness is somewhat mitigated by a marginal note. This is the poem, which Coleridge did not publish:

W. H. *EHEU*
Beneath this stone does William Hazlitt lie,
Thankless of all that God or man could give.

> He lived like one who never thought to die,
> He died like one who dared not hope to live.

The note reads:

> With a sadness at heart, and an earnest hope grounded on his misanthropic strangenesses when I first knew him in his 20 or 21st year, that a something existed in his bodily organism that in the sight of the All-Merciful lessened his responsibility, & the moral imputation of his acts & feelings.[21]

Coleridge also anatomized Southey during the course of this conversation of 19 September: 'Southey picked Nature's pockets, as a poet, instead of borrowing from her. He went out and took some particular image, for example a water-insect – and then exactly copied its make, colors and motions. This he put in a poem. The true way for a poet is to examine Nature, but write from your recollection, and trust more to your imagination than your memory.'[22]

A week later, on 26 September, Coleridge turned his attention to Wordsworth. A trace of happier times in his own life appears as Coleridge remembers his early married life in Nether Stowey and the birth of his beloved Hartley, while accusing Wordsworth, not entirely fairly, of not understanding what love is: 'Wordsworth said he could make nothing of Love except that it was Friendship accidentally combined with Desire. Whence I conclude that Wordsworth was never in love. For what shall we say of the feeling which a man of sensibility has towards his wife with her baby at her breast? How pure from sensual Desire – yet how different from Friendship!'[23]

Coleridge probably did not know how desperate his son Hartley's situation now was. Dorothy, whose 'sad office' it was to report to Mrs Coleridge in Cornwall about his doings, did not flinch from sending accounts of his vagabond existence and accumulation of drinking debts. In February 1830 he was wandering about, sleeping in barns, avoiding his friends at Grasmere. Dorothy wrote at length to his mother, for whom she now felt some respect as well as pity. She told of Wordsworth's efforts to ensure that Hartley's bills were paid and attempts to find a family to take him in 'to guard him from perishing of cold and hunger'.[24]

Hartley's behaviour followed a pattern. He would settle down in the house of some hospitable farmer, writing articles for *Blackwood's* and the annuals, then when he had some money in his pocket he would wander from inn to inn, drinking until his money ran out, when he drank on credit. Occasionally he visited the Wordsworths, who were kind to him, as he told Derwent in a long, rambling letter at the end of August. But his gratitude was not untempered by criticism. Like his father before him, he thought that Wordsworth was absurdly 'parsimonious of praise to contemporary authors' and extremely irritable about any dispraise of himself. The Rydal Mount family, he told Derwent, 'were all hugely belly-ached with

Townshend's articles in *Blackwood*, articles which Hartley thought too silly to be worth noticing.[25] He came and went from their house, and by November Dorothy had to tell Mrs Coleridge, now living with Sara and Henry in Hampstead, that he had disappeared again.[26]

Poor Mrs Coleridge. She had left Derwent's house for Hampstead to be with Sara during the birth of her first child, Herbert, born on 7 October 1830. She wrote to Poole on 12 September that she had not yet seen her husband, who was 'very poorly at this time', though he hoped to be able to visit his daughter after the birth.[27] The successful confinement was a relief to all those who knew Sara's physical and nervous weaknesses. Hartley talked of her 'morbid delicacy' and gave in his letter to Derwent an insight into the difficulties, partly self-induced, under which she had lived all those years at Greta Hall, 'the house of bondage', as he dramatically called it. She and her mother were under a constant sense of obligation, of which Edith Southey seems to have reminded them by her demeanour: 'They were afraid to move, to speak, every wrinkle of that blood-ill-temper which disorders not diminishes Aunt S.'s benevolence, even sometimes the young lady airs of our Lady Cousins, seem'd to their feverish apprehensions like a warning to depart. But *N'importe*, she is, I hope, a happy wife, and will be ere long a happy mother.'[28]

Sara's nervousness and exhaustion, combined with the fact that Henry was not yet established enough in his profession to be able to afford a carriage, meant that she was unable to visit her father, only a short distance away in Highgate. And he was so frequently ill from 1830 on that he spent most of his time confined to his room, if not to his bed. So father and daughter saw much less of one another than they had hoped, though of course Henry continued to visit Highgate, notebook in hand. In January 1831 Coleridge had a rare sight of Derwent, up from Cornwall to consider taking on a school in Harrow, a plan which came to nothing.[29]

Coleridge's finances, always precarious, took a serious knock in the summer of 1831, and so did his pride. Since he had been made an Associate of the Royal Society of Literature in 1824, the hundred guineas he received every year had been almost his only income. Now, with the accession of William IV on a much reduced budget – only about half that of George IV – an immediate saving was made by the discontinuation of the ten Associateships. Sotheby, Lamb, and the ever well-disposed Daniel Stuart used their influence to plead for some relief for Coleridge. The result was a gift of £200, to be paid in two instalments. Coleridge was insulted, feeling this to be a reluctant handout on account of his extreme poverty rather than an acknowledgment of his services to literature.

He declined the grant. But he had to endure the publicizing of his plight, as well-meaning articles appeared in June in *The Times* and other newpapers.[30] With the loss of the hundred guineas, Coleridge did not know how he could pay Gillman for his board, which was owing from May 1830. Fortunately, Sotheby stepped in with an immediate gift of £50.[31]

During 1831 Reform agitation reached fever pitch. Grey's first Bill, presented to Parliament in March, was narrowly defeated, and Grey resigned, forcing an election, which returned him with an increased majority. Thus bolstered, and with agitation throughout the country ranging from mass open-air meetings to numerous petitions to Parliament (over 3,000 between October 1830 and April 1831), Grey introduced the Bill again in June. This one went through its three readings in the Commons, but was rejected in October by a small majority in the Lords.[32] The violent response across the country caused widespread fear, among Whigs and Tories alike, of bloody revolution.

Coleridge and his associates were not exempt from this fear. Southey's view was that the Whigs had 'raised the devil' and were now 'heartily afraid of the democracy' they had espoused.[33] Sara Hutchinson 'rejoiced that The Lords Spiritual & Temp. have done their duty' in rejecting the Bill, though she accepted that a Bill of some sort was now inevitable.[34] Wordsworth was apocalyptic in his gloom: 'The Constitution of England which seems about to be destroyed, offers to my mind the sublimest contemplation which the History of Society and Govern[ment] have ever presented to it.' He even told Crabb Robinson that he was considering leaving the country.[35]

Coleridge, too, was alarmed by the 'hellish Licence' he perceived in the country and the press at this volatile moment in British history, though his views were mild in comparison to those of his friends.[36] Still, he was no supporter of the Bill, blaming Grey for appealing 'to the argument of the greater number of voices – no matter whether those voices were drunk or sober, competent or not competent'.[37] On 22 April 1831, the day Parliament was dissolved, he announced hyperbolically in his notebook that 'the first day of the first Year of the British (?Brutish) Revolution' had dawned.[38] A year later, with the Bill about to become law, he was more relaxed, joking in conversation that he had heard only 'two arguments of any weight adduced for the passing of this Reform Bill'. These were: '1. We will blow your brains out if your don't pass it. 2. We will drag you through a horsepond if you don't pass it; and there is some cogency in both'.[39]

These fears and anti-democratic statements of Coleridge and his friends seem strange to us now, with universal adult suffrage established and no armed revolution having been necessary to bring it about. In any case, the Reform Act of 1832 fell far short of full electoral reform. Though many abuses of the system were swept away – small pocket boroughs, for example – and seats were allocated for the first time to the new industrial and commercial towns of the Midlands and North of England, still only 20 per cent of adult males were enfranchised by the £10 householder rule. Nevertheless, it was the first major piece of reform legislation the country had known, and was therefore a huge step for any Government to take.

It is not surprising that for Coleridge Reform represented a shift in the ideal balance he had envisaged between the forces of Permanence and those of Progression, a shift which might take the country too far from the first of these two magnetic poles. 'We are now, I think, on the turning point', he said in April 1832:

> This Reform is the ne plus ultra of that tendency of the public mind which substitutes its own undefined notions or passions for real objects and histori-cal actualities. There is not one of the Ministers, except the one or two revolutionists among them, who have ever given a hint throughout this long struggle as to *what* they really do believe will be the product of this Bill . . . No! they have actualized for a moment a wish – or a fear – a passion – but not an Idea.[40]

Just as Huskisson's sudden death at the celebration of that great emblem of progress, the railway, had seemed ominous, so now another phenom-enon sweeping Britain appeared to comment ironically on the long and bitter struggle to pass the Reform Bill. This was cholera, which had spread from Asia to Europe, reaching England in November 1831 and London in February 1832. In July Coleridge wrote some grimly comic lines addressed to the poor of St Giles's, Saffron Hill and Bethnal Green, exhorting them to leave off agitating for their political rights and turn their efforts instead to fighting off the fatal disease:

> Quit Cobbett's, O'Connell's and Beelzebub's banners,
> And whitewash at once bowels, rooms, hands, and manners![41]

Coleridge was now constantly ill, though he appears to have given up opium for about six weeks between the end of March and some time in May 1832, resuming it, he told William Worship, at the request of Green and Gillman, who thought his doing without it completely was 'a step bordering too near on suicidal'.[42] He wrote to Green expressing his disgust at his reliance on 'the Poison, which for more than 30 years has been the guilt, debasement, and misery of my Existence'.[43] It is abundantly clear that, horrific and debilitating though the physical effects of his addiction were, it was the moral and pyschological damage which caused him much the most misery.

He now thought that his intellectual powers had begun to decay 'pro-portionate to the decay of the Organs',[44] a view not at all supported by the evidence of his letters or conversation. Indeed, he was sprightly enough in a letter of 7 May 1832 to Henry Nelson Coleridge, who was preparing Coleridge's poems for a new three-volume edition (eventually published in 1834), to point out that in the Parisian and American editions of his poetry the first line of 'Work Without Hope' –

> All Nature seems at work. Slugs leave their lair –

carries a comic misprint, 'dignifying' his slugs into stags, 'which is really so much grander that I grieve, it should be senseless'.[45]

In May Coleridge's older brother, the Colonel, in town to seek medical advice, called in his carriage, but 'I would not expose him to the fatigue of getting out', Coleridge told Green, '& climbing 5 flights of Stairs, in order to behold a Mask of Syphilis . . . when he had expected to see the Son of his Father'.[46] Crabb Robinson, who had not seen him recently, recorded a visit on 29 September, when Coleridge 'was horribly bent and looked seventy years of age'.[47] A portrait, done by Moses Haughton at this time, shows him looking white-haired and venerable, but with an ideal absence of wrinkles on his round face (see plate 22).

Because of his declining health he was not told about the 'uncertain state' of Dorothy Wordsworth (she was in the early stages of senile dementia).[48] Nor did the family tell him that Hartley had left the Lakes for a two-year stay in Leeds, where he had gone to write a series of biographical portraits of Northern worthies for the publisher F. E. Bingley. He had not seen his mother when she paid a visit to the Wordsworths in the summer of 1831, and he had not written to his father, though she constantly urged him to do so.[49] Though he never did bring himself to write to Coleridge, he prefaced his volume of poetry, published in 1833, with a touching dedicatory sonnet, which he intended as the tribute he was too ashamed to offer personally:

> Father, and Bard revered! to whom I owe,
> Whate'er it be, my little art of numbers,
> Thou, in thy night-watch o'er my cradled slumbers,
> Didst meditate the verse that lives to shew,
> (And long shall live, when we alike are low)
> Thy prayer how ardent, and thy hope how strong,
> That I should learn of Nature's self the song,
> The lore which none but Nature's pupils know.
>
> Thy prayer was heard: I 'wander'd like a breeze',
> By mountain brooks and solitary meres,
> And gather'd there the shapes and phantasies
> Which, mixt with passions of my sadder years,
> Compose this book. If good therein there be,
> That good, my sire, I dedicate to thee.[50]

According to Mrs Coleridge, her husband was 'much affected' by this dedication from the son he had not seen for ten years.[51]

Coleridge roused himself to go to Hampstead for the christening of Sara's second child, Edith, on 9 August 1832. He told Green that he wished 'to stand beside Mrs Coleridge at this second birth of our common Offspring – in proof that the lack of oil or Anti-friction Powder in our Conjugal Carriage-wheels did not extend to our parental relations – (– and in fact, bating living in the same house with her there are few women, that I have a greater respect & *ratherish* liking for, than Mrs C —)'.[52]

If he felt thus warmly towards his wife on the occasion, she too had renewed positive feelings towards him, which she expressed with something between amusement and bemusement to Poole:

The grandfather came from Highgate to be present, and to pass the rest of the day here! – You have probably heard that S.T.C. has intirely left off the use of Laudanum; he has suffered greatly by the effort . . . His power of continuous talking seems unabated, for he talked incessantly for full 5 hours to the great entertainment of Mrs May and a few other friends who were present, and did not leave us till 10, when he was accompanied home by the Revd James Gillman, (son of his friends,) who performed the ceremony, and when Henry called to see him yesterday he appeared no worse for the exertion he had made.[53]

Only a week after the christening a young friend and disciple of Coleridge's, Adam Steinmetz, died, leaving him £300. According to Mrs Coleridge, Coleridge wrote to the young man's father asking him if his son was 'of *sound mind*' when he made his will. The answer was, 'perfectly'.[54] Coleridge may also have received something from the will of Dr Andrew Bell, whose educational system he had defended so vigorously, and in breach of the rules, at the Royal Institution in 1808. Southey had read the will in 1831 and reported to his wife that he and Wordsworth were to get more than £100 and Coleridge somewhat less. 'Schools, schools swallow up all the rest.'[55] Hartley exercised his wit on hearing of Bell's death in February 1832: 'Poor old Dr. Bell. What will he do in Heaven, where I suppose all Education is suspended.'[56]

Then in September 1832 Walter Scott, with whom he had had such an ambivalent relationship, died. Coleridge's thoughts were now kinder than they had been, though he still rated Scott's poetry rather low. He made an interesting comparison between himself and Scott in conversation in August 1833, one which was naturally in his own favour, but which betrays his fascination with Scott's busy historical mind:

Dear Sir Walter Scott and myself were exact, but harmonious, opposites in this – that every old ruin or hill or river called up in his mind a host of historical or biographical associations – just as a bright plate of brass, when beaten, attracts the swarming bees; whilst, notwithstanding Dr Johnson, I really believe I should walk over the plain of Marathon wihout taking more interest in it than any other plain of similar features. Yet I receive as much pleasure in reading the account of the battle in Herodotus, as any one can. Charles Lamb wrote an essay on a man who lived in past time; I thought of adding another to it of one, who lives not in *time* at all, past, present or future.[57]

By April 1833 Coleridge's health was wretched. Henry Nelson Coleridge noticed that he had 'a good deal lost his articulation; – *He* thinks from a paralysis in the jaw – Green says it is from his teeth being loose'.[58] Coleridge and Green were working hard on the manuscript of 'Logic', which Coleridge intended his friend to complete and publish. And he was using Green, as he had used Allsop, as a recipient of personal confidences. It was to Green that he wrote more than once about his enslavement to opium. In April 1833 he confessed that if such a thing as a 'Maison de Santé' for

'Lunacy & Ideocy of the *Will*' had then existed, 'I know who would have entered himself as a Patient some five & 20 years ago'.[59]

Trouble with his articulation notwithstanding, Coleridge went on talking as brilliantly as ever. Abraham Hayward sent him a copy of his translation of *Faust*, in which he praised Coleridge's 'magnificent' translation of *Wallenstein*[60], and this set Coleridge off on his long verbal critique of Goethe's play, his own early plans to write about Michael Scott, and his near-translation of *Faust* itself in 1814.[61] His mind was still active on Shakespeare; indeed some of his most brilliant insights were recorded in 1833–4. He elaborated on the idea of Shakespeare as God or Jove in April 1833:

> In Shakspeare one sentence begets the next naturally: the meaning is all inwoven. He goes on kindling like a meteor through the dark atmosphere – yet when the creation in its outlines is once perfect, then he seems to rest from his Labor and to smile upon his work and tell himself it is very good. You see many scenes and parts of scenes, which are simply Shakspeare's disporting himself in joyous triumph and vigorous fun after a great achievement of his highest genius.[62]

As late as March 1834, when his last illness was upon him, Coleridge exercised his comparative facility in an extended remark on Shakespeare and Chaucer, to the illumination of both: 'The sympathy of the poet with the subjects of his poetry is equally remarkable in Shakspeare and Chaucer; but what the first effects by a strong act of imagination, of mental metamorphosis, the last does without any effort merely by the inborn kindly joyousness of his nature. How well we seem to know Chaucer! how absolutely nothing do we know of Shakspeare!' Shakespeare's words, he added, 'came out of the unfathomable depths of his own oceanic mind – his observation and reading supplied him with the drapery of his figures'.[63]

In his last years Coleridge more than once described with admirable clarity the philosophical conclusions of a lifetime of study. In August 1831 he deftly illustrated the vital difference between Reason and Understanding, enunciated – though often obscurely – in many of his prose works. He drew once more on the argument between Hume and Kant, which he adapted to his own purposes:

> A man having seen a million moss roses all red concludes from his own experience and that of others that all moss roses are red. That is a maxim with him – the greatest amount of his knowledge on the subject. But it is only true until some gardener has produced a white moss rose; after which the maxim is good for nothing . . . Compare this in its highest degree with the assurance which you have that the two sides of any triangle are greater than the third. This demonstrated of one triangle is seen to be eternally true of all imaginable triangles. This is the truth perceived at once by the Reason, wholly independently of experience. It is and must ever be so, multiply the shapes and sizes of triangles as you may.[64]

He was, in general, at least as reported by his son-in-law, less convoluted in his sentence structure in conversation than in his written sentences, which even he had likened in a letter to Sotheby of 1808 to a series of 'Surinam Toads' with little toads 'vegetating out from back and side'.[65] Peacock had guyed him mercilessly for this in *Nightmare Abbey*, reproducing Mr Flosky's endless sentences explaining his delight in 'synthetical reasoning' with its tendency 'at every step' to strike out 'into two branches, in a compound ratio of ramification; so that you are perfectly sure of losing your way, and keeping your mind in perfect health, by the perpetual exercise of an interminable quest; and for these reasons I have christened my eldest son Emanuel Kant Flosky.'[66]

This had been in response to the obscurities in *Biographia Literaria*, to which Coleridge alluded in conversation in June 1834, admitting that 'all that metaphysical disquisition' in chapters thirteen and fourteen was 'unformed and immature'.[67] He now reiterated the famous distinction between Fancy and Imagination, avoiding jargon and unnecessary complexity. 'The fancy brings together images which have no connection natural or moral, but are yoked together by the poet by some accidental coincidence', the example he gives being a comparison of dawn to 'a lobster boyl'd' in Samuel Butler's *Hudibras*. By contrast, 'the imagination modifies images and gives unity to variety; it sees all things in one':

There is an epic imagination, the perfection of which is in Milton; and the dramatic, of which Shakspeare is the absolute master. The first gives unity by throwing back into the distance, as after the magnificent approach of the Messiah to battle, the poet by one touch – 'far off their coming shone!' – makes the whole one image: and so at the conclusion of Satan's address to the entranced angels in which every sort of image from all the regions of earth and air is introduced to diversify and illustrate, the reader is brought back to the single image by

> He called so loud that all the hollow deep
> Of Hell resounded.

The dramatic imagination does not throw back, but brings close; all nature is stamped with one meaning, as in Lear, &c.[68]

This was his last recorded word on the subject which had possessed him for over thirty years. It is utterly free of Floskyism.

Though in October 1833 Coleridge wrote that he had been 'a prisoner for nearly 3 years to my Bedroom, and for the far larger portion to my *bed*',[69] his talk flowed on. He talked of 'Christabel' and how he had been unable to carry on its 'witchery by daylight'. He talked of the eighteeenth-century novel, of how wholesome Fielding is compared to Richardson: 'To take him up after Richardson is like emerging from a sick room heated by stoves into an open lawn on a breezy day in May'.[70]

Responding to a Bill put before Parliament in March 1834 'to promote the better observance of the Lord's Day' and mercifully dropped in May, he gave his interesting and independent view: 'I would prohibit compulsory labor, and put down operas, theatres &c., for this plain reason, that if the rich be allowed to *play*, the poor will be forced, or be induced, to work. I am not for a Paris Sunday. But to stop coaches and to let the gentleman's carriage run – is monstrous'.[71]

During the summer of 1833 Coleridge experienced one of those miraculous recoveries at which Dorothy Wordsworth used to marvel. To everyone's astonishment he was fit enough to visit Cambridge for three days in June and to enjoy a summer holiday with the Gillmans in their old haunt, Ramsgate, in July. The visit to Cambridge was a triumph. He went with Gillman and Green for the third annual meeting of the British Association for the Advancement of Science. Derwent was in Cambridge, and was 'surprised & highly gratified at the unexpected arrival of his father', who received a flattering reception from the assembled scientists.[72]

Coleridge himself said his emotions on revisiting Cambridge were 'at first overwhelming'. He was lionized by the young men of Trinity, and met Michael Faraday, the erstwhile disciple of Davy, by whom he was favourably impressed.[73] On his return he talked energetically about the subjects which had been discussed at the conference, including electricity, light, and the newly published geological studies of Charles Lyell, *Principles of Geology* (1830–3), so influential in the next generation, especially on Tennyson's writing of *In Memoriam*. He also talked about architecture, marvelling at the 'sublimity and transcendent beauty' of King's College Chapel, and about the paintings he had seen at the Fitzwilliam Museum in Cambridge.[74]

After three weeks in Ramsgate, he returned to Highgate, where in August he settled perhaps his last clandestine debt with Dunn the chemist.[75] He was visited by Ralph Waldo Emerson, who recorded that he 'burst into a declamation on the folly and ignorance of Unitarianism'. Emerson, a Unitarian himself, sensibly refused to be offended by the tactlessness of a man now 'old and preoccupied', who 'could not bend to a new companion and think with him'. Emerson nevertheless recognized his 'hunger for ideas' and later declared that he wrote and spoke 'the only high criticism in his time'.[76]

Though Coleridge was largely cheerful, his bodily health continued to decline. On 28 October he wrote 'My Baptismal Birth-Day', subtitled 'Lines composed on a sick-bed', which end on an accepting couplet:

> Is that a death-bed where a Christian lies?-
> Yes! but not his – 'tis Death itself there dies.[77]

Possibly on the same day he wrote his last poem of all in the back of one of his notebooks. Appropriately, it was an epitaph for himself, alluding one last time to 'The Ancient Mariner':

> A Tombstone
> ΕΣΤΗΣΕ

Stop, Christian Passer-by! Stop, child of God!
And read with gentle heart. Beneath this sod
A Poet lies; or that which once was he.
O lift one thought in prayer for S. T. C.
That he, who many a year with toil of breath,
Found Death in Life, may here find Life in Death.
Mercy for Praise, *to be forgiven* for Fame
He ask'd, and hop'd thro' Christ. Do thou the Same![78]

This pious piece was enclosed in a letter to Green. To Mrs Aders he sent a more frivolous, self-mocking epitaph, accompanied by a crude drawing of a tombstone labelled 'S. T. C.' and, as ever, getting his age wrong by two years:

S.T. Coleridge Aetat, suae 63.
Not/ handsome/ was/ but was/ eloquent
Non formosus erat, sed erat facundus Ulysses.
Translation
'In truth, he's no beauty!' cry'd Moll, Poll, and Tab,
But they all of them owned He'd the gift of the Gab.[79]

The last portrait of Coleridge was done at this time, a pencil sketch by the young German artist J. Kayser, which Coleridge admitted to be 'a Likeness, certainly; but with such unhappy Density of the Nose & ideotic Drooping of the Lip' and a 'pervading *Woodenness* of the whole Countenance' that his friends told him it hardly flattered him.[80]

In January 1834 Sara Coleridge gave birth to twins, Berkeley and Florence, who survived only two days. She was plunged into greater depression than ever, and resorted to high doses of opium and all the guilt and misery these brought. In September 1834 her volume of children's verses, *Pretty Lessons in Verse for Small Children*, appeared, including an extraordinary and incongruous poem addressed to her son Herbert about poppies and the relief their juice brings to his 'poor mama'. The last stanza reads:

O then my sweet my happy boy
Will thank the poppy flow'r
Which brings the sleep to dear mamma
At midnight's darksome hour.[81]

Coleridge himself was growing weaker. In March he was suffering from a tumour in the cheek and neck and another outbreak of erysipelas. He wrote to Green that he would like to see him before he died, to 'leave with you, the sole Depositarium of my Mind & Aspirations, what God may suggest to me'.[82]

The three volumes of his *Poetical Works*, edited by Henry, came out during the first half of 1834 to a chorus of critical approval. The writer in the *Gentleman's Magazine* praised his 'truly poetical mind', comparing it to 'his great contemporary, the poet of Rydal Mount'. Wordsworth and Coleridge had finally, albeit late in the day, succeeded in creating the taste by which their works were to be enjoyed. Henry Nelson Coleridge himself wrote a long panegyric which was published in the *Quarterly Review* in August, shortly after Coleridge's death.[83]

Sara Hutchinson, on whom Coleridge had so destructively fixed his notion of ideal womanhood, visited him before his death. She came to London in May, hoping to rouse young Sara Coleridge from her 'fanciful despondency'.[84] On 8 May she went to Highgate, '& greatly was I shocked with the changed appearance of my dear old Friend'. 'He will never rise from his bed more I fear', she added.[85]

This plain, straightforward, slightly acerbic woman, who had been so burdened with the weight of Coleridge's fancied love, still felt some warmth towards him. Her last sharp comment in connection with him was made shortly after his death, when she said, with some justice, that his own relations had 'more pride in him than Love for him – at least Pride was the foundation of their Love'.[86] She and the Wordsworths, on the other hand, though they had moved apart from him over twenty years before, could claim to have loved him for himself. Sara outlived Coleridge by less than a year, dying in June 1835 after wearing herself out with nursing Dorothy and helping Southey, whose irritable wife was committed to a lunatic asylum in September 1834.[87]

An extraordinary thing happened in July 1834. A Mrs Dashwood wrote out of the blue to Mrs Gillman, expressing her admiration for Coleridge's genius and offering him a small annuity. Almost the last letter he wrote was a reply to this would-be benefactor, graciously acknowledging the offer. It was, of course, too late for annuities. On 25 July Coleridge died, as nearly at peace with himself as was possible, concerned about his friends, and glad to be leaving behind a life of suffering. It had not been a happy life for many of the sixty-one years it lasted. But it had been an extraordinary one. It seems utterly appropriate that Coleridge should have died still able to talk brilliantly on all the subjects under the sun, and still able so to impress others with his genius that they automatically opened their hearts, their minds, and their purses to him.

Coleridge was buried in Highgate, in a vault next to Highgate School, on 2 August 1834. Henry and Edward Coleridge attended, as did Green and James Gillman junior, whose father was too ill to go. John Sterling came from Cambridge. The vault filled up, in due course, with other family members: Henry Nelson Coleridge in 1843, Coleridge's unfortunate wife in 1845, his beloved daughter in 1852, and her brilliant son Herbert in 1861.

Highgate School subsequently built a new chapel which extended over the graveyard, and the Coleridge family vault was neglected. In 1961, after efforts by his descendants and other interested people, Coleridge's remains were moved to St Michael's Church, just opposite No. 3, The Grove, where he had spent his last years with the Gillmans. A service was held, attended by luminaries who included John Masefield, T. S. Eliot and I. A. Richards.[88] It was testimony to the hold Coleridge has enduringly and increasingly had over the imaginations of fellow poets and critics.

Wordsworth, in some table talk of his own which the indefatigable Henry Nelson Coleridge noted down in October 1829, summed up his friend's talk and his intellect: 'S. T. C. never did *converse* in the common sense of the word; he would lay hold of another person's suggestion, then refine upon it, divide & subtilize it till he had made it entirely his own. He borrowed largely, but he had a right to do so, for he gave away as largely.' No epitaph could be better adapted to its subject, of whom Wordsworth also said, simply:

> Many men have done wonderful things – Newton, Davy &c., but S. T. C. is the only wonderful man I ever knew.[89]

Notes

ABBREVIATIONS USED IN REFERENCES

For Coleridge's works, I refer to the excellent *Collected Works* in the Bollingen series published by Routledge and Princeton University Press. Most of the sixteen volumes (many of them subdivided into two or more part-volumes) have been published, edited and annotated by different scholars. These are referred to in the notes, where full bibliographical details are given, as *CW*. For the poetry, not yet published in *CW*, I use *Complete Poetical Works*, ed. Ernest Hartley Coleridge, 2 vols, Oxford, 1912 (referred to as *PW*).

The Collected Letters, ed. Earl Leslie Griggs, 6 vols, Oxford, 1956–71, are abbreviated as *CL*. Coleridge's notebooks up to 1826 have been published in four double volumes, ed. Kathleen Coburn, London, 1957–90. These are referred to as *CN*. Kathleen Coburn also edited *Inquiring Spirit: A New Presentation of Coleridge from his Unpublished Prose Writings*, London, 1951, reprinted Toronto, 1979, and *The Philosophical Lectures of Samuel Taylor Coleridge*, London, 1949. Other collections and editions of Coleridge's conversation and miscellaneous criticism are referred to under the editor's name.

INTRODUCTION

1 E. M. Forster, 'Trooper Silas Tomkyn Comberbacke' (1931), in *Abinger Harvest* (1936, repr. Harmondsworth, 1974), p. 247.
2 John Rickman to Southey, 26 March 1804, Orlo Williams, *Life and Letters of John Rickman* (London, 1912), pp. 107–8.
3 STC to William Godwin, 25 March 1801, *CL*, II, 714.
4 Southey to Grosvenor Charles Bedford, 22 December 1810, *New Letters of Robert Southey*, ed. Kenneth Curry, 2 vols. (New York and London, 1965), I, 548.
5 Lamb to Wordsworth, 26 April 1816, *The Letters of Charles and Mary Lamb*, ed. Edwin W. Marrs. Jr, 3 vols. (Ithaca, New York, and London, 1975–8), III, 215.
6 For previous biographies of Coleridge see Bibliography.

7   See *Coleridge the Talker: A Series of Contemporary Descriptions and Comments*, ed. R. W. Armour and R. F. Howes (New York, 1940).
8   *New Monthly Magazine*, XXXII (July 1831), 330.
9   Southey to STC, 4 August 1802, *The Life and Correspondence of the late Robert Southey*, ed. C. C. Southey, 6 vols. (London, 1849–50), II, 190.
10   Byron, Dedication to *Don Juan*, *Poetical Works* (London, 1904, reprinted 1967), p. 635.
11   Forster, 'Silas Tomkyn Comberbacke', p. 246.
12   Lamb to STC, 8 November 1796, *Letters*, ed. Marrs, I, 58.
13   Lamb, 'The Death of Coleridge' (1834), *The Works of Charles and Mary Lamb*, ed. E. V. Lucas, 7 vols. (London, 1903–5), I, 351.
14   Wordsworth, 'Extempore Effusion upon the Death of James Hogg', *Poetical Works*, ed. Thomas Hutchinson, rev. Ernest de Selincourt (London, 1904, repr. 1965), p. 459.
15   See Christopher Wordsworth, *Memoirs of William Wordsworth, Poet Laureate, D.C.L.*, 2 vols. (London, 1851), II, 288–9.
16   See *Coleridge: The Critical Heritage*, ed. J. R. de J. Jackson (London, 1970).
17   See Rosemary Ashton, *The German Idea: Four English Writers and the Reception of German Thought, 1800–60* (Cambridge, 1980, repr. London, 1994).
18   STC to Francis Wrangham, 19 December 1800, *CL*, I, 658.
19   STC to William Sotheby, 13 July 1802, *CL*, II, 810.
20   See C. R. Sanders, *Coleridge and the Broad Church Movement* (New York, 1942, repr. 1972), and Stephen Prickett, *Romanticism and Religion: The Tradition of Coleridge and Wordsworth in the Victorian Church* (Cambridge, 1976).
21   J. S. Mill, 'Coleridge', *London and Westminster Review*, XXXIII (March 1840), 263.
22   *Memoir and Letters of Sara Coleridge*, ed. Edith Coleridge, 2 vols. (London, 1873), I, 166.
23   *Collected Poems of Stevie Smith* (Harmondsworth, 1985), pp. 385, 386.
24   See Elisabeth Schneider, *Coleridge, Opium and 'Kubla Khan'* (Chicago, 1953), Alethea Hayter, *Opium and the Romantic Imagination* (London, 1968) and Molly Lefebure, *Samuel Taylor Coleridge: A Bondage of Opium* (London, 1974).
25   *Athenaem*, 17 June 1893, in *Coleridge: The Critical Heritage Volume 2: 1834–1900*, ed. J. R. de J. Jackson (London, 1991), p. 189.
26   STC to John Thelwall, 17 December 1796, *CL*, I, 277.
27   Virginia Woolf, 'The Man at the Gate' (1940), in *The Death of the Moth and Other Essays* (London, 1942, repr. 1981), p. 70.
28   Wordsworth, 'A Character', *Lyrical Ballads* (1800), ed. R. L. Brett and A. R. Jones (London, 1963, repr. 1978), pp. 214–15.

CHAPTER 1   INSPIRED CHARITY BOY 1772–1791

1   Lord Coleridge, *The Story of a Devonshire House* (London, 1906). See also *Coleridge: The Early Family Letters*, ed. James Engell (Oxford, 1994), in which letters collected by Lord Coleridge, but not previously published in full, are now reprinted.
2   STC to Tom Poole, 6 February 1797, *CL*, I, 302.
3   William Godwin's account of STC's early life, as told him by STC *circa*

December 1799, mentions his grandfather's illegitimacy, MS Abinger – Shelley Papers, Bodleian Library.

4 Abinger–Shelley Papers.
5 *Story of a Devonshire House*, pp. 12–13.
6 See Southey to J. G. Lockhart, 14 December 1828, *New Letters*, II, 331.
7 STC to Poole, 6 February 1797, *CL*, I, 302.
8 See John A. Whitham, *The Church of St. Mary of Ottery: A Short History and Guide*, 8th edn. (Ottery St Mary, 1982), pp. 8–12.
9 STC to Poole, March 1797, 16 October 1797, *CL*, I, 310, 355. See also James Gillman, *The Life of Samuel Taylor Coleridge* (London, 1838), p. 2.
10 Gillman, *Life*, pp. 3–4.
11 *Story of a Devonshire House*, pp. 24ff.
12 Gillman, *Life*, pp. 6–7.
13 STC to Poole, March 1797, 16 October 1797, *CL*, I, 310, 354.
14 STC to Poole, 9 October 1797, *CL*, I, 348.
15 Abinger –Shelley Papers.
16 STC to Poole, 16 October 1797, *CL*, I, 352–4.
17 Notebook for 19 July 1803, *CN*, I, 1416.
18 See Richard Holmes, *Coleridge: Early Visions* (London, 1989), p. 17.
19 STC, *PW*, I, 125.
20 See 'Resolution and Independence' (1802), *Poetical Works*, p. 155.
21 See Lefebure, *A Bondage of Opium*, p. 74: 'The adventure . . . laid down the blueprint, as it were, of his lifelong pattern as an incurable bolter.'
22 Basil Willey, *Samuel Taylor Coleridge* (London, 1972), p. 32.
23 STC to Poole, 16 October 1797, *CL*, I, 354.
24 *Story of a Devonshire House*, p. 23ff; STC to Poole, March 1797, *CL*, I, 311. John Coleridge, the oldest brother, seems also to have taken his own life, see *Coleridge: The Early Family Letters*, p. 91, though it is not clear whether Coleridge knew this.
25 STC to Poole, March 1797, *CL*, I, 310–11.
26 STC to Luke Coleridge, 12 May 1787, *CL*, I, 3.
27 *PW*, I, 20 and note.
28 STC to Poole, March 1797, *CL*, I, 311.
29 John Coleridge to James Coleridge, August 1783, *Story of a Devonshire House*, p. 29.
30 See Molly Lefebure, *The Bondage of Love: A Life of Mrs Samuel Taylor Coleridge* (London, 1986), pp. 24–5, 30–1.
31 See *Henry Crabb Robinson On Books and Their Writers*, ed. Edith J. Morley, 3 vols. (London, 1938), I, 105–6 (diary 4 August 1812). Robinson is reporting what he has heard from the Morgans, with whom Coleridge was living in 1812.
32 STC to Poole, 9 October 1797, *CL*, I, 347–8.
33 Joseph Cottle, *Early Recollections; chiefly relating to the late Samuel Taylor Coleridge*, 2 vols. (London, 1837), I, 241. Cottle is a notoriously unreliable writer. He prints letters of Coleridge's in mangled, transposed, and inaccurate form, and his vanity ensures that he himself is much at the centre of his narrative. Yet his is the fullest account we have of Coleridge's life in Bristol in 1795–6; it is therefore invaluable.
34 See *Christ's Hospital: Recollections of Lamb, Coleridge, and Leigh Hunt*, ed. R. Brimley Johnson (London, 1896), p. 69.
35 STC to Poole, 19 February 1798, *CL*, I, 388.
36 Lamb, 'Recollections of Christ's Hospital' (1818), *Works*, I, 149.

37 Ibid., I, 140, 148.
38 Leigh Hunt, *Autobiography* (1859), ed. J. E. Morpurgo (London, 1949), p. 56.
39 STC to the Court of Assistants of the Worshipful Company of Haberdashers, 27 May 1834, *CL*, VI, 983.
40 *Biographia Literaria* (1817), ed. James Engell and W. Jackson Bate (London, 1983) in *CW*, 7:I, 8–10, 11.
41 Lamb, 'Christ's Hospital Five and Thirty Years Ago' (1820), *Works*, II, 19–20. See also Leigh Hunt, *Autobiography*, p. 67.
42 Conversation of 27 May 1830, *Table Talk*, ed. Carl Woodring (London, 1990) in *CW*, 14:I, 143–4.
43 See R. A. Foakes, ' "Thriving Prisoners": Coleridge, Wordsworth and the Child at School', *Studies in Romanticism*, XXVIII (1989), 187ff. See also STC, *Lectures 1808–1819: On Literature*, ed. R. A. Foakes (London, 1987) in *CW*, 5:I and II. See also *Blake, Coleridge, Wordsworth, Lamb, Etc. Being Selections from the Remains of Henry Crabb Robinson*, ed. Edith J. Morley (London, 1922), p. 105.
44 Lecture of 3 May 1808, *CW*, 5:I, 106.
45 Lamb, 'Christ's Hospital Five and Thirty Years Ago', *Works*, II, 13.
46 Godwin's biographical notes on STC, Abinger–Shelley Papers.
47 Lamb, *Works*, II, 13, 14.
48 *CN*, I, 1176 (April–May 1802).
49 See *CL*, IV, 663n.
50 STC to Ann Coleridge, 4 February 1785, *CL*, I, 1.
51 Gillman, *Life*, p. 23.
52 STC to Luke Coleridge, 12 May 1787, *CL*, I, 2.
53 STC, *PW*, I, 1.
54 STC to Luke Coleridge, 12 May 1787, *CL*, I, 2.
55 STC to Godwin, 22 January 1802, *CL*, II, 782.
56 STC to George Coleridge, 17 May 1791, *CL*, I, 10.
57 Gillman, *Life*, p. 20.
58 Dickens, *David Copperfield* (1850, reprinted Harmondsworth, 1977), pp. 105, 106.
59 *CW*, 7:I, 15.
60 Lamb, 'Christ's Hospital', *Works*, II, 21.
61 Lamb, 'The Death of Coleridge', *Works*, I, 352.
62 Gillman, *Life*, p. 28.
63 STC to George Coleridge, 24 January 1792, *CL*, I, 19–20.
64 STC to Mrs Evans, 13 February 1792, *CL*, I, 21–2.
65 *CL*, I, 22–4.
66 *CL*, I, 24.
67 *CN*, II, 2516 (1 April 1805).
68 STC to Morgan, 23 February 1812, *CL*, III, 377.
69 For example, Thomson's 'Liberty' (1735–6), Collins's 'Ode to Liberty' (1747), and Gray's 'Bard' (1757). See William Levine, 'The Progress Poem in Coleridge's Political Lyrics', *The Wordsworth Circle*, XX (Spring 1989), 68–74.
70 The examples are taken from the following early poems: 'Easter Holidays' (1787), 'Dura Navis' (1787), 'Sonnet to the Autumnal Moon' (1788), 'Anthem for the Children of Christ's Hospital' (1789), 'The Nose' (1789), *PW*, I, 1–9. See Jack Stillinger, 'Pictorialism and Matter-of-Factness in Coleridge's Poems of Somerset', *The Wordsworth Circle*, XX (Spring 1989), 62–7.
71 *Biographia Literaria*, *CW*, 7:I, 10.
72 *PW*, I, 2.

73 See Donald H. Reiman, 'Coleridge and the Art of Equivocation', *Studies in Romanticism*, XXV (1986), 328–9.
74 *PW*, I, 10–11.
75 Gillman, *Life*, p. 33.
76 *PW*, I, 17.
77 STC to George Coleridge, 28 November 1791, *CL*, I, 18.
78 See the opening pages of Molly Lefebure, *A Bondage of Opium*; also Schneider, *Coleridge, Opium and 'Kubla Khan'*, and Hayter, *Opium and the Romantic Imagination*.
79 STC to George Coleridge, c.10 March 1798, *CL*, I, 394.
80 See STC to Cottle, 26 April 1814, and to Gillman, 13 April 1816, *CL*, III, 476, IV, 630; also *Biographia Literaria*, *CW*, 7:I, 17.
81 *PW*, I, 84.
82 *CW*, 7:I, 25.
83 STC to Thelwall, 17 December 1796, *CL*, I, 279. Mark Akenside was the author of *The Pleasures of Imagination* (1744), a blank verse poem of a moral-reflective cast. See Harriet Devine Jump, 'High Sentiment of Liberty: Coleridge's Unacknowledged Debt to Akenside', *Studies in Romanticism*, XXVIII (1989), 207–24.
84 *PW*, I, 29.
85 See *CN*, I, 1250 (3 October 1802), and 1726 (13 December 1803).
86 STC to Sara Hutchinson, 4 April 1802, *CL*, II, 791–2.

CHAPTER 2   CAMBRIDGE AND PANTISOCRACY 1791–1794

1 STC to George Coleridge, 16 October 1791, *CL*, I, 15.
2 Gillman, *Life*, pp. 41–2.
3 Ibid., p. 44.
4 *Biographia Literaria*, *CW*, 7:I, 13.
5 STC to George Coleridge, early November 1791, *CL*, I, 16–17.
6 See STC to George Coleridge, 13 January 1793, *CL*, I, 45.
7 STC to George Coleridge, 28 November 1791, *CL*, I, 18.
8 STC to Mrs Evans, 22 February 1792, and to Anne Evans, 14 February 1792, *CL*, I, 33, 31.
9 STC to Mary Evans, 13 February 1792, *CL*, I, 26, 27.
10 STC to George Coleridge, 24 July 1793, *CL*, I, 57.
11 See Albert Goodwin, *The Friends of Liberty* (London, 1979), pp. 19–25.
12 Ibid., pp. 271–2.
13 See *British Pamphleteers*, ed. George Orwell and Reginald Reynolds, 2 vols. (London, 1948 and 1951), II, 38.
14 STC to George Coleridge, 24 August 1792, *CL*, I, 40.
15 *CL*, I, 40.
16 STC to George Coleridge, 13 January 1793, *CL*, I, 45–6.
17 See Lord Coleridge, *The Story of a Devonshire House*, p. 265.
18 Ibid., pp. 169–70.
19 STC to Mary Evans, 7 February 1793, *CL*, I, 49.
20 STC to Humphry Davy, 20 May 1801, *CL*, II, 734.
21 See Lefebure, *A Bondage of Opium*, pp. 83–4, and *The Bondage of Love*, pp. 76, 107, 265.

22 *CN*, I, 1726. See also *CN*, III, 3429.
23 Full repeal of the Test Acts came finally in 1828, see Goodwin, *Friends of Liberty*, p. 97.
24 See *CL*, I, 20n; also P. M. Zall, 'The Trials of William Frend', *The Wordsworth Circle*, II (Winter 1971), 26–31; and Nicholas Roe, *Wordsworth and Coleridge: The Radical Years* (Oxford, 1988), pp. 15–19, 94ff.
25 Valentine Le Grice, 'College Reminiscences of Mr. Coleridge', *Gentleman's Magazine*, new series II (December 1834), 606. See also Gillman, *Life*, p. 54ff.
26 STC to George Coleridge, 24 January 1792, *CL*, I, 20.
27 STC to George Coleridge, 9 February 1793, *CL*, I, 53–4.
28 STC to George Coleridge, 18 February 1793, *CL*, I, 56–7.
29 STC to George Coleridge, 24 July 1793, *CL*, I, 58.
30 *PW*, I, 42.
31 *PW*, I, 55.
32 *Poems on Various Subjects* (Bristol, 1796), p. 183; *PW*, I, 52.
33 Christopher Wordsworth, *Social Life at the English Universities in the Eighteenth Century* (Cambridge, 1874), II, 589–90. See also E. K. Chambers, *Samuel Taylor Coleridge: A Biographical Study* (Oxford, 1938), p. 22.
34 STC to George Coleridge, 23 February 1794, *CL*, I, 68.
35 STC to James Coleridge, 20 February 1794, *CL*, I, 65.
36 STC to George Coleridge, 23 February 1794, *CL*, I, 67–8.
37 Gillman, *Life*, p. 64.
38 Cottle, *Early Recollections*, II, 54.
39 STC to James Coleridge, 20 February 1794, *CL*, I, 66.
40 Gillman, *Life*, pp. 59–60.
41 Cottle, *Early Recollections*, II, 58.
42 Charles Lloyd, *Edmund Oliver* (Bristol, 1798), I, x, 41, 42–3.
43 See *CL*, I, 63–9.
44 STC to John Colson, 8 December 1796, *CL*, I, 265.
45 *CL*, I, 75n.
46 STC to George Coleridge, 3 March 1794, *CL*, I, 70, 72–3.
47 *CL*, I, 76n.
48 *CL*, I, 77n.
49 MS Abinger–Shelley Papers.
50 STC to George Coleridge, 11 April 1794, *CL*, I, 79.
51 STC to George Coleridge, 1 May 1794, *CL*, I, 80.
52 See *New Letters of Robert Southey*, I, 3n.
53 Southey to Horace Bedford, 11 December 1793, ibid., I, 37.
54 Southey to Horace Bedford, 12 December 1793, ibid., I, 40.
55 Southey to Horace Bedford, 11 December 1793, ibid., I, 36.
56 Ibid., I, 37.
57 See Lefebure, *A Bondage of Love*, pp. 23–5; and Southey to Horace Bedford, 22 August 1794, *New Letters*, I, 71.
58 See John Ruskin Clark, *Joseph Priestley: A Comet in the System* (San Diego, California, 1990), pp. 11ff., and P. M. Zall, 'Joseph Priestley, Firebrand Philosopher', *The Wordsworth Circle*, IX (Winter 1978), 64–70.
59 See P. M. Zall, 'Up Loyal Sock Creek', *The Wordsworth Circle*, III (Summer 1972), 161–7.
60 STC to Southey, 21 October 1794, *CL*, I, 115; Southey to Horace Bedford, 22 August 1794 and 12 December 1793, *New Letters*, I, 71, 39.

61 STC to Southey, 6 July 1794, *CL*, I, 83–4.
62 Wordsworth, two-part *Prelude*, Part II, lines 506–7, see *The Prelude*, Norton Critical Edition, ed. Jonathan Wordsworth, M. H. Abrams and Stephen Gill (New York, 1979), p. 27.
63 'The Pains of Sleep' (1803), *PW*, I, 391.
64 Southey to Grosvenor Bedford, 12–19 June 1794, *New Letters* I, 56.
65 'To the exiled patriots Muir and Palmer', published in an unauthorized edition of Southey's *Poetical Works* (Paris, 1829), p. 698.
66 Henry Cockburn, *Memorials of His Time* (Edinburgh, 1856), p. 117.
67 For an excellent account of the Edinburgh trials see Goodwin, *Friends of Liberty*, p. 287ff.
68 See STC, *Lectures 1795 On Politics and Religion*, ed. Lewis Patton and Peter Mann (London, 1971) in *CW*, 1, 14–15n.
69 See Philip Anthony Brown, *The French Revolution in English History* (London, 1918, reprinted 1965), p. 97.
70 *CW*, 1, 2, 16–17.
71 STC to Southey, 13 July 1794, *CL*, I, 85.
72 *CL*, I, 86; *PW*, I, 32.
73 STC to Southey, 13 July 1794, *CL*, I, 87–8.
74 *CL*, I, 89.
75 Southey to Grosvenor Bedford, 21 August 1794, *New Letters*, I, 68–9.
76 See *Paupers and Pig Killers: The Diary of William Holland, A Somerset Parson, 1799–1818*, ed. Jack Ayres (Gloucester, 1984), pp. 15, 35.
77 See David Knight, *Humphry Davy: Science and Power* (Oxford, 1992), p. 45; P. M. Zall, 'Do Ye Ken Tom Poole?', *The Wordsworth Circle*, VIII (Winter 1977), 56–61; *Paupers and Pig Killers*, p. 57.
78 See Mrs Henry Sandford, *Thomas Poole and His Friends*, 2 vols. (London, 1888), I, 103.
79 Ibid., I, 97.
80 Ibid., I, 96–7.
81 Ibid., I, 98.
82 Southey to Horace Bedford, 22 August 1794, *New Letters*, I, 70–1.
83 Ibid., I, 72, 73.
84 Southey to Grosvenor Bedford, 4 September 1794, ibid., I, 74.
85 STC to Charles Heath, 29 August 1794, *CL*, I, 97.
86 See Carl Woodring, *Politics in the Poetry of Coleridge* (Madison, Wisconsin, 1961), pp. 194–8.
87 STC to Southey, 19 September 1794, *CL*, I, 106.
88 See Brian Morris, 'Coleridge and Other People', *The Wordsworth Circle*, X (Autumn 1979), 357–8 for an interesting criticism of the play.
89 *The Fall of Robespierre*, Act I, lines 198–201, *PW*, II, 501.
90 Act I, lines 170–2, *PW*, II, 500.
91 *British Critic*, V (May 1795), *Critical Heritage*, p. 23.
92 Clement Carlyon, *Early Years and Late Reflections*, 4 vols. (London, 1836–58), I (1836), 28.
93 See L. G. Mitchell, *Charles James Fox* (Oxford, 1992), pp. 119–35.
94 See James McKusick, 'Coleridge and Horne Tooke', *Studies in Romanticism*, XXIV (1985), 85–111; P. M. Zall, 'Thomas Holcroft, Hyperhack', *The Wordsworth Circle*, XI (Autumn 1980), 212–14; P. M. Zall, 'Citizen John Up Against the Wall', *The Wordsworth Circle*, III (Spring 1972), 111–16. For a full account of the trials see Goodwin, *Friends of Liberty*, pp. 216–19, 307ff.

95   See S. Maccoby, *English Radicalism 1786–1832* (London, 1955), p. 86; Goodwin, *Friends of Liberty*, pp. 355–6.

96   The suspension of Habeas Corpus was not removed until 1801, see Goodwin, *Friends of Liberty*, p. 367. For Thelwall, see Mrs Thelwall, *The Life of John Thelwall* (London, 1837), I, 224ff. (Two volumes were announced, but only one appeared.)

97   See Goodwin, *Friends of Liberty*, pp. 272–3.

98   See Roe, *Wordsworth and Coleridge*, pp. 207–8; see also Roe's essay, 'Coleridge and John Thelwall' in *The Coleridge Connection: Essays for Thomas McFarland*, ed. Richard Gravil and Molly Lefebure (London, 1990).

99   Southey to Thomas Southey, 7 September 1794, *New Letters*, I, 75.

100 Southey to Sara Fricker, 25 October 1794, ibid., I, 85.

101 Southey to Thomas Southey, 19 October 1794, *Life and Correspondence*, I, 223.

102 Southey to Sara Fricker, 25 October 1794, and to Horace Bedford, 12 November 1794, *New Letters*, I, 85, 87.

103 STC to Southey, 1 September 1794, *CL*, I, 99.

104 STC to George Dyer, 11 September 1794, *CL*, I, 100–1.

105 STC to Southey, 18 September 1794, *CL*, I, 103.

106 Southey to Sara Fricker, 25 October 1794, *New Letters*, I, 85.

107 STC to Southey, 19 September 1794, *CL*, I, 105.

108 See STC to Southey, 13 July 1794, *CL*, I, 85; also Godwin's account of Coleridge, Abinger–Shelley Papers ('Southey never knew a woman').

109 STC to Southey, 19 September 1794, *CL*, I, 106.

110 'To a Young Lady with a Poem on the French Revolution' and 'To Miss Brunton', *PW*, I, 64–6, 67–8.

111 STC to Southey, 26 September 1794, *CL*, I, 109, 110.

112 STC to Southey, 21 October 1794, *CL*, I, 112, 113.

113 *CL*, I, 118.

114 STC to Southey, 3 November 1794, *CL*, I, 123.

115 'The Sigh', *CL*, I, 124; *PW*, I, 63.

116 STC to Southey, 9 and 29 December 1794, *CL*, I, 132, 145.

CHAPTER 3   BRISTOL AND MARRIAGE 1795–1796

1   *Die Räuber* was translated by A. F. Tytler in 1792, see Bayard Quincy Morgan, *A Critical Bibliography of German Literature in English Translation 1481–1927*, second edition revised (New York, 1965).

2   STC to Southey, 3 November 1794, *CL*, I, 122.

3   'The Man at the Gate', p. 70.

4   See Richard Holmes, *Shelley: The Pursuit* (London, 1974), pp. 328–9 (quoting from Dr Polidori's diary for 18 June 1816).

5   See *The Journals of Mary Shelley 1814–44*, ed. Paula R. Feldman and Diana Scott-Kilvert, 2 vols. (Oxford, 1987), II, 474, 573 (18 January 1824, 16 April 1841).

6   *PW*, I, 72–3.

7   'To the Rev. W. L. Bowles', STC to Southey, 11 December 1794, *CL*, I, 136; *PW*, I, 84.

8   See A. Aspinall, *Politics and the Press circa 1780–1850* (London, 1949). p. 69.

9   See STC to Southey, 17 December 1794, *CL*, I, 138; also P. H. Marshall, *William Godwin* (New Haven, Connecticut, 1984), p. 125.

10 'William Godwin', *Complete Works of William Hazlitt*, ed. P. P. Howe, 21 vols. (London, 1930–4), XI, 17.

11 STC to Southey, 11 September 1794, *CL*, I, 102.

12 STC to Southey, 17 December 1794, *CL*, I, 138–9. See also Carlyon, *Early Years*, I, 245.

13 Note by Godwin, C. Kegan Paul, *William Godwin: His Friends and Contemporaries*, 2 vols. (London, 1876), I, 357.

14 'To William Godwin', *Morning Chronicle*, 10 January 1795; *PW*, I, 86.

15 See Goodwin, *Friends of Liberty*, pp. 345ff.

16 'Sonnets on Eminent Characters', *PW*, I, 79–90.

17 STC to Southey, 29 December 1794, *CL*, I, 146.

18 STC to Southey, 2 January 1795, *CL*, I, 148.

19 *CL*, I, 148n.

20 Southey to Edith Fricker, 12 January 1795, *New Letters*, I, 91.

21 Sara Coleridge in a memoir dictated to her daughter in 1843, Lefebure, *Bondage of Love*, p. 41.

22 *Memoir and Letters of Sara Coleridge*, I, 11.

23 STC to George Dyer, late February 1795, *CL*, I, 151.

24 STC to Southey, 29 December 1794, *CL*, I, 147.

25 See Lefebure, *Bondage of Love*, p. 24.

26 See STC, *Lectures on Politics and Religion*, *CW*, 1, 232, 244–5n.

27 Southey, Preface to *Joan of Arc, Poetical Works*, 10 vols. (London, 1837–8), I, xviii.

28 Cottle, *Early Recollections*, I, 7.

29 Ibid., I, 10.

30 For details of Cottle's connection with Coleridge and his mishandling of documents, see *CL*, I, 153; also Lewis Patton, Introduction to *Lectures on Politics and Religion*, *CW*, 1, xxvii.

31 STC to Dyer, late February 1795, *CL*, I, 152.

32 Hazlitt, *Spirit of the Age, Complete Works*, XI, 34.

33 See STC, *The Friend* (1818), ed. Barbara E. Rooke, 2 vols. (London, 1969), in *CW*, 4:I, 326.

34 STC to Sir George and Lady Beaumont, 1 October 1803, *CL*, II, 1000–1.

35 Virginia Woolf, 'The Man at the Gate', p. 70.

36 *CW*, 1, 4.

37 *CW*, 1, 10–14.

38 See Mrs Thelwall, *Life*, p. 310; also STC, *CW*, 1, xxxi.

39 Cottle, *Early Recollections*, I, 20; *Monthly Magazine*, XLVIII (October 1819), 203.

40 For the complicated story of the lectures and pamphlet see *CW*, 1, 22–3.

41 *CW*, 1, xxi, 29n.

42 See Mrs Sandford, I, 135.

43 *Conciones*, *CW*, 1, 54–5.

44 *CW*, 1, 63. See Mary Dorothy George, *Catalogue of Political and Personal Satires*, VI (London, 1978), 833–4.

45 *CW*, 1, 64.

46 *CW*, 1, 69.

47 See Mrs Sandford, I, 111n; also Mrs Thelwall, p. 321.

48 STC, 'Lecture on the Slave Trade', *CW*, 1, 241–2, 243.

49 *CW*, 1, 248, 250–1.

50 See Goodwin, *Friends of Liberty*, pp. 387–8.

51 *Friend*, 8 June 1809, *CW*, 4:II, 25 and n.
52 Southey to Charles Danvers, 15 June 1809, *New Letters*, I, 511.
53 STC, 'Lecture on the Two Bills', *CW*, 1, 262.
54 *CW*, 1, 268–9.
55 For a discussion of the probable date of publication see *CW*, 1, 278.
56 *CW*, 1, 285–6.
57 *CW*, 1, 296–7.
58 *The Observer. Part 1st. Being a Transient Glance at about Forty Youths of Bristol* (Bristol, 1795), p. 15.
59 Cottle, *Early Recollections*, I, 178.
60 *The Observer*, p. 15.
61 Samuel Johnson in conversation, 24 May 1763, see James Boswell, *Life of Johnson*, ed. G. B. Hill, revised L. F. Powell, 6 vols. (Oxford, 1971–5), I, 397.
62 Cottle, *Early Recollections*, I, xxxi.
63 STC to Thelwall, 19 November 1796, *CL*, I, 259–60.
64 Cottle, *Early Recollections*, I, 146.
65 STC to Sir George and Lady Beaumont, 1 October 1803, *CL*, II, 1000.
66 See *CW*, 1, xxv.
67 *CW*, 1, 89–92.
68 David Hartley, *Observations on Man, His Frame, His Duty, and His Expectations* (1749, reprinted ed. Hermann Pistorius, 1791); see *CW*, 1, lix–lx. See also STC to Southey, 11 December 1794, *CL*, I, 137.
69 *CW*, 1, 105–6. See the long editorial notes on STC's various utterances on the problem of evil, ibid., 105–8n.
70 *CW*, 1, 207–8.
71 *CN*, II, 2448.
72 See STC, 'Superstition, Religion, Atheism (An Allegoric Vision)', *Courier*, 31 August 1811, *Essays on His Times*, ed. David V. Erdman, 3 vols. (London, 1978) in *CW*, 3:II, 262ff.
73 Southey to Grosvenor Bedford, 8 February 1795, *Life and Correspondence*, I, 231.
74 Ibid., I, 231, 232.
75 Southey to Grosvenor Bedford, 27 May 1795, ibid., I, 239.
76 Cottle, *Early Recollections*, I, 41–9.
77 See STC, *CL*, I, 157n; Southey, *Life and Correspondence*, I, 250.
78 STC to Southey, early August 1795, *CL*, I, 158.
79 STC to Southey, 13 November 1795, *CL*, 163–5.
80 See *New Letters*, I, xvi, xvii.
81 STC to Southey, 13 November 1795, *CL*, I, 165–6.
82 *CL*, I, 168.
83 *CL*, I, 171.
84 *CL*, I, 172, 173.
85 See Lefebure, *Bondage of Love*, p. 17.
86 *PW*, I, 100. See Paul Magnuson, ' "The Eolian Harp" in Context', *Studies in Romanticism*, XXIV (1985), 3–20, for an account of the different versions of this poem from its beginnings as 'Effusion XXXV' in Coleridge's *Poems* of 1796.
87 Carlyon, *Early Years*, I, 180.
88 *PW*, I, 99–100.
89 Forster, 'Trooper Silas Tomkyn Comberbacke'. p. 250.

90   *Table Talk, CW*, 14:I, 208 (26 September 1830).
91   *Westminster Review*, January 1830, in *Critical Heritage*, p. 539.
92   *PW*, I, 100–1.
93   See M. H. Abrams, *The Mirror and the Lamp: Romantic Theory and the Critical Tradition* (Oxford, 1953, reprinted 1958), p. 51.
94   *The Statesman's Manual, Lay Sermons*, ed. R. J. White (London, 1972) in *CW*, 6, 30.
95   STC to Poole, 7 October 1795, *CL*, I, 160.
96   STC to Cottle, 5 October 1795, *CL*, I, 160.
97   STC to Poole, 7 October 1795, *CL*, I, 161.
98   Poole to STC, 10 October 1795, Mrs Sandford, I, 121–2.
99   See Stephen Gill, *William Wordsworth: A Life* (Oxford, 1989), pp. 83–4, 92.
100 The house, in Great George Street, Bristol, is now a museum.
101 Wordsworth to William Mathews, 24 October 1795, *Letters of William and Dorothy Wordsworth*, ed. E. De Selincourt, *The Early Years, 1787–1805*, revised Chester L. Shaver (Oxford, 1967), p. 153 (henceforth referred to as *EY*).
102 *PW*, I, 97.
103 Wordsworth, *Poetical Works*, pp. 466, 467.
104 See Dorothy A. Stansfield, *Thomas Beddoes M. D.: Chemist, Physician, Democrat* (Boston, Massachusetts, 1984), pp. 74–9.
105 Report of the meeting in the *Star*, 23 November 1795, *CW*, 1, 359.
106 *CW*, 1, 361, xlvi and n. See also STC's note to 'Religious Musings', line 159, in which he quotes Lord Abingdon in Parliament on 30 May 1794 saying 'the best road to Peace, my Lords, is WAR!', *PW*, I, 115n.
107 *CW*, 1, xlv–xlvi, 370ff.
108 STC to Poole, 7 October 1795, *CL*, I, 161.
109 See STC, *The Watchman*, ed. Lewis Patton (London, 1970) in *CW*, 2, xxix.
110 STC to Josiah Wade, 18 January 1796, *CL*, I, 176.
111 See *Biographia Literaria*, *CW*, 7:I, 179.
112 STC to Wade, 2 February 1796, *CL*, I, 180.
113 Cottle, *Early Recollections*, I, xxxi, 179.
114 STC to Wade, 27 January 1796, *CL*, I, 177.
115 STC to Wade, 10 January 1796, *CL*, I, 175.
116 STC to Wade, *circa* 10 February 1796, *CL*, I, 184.
117 De Quincey, *Confessions of an English Opium-Eater* (London, 1822, reprinted in facsimile, Oxford, 1989), p. 156.
118 *Monthly Magazine*, II (October 1796), 712; *PW*, I, 107.
119 *The Watchman*, *CW*, 2, xxxiii, 5.
120 *Watchman*, 1 March 1796, *CW*, 2, 10.
121 *Watchman*, 9 March 1796, *CW*, 2, 54–5.
122 STC to John Edwards, 20 March 1796, *CL*, I, 191.
123 *Biographia Literaria*, *CW*, 7:I, 184, 179.
124 *Watchman*, 13 May 1796, *CW*, 2, 375.
125 STC to Edwards, 20 March 1796, *CL*, I, 192.
126 See STC to Cottle, *circa* 12 March 1796, and to Poole, 30 March 1796, *CL*, I, 189, 194.
127 See Mrs Sandford, II, 133, 137n.
128 See *CW*, 4:II, 497.
129 STC to Poole, 5 May 1796, *CL*, I, 208–9.
130 See *CL*, I, 195n.
131 STC to Poole, 11 April 1796, *CL*, I, 203.

132　See John Thelwall, *Prospectus of a Course of Lectures* (London, 1796), pp. 19–20.

133　STC to Thelwall, late April 1796, *CL*, I, 205.

134　'Religious Musings' (1796), *PW*, I, 114n, 116, 121.

135　STC to Edwards, 20 March 1796, *CL*, I, 192.

136　*PW*, I, 108–9n (version of 1796).

137　*Table Talk*, *CW*, 14:I, 442 (2 September 1833). For a detailed critical discussion of the Unitarianism of 'Religious Musings' see Ian Wylie, *Young Coleridge and the Philosophers of Nature* (Oxford, 1989), pp. 95–6.

138　*PW*, I, 117, 122–3, 118 (version of 1796).

139　STC to John Prior Estlin, 4 July 1796, *CL*, I, 224.

140　*Poems by S. T. Coleridge. Second Edition, to which are now added Poems by Charles Lamb and Charles Lloyd* (Bristol, 1797), p. xvii.

141　STC to Poole, 5 May 1796, *CL*, I, 209–10.

142　Poole's copybook, 28 March 1796, Mrs Sandford, I, 142–3.

143　STC to Estlin, 4 July 1796, *CL*, I, 222.

144　See *CL*, I, 228n; STC to Poole, 22 August 1796, *CL*, I, 231.

145　STC to Estlin, 22 August 1796, *CL*, I, 232.

146　STC to Poole, 24 September 1796, *CL*, I, 234.

147　*CL*, I, 236.

148　'Sonnet to a Friend who asked, how I felt when the Nurse first presented my Infant to Me', *PW*, I, 154.

CHAPTER 4　NETHER STOWEY AND *KUBLA KHAN* 1796–1797

1　Lamb to STC, 27 May 1796, *Letters*, ed. Marrs, I, 3–4.

2　Ibid., I, xxxiv.

3　Lamb to STC, 31 May 1796, ibid., I, 10–11.

4　Ibid., I, 10.

5　Lamb to STC, 8–10 June 1796, ibid., I, 23.

6　Lamb to STC, 27 September 1796, ibid., I, 44.

7　Lamb to STC, 1 December 1796, ibid., I, 66.

8　Lamb to STC, 27 September 1796, ibid., I, 44. Only the first of Coleridge's letters survives. In December 1796 Lamb confessed to having burnt many of his papers and to having lent Coleridge's letters to a friend and not got them back, ibid., I. 78.

9　STC to Lamb, 28 September 1796, *CL*, I, 239.

10　Lamb to STC, 17 October 1796, *Letters*, I, 51–2.

11　Lamb to STC, 7–10 January 1797, ibid., I, 90.

12　STC to Lloyd senior, 15 October 1796, *CL*, I, 240; see also I, 397.

13　See *CL*, I, 288n. Coleridge's cottage is now a National Trust property.

14　Mrs Sandford, I, 202.

15　STC to Poole, 5 November 1796, *CL*, I, 249–50.

16　STC to Poole, 7 November 1796, *CL*, I, 251.

17　STC to Poole, 15 November 1796, *CL*, I, 257.

18　STC to Poole, 13 December 1796, *CL*, I, 271–2.

19　*CL*, I, 272–3, 275.

20　Lamb to STC, 1 December 1796, and 7–10 January 1797, *Letters*, I, 65, 87.

21　Lamb to STC, 8 November 1796, and 7–10 January 1797, ibid., I, 60, 87.

22　*CN*, I, 161.

23 STC to Thelwall, 13 May 1796, *CL*, I, 216.
24 *CL*, I, 215–16.
25 *Watchman*, 17 March 1796, *CW*, 2, 98–9 and n.
26 STC to Thelwall, 13 May 1796, *CL*, I, 213.
27 Gerrald appears to have been a Jekyll and Hyde figure, agitating for reform while secretly working on behalf of slave owners, see Peter Mann, 'Coleridge, Joseph Gerrald, and the Slave Trade', *The Wordsworth Circle*, VIII (Winter 1977), 38–46.
28 STC to Benjamin Flower, 11 December 1796, *CL*, I, 267.
29 Unpublished notebook, dated 7 October 1833, in British Library (Add. MS 47,548, ff. 25v–26).
30 STC to Thelwall, 22 June 1796, *CL*, I, 221.
31 STC to Thelwall, 19 November 1796, *CL*, I, 259–60.
32 STC to Thelwall, 17 December 1796, *CL*, I, 280–1, 278.
33 *Biographia Literaria*, *CW*, 7:I, 117, 120 (chapter 7).
34 *Table Talk*, *CW*, 14:I, 312 (21 July 1832).
35 See *CL*, I, 294n.
36 Lamb to STC, 28 October 1796, *Letters*, I, 57.
37 STC to Southey, 27 December 1796, *CL*, I, 290, 291.
38 STC to Thelwall, 31 December 1796, *CL*, I, 294.
39 STC to Cottle, 6 January 1797, to Estlin, January 1797, and to Thelwall, 6 February 1797, *CL*, I, 296–7, 301, 308.
40 See, for example, *EY*, p. 180.
41 *CN*, I, 161, 162 (1796).
42 *Poems* (Bristol, 1797), p. 244.
43 Ibid., p. xvii.
44 'Ode on the Departing Year', *PW*, I, 166.
45 Cottle, *Early Recollections*, I, 147.
46 Lamb to STC, 14 November 1796, *Letters*, I, 64.
47 'To the Rev. George Coleridge', *PW*, I, 174. Coleridge remembered Boyer's injunction in *Biographia Literaria*, *CW*, 7:I, 10 and n.
48 *PW*, I, 173n.
49 *Critical Review*, XXIII (July 1798), in *Critical Heritage*, p. 42.
50 Southey to John May, 11 July 1797, *Life and Correspondence*, I, 319.
51 STC to Poole, 6 February 1797, *CL*, I, 302.
52 STC to Poole, 16 October 1797, *CL*, I, 354.
53 Lamb to STC, 5 February 1797, *Letters*, I, 94.
54 'The Destiny of Nations', *PW*, I, 135 and n.
55 *Critical Review*, XIX (February 1797), 194–7.
56 STC to Richard Brinsley Sheridan, 6 February 1797, *CL*, I, 304.
57 STC to Bowles, 16 March 1797, *CL*, I, 318.
58 See Southey to C. W. Williams Wynn, 16 August 1797, and to Charles Danvers, 5 September 1797, *New Letters*, I, 141, 144.
59 Ibid., I, 144.
60 STC to Cottle, early April 1797, *CL*, I, 319.
61 Lamb to STC, 7 April 1797, *Letters*, I, 105.
62 Lamb to STC, 15 April 1797, ibid., I, 109.
63 Lamb to STC, 12 June 1797, ibid., I, 110.
64 STC to Cottle, early April 1797, *CL*, I, 319.
65 *CL*, I, 320.

66 See Gill, pp. 115–19, for Wordsworth's financial position in the spring of 1797.
67 Mary Wordsworth to Sara Coleridge junior, 7 November 1845, *Letters of William and Dorothy Wordsworth*, ed. E. De Selincourt, *The Later Years 1821–53*, revised Alan G. Hill, 4 vols. (Oxford, 1987–8), IV, 719 (henceforth referred to as *LY*).
68 Dorothy Wordsworth to Mary Hutchinson, June 1797, *EY*, pp. 188–9.
69 STC to Cottle, 8 June 1797, and to Estlin, 10 June 1797, *CL*, I, 325, 327.
70 STC to Estlin, 8 June 1797, *CL*, I, 325.
71 STC to Cottle, 8 June 1797, *CL*, I, 325.
72 For discussions of *Osorio* and its reworking as *Remorse* see G. Wilson Knight, *The Starlit Dome* (London, 1941, reprinted 1959), pp. 143ff; Katharine Cooke, *Coleridge* (London, 1979), pp. 46–9; and Brian Morris, 'Coleridge and Other People', *The Wordsworth Circle*, X (Autumn 1979), 356–64.
73 *Osorio*, V, lines 303–6, *PW*, II, 596.
74 *PW*, II, 1114 (Appendix IV); Carlyon, *Early Years*, I, 143–4.
75 STC to Cottle, 3 July 1797, *CL*, I, 330–1.
76 De Quincey, 'The Lake Poets: William Wordsworth', *Tait's Magazine* (January–April 1839), in *Collected Writings*, ed. David Masson, 14 vols. (Edinburgh, 1889–90), II, 238–9.
77 Dorothy Wordsworth to Mary Hutchinson, 4 July 1797, *EY*, p. 189.
78 Dorothy Wordsworth to Mary Hutchinson, 14 August 1797, ibid., p. 190 and n.
79 STC to Southey, *circa* 17 July 1797, *CL*, I, 334.
80 Lamb to STC, 24 June 1797, *Letters*, I, 113.
81 Lamb to STC, 29 June 1797, ibid., I, 113, 114.
82 STC to Southey, *circa* 17 July 1797, *CL*, I, 334.
83 STC to Thelwall, 17 December 1796, *CL*, I, 279.
84 William Cowper, *The Task*, *Poetical Works*, ed. William Benham (London, 1924), pp. 231, 186, 189.
85 STC to Southey, *circa* 17 July 1797, *CL*, I, 334–6.
86 *Lyrical Ballads*, ed. Brett and Jones, p. 251.
87 STC to Wade, 1 August 1797, and to John Chubb, 20 August 1797, *CL*, I, 339, 343.
88 Thelwall to his wife, 18 July 1797, Mrs Sandford, I, 232–3.
89 Ibid., I, 223.
90 Thelwall, *Poems, chiefly written in Retirement* (London, 1801), pp. 127, 129, 130, 131.
91 Cottle, *Early Recollections*, I, 275–7.
92 *Table Talk*, *CW*, 14:I, 180–1 (24 July 1830).
93 STC to Thelwall, 21 August 1797, *CL*, I, 343.
94 See *Biographia Literaria*, *CW*, 7:I, 193–7, For Coleridge and Thelwall see E. P. Thompson, 'Disenchantment or Default? A Lay Sermon', in *Power and Consciousness*, ed. Conor Cruise O'Brien and William Dean Vanech (London, 1969), pp. 149–81; and Roe, 'Coleridge and John Thelwall', in *The Coleridge Connection*, pp. 60ff.
95 Quoted in Roe, *Wordsworth and Coleridge*, p. 248. Roe gives the fullest account of the episode, quoting from Home Office documents, pp. 248–62.
96 Ibid., pp. 258, 260, 261.
97 See Roe, 'Coleridge and Thelwall', p. 76.

98 STC to Wade, 1 August 1797, *CL*, I, 339.
99 Dorothy Wordsworth to Mary Hutchinson, *EY*, p. 194.
100 There is one puzzling exception. Dorothy Wordsworth talks in her journal in Germany in October 1798 of 'carrying *Kubla* to a fountain' to drink water, which may be a play on the German word for bucket (Kübel). See Schneider, *Coleridge, Opium and 'Kubla Khan'*, pp. 216–18.
101 STC, *PW*, I, 295.
102 Hazlitt, *Examiner* (June 1816), in *Critical Heritage*, p. 208.
103 See E. H. Coleridge's editorial note, STC, *PW*, I, 295.
104 See T. C. Skeat, 'Kubla Khan', *British Museum Quarterly*, XXVI (1962–3), 77–83, for a good summing up of the problems surrounding the poem's composition. See also Holmes, *Coleridge*, pp. 162–7. Hilton Kelliher, in 'The *Kubla Khan* Manuscript and its First Collector', *The British Library Journal*, XX (Autumn 1994), 184–98, brings evidence to suggest that the manuscript was given by Southey to Mrs Elizabeth Smith in February 1804.
105 STC to Thelwall, 14 October 1797, *CL*, I, 350–1.
106 See Schneider, *Coleridge, Opium and 'Kubla Khan'*, pp. 272ff, for a discussion of the rhyming of the poem and a comparison with Milton's *Lycidas*.
107 The most famous and exhaustive study of sources is J. Livingston Lowes, *The Road to Xanadu: A Study in the Ways of the Imagination* (Cambridge, Massachusetts, 1927).
108 STC to George Coleridge, *circa* 10 March 1798, *CL*, I, 394.
109 Southey to John May, 6 October 1797, *New Letters*, I, 152.
110 STC to Cottle, *circa* 20 November 1797, *CL*, I, 357.
111 Dorothy Wordsworth to Mary Hutchinson, 20 November 1797, *EY*, p. 194.
112 STC to Estlin, 9 June 1797, *CL*, I, 326.
113 STC to Estlin, 23 July 1797, *CL*, I, 337–8.
114 See R. B. Litchfield, *Tom Wedgwood: The First Photographer* (London, 1903), and Barbara and Hensleigh Wedgwood, *The Wedgwood Circle 1730–1897* (London, 1980).
115 See Stansfield, *Thomas Beddoes*, pp. 145ff.
116 See Ian Wylie, 'Coleridge and the Lunaticks', *The Coleridge Connection*, pp. 25ff.
117 See Stansfield, p. 159.
118 See Litchfield, pp. 45ff.
119 James Mackintosh to STC, 17 November 1797, *CL*, I, 359–60n.
120 See STC to Estlin, 30 December 1797, *CL*, I, 363.
121 See STC, *Essays on His Times*, *CW*, 3:III, 286.
122 See *CL*, I, 363.
123 STC to Josiah Wedgwood, 27 December 1797, *CL*, I, 361.
124 STC to Josiah Wedgwood, 5 January 1798, *CL*, I, 364–5.
125 *CL*, I, 366–7.
126 STC to Estlin, 6 January 1798, *CL*, I, 368.
127 Tom and Josiah Wedgwood to STC, 10 January 1798, *CL*, I, 373–4n.
128 Mrs Sandford, I, 259–61.
129 Southey in conversation with Henry Crabb Robinson, 24 July 1811, *Blake, Coleridge, Wordsworth etc.*, p. 43.
130 STC to Estlin, 16 January 1798, *CL*, I, 371.
131 *The Liberal* (April 1823). This is an enlarged version of a letter Hazlitt published in the *Examiner* on 12 January 1817. Both are republished in *Complete Works*.
132 Lamb to Wordsworth, 23 September 1816, *Letters*, III, 224–5.

133 Hazlitt, *Complete Works*, XVII, 107.
134 Ibid., XVII, 108–9. The passage in French, celebrating passages from youth which can never be effaced from the memory, is from Rousseau's *Confessions*; the description of Coleridge's voice rising 'like a steam of rich distilled perfumes' is from Milton's *Comus*; the quotation about the 'once-lov'd poet' is from Pope's 'Epistle to Robert, Earl of Oxford'.

CHAPTER 5 *THE ANCIENT MARINER* 1798

1 See Jonathan Bate, *Shakespeare and the English Romantic Imagination* (Oxford, 1986).
2 'Fire, Famine, and Slaughter', *PW*, I, 237, 239.
3 STC to Wordsworth, 23 January 1798, *CL*, I, 378.
4 See Wordsworth, *Letters, EY*, p. 211n.
5 STC to Wordsworth, 23 January 1798, *CL*, I, 379 and n. For 'Sir Cauline' see *Reliques of Ancient English Poetry*, ed. Thomas Percy, 3 vols. (London, 1765), I, 35ff.
6 See Ashton, *The German Idea*, pp. 5, 10.
7 *Courier*, 29 August 1916, reprinted in *Biographia Literaria*, *CW*, 7:II, 211, 212.
8 Ibid., 7:II, 211.
9 See *CL*, I, 411n.
10 STC, prefatory note to 'The Wanderings of Cain' (1828), *PW*, I, 287.
11 Hazlitt, 'My First Acquaintance with Poets', *Complete Works*, XVII, 120.
12 'The Wanderings of Cain', *PW*, I, 287, 289.
13 Genesis 4. 12–16.
14 See Mary Moorman, *William Wordsworth: A Biography*, 2 vols. (Oxford, 1957, 1965), I, 347–8.
15 STC to George Coleridge, *circa* 10 March 1798, *CL*, I, 396.
16 See Lowes, *The Road to Xanadu*, pp. 221ff.
17 'The Rime of the Ancyent Marinere' (1798), *PW*, II, 1031–2.
18 *PW*, II, 1037, 1041.
19 *Paradise Lost*, Book IX, lines 445–57.
20 *PW*, II, 1033.
21 *PW*, II, 1033.
22 Leigh Hunt, *Autobiography*, p. 301.
23 See *CN*, I, 174 (Notes).
24 *PW*, II, 1038.
25 *PW*, II, 1047.
26 *Table Talk*, *CW*, 14:I, 272–3 (31 March 1832).
27 *Table Talk*, *CW*, 14:I, 149 (30 May 1830).
28 *Table Talk*, *CW*, 14:I, 273–4 (31 March 1832).
29 *Biographia Literaria*, *CW*, 7:II, 6 (chapter 14). Some of the most influential of the many critical studies of 'The Ancient Mariner' are Robert Penn Warren, 'A Poem of Pure Imagination', *Selected Essays* (New York, 1941, revised 1958); Humphry House, 'The Ancient Mariner', *Coleridge: The Clark Lectures 1951–2* (London, 1953); Paul Magnuson, *Coleridge's Nightmare Poetry* (Charlottesville, Virginia, 1974); and John Beer, *Coleridge's Poetic Intelligence* (London, 1977). Beer points out in a recent essay that Coleridge was aware of his tendency to add morals to his poems, attributing it to 'cowardly fear of the Goody!', 'How Far Can We Trust Coleridge?', *The Wordsworth Circle*, XX (Spring 1989), 82.

30 Leslie Stephen, 'Coleridge', *Hours in a Library*, 3 vols. (London, 1892), III, 358–9.
31 See Dorothy Wordsworth, 'Alfoxden Journal', *Journals*, ed. Mary Moorman (Oxford, 1971, reprinted 1974), p. 11.
32 STC to Cottle, *circa* 20 November 1797, *CL*, I, 357–8.
33 STC to Lamb, early May 1798, *CL*, I, 404.
34 Lloyd, *Edmund Oliver*, I, x, xii.
35 Ibid., I, 210.
36 Ibid., II, 55, 57.
37 See Litchfield, p. 139, and Barbara and Hensleigh Wedgwood, p. 126.
38 Hazlitt, 'My First Acquaintance with Poets', *Complete Works*, XVII, 112.
39 STC to Cottle, *circa* 13 March 1798, and to Lamb, early May 1798, *CL*, I, 399, 405.
40 *PW*, II, 964.
41 See STC *PW*, I, 243.
42 Note by Coleridge on a copy of the poem, *PW*, I, 257n. See Richard T. Martin, 'Coleridge's Use of *sermoni propriora*', *The Wordsworth Circle*, III (Spring 1972), 71–5.
43 *PW*, I, 263.
44 *PW*, I, 240. See Cowper, *The Task*, Book IV, lines 291–310, *Poetical Works*, p. 237.
45 *PW*, I, 242.
46 STC to Sara Coleridge, 18 September 1798, *CL*, I, 417–18.
47 See P. M. Zall, 'Joseph Johnson, or the Perils of Publishing', *The Wordsworth Circle*, III (Winter 1972), 25–30; and Gerald P. Tyson, *Joseph Johnson: A Liberal Publisher* (Iowa, 1979), pp. 135ff.
48 Undated note, *CN*, I, 219.
49 *PW*, I, 267.
50 STC to Wordsworth, 10 May 1798, *CL*, I, 406.
51 For an interesting account of 'The Nightingale' and its sources see Fred V. Randel, 'Coleridge and the Contentiousness of Romantic Nightingales', *Studies in Romanticism*, XXI (1982), 33–55.
52 Thomas Love Peacock, *Nightmare Abbey* (London, 1818, reprinted Harmondsworth, 1969), p. 67.
53 Wordsworth to Losh, 11 March 1798, *EY*, p. 213.
54 Dorothy Wordsworth to Mrs Rawson, 13 June 1798, *EY*, p. 221.
55 Southey to John May, 8 July 1798, *New Letters*, I, 170.
56 See STC to Poole, 3 August 1798, *CL*, I, 414.
57 STC to Cottle, 28 May 1798, *CL*, I, 412.
58 See Paul Magnuson, '"The Eolian Harp" in Context', *Studies in Romanticism*, XXIV (1985), 15.
59 See R. Mayo, 'The Contemporaneity of the *Lyrical Ballads*', *Publications of the Modern Languages Association of America*, LXIX (1954), 486–522.
60 Wordsworth to James Tobin, 6 March 1798, *EY*, p. 212.
61 STC to George Coleridge, 10 March 1798, *CL*, I, 397.
62 See *Lyrical Ballads*, ed. Brett and Jones, p. xviii.
63 Advertisement to 1798 *Lyrical Ballads*, ibid., pp. 7, 8.
64 *CW*, 7:I, 5–7 and notes.
65 *The Prelude* (1805), Book XIII, lines 392–410, Norton edition, p. 480.
66 Cottle, *Early Recollections*, II, 23, 26–7.
67 *Gentleman's Magazine*, LXVIII (September 1798), 774. The article on Coleridge

was in [David Rivers], *Literary Memoirs of Living Authors of Great Britain*, 2 vols. (London, 1798), I, 105–7.

68 *The Anti-Jacobin; or, Weekly Examiner*, no. 36 (9 July 1798), 286.
69 The cartoon appeared as a fold-out page in the *Anti-Jacobin Review and Magazine*, I (July 1798), 115.
70 Southey to Wynn, 15 August 1798, *Life and Correspondence*, I, 345.
71 Lamb to Southey, 28 July 1798, *Letters*, I, 130.
72 Lamb to Coleridge, late May/early June 1798, ibid., I, 128–9.
73 STC to Poole, 3 August and 15 September 1798, *CL*, I, 414, 415.

CHAPTER 6 TO GERMANY AND BACK 1798–1800

1 Hazlitt, 'My First Acquaintance with Poets', *Complete Works*, XVII, 119.
2 Beddoes translated a long passage from *The Critique of Pure Reason* in 'Observations on the Nature of Demonstrative Evidence' (1793), see Stansfield, pp. 93–4. For details of translations of Kant's works in England see Morgan, *Critical Bibliography*, pp. 257–60.
3 STC to Poole, 5 May 1796, and to Thelwall, 17 December 1796, *CL*, I, 209, 284n.
4 For an account of Coleridge's German studies see *CN*, I, 451–4 (Notes, Appendix A).
5 STC to Poole, 15 September 1798, *CL*, I, 415.
6 STC to Sara Coleridge, 18 September 1798, *CL*, I, 415–16.
7 *CL*, I, 416.
8 STC to Sara Coleridge, 3 October 1798, *CL*, I, 424–6.
9 Ibid., I, 421.
10 STC to Sara Coleridge, 20 October 1798, *CL*, I, 429.
11 Ibid., I, 429, 430.
12 Poole to STC, 8 October 1798, Mrs Sandford, I, 278.
13 STC to Poole, 26 October 1798, *CL*, I, 435.
14 STC to Poole, 20 November 1798, *CL*, I, 442, 443.
15 Ibid., I, 445.
16 Lamb to Southey, 28 November 1798, *Letters*, I, 152.
17 Poole to STC, 8 October 1798, Mrs Sandford, I, 278.
18 Josiah Wedgwood to Poole, 1 February 1799, unpublished Correspondence of Thomas Poole, BL Add. MS 35,345, f. 122.
19 Poole to STC, 8 October 1798, Mrs Sandford, I, 279–80.
20 STC to Poole, 4 January 1799, *CL*, I, 454–5.
21 STC to Wordsworth, early December 1798, *CL*, I, 451–2; *PW*, I, 304–5.
22 *CN*, I, 372–3 (1798–9).
23 See STC to Poole, 20 November 1798, and to Sara Coleridge, 14 January 1799, *CL*, I, 445, 459.
24 Wordsworth and Dorothy Wordsworth to STC, 14 or 21 December 1798, *EY*, pp. 236–42.
25 STC to Wordsworth, 10 December 1798, *CL*, I, 452–3.
26 STC to Sara Coleridge, 26 November 1798, *CL*, I, 446.
27 MS The Wordsworth Trust, Dove Cottage, Grasmere. Published, with variations, and with 'Frederic' for 'Hartley' in the last verse, in the *Morning Post*, 19 October 1802; *PW*, I, 387.

28 Sara Coleridge to STC, 1 November 1798, Lefebure, *Bondage of Love*, pp. 105–7.

29 Sara Coleridge to STC, 13 December 1798, ibid., p. 108.

30 STC to Sara Coleridge, 2 December 1798, *CL*, I, 449.

31 Poole to STC, 22 November 1798, Mrs Sandford, I, 281–2.

32 Sara Coleridge to STC, 13 December 1798, *Bondage of Love*, p. 109.

33 Poole to STC, 24 January 1799, Mrs Sandford, I, 284–5.

34 Sara Coleridge to Poole, 11 February 1799, *Minnow Among Tritons: Mrs S. T. Coleridge's Letters to Thomas Poole 1799–1834*, ed, Stephen Potter (London, 1934), p. 1.

35 Lamb in conversation with Henry Crabb Robinson, 8 January 1823, *Henry Crabb Robinson On Books*, I, 289.

36 STC to Sara Coleridge, 10 March 1799, *CL*, I, 470.

37 Poole to Josiah Wedgwood, February or March 1799, Litchfield, *Tom Wedgwood*, pp. 66–7.

38 Poole to STC, 15 March 1799, Mrs Sandford, I, 292–3.

39 Sara Coleridge to STC, 25 March 1799, MS Coleridge Collection, Harry Ransom Humanities Research Center, University of Texas at Austin.

40 Sara Coleridge to STC, 15 May 1799, MS Harry Ransom Humanities Research Center.

41 STC to Sara Coleridge, 8 April 1799, *CL*, I, 482–3.

42 *CN*, I, 377 (1798–9). For a succinct account of the similarities between Coleridge and Lessing see Basil Willey, *Samuel Taylor Coleridge* (London, 1972), pp. 75–6.

43 STC to Sara Coleridge, 8 November 1798, *CL*, I, 437.

44 STC to Poole, 4 January 1799, *CL*, I, 455; Carlyon, *Early Years*, I, 100.

45 STC to Sara Coleridge, 23 April 1799, *CL*, I, 484.

46 *Anti-Jacobin; or, Weekly Examiner*, nos 30–1 (4 and 11 June 1798), 237–9, 243–6.

47 STC to Sara Coleridge, 23 April 1799, *CL*, I, 484.

48 STC to John Morgan, 14 May 1814, *CL*, III, 489–90.

49 Carlyon, *Early Years*, I, 191; see also E. S. Shaffer, *'Kubla Khan' and The Fall of Jerusalem* (Cambridge, 1975).

50 Quoted in Carlyon, *Early Years*, I, 100–1.

51 Ibid., I, 101, 162.

52 STC to Poole, 6 May 1799, *CL*, I, 490–1.

53 STC to Sara Coleridge, 6 May 1799, *CL*, I, 496.

54 STC to Sara Coleridge, 17 May 1799, *CL*, I, 503.

55 Carlyon, I, 43; see also Gillman, *Life*, pp. 140–1n.

56 STC to Sara Coleridge, 17 May 1799, *CL*, I, 504–5; *PW*, I, 315–16.

57 Carlyon, I, 29, 33, 51, 127, 138, 141.

58 STC to Josiah Wedgwood, 21 May 1799, *CL*, I, 518–19.

59 Wordsworth to Cottle, 24 June 1799, *EY*, p. 264.

60 See *The Critical Heritage*, pp. 51–9; Wordsworth, *EY*, pp. 267–8n.

61 Southey to Wynn, 17 December 1798, *New Letters*, I, 177.

62 Wordsworth to Cottle, summer 1799, *EY*, pp. 267–8.

63 *The Critical Heritage*, p. 53.

64 Sara Coleridge to Poole, March 1799, *Minnow*, p. 4.

65 *The Critical Heritage*, pp. 52, 56.

66 Francis Jeffrey to George Bell, 21 March 1799, *Memorials of the Life and Writings of the Rev. Robert Morehead, D. D.*, ed. Charles Morehead (Edinburgh, 1875), p. 102.

67 Lamb to Southey, 8 November 1798, *Letters*, I, 142–3.
68 Southey to Tom Southey [October 1798], Southey Correspondence, BL Add. MS 30,927, ff.34–5. Southey published the poem in the 1837–8 edition of his *Poetical Works*, II, 61–6. See Chris Rubinstein, 'A New Identity for the Mariner', *The Coleridge Bulletin*, III (Winter 1990), 16–29.
69 STC to Southey, 29 July 1799, *CL*, I, 523.
70 STC to Southey, 8 August 1799, *CL*, I, 524; Southey to Tom Southey, 6 September 1799, *New Letters*, I, 199 and n.
71 Southey to John May, 3 September 1799, *Selections from the Letters of Robert Southey*, ed. John Wood Warter, 4 vols. (London, 1856), I, 81, 82–3.
72 STC to Poole, 16 September 1799, *CL*, I, 528.
73 Southey to Charles Danvers, 20 August 1799, *Selected Letters*, ed. Warter, I, 78.
74 See Wilfrid Hindle, *The Morning Post 1772–1937: Portrait of a Newspaper* (London, 1937), pp. 89–92.
75 Southey, *Poetical Works*, III, 84.
76 'The Devil's Thoughts', STC, *PW*, I, 321, 322.
77 Southey to Tom Southey, 6 September 1799, *New Letters*, I, 200.
78 STC to George Coleridge, 29 September 1799, *CL*, I, 532.
79 See *PW*, I, 327 and n.
80 Southey to William Taylor, *A Memoir of the Life and Writings of the late William Taylor of Norwich*, ed. J. W. Robberds, 2 vols. (London, 1843), I, 294.
81 *PW*, I, 329.
82 Southey to Wynn, 30 March 1799, *New Letters*, I, 183.
83 Cottle, *Early Recollections*, II, 33.
84 Southey to William Taylor, *A Memoir*, I, 293.
85 Humphry Davy, *Researches, Chemical and Philosophical; chiefly concerning Nitrous Oxide, or Dephlogisticated Nitrous Air, and its Respiration* (London, 1800), p. 516.
86 David Knight, *Humphry Davy*, p. 30.
87 For Davy and Coleridge see David Knight, pp. 26–41, and Molly Lefebure, 'Consolations in Opium: The Expanding Universe of Coleridge, Humphry Davy and "The Recluse"', *The Wordsworth Circle*, XVII (Spring 1986), 51–60.
88 See Lefebure, *Bondage of Love*, p. 122.
89 STC to Southey, 25 September 1799, *CL*, I, 530.
90 STC to Southey, 30 September 1799, *CL*, I, 534.
91 *CL*, I, 534, 536.
92 See Southey to STC, 11 October 1799, *New Letters*, I, 203.
93 STC to Southey, 15 October 1799, *CL*, I, 540.
94 Sara Coleridge to Mrs George Coleridge, 2 November 1799, Lefebure, *Bondage of Love*, p. 123.
95 See STC to Southey, 10 November 1799, *CL*, I, 545.
96 STC to Southey, 30 September 1799, *CL*, I, 533.
97 *CN*, I, 493 (October 1799).
98 STC to Dorothy Wordsworth, *circa* 10 November 1799, *CL*, I, 543.
99 Wordsworth to Dorothy Wordsworth, 8 November 1799, *EY*, p. 272.
100 *CN*, I, 523, 556 (November 1799).
101 STC to Southey, 10 November 1799, *CL*, I, 545.
102 *CN*, I, 578, 1575 and Notes (November 1799, October 1803).
103 Sara Coleridge junior to Edith Coleridge, 8 September 1851, *Memoir and Letters*, I, 19–20.

104 *PW*, II, 1053–9.
105 See STC to Cottle, *circa* 1 December 1799, *CL*, I, 547.
106 See STC to Southey, 19 December 1799, *CL*, I, 547–8; and Southey to STC, 27 December 1799 and 8 January 1800, *Life and Correspondence*, I, 36, 40.
107 STC to Southey, 19 December 1799, *CL*, I, 549.
108 *Beauties of the Anti-Jacobin* (London, 1799), p. 306.
109 See *CW*, 4:II, 22–3 and n., and 7:I, 67–8n.
110 Daniel Stuart to Sara Coleridge, 9 February 1799, *Essays on His Times*, *CW*, 3:III, 165.
111 Ibid., 3:III, 288–9.
112 Ibid., 3:I, lxxxviff.
113 *PW*, I, 339.
114 STC to Josiah Wedgwood, 4 February 1800, *CL*, I, 568–9.
115 For a detailed discussion of the row see Erdman's introduction to *Essays on His Times*, *CW*, 3:I; see also Chambers, *Samuel Taylor Coleridge*, pp. 120–4.
116 See STC to Poole, 21 March 1800, *CL*, I, 582.
117 *Morning Post*, 19 March 1800, *CW*, 3:I, 220–1.
118 Ibid., 3:I, 225.
119 Lamb to STC, 16 or 17 April 1800, *Letters*, I, 198.
120 STC to Southey, 24 December 1799, *CL*, I, 553.
121 Lamb to Thomas Manning, 8 and 18 February 1800, *Letters*, I, 183, 185–6.
122 See Marshall, *William Godwin*, pp. 209, 238.
123 STC to Southey, 12 February 1800, *CL*, I, 570.
124 STC to Godwin, 21 May 1800, *CL*, I, 588.
125 Godwin, undated note, Charles Kegan Paul, *William Godwin*, I, 357–8.
126 STC to Estlin, 1 March 1800, *CL*, I, 577.
127 *CN*, I, 467 (autumn 1799).
128 See Carlyon, *Early Years*, I, 193–4; *CN*, I, 556 (November 1799).
129 STC to Davy, 1 January 1800, *CL*, I, 557.
130 Davy notebooks, quoted in Molly Lefebure, 'Humphry Davy: Philosophic Alchemist', *The Coleridge Connection*, pp. 102–3.
131 STC to Tom Wedgwood, 2 January 1800, *CL*, I, 559.
132 STC to Southey, 12 February 1800, *CL*, I, 570.
133 Poole to STC, 21 January 1800, Mrs Sandford, II, 3; STC to Poole, 14 February 1800, *CL*, I, 572.
134 STC to Poole, January 1800, *CL*, I, 562.
135 STC to Josiah Wedgwood, 4 February 1800, and to Southey, 12 February 1800, *CL*, I, 569, 571.
136 STC to Southey, 25 January and 12 February 1800, *CL*, I, 563, 570.
137 STC to Poole, 21 March 1800, *CL*, I, 582.
138 STC to Samuel Purkis, 15 March 1800, *CL*, I, 580.
139 STC to Poole, 25 February 1800, *CL*, I, 574.
140 Lamb to STC, 6 August 1800, *Letters*, I, 217, and STC to Godwin, 3 March 1800, *CL*, I, 579–80.
141 STC to Southey, 28 February 1800, *CL*, I, 575.
142 STC to Daniel Stuart, 1 March 1800, *CL*, I, 579.
143 Lamb to Manning, 17 March 1800, *Letters*, I, 189.
144 Lamb to Manning, 5 April 1800, ibid., I, 191.
145 STC to Poole, 31 March 1800, *CL*, I, 584–5.
146 *CN*, I, 718 (March–April 1800).

CHAPTER 7 GRETA HALL 1800–1802

1 See Dorothy Wordsworth, *Journals*, p. 23 (4 June 1800).
2 STC to Josiah Wedgwood, 1 November 1800, *CL*, I, 644–5.
3 STC to Purkis, 29 July 1800, *CL*, I, 614–15.
4 See *CN*, I, 804 (9 September 1800).
5 STC to Davy, 25 July 1800, *CL*, I, 612.
6 STC to James Tobin, 25 July 1800, *CL*, I, 614.
7 STC to Poole, 6 December 1800, *CL*, I, 650.
8 Wordsworth, *Poetical Works*, p. 70.
9 See STC to Poole, 14 October 1803, *CL*, II, 1014.
10 See STC to Josiah Wedgwood, 24 July 1800, *CL*, I, 609.
11 Sara Coleridge to Mrs George Coleridge, Lefebure, *Bondage of Love*, p. 127.
12 Dorothy Wordsworth, *Journals*, p. 35 (22 August 1800).
13 See *CL*, I, 592n.
14 See Wordsworth to Richard Wordsworth, 8 June 1800, *Letters, EY*, p. 283.
15 Lamb to Wordsworth, 30 January 1801, *Letters*, I, 266.
16 Ibid.
17 See *CL*, I, 631n.
18 Wordsworth's note to 'The Ancient Mariner', *Lyrical Ballads* (1800), ed. Brett and Jones, pp. 276–7.
19 See Dorothy Wordsworth, *Journals*, pp. 37, 43 (29 August, 4–6 October 1800).
20 STC to Tobin, 17 September 1800, *CL*, I, 623.
21 STC to Davy, 9 October 1800, *CL*, I, 631 and n.
22 See STC to Southey, 29 July 1802, *CL*, II, 830.
23 See Marilyn Katz, 'Early Dissent between Wordsworth and Coleridge: Preface Deletion of October 1800', *The Wordsworth Circle*, IX (Winter 1978), 50–6.
24 STC to Josiah Wedgwood, 1 November 1800, *CL*, I, 643.
25 *CN*, I, 834 (30 October 1800).
26 See James Kissane, ' "Michael", "Christabel", and the *Lyrical Ballads* of 1800', *The Wordsworth Circle*, IX (Winter 1978), 57–63.
27 See STC to Godwin, 22 January 1802, *CL*, II, 784.
28 *Lyrical Ballads* (1800), ed. Brett and Jones, p. 214.
29 STC to Thelwall, 17 December 1800, *CL*, I, 656.
30 STC to Francis Wrangham, 19 December 1800, *CL*, I, 658.
31 STC to Poole, 14 August 1800, *CL*, I, 618–19.
32 See E. H. Coleridge's notes to 'Christabel', *PW*, I, 213–14.
33 Some useful essays on 'Christabel' are Jo Ann Citron, 'Two Unrecorded Manuscripts of "Christabel"', *The Wordsworth Circle*, XIII (Autumn 1982), 214–18; Kathleen M. Wheeler, 'Disruption and Displacement in Coleridge's "Christabel"', *The Wordsworth Circle*, XX (Spring 1989), 85–90; Norman Fruman, 'Creative Process and Concealment in Coleridge's Poetry', in *Romantic Revisions*, ed. Robert Brinkley and Keith Hanley (Cambridge, 1992), pp. 154–68; Holmes, *Coleridge: Early Visions*, pp. 286–90.
34 See Norman Fruman, 'Creative Process and Concealment', p. 162.
35 See Gillman, *Life*, pp. 301ff.; also *PW*, I, 213n.
36 *PW*, I, 224.
37 *Examiner* (1816), *Critical Heritage*, p. 207.
38 'Christabel, Part Third', *Blackwood's Magazine*, V (June 1819), 288.

39   STC, *Critical Review*, XIV (February 1797), 197.
40   STC to Mary Robinson, 27 December 1802, *CL*, II, 905.
41   *CN*, I, 848 and Notes (28 November 1800).
42   See *Critical Heritage*, p. 233.
43   See E. M. Wilkinson, 'Coleridge's Knowledge of German as Seen in the Early
      Notebooks', *CN*, I, 451–4 (Notes, Appendix A).
44   See *Scott: The Critical Heritage*, ed. John O. Hayden (London, 1970), p. 6.
45   John Stoddart to Walter Scott, 26 December 1800, *Sir Walter Scott's Postbag*, ed.
      Wilfrid Partington (London, 1932), p. 12.
46   See *CL*, II, 1191–2n.
47   See Walter Scott, *Poetical Works*, ed. J. Logie Robertson (London, 1904,
      reprinted 1971), pp. 52–3.
48   Ibid., p. 1.
49   Byron, *Poetical Works*, p. 299.
50   See Byron to STC, 27 October 1815, *Letters and Journals*, ed. Leslie Marchand,
      12 vols. (London, 1973–82), IV, 321 and n.
51   STC to Godwin, 8 September 1800, *CL*, I, 621.
52   For a detailed account of the *Wallenstein* publication and Coleridge's trans-
      lation see Joyce Crick, 'Some Editorial and Stylistic Observations on
      Coleridge's Translation of Schiller's *Wallenstein*', *Publications of the English
      Goethe Society*, new series LIV (1985), 37–75.
53   See Ashton, pp. 33–5, 189.
54   STC to William Sotheby, 10 September 1802, *CL*, II, 863.
55   STC to the Editor of the *Monthly Review*, 18 November 1800, *CL*, I, 648.
56   Preface to *The Death of Wallenstein*, *PW*, II, 724–5.
57   See Joyce Crick, 'Editorial Observations', pp. 61–5.
58   STC, *PW*, II, 799–800.
59   *Table Talk*, *CW*, 14:I, 340–1 (16 February 1833).
60   *PW*, II, 598–9n.
61   See *Henry Crabb Robinson On Books*, I, 107.
62   Southey to Charles Danvers, 18 December 1800, *New Letters*, I, 233.
63   *CN*, I, 813 (27 September 1800).
64   *CN*, I, 828 (October 1800).
65   Dorothy Wordsworth, *Journals*, pp. 51–4.
66   STC to Poole, 6 January 1801, *CL*, II, 661.
67   See Lefebure's biography of Coleridge, *Bondage of Opium*, pp. 493–5 (Appen-
      dix I).
68   STC to Davy, 11 January 1801, *CL*, II, 662–3.
69   STC to Poole, 1 February 1801, *CL*, II, 668–9.
70   Wordsworth, *Poetical Works*, p. 460.
71   See *Essays on His Times*, *CW*, 3:III, 291n.
72   STC to Poole, 1 February 1801, *CL*, II, 669.
73   See *Essays on His Times*, *CW*, 3:III, 291; *PW*, I, 350–2 and n.
74   See *Memoirs of the late Mrs Robinson, written by herself*, ed. M. E. Robinson, 4 vols.
      (London, 1801), IV, 145.
75   STC to Poole, 1 February 1801, *CL*, II, 669.
76   *Memoirs of the late Mrs Robinson*, II, 129–32; see also Schneider, p. 86.
77   Poole to STC, 14 November 1800, Mrs Sandford, II, 20.
78   Poole to STC, 11 January 1801, ibid., II, 23.
79   STC to Davy, 3 February 1801, *CL*, II, 671–2.
80   STC to Poole, 13 February 1801, *CL*, II, 675–6.

81 STC to Dorothy Wordsworth, 9 February 1801, *CL*, II, 673.
82 Josiah Wedgwood to Poole, 31 March 1801, *CL*, II, 677n.
83 *CW*, 7:I, 121.
84 Ibid., 7:I, 117, 119.
85 *Table Talk*, *CW*, 14:I, 312 (21 July 1832).
86 *CW*, 7:I, 153.
87 STC to Poole, 23 March 1801, *CL*, II, 709. For STC and Kant see Elisabeth Winkelmann, *Coleridge und die Kantische Philosophie* (Leipzig, 1933) and Ashton, *The German Idea.*
88 *CW*, 7:I, 142.
89 *CN*, I, 923 (17 March 1801).
90 See STC to Josiah Wedgwood, 18 February 1801, *CL*, II, 679.
91 Hazlitt, 'On the Qualifications necessary to Success in Life' (June 1820), *Complete Works*, XII, 198–9.
92 *Memoir and Letters*, I, 346–7.
93 STC to Poole, 16 March 1801, *CL*, II, 707.
94 STC to Poole, 23 March 1801, *CL*, II, 708.
95 STC to Poole, 16 March 1801, *CL*, II, 707.
96 STC to Godwin, 25 March 1801, *CL*, II, 714.
97 Ibid.
98 STC to Thelwall, 23 April 1801, *CL*, II, 724.
99 See *CN*, I, 994 (September–October 1801).
100 STC to Southey, 6 May 1801, *CL*, II, 727.
101 *CN*, I, 979 (August–September 1801).
102 STC to Southey, 6 May 1801, *CL*, II, 728.
103 STC to Southey, 22 July 1801, *CL*, II, 746.
104 *CN*, I, 984–6 (September 1801).
105 E.g., STC to Godwin, 22 September 1801, and to Southey, 21 October 1801, *CL*, II, 762 and n, 767.
106 STC to Southey, 9 November 1801, *CL*, II, 774–5.
107 See Wordsworth, *EY*, p. 350n.
108 Dorothy Wordsworth to Mary Hutchinson, 29 April 1801, ibid., pp. 330–1.
109 Southey to John Rickman, April 1807, *New Letters*, I, 449.
110 Poole to STC, 21 July 1801, Mrs Sandford, II, 61–2.
111 STC to Poole, 7 September 1801, *CL*, II, 756.
112 See *Essays on His Times*, *CW*, 3:I, 265 and n.
113 STC to Godwin, 22 January 1802, *CL*, II, 782.
114 *CN*, I, 1098 (January–February 1802).
115 *CN*, I, 1099 (January–February 1802).
116 STC to Sara Coleridge, 19 February 1802, *CL*, II, 786.
117 Southey to Charles Danvers, 10 May 1802, *New Letters*, I, 277.
118 *CN*, I, 1152, 1156, 1157 (March–April 1802).
119 *CN*, III, 3304 (12 May 1808).
120. J. S. Mill, *Autobiography* (London, 1873, reprinted, ed. John Robson, Harmondsworth, 1989), p. 112.
121 *Lyrical Ballads* (1798), ed. Brett and Jones, p. 104.
122 See Dorothy Wordsworth, *Journals*, p. 106.
123 See Lefebure, *Bondage of Love*, p. 148.
124 STC to Sara Hutchinson, 4 April 1802, *CL*, II, 790–8.
125 STC to Sotheby, 10 September 1802, *CL*, II, 867 and n.
126 STC to Poole, 7 May 1802, *CL*, II, 799.

127   Poole to STC, 2 May 1802, Mrs Sandford, II, 79. The portrait is reproduced in *CL*, I, 470.
128   Dorothy Wordsworth to Sara Hutchinson, 14 June 1802, *EY*, p. 362.
129   See Alan Hankinson, *Coleridge Walks the Fells: A Lakeland Journey Retraced* (London, 1991), for a reconstruction of Coleridge's walk.
130   STC to Sara Hutchinson, 1–5 August 1802, *CL*, II, 834–5.
131   STC to Sara Hutchinson, 6 August 1802, *CL*, II, 841–2.
132   *CN*, I, 1233 (August–September 1802).
133   STC to George Coleridge, 3 June and 1 July 1802, *CL*, II, 802–3, 805–7.
134   STC to Tom Wedgwood, 20 October 1802, *CL*, II, 876.
135   STC to Sara Coleridge, 23 November 1802, *CL*, II, 887–8.
136   *CN*, I, 1250 (3 October 1802).
137   See Dorothy Wordsworth, *Journals*, p. 154.
138   See STC to Sara Hutchinson, 10 August 1802, *CL*, II, 849. See also Gill, *William Wordsworth*, p. 435, n.107.
139   STC to Sotheby, 13 July 1802, *CL*, II, 812.
140   STC to Southey, 29 July 1802, *CL*, II, 830.
141   STC to Sotheby, 10 September 1802, *CL*, II, 865–6.
142   STC to Tom Wedgwood, 20 October 1802, *CL*, II, 879.
143   STC to Sotheby, 13 July 1802, *CL*, II, 808 and n.
144   STC to Sotheby, 10 September 1802, *CL*, II, 864–5 and n.; *PW*, I, 376–80.
145   4 and 9 November 1802, *Essays on His Times*, *CW*, 3:I, 376–90, 391–400.
146   Poole to STC, 22 August 1802, Mrs Sandford, II, 88.
147   See *Essays on His Times*, *CW*, 3:III, 295 and n.
148   Ibid., 3:I, 403–15; *The Prelude* (1805), Book VII, lines 347ff.
149   STC to Sara Coleridge, 16 and 23 November 1802, *CL*, II, 884, 889.
150   STC to Sara Coleridge, 5 December 1802, *CL*, II, 892.
151   *PW*, I, 282. See also *Letters, Conversations, and Recollections of S. T. Coleridge*, ed. Thomas Allsop, 3rd edition (London, 1864), p. 101.
152   Goethe, *Wilhelm Meisters Lehrjahre* (1795–6) and *Wilhelm Meisters Wanderjahre* (1821).

Chapter 8   In Search of Health: To Malta and Back 1803–1806

1   STC to Southey, 15 February 1803, *CL*, II, 925–6.
2   Southey to William Taylor, 14 February 1803, Robberds, I, 455.
3   Southey to William Taylor, 23 June 1803, ibid., I, 462.
4   STC to Tom Wedgwood, 17 February 1803, *CL*, II, 934.
5   STC to Purkis, 1 February 1803, *CL*, II, 920.
6   See Litchfield, *Tom Wedgwood*, pp. 140–1.
7   Ibid., p. 139.
8   Rickman to Southey, 30 March 1803, Williams, *Life and Letters of John Rickman*, p. 88.
9   STC to Sara Coleridge, 4 April 1803, *CL*, II, 941.
10   STC to Southey, 17 May 1803, *CL*, II, 943.
11   STC to Poole, 14 October 1803, *CL*, II, 1011.
12   STC to Godwin, 4 June 1803, *CL* II, 947–8.
13   Southey to Wynn, 18 July 1803, *New Letters*, I, 319 and n.; STC to Southey, July 1803, *CL*, II, 955–6.
14   See *Essays on His Times*, *CW*, 3:I, cxvii–cxviii.

15 20 August 1803, *Essays on His Times*, *CW*, 3:I, 431 and n.
16 'France: An Ode', *PW*, I, 247n.
17 See Lamb to STC, June 1803, *Letters*, II, 116; STC to Southey, 14 August 1803, *CL* II, 977.
18 See Dorothy Wordsworth to Mrs Clarkson, 17 July 1803, *EY*, p. 396; STC to Wordsworth, 23 July 1803, *CL*, II, 957 and n.
19 STC to Tom Wedgwood, 16 September 1803, *CL*, II, 990–1.
20 *CL*, II, 991n.
21 STC to George Coleridge, 2 October 1803, *CL*, II, 1006.
22 See *CL*, II, 975n.
23 STC to Sara Coleridge, 2 September 1803, *CL*, II, 978–9.
24 STC to Southey, 11 September 1803, *CL*, II, 982–4.
25 See *EY*, pp. 412n, 414 and n.
26 STC to Tom Wedgwood, 16 September 1803, *CL*, II, 992.
27 STC to Poole, 14 October 1803, *CL*, II, 1012–13.
28 Mary Lamb to Sara Hutchinson, ?November 1816, *Letters*, III, 233.
29 *CN*, I, 1577 (19 October 1803). See also *CN*, I, 1646 (November 1803).
30 Derwent Coleridge, 'Early Recollections', MS Harry Ransom Humanities Research Center. Quoted in Cherry Durrant, 'The Lives and Works of Hartley, Derwent and Sara Coleridge', unpublished PhD thesis, Birkbeck College, London, 1994.
31 STC to Sir George and Lady Beaumont, 1 October 1803, *CL*, II, 999–1003.
32 Wordsworth to Richard Wordsworth, 12 December 1803, *EY*, p. 427.
33 STC to Poole, 3 October 1803, *CL*, II, 1010.
34 STC to Poole, 14 October 1803, *CL*, II, 1014–15.
35 STC to Thelwall, 25 November 1803, *CL*, II, 1019.
36 STC to Matthew Coates, 5 December 1803, *CL*, II, 1022.
37 See STC to Sara Coleridge, early January 1804, *CL*, II, 1025.
38 Dorothy Wordsworth to Mrs Clarkson, *EY*, p. 428.
39 *CN*, I, 1801 (4 January 1804).
40 STC to Richard Sharp, 15 January 1804, *CL*, II, 1034.
41 See STC to Wordsworth, 8 February 1804, and to Southey, 20 February 1804, *CL*, II, 1058–9, 1071–3; Southey to John King, 5 March 1804, *New Letters*, I, 354–5.
42 See *Memoirs of the Life of the Rt. Hon. Sir James Mackintosh*, ed. Robert James Mackintosh, 2 vols. (London, 1835), I, 203.
43 See STC to Poole, 13 February 1801, to Godwin, 23 June 1801, and to Poole, 26 January 1804, *CL*, II, 675, 737, 1041.
44 STC to Rickman, 18 February 1804, and to Southey, 8 January 1803, *CL*, II, 1068, 910.
45 See *Essays on His Times*, *CW*, 3:II, 5–27.
46 STC to Sotheby, 13 March 1804, *CL*, II, 1086; *CL*, II, 1087n.
47 STC to the Wordsworths, 8 February 1804, and to Greenough, 31 January 1804, *CL*, II, 1059, 1050.
48 See *CL*, II, 1103n.
49 STC to Southey, 7 April 1804, *CL*, II, 1124.
50 See *CL*, II, 1107n.
51 See STC to Davy, 25 March 1804, *CL*, II, 1101 and n.
52 *CN*, II, 1977 (March 1804).
53 STC to Sara Hutchinson, 10 March 1804, *CL*, II, 1081.
54 STC to Sara Coleridge, 1 April 1804, *CL*, II, 1114.

55 Southey to Miss Barker, 3 April 1804, *Selected Letters*, ed. Warter, I, 270–1.
56 See William and Dorothy Wordsworth to STC, 29 March 1804, *EY*, pp. 462–3.
57 *The Prelude* (1805), Book VI, lines 249–60.
58 *CN*, II, 1993 (9 and 10 April 1804).
59 *CN*, II, 2001 (April 1804).
60 *CN*, II, 2055 (April 1804).
61 *CN*, II, 1997 (11 April 1804).
62 See Donald Sultana, *Samuel Taylor Coleridge in Malta and Italy* (New York, 1969), pp. 117, 129, 133–4.
63 *CN*, II, 2090 (May 1804).
64 *CN*, II, 2085 (9 May 1804).
65 *CN*, II, 2091 (13 May 1804).
66 STC to Sara Coleridge, 5 June 1804, *CL*, II, 1135–40.
67 See Wordsworth to Sir George Beaumont, 31 August 1804, *EY*, p. 497.
68 Mary Lamb to Sarah Stoddart, mid-June 1804, *Letters*, II, 141.
69 *CN*, II, 2099 (18 May 1804).
70 *Table Talk*, *CW*, 14:I, 474 (16 April 1834).
71 Ibid., 14:I, 358 (5 April 1833).
72 See STC to Sotheby, 5 July 1804, *CL*, II, 1140–2.
73 See Sultana, pp. 137, 178.
74 Cottle, *Early Recollections*, II, 82–3n.
75 STC to Southey, 4 August 1804, *CN*, II, 1148.
76 *CN*, II, 2193 (5 October 1804).
77 *CN*, II, 2196, III, 3404 (11 October 1804, 22 October 1808).
78 *CN*, II, 2237 (21 October 1804).
79 *CN*, II, 2241, 2251 (26 October 1804, November 1804).
80 Dorothy Wordsworth to Mrs Clarkson, 15 October 1804, *EY*, p. 510.
81 Dorothy Wordsworth to Lady Beaumont, 7 October 1804, ibid., p. 506.
82 See Dorothy Wordsworth to Mrs Clarkson, 9 December 1804, ibid., p. 516.
83 STC to Southey, 2 February 1805, *CL*, II, 1162.
84 Southey to Danvers, 15 January 1805, *Selected Letters*, I, 311.
85 *See CL*, II, 1160n, 1163.
86 *CN*, II, 2368 (23 December 1804).
87 *CN*, II, 2387 (27 December 1804). See also *CN*, II (Notes), Appendix C.
88 *CN*, II, 2372 (25 December 1804).
89 See *CN*, II, 2420 (28 January 1805).
90 *CN*, II, 2398 (11 January 1805).
91 See STC to Southey, 2 February 1805, *CL*, II, 1163.
92 *CN*, II 2428 (February 1805).
93 *CN*, II, 2448 (12 February 1805).
94 *CN*, II, 2495 (20 March 1805).
95 See Wordsworth, *EY*, pp. 539–40n.
96 Wordsworth to Sir George Beaumont, 11 February 1805, *EY*, p. 542.
97 See STC to Daniel Stuart, 18 February 1808, *CL*, III, 76.
98 *CN*, II, 2517 (31 March 1805).
99 STC to Stuart, 1 May 1805, *CL*, II, 1168.
100 See *CN*, II, 2542 (Notes).
101 STC to Sara Coleridge, 21 July 1805, *CL*, II, 1169.
102 Sara Coleridge to Josiah Wedgwood, 13 October 1805, *CL*, III, 20n.
103 *CN*, II, 2610, 2613 (3 and 20 July 1805).
104 *CN*, II, 2647 (summer 1805).

105 Wordsworth to Sir George Beaumont, 17 October and 3 June 1805, *EY*, pp. 628, 594.
106 See Sultana, p. 366.
107 Ibid., p. 374.
108 *CN*, II, 2701 (15 October 1805).
109 Dorothy Wordsworth to Lady Beaumont, 27 October 1805, *EY*, p. 634.
110 See Sultana, p. 376.
111 *CN*, II, 2731 (November–December 1805).
112 See STC to Stuart, 18 August 1806, *CL*, II, 1175.
113 *CN*, II, 2785 (1 January 1806).
114 Edgar Preston Richardson, *Washington Allston: A Study of the Romantic Artist in America* (Chicago, 1948), p. 75.
115 See *CN*, II, 2808, 2828 (March–April 1806).
116 *CN*, II, 2831 (April–May 1806).
117 See Sultana, p. 394.
118 STC to Washington Allston, 17 June 1806, *CL*, II, 1173.
119 *CN*, II, 2860 (7 June 1806).
120 *PW*, I, 188.
121 See STC to Southey, 20 August 1806, *CL*, II, 1176.
122 STC to Southey, 20 August 1806, *CL*, II, 1177.
123 See STC to Daniel Stuart, 22 August 1806, *CN*, II, 1177.
124 STC to Sara Coleridge, 9 October 1806, *CL*, II, 1190.
125 Mary Lamb to Dorothy Wordsworth, 29 August 1806, *Letters*, II, 238.
126 STC to Stuart, 22 August 1806, *CL*, II, 1177.
127 Wordsworth to Sir George Beaumont, 8 September 1806, *Letters, The Middle Years, 1806–11*, revised Mary Moorman (Oxford, 1969), p. 78. Henceforth referred to as *MY*, I.
128 *PW*, I, 403.
129 STC to Sara Coleridge, 16 September 1806, *CL*, II, 1181–2.
130 STC to Sara Coleridge, 2 October 1806, *CL*, II, 1186.
131 STC to George Fricker, 4 and 9 October 1806, *CL*, II, 1189, 1192.
132 STC to Sara Coleridge, 9 October 1806, *CL*, II, 1191.
133 STC to Thomas Clarkson, 13 October 1806, *CL*, II, 1193–8.
134 *CN*, II, 2894 (October 1806).
135 Dorothy Wordsworth to Mrs Clarkson, 5 November 1806, *MY*, I, 86–7.
136 See *CL*, II, 1199n.
137 STC to the Wordsworths, *circa* 19 November 1806, *CL*, II, 1200.
138 Wordsworth to STC, 7 November 1806, *MY*, I, 90.
139 Dorothy Wordsworth to Lady Beaumont, 7 December 1806, ibid., I, 107.
140 STC to Sara Coleridge, 25 December 1806, *CL*, II, 1205.

CHAPTER 9 FRIENDSHIPS AND *THE FRIEND* 1807–1810

1 Dorothy Wordsworth to Lady Beaumont, 19 December 1806, *MY*, I, 110.
2 Southey to Henry Southey, 30 December 1806, *New Letters*, I, 433.
3 *PW*, I, 403n.
4 *PW*, I, 404 and n. I quote here from the MS given to Wordsworth, which differs slightly from the published version.
5 *PW*, I, 365.
6 *CN*, II, 2975 (27 December 1806). His later memorandum accepted that it was

'a mere phantasm: and yet what anguish, what gnawings of despair, what throbbings and lancinations of positive Jealousy!', ibid., II, 2975 (Notes).

7 *CN*, II, 3148 (13 September 1807).
8 STC to Derwent Coleridge, 3 March 1807, *CL* III, 5–6.
9 See *CL*, III, 22n.
10 George Coleridge to STC, 6 April 1807, *CL*, III, 8–9n.
11 Sara Coleridge to Mary Lovell, *circa* June 1843, Lefebure, *Bondage of Love*, p. 182.
12 STC to Hartley Coleridge, 3 April 1807, *CL*, III, 10.
13 Josiah Wedgwood to Tom Poole, January 1807, Mrs Sandford, II, 178–9.
14 STC to Josiah Wedgwood, 25 June 1807, *CL* III, 19–20.
15 See Grevel Lindop, *The Opium-Eater: A Life of Thomas De Quincey* (London, 1981), pp. 102–4.
16 Ibid., pp. 105, 140.
17 De Quincey, 'Samuel Taylor Coleridge', *Tait's Magazine*, September 1834–January 1835, reprinted *Collected Writings*, II, 150.
18 Ibid., II, 146–7.
19 See *CL*, III, 33–4 and n.
20 Davy to Poole, August 1807, Mrs Sandford, II, 193.
21 STC to Davy, 9 September 1807, *CL*, III, 30.
22 Sara Coleridge to Poole, 28 December 1807, *Minnow*, pp. 8–9.
23 Ibid., p. 10.
24 STC to Dorothy Wordsworth, 24 November 1807, *CL*, III, 37–8; *PW*, I, 410.
25 De Quincey, 'Samuel Taylor Coleridge', *Collected Works*, II, 189.
26 STC to Mrs Morgan, 10 February 1808, *CL*, III, 61.
27 STC to the Morgans, 17 February 1808, *CL*, III, 73–4.
28 *CN*, II, 3094 (1807).
29 *CN*, II, 3148 (13 September 1807).
30 *CN*, II, 3189 (November–December 1807).
31 For the complicated history of the 1808 lectures, see Introduction to *Lectures 1808–1819, CW*, 5:I, 12, 17.
32 James Coleridge to John Taylor Coleridge, 25 January 1808, *Story of a Devonshire House*, p. 169.
33 *CW*, 5:I, 27, 30.
34 *CW*, 5:I, 56.
35 Wordsworth to Sir George Beaumont, 8 April 1808, *MY*, I, 208.
36 STC to Stuart, *circa* 18 April 1808, *CL*, III, 91.
37 *CN*, III, 3304 (12 May 1808).
38 Wordsworth to STC, late May or early June 1808, *MY*, I, 240, 244.
39 See *CL*, III, 72–4, 94–6, 102–5.
40 *CN*, III, 3314 (16 May 1808).
41 *CN*, III, 3325, 3328 (May 1808).
42 Mary Lamb to Mrs Clarkson, 10 December 1808, *Letters*, II, 289.
43 *CW*, 5:I, 96; Wordsworth, *MY*, I, 269n.
44 For accounts of the Bell–Lancaster controversy see *CW*, 5:I, 96–104; P. M. Zall, 'Joseph Lancaster's System', *The Wordsworth Circle*, XIII (Winter 1982), 91–3; and R. A, Foakes, ' "Thriving Prisoners": Coleridge, Wordsworth and the Child at School', *Studies in Romanticism*, XXVIII (1989), 187–200.
45 *CW*, 5:I, 106.
46 STC to Sara Coleridge, 5 May 1808, *CL*, III, 98.
47 *Edinburgh Review*, XII (April 1808), 133.

48 STC to Jeffrey, 23 May 1808, *CL* III, 116–17.
49 Jeffrey to STC, 27 May 1808, Deirdre Coleman, 'Jeffrey and Coleridge: Four Unpublished Letters', *The Wordsworth Circle*, XVIII (Winter 1987), 41–2.
50 Jeffrey to STC, 22 July 1808, ibid., pp. 42–3.
51 STC to Street, 19 September 1808, *CL*, III, 124–5.
52 *Edinburgh Review*, XII (July 1808), 355–79.
53 *HCR On Books*, I, 35. See also STC to Stuart, 11–16 February 1809, *CL*, III, 179.
54 STC to Jeffrey, 14 December 1808, *CL*, III, 148.
55 STC to Sara Coleridge, 9 September 1808, *CL*, III, 120–1.
56 *Memoir and Letters*, pp. 25, 18–19.
57 STC to Davy, 7 December 1808, *CL*, III, 135.
58 STC to Stuart, *circa* 14 December 1808, *CL*, III, 141.
59 STC to Sir George Beaumont, *circa* 14 December 1808, *CL*, III, 146.
60 STC to Clarkson, 13 October 1806, CL, II, 1198.
61 See Ashton, *The German Idea*, pp. 36–48.
62 See Deirdre Coleman, 'Coleridge, Quakerism and *The Friend*', *The Wordsworth Circle*, XVII (Summer 1986), 134–42.
63 See Wordsworth, *MY*, I, 275n.
64 See Grevel Lindop, pp. 166ff, for an account of De Quincey's labours; also John E. Jordan, *De Quincey to Wordsworth: A Biography of a Relationship* (Berkeley, California, 1962).
65 Dorothy Wordsworth to Mrs Clarkson, 8 December 1808, *MY*, I, 282–3.
66 See *CW*, 4:II, 407 (Appendix E).
67 See *CW*, 4:I, xxxix–xli, and 4:II, 474ff (Appendix F).
68 STC to Stuart, 13 June 1809, *CL*, III, 211.
69 Southey to Rickman, 18 January 1809, *Selected Letters*, II, 120.
70 Jeffrey to STC, 28 December 1808, Deirdre Coleman, 'Jeffrey and Coleridge', p. 44.
71 Prospectus to *Friend*, *CW*, 4:II, 16.
72 *CW*, 4:II, 22–6n.
73 Southey to Charles Danvers, 15 June 1809, *New Letters*, II, 511.
74 Dorothy Wordsworth to Mrs Clarkson, 15 June 1809, *MY*, I, 355–6.
75 *Friend*, 7 September 1809, *CW*, 4:II, 59.
76 *Friend*, 5 October 1809, *CW*, 4:II, 116–17.
77 *Examiner*, 8 September 1816, reprinted Hazlitt, *Complete Works*, VII, 115.
78 *Friend*, 14 December 1809, *CW*, 4:II, 222–9.
79 See STC to Poole, 12 January 1810, *CL*, III, 271.
80 STC to George Coleridge, 9 October 1809, *CL*, III, 237.
81 Southey to Miss Barker, 29 January 1810, *Selected Letters*, II, 190.
82 Sara Coleridge to Poole, 3 August 1810, *Minnow*, pp. 11, 14.
83 See *Essays on His Times*, *CW*, 3:II, 37–100.
84 See Introduction, *Essays on His Times*, *CW*, 3:I, cxxviii and n.
85 STC to Purkis, 11 October 1809, *CL*, III, 244–5.
86 *Courier*, 7 December 1809, *CW*, 3:II, 39.
87 STC to Southey, 20 October 1809, *CL*, III, 254.
88 *Friend*, 26 October 1809, *CW*, 4:II, 150.
89 STC to Southey, early November 1809, *CL*, III, 261.
90 James Coleridge to John Taylor Coleridge, 5 November 1809, *Story of a Devonshire House*, p. 178.
91 Southey to STC, 26 October 1809, *Friend*, *CW*, 4:II, 497 (Appendix F).

92 STC to Sara Coleridge, *circa* 19 February and *circa* 14 April 1810, *CL*, III, 284, 286.
93 *CN*, III, 3858 (June 1810).
94 *CN*, III, 3510 (summer 1809).
95 *CN*, III, 3869 (June 1810).
96 For example, *CN*, III, 3539, 3874 (July –September 1809, June 1810).
97 *CN*, III, 3864 (probably June 1810).
98 *CN*, III, 3648 (November–December 1809).
99 *CN*, III, 3404 (22 October 1808).
100 *CN*, III, 3912 (June 1810).
101 Dorothy Wordsworth to Mrs Clarkson, *circa* 12 April 1810, *MY*, I, 398–400.
102 Southey to Grosvenor Bedford, 22 December 1810, *New Letters*, I, 548.
103 Southey to Rickman, 1 August 1810, ibid., I, 537.
104 See John Sutherland, *The Life of Walter Scott: A Critical Biography* (Oxford, 1995).
105 STC to Wordsworth, early October 1810, *CL*, III, 291–5.
106 See *CL*, III, 291n.
107 *Edinburgh Annual Register for 1808*, II (July 1810), 427.
108 *CN*, III, 3952 (7 July 1810). See also *CN*, III, 3970 (September 1810).
109 The review appeared in the *Quarterly Review*, V (February 1811), 40–61.
110 Southey to Scott, 17 September 1810, *Life and Correspondence*, III, 291.
111 Scott to Southey, 19–20 September 1810, *The Letters of Sir Walter Scott*, ed. H. J. C. Grierson, 12 vols. (London, 1932–7), II, 373.
112 *Essays on His Times*, *CW*, 3:II, 105.
113 See Southey, *New Letters*, I, 549–50 and n.: Marshall, *William Godwin*, p. 209.
114 *CN*, III, 3391, 3397 (October 1810, 28 October 1810).
115 Wordsworth to John Edwards, 27 March 1811, *MY*, I, 470.
116 See *CL*, III, 296–7n.
117 See Lucy Watson, *Coleridge at Highgate* (London, 1925), p. 124.

CHAPTER 10   LIFE-IN-DEATH: LONDON 1810–1814

1 Southey to Danvers, 13 November 1810, in *CL*, III, 298n.
2 STC to Wordsworth, 4 May 1812, *CL*, III, 399.
3 STC to the Morgans, 21 December 1810, *CL*, III, 301.
4 See, for example, *CN*, III, 4006, 4036 (November 1810).
5 Lamb to Dorothy Wordsworth, 13 November 1810, *Letters*, III, 62.
6 See *CL*, III, 309n.
7 Crabb Robinson to Dorothy Wordsworth, 23 December 1810, *The Correspondence of Henry Crabb Robinson with the Wordsworth Circle 1808–66*, ed. Edith J. Morley, 2 vols. (Oxford, 1927), I, 63–4.
8 15 November 1810, *Blake, Coleridge, Wordsworth etc.*, p. 31.
9 See *Table Talk*, *CW*, 14:I, 381n for Coleridge's attempts to obtain a set of Goethe's works between 1812 and 1816; also *CW*, 14:I, 341 and n for a brief mention of *Wilhelm Meister* on 16 February 1833.
10 E. H. Coleridge suggests a date of 1799 in *PW*, I, 311, but there is no evidence in the notebooks written in Germany in 1798–9 of his having read *Wilhelm Meister* then.
11 *Table Talk*, *CW*, 14:II, 61 (24 June 1827). The editor points out that though the

remark was published in H. N. Coleridge's edition of *Table Talk* in 1835, it does not appear in the manuscript on which he based his edition (see *CW*, 14:I, 77n.).

12 *Blake, Coleridge, Wordsworth etc.*, p. 35 (23 December 1810).
13 Ibid., p. 32. See also *CN*, III, 4066 (April 1811).
14 See Colley, *Britons*, pp. 217–19.
15 *Blake, Coleridge, Wordsworth etc.*, pp. 34, 36–7 (23 December 1810 and 23 January 1811).
16 *Examiner*, 25 November 1810, quoted in *Essays on His Times*, *CW*, 3:I, cxliv.
17 *CW*, 3:I, cxlv–vii.
18 See *CW*, 3:I, cxlvii.
19 See *CW*, 3:II, 110–21, 122–4, 152–3 (April–May 1811).
20 See *CW*, 3:III, 220–35.
21 See Colley, *Britons*, pp. 217–18.
22 *HCR On Books*, I, 37 (12 July 1811).
23 Southey to Grosvenor Bedford, 14 January 1811, *New Letters*, II, 3–4.
24 Southey to Danvers, 31 March 1811, ibid., II, 7–8.
25 See STC to Crabb Robinson, 12 March 1811, *CL*, III, 306 and n; Lamb, *Letters*, III, 73n.
26 Lamb to Morgan, 8 March 1811, *Letters*, III, 74.
27 For a full account of John Taylor Coleridge's career see *Story of a Devonshire House*, pp. 151–357.
28 John Taylor Coleridge to James Coleridge junior, ?April 1811, *Story of a Devonshire House*, pp. 191–2. See also *Table Talk*, *CW*, 14:I, 5–15.
29 STC to Longman, 2 May 1811, and to Stuart, 5 May 1811, *CL*, III, 325, 327–8.
30 See STC to Godwin, 29 March 1811, *CL*, III, 317.
31 *HCR On Books*, I, 48 (20 October 1811).
32 See *Blake, Coleridge etc.*, p. 45; R. A. Foakes, Introduction to *Lectures 1808–19*, *CW*, 5:I, 156 and n, 159–60 and n.
33 Southey to John Morgan, 13 November 1811, *New Letters*, II, 12, and to John May, 24 November 1811, *Selected Letters*, II, 247.
34 See *Lectures 1808–1819*, *CW*, 5:I, lxxxiv–v, 163–6.
35 Prospectus, *CW*, 5:I, 179–80.
36 *HCR On Books*, I, 60.
37 *CW*, 5:I, 190.
38 *CW*, 5:I, 194; *HCR On Books*, I, 51.
39 See Sara Hutchinson to Mary Monkhouse, 3 December 1811, *The Letters of Sara Hutchinson from 1800 to 1835*, ed. Kathleen Coburn (London, 1954), p. 37.
40 STC to Robinson, 18 November 1811, *CL*, III, 347.
41 *CW*, 5:I, 203.
42 *CW*, 5:I, 205–7.
43 *CW*, 5:I, 208–9.
44 *HCR On Books*, I, 52 (28 November 1811).
45 *CN*, III, 3342 (May 1808).
46 *CW*, 5:I, 277, 278, 285–6.
47 *HCR On Books*, I, 53 (5 December 1811).
48 *CW*, 5:I, 316.
49 Robinson to Mrs Clarkson, 13 December 1811, *Blake, Coleridge etc.*, pp. 124–5; *CW*, 5:I, 339–40.

50 The most detailed discussion of Coleridge's plagiarism is Norman Fruman's *Coleridge: The Damaged Archangel* (London, 1972). For a summary of the arguments, see Frederick Burwick, 'On Stage Illusion: From Wordsworth's Marginalia to Coleridge's Lectures', *The Wordsworth Circle*, XIX (Winter 1988), 29, 36.

51 STC to Robinson, 6 November 1811, *CL*, III, 343.

52 *CW*, 5:I, 353–4.

53 I. A. Richards certainly thought so; see his appreciative study, *Coleridge on Imagination* (London, 1934), and his *Principles of Literary Criticism* (London, 1924).

54 STC to unknown correspondent, *circa* 15–21 December 1811, *CL*, III, 355–61.

55 See *CN*, III, 3952 (7 July 1810).

56 Samuel Johnson, *Preface to the Edition of Shakespeare's Plays* (1765), in *Samuel Johnson on Shakespeare*, ed. H. R. Woudhuysen (Harmondsworth, 1989), pp. 134–5.

57 Lecture XVII, *Lectures on Dramatic Art and Literature*, trans. John Black (London, 1815, reprinted 1861), p. 246. For the original German see A. W. Schlegel, *Kritische Schriften und Briefe*, ed. Edgar Lohner, 7 vols. (Stuttgart, 1962–74), VI, 22.

58 *Lectures 1808–19, CW*, 5:I, 134.

59 See *CW*, 5:I, 134n.; also Burwick, 'On Stage Illusion', pp. 28–37.

60 *CW*, 7:II, 6 (*Biographia Literaria*, chapter 14).

61 *CW*, 5:I, 388.

62 *CW*, 5:I, 391.

63 *HCR On Books*, I, 58 (16 January 1812).

64 *CW*, 5:I, 407.

65 See STC to Mrs Sotheby, 6 February 1812, *CL*, III, 364.

66 STC to Sara Coleridge, 7 February 1812, *CL*, III, 365.

67 Southey to Bedford, 4 January 1812, *The Letters of Percy Bysshe Shelley*, ed. Frederick L. Jones, 2 vols. (Oxford, 1964), I, 219n.

68 Shelley to Peacock, 17 July 1816, ibid., I, 490. For Coleridge's works owned by Shelley see II, 471–2.

69 Shelley to Elizabeth Hitchener, 2 January 1812, ibid., I, 219.

70 STC to Morgan, 23 February 1812, *CL*, III, 375–7.

71 Sara Coleridge to Poole, 30 October 1812, *Minnow*, p. 16.

72 STC to Morgan, 24 March 1812, *CL*, III, 380.

73 Sara Coleridge to Poole, 30 October 1812, *Minnow*, p. 17.

74 Ibid., p. 19.

75 *CW*, 5:I, 418.

76 See letters of STC and Wordsworth April–May 1812, especially *CL*, III, 403–6n; *HCR On Books*, I, 70–81; *Correspondence of HCR with the Wordsworth Circle*, I, 68–72.

77 *HCR On Books*, I, 78, 80.

78 Robinson to Thomas Robinson, 20 May 1812, *Correspondence of HCR with the Wordsworth Circle*, I, 70.

79 See *CL*, III, 401n.

80 Mrs Clarkson to Robinson, 22 April 1812, *Correspondence of HCR with the Wordsworth Circle*, I, 68.

81 See STC to Sir George Beaumont, 7 December 1811, and to Sara Coleridge, 21 April 1812, *CL*, III, 350 and n, 386.

82 STC to Wordsworth, 4 May 1812, *CL*, III, 397–402.
83 See Wordsworth to Mrs Clarkson, 4 June 1812, *Letters, The Middle Years, 1812– 20*, revised Mary Moorman and Alan G. Hill (Oxford, 1970), p. 22. (Henceforth referred to as *MY*, II.)
84 STC to Southey, 12 May 1812, *CL*, III, 410; see also *CW*, 3:II, 347–9 for the article on Perceval in the *Courier*.
85 *HCR On Books*, I, 85, 87 (23 and 26 May 1812).
86 Ibid., I, 63 (11 February 1812).
87 STC to Mrs Morgan, 25 October 1813, *CL*, III, 446; *CW*, 5:I, 479–83.
88 *CW*, 5:I, 492.
89 *HCR On Books*, I, 117.
90 Josiah Wedgwood to Coleridge, 9 November and 5 December 1812, and STC to Josiah Wedgwood, 1 December 1812, *CL*, III, 420–1 and n.
91 STC to Stuart, 22 December 1812, *CL*, III, 426.
92 See STC to Josiah Wedgwood, 1 December 1812, *CL*, III, 421.
93 STC to Wordsworth, 7 December 1812, *CL*, III, 423.
94 STC to Poole, 13 February 1813, *CL*, III, 437.
95 See Dorothy Wordsworth to Mrs Clarkson, 6 April 1813, *MY*, II, 90–1.
96 STC to Sara Coleridge, 27 January 1813, *CL*, III, 431.
97 See Richard Lansdown, *Byron's Historical Dramas* (Oxford, 1992), pp. 5, 11–18.
98 *Remorse*, Act III, scene i, *PW*, II, 851.
99 *Remorse*, Act V, scene i, *PW*, II, 881. See Wilson Knight, *The Starlit Dome*, pp. 145ff for a study of the language of *Remorse*.
100 *HCR On Books*, I, 117 (23 January 1813).
101 *Examiner*, 31 January 1813, in *Critical Heritage*, p. 123.
102 *HCR On Books*, I, 107 (13 August 1812).
103 See *PW*, II, 732, 853.
104 STC to Southey, 9 February 1813, *CL*, III, 435.
105 *Leigh Hunt's Dramatic Criticism 1808–1831*, ed. L. H. and C. W. Houtchens (London, 1950), p. 103.
106. Southey to Thomas Southey, 20 January 1813, *New Letters*, II, 43.
107 *Quarterly Review*, XI (April 1814), in *Critical Heritage*, pp. 175–88.
108 *Osorio*, Act IV, scene i, *PW*, II, 562.
109 Mrs Clarkson to Robinson, 10 March 1813, *Correspondence of HCR with the Wordsworth Circle*, I, 72.
110 Dorothy Wordsworth to Sara Hutchinson, 10 October 1813, *MY*, II, 127.
111 See *CW*, 5:I, 501–97.
112 Sara Coleridge to Poole, February 1814, *Minnow*, p. 28.
113 STC to Morgan, 14 May 1814, *CL*, III, 490.
114 STC to Morgan, 15 May 1814, *CL*, III, 491.
115 Cottle to STC, 25 April 1814, *Early Recollections*, II, 151–2, 154.
116 STC to Cottle, 26 April 1814, *CL*, III, 477.
117 STC to Cottle, 26 April 1814, *CL*, III, 478.
118 STC to Wade, 26 June 1814, *CL*, III, 511.
119 See *CW*, 5:II, 19.
120 Dorothy Wordsworth to Wade, 27 March 1814, *MY*, II, 133.
121 Southey to Cottle, 17 April 1814, *New Letters*, II, 94.
122 Southey to Cottle, April 1814, ibid., II, 98.
123 *Story of a Devonshire House*, pp. 214–15.
124 See Southey to Cottle, 27 October 1814, *New Letters*, II, 107 and n.

125 Southey to Cottle, 2 March 1815, ibid., II, 117.
126 Southey to John Taylor Coleridge, 14 March 1814, *Letters of Hartley Coleridge*, ed. Grace Evelyn Griggs and Earl Leslie Griggs (London, 1937, reprinted 1941), p. 10.
127 Lamb to STC, 13 August 1814, *Letters*, III, 101.
128 STC to Morgan, 16 August 1814, *CL*, VI, 1030.
129 STC to Morgan, 30 June 1814, *CL*, III, 515.

CHAPTER 11   RISEN AGAIN: *BIOGRAPHIA LITERARIA* 1814–1817

1 STC to Stuart, 12 September 1814, *CL*, III, 532.
2 See *HCR On Books*, I, 448 (7 October 1834).
3 STC to Murray, 23 August 1814, *CL*, III, 521–2.
4 STC to Murray, 31 August 1814, *CL*, III, 523–5.
5 Lamb to STC, 26 August 1814, *Letters*, III, 107.
6 See Southey, *Selected Letters*, II, 332n.
7 STC to Murray, 10 September 1814, *CL*, III, 528. For a full discussion of Coleridge's relations with German literature, especially Goethe, see Ashton, *The German Idea*.
8 *HCR On Books*, I, 107 (13 August 1812).
9 See Ashton, *The German Idea*, passim.
10 See Shelley, *Poetical Works*, ed. Thomas Hutchinson (Oxford, 1905, reprinted 1967), pp. 748–62.
11 Thomas Medwin, *Conversations of Lord Byron* (London, 1824, revised and edited Ernest J. Lovell Jr, Princeton, New Jersey, 1966), p. 261.
12 See Shelley, *Letters*, II, 676 and n.
13 *Table Talk*, *CW*, 14:I, 337–8 (16 February 1833).
14 *CW*, 14:I, 343.
15 STC to R. H. Brabant, 10 March 1815, *CL*, IV, 548.
16 *PW*, I, 425–6.
17 STC to Brabant, 10 March 1815, *CL*, IV, 549.
18 STC to Brabant, 13 March 1815, *CL*, IV, 554.
19 Sara Coleridge to Poole, 20 September 1815, *Minnow*, p. 39.
20 Sara Coleridge to Poole, 2 January 1815, ibid., p. 32.
21 Southey to J. N. White, 8 May 1815, *Selected Letters*, II, 408–9.
22 Sara Coleridge to Poole, 2 January 1815, *Minnow*, p. 32.
23 STC to Byron, 29 March 1815, *CL*, VI, 1033–5.
24 Byron to STC, 31 March 1815, *Letters and Journals*, IV, 286.
25 See *CL*, IV, 634n.
26 Sara Coleridge to Poole, 24 May 1816, *Minnow*, p. 48.
27 Byron to STC, 18 and 17 October 1815, *Letters and Journals*, IV, 318–19, 321. See also *CL*, IV, 603n.
28 Byron to Moore, 28 October 1815, *Letters and Journals*, IV, 324.
29 See STC to Byron, 15 February 1816, *CL*, IV, 622.
30 For the authorship of the review, and the review itself, see *Critical Heritage*, pp. 226ff.
31 *Edinburgh Review*, XXVII (September 1816), in *Critical Heritage*, pp. 227, 234.
32 See STC to Edward Cole, 11 November 1825, *CL*, V, 509.
33 See *HCR On Books*, I, 156 (19 December 1814). See also William E. A. Axon, 'Anna Vardill Niven, the Authoress of "Christobell", the Sequel to Coleridge's

"Christabel". With a Bibliography', *Transactions of the Royal Society of Literature* (London, 1908); Donald H. Reiman, 'Christobell; or, The Case of the Sequel Preemptive', *The Wordsworth Circle*, VI (Autumn 1975), 283–9; and Richard Haven, 'Anna Vardill Niven's "Christobell": An Addendum', *The Wordsworth Circle*, VII (Spring 1976), 117–18.

34 For a sample of parodies of 'Christabel' see *Parodies of the Works of English and American Authors*, ed. Walter Hamilton, 6 vols. in 3 (London, 1884–9), volume III.
35 Hazlitt to Editor of the *Examiner*, 29 October 1815, *The Letters of William Hazlitt*, ed. H. M. Sikes, W. H. Bonner, and G. Lahely (London, 1979), p. 146.
36 *HCR On Books*, I, 169 (15 June 1815).
37 STC to Francis Wrangham, 5 June 1817, and to R. H. Brabant, 5 December 1816, *CL*, IV, 735, 693.
38 *HCR On Books*, I, 197 (2 November 1816).
39 See *CL*, IV, 621n.
40 STC to Byron, 10 April 1816, and to Gillman, 13 April 1816, *CL*, IV, 626, 628, 629–30.
41 STC to Murray, 23 April 1816, *CL*, IV, 633.
42 STC to Gillman, 13 April 1816, *CL*, IV, 630.
43 *CN*, III, 4269 (3 November 1815) and Notes.
44 *CN*, III, 4272 (December 1815).
45 Southey to Wordsworth, 5 May 1817, *New Letters*, II, 156.
46 Lamb to Wordsworth, 26 April 1816, *Letters*, III, 215.
47 Lamb to Wordsworth, 23 September 1816, ibid., III, 225.
48 *HCR On Books*, I, 185 (14 July 1816). For an astute fictional reconstruction of the Coleridge–Gillman relationship see Henry James, *The Coxon Fund* (1894).
49 See STC to Morgan, 24 June 1816, *CL*, VI, 1041–2.
50 Lamb to Wordsworth, 26 April 1816, *Letters*, III, 215.
51 See *CL*, IV, 636n.
52 *Examiner*, 8 September 1816, in *Critical Heritage*, pp. 248–53.
53 *Examiner*, 29 December 1816, ibid., pp. 253, 256.
54 *Edinburgh Review*, XXVII (December 1816), ibid., p. 263.
55 *Lay Sermons*, *CW*, 6, xlix.
56 *CW*, 6, 69.
57 *CW*, 6, 22ff., 40.
58 *CW*, 6, 30.
59 *CW*, 6, 243.
60 *Critical Review*, January 1817, in *Critical Heritage*, p. 280.
61 *CW*, 6, 131ff.
62 *CW*, 6, 145.
63 *CW*, 6, 228.
64 STC to Rest Fenner, 22 September 1816, *CL*, IV, 679.
65 Dorothy Wordsworth to Mrs Clarkson, 2 March 1817, *MY*, II, 373.
66 Sara Hutchinson to Tom Monkhouse, 17 February 1817, *Letters*, p. 105.
67 Southey to Humphrey Senhouse, 22 March 1817, *Life and Correspondence*, IV, 258.
68 *British Pamphleteers*, II, 67.
69 STC to Editor of *Morning Chronicle*, 25 January 1818, *CL*, IV, 814–15.
70 See *CL*, IV, 712n.; Southey, *New Letters*, II, 150–1n.
71 Dorothy Wordsworth to Mrs Clarkson, 13 April 1817, *MY*, II, 380.

72   Hazlitt to Editor of the *Examiner*, 12 January 1817, *Letters*, p. 166.
73   Southey to Grosvenor Bedford, 29 October 1817, *New Letters*, II, 176.
74   STC to Brabant, 21 September 1816, *CL*, IV, 673.
75   *HCR On Books*, I, 189–90 (9 September 1816).
76   STC to Poole, 22 July 1817, *CL*, IV, 755.
77   See *CL*, IV, 767n., 800n.
78   STC to Poole, 22 July 1817, *CL*, IV, 755–6.
79   Poole to STC, 31 July 1817, Mrs Sandford, II, 257.
80   Ibid., II, 258.
81   *Paupers and Pig Killers*, p. 287.
82   For details see *Biographia Literaria*, *CW*, 7:I, lviiiff and 7:II, 283ff; also *CL*, IV, 650n, 657–8n.
83   See *CW*, 7:I, lxii.
84   *CW*, 7:I, 16.
85   *CW*, 7:I, 193ff.
86   See, for example, *CN*, III, 4301 (1815–16).
87   *Edinburgh Review*, August 1817, in *Critical Heritage*, p. 300.
88   *CW*, 7:I, 17.
89   *CW*, 7:II, 247–8.
90   *CW*, 7:I, 263 (chapter twelve). See also ibid., 7:I, 136, 304.
91   *Nightmare Abbey*, p. 83.
92   See *CW*, 7:I, xli.
93   See *CW*, 7:II, 253–4; also Introduction to Volume I and excellent footnotes to both volumes.
94   See Bradford K, Mudge, 'Sara Coleridge and "The Business of Life"', *The Wordsworth Circle*, XIX (Winter 1988), 55–64.
95   *CN*, III, 4265 and Notes (September 1815).
96   *CW*, 7:I, 153, 161, 163–4.
97   See *CW*, 7:I, 124n.
98   *CW*, 7:I, 124–5 (chapter seven). See Kathleen Wheeler, *Sources, Processes and Methods in Coleridge's Biographia Literaria* (Cambridge, 1980), and Catherine Miles Wallace, *The Design of Biographia Literaria* (London, 1983).
99   *CW*, 7:I, 120, 117 (chapter seven).
100 *CW*, 7:I, 142 (chapter nine).
101 See Introduction to *Biographia Literaria*, *CW*, 7:I, lxxxi–xcvii.
102 *CW*, 7:I, 304–5 (chapter thirteen).
103 *CW*, 7:II, 19.
104 *Principles of Literary Criticism*, p. 191. See also *Coleridge on Imagination*, passim.
105 STC to Daniel Stuart, 13 May 1816, *CL*, IV, 642.
106 See his note to chapter two of *Biographia Literaria*, *CW*, 7:I, 34.
107 *CW*, 7:II, 26–7.
108 Wordsworth, 'It is not to be thought of that the Flood', *Poems Dedicated to National Independence and Liberty*, Part I, no. xvi.
109 *CW*, 7:II, 150–1 (chapter twenty-two).
110 *CW*, 7:I, 85 and n; *CN*, III, 3290 (March 1808).
111 *CW*, 7:II, 136–7 (chapter twenty-two).
112 See *CW*, 7:II, 135, 59.
113 *CW*, 7:II, 126.
114 See *CW*, 7:I, 37, 66, 82, 127, 143, 181, 204, 287; 7:II, 126.
115 *CW*, 7:II, 148–9 (chapter twenty-two).
116 Wordsworth, *Poetical Works*, pp. 734, 735.

117 See STC to Southey, 29 July 1802, and to William Sotheby, 13 July 1802, *CL*, II, 830, 811–12.
118 Shelley, 'A Defence of Poetry' (1821), in *English Critical Texts*, ed. D. J. Enright and Ernst de Chickera (Oxford, 1962, reprinted 1983), p. 233.
119 *CW*, 7:II, 6.
120 Wordsworth, *Poetical Works*, p. 750.
121 Ibid., p. 745.
122 *CW*, 7:I, 34n. (chapter two).
123 STC to Brabant, 29 July 1815, *CL*, IV, 579.
124 STC to William Sotheby, 31 January 1816, *CL*, IV, 620.
125 *CW*, 7:II, 14.
126 Wordsworth to Gillies, 19 September 1817, *MY*, II, 399.
127 *HCR On Books*, I, 213 (4 December 1817).
128 Ibid., I, 214 (27 December 1817).
129 Ibid., I, 215–16.
130 See *CW*, 7:II, 50–1n., 123–4n., 140n.
131 *Edinburgh Review*, August 1817, in *Critical Heritage*, pp. 295–322.
132 *HCR On Books*, I, 209–10 (6 October 1817).
133 *Blackwood's Magazine*, October 1817, in *Critical Heritage*, pp. 325–50.
134 See *HCR On Books*, I, 213 (6 December 1817).
135 See P. P. Howe, *The Life of William Hazlitt* (London, 1922), pp. 262ff.
136 Keats to George and Tom Keats, 21 December 1817, *The Letters of John Keats*, ed. Hyder Edward Rollins, 2 vols. (Cambridge, Mass., 1958, reprinted 1980), I, 193–4.

Chapter 12 Highgate 1818–1821

1 For a summary of changes made to the poem between 1798 and 1817 see *Lyrical Ballads*, ed. Michael Mason (London, 1992), p. 177.
2 See *CL*, IV, 650n., 703–4n., 710n.
3 Byron to Murray, 17 September 1817, *Letters and Journals*, V, 267.
4 See *CL*, IV, 723–5n.
5 See STC to Derwent Coleridge, 8 January 1818, *CL*, IV, 799.
6 *Champion*, 26 January 1818, see *Lectures 1808–19*, *CW*, 5:II, 28.
7 Sara Hutchinson to Monkhouse, 6 February 1818, *Letters*, p. 122.
8 *CN*, III, 4480 (25 February 1819).
9 STC to Perry, 5 February 1818, and to Mudford, 18 February 1818, *CL*, IV, 830–1, 839–40.
10 Hazlitt, 'Lectures on the English Poets', *Complete Works*, V, 47.
11 Ibid., V, 166–7.
12 *CN*, III, 4248 (1815).
13 See Introduction by J. R. de J. Jackson, *Logic* (London, 1981), *CW*, 13.
14 See *CL*, IV, 738n. See also Walter Jackson Bate, *Coleridge* (New York, 1968, reprinted 1970), pp. 205–6.
15 See H. J. Jackson, 'Coleridge's Collaborator, Joseph Henry Green', *Studies in Romanticism*, XXI (1982), 161–79.
16 STC to J. H. Green, 13 December 1817 and 30 September 1818, *CL*, IV, 791–2, 874.
17 STC to William Hart Coleridge, 1 April 1818, *CL*, IV, 847.

18 George Coleridge to John Taylor Coleridge, 14 February 1818, *Story of a Devonshire House*, p. 273.

19 See, for example, STC to Tulk, September 1817, *CL*, IV, 767–76. For Tulk's career see *CL*, V, 9–10n.

20 *PW*, I, 436.

21 See *CL*, IV, 778n.

22 STC to H. F. Cary, 6 February 1818, *CL*, IV, 833–4.

23 STC to Green, 30 April 1818, *CL*, IV, 853.

24 *Courier*, 31 March 1818, *Essays on His Times*, *CW*, 3:II, 488.

25 *Remarks on the Ojections which have been urged against the Principles of Sir Robert Peel's Bill*, in *Inquiring Spirit: A New Presentation of Coleridge from his Published and Unpublished Prose Writings*, ed. Kathleen Coburn (London, 1951, reprinted 1979), pp. 351, 353, 358.

26 See *CN*, III, 4482 (25 February 1819) and Notes.

27 Lamb, Dedication to *Works*, 2 vols (London, 1818), vol. I.

28 For details of the revisions see Introduction, *Friend*, *CW*, 4:I, xciiff.

29 *CW*, 4:I, 457.

30 *CW*, 4:I, 472.

31 *Edinburgh Magazine*, January 1821, in *Critical Heritage*, p. 428.

32 Sara Coleridge to Poole, September 1818, *Minnow*, pp. 67–8.

33 STC to Charlotte Brent, 4 November 1818, and to William Collins, 4 December 1818, *CL*, IV, 878, 891.

34 See Dorothy Wordsworth to Sara Hutchinson, *circa* 17 March 1819, *MY*, II, 528; *CL*, IV, 878–9n.

35 Southey to Wade Browne, 31 December 1818, *New Letters*, II, 194.

36 Hartley Coleridge to George Coleridge, 6 December 1818, *Letters*, p. 19.

37 Sara Coleridge to Poole, April 1819, *Minnow*, p. 70.

38 STC to William Davies, 20 April 1819, *CL*, IV, 936–7.

39 Southey to Edith Southey, 16 June 1820, *New Letters*, II, 215.

40 See *CW*, 5:II, 279 and n.

41 *CW*, 5:II, 294.

42 See *CW*, 5:II, 301–2.

43 See Introduction to *The Philosophical Lectures of Samuel Taylor Coleridge*, ed. Kathleen Coburn (London, 1949), pp. 34–5.

44 See STC to Southey, 31 January 1819, *CL*, IV, 917.

45 Prospectus, *Philosophical Lectures*, p. 66.

46 *Philosophical Lectures*, pp. 186–7.

47 See STC to Tieck, 4 July 1817, and to Green, 16 January 1819, *CL*, IV, 750, 911.

48 Lecture thirteen, *Philosophical Lectures*, pp. 388–9.

49 Ibid., p. 390.

50 See *CW*, 5:II, 343ff.

51 See *CW*, 5:II, 376; *Coleridge's Shakespearean Criticism*, ed. Thomas Middleton Raysor, 2 vols. (London, 1930, reprinted 1960), I, 102.

52 *Table Talk*, *CW*, 14:I, 73 (24 June 1827).

53 See Raysor, *Coleridge's Shakespearean Criticism;* Terence Hawkes's selection, *Coleridge on Shakespeare* (Harmondsworth, 1969); and *Coleridge's Criticism of Shakespeare: A Selection*, ed. R. A. Foakes (London, 1989).

54 Note on his edition of Shakespeare, probably for a lecture of 7 January 1819, see *CW*, 5:II, 295.

55 Lecture of 2 January 1812, *CW*, 5:I, 386.

56 *Table Talk*, *CW*, 14:I, 83 (8 July 1827).

57 *CW*, 5:II, 315.
58 *Table Talk, CW*, 14:I, 26–7 (6 January 1823).
59 Keats to George and Georgiana Keats, 15 April 1819, *Letters*, II, 88–9.
60 Sara Coleridge to Poole, 4 June 1819, *Minnow*, pp. 77, 78.
61 Sara Coleridge to Poole, 20 September 1819, ibid., pp. 81, 84.
62 STC to Francis Wrangham, 28 September 1819, *CL*, IV, 951.
63 *CN*, IV, 4542 (June 1819).
64 *CN*, IV, 4512–13 (April 1819).
65 *CN*, IV, 4537 (6 May 1819).
66 *CN*, IV, 4537 (Notes).
67 Southey to Wordsworth, quoting Morgan, 5 and 8 May 1817, *New Letters*, II, 155.
68 *Don Juan*, Canto I (1819), stanza ccv, lines 1–4.
69 STC to Byron, 4 September 1819, *CL*, IV, 948.
70 Byron to Murray, 24 November 1818, *Letters and Journals*, VI, 82–3.
71 Byron, *The Complete Miscellaneous Prose*, ed. Andrew Nicholson (Oxford, 1991), p. 375.
72 *Don Juan*, Canto III (1821), stanza xciii.
73 See Eric Partridge, *A Dictionary of Slang and Unconventional English* (London, 1937, revised 1984).
74 Byron to Murray, 11 September 1822, *Letters and Journals*, IX, 206–7.
75 Sara Hutchinson to Tom Monkhouse, 25 July 1819, *Letters*, p. 157.
76 See David V. Erdman, 'Coleridge and the "Review Business": An Account of His Adventures with the *Edinburgh*, the *Quarterly*, and *Maga*,' *The Wordsworth Circle*, VI (Winter 1975), 3–50.
77 STC to Mudford, 19 March 1819, *CL*, IV, 928.
78 STC to Blackwood, 12 April 1819, *CL*, IV, 932, 933n.
79 Lockhart to STC, 8 June 1819, *CL*, IV, 943–4n.
80 STC to Blackwood, 30 June 1819, *CL*, IV, 944 and n.
81 [J. G. Lockhart], *Peter's Letters to his Kinsfolk*, 3 vols. (Edinburgh, 1819), II, 218–21.
82 Sara Hutchinson to John Monkhouse, November–December 1819, *Letters*, p. 166.
83 See STC to Lockhart, November 1819, *CL*, IV, 966–7 and n.
84 *Blackwood's Magazine*, October 1819, in *Critical Heritage*, pp. 436–51.
85 *Blackwood's Magazine*, XIV (October 1823), 377. Abraham Hayward praises STC's translation of *Wallenstein* in the preface to his translation of *Faust* (London, 1833), p. xiii.
86 See *CL*, IV, 123–4n.
87 STC to Lockhart, December 1820, *CL*, V, 127.
88 See Erdman, 'Coleridge and the "Review Business"', pp. 35ff.
89 STC to Blackwood, *circa* 19 September 1821, *CL*, V, 167–71.
90 *CL*, V, 169.
91 See Raymond Williams, *Keywords: A Vocabulary of Culture and Society* (London, 1976), p. 27.
92 See STC to John Taylor Coleridge, 3 May 1824, *CL*, V, 361.
93 STC to Allsop, 30 March 1820, *CL*, V, 24.
94 STC to Allsop, 8 April 1820, *CL*, V, 33.
95 *Coleridge's Miscellaneous Criticism*, ed. Thomas Middleton Raysor (London, 1936), pp. 329, 335.
96 See *CL*, V, 379.

97 See *CL*, V, 59n.
98 See John Taylor Coleridge to Gillman, 29 June 1820, *CL*, V, 67.
99 Sara Coleridge to Poole, 11 March 1821, *Minnow*, p. 85.
100 See *CL*, V, 81.
101 *CN*, IV, 4689 (30 June 1820).
102 STC to Allsop, 1 July 1820, *CL*, V, 79–80.
103 STC to Derwent Coleridge, 3 July 1820, *CL*, V, 84.
104 See *Letters of Hartley Coleridge*, ed. Griggs, p. 36.
105 See STC to Allsop, 8 August 1820, *CL*, V, 96.
106 STC to Allsop, 8 August 1820, *CL*, V, 95.
107 Hazlitt, 'The Drama', *London Magazine*, December 1820, *Complete Works*, XVIII, 370.
108 Lamb, 'Christ's Hospital Five and Thirty Years Ago', *London Magazine*, November 1820, *Works*, II, 12ff.
109 See Colley, *Britons*, p. 264, and Maccoby, *English Radicalism*, pp. 357ff.
110 *Table Talk*, *CW*, 14:I, 48 (27 April 1823).
111 See *CL*, V, 116n; Colley, *Britons*, pp. 265–6.
112 See Maccoby, *English Radicalism*, p. 374.
113 *HCR On Books*, I, 258 (8 December 1820).
114 STC to Allsop, 11 October 1820, *CL*, V, 117.
115 STC to Allsop, 25 October 1820, *CL*, V, 118–19.
116 STC to Derwent Coleridge, 16 May 1821, *CL*, V, 141.
117 STC to Francis Wrangham, 28 September 1819, *CL*, IV, 951.
118 See *Letters of Hartley Coleridge*, p. 56.
119 Hartley Coleridge to Lady Beaumont, December 1820, ibid., pp. 52–3.
120 Hartley Coleridge to Derwent Coleridge, 2 May 1821, ibid., p. 61.
121 STC to George Coleridge, 11 June 1821, *CL*, V, 145–8.
122 STC to Mrs Montagu, 12 June 1821, *CL*, V, 149.

CHAPTER 13   COLERIDGE THE SAGE: *AIDS TO REFLECTION* 1821–1825

1 STC to Allsop, probably June 1821, *CL*, V, 152–4.
2 STC to Allsop, 1 March 1822, *CL*, V, 218.
3 STC to Derwent Coleridge, 11 January 1822, *CL*, V, 192.
4 STC to Derwent Coleridge, 15 January 1822, *CL*, V, 197.
5 STC to Derwent Coleridge, 11 January 1822, *CL*, V, 193–4.
6 John Taylor Coleridge, Journal, 1 December 1821, *CL*, V, 195n.
7 STC, draft letter to John Dawes, late May 1822, *CL*, V, 229, 233.
8 Southey to Wordsworth, 11 April 1822, *New Letters*, II, 234.
9 Hartley Coleridge to STC, [1822], *Letters*, p. 75.
10 See STC to John Taylor Coleridge, 15 July 1822, *CL*, V, 246–7.
11 STC to Allsop, 3 August 1822, *CL*, V, 248.
12 STC to Allsop, 8 October 1822, *CL*, V, 249–51.
13 See *CL*, V, 203n.
14 STC to Murray, 18 January 1822, *CL*, V, 197–200.
15 See STC to C. A. Tulk, July 1823, *CL*, V, 281–4.
16 See Bradford K. Mudge, *Sara Coleridge: A Victorian Daughter* (New Haven, Conn., 1989), pp. 21ff, 55ff.
17 Ibid., p. 37.
18 See Sara Coleridge to Poole, 7 November 1822, *Minnow*, pp. 88–90.

19   Sara Hutchinson to John Monkhouse, 22 February 1822, *Letters*, p. 237.
20   *Table Talk*, *CW*, 14:II, 182–3 (4 August 1832).
21   STC to Charles Aders, 3 January 1823, *CL*, V, 267.
22   Sara Coleridge to Poole, 29 March 1823, *Minnow*, p. 99.
23   Lamb to Bernard Barton, 11 March 1823, *Letters of Charles Lamb, to which are added those of his Sister, Mary Lamb*, ed. E. V. Lucas, 3 vols. (London, 1935), II, 374.
24   *Table Talk*, *CW*, 14:I, 61 (2 June 1824).
25   *Etonian*, 1821, in *Critical Heritage*, pp. 463, 466.
26   *Examiner*, 21 October 1821, in *Critical Heritage*, pp. 471–5.
27   *Table Talk*, *CW*, 14:I, 26 (5 January 1823).
28   *Table Talk*, *CW*, 14:I, 16 (9 January 1823).
29   *CW*, 14:I, 16–17.
30   James Coleridge to John Taylor Coleridge, 22 March 1823, *Story of a Devonshire House*, p. 282.
31   STC to Mrs Aders, 25 March 1823, *CL*, V, 271.
32   Lamb to Barton, 5 April 1823, *Letters*, ed. Lucas, II, 376–7.
33   See *HCR On Books*, I, 293 (5 April 1823).
34   *Table Talk*, *CW*, 14:I, 42 (27 April 1823).
35   *CW*, 14:I, 52 and n (1 May 1823).
36   *PW*, I, 441–3.
37   *PW*, I, 439–41.
38   *CN*, IV, 4986 (July–September 1823); *PW*, II, 982–3.
39   STC to Taylor and Hessey, 8 August 1823, *CL*, V, 290.
40   STC to John Anster, 18 February 1824, *CL*, V, 336–7.
41   Lamb to Barton, 23 January 1824, *Letters*, ed. Lucas, II, 416.
42   See STC to Allsop, 17 November 1821, *CL*, V, 187.
43   See STC to Richard Cattermole, Secretary of the Royal Society of Literature, 16 March 1824, *CL*, V, 343 and n.
44   STC to Anster, 18 February 1824, *CL*, V, 335–6.
45   *CL*, V, 335–7.
46   Hartley Coleridge to STC, 12 March 1824, *Letters*, pp. 85–6; *CN*, IV, 5113 (January–February 1824).
47   STC to Wordsworth, 12 April 1824, *CL*, VI, 1052–3.
48   See *CL*, V, 354n.
49   Hartley Coleridge to STC, 12 March 1824, *Letters*, p. 87.
50   STC to T. H. Dunn, 10 March 1824, *CL*, V, 342. See also V, 362, 373 and n.
51   De Quincey, *Confessions*, p. 88.
52   Quoted in Gillman, *Life*, pp. 247–8.
53   *Confessions*, p. 4.
54   Ibid., p. 155.
55   Ibid., p. 158.
56   Ibid., pp. 163–4.
57   See *CN*, IV, 5163 (Notes); *CL*, III, 541.
58   See *CN*, IV, 5164 and Notes (29 September 1824).
59   STC to De Quincey, 8 August 1821, *CL*, V, 161–4. See also Lindop, *The Opium-Eater*, p. 246.
60   Mrs Gillman to STC, 7 April 1824, *CL*, V, 346.
61   STC to Green, 9 April 1824, *CL*, V, 348.
62   STC to Allsop, 10 February 1825, *CL*, V, 411.
63   Lamb to Robinson, 29 November 1824, *Letters*, ed. Lucas, II, 445.

64 STC to Charlotte Brent, 7 July 1823, *CL*, V, 280.
65 Lamb to Leigh Hunt, [early 1825], *Letters*, ed. Lucas, II, 457.
66 See *Table Talk*, *CW*, 14:I, 127–8n.
67 *CN*, IV, 5192 (21 February 1825); see also *CL*, V, 414–15.
68 *PW*, I, 447.
69 *PW*, I, 451–3 (first published in 1834).
70 See Jones, *Hazlitt*, pp. 319ff, 343, 359ff.
71 *Spirit of the Age, Complete Works*, XI, 28–38.
72 Medwin, *Conversations*, pp. 178–9.
73 STC to John Taylor Coleridge, 8 April 1825, *CL*, V, 421–2 and n.
74 STC to Stuart, 8 July 1825, *CL*, V, 475.
75 STC to Edward Coleridge, [11 November 1825], *CL*, V, 509.
76 See John Beer's Introduction to *Aids to Reflection* (London 1993), *CW*, 9, xcvi.
77 See the useful notes in *CW*, 9, passim.
78 *Aids to Reflection*, *CW*, 9, 106–7.
79 Mill, 'Coleridge', *London and Westminster Review*, XXXIII (March 1840), 266–7.
80 *CW*, 9, 5–6.
81 See Index to *CW*, 9, 594.
82 *CW*, 9, 8.
83 *CW*, 9, 8–9.
84 *CW*, 9, 216–18, 223.
85 *HCR On Books*, I, 335 (20 May 1826).
86 Mill, 'Coleridge', p. 263.
87 *British Critic*, October 1826, in *Critical Heritage*, p. 487.
88 Southey to Lockhart, 2 January 1826, *New Letters*, II, 299–300.
89 *Fraser's Magazine*, June 1832, in *Critical Heritage*, pp. 585–6.
90 See John Beer, Introduction to *Aids to Reflection*, *CW*, 9, cxiv–cxvi; also C. R. Sanders, *Coleridge and the Broad Church Movement* (Durham, North Carolina, 1942, reprinted New York, 1972).
91 See *CW*, 9, cxxiii.
92 F. D. Maurice, *The Kingdom of Christ*, quoted in *Coleridge: The Critical Heritage*, vol. 2, ed. J. R. de J. Jackson (London, 1991), p. 121.

CHAPTER 14   PROGRESS AND PERMANENCE 1826–1829

1 See Negley Harte and John North, *The World of UCL 1828–1990* (London, 1978, revised 1991).
2 STC to Allsop, 10 May 1825, and to Green, 10 May 1825, *CL*, V, 446, 447–8.
3 STC to John Taylor Coleridge, 17 May 1825, *CL*, V, 457.
4 See Harte and North, p. 31.
5 STC to Hessey, 7 May 1825, *CL*, V, 435 and n.
6 Carlyle to John Carlyle, 24 June 1824, *The Collected Letters of Thomas and Jane Welsh Carlyle*, ed. C. R. Sanders and K. J. Fielding et al., 21 vols so far (Durham, North Carolina, 1970–), III, 90.
7 Carlyle, *Life of John Sterling, Works*, ed. H. D. Traill, 31 vols. (London, 1896–1901), XI, 56.
8 Ibid., XI, 59.
9 Carlyle to Emerson, 8 December 1837, *Collected Letters*, IX, 360–1.
10 STC to Hessey, 23 May 1825, *CL*, V, 464–5.
11 See STC to John Taylor Coleridge, 20 December 1825, *CL*, V, 525.

12 STC to Edward Coleridge, 14 April 1825, *CL*, V, 424.
13 STC to Edward Coleridge, 15 July 1825, and to the Gillmans, *circa* 24 July 1825, *CL*, V, 482–3, 487.
14 STC to Edward Coleridge, 18 October 1825, *CL*, V, 501–2.
15 STC to Gillman, 22 October 1825, *CL*, V, 505–7.
16 STC to Derwent Coleridge, 21 December 1825, *CL*, V, 527.
17 See STC to George Skinner, 26 January 1826, *CL*, VI, 547.
18 Sara Coleridge to Derwent Coleridge, 30 January 1826, *CL*, VI, 546n.
19 STC to Derwent Coleridge, [January 1826], *CL*, VI, 546–7.
20 Hartley Coleridge to John Taylor Coleridge, 12 February 1825, *Letters*, pp. 89, 95.
21 Hartley Coleridge to Sara Coleridge, 6 February 1831, ibid., pp. 127–8.
22 Ibid., pp. 90, 95.
23 Hartley Coleridge to Derwent Coleridge, [1826], ibid., p. 92.
24 Dorothy Wordsworth to Mary Laing, 29 March 1826, and to Crabb Robinson, 18 December 1826, *Letters, The Later Years, 1821–53*, revised Alan G. Hill, 4 vols. (Oxford, 1978–88), I, 434, 500. Henceforth referred to as *LY*.
25 Sara Coleridge to Poole, 28 August 1826, *Minnow*, p. 133.
26 *Letters of Hartley Coleridge*, p. 96
27 STC to Gillman, [probably May 1825], *CL*, V, 466.
28 *PW*, I, 457, 458.
29 *CN*, IV, 5275 (November 1825).
30 *CN*, IV, 5318 (January–February 1826).
31 STC to Derwent Coleridge, 11 January 1826, *CL*, VI, 537.
32 STC to Edward Coleridge, 15 July 1825, *CL*, V, 481.
33 STC to Stuart, 18 April 1826, *CL*, VI, 577.
34 *CN*, IV, 5322 (January–February 1826).
35 *CN*, IV, 5323 (8 February 1826).
36 Unpublished notebook, BL Add. MS 47,528, f. 11v (July 1827).
37 *CN*, IV, 5334 and Notes (13 March 1826).
38 *CN*, IV, 5360 (26 April 1826).
39 Ibid.
40 See Introduction to Scott's *Journal*, ed. W. E. K. Anderson (Oxford, 1972), pp. xxiii–xxviii.
41 STC to Edward Coleridge, 8 February 1826, *CL*, VI, 562.
42 See *CL*, VI, 602–3n.
43 See *CN*, IV, 5402 (Notes).
44 STC to Edward Coleridge, 8 February 1826, *CL*, VI, 560.
45 Hartley Coleridge to Derwent Coleridge, [1826], *Letters*, p. 93.
46 *CN*, IV, 5402 (17 June 1826).
47 STC to Edward Coleridge, 27 July 1826, *CL*, VI, 589 and n.
48 STC to Edward Coleridge, 27 July 1826, *CL*, VI, 590–1.
49 Sara Coleridge to Poole, 28 August 1826, *Minnow*, p. 132.
50 Sara Hutchinson to Edward Quillinan, 23 August 1826, *Letters*, pp. 322–3.
51 *CN*, IV, 5419 (30 July 1826).
52 Southey to Richard White, 1 July 1826, *Life and Correspondence*, V, 262.
53 *Table Talk*, *CW*, 14:I, 66 (10 March 1827).
54 Unpublished notebook, BL Add. MS 47,549, f. 18 (early 1834).
55 Henry Nelson Coleridge to Sara Coleridge, 2 January 1827, *Table Talk*, *CW*, 14:I, 62n.
56 STC to Edward Coleridge, 28 October 1826, *CL*, VI, 643.

57 See STC to Edward Coleridge, 19 November 1826, *CL*, VI, 647.
58 STC to Mrs Aders, [December 1826], *CL*, VI, 652.
59 STC to William Worship, 29 December 1826, *CL*, VI, 659.
60 'To Mary Pridham', *PW*, I, 468–9.
61 See *HCR On Books*, I, 350 (9 December 1827).
62 'Homeless', *PW*, I, 460.
63 STC to Frere, [January 1826], and to Daniel Stuart, 20 February 1827, *CL*, VI, 539 and n, 669–70 and n.
64 STC to Henry Nelson Coleridge, 8 May 1827, *CL*, VI, 680–1, 682.
65 Sara Coleridge to Poole, summer 1827, *Minnow*, p. 137.
66 STC to Derwent Coleridge, [October 1827], *CL*, VI, 705.
67 STC to Mrs Alaric Watts, 2 July 1827, *CL*, VI, 695.
68 See *Table Talk*, *CW*, 14:I, 73–8.
69 STC to George May Coleridge, 14 January 1828, *CL*, VI, 720.
70 Unpublished notebook, BL Add. MS 47,531, f. 47 (13 January 1828).
71 Leigh Hunt, *Lord Byron and Some of His Contemporaries* (London, 1828), pp. 300, 301.
72 Ibid., p. 304.
73 STC to Henry Nelson Coleridge, 20 February 1828, *CL*, VI, 729–30.
74 *PW*, I, 468.
75 *CL*, VI, 731n.
76 *PW*, I, 476.
77 *Westminster Review*, January 1830, in *Critical Heritage*, pp. 548, 550–1, 552, 554.
78 See Mudge, *Sara Coleridge*, p. 47.
79 See STC to William Sotheby, 28 April 1828, *CL*, VI, 736.
80 James Fenimore Cooper, *Gleanings in Europe: England (1837)*, ed. Donald A. Ringe and Kenneth W. Staggs (Albany, New York, 1982), p. 127.
81 Scott, *Journal*, p. 462 (22 April 1828).
82 *HCR On Books*, I, 359–60 (18 June 1828).
83 Ibid., I, 357 (28 May 1828).
84 See Colley, *Britons*, pp. 324ff.
85 Sara Coleridge to Poole, 15 July 1829, *Minnow*, p. 148.
86 Southey to Landor, 14 April 1829, *Life and Correspondence*, VI, 44.
87 See Gill, *William Wordsworth*, p. 403.
88 See Dora Wordsworth to Edward Quillinan, 1 August 1828, *LY*, I, 620.
89 Ibid., I, 620, 621n.
90 Charles Aders to Crabb Robinson, August 1828, *Correspondence of HCR with the Wordsworth Circle*, I, 190.
91 Thomas Colley Grattan, *Beaten Paths; and Those Who Trod Them*, 2 vols. (London, 1862), II, 109–10.
92 See Wordsworth, *LY*, I, 616n.
93 *Correspondence of HCR with the Wordsworth Circle*, I, 190.
94 Julian Charles Young, *A Memoir of Charles Mayne Young*, 2 vols. (London, 1871), I, 174.
95 Unpublished notebook, BL Add. MS 47,535, f. 8ff (14 July 1828). Coleridge's rather rusty German reads: 'Kurzlich, alle Fehlerhaften, die in seinen frühen männlichen Jahren ihn auszeichnete, haben sich erstaunlich vergrössert – die grandiöse Riesenblümen seines philosophischen und dichterischen Genies sind verblüht und austrocknet.'
96 STC to F. M. Reynolds, 8 August 1828, *CL*, VI, 748.

97 See Wordsworth, *LY*, II, 15n; see also *CL*, VI, 752 and n, 759–60 and n, 776 and n.
98 STC to Reynolds, 25 August 1828, *CL* 754 and n.
99 *CL*, VI, 763–4n.
100 STC to Stuart, 14 October 1828, *CL*, VI, 765–6 and n.
101 STC to Hall, 4 December 1828, *CL*, VI, 775; see also *CL*, VI, 752n.
102 STC to Thomas Hurst, 19 January 1829, and to William Pickering, [probably January 1829], *CL*, VI, 780–1 and n, 782 and n.
103 See Sara Coleridge to Poole, 15 July 1829, *Minnow*, p. 147.
104 Sara Coleridge to Poole, 15 July 1829, ibid., pp. 147, 148.
105 Southey to Mrs Septimus Hodson, 10 September 1829, *New Letters*, II, 344.
106 STC to Derwent Coleridge, 28 August 1829, *CL*, VI, 814–15.
107 Hartley Coleridge to Sara Coleridge, [July] 1829, *Letters*, pp. 99, 101.
108 See *Minnow*, p. 146.
109 See Sara Coleridge to Poole, 26 September 1829, ibid., p. 153.
110 Southey to Bedford, 28 September 1829, *New Letters*, II, 345.
111 See Mudge, *Sara Coleridge*, p. 55.
112 See Dorothy Wordsworth to Derwent Coleridge, 27 September 1829, *LY*, II, 153.
113 Sara Coleridge to Poole, 26 September 1829, *Minnow*, p. 153.
114 STC to Thomas Dunn, [August 1829], *CL*, VI, 813.
115 *CL*, VI, 692n.
116 Unpublished notebook, BL Add. MS 47,536, f. 54v. (2 September 1829).
117 See *CL*, VI, 1000–1 (Appendix A).
118 *CL*, VI, 1000.
119 Unpublished notebook, BL Add. MS 47,535, ff. 24–24v (?early May 1829).
120 See Editor's Introduction to *On the Constitution of Church and State*, ed. John Colmer (London, 1976), *CW*, 10, xliiff.
121 *On the Constitution of Church and State*, *CW*, 10, 156.
122 *CW*, 10, 107, 108.
123 *CW*, 10, 91, 93.
124 *CW*, 10, 92–3n.
125 See Sara Coleridge to Poole, 25 June 1830, *Minnow*, pp. 155–6.
126 *CW*, 10, 46.
127 See *CW*, 10, lxiiff.
128 John Sterling, *Essays and Tales*, ed. J. C. Hare, 2 vols. (London, 1848), I, xv.
129 *CW*, 10, 66–7.
130 Unpublished notebook, BL Add. MS 47,530, f. 9 (1827).

CHAPTER 15 LAST YEARS: *CHURCH AND STATE* 1830–1834

1 STC to Henry Nelson Coleridge, 11 September 1830, and to Cary, 29 November 1830, *CL*, VI, 846–7, 847.
2 *Eclectic Review*, July 1831, in *Critical Heritage*, pp. 562–4.
3 *Edinburgh Review*, April 1835, in *Critical Heritage*, II, 36–7.
4 *Table Talk*, *CW*, 14:I, 157 (4 June 1830).
5 *CW*, 14:I, 276–7 (31 March 1832).
6 See *CL*, VI, 285n.
7 *Table Talk*, *CW*, 14:I, 187–8 (8 September 1830).

8 *CW*, 14:I, 214–15 (8 October 1830).
9 STC to William Blackwood, 15 May 1830, *CL*, VI, 836.
10 Lamb to Southey, 10 May 1830, *Letters*, ed. Lucas, II, 270.
11 Henry Nelson Coleridge to Colonel James Coleridge, 8 June 1830, *Table Talk*, *CW*, 14:I, 162–3n.
12 *CW*, 14:I, 200 (19 September 1830).
13 *CW*, 14:I, 106 (20 April 1830).
14 *CW*, 14:I, 174–5 (7 July 1830).
15 George Eliot, 'The Natural History of German Life', *Selected Critical Writings*, ed. Rosemary Ashton (Oxford, 1992), p. 295.
16 Dorothy Wordsworth to Mrs Clarkson, *circa* 5 November 1830, *LY*, II, 336.
17 *Table Talk*, *CW*, 14:I, 126–7 (9 May 1830).
18 Unpublished notebook, BL Add. MS 47,539, ff. 3v–5.
19 *Table Talk*, *CW*, 14:I, 197 (19 September 1830).
20 Unpublished notebook, BL Add. MS 47,541, f. 9 (30 August 1830).
21 STC, *PW*, II, 962 and n. Text corrected from unpublished notebook, BL Add. MS 47,542, f. 1v.
22 *Table Talk*, *CW*, 14:I, 194 (19 September 1830).
23 *CW*, 14:I, 206 (26 September 1830).
24 Dorothy Wordsworth to Sara Coleridge, 5 March 1830, *LY*, II, 208–12.
25 Hartley Coleridge to Derwent Coleridge, 30 August 1830, *Letters*, p. 111.
26 Dorothy Wordsworth to Sara Coleridge, 8 November 1830, *LY*, II, 344.
27 Sara Coleridge to Poole, 12 September 1830, *Minnow*, p. 160.
28 Hartley Coleridge to Derwent Coleridge, 30 August 1830, *Letters*, p. 109.
29 See *CL*, VI, 854 and n.
30 See *CL*, VI, 854–7n.
31 See STC to Henry Nelson Coleridge, 27 May 1831, *CL*, VI, 860; also ibid., 856n.
32 See Colley, *Britons*, pp. 342–5.
33 Southey to J. W. Warter, 12 January 1831, *Life and Correspondence*, VI, 127.
34 Sara Hutchinson to Elizabeth Hutchinson, 11 October 1831, *Letters*, p. 385.
35 Wordsworth to William Rowan Hamilton, 22 November 1831, *LY*, II, 455; *HCR On Books*, I, 405 (24 March 1832).
36 STC to Green, 13 September 1831, *CL*, VI, 871.
37 *Table Talk*, *CW*, 14:I, 254 (20 November 1831).
38 Unpublished notebook, BL Add. MS 47,545, f. 9v (22 April 1831).
39 *Table Talk*, *CW*, 14:I, 270 (31 March 1832).
40 *CW*, 14:I, 281–2 (4 April 1832).
41 'Cholera Cured Before-Hand', *PW*, II, 986; See also *CL*, VI, 924.
42 STC to Worship, May 1832, *CL*, VI, 911; also STC to Green, 7 April 1832, *CL*, VI, 899.
43 STC to Green, 29 March 1832, *CL*, VI, 894.
44 *CL*, VI, 895.
45 STC to Henry Nelson Coleridge, 7 May 1832, *CL*, VI, 903–4.
46 STC to Green, 18 May 1832, *CL*, VI, 909.
47 *HCR On Books*, I, 413 (29 September 1832).
48 See Wordsworth, *LY*, II, 538; Gill, *Wordsworth*, p. 375; Sara Coleridge to Poole, 16 August 1832, *Minnow*, p. 165.
49 See Hartley Coleridge to Sara Coleridge, 16 April and 10 October 1831, 17 February and 24 July 1832, *Letters*, pp. 132–8, 143.
50 See Hartley Coleridge, *New Poems*, ed. E. L. Griggs (Oxford, 1942), p. 3.
51 Sara Coleridge to Poole, 24 July 1833, *Minnow*, p. 177.

52 STC to Green, 6 August 1832, *CL*, VI, 918.
53 Sara Coleridge to Poole, 16 August 1832, *Minnow*, p. 165.
54 Sara Coleridge to Poole, 18 October 1832, ibid., p. 172.
55 Southey to Edith Southey, 18 June 1831, *New Letters*, II, 369.
56 Hartley Coleridge to Sara Coleridge, 17 February 1832, *Letters*, p. 137.
57 *Table Talk, CW*, 14:I, 412–13 (4 August 1833).
58 Henry Nelson Coleridge to John Taylor Coleridge, 2 April 1833, *CW*, 14:I, 350n.
59 STC to Green, 7 April 1833, *CL*, VI, 934.
60 Hayward, *Faust*, p. xiii; see STC to John Sterling, 11 April 1833, *CL*, VI, 935.
61 *Table Talk, CW*, 14:I, 336–43 (16 February 1833).
62 *CW*, 14:I, 356–7 (5 April 1833).
63 *CW*, 14:I, 466–8 (15 March 1834).
64 *CW*, 14:I, 244–5 (14 August 1831).
65 STC to Sotheby, 28 April 1808, *CL*, III, 95.
66 *Nightmare Abbey*, p. 67.
67 *Table Talk, CW*, 14:I, 492 (28 June 1834).
68 *CW*, 14:I, 489–90 (23 June 1834).
69 STC to Gioacchino de' Prati, 29 October 1833, *CL*, VI, 966.
70 *Table Talk, CW*, 14:I, 410, 496 (1 and 5 July 1833).
71 *CW*, 14:I, 479 (19 May 1834).
72 See Sara Coleridge to Poole, 24 July 1833, *Minnow*, p. 176.
73 *Table Talk, CW*, 14:I, 392–3 and n (29 June 1833).
74 *CW*, 14:I, 394–7 (29 June 1833).
75 STC to Dunn, 14 August 1833, *CL*, VI, 953.
76 Ralph Waldo Emerson, *English Traits* (1856), ed. Howard Mumford Jones (Cambridge, Mass., 1966), pp. 6, 8, 160.
77 *PW*, I, 491.
78 Unpublished notebook, BL Add. MS 47,547, f. 26. See also the version in STC to Green, 28 October 1833, *CL*, VI, 963, and *PW*, I, 491–2.
79 STC to Mrs Aders [November 1833], *CL*, VI, 969.
80 STC to E. F. Finden, 6 November 1833, *CL*, VI, 974.
81 See Mudge, *Sara Coleridge*, p. 66.
82 STC to Green, 17 March 1834, *CL*, VI, 977.
83 *Critical Heritage*, pp. 613, 620–51.
84 See Sara Hutchinson to Mary Hutchinson, August 1834, *Letters*, p. 428.
85 Sara Hutchinson to Quillinan, 9 May 1834, ibid., p. 414.
86 Sara Hutchinson to Mary Hutchinson, August 1834, ibid., p. 428.
87 See Sara Hutchinson to Sara Coleridge, 28 September 1834, ibid., p. 430.
88 See *CL*, VI, 994–7 (Appendix A).
89 See Appendix E of *Table Talk, CW*, 14:I, 546 (15 October 1829).

Bibliography

Manuscript Sources

British Library, Add. MSS 47,525–47,550 (Coleridge notebooks not yet published in *CN*).
British Library, Add. MS 35,345 (Correspondence of Thomas Poole).
British Library, Add. MS 30,927 (Southey Correspondence).
Bodleian Library, Oxford, MS Dep. c. 604/3 (Abinger–Shelley Papers).
The Wordsworth Trust, Dove Cottage, Grasmere, Cumbria (MS of STC poem 'The Day-Dream').
Harry Ransom Humanities Research Center, University of Texas at Austin (letters of Sara Coleridge and other members of the Coleridge family).

Biographies of Coleridge

Gillman, James, *The Life of Samuel Taylor Coleridge*, London, 1838.
Chambers, E. K., *Samuel Taylor Coleridge: A Biographical Study*, Oxford, 1938.
Bate, Walter Jackson, *Coleridge*, New York, 1968, reprinted 1970.
Willey, Basil, *Samuel Taylor Coleridge*, London, 1972.
Fruman, Norman, *Coleridge, The Damaged Archangel*, London, 1972.
Cornwell, John, *Coleridge, Poet and Revolutionary 1772–1804*, London, 1973.
Lefebure, Molly, *Samuel Taylor Coleridge: A Bondage of Opium*, London, 1974.
Holmes, Richard, *Coleridge: Early Visions*, London, 1989.

Abrams, M. H., *The Mirror and the Lamp: Romantic Theory and the Critical Tradition*, Oxford, 1953.
Allsop, Thomas (ed.), *Letters, Conversations, and Recollections of S. T. Coleridge*, 3rd edition, London, 1864.
Armour, R. W. and Howes, R. F. (eds), *Coleridge the Talker: A Series of Contemporary Descriptions and Comments*, New York, 1940.

Ashton, Rosemary, *The German Idea: Four English Writers and the Reception of German Thought, 1800–60*, Cambridge, 1980, reprinted London, 1994.

Aspinall, A., *Politics and the Press ca 1780–1850*, London, 1949.

Axon, William E. A., 'Anna Jane Vardill Niven, the Authoress of "Christobell", the Sequel to Coleridge's "Christabel". With a Bibliography', *Transactions of the Royal Society of Literature*, London, 1908.

Bate, Jonathan, *Shakespeare and the English Romantic Imagination*, Oxford, 1986.

Beer, John, *Coleridge's Poetic Intelligence*, London, 1977.

Beer, John, 'How Far Can We Trust Coleridge?', *The Wordsworth Circle*, XX, Spring 1989.

British Pamphleteers, ed. George Orwell and Reginald Reynolds, 2 vols, London, 1948 and 1951.

Brown, Philip Anthony, *The French Revolution in English History*, London, 1918, reprinted 1965.

Burwick, Frederick, 'On Stage Illusion: From Wordsworth's Marginalia to Coleridge's Lectures', *The Wordsworth Circle*, XIX, Winter 1988.

Byron, George Gordon, 6th Baron, *The Complete Miscellaneous Prose*, ed. Andrew Nicholson, Oxford, 1991.

Byron, George Gordon, 6th Baron, *Letters and Journals*, ed. Leslie Marchand, 12 vols, London, 1973–82.

Byron, George Gordon, 6th Baron, *Poetical Works*, London, 1904, reprinted 1967.

Carlyle, Thomas, *The Collected Letters of Thomas and Jane Welsh Carlyle*, ed. C. R. Sanders, K. J. Fielding et al., 21 vols so far, Durham, North Carolina, 1970– .

Carlyle, Thomas, *Works*, Centenary Edition, ed. H. D. Traill, 31 vols, London, 1896–1901.

Carlyon, Clement, *Early Years and Late Reflections*, 4 vols, London, 1836–58.

Christ's Hospital: Recollections of Lamb, Coleridge, and Leigh Hunt, ed. R. Brimley Johnson, London, 1896.

Citron, Jo Ann, 'Two Unrecorded Manuscripts of "Christabel"', *The Wordsworth Circle*, XIII, Autumn 1982.

Clark, John Ruskin, *Joseph Priestley: A Comet in the System*, San Diego, California, 1990.

Cockburn, Henry, *Memorials of His Time*, Edinburgh, 1856.

Coleman, Deirdre, 'Coleridge, Quakerism, and *The Friend*', *The Wordsworth Circle*, XVII, Summer 1986.

Coleman, Deirdre, 'Jeffrey and Coleridge: Four Unpublished Letters', *The Wordsworth Circle*, XVIII, Winter 1987.

Coleridge, The Critical Heritage, ed. J. R. de J. Jackson, London, 1970.

Coleridge, The Critical Heritage Volume 2: 1834–1900, ed. J. R. de J. Jackson, London, 1991.

Coleridge, Lord, *The Story of a Devonshire House*, London, 1906.

Coleridge, Hartley, *Letters*, ed. Grace Evelyn Griggs and Earl Leslie Griggs, Oxford, 1937, reprinted 1941.

Coleridge, Hartley *New Poems*, ed. Earl Leslie Griggs, Oxford, 1942.

Coleridge Sara (junior), *Memoir and Letters of Sara Coleridge*, ed. Edith Coleridge, 2 vols, London, 1873.

Colley, Linda, *Britons: Forging the Nation 1707–1837*, New Haven, Connecticut, 1992.

Cooke, Katharine, *Coleridge*, London, 1979.

Cooper, James Fenimore, *Gleanings in Europe: England (1837)*, ed. Donald A. Ringe and Kenneth W. Staggs, Albany, New York, 1982.

Cottle, Joseph, *Early Recollections; chiefly relating to the late Samuel Taylor Coleridge*, 2 vols, London, 1837.

Cowper, William, *Poetical Works*, ed. William Benham, London, 1924.

Crick, Joyce, 'Some Editorial and Stylistic Observations on Coleridge's Translation of Schiller's *Wallenstein*', *Publications of the English Goethe Society*, new series LIV, 1985.

Critical Heritage, for references concerning STC see under Coleridge.

Davy, Humphry, *Researches, Chemical and Philosophical; chiefly concerning Nitrous Oxide, or Dephlogisticated Nitrous Air, and its Respiration*, London, 1800.

De Quincey, Thomas, *Collected Writings*, ed. David Masson, 14 vols, Edinburgh, 1889–90.

De Quincey, Thomas, *Confessions of an English Opium-Eater*, London, 1822, reprinted in facsimile, Oxford, 1989.

Dickens, Charles, *David Copperfield*, Harmondsworth, 1977.

Durrant, Cherry, 'The Lives and Works of Hartley, Derwent and Sara Coleridge', unpublished PhD thesis, University of London, 1994.

Eliot, George, *Selected Critical Writings*, ed. Rosemary Ashton, Oxford, 1992.

Emerson, Ralph Waldo, *English Traits* (1856), ed. Howard Mumford Jones, Cambridge, Mass., 1966.

Engell, James (ed.), *Coleridge: The Early Family Letters*, Oxford, 1994.

D. J. Enright and Ernst de Chickera, (eds), *English Critical Texts*, Oxford, 1962, reprinted 1983.

Erdman, David V., 'Coleridge and the "Review Business": An Account of his Adventures with the *Edinburgh*, the *Quarterly*, and *Maga*', *The Wordsworth Circle*, VI, Winter 1975.

Foakes, R. A. (ed.), *Coleridge's Criticism of Shakespeare: A Selection*, London, 1989.

Foakes, R. A., '"Thriving Prisoners": Coleridge, Wordsworth and the Child at School', *Studies in Romanticism*, XXVIII, 1989.

Forster, E. M., 'Trooper Silas Tomkyn Comberbacke', *Abinger Harvest*, London, 1936, reprinted Harmondsworth, 1974.

Fruman, Norman, 'Creative Process and Concealment in Coleridge's Poetry', *Romantic Revisions*, ed. Robert Brinkley and Keith Hanley, Cambridge, 1992.

George, Mary Dorothy, vol. VI of *Catalogue of Political and Personal Satires*, London, 1978.

Gill, Stephen, *William Wordsworth: A Life*, Oxford, 1989.

Goodwin, Albert, *The Friends of Liberty*, London, 1979.

Grattan, Thomas Colley, *Beaten Paths; and Those Who Trod Them*, 2 vols, London, 1862.

Hamilton, Walter (ed.), *Parodies of the Works of English and American Authors*, 6 vols in 3, London, 1884–9.

Hankinson, Alan, *Coleridge Walks the Fells: A Lakeland Journey Retraced*, London, 1991.

Harte, Negley and North, John, *The World of UCL 1828–1990*, London, 1978, revised 1991.

Hartley, David, *Observations on Man, His Frame, His Duty, and His Expectations*, London, 1749, reprinted, ed. Hermann Pistorius, 1791.

Haven, Richard, 'Anna Vardill Niven's "Christobell": An Addendum', *The Wordsworth Circle*, VII, Spring 1976.

Hawkes, Terence (ed.), *Coleridge on Shakespeare*, Harmondsworth, 1969.

Hayter, Alethea, *Opium and the Romantic Imagination*, London, 1968.

Hayward, Abraham (tr.), *Faust, a Dramatic Poem, by Goethe*, London, 1833.

Hazlitt, William, *Complete Works*, ed. P. P. Howe, 21 vols, London, 1930–4.

Hazlitt, William, *Letters*, ed. H. M. Sikes, W. H. Bonner, and G. Lahely, London, 1979.

Hindle, Wilfred, *The Morning Post 1772–1937: Portrait of a Newspaper*, London, 1937.

Holmes, Richard, *Shelley: The Pursuit*, London, 1974.

House, Humphry, *Coleridge: The Clark Lectures 1951–1952*, London, 1953.

Hunt, Leigh, *Lord Byron and Some of His Contemporaries*, London, 1828.

Hunt, Leigh, *Autobiography*, ed. J. E. Morpurgo, London, 1949.

Hunt, Leigh, *Dramatic Criticism 1808–1831*, ed. L. H. Houtchens and C. W. Houtchens, London, 1950.

Hutchinson, Sara, *Letters from 1800 to 1835*, ed. Kathleen Coburn, London, 1954.

Jackson, H. J., 'Coleridge's Collaborator, Joseph Henry Green', *Studies in Romanticism*, XXI, 1982.

James, Henry, *The Coxon Fund*, London, 1894.

Johnson, Samuel, *Preface to the Edition of Shakespeare's Plays*, in *Samuel Johnson on Shakespeare*, ed. H. R. Woudhuysen, Harmondsworth, 1989.

Jones, Stanley, *Hazlitt: A Life*, Oxford, 1989.

Jordan, John E., *De Quincey to Wordsworth: A Biography of a Relationship*, Berkeley, California, 1962.

Jump, Harriet Devine, 'High Sentiment of Liberty: Coleridge's Unacknowledged Debt to Akenside', *Studies in Romanticism*, XXVIII, 1989.

Kant, Immanuel, *Werke*, ed. Wilhelm Weischedel, 6 vols, Wiesbaden, 1956–64.

Katz, Marilyn, 'Early Dissent between Wordsworth and Coleridge: Preface Deletion of October 1800', *The Wordsworth Circle*, IX, Winter 1978.

Keats, John, *Letters*, ed. Hyder Edward Rollins, 2 vols, Cambridge, Mass., 1958, reprinted 1980.

Kelliher, Hilton, 'The *Kubla Khan* Manuscript and its First Collector', *The British Library Journal*, XX, Autumn 1994.

Kissane, James, ' "Michael", "Christabel", and the *Lyrical Ballads* of 1800', *The Wordsworth Circle*, IX, Winter 1978.

Knight, David, *Humphry Davy: Science and Power*, Oxford, 1992.

Knight, G. Wilson, *The Starlit Dome: Studies in the Poetry of Vision*, 1941, reprinted London, 1959.

Lamb, Charles, *Works*, 2 vols, London, 1818.

Lamb, Charles, *The Works of Charles and Mary Lamb*, ed. E. V. Lucas, 7 vols, London, 1903–5.

Lamb, Charles, *The Letters of Charles Lamb, to which are added those of his Sister, Mary Lamb*, ed. E. V. Lucas, 3 vols, London, 1935.

Lamb, Charles, *The Letters of Charles and Mary Lamb*, ed. Edwin W. Marrs Jr, 3 vols, Ithaca, New York, and London, 1975–8.

Lansdown, Richard, *Byron's Historical Dramas*, Oxford, 1992.

Lefebure, Molly, '*The Bondage of Love: A Life of Mrs Samuel Taylor Coleridge*, London, 1986.

Lefebure, Molly, 'Consolations in Opium: The Expanding Universe of Coleridge, Humphry Davy, and "The Recluse"', *The Wordsworth Circle*, XVII, Spring 1986.

Lefebure, Molly, 'Humphry Davy: Philosophic Alchemist', in *The Coleridge Connection: Essays for Thomas McFarland*, ed. Richard Gravil and Molly Lefebure, London, 1990.

Le Grice, Valentine, 'College Reminiscences of Mr Coleridge', *Gentleman's Magazine*, new series II, December 1834.

Levine, William, 'The Progress Poem in Coleridge's Political Lyrics', *The Wordsworth Circle*, XX, Spring 1989.

Lindop, Grevel, *The Opium-Eater: A Life of Thomas De Quincey*, London, 1981.

Litchfield, R. B., *Tom Wedgwood: The First Photographer*, London, 1903.

Lloyd, Charles, *Edmund Oliver*, Bristol, 1798.

Lockhart, J. G., *Peter's Letters to his Kinsfolk*, 3 vols, Edinburgh, 1819.

Lowes, J. Livingston, *The Road to Xanadu: A Study in the Ways of the Imagination*, Cambridge, Mass., 1927.

Maccoby, S., *English Radicalism 1786–1832*, London, 1955.

Mackintosh, Sir James, *Memoirs of the Life of the Rt. Hon. Sir James Mackintosh*, ed. Robert James Mackintosh, 2 vols, London, 1835.

McFarland, Tom, *Coleridge and the Pantheist Tradition*, Oxford, 1969.

McKusick, James, 'Coleridge and Horne Tooke', *Studies in Romanticism*, XXIV, 1985.

Magnuson, Paul, *Coleridge's Nightmare Poetry*, Charlottesville, Virginia, 1974.

Magnuson, Paul, ' "The Eolian Harp" in Context', *Studies in Romanticism*, XXIV, 1985.

Mann, Peter, 'Coleridge, Joseph Gerrald, and the Slave Trade', *The Wordsworth Circle*, VIII, Winter 1977.

Marshall, P. H., *William Godwin*, New Haven, Conn., 1984.

Martin, Richard T., 'Coleridge's Use of *sermoni propriora*', *The Wordsworth Circle*, III, Spring 1972.

Mayo, R., 'The Contemporaneity of the *Lyrical Ballads*', *Publications of the Modern Languages Association of America*, LXIX, 1954.

Medwin, Thomas, *Conversations of Lord Byron*, London, 1824, revised and ed. Ernest J. Lovell, Jr, Princeton, New Jersey, 1966.

Mill, John Stuart, 'Coleridge', *London and Westminster Review*, XXXIII, March 1840.

Mill, John Stuart, *Autobiography*, London, 1873, reprinted, ed. John Robson, Harmondsworth, 1989.

Minnow Among Tritons: Mrs. S. T. Coleridge's Letters to Thomas Poole 1799–1834, ed. Stephen Potter, London, 1934.

Mitchell, L. G., *Charles James Fox*, Oxford, 1992.

Morehead, Robert, *Memorials of the Life and Writings of the Rev. Robert Morehead, DD*, ed. Charles Morehead, Edinburgh, 1875.

Moorman, Mary, *William Wordsworth: A Biography*, 2 vols, Oxford, 1957, 1965.

Morgan, Bayard Quincy, *A Critical Bibliography of German Literature in English Translation 1481–1927*, 2nd edition revised, New York, 1965.

Morris, Brian, 'Coleridge and Other People', *The Wordsworth Circle*, X, Autumn 1979.

Mudge, Bradford K, 'Sara Coleridge and "The Business of Life"', *The Wordsworth Circle*, XIX, Winter 1988.

Mudge, Bradford K., *Sara Coleridge: A Victorian Daughter*, New Haven, Conn., 1989.

The Observer. Part 1st. Being a Transient Glance at about Forty Youths of Bristol, Bristol, 1795.

Partridge, Eric, *A Dictionary of Slang and Unconventional English*, London, 1937, revised 1984.

Paul, Charles Kegan, *William Godwin: His Friends and Contemporaries*, 2 vols, London, 1876.

Paupers and Pig Killers: The Diary of William Holland, a Somerset Parson, 1799–1818, ed. Jack Ayres, Gloucester, 1984.

Peacock, Thomas Love, *Nightmare Abbey*, London, 1818, reprinted Harmondsworth, 1969.

Prickett, Stephen, *Romanticism and Religion: The Tradition of Coleridge and Wordsworth in the Victorian Church*, Cambridge, 1976.

Randel, Fred V., 'Coleridge and the Contentiousness of Romantic Nightingales', *Studies in Romanticism*, XXI, 1982.

Raysor, Thomas Middleton (ed.), *Coleridge's Miscellaneous Criticism*, London, 1936.

Raysor, Thomas Middleton, *Coleridge's Shakespearean Criticism*, 2 vols, London, 1930, reprinted 1960.

Reliques of Ancient English Poetry, ed. Thomas Percy, 3 vols, London, 1765.

Reiman, Donald H., 'Christobell; or, the Case of the Sequel Preemptive', *The Wordsworth Circle*, VI, Autumn 1975.

Reiman, Donald H., 'Coleridge and the Art of Equivocation', *Studies in Romanticism*, XXV, 1986.

Richards, I. A., *Coleridge on Imagination*, London, 1934.

Richards, I. A., *Practical Criticism*, London, 1929.

Richards, I. A., *The Principles of Literary Criticism*, London, 1924.

Richardson, Edgar Preston, *Washington Allston: A Study of the Romantic Artist in America*, Chicago, 1948.

[Rivers, David], *Literary Memoirs of Living Authors of Great Britain*, 2 vols, London, 1798.

Robinson, Henry Crabb, *Blake, Coleridge, Wordsworth, Lamb, Etc.. Being Selections from the Remains of Henry Crabb Robinson*, ed. Edith J. Morley, London, 1922.

Robinson, Henry Crabb, *The Correspondence of Henry Crabb Robinson with the Wordsworth Circle (1808–1866)*, ed. Edith J. Morley, 2 vols, Oxford, 1927.

Robinson, Henry Crabb, *Henry Crabb Robinson On Books and Their Writers*, ed. Edith J. Morley, 3 vols, London, 1938.

Robinson, Mary, *Memoirs of the late Mrs Robinson, written by herself*, ed. M. E. Robinson, 4 vols, London, 1801.

Roe, Nicholas, *Wordsworth and Coleridge: The Radical Years*, Oxford, 1988.

Roe, Nicholas, 'Coleridge and John Thelwall: The Road to Nether Stowey', in *The Coleridge Connection: Essays for Thomas McFarland*, ed. Richard Gravil and Molly Lefebure, London, 1990.

Rubinstein, Chris, 'A New Identity for the Mariner', *The Coleridge Bulletin*, III, Winter 1990.

Sanders, C. R., *Coleridge and the Broad Church Movement*, Durham, North Carolina, 1942, reprinted New York, 1972.

Sandford, Mrs Henry, *Thomas Poole and His Friends*, 2 vols, London, 1888.

Schlegel, August Wilhelm, *Lectures on Dramatic Art and Literature*, trans. John Black, London, 1815, reprinted 1861.

Schlegel, August Wilhelm, *Kritische Schriften und Briefe*, ed. Edgar Lohner, 7 vols, Stuttgart, 1962–74.

Schneider, Elisabeth, *Coleridge, Opium and 'Kubla Khan'*, Chicago, 1953.

Scott, Sir Walter, *Journal*, ed. W. E. K. Anderson, Oxford, 1972.

Scott, Sir Walter, *Letters*, ed. H. J. C. Grierson, 12 vols, London, 1932–7.

Scott, Sir Walter, *Poetical Works*, ed. J. Logie Robertson, London, 1904, reprinted 1971.

Scott, Sir Walter, *Scott: The Critical Heritage*, ed. John O. Hayden, London, 1970.

Scott, Sir Walter, *Sir Walter's Postbag*, ed. Wilfred Partington, London, 1932.

Shaffer, E. S., '*Kubla Khan' and The Fall of Jerusalem*, Cambridge, 1975.

Shelley, Mary, *Journals 1814–1844*, ed. Paula R. Feldman and Diana Scott-Kilvert, 2 vols, Oxford, 1987.

Shelley, Percy Bysshe, *Letters*, ed. Frederick L. Jones, 2 vols, Oxford, 1964.

Shelley, Percy Bysshe, *Poetical Works*, ed. Thomas Hutchinson, Oxford, 1905, reprinted 1967.

Skeat, T. C., 'Kubla Khan', *British Museum Quarterly*, XXVI, 1962–3.

Smith, Stevie, *Collected Poems*, Harmondsworth, 1985.

Southey, Robert, *The Life and Correspondence of the late Robert Southey*, ed. C. C. Southey, 6 vols, London, 1849–50.

Southey, Robert, *New Letters*, ed. Kenneth Curry, 2 vols, New York and London, 1965.

Southey, Robert, *Poetical Works*, 10 vols, London, 1837–8.

Southey, Robert, *Selections from the Letters of Robert Southey*, ed. John Wood Warter, 4 vols, London, 1856.

Stansfield, Dorothy A., *Thomas Beddoes M. D.: Chemist, Physician, Democrat*, Boston, Mass., 1984.

Stephen, Leslie, 'Coleridge', *Hours in a Library*, 3 vols, London, 1892.

Sterling, John, *Essays and Tales*, ed. J. C. Hare, 2 vols, London, 1848.

Stillinger, Jack, 'Pictorialism and Matter-of-Factness in Coleridge's Poems of Somerset', *The Wordsworth Circle*, XX, Spring 1989.

Sultana, Donald, *Samuel Taylor Coleridge in Malta and Italy*, New York, 1969.

Sutherland, John, *The Life of Walter Scott: A Critical Biography*, Oxford, 1995.

Taylor, William, *A Memoir of the Life and Writing of the late William Taylor of Norwich*, ed. J. W. Robberds, 2 vols, London, 1843.

Thelwall, John, *Poems, chiefly written in Retirement*, London, 1801.

Thelwall, John, *Prospectus of a Course of Lectures*, London, 1796.

Thelwall, Mrs, *The Life of John Thelwall*, London, 1837.

Thompson, E. P., 'Disenchantment or Default? A Lay Sermon', *Power and Consciousness*, ed. Conor Cruise O'Brien and William Dean Vanech, London, 1969.

Tyson, Gerald P., *Joseph Johnson: A Liberal Publisher*, Iowa, 1979.

Wallace, Catherine Miles, *The Design of Biographia Literaria*, London, 1983.

Warren, Robert Penn, 'A Poem of Pure Imagination', *Selected Essays*, New York, 1941, revised 1958.

Watson, Lucy, *Coleridge at Highgate*, London, 1925.

Wedgwood, Barbara and Hensleigh, *The Wedgwood Circle 1730–1897*, London, 1980.

Wheeler, Kathleen M., *Sources, Processes, and Methods in Coleridge's Biographia Literaria*, Cambridge, 1980.

Wheeler, Kathleen M., 'Disruption and Displacement in Coleridge's "Christabel"', *The Wordsworth Circle*, XX, Spring 1989.

Whitham, John A., *The Church of St. Mary of Ottery: A Short History and Guide*, 8th edition, Ottery St Mary, 1982.

Wilkinson, E. M., 'Coleridge's Knowledge of German as Seen in the Early Notebooks', *The Notebooks of Samuel Taylor Coleridge*, ed. Kathleen Coburn, vol I (London, 1957), Notes, Appendix A.

Williams, Orlo, *Life and Letters of John Rickman*, London, 1912.

Williams, Raymond, *Keywords: A Vocabulary of Culture and Society*, London, 1976.

Winkelmann, Elisabeth, *Coleridge und die Kantische Philosophie*, Leipzig, 1933.

Woodring, Carl R., *Politics in the Poetry of Coleridge*, Madison, Wisconsin, 1961.

Woolf, Virginia, 'The Man at the Gate', *The Death of the Moth and Other Essays*,

London, 1942, reprinted 1981.

Wordsworth, Christopher, *Memoirs of William Wordsworth, Poet Laureate, DCL*, 2 vols, London, 1851.

Wordsworth, Christopher, *Social Life at the English Universities in the Eighteenth Century*, Cambridge, 1874.

Wordsworth, Dorothy, *Journals*, ed. Mary Moorman, Oxford, 1971, reprinted 1974.

Wordsworth, William, *Letters of William and Dorothy Wordsworth*, ed. E. De Selincourt; *The Early Years, 1787–1805*, revised Chester L.Shaver, Oxford, 1967; *The Middle Years, 1806–11*, revised Mary Moorman, Oxford, 1969; *The Middle Years, 1812–20*, revised Mary Moorman and Alan G. Hill, Oxford, 1970; *The Later Years, 1821–53*, revised Alan G. Hill, 4 vols, Oxford, 1978–88.

Wordsworth, William, *Poetical Works*, ed. Thomas Hutchinson, revised Ernest De Selincourt, London, 1904, reprinted 1965.

Wordsworth, William, *The Prelude 1799, 1805, 1850*, ed. Jonathan Wordsworth, M. H. Abrams, and Stephen Gill, New York, 1979.

Wordsworth and Coleridge, *Lyrical Ballads*, ed. R. L. Brett and A. R. Jones, London, 1963, reprinted 1978.

Wordsworth and Coleridge, *Lyrical Ballads*, ed. Micahel Mason, London, 1992.

Wylie, Ian, *Young Coleridge and the Philosophers of Nature*, Oxford, 1989.

Wylie, Ian, 'Coleridge and the Lunaticks', *The Coleridge Connection: Essays for Thomas McFarland*, ed. Richard Gravil and Molly Lefebure, London, 1990.

Young, Julian Charles, *A Memoir of Charles Mayne Young*, 2 vols, London, 1871.

Zall, P. M., 'Citizen John Up Against the Wall', *The Wordsworth Circle*, III, Spring 1972.

Zall, P. M., 'Do Ye Ken Tom Poole', *The Wordsworth Circle*, VIII, Winter 1977.

Zall, P. M., 'Joseph Johnson, or the Perils of Publishing', *The Wordsworth Circle*, III, Winter 1972.

Zall, P. M., 'Joseph Lancaster's System', *The Wordsworth Circle*, XIII, Winter 1982.

Zall, P. M., 'Joseph Priestley, Firebrand Philosopher', *The Wordsworth Circle*, IX, Winter 1978.

Zall, P. M., 'Thomas Holcroft, Hyperhack', *The Wordsworth Circle*, XI, Autumn 1980.

Zall, P. M., 'The Trials of William Frend', *The Wordsworth Circle*, II, Winter 1971.

Zall, P. M., 'Up Loyal Sock Creek', *The Wordsworth Circle*, III, Summer 1972.

Index

Specific discussion of an entry is indicated by page numbers in italic.